LOLLARDS AND THEIR INFLUENCE
IN LATE MEDIEVAL ENGLAND

Who were the Lollards? What did Lollards believe? What can the manuscript record of Lollard works teach us about the textual dissemination of Lollard beliefs and the audience for Lollard writings? What did Lollards have in common with other reformist or dissident thinkers in late medieval England, and how were their views distinctive? These questions have been fundamental to the modern study of Lollardy (also known as Wycliffism). The essays in this book reveal their broader implications for the study of English literature and history through a series of closely focused studies that demonstrate the wide-ranging influence of Lollard writings and ideas on later medieval English culture. Introductions to previous scholarship, and an extensive Bibliography of printed resources for the study of Wyclif and Wycliffites, provide an entry to scholarship for those new to the field.

LOLLARDS AND THEIR INFLUENCE IN LATE MEDIEVAL ENGLAND

Edited by

Fiona Somerset, Jill C. Havens, and Derrick G. Pitard

THE BOYDELL PRESS

First published 2003
The Boydell Press, Woodbridge
Reprinted in paperback 2009

ISBN 978-0-85115-995-9 hardback
ISBN 978-1-84383-508-0 paperback

Transferred to digital printing

The Boydell Press is an imprint of Boydell & Brewer Ltd
PO Box 9, Woodbridge, Suffolk IP12 3DF, UK
and of Boydell & Brewer Inc.
668 Mt. Hope Avenue, Rochester NY 14620, USA
website: www.boydellandbrewer.com

A CIP catalogue record for this title is available
from the British Library

This book is printed on acid-free paper

Contents

Acknowledgements

This volume has grown out of the scholarship presented in Lollard Society sessions in Kalamazoo and Leeds over the past five years. We thank all participants in those sessions, and most especially the contributors whose essays are included here.

Anne Hudson's continuing energetic scholarship has been a major force in creating the modern field of Lollard Studies. The publication of this collection will coincide with her retirement (from teaching, though assuredly not from active research), and while this volume is not formally a festschrift, it is nonetheless a celebration of her work. All of us are grateful to her for her support and help with this project.

Fiona Somerset would in addition like to thank those who have commented on her contributions and helped in formulating the volume as a whole: along with her fellow contributors, David Aers, Andrew Cole, Richard F. Green, Glending Olson, Paul Remley, Paul Strohm, Míceál Vaughan, Jim Weldon, and Nicholas Watson.

Jill C. Havens would like to thank her co-editors, Derrick Pitard and Fiona Somerset, as well as Margaret Aston, Simon Forde, Ralph Hanna, Wendy Scase, and Christina von Nolcken for their continuing support of the Lollard Society.

Derrick Pitard would especially like to thank all of those who have patiently helped with the Bibliography. Mishtooni Bose, Rita Copeland, Andrew Cole, Ralph Hanna, Jill Havens, Anne Hudson, Stephen Lahey, Ian Levy, Fiona Somerset, Georgi Vassilev and David Watt have at various times suggested additional sources, tracked down obscure and recalcitrant references, helped with unfamiliar languages, found more than a few errors, and extended my knowledge to new and unfamiliar areas. It is to be hoped that the result will be both worthy of their help and an aid to other scholars, both novice and experienced, interested in late medieval religion and culture.

We would also like to thank the staff at Boydell & Brewer, in particular Caroline Palmer for first suggesting the project, our anonymous reviewer for his/her very helpful comments on individual essays, Phillip Judge for his work on the map, and Pru Harrison for her efficient work on the volume's production.

Abbreviations

BIHR	*Bulletin of the Institute of Historical Research*
BJRL	*Bulletin of the John Rylands Library*
BL	British Library London
BRUO	A.B. Emden, *A Biographical Register of the University of Oxford to AD 1500* (6)
Cal. Inq. Misc.	*Calendar of Inquisitions Miscellaneous* [1219–1422] 7 vols. (London, 1916–1968)
CCCA	Corpus Christi College Archives, Oxford
CChR	*Calendar of Charter Rolls* [1226–1517] 6 vols. (London, 1903–1927)
CCR	*Calendar of the Close Rolls* [1272–1509] 47 vols. (London, 1902–1938)
CFR	*Calendar of the Fine Rolls* [1272–1509] 22 vols. (London, 1911–1962)
CIPM	*Calendar of Inquisitions Post Mortem* [1236–1422] 21 vols. (London, 1904–2002)
Complete Peerage	*The Complete Peerage*, ed. G.E. Cokayne et al. 12 vols. in 13 (London, 1910–57)
CPR	*Calendar of the Patent Rolls* [1232–1509] 52 vols. (London, 1891–1916)
CUL	Cambridge University Library
DMBL	A.G. Watson, *Catalogue of Dated and Datable Manuscripts c.700–1600 in the Department of Manuscripts, The British Library* 2 vols. (London, 1979)
DMC	P.R. Robinson, *Catalogue of Dated and Datable Manuscripts c.737–1600 in Cambridge Libraries* 2 vols. (Cambridge, 1988)
DMO	A.G. Watson, *Catalogue of Dated and Datable Manuscripts c.435–1600 in Oxford Libraries* 2 vols. (Oxford, 1984)
EETS	Early English Text Society (London, 1864–); o.s. original series, e.s. extra series
FDR	*Friar Daw's Reply* in *Jack Upland, Friar Daw's Reply and Upland's Rejoinder*, ed. P.L. Heyworth (159)
FZ	*Fasciculi Zizaniorum*, ed. W.W. Shirley (139)
Hist. Parl.	J.S. Roskell, L. Clark, C. Rawcliffe, *The History of*

	Parliament. The House of Commons 1386–1421 4 vols. (Stroud, 1992)
IMEV	C. Brown, R.H. Robbins, *Index of Middle English Verse* (New York, 1953)
IPMEP	R.E. Lewis et al., *Index of Printed Middle English Prose* (*18*)
JU	*Jack Upland* in *Jack Upland, Friar Daw's Reply and Upland's Rejoinder,* ed. P.L. Heyworth (*159*)
LFC	*The Lay Folks' Catechism*, ed. T.F. Simmons, H.E. Nolloth, EETS 118 (*176*)
ME	Middle English
MED	Middle English Dictionary, ed. H. Kurath, S.M. Kuhn et al. (Ann Arbor, 1952–)
Op. Min.	*Johannis Wyclif Opera Minora*, ed. J. Loserth. Wyclif Society (London, 1913)
Oxon. Hist. Soc.	Oxford Historical Society (Oxford, 1885–)
PL	*Patrologia Latina*, ed. J.P. Migne (Paris, 1841–)
Pol. Wks.	*John Wiclif's Polemical Works in Latin*, ed. R. Buddensieg 2 vols. Wyclif Society (London, 1883)
PRO	Public Record Office
RS	Rolls Series (London, 1858–1911)
ST	Thomas Aquinas, *Summa Theologiae*
STC	*A Short-Title Catalogue of Books printed in England, Scotland, and Ireland and of English Books printed abroad 1475–1640*, ed. A.W. Pollard, G.R. Redgrave, revised W.A. Jackson, F.S. Ferguson, K.F. Pantzer 2 vols. (London, 1976–86)
UR1, UR2	Respectively *Upland's Rejoinder* and the portions of the *Rejoinder* Heyworth relegated to his notes. In *Jack Upland, Friar Daw's Reply and Upland's Rejoinder,* ed. P.L. Heyworth (*159*)
VCH	Victoria County History

Preface

Anne Hudson

Matthew Paris reported that Robert Grosseteste, the "seint Roberd" of later English sectarian language, asked to define heresy, replied "Heresy in its Greek etymology means 'choice': it is a choice made for human ends, contrary to Holy Scripture, openly declared, and stubbornly maintained."[1] Such a definition, one which diverged slightly from the normal canonists' formulation,[2] is worth pondering in regard to the "heresy" which was discerned in England, and subsequently in Bohemia, following (*post hoc* or *propter hoc* remaining an issue of contention) the teaching of John Wyclif. Two elements are notable: first a presence, namely, the declared stress on "choice," a choice made in Grosseteste's formulation by the perpetrator; and second an absence, the lack of any specification of agency responsible for the definition of what is "contrary to Holy Scripture," or of deciding whether it has been "openly declared and stubbornly maintained."

Grosseteste's implication in regard to the second, the absence, is perhaps clearer than in regard to the first: though no unquestioning servant of his ecclesiastical superiors, Grosseteste would surely have defined the agency of discernment to have been the Church, as embodied in the pope, ecclesiastical law and its ministers. Heresy, as has long been a truism, is defined by its opponents.[3] An example from the earlier period makes this particularly clear: the kind of mission envisaged by Francis of Assisi was given papal approval and acceptance, whilst the ostensibly similar aims of Peter Waldes of Lyons were first questioned and finally hereticated.[4] The fluctuating fortunes of the "rigorist" understanding of Francis's *Rule* and *Testament* (mentioned here by Clopper) provide another instructive example. For the heresy which came to be regarded as characteristically English this is particularly clear: from the Blackfriars' Council of 1382 onwards, the ecclesiastical authorities produced lists of condemned conclusions which formed the basis for enquiry into a suspect's orthodoxy – those authorities

---

[1] Reported in R.W. Southern, *Robert Grosseteste: the Growth of an English Mind in Medieval Europe* (Oxford: Clarendon, 1986), 292–3.

[2] Southern gives the example of Hostiensis in *Aurea summa* where a heretic is one "qui aliter sentit de articulis fidei quam Romana ecclesia."

[3] This has been stressed recently, for instance by R.N. Swanson (*1166*) [the italicized number refers to the numbered reference in the Selected Bibliography, 251–310 below].

[4] See E. Cameron, *Waldenses: Rejections of Holy Church in Medieval Europe* (Oxford: Blackwell, 2000), 20–1.

defined the heresy, accused the suspect and acted as judge in any ensuing trial, and also laid down the practices which were to be regarded as unacceptable.[5] The name given to that heresy, whether Wycliffite or Lollard, derives essentially from those who opposed the unorthodoxy, even if adherents in time came to use the same vocabulary (cf. Scase, Cole).

These origins have numerous implications. Perhaps most important is that the vocabulary of heresy is primarily emotive: whether deriving from foe or friend, it aims to arouse a reaction, as well as – or even to the exclusion of – intellectual analysis. In this there is an obvious modern analogy in the language of political discourse: terms such as "fascist," "communist," "socialist," "terrorist," "freedom-fighter" are commonly bandied around as tokens in a polemical debate, not as defining the precise ideological outlook of the people or programmes to which they are applied. Netter reveals exactly the same sort of linguistic usage in his huge *Doctrinale fidei catholici* when he designates Wyclif at various times as an adherent of the heresies of Donatus, Arius, Julian, Pelagius, Mani, Petilian, Peter Abelard, the Cathars, the Waldensians: he is not making any exact attribution of descent, but merely using all the abusive terms he can muster to condemn an heresiarch he sees as worse than each.[6] This example is blatant, but its significance for our understanding of other, less outrageous contemporary claims should not be forgotten. Netter's hysteria is also revealing: however much recent critics have attempted to reduce Lollardy to a "little, local difficulty," even to a mere tool in the armoury of Lancastrian propaganda, contemporary ecclesiastical legislation makes it clear that this was not how it seemed on the ground in England between the 1380s and 1530s.[7] The vexed question of Wyclif's influence on Jan Hus and his followers is not relevant to the present volume, but Netter's assertion of the Englishman's originating role certainly finds support in the deliberations of the church fathers at the Councils of Constance and of Basel.[8]

The paramount role of the prosecution in the definition of heresy is also central to an understanding of the documentary sources for Lollardy. Those sources are primarily the records of the various diocesan bishops and their officials, surviving usually within the main episcopal registers but in a few cases in separate books or sets of quires.[9] In almost every instance the minimum information for sentence is set down: the name and place of residence of the suspect, the view(s) and sometimes the practice(s) which are

---

[5] For the Blackfriars conclusions see *Fasciculi zizaniorum* (*139*, 277–82); for later lists see my *Lollards and their Books* (*67*, 125–40).

[6] See the edition by B. Blanciotti (*188*); I have discussed Netter's analysis of Wyclif and Lollardy further in a paper to be published in a collective volume on the Carmelite writer edited by Richard Copsey.

[7] Notably by E. Duffy (*512*); P. Strohm (*1159*). The major stages of the legislation against heresy to 1414 can be seen in the documents printed in *Concilia Magnae Britanniae et Hiberniae* (*228*, 3.116–360); the subsequent efforts of Archbishop Chichele are discussed in *The Register of Henry Chichele*, ed. E.F. Jacob (Oxford: Clarendon, 1938–47), 1.cxxix–cxliv.

[8] For a number of recent continental views about Hus's debt, with citation of older discussions, see *Jan Hus: Zwischen Zeiten, Volkern, Konfessionen* (*81*); see also G. Christianson (*389*).

[9] See the summary of these sources, and of the difficulties of their interpretation, in my *The Premature Reformation: Wycliffite Texts and Lollard History* (*713*, 32–42).

censured, and the penalty. When a sequence of investigations by the same bishop within a limited period of time and a restricted area is available, it may be possible to infer a little more about the *modus procedendi* of the investigations; but, in the absence of such comparative material, it would be rash to conclude that a suspect's unusual views or habits were all declared in the written record. The rare courtbooks, of Alnwick of Norwich or of Blythe of Coventry and Lichfield, reveal more about the networks of association and the nuances of opinion that might be found – and reveal how much has been suppressed in the usual formulaic record.[10] Even less frequent is any attempt to record the full process of enquiry: Bishop Trefnant's dealings with William Swinderby and Walter Brut in the Hereford diocese in 1393 are set out with unparalleled amplitude, though even there the record is fairly certainly incomplete.[11] The irregularity of record uncovered by the Alnwick courtbook – only one case of unorthodoxy is recorded in Alnwick's main register – should also make us beware of drawing conclusions from silence; that Alnwick was not alone in relegating heresy material to a file separate from his register is indicated by Bishop Russell of Lincoln, who, "worn out" by heresy investigations, in 1492 abbreviated book VI of Netter's *Doctrinale* for the assistance of other bishops similarly afflicted, though there is no known heresy case within the records of his episcopacy.[12] Here certainly the vagaries of documentary survival are at stake, but they do not make the interpretation of the usual bare account of conviction that does still exist any the easier to interpret.

Those bare records do, however, provide clues that need to be recalled in dealing with manuscripts and texts that may, or may not, have Lollard affiliations. Ownership of vernacular books clearly became a serious contributory factor in the official discernment of a "heretic," especially in the course of the fifteenth and sixteenth centuries. It was, therefore, wise not to enter marks of ownership in any manuscript owned, not to betray in titles or colophons the origin of a text, to hide or even destroy incriminating materials – the late suspect who declared that "he would rather burn his books than that his books burn him" is hardly likely to have been unique even if he was unusually candid.[13] The possibility that it was deliberate concealment, rather than inadvertent confusion, to intersperse unequivocally heterodox texts with others of less controversial outlook should be borne in mind (see Steiner). From a very early stage, however, the Wycliffite movement had declaredly utilized older, uncontentious works as the foundation for its own productions: the revisions of Rolle's Psalter

[10] For the first see N. Tanner (*208*); a full edition of the Blythe courtbook is being produced by Norman Tanner and Shannon McSheffrey.

[11] *Registrum Johannis Trefnant* (*213*, 231–411); the possibility of incompleteness in the case of Brut derives from the fact that the charges listed on pp. 361–5 cannot all be matched against the declarations of Brut included in the previous material.

[12] See Oxford, University College MS 156, f.i.

[13] John Phip, a suspect during Bishop Longland of Lincoln's persecution between 1518 and 1521, reported in Foxe, *The Actes and Monuments*, ed. S.R. Cattley and J. Pratt (London, 1853–70), 4.237.

commentary or the so-called *Glossed Gospels*, the latter taking Aquinas's
Catena aurea as their basis, are well-known examples;[14] the possibility that
the work of biblical translation that culminated in the Late Version of the
Wycliffite Bible consciously developed earlier English attempts at scriptural
rendering is an area still awaiting full investigation (see Hanna).

This acknowledged annexation of earlier texts is, of course, the most
manifest demonstration of another factor that complicates the modern
analysis of heresy in later medieval England. Wyclif himself, despite his
conviction that the Gospels and Epistles must form the touchstone for all
Christian teaching, quoted innumerable passages from the fathers of the
church, from some of their medieval successors (notably Bernard and
Grosseteste) and from canon law; his quotations, often lengthy, are largely
accurate and are regularly provided with precise references (including for
canon law the patristic source of the chapter). His followers, especially in
the earlier texts, emulated that example.[15] Not surprisingly, therefore, many
of the views propounded in texts that might be described as "Wycliffite" are
traceable to writers that antedate Wyclif, writers who themselves were
accepted as entirely orthodox. To put it at its most extreme, why should a
series of authorities on the eucharist, declaredly (and correctly) derived
from Augustine, Jerome, Ambrose and so forth, be described as "Wycliffite"?[16] If the answer may be suspected to lie in the selection, then that can
be an extraordinarily difficult thesis to prove: the *Glossed Gospels* consist
entirely in attributed quotations, but it would be a bold critic who claimed
to have established beyond doubt that the expansion of Aquinas's extracts
from the *originalia* that he was using had been designed to prove
unorthodox conclusions. Similarly, Wyclif(fite) polemic drew heavily on
existing traditions: much of the antifraternal satire is traceable to the earlier
opposition of men such as William of St. Amour or FitzRalph, many of the
tropes of more general anticlericalism to centuries of hostility to the
temporalities of the clergy, the vices (real or alleged) of the monastic
orders, the pretensions of the papacy to universal spiritual, and often
temporal, jurisdiction.[17] But further such polemical language was, of
course, available to many who would not have given unacceptable answers
to the lists of questions drawn up early in the fifteenth century for
administration to those suspect of heresy. To discriminate between orthodox and heterodox anticlericalism can be an impossible task. Furthermore,
some of the recurrent language is biblical: Christ's condemnation of the
pharisees and saducees of his day provided a rich source of abusive
language for all parties to the later medieval debates. What's new? we
may often feel, as we try, perhaps arrogantly, to pin down fifteenth-century
satire (see Scase).

---

[14] See *713*, 259–64, 247–59 and references there given.

[15] Notable examples are *The Lanterne of Liȝt* (*174*) and *The Thirty-Seven Conclusions of the Lollards*
(*140, 210*).

[16] For the sequence in question see Cambridge, University Library MS Ff.6.31(3), ff.27v–35v.

[17] For some of the background see J.A. Yunck, *The Lineage of Lady Meed* (Notre Dame Univ.
Press, 1963), P. R. Szittya (*1169*), W. Scase (*1081*).

To return to Grosseteste's definition of heresy: "Heresy . . . means 'choice': it is a choice made for human ends." Modern analysis has stressed that the "choice" is that of the opponent, rather than, as Grosseteste certainly envisaged, that of the suspect – certain beliefs, notably in the present case those concerning the eucharist, are seen as unacceptable by the ecclesiastical authorities and are pursued as such. Certainly, this says much of relevance to the Wycliffite heresy: Southern, that most perceptive of historians, commented back in 1962 that "for several years, until it became too dangerous to agree with him, probably a majority of that not notably revolutionary body, the University of Oxford, would have gone most of the way in most of what [Wyclif] said";[18] if that verdict needs modification in the light of more recent research, it is to emphasise the underlying message – that Wyclif and his followers picked up numerous strands of contemporary discontents, and that many people, even after Archbishop Arundel had done his worst, continued to see elements in the Lollard programme with which they could sympathise.[19] As has often been urged, had Wyclif kept off the subject of the sacrament, or at least (or most of all?) had kept discussion of the issue within the decently obscure confines of academic Latin, his views might have escaped condemnation. However, it may be argued that it was his views on dominion that set the ecclesiastical hierarchy to the search for an issue on which they could with less equivocation bring about his censure.[20] In any event, it is clear that the heretication of views concerning issues such as private religion, images, pilgrimages or vernacular scriptures was the "choice" of Lollardy's opponents. Was Grosseteste then mistaken in seeing "choice" as lying with the adherent to the heresy?[21] Is the modern critic the more perceptive when he argues that no-one chose to be a heretic? – or, to put it another way, was heresy always thrust upon a person, rather than being a mark of birth or of conscious achievement? Using Malvolio's trinity perhaps reveals the questionableness of the modern assumption: given the undoubted importance of the family in the fostering of Lollardy, many later suspects plainly became "heretics" by accident of birth or upbringing.[22] Equally, choice must be accepted in the case of those suspects who reverted to Lollardy after recanting: after 1401 that reversion carried the known risk of an agonising death. It is, surely, deplorable arrogance on the part of the modern inhabitant of a western world where capital punishment is almost unknown to denigrate the convictions that led men and women to stand by their opinions to such an end. Even if the number of those who are known to have suffered such a death is by modern standards of atrocity small, it is not negligible; their convictions must be accepted as choice just as the decision of the authorities, ecclesiastical and secular, to exact that death is equally a choice. Yet the present-day observer should

[18] R.W. Southern, *Western Views of Islam in the Middle Ages* (Cambridge, Mass.: Harvard University Press, 1962), 77.
[19] For continuing interest in Wyclif in Oxford see M. Jurkowski (*762*).
[20] See my paper "*Peculiaris regis clericus*: Wyclif and the Issue of Authority" (*732*).
[21] See above, n.3.
[22] See, for example, the families involved in archbishop Warham's investigations in Kent (*209*).

surely give the Green Knight's verdict on those who recanted: "þe lasse I yow blame," and concede agnosticism on the question of underlying motive for the act – it need not be conviction of error.

As Fiona Somerset indicates in her Introduction, much has changed in the field of Lollard studies in the past thirty or so years. In the late 1960s the standard written account of Wyclif and his followers was that of K.B. McFarlane's book *John Wycliffe and the Beginnings of English Nonconformity*, published first in 1952; masterful and greatly influential though it has been, it was written to the depressing conclusion that when Wyclif died in 1384 "most of the causes for which he had fought so vigorously had been lost," and that the Lollard sect was "hopelessly outmatched," and it was included in a series "Teach yourself History" which permitted no footnotes or other documentation.[23] McFarlane substantially modified some of his views in lectures, published posthumously in 1972, but these did not cover the full range of the earlier book.[24] One pupil, John Thomson, in his thesis issued in 1965 as *The Later Lollards 1414–1520*, had produced the groundbreaking initial survey of episcopal records of the heresy.[25] Another, Margaret Aston, published in the '60s three more adventurous papers, the first of which, "Lollardy and Sedition, 1381–1431" was (and remains) one of the most innovative and influential of all modern studies.[26] A little had recently been done on Wyclif himself: J.A. Robson's book *Wyclif and the Oxford Schools* (Cambridge, 1961) placed the logical and philosophical writings within the context of contemporary academic study, whilst Michael Wilks had begun his long series of explorations of Wyclif's thought.[27] James Crompton had published only a small amount of his erudite findings before his untimely death.[28] Otherwise most of the editions that the incipient Wyclif(fite) scholar needed to consult, and most of the analyses of evidence for the movement, had been produced thirty years or more previously, and might be thought to need serious revision. A glance at the dates in the bibliography at the end of this volume reveals how much, at least in terms of quantity, the past thirty years have added. The contents of the present

---

[23] Originally published London: English Universities Press Ltd, 1952, and several times reprinted; it was reissued under the abbreviated title *Wycliffe and English Nonconformity* by Penguin Books in 1972.

[24] *Lancastrian Kings and Lollard Knights* (*934*); the book was put together by G.L. Harriss from McFarlane's notes, and the second half on the Lollard knights derives principally from a version of the lectures given in 1966.

[25] The thesis was submitted in 1960, and was published in London by Oxford University Press, 1965 (*1189*).

[26] Produced first in *Past and Present* 17 (1960): 1–44, reprinted on various occasions but most notably in her *Lollards and Reformers: Images and Literacy in Late Medieval Religion* (*43*, 1–47). The other two papers are "Lollardy and the Reformation: Survival or Revival?" (*270*, originally published in 1964), and "John Wycliffe's Reformation Reputation" (*271*, originally published in 1965), there pp. 243–72.

[27] Now most conveniently collected in his *Wyclif: Political Ideas and Practice* (*92*), where the pre-1970 papers are "Predestination, Property and Power: Wyclif's Theory of Dominion and Grace" (*1285*, first published in 1965), there pp. 16–32, and "The Early Oxford Wyclif: Papalist or Nominalist?" (*1286*, first published in 1969), there pp. 33–62.

[28] Notably his "Fasciculi zizaniorum" (*438*); and "Leicestershire Lollards" (*440*).

book may give an idea of the range of issues that are currently being confronted.

What remains to be done? A vast deal, I would suggest, on Wyclif himself. First, and most crucially, we have no edition of some of his works (notably of any part of the *Postilla in totam Bibliam*); the editions produced between 1883 and 1921 by the Wyclif Society, indispensible though they are to the modern student, are in varying degrees inadequate by modern standards and need, as a minimum, substantial revision and supplementation. Equally, Wyclif's lengthy, often digressive and sometimes contorted, Latin writings, writings that were often perceptibly subject to revision in his later years, do not lend themselves to easy or summary conclusions; as more is done, it becomes increasingly obvious that Wyclif wrote, and revised, to meet changing circumstances and interests, often breaking off the declared structure of a work to discuss a contemporary issue that had arisen. The modern critic needs assistance in contextualising these discussions.[29] Much the same situation exists with the longer writings of his followers. Despite the appearance of some new editions, many crucial texts remain out of sight without access to manuscripts: nothing has yet been printed (beyond the briefest snippets) of the *Glossed Gospels* or of the revisions of Rolle's Psalter commentary, let alone of the Latin *Opus arduum*.[30] The only edition of the *Thirty-Seven Conclusions of the Lollards* is hidden under a strange title published in 1851, of the so-called *Apology for Lollard Doctrines* in a Camden Series volume of 1842; amongst the shorter works, properly annotated editions from all manuscripts now known are badly needed for many of the texts edited by T. Arnold in *Select English Works of John Wyclif* (1871) and by F.D. Matthew in his 1884 anthology.[31] And, whilst we are deeply indebted to the resilience of Conrad Lindberg in producing a new edition of the Early Version of the Wycliffite Bible (and now starting on a more limited project to print one manuscript of the Later Version), many questions concerning that major undertaking remain unanswered.[32] Equally, editorial work is badly needed to produce editions of many works written by opponents of the Lollards: Netter is accessible thanks to a reprint of the 1757–59 Venice edition, but most of Woodford's ripostes to Wyclif and early disciples such as Brut remain unedited, as do the shorter contributions of men such as Nicholas Radcliffe, Richard Ullerston, William Rymington and the anonymous Dominican author of the *Pharetra sacramenti*.[33] Analytical criticism may seem more appealing, but it may be salutary to consider the longevity of editions in this field.

---

[29] For a recent example of such work see K. Ghosh (*598*).

[30] For many years Dr. Henry Hargreaves worked on the first, but has not yet produced any edition; I have just begun editorial work on the second; Dr. Curt Bostick has plans for an edition of the third.

[31] The second is EETS o.s. 74, originally produced in 1884 but revised for a second edition in 1902 (*182*).

[32] See bibliography nos. *109–12, 114, 116*.

[33] For the first three see R. Sharpe (*34*), nos. 1110, 1400 and 2157; the fourth is entered under 665 John Deverose, but this cannot be correct since Deverose was a secular, whilst the author of this text states himself to have been a Dominican.

The essays in the present collection give a good idea of some of the analytical work that can be done on vernacular texts associated with the Lollard movement, whether their authors' ideological affiliations can clearly be traced or not. As is becoming increasingly evident in this area, simple binarism is not adequate: there is a vast range of material that shows some sympathy with viewpoints that are characteristic of Lollardy but are not peculiar to that sect, of knowledge of Wycliffite positions without full agreement with them, of allusion (whether mocking or not) to Lollard phraseology and idiom. Much analysis remains to be done, much refinement of critical discernment to be achieved. As recent advances in the understanding of medieval romance have underlined, investigation of individual manuscript contents, contexts and ownerships can reveal much; more remains to be done in this area. Unreflected in the present volume are the exciting possibilities for orthographic and vocabulary studies opened up by the rapid analysis of large quantities of data by computing programmes:[34] until scanners can read medieval manuscripts as well as modern typescript, these possibilities reinforce the urgent need for more printed editions. Studies of vocabulary, using such tools, should range over Latin as well as English, texts whose affiliations can be surely mapped as well as those which do not wear their hearts on their sleeves. Central to all of these desirable projects is the need for researchers who are familiar with historical *and* literary techniques, with the theological, philosophical and legal contexts within which the texts and documents were written, with Latin as well as Middle English – a tall order maybe, but surely an exhilarating one!

---

[34] For a recent example see M. Peikola (*1031*).

Introduction

Fiona Somerset

Since the late 1960s, the field of Lollard (or Wycliffite[1]) studies has undergone nothing less than an explosion in scholarly activity. The current vitality in the field began from the pioneering researches of scholars such as Anne Hudson, who first began to investigate in detail the large volume of mostly vernacular texts left behind by the movement, in the process doing no less than to establish Wycliffite studies as a sub-specialty within the field of medieval English literature, and Margaret Aston, who has undertaken wide-ranging studies of the beliefs and practices of Lollards based in detailed study of their own writings as well as those of their contemporary observers and opponents, in the process helping to increase historians' respect for Wycliffite ideas.[2] Many scholars in both disciplines have by now followed their lead, both in their willingness to draw upon the methodologies of both history and literary study in order to address their topic, and in their revisionist bent: as is appropriate to the study of a heresy, this is a field in which established ideas are always open to question.

New work on Wycliffism has not merely revolutionised an existing field of study: it has created a new one, where scholars of history and literature have met, and drawn upon one another's methods, in order to edit, study, and interpret a body of texts and records which had previously, especially in English departments, received little attention. The field is now firmly established as an important aspect of the study of medieval England, and within the past ten years or so in particular, Lollard studies have not only entered the mainstream, but come to occupy a central place. Not only is it common now for graduate students to write theses focused in whole or in part on Wycliffite texts or manuscripts, but many well-known scholars not originally trained in this area have become interested in exploring what our

---

[1] The terms "Lollard" and "Wycliffite" have sometimes been used to distinguish unlearned lay followers at greater remove from the movement's core from university-trained followers of Wyclif; but in this book, as in nearly all recent scholarship, the terms will be used interchangeably. Scase's and Cole's new investigations of the early history of the words "loller" and "lollard" (see below, 19–36 and 37–58) may bring some reconsideration of this practice, which has been standard for some time: see Anne Hudson (*713*, 2–4).

[2] Readers curious about early developments in the years from the mid-sixties to the present are directed especially to these collected essays: Margaret Aston (*43*), Anne Hudson (*67*). Other significant early contributions include James Crompton (*440*); James Crompton (*438*); Steven Halasey (*623*); K.B. McFarlane (*934*); J.A.F. Thompson (*1189*). See also Anne Hudson's Preface to this volume, 1–8.

knowledge of Lollardy can contribute to our understanding of late medieval English vernacular writing and book production more generally. Now that Lollard writings have been extensively studied in isolation in order to identify their specific qualities, efforts are increasingly being made to integrate this new knowledge into our larger picture of the period – a picture they alter, sometimes greatly, through their new presence.

The present volume aims to present something of the range and excitement of the new work on Lollardy now being produced by both literary scholars and historians, and by both younger and more established scholars. We hope to provide an introduction to the latest scholarship in this area, and to how it has developed, that will be useful for graduate students and others contemplating research in this area for the first time. This is the logic behind the extensive bibliography and lists of suggested introductory readings by Derrick Pitard, and it is also the reason why each of the four sections within the collection is organized around one of the fundamental, longstanding questions in the field. But in providing an introduction, our goal is not to impose an orthodoxy. Instead, the contributors each bring new perspectives and methods to bear on their subjects. Rather than always agreeing with one another, they often propose alternatives, and point toward a variety of new directions for future research.

Who were the Lollards? Trial records and chronicles suggest that a wide range of people espoused Lollard beliefs, from university-educated scholars to members of the gentry to village artisans. Past scholarship was sometimes quick to dissociate scholars from lower-class artisans, emphasizing the incoherence and confusion in the latter's beliefs and reserving the label "Wycliffite" to designate university men with especially close links to Wyclif. More recent scholarship has emphasized that Lollards and Wycliffites were not so readily distinguishable. Instead, there was some identifiable continuity in the content of belief and even in membership between the earliest university followers and later communities in far-flung villages and towns, stretching even up to the sixteenth century. What is more, the term "Lollard" was used from very early on within the university, rather than being a later coinage used to designate uneducated, lower-class heretics.[3] In Part I, "Lollers in the Wind," two literary critics and two historians address anew the question of what we can learn about the people who were called Lollards by examining records describing them.

Wendy Scase and Andrew Cole move beyond the view of Lollardy we derive from trial records, chronicles, and other hostile records. Each compares these hostile reports with writings produced by Lollards themselves, or by other witnesses not actively engaged in the persecution of Lollards, in order to reconsider how it was that followers of Wyclif came to be called Lollards. For Scase, this approach leads to new insight into controversies going on within the university, and points attention to a range

---

[3] See above, n.1.

of literary and other texts, mostly in Latin, that have remained largely unexamined. A revisionist reading of the poem "On the Council of London" helps to disclose a discursive space, constructed amidst fast-flying satirical poetic exchanges which refer in turn to a web of other writings in Latin and the vernacular, within which the Wycliffite masters in Oxford can see themselves as victors. For Cole, adjustments to our account of how the terminology for labelling Lollards developed prompt a new assessment of Langland's role in the invention of Lollardy. Unconvinced by the current critical view that Langland's "lollares" have nothing to do with Lollards, Cole employs newly discovered contemporary usages of "loller" to paint a different picture. This is not, however, to say that Langland is a Wycliffite, but only that he is "not seeing 'lollardy' through the eyes of orthodoxy."[4] The impulse to affirm or deny that every writer or at the very least his characters is either Wycliffite or antiWycliffite was at one stage common in articles that mention major literary authors and Wycliffism in the same breath.[5] But as Cole's contribution helps to show, this impulse can lead to distortions.

Andrew Larsen and Maureen Jurkowski are also concerned to move beyond the limitations of the evidence provided by trial records. Larsen prompts us to reconsider how Lollards and their beliefs have been defined. Often, he suggests, the assertion that Wycliffism was the first English heresy becomes a self-fulfilling prophecy, in that any behaviour or beliefs thought heretical at the time or appearing heretical to a historian may be labelled "Lollard" if indigenous to England. But is this definition of Lollardy adequate, or even workable, for investigating the Lollard movement? Larsen thinks not, and proposes a new approach grounded in careful analysis of the information that trial records, together with other sources, can provide. Maureen Jurkowski's essay, too, prompts reconsideration of historiographic method, this time with a test case which shows how prosopography can contribute to, and prompt revision of, the notions of the heresy's development that we have derived from examining hostile contemporary accounts of it. Jurkowski uses new archival findings to examine the case of Thomas Compworth, the first layman convicted of the Lollard heresy, and often confused with his son of the same name. A member of the gentry with links to heretics in Oxford as well as to unrest and even dissidence of a more secular sort, Compworth gives us new insight into these forms of association.

What did Lollards believe, and how did their beliefs create a sense of community? Although any account of Lollard thought cannot ignore what hostile contemporaries thought Lollards thought – as must be true in the study of any social movement formed through adversity and opposition – scholarship has increasingly placed emphasis on what Lollards themselves had to say about their beliefs, rather than concentrating mainly on what the

---

[4] See below, 58.
[5] See, for example Alcuin Blamires (327); Pamela Gradon (608); and David Lawton (827).

authorities accused them of believing. Whereas some past scholars concluded that trial records revealed inconsistency of belief among Lollard
communities, more recently scholars have stressed the remarkable consistency over time that may be found amongst Wycliffite writings, and even
(with the writings to explain depositions more thoroughly) between written
explanations of specific beliefs on key issues and trial depositions that might
have looked incoherent out of context.[6] The essays in Part II, "Lollard
Thought," shift away from Part I's emphasis on outsiders' descriptions of
Lollardy toward Lollards' own accounts of their theology and social ideas.
The essays re-examine two of the Lollards' most fiercely held beliefs, ones
that most sharply divided them from orthodoxy and contributed most
strongly to forming their sense of community: the theology of the Eucharist,
and that of adoration of the cross.

Margaret Aston addresses a central issue where theology and ideas of
community converge in her investigation of controversies over adoration of
the cross and crucifix. In challenging the role of the cross and crucifix in
worship, Lollards drew on earlier theological controversies, but also
brought the issue out into a wider world of less learned believers, and
affected contemporary consciousness far beyond the bounds of the movement itself. Surveying an array of different kinds of evidence for Lollard
belief and practice, Aston discovers remarkable consistency in views among
a wide range of heretics across time up to the sixteenth century. While
David Aers is also interested in Lollard ideas of community, he thinks that
the consistency among their views needs closer examination. He shows that
amidst reasonable consistency on key points of belief there can be
considerable difference in emphasis and approach, and that these differences merit attention: the careful study of individual Wycliffites' beliefs,
especially where they seem unusual, can enrich our understanding of the
movement. Aers examines the self-styled "literate layman" Walter Brut's
extensive explanation of his theology of the Eucharist provided in the
context of his trial for heresy. For Walter Brut, Aers contends, the precise
shades of meaning of the terminology involved in scholastic debates over
explaining the Eucharist are not nearly as important as the Eucharist's
significance as a participatory act of faith sustaining Christian community
through salvation history to the end of time. This emphasis is no less
heretical, as it turns out, than the more ordinary emphasis on the theology
of consecration, since Brut's vision of Christian community is inconsistent
with that of the contemporary Church – though also, possibly, with itself.

Brut insists that he is a layman, even though he evidently knew a great
deal about theology. Fiona Somerset's essay suggests another way in which
information about the Eucharist even of a highly technical sort was
available to at least some of the laity. In the process she suggests that we
should reconsider our ideas about the range of possible relationships
between Lollard groups and the larger communities within which they

[6] For the former view, see J.A.F. Thompson (*1189*); for a striking example of trial testimony which
comes into focus when placed in context, see Hudson (*713*, 5) on John Harris.

found themselves. Somerset traces the presence of one dominant strand of Lollard eucharistic thinking through a variety of vernacular as well as Latin texts, Lollard and otherwise, including even one of Chaucer's *Canterbury Tales*. Whereas literary scholars have recently tended to believe that English literate culture was divided among Wycliffites, antiWycliffites, and other vernacular readers and writers who were cowed into silence and ignorance by draconian censorship,[7] it seems likely that instead, outside the Wycliffite/ antiWycliffite nexus, there was a wider noncombatant audience of readers and writers knowledgeable about the heresy, but neither engaged in its persecution, nor (perhaps thanks to their relatively secure social position) vulnerable to reprisal for their interest in it.

How were Lollard beliefs disseminated, and to whom? Increased attention to Wycliffite writings has brought with it increased attention to the manuscripts in which they are preserved. Part III, "Lollards and their Books," includes essays which use manuscript evidence to consider issues of production, audience, and reception.[8] From the earliest work on manuscripts that contain writings identified as Lollard, it has been clear that Lollard writings are in many ways imbricated with the writings of the broader culture within which they were produced: Lollard and orthodox texts appear together in the same manuscripts; works are extant in both orthodox and Lollard (or Lollard-interpolated) versions, and Lollard works (especially versions of their Bible translation) are known to have been owned by members of the gentry and nobility who were not Lollards themselves – or were they? Examples such as these have led to lively debate about whether such cases should be interpreted in terms of competition, contamination, or convergence; over what audiences Lollard writings did have; and about modes of Lollard book production. Heresy and orthodoxy may not always be as separate and clearly demarcated as some previous scholars have assumed.

Hanna's re-evaluation of the part Wycliffite Bible manuscripts played in both the development of Middle English and that of London book production comes to thought-provoking conclusions. He uncovers an alternative mid-fourteenth-century London literary canon, alongside and previous to the much-studied Auchinleck manuscript's romances, consisting of vernacular prose texts of biblical translation and commentary. Focusing on Cambridge, Magdalene College Pepys 2498, Hanna suggests that this manuscript and others related to it, although containing a different (and apparently, for contemporary tastes, inferior) sort of biblical reading than the Wycliffite Bible would soon present, appealed to the same lay appetites for biblical reading. When the Wycliffite Bible supplanted this canon, it too was widely read among orthodox audiences, despite Arundel's attempts at prohibition. This neglected sequence of development suggests that Lollardy was not so marginal or oppositional as has sometimes

---

[7] See, for example, Nicholas Watson (*1265*); and Kathryn Kerby-Fulton (*789*).
[8] The title of this section is drawn from Anne Hudson's collection of early essays on Lollard manuscripts and texts (*67*).

recently been claimed: instead, Lollard books play a central role in the development of vernacular literate culture.[9]

Emily Steiner, on the other hand, lends support to the claim that Lollard books are central to the development of vernacular literate culture precisely through examining their oppositional role. She focuses on a text whose varying versions reveal strong partisan competition between Lollards and anti-Lollards – competition over not only doctrine, but lay reading practices. She shows that different versions of the *Charter of Christ* could and did serve both orthodox and heterodox agendas. Revisions and expansions to the version known as the *Long Charter* after 1400 are designed, she suggests, to "insulate the poem from misreadings and appropriations" by Lollards through the addition of a narrator/mediator who explains how to understand Christ's words.[10]

How were Lollard ideas related to those of their contemporaries? This question has been prominent throughout this collection of essays, and the essays in Part IV, "Heresy, Dissidence, and Reform," turn to confront it squarely by examining dissenting and reformist Lollard ideas within a broader context. These essays reply to the concerns found in the essays in Part I: they help to demonstrate which reformist and dissenting ideas of the Lollards were shared by their predecessors and contemporaries, and they suggest ways in which these commonalities can profitably be examined, as well as ways in which Lollards and their contemporaries need to be more carefully distinguished.

Lawrence Clopper aims to centre his investigation before Lollardy, repositioning texts that present anti-poverty, pro-poverty, or anti-fraternal views, long considered to have been produced by Lollards, in the same earlier period. He shows that texts such as the commentary on the Franciscan *Rule* and *Testament* or the *Fifty Errors and Heresies of the Friars* may actually originate from conflicts within and between fraternal orders, even if they were later put to use by Lollards. His argument has implications for studies that have based large claims on the presence of "Lollard sect vocabulary" in Lollard and other texts: we should instead, he says, think in terms of a broader reformist vocabulary which has more or less specific content depending on the user and his or her purposes.[11]

Orthodox opponents to Lollardy frequently accused its adherents of plotting unrest and even insurrection, as well as of heterodoxy. Barr's essay considers whether there are in fact any links between Lollardy and contemporary civil dissent: after all, in their writings Wycliffites frequently trumpet their obedience to secular authority. Nonetheless, Barr shows that

---

[9] See below, 152–3.

[10] See below, 174.

[11] Anne Hudson's article "A Lollard Sect Vocabulary?" (*698*) has sometimes been cited as if it authorized the classification of any text containing a word the Lollards used as potentially Lollard: scholars such as Clopper (see 187–96) and Matti Peikola (*1031*) are now proceeding more cautiously to consider what sorts of analyses are made possible by the presence of specialized vocabulary.

Lollard attitudes toward the third estate do exhibit distinctive reformist tendencies stemming from their ecclesiology. Wycliffites are far less condemnatory of the poor, and particularly the labouring poor, than is the norm; and they transfer the negative representations of the poor that appear widely in the writing of their predecessors and contemporaries to friars, monks, and prelates. Thus far some of their contemporaries – such as Langland – might follow them. But only Wycliffites go so far as to call for no less than the abolition of the second estate – and this is also where they come closest to converging with the 1381 rebels.

Along with being affected by their reforming and dissenting predecessors and contemporaries, Lollards also affected would-be reformers who came later, although not always in the ways we might assume. Mishtooni Bose positions herself in the mid-fifteenth century in order to consider anew the vernacular ouevre of Bishop Reginald Pecock, whose writings were famously burned as heretical despite his intention to provide an orthodox reforming alternative to Wycliffism. Some critics have claimed that Pecock, drawn into answering the Wycliffites on their own terms, became so infected with Wycliffite discourse that his own writing is difficult to distinguish from theirs.[12] Bose instead pursues a more searching investigation of how Wycliffite as well as other writers influenced Pecock. Surveying Pecock's rhetoric, his experiments with genre, and his use of terminology shared with the Wycliffites, Bose shows that Pecock tries to seal up Wycliffite experimentation with argumentation in the vernacular by imposing a conservative character on it. She suggests that what Pecock can partly reveal to us is the impact of Wycliffite controversies on later attempts to formulate new and separate discourses of reform.

Last, Geoffrey Martin provides a postlude to the volume's revisionist impulses by means of a survey, stretching from Wyclif's near contemporaries up through the work of twentieth-century scholars, of how historians have viewed Wyclif and his followers. Martin's perspective on the preconceptions and assumptions of many of these writers may be especially useful to those trained in literary study, for whom the practice of measuring the distance between historians and their objects of study is relatively new. In the process Martin's essay also provides a prolegomenon to Derrick Pitard's bibliography of every aspect of the past and present study of Lollards and Lollardy.

In introducing readers to the vitality of current work in the field of Wycliffite studies, this volume aims to show the ferment of new ideas and interpretations being discussed among critics in the field rather than to assert fixed conclusions. These essays can serve to bring readers into the field with a sense of how conclusions about the membership of the Lollard movement and their precise beliefs are still open to discussion; to encourage them to be more attentive to the context, genre, and expectations of both Wycliffite and antiWycliffite sources; to consider the significant impact

---

[12] See Bose's n.17.

Lollards may have had on the vernacular book trade in general; and even to expand our notions of reform in the medieval church and of audiences' receptivity to such reform. The contributors offer new methodologies and perspectives, as well as new uses of such traditional approaches as codicology and prosopography, that will provide a gateway to further research in the field. But despite the diversity of new directions represented here, an overall emphasis that emerges with apparent unanimity from the essays in this collection demands the attention of all scholars working in the late medieval field, and beyond. Each of the contributors has stressed how Wycliffites and their writings had influences far beyond the scope, and the membership, of the movement itself. Of course Wycliffites drew the sustained attention of their opponents, and that of their adherents; but their writings were also widely read and their ideas known by a broader audience of lay noncombatants – the same audience, or at least an over-lapping one, that read works of prose devotion, romances, vernacular scientific writings, Chaucer, Langland, Gower, Hoccleve, Lydgate . . . the list goes on. It follows that no scholar of these writings can afford to ignore what else their audience or audiences were also reading. Now that Lollard studies are on the map, everything else seems to have moved.

System of Reference

Italicized numbers that occur in the list of Abbreviations and in notes refer to the numbered references in the Selected Bibliography for Lollard Studies at the end of the volume.

Part I

LOLLERS IN THE WIND

"Heu! quanta desolatio Angliae praestatur":
A Wycliffite Libel and
the Naming of Heretics, Oxford 1382

Wendy Scase

It has become an accepted fact in Wycliffite studies that the first datable use of the term *lollardi* to refer to Wycliffites occurred in Oxford in 1382.[1] The source upon which this claim is based has many times been cited and quoted by students of Lollardy. It is a passage in the Carmelite *Fasciculi Zizaniorum*. The text relates to events associated with the "Earthquake Council" held that year at London's Blackfriars. The Chancellor of the University of Oxford, Robert Rigg, was ordered by the archbishop of Canterbury to publish the Earthquake Council's list of condemned propositions and to prohibit their teaching in Oxford. At first Rigg resisted, but the list was eventually published in Oxford, in English and Latin, on 15 June 1382. Rigg was instructed to prevent Nicholas Hereford, Philip Repingdon, and other named persons from teaching, preaching, and defending these propositions, either in the schools or outside them. Protest and hostility were expected, so Rigg was also ordered to prevent reprisals being taken against those persons who had been involved in helping the archbishop with the matter.[2] The *Fasciculi Zizaniorum* records that, despite this provision, the Cistercian monk Henry Crumpe was suspended from scholastic acts, "quia vocavit haereticos Lollardos":

> ... non obstantibus illis praeceptis, suspenditur Henricus Crumpe, magister in theologia, ab actibus suis, publice, in ecclesia B. Virginis; et imponunt sibi perturbationem pacis, quia vocavit haereticos Lollardos.[3]

Translating this last phrase, in a tradition that goes back at least as far as Foxe, "because he called the heretics 'Lollards,'" scholars have seen this

---

[1] For example, Margaret Aston (*269*, 1, n.1); J.I. Catto (*378*, 216); A.B. Emden (*6*, entry on Crumpe); Anne Hudson (*713*, 2). I followed this interpretation in Scase (*1081*), but found the use of *lollardi* in this context "hard to account for" (154).

[2] W.W. Shirley (*139*, 309–11) gives the text of the archbishop's mandate to Rigg. Also specifically named as suspected of heresy were Wyclif, John Aston and Laurence Bedeman. For a narrative of these events see Catto (*378*, 214–7) and Hudson (*709*, 70–3).

[3] Shirley (*139*, 311–12). ("Notwithstanding the mandate, Henry Crumpe, Master of Theology, was publicly suspended from scholastic acts in the Church of the Blessed Virgin, and he was cited for disturbance of the peace, 'quia vocavit haereticos Lollardos'.")

text as recording a key moment in the early history of Lollardy.[4] In this essay I shall dispute this translation and interpretation of the *Fasciculi* passage. I shall propose that, read critically and in context in the *Fasciculi*, the passage means something rather different. I shall also suggest that there are a number of other texts which can shed light on, and are informed by, what was at stake here. This essay is about some of the broader discursive and textual dimensions of the event mentioned in this passage.

A critical reading of the *Fasciculi* passage alone is enough to cast considerable doubt on it as evidence for the earliest datable use of the word *lollard*. First, it might be objected that this is the statement of a hostile chronicler writing some years distant from the events related. Second, grammatically, there are two possible interpretations of the phrase "quia vocavit haereticos Lollardos": "because he called the heretics 'Lollards,'" *or* "because he called the Lollards 'heretics.'" To the first objection it might be said that we should doubt the interpretation but not the factual claim; to the second that this is an undecidable problem of grammatical ambiguity. There is, however, further material in the *Fasciculi* that provides a check on the statement. The *Fasciculi Zizaniorum* is a narrative of events that is based upon and links together official documents. The narrative here appears to be based principally on a document which calls for Crumpe's reinstatement.[5] This document says that Crumpe had supported the archbishop of Canterbury by condemning the Wycliffites' conclusions as erroneous or heretical. It does not use the word *lollardus*. The word must be that of the Carmelite compiler. Writing some years after the events reported occurred, by which time the term was regularly used to denote Wycliffites, the compiler routinely uses *lollardus*. Moreover, it is clear that the compiler uses *lollardus* when the actors in his narrative are using other terms. For example, relating how Repingdon claimed that John of Gaunt would support the Wycliffites, the Carmelite writes:

> Et inter cetera dixit quod dominus dux Lancastriae multum afficiebatur, et defendere vellet omnes Lollardos; ipsos tamen nominavit sanctos sacerdotes.[6]

This seems to mean that Repingdon said that John of Gaunt called the Lollards "holy priests." Here "sanctos sacerdotes" are the Duke's words (as reported by Repingdon) and "Lollardos" is the narrator's term.

If we examine further the documentary sources that the Carmelite compiler was using, we may strengthen the argument against the traditional interpretation of the *Fasciculi* passage. The documents quoted in the *Fasciculi* support an inference that Crumpe condemned the Wycliffites as heretics. First, there is the evidence of the archbishop's mandate to Rigg.

---

[4] Josiah Pratt, ed., *The Acts and Monuments of John Foxe*, 8 volumes (London: The Religious Tract Society, 1877), 3.30.

[5] Shirley (*139*, 314–17). The *Fasciculi* compiler is writing in the knowledge that Crumpe himself was convicted of unorthodoxy a decade later; see Shirley (*139*, 343–59).

[6] Shirley (*139*, 300). ("And among other things he said that the lord Duke of Lancaster was much moved, and wished to defend all Lollards; notwithstanding he called them 'holy priests.'")

The archbishop anticipated that the denunciation of Hereford and the others as *heretics* would lead to protest and reprisals in Oxford. From the reinstatement document it may be inferred that Crumpe had complained to the king that he had been the victim of just such a reprisal: he was accused of having caused a breach of the peace in an Oxford lecture and suspended. It is less clear whether he had repeated the condemnation in Oxford, and, indeed, whether this is what the compiler means by the statement "imponunt sibi perturbacionem pacis, quia vocavit haereticos Lollardos." By being one of those who drew up the list of condemned propositions, Crumpe had called the Wycliffites heretics: this would have been enough to attract the reprisal and to underpin the *Fasciculi* compiler's statement that he was cited for causing a breach of the peace because he called the Wycliffites heretics. (Note that "quia" is ambiguous too: the compiler could be explaining the motives for the citation of Crumpe (making an inference from the king's letter to Rigg) rather than the reasons for the disturbance of the peace.) But the fact that the king orders Rigg henceforth not to prevent condemnation of the heresies and their perpetrators in the university implies that this is what Crumpe had done. Crumpe *could* have called the Wycliffites *lollardi* in order to offend them. The *lollardus* label would undoubtedly have offended (especially if, as seems likely, some opponents were using the "*lollia*" image when they charged Wycliffites with inciting the Peasants' Revolt, and the Wycliffites were using the term *loller* against the friars).[7] But the *Fasciculi* passage does not provide evidence that he did.

The archbishop's fears of reprisal from the Wycliffites were well-founded. The attack on Crumpe for his part in the denunciation of the heretics was part of a vigorously aggressive Oxford defence of the Wycliffite masters. In defending the heretics by openly disobeying the archbishop's mandate, Rigg's action against Crumpe is typical. Rigg was accused of favouring the Wycliffites by allowing them to preach, and to engage in disputations, even after the Earthquake Council had condemned their propositions. Philip Repingdon preached against the mendicants on 5 June 1382, with Rigg's permission, despite the archbishop's prohibition of further preaching or teaching by the Wycliffites at Oxford.[8] Rigg's and Repingdon's robust responses are characteristic of the way that the Oxford seculars resisted the charge of heresy. The issue became one of university freedom and academic dominance. In reply to the claim that they were heretics (and therefore had no authority to preach and teach in Oxford), the Wycliffites used a number of linked textual strategies to assert their hegemony in the schools. Weaving a web of interlinked texts, they constructed a discursive space in which they were the masters. In the rest of this essay I want to examine a number of different kinds of text, and records of texts, vernacular and Latin, sermon, sermon record, verse, and verse quotation, from which this web was woven. These include the Wycliffite poem "Heu! quanta desolatio Angliae praestatur," edited by Thomas Wright under the title "On the Council of

[7] See further below, and note 20.
[8] Hudson (*709*, 71).

London" and other texts to which, I shall propose, that poem is closely related.[9] "Heu! quanta desolatio" has previously been regarded as being an account of the Blackfriars Council. I propose to argue that the scene it imagines is that of the Oxford schools, and that among the people it satirises we should identify that would-be silencer of the Wycliffites, Henry Crumpe.

A very detailed record of a sermon preached by Nicholas Hereford in Oxford on Ascension Day, 1382 (15 May), not quite a week before the first condemnation was issued at the London Blackfriars, permits us to begin to piece together the textual and polemical context in which Crumpe attracted hostile fire.[10] Hereford's Ascension Day sermon deals with the estates in turn, with, if one may judge from the record, most attention being given to the monks and the friars. Together with the possessioners, the friars built lofty houses and churches and had food and clothing to excess. They begged from the poor, saying that they could not live without their support, and when they had begged enough for their order, then they begged for themselves. They among all men were the most burdensome to the realm; they of all men most perturbed the tranquillity and peace of the kingdom. Only when they remained in their cloisters and lived as they should would peace and tranquillity arise. If the king would take away the goods of the possessioners, it would not be necessary to tax the people so heavily.[11]

The surviving record of the sermon was made not by Hereford himself, but by a public notary who was working for the Carmelite friar Peter Stokes.[12] Stokes himself served as a messenger between the archbishop of Canterbury and Robert Rigg.[13] The record is an abbreviated account of the sermon. More clues about the implications (perceived or alleged) of Hereford's position can be gathered from a complaint about him to John of Gaunt. In February 1382 representatives of the four orders of friars in Oxford wrote to the Duke of Lancaster complaining that Nicholas Hereford was their chief enemy. He and others had been preaching that the friars had caused the Peasants' Revolt of 1381, the previous year. According to these preachers, the people had rebelled because the friars' begging had pauperised the community. Another ground for the charge was that the friars' mendicancy had given a perverse example to serfs and rustics

---

[9] Thomas Wright (*235*, 1.253–63). The poem is item number 7791 in Hans Walther, *Initia Carminum ac Versuum Medii Aevi Posterioris Latinorum* (Göttingen, 1969). Wright's edition is based on London, British Library MS Cotton Cleopatra B. ii. ff. 60r–63r. Four more manuscripts of the poem are now known: Oxford, Bodleian Library, MS Digby 98 ff. 195r–v; Vienna, Österreichische Nationalbibliothek MS 3929, ff. 223v–225; Prague, Metropolitan Chapter MS D.12, ff. 217v–222; and Rome, Vatican Library Pal. lat. 994, ff. 159v–160. The survival of the last three manuscripts was noticed by Anne Hudson (*727*, 656 n.50). I am grateful to Professor Hudson for allowing me to consult her copies of these three continental manuscripts. In this essay I have quoted from Wright's edition, with comments and emendations where manuscript variation is relevant to my arguments. I propose to examine the textual issues in more detail elsewhere in the context of further work on this and other libels.

[10] Simon Forde (*151*). For the date of the condemnation (21 May 1382) see Hudson (*709*, 71 n.19).

[11] Forde (*151*, 239–40).

[12] Forde (*151*, 206).

[13] Hudson (*709*, 68).

who, having become contemptuous of labour, rebelled against their lords. The third ground for the charge was that, as they were responsible for the care of many people's souls, they could have prevented the revolt. However, they did not, and therefore caused lords to turn against people and people to turn against lords.[14]

Nicholas Hereford's Ascension Day sermon seems to have been one of a series of public disputations and sermons calculated to discredit the religious orders. Hereford presented mendicancy as an incitement to the 1381 revolt. The lazy rebels had taken the lazy friars as their model: the rebels were like the friars. The records of the sermon suggest that in May 1382 at least, Hereford used a related image to characterise the friars. This is a matter that I have discussed elsewhere, but I need to summarise my suggestions here for the sake of the argument.[15] The record tells us that he described the friars as "lurdici et loselli."[16] "Lurdici" is an odd word: it must derive from the verb "lordicare" which, in the Benedictine rule known as the Master's Rule, is used to denote the way that a false beggar moves with a bent back in order to feign infirmity and excite the sympathy of patrons.[17] The image used by Hereford, then, was that of the false beggar who feigned infirmity. Wyclif used a similar image in connection with the friars, using the word *trutanni* ("rascally beggars").[18] Hereford's sermon itself was delivered in English, so this raises the question of what English words lie behind the expression "lurdici et loselli" in the Latin record. I propose that Hereford called the friars "lollers and losels." The Middle English verb *lollen*, according to a passage in *Piers Plowman*, denoted the way that a maimed man carried himself. "Loller" then, could be an equivalent for the Latin *lurdicus*. "Lurdici et loselli" is alliterative and one word of the two, *loselli*, is already Latinised Middle English. The C Version of *Piers Plowman*, almost certainly of later date, attests to the alliterative collocation "lollers and losels" and its application to friars:

> . . . frere faytour and folk of þat order,
> That lollares and loseles lele men holdeth . . .[19]

Reversing Hereford's charge against him, the friars accused Hereford of inciting rebellion through his inflammatory preaching. Serf having been turned against lord and man against God, at the suggestion of the serpent, now at the suggestion of the serpent the populace was rising against religious orders. Having failed to prevail against the king, lords and prelates, now the people were turning against simple religious and especially

[14] Shirley (*139*, 292–5).
[15] See a fuller discussion in Scase (*1081*, 152–3).
[16] Forde (*151*, 240/111–12).
[17] R.E. Latham and D.R. Howlett, eds., *Dictionary of Medieval Latin from British Sources* (London, 1975–) oddly glosses this use of *lurdicus* in Hereford's sermon "? fool, dolt," though it cross-refers to *lurdus* "stooped, limping."
[18] Johann Loserth, ed., *Iohannis Wyclif Sermones*, 4 volumes (London: Wyclif Society, 1888), 2.342. This sermon is item no. 161 in Williell R. Thomson (*39*).
[19] *170*, 8.69–74: " . . . friar pretender and folk of that order, Whom loyal men call lollers and losels . . .". Cf. *170*, 9.213–18.

mendicant friars.[20] Because it was preached in English, Hereford's Ascension Day sermon must have been accessible to a large number of Oxford people – this wide appeal, indeed, was clearly the basis of the friars' objections to the Wycliffites' preaching.[21]

This conflict between the Wycliffites and the religious orders was carried on in the schools and the pulpit, and it was also expressed, to an extent and in ways that have not previously been recognised, in satirical verse, including the Wycliffite satire "Heu! quanta desolatio Angliae praestatur." This poem has not previously been associated with the naming and defence of heretics in Oxford, 1382. In my reading, the poem stakes out an alternative discursive space to that of the London Council, a place morally and discursively distant from the Council, a space in which, rather than being silenced as heretics, the Wycliffite masters silence their opponents.

First, a resumé of the poem. "Heu! quanta desolatio" has 49 six-line stanzas, each of them a quatrain followed by a two-line couplet beginning with the vernacular refrain "With an o and an i." Structurally, the poem falls into four sections. The opening six stanzas begin with a lament about the disasters that have befallen England. Plague is weakening the health of the population. Serfs rage wildly. Christ is not known among English people. None of the religious is devout. On account of the sins of the people, an earthquake has occurred. The next section of the poem is a survey of failings in each of the estates. Traders give false measure. Clerics, who should be lights and mirrors to the laity, are immersed in the darkness of rapacity. Prelates are promoted by means of gift, quill, and entreaty. Seventeen stanzas are devoted to failings of members of the religious orders, including, specifically, Franciscan friars and Benedictine monks. Their sins include building fine houses, begging, currying favour with the rich and mistreating the poor. This section closes with a claim by the poet that he used to be a monk, but is one no longer. The final section of 22 stanzas is concerned with disputations over religious poverty, and a series of disputants are named and caricatured. Those named include Wyclif and some prominent followers and their opponents: in the spelling of Wright's edition (based on London, British Library MS Cotton Cleopatra B. ii. ff. 60–63) Johannes Wellis, Nichol Herford, Goydoun, Crophorne, Mertoun, Whappelode, Stokis, and Philippus Repyndoun; one Pers is also mentioned.

"Heu! quanta desolatio Angliae praestatur" was edited by Thomas Wright in *Political Poems and Songs* under the title "On the Council of London" because Wright took the poem to be an account of the London

---

[20] Shirley (*139*, 292–3). It seems to have been first in *this* connection that the term *lollardus* was turned against the Wycliffites. An undated Latin poem on the Peasants' Revolt describes Wyclif's followers as the cause of dissension among clerics and the people and of disturbance in the kingdom. John Ball, the rebel leader, is named in this poem as one who, executed for his part in the rebellion, made manifest the fact that Wyclif's "familia" was the primary cause of the strife (Wright [*235*, 1.235]). This poem labels the Wycliffites "lollardi." The name is explained because they are "zizannia . . . ac lollia" (232, "cockle or tares") spewed out by the enemy of the people, the author of all peril, into the garden of Christ's Church.

[21] Cf. Hudson (*709*, 74–5).

Blackfriars Council which condemned Wyclif and other named followers in 1382. In his introduction, Wright pointed out that the reference to an earthquake in "Heu! quanta desolatio" is to an earthquake that took place on Wednesday, 19 May, 1382.[22] It was a widely-recorded event. At the end of the opening section of the poem, the poet describes the time of its occurrence in extremely revealing terms:

> In hoc terraemotu ab hora diei,
> Quia tunc convenerant scribae, Pharisaei,
> Cum summis sacerdotibus contra Christum Dei,
> Vultus irae patuit divinae faciei.[23]

Wright pointed out that what the poet calls an assembly of scribes and pharisees must be the Council at which the propositions of Wyclif and other named followers were condemned, which took place in London in May and June 1382. The earthquake took place while the Council was in session. Wyclif himself styled the proceedings the "concilium terraemotus."[24] Wright found additional confirmation for this identification of the poem's subject in the closing section of the poem, the section where the poet names names, caricaturing various clerical disputants. Wright read the last section of the poem as a satirical narrative of the proceedings of the Earthquake Council.[25] The poem has not found many commentators, but those who have mentioned it have followed Wright. In his study of antifraternal

---

[22] Wright (*235*, 1.lxiv).

[23] Wright (*235*, 1.254). ("The face of anger appeared in God's divine countenance, in this earthquake, from the hour of the day because then the scribes and pharisees gathered against Christ with the highest priests . . .")

[24] Shirley (*139*, 283), citing Wyclif's *Trialogus*.

[25] Paraphrasing this section in his introduction, Wright wrote: ". . . they were now assembled in council, and the monk of Ramsey, John Welles, began the attack, in a windy and stormy discourse, with a face the colour of gall, which displayed the temper it covered. Wycliffe himself was not present, but his disciple, Nicholas Hereford, replied to Welles, and soon brought him to a stand in his arguments. Then rose another pompous monk, named Goydoun – who was not a regular monk, but a layman in monk's clothing – and undertook to prove that monks ought not to labour, and that friars, though able-bodied men, and capable of earning their living, ought to beg. Crophorne, a man of no fame, spoke less to the purpose than his predecessors, and his arguments were not worth *unum stercus canis* [i.e. 'a dog's turd': Wright delicately does not translate, presumably because any Victorian reader who did not know Latin would be either female or lower-class and so would be in need of moral protection]; he [i.e. Crophorne] and the rest of the monks did no more than 'croak like frogs.' After the monks had done, the friars began, and a Minorite doctor named Merton rose to speak, but only babbled like a raven. Whappelode, who followed, was a notorious liar, a hair-brained fellow, who only proved himself an empty talker. Stokes, who spoke next, displayed a bilious-looking face and an equally bilious temper, yet he laboured through several days to convict the reformers of heresy, though to little purpose. On the last day Nicholas Hereford replied, and, with the assistance of Philip Repingdon, so confuted his accusers that they held down their heads in confusion. Nevertheless, the monks and friars, having filled their purses with the money of the poor, hastened to London, prepared, as the writer says 'to give large thongs out of other people's leather.' They presented themselves before the archbishop, and proclaimed Nicholas Hereford a heretic and Philip Repingdon a madman, while they anointed the prelate's hand with money. The archbishop, thus propitiated, assented to all that the friars demanded. Then the bishop and the friars cited Hereford and Repingdon to appear before them; but when they came they merely abused them, without alleging any substantial charges; and the two subjects of their persecution, perceiving their danger, appealed to the pope." (Wright [*235*, 1.lxvi–ii.])

writing, Penn Szittya says that the poem "denounces the 'Earthquake Council' of 19 May 1382 for its condemnation of the doctrines of Wyclif."[26] George Rigg says much the same as Wright in his *History of Anglo-Latin Literature*.[27]

One problem with Wright's interpretation is that the names in the poem only correspond partially with those of members of the Council. Listed in the *Fasciculi* as having been in attendance at the first session of the Council are ten bishops, six Carmelites, six Dominicans, four Augustinians, five Franciscans, one Benedictine monk, an Oxford bachelor of theology, two bachelors of law, and eleven doctors of canon and civil law. They were joined at the second convocation by eleven more people, and at the fifth session by a further nine persons. Of the persons named as the Wycliffites' opponents in the poem, only two, or possibly three, appear on the lists. The names Whappelode, Goydoun and Mertoun are not listed.[28] John Wells, Benedictine monk, and Peter Stokes, Carmelite friar, do appear on the lists. A manuscript variant possibly conceals the name of a third Council member. Where the manuscript on which Wright based his edition, London, British Library BL MS Cotton Cleopatra B. ii., names "Crophorne," Oxford, Bodleian Library, MS Digby 98, has "Crumphorn," Vienna, Österreichische Nationalbibliothek MS 3929 has "Cromphorn," Prague, Metropolitan Chapter MS D.12 has "Cromphorn," and Vatican Library Pal. lat. 994 has "Cromphorne."[29] Arguably this form of the name – possibly jocular – and the poem's description of this person "Non Anglicus nec Gallicus, nec Francus nec Scotus, Non claustro, sed saeculo se donabat totus" are satirical references to the Irish Cistercian monk, Henry Crumpe.

One explanation for the mismatch in the lists might be that the names of these people mentioned in the poem are concealed under the general phrase "cum aliis pluribus" that appears at the end of the first list of Council members.[30] But, given the care with which the names of members of the orders, lawyers and so on are listed in categories and with other information about them, arguably this general designation is more likely to apply to notarial and secretarial officials who were present at the Council, rather than to those who took part. A second problem with Wright's reading is

---

[26] Penn R. Szittya (*1169*, 194).

[27] A. G. Rigg, *A History of Anglo-Latin Literature 1066–1422* (Cambridge: Cambridge Univ. Press, 1992), 281–2.

[28] Of these, only Mertoun has an entry in Emden (*6*), and that is based on this source. For "Whappelode," Vienna, Österreichische Nationalbibliothek MS 3929, Prague, Metropolitan Chapter MS D.12, and Rome, Vatican Library Pal. lat. 994 read "Fabulot" and Oxford, Bodleian Library, MS Digby 98 reads "Waplode." For "Mertoun," Vienna, Österreichische Nationalbibliothek MS 3929, and Prague, Metropolitan Chapter MS D.12 read "Morton" and Oxford, Bodleian Library, MS Digby 98 reads "Martoun." For "Goydoun," Vienna, Österreichische Nationalbibliothek MS 3929, and Prague, Metropolitan Chapter MS D.12 read "Gaydon"; Oxford, Bodleian Library, MS Digby 98 reads ?"Goyder" for the second instance of the name; and "Goyd[. . .]" (with possible deliberate erasure) for the first instance.

[29] The reading in London, British Library MS Cotton Cleopatra B. ii. has presumably resulted from the omission of a macron.

[30] Shirley (*139*, 288). The delegates who attended the first session are also listed in Oxford, Bodleian Library, MS Bodley 703, ff. 66r–v.

that Hereford and Repingdon were convicted of heresy by the Council; they did not win their arguments as is suggested by the poem.

A solution to the difficulty, I propose, is suggested by the language used to describe the exchanges between the Wycliffites and their opponents. The poet describes how friars preach, and doctors of the orders teach, false fables in the schools, soon spreading false rumours. Another reference to the schools occurs in the stanza after this, which describes John Wells as "determinans," determining. This term, of course, has a precise academic meaning, referring to an act of scholastic disputation. Following lines specify that the setting for debate is "in scholis;" this and the verbs "respondebat," "solvebat," and "argumentare" are all words associated with the university. The frame of reference, I propose, is academic: the exchanges between the Wycliffites and their opponents are imagined in the language and environment of scholastic disputation. As we have seen, many of those named were active in Oxford. Nicholas Hereford and Philip Repingdon were prominent Wycliffite disputants in Oxford. Crumpe, as the *Fasciculi* text shows, was prominent in Oxford as an opponent of the Wycliffites and a public supporter of the Council's condemnation of them as heretics. Wells and Stokes, present at the Council, were also active in Oxford: in acting as an intermediary between Archbishop Courtenay and Robert Rigg, commissioning the report of Hereford's sermon and transmitting the archbishop's mandates, Stokes was assisted by the Benedictine monk John Wells.[31] The poem describes a geographical and discursive distance between Oxford, where the Wycliffites dominate discourse through the power of their argumentation, and London. The imagined scene only shifts to London at the very end of the poem. Having been unable to prevail against the Wycliffites in disputation and preaching, the friars and monks run to London and use the power of others' money to have their opponents condemned:

> Pauperum pecuniis loculos replentes,
> Quantum possunt properant Londonias currentes . . .[32]

"Heu! quanta desolatio" views London and the Council from an imagined position of superiority in Oxford; it also describes and engages with Oxford discursive practices by means of complex modes of intertextuality. In the rest of this essay I propose to use "Heu! quanta desolatio" as a starting-point from which to trace the dense web of intertextuality which the Wycliffites used to capture this discursive space.

"Heu! quanta desolatio" owes a great deal in structure and themes to the genre of estates satire. Poems in this genre satirised each estate in turn, drawing on a common and recurrent stock of satirical topics.[33] The poet's claim that traders give false measure was the usual gripe against this group.

---

[31] Shirley (*139*, 305). Wells was a member of a committee of twelve that had condemned Wyclif's views on the eucharist in 1381 (Hudson [*709*, 68]).

[32] Wright (*235*, 1.263). ("Filling their purses as much as they can with the money of the poor, they hasten running to London . . .")

[33] The classic study is Jill Mann (*914*).

His claim that religious exclude the poor and seduce the rich can be paralleled in many poems. For example, there are close parallels between "Heu! quanta desolatio" and the Middle English poem known as *The Simonie*.[34] Estates satire was a clerical tradition of writing, and usually, as here, the poet made only brief reference to the failings of those who were not clergy. But because in theory all estates of society were at fault, then the poet could not claim to be free from guilt himself. This meant that he had no authority to criticise others. Poets got round this problem of authority by claiming that natural disasters were God's judgement on the sins of the people. The "Heu! quanta desolatio" poet claims that earthquake and plague have come about because of sin. It is God who has passed judgement, not him. This rather closely parallels *The Simonie*, where poor harvests, plague, and disease among livestock are read as signs of God's moral judgement on sin.

However, the contrasts between "Heu! quanta desolatio" and *The Simonie* are perhaps more revealing than the similarities. Poems like *The Simonie* proved highly long-lived. There are redactions of *The Simonie* from the early fourteenth century, the late fourteenth century and the fifteenth century. Doubtless readers continued to find in its prophetic complaints ways of reading and making moral sense of the discomforts and afflictions of their own particular present. A few topical allusions to particular taxes were changed, but the later redactions, studied by Derek Pearsall, show little attempt to update the poem by adding new, specifically topical references.[35] "Heu! quanta desolatio" is rather different. If one can detect in this poem the thematic and rhetorical structures of the estates satire, it is also the case that they have been used as a vehicle for a poem with topical specificity and an identifiable agenda. In its emphasis on the religious orders and in its general order, the treatment of the estates in "Heu! quanta desolatio" parallels that in Hereford's Ascension Day sermon. Like the poet, Hereford dealt first with the laity, then with secular clerics and prelates, then at greater length with possessioners and finally, at even greater length, with the failings of the friars. Hereford's charge that the friars, responsible for people's souls, could and should have prevented the Peasants' Revolt is echoed in "Heu! quanta desolatio," which prefaces its account of pestilence, the wild raging of serfs and the earthquake by praying for divine guidance of the king's mind so that he should recognise the serpent of hypocrisy among the monks and friars. But this allusion to the theme of Hereford's sermon is only one of the poem's many modes of intertextual reference.

"Heu! quanta desolatio" shows awareness that Wycliffites were being labelled heretics, through its defence of named Wycliffite preachers and teachers, and also through the terms applied to them. The term "sanctos sacerdotes," which, according to the *Fasciculi Zizaniorum*, Repingdon

[34] Dan Embree and Elizabeth Urquhart, eds., *The Simonie: A Parallel Text Edition* (Heidelberg, 1991).

[35] See Derek Pearsall, "The Timelessness of *The Simonie*," in *Individuality and Achievement in Middle English Poetry*, ed. O.S. Pickering (Cambridge, 1997), 59–72.

claimed John of Gaunt used as an epithet for Wycliffites, was not a usual one for Lollards – the editor Shirley suggests it is a copyist's error for "simplices sacerdotes" – the more usual term simple (or poor) priests.[36] However, "sanctos sacerdotes" finds an echo in "Heu! quanta desolatio," where the poet asserts that the scribes and pharisees "defame the saints" by imputing them heretics.[37] Continuing on this theme, the poet alludes to and reverses the "cockle/tares" image when he laments that threshed grain is thrown to the winds and the waters.[38] The common Lollard name "trew men" appears in the poem as "viri veritatis."[39] The "Heu! quanta desolatio" poet therefore engages with the battle over labelling the Wycliffites heretics by using terms with which the Wycliffites chose to name themselves.

The work of George Rigg in particular has led to the recognition that debates among clerics generated the circulation in Oxford of short satirical poems that named prominent figures who were important to or actually active in controversies at the university.[40] The Franciscan friar Richard Tryvytlam issued a poem called "De laude universitatis Oxonie." Ostensibly in praise of the university of Oxford, this poem is actually an attack on monks who have been permitted by the university to criticise friars, including Cistercian monk Richard de Lincoln, whose lecherous gluttony rather spoils the reputation of his order for abstinence, and the Benedictine monk Uthred of Boldon, who, the poet says, is aptly named "owt-rede" – "without counsel."[41] George Rigg suggests that an antifraternal poem called "De supersticione phariseorum" was probably composed as a reply to Tryvytlam's verse. Another antifraternal poem, "Sedens super flumina," describes how, like one sitting by the waters of Babylon, the poet laments. He has been deceived by friars but now recognises their evil ways.[42] "Quis dabit meo capiti" opens with a similar reference to biblical lament (this time Jeremiah) and uses the same stanza-form and metre to attack the antimendicant poets.[43] One point of the attack is that those who oppose the friars issue verses against them – but because they are stupid they make mistakes in the metre. Here then, is a reference to the circulation of short polemical verses *and* some possible examples of the genre.

There is good reason for situating "Heu! quanta desolatio" in a similar context, that is, for seeing it as the product of clerical conflict at the

[36] Shirley (*139*, 300n.).
[37] Wright (*235*, 1.254).
[38] Wright (*235*, 1.254).
[39] Wright (*235*, 1.259).
[40] A. G. Rigg, "Two Latin Poems against the Friars," *Mediaeval Studies* 30 (1968): 106–18; and Rigg, *Anglo-Latin Literature*, 269–76.
[41] Rigg, *Anglo-Latin Literature*, 273–4.
[42] Discussed and edited by Penn R. Szittya, " 'Sedens super flumina': A Fourteenth-Century Poem against the Friars," *Mediaeval Studies* 41 (1979): 30–43. See also Rigg, *Anglo-Latin Literature*, 270–1.
[43] Rigg, *Anglo-Latin Literature*, 272. Fiona Somerset has pointed out to me that the use of Jeremiah 9.1 in a sermon attributed to Bernard was an issue in the mid-century conflict between FitzRalph and the friars, as is evidenced by FitzRalph's *Quia in proposicione nuper facta* (Oxford, Bodleian Library, MS Bodley 144, f. 277v). FitzRalph gives Bernard's use of the text as an example of *excitatiue* language use; there were many subsequent polemical and satirical uses of the text. I am grateful to Professor Somerset for this reference.

University of Oxford, and as alluding to this tradition, perhaps even to some of these very poems. Like these poems just mentioned, "Heu! quanta desolatio" names disputants and takes a stand on polemical issues (perhaps playing on the names of Crumpe ("Crumphorn") and others as the earlier poet played with "owt-rede"). It uses precisely the same stanza-form as "Sedens super flumina" and "Quis dabit," including the vernacular o and i refrain. In addition, it shares a satirical device with these poems. The "Sedens" poet claims that he used to be a friar but left the order once he recognised their evil.[44] Likewise, the "Heu! quanta desolatio" poet claims that he was once a novice monk, who had been given a tonsure but had not yet made his profession. Now he has entered into the rule of Christ.[45]

The person who composed "Heu! quanta desolatio" could have had access to "Sedens" in late fourteenth-century Oxford. "Sedens" was collected by one Peter Partriche at Oxford in the early fifteenth century.[46] John Bale saw a copy at Queen's College.[47] Queen's was the college where both John Wyclif and Nicholas Hereford resided. John Wyclif himself quoted "Sedens" in a sermon. The poet laments the friars' desire to be like kings, even though they situate their monastery on the foundations of the seven deadly sins:

> Heu per septem stipites fratres supportantur
> Qui septem mortalia clare designantur,
> Per que monasteria sua situantur.
> Ac venusta pereunt et redintegrantur.
> With an o and an i, vellent esse reges;
> Quod absit a seculo ne confundant leges.[48]

Quoting these lines ("ut dicit metricus"), Wyclif uses a similar image to support his contention that the friars aspire to regal status:

> Et videtur multis fidelibus quod fratres tam singulariter a templo Salomonis et factis suis culpabilibus in suis edificiis exemplum accipiunt, quia vellent ad status regios aspirare, ut dicit metricus:
>> Quod in suo animo
>> Vellent esse reges,
>> Sed absit hoc a seculo
>> Ne confundant leges.[49]

---

[44] Szittya, "Poem against the Friars," 11–12.

[45] Wright (235, 1.258).

[46] For Partriche see the entry in Emden (6).

[47] Szittya (1169, 193); this copy is now lost.

[48] Szittya, "Poem against the Friars," 37–42; Szittya (1169, 193). ("Alas, the friars are supported by seven pillars, which clearly represent the seven mortal sins on which their convents are founded. But beauties pass away and are restored. With an o and an i, they wish to be kings; [?]May that be absent from the world lest they mix up the laws.")

[49] Loserth, *Wyclif Sermones*, 2.121, from Cambridge, Trinity College, MS B.16.2. This is an editorial compilation of Wyclif's sermons, produced between 1382 and 1384 (Thomson [39, 99]); the sermon is item number 130 in Thomson's catalogue (128). Wyclif has "Quod in suo animo" where "Sedens super flumina" has the refrain "With an o and an i"; possibly the scribe has misread the vernacular refrain as abbreviated Latin words. See n. 64 below for another instance of miscopying of the vernacular. ("And it seems to many believers that the friars have taken their

Bale proposed that the author of "Sedens" was the apostate Augustinian friar Peter Pateshull. Possibly the reason Bale attributed the poem to Pateshull was that Thomas Walsingham described how Pateshull, a Wycliffite sympathiser, caused uproar by preaching against his order in London in 1387. Afterwards, at the instigation of some Wycliffites, he wrote down his charges and nailed them to St Paul's in London; copies were made and circulated by knights.[50] Bale may have thought that "Sedens" was one of Pateshull's libels because the poet describes himself as an apostate friar.[51] Overturning Bale's attribution of "Sedens" to Peter Pateshull, Penn Szittya argued that it should be associated with the conflict between the friars and Richard FitzRalph (d.1360). His grounds for this claim were his reading of "Sedens" as a "companion poem" to "Quis dabit capiti" which attacks FitzRalph.[52] Even if this mid-century dating is correct, it is clear that "Sedens" seemed highly meaningful to Oxford Wycliffites in the 1380s. Given too, the composition of "Heu! quanta desolatio" in this tradition in the 1380s and the absence of any explicit reference to the 1360s controversy or its protagonists in "Sedens," it may be time to relocate "Sedens" as part of a tissue of texts and intertexts that made up the Wycliffites' claimed discursive territory in the 1380s – to relocate it, not to London, 1387, but to Oxford, 1382.[53] This reading would fit particularly well with stanzas which complain that the friars say that the secular clerics' books are full of error; when the friars cannot prevail in disputation ("arte"), they defame and berate the seculars publicly:

> Isti fratres disputant de libris clericorum,
> Dicentes quod sunt pessimi ac pleni errorum.
> Quid mirum si nesciant intellectum horum
> Cum carent principiis hii philosophorum.
> With an o and an i, discant sua prima
> Et sic demum disputent horum de doctrina.
>
> Clericos cum nequeunt fratres superare
> Hos detraccionibus querunt impugnare
> Atque in sermonibus illos depravare.
> Et sic nituntur nequiter clerum defamare.

example from the temple of Solomon and his blameworthy deeds in their buildings, because they wish to aspire to regal status, as the verse says: 'Because they wish in their heart to be kings; [?]But may this be absent from the world lest they mix up the laws.'")

[50] Walsingham (*221*, 2.157–9).

[51] Szittya, "Poem against the Friars," 33.

[52] Szittya, "Poem against the Friars," 34–5. Rigg too sees "Quis dabit" as a reply to "Sedens": *Anglo-Latin Literature*, 272.

[53] On this point about the relationship between the Oxford verse and Pateshull's and other Lollard bill campaigns see further below. A text which might resemble part of one of the Pateshull bills as described by Walsingham survives in the *Fasciculi Zizaniorum* (Shirley [*139*, 369]), where it is associated with the "Twelve Conclusions of the Lollards" of 1395, and in London, British Library, MS Cotton Vespasian D.ix, f. 48. I propose to discuss this elsewhere. On the question of the date of "Sedens" and its links with the 1360s dispute between the friars and the secular clergy, it should be noted that reference to FitzRalph is not in any case necessarily an indication of a mid-century date: "Heu! quanta desolatio" explicitly refers to Richard FitzRalph, as does Hereford's Ascension Day sermon; clearly FitzRalph's polemic was of great interest to those involved in the mendicant controversies of the 1380s.

With an o and an i, cum non possunt arte
Superare clericos, rixantur aperte.[54]

A similar claim is made in "Heu! quanta desolatio," where it is said that friars preach and the doctors of the orders teach fictions in the schools: true men are greatly defamed by their abridged sayings:

. . . falsas fabulas fratres praedicarent,
Et doctores ordinum scholis doctrinarent,
Per quas famas floridas in sonitum [n]igrarent.
With an o and an i, viri veritatis
Multum diffamati sunt dictis contractatis.[55]

These are further examples of close intertextual relations between sermons and poems like that between Hereford's sermon and "Heu! quanta desolatio." Another example of sermon-poem intertextuality concerns one of Wyclif's sermons. In a sermon attacking "private religions," that is, the orders of monks and friars, Wyclif defended himself against the charge of a Carmelite friar who had called him a fox in a public sermon: he himself called the Carmelite and the black monks alike great dogs, and he rejoiced that the friars and the monks were brought together like Herod and Pilate:

Voco autem istum dompnum et sibi similes canes magni, quia sic vocavit Carmelita publice predicando me vulpem et ipsos canes vulpem illam usque ad exitum insequentes. Et gaudeo quod sunt adeo concordati tamquam Herodes et Pilatus quod omnes iste religiones private sunt, ut idem niger canis asserit, essencialiter idem ordo.[56]

The same point and image are associated in "Heu! quanta desolatio"; here

---

[54] Szittya, "Poem against the Friars," 85–96. ("These friars dispute about the books of clerics, saying that they are very bad and full of errors. What wonder if they do not know their meaning, when they lack the principles of philosophers. With an o and an i, let them learn first principles and thus at last let them dispute about doctrine. When friars cannot prevail over clerics, they seek to impugn them with detraction and to slander them in sermons. And thus shamefully they try to defame the clergy. With an o and an i, when they cannot overcome clerics with skill, they quarrel openly.")

[55] Wright (235, 1.259). Wright reads "migrarent" in line 3. I have emended to the reading in Vienna, Österreichische Nationalbibliothek MS 3929; Prague, Metropolitan Chapter MS D.12 and Rome, Vatican Library Pal. lat. 994. The Wycliffites' opponents' practice of making a notarial record of their sermons – as Peter Stokes did of Hereford's sermon – would be one possible interpretation of the poet's claim that their enemies defame true men "dictis contractatis" – with abridged sayings – this expression would also include the drawing up of series of condemned propositions, as the Blackfriars Council did. (". . . friars preached false fictions and doctors of the orders taught in the schools, through which they blackened their fair reputation in sound. With an o and an i, men of truth are much defamed by abridged statements.")

[56] Loserth, *Wyclif Sermones*, 3.246–7; Thomson (39, 156, item no. 205). Thomson followed Loserth in identifying the black monk as John Wells but doubted Loserth's identification of the Carmelite as Peter Stokes. The passage is quoted in the *Fasciculi Zizaniorum*, where Bale identified the monk as Wells; the heading however has "Willielmi monachi de Ramseye" (Shirley [139, 239]). ("But I call this master and those like him 'great dogs,' because by preaching the Carmelite publicly called me a fox, and themselves dogs, pursuing that fox to the end. And I rejoice that they are united to such an extent as Herod and Pilate, in that, as the same black dog asserts, all these private religious orders are essentially the same order.")

Wyclif is praised as the principal agent of concord between the friars and the monks:

> With an o and an i, sit Deus beatus,
> His amici facti sunt Herodes et Pilatus.
> Armacan, quem coelo Dominus coronavit,
> Discordes tantomodo fratres adunavit;
> Sed magno miraculo Wyclif coruscavit,
> Cum fratres et monachos simul collocavit.
> With an o and an i, consortes effecti,
> Quovis adversario dicunt sunt protecti.[57]

God has crowned FitzRalph in heaven for uniting the orders of friars, but Wyclif has performed a great miracle by bringing together Herod and Pilate: the friars and the monks.

It has recently been suggested that "Heu! quanta desolatio" names Piers Plowman. If this is the case, this suggests a further layer of intertextuality. The suggestion is based on an interpretation of a line against the friars that runs:

> With an o and an i, fuerunt pyed freres;
> Quomodo mutati sunt rogo dicat Pers.[58]

George Rigg translates:

> With an O and an I – they wore motley habit;
> For the tale of how they've changed, ask Piers – he will have it.[59]

Rigg makes a convincing case that the reference is to the Carmelites, whose habit *was* "pied," being two colours – brown and white, saying that the "poet notes that Piers (presumably Piers Plowman) can testify to the degeneracy of modern friars."[60] Rigg does not explain the reasons for his assumption, but he does cite *Pierce the Plowman's Crede*, a poem in which the Carmelites are criticised and the ploughman Pierce is the only person who can teach the narrator his creed. This poem is dated too late for it to explain the possible allusion here, however.[61] But there are, of course, earlier possibilities. *Piers Plowman* was in circulation in some form by this date. In 1381, as is well-known, the rebels used the name of Piers Plowman in some of their cryptic vernacular letters, and Piers became identified as a leader of the Peasants' Revolt – a belief witnessed by the *Dieulacres Chronicle*.[62] By 1382, Piers was an antifraternal name.

---

[57] Wright (*235*, 1.259). ("With an o and an i, may God be blessed, Herod and Pilate are made friends by these. Armacan [Richard FitzRalph] whom the Lord has crowned in heaven, only united the quarrelling friars, but Wyclif dazzled us with a great miracle when he brought together friars and monks. With an o and an i, they have been made partners: they say they are protected from any adversary.")

[58] Wright (*235*, 1.262).

[59] Rigg, *Anglo-Latin Literature*, 282.

[60] Rigg, *Anglo-Latin Literature*, 281.

[61] Cf. Kathryn Kerby-Fulton (*789*, 336 n.82).

[62] For texts of the rebels' letters see Steven Justice (*765*, 13–15). For the passage in the *Dieulacres Chronicle* see M.V. Clarke and V.H. Galbraith, "The Deposition of Richard II," *Bulletin of the John Rylands Library* 14 (1930), 125–81: 164.

There is, however, another possible interpretation. The passage on the Carmelites begins with a description of a disputant "Stokis nominatus." This of course is a clear reference to Hereford's Carmelite enemy. Stokes's Christian name was Peter. So an interpretation might be – "Let Peter [i.e. Stokes] tell how the friars have changed [that is, have degenerated from the time of their earliest foundation]." Indeed, the poet goes on to discuss the Carmelites' foundation stories.[63] But there is a further possibility: arguably the two readings co-exist productively.

In "Heu! quanta desolatio," the name "Pers" is clearly vernacular; its vernacularity is confirmed by the chime of the rhyme with "Pyed freres," also vernacular.[64] This code-switching is a feature of the poem. The refrain "with an o and an i" is a vernacular jingle, repeatedly reminding the reader of those others beyond the discursive space of the schools: not the members of the London Council, but the laity to whom the Wycliffites' sermons appeal. (As I noted in connection with the friars' letter to Gaunt, it was the power of the Wycliffites' appeal to the laity that the friars seemed to fear most.) Advertising this ability to code-switch (and to appeal to a lay audience), the poet invites the reader to imagine rich mendicant Peter Stokes from the perspective of poor Piers.

The manuscript environment of "Heu! quanta desolatio" gives further evidence of the textual cultures with which it is associated and the intertextual space that it occupies. One of the surviving copies of "Heu! quanta desolatio" is in Partriche's manuscript, Oxford, Bodleian Library, MS Digby 98, the manuscript containing the sole surviving copy of "Sedens." This in itself suggests that the poem belongs with Oxford polemical verse of the "Sedens" variety.[65] But the manner of the poem's preservation in this manuscript also suggests much about the method of its dissemination in Oxford. "Heu! quanta desolatio" survives on a single leaf of vellum that has been sewn into the manuscript book sideways.[66] That is,

---

[63] Kerby-Fulton (789, 336 n.82) argues against identification of "Pers" with Peter Stokes and in favour of a reference to Piers Plowman on the grounds that the Carmelite friar "would hardly have been represented as uttering the antimendicant comment attributed in the poem to 'Pers,'" without mentioning the reference to "Stokis," or the possibility of irony here.

[64] The vernacular name would not, presumably, have meant much – either as a name or as a poetic reference – to the copyists of the continental manuscripts of the poem, hence, presumably, the readings "peris" (Vienna, Österreichische Nationalbibliothek MS 3929), "perijs" (Prague, Metropolitan Chapter MS D.12), and "pere" (Rome, Vatican Library Pal. lat. 994).

[65] Cf. Szittya (1169, 194).

[66] Oxford, Bodleian Library, MS Digby 98, f. 195. The top of the piece of vellum has been folded back 9mm and the vellum has been sewn along this fold into the codex between quires 9 and 10. The sheet of vellum measures 282mm long, plus the stub of 9mm, and 193mm wide at the loose end tapering to 180mm wide at the sewn end. It has been folded in half widthways in order to fit into the book. The poem is set out in three columns and there is text on both sides of the vellum. A later hand wrote some notes on the vellum, including a line from "Sedens super flumina" (line 113). This hand is not Partriche's, but also occurs on ff. 1 and 3v so the notes must have been written after the bill was sewn into the volume. For a description of this manuscript see the entries in G.D. Macray, *Catalogi Codicum Manuscriptorum Bibliothecae Bodleianae* (Oxford, 1883), and R.W. Hunt and A.G. Watson, *Bodleian Library Quarto Catalogues IX Digby Manuscripts 2 Notes on Macray's Description of Manuscripts* (Oxford, 1997), 53–4. I am indebted to Dr. Bruce Barker-Benfield of the Bodleian Library for permitting and helping me to examine this very fragile manuscript.

this is a little piece of vellum designed to be circulated separately from a book, as a single sheet to be passed around and perhaps displayed; a form often called a "libel," "bill" or "broadside."[67] It is a very rare physical survival of the method of circulation that Pateshull and his knightly accomplices allegedly used in London, and that "Quis dabit" claims was used in Oxford.

Another poem which may be textually related to the Oxford controversy is "Vox in Rama." This text is extremely hard to situate because it includes only the most coded of allusions. It is clearly a poem written in favour of the possessioners, however. George Rigg suggests that absence of mention of Wyclif's views must mean that it predates 1377.[68] Another possibility, however, is that it is closely associated with the texts of 1382. It has the same metre and o and i refrain as "Heu! quanta desolatio," it begins with an allusion to a biblical lamentation – this time that of Rachel in Rama – and it suggests that a serpent is deceiving the people, using an image shared by "Heu! quanta desolatio," and the polemic between Hereford and the friars.[69] But by contrast with "Heu! quanta desolatio" it is notably circumspect about labelling sects and naming names:

> Reprehendo genera tamen singulorum
> Et nequaquam singula generum ipsorum.
> Non est secta integra de sectis cunctorum
> Que non ponat lolium inter grana morum.[70]

The reference to cockle and tares ("lolia") is here, but it is not attached to any individual. Such circumspection would have been wise in the climate faced in Oxford by religious opponents of the Wycliffites. Peter Stokes, named in "Heu! quanta desolatio" as a disputant whom Repingdon demolished, was too frightened to appear at Repingdon's sermon where town and gown supported the Wycliffite, and armed men were present.[71] As we have seen, Crumpe met with reprisal for his part in the condemnation of the Wycliffites as heretics and was suspended from preaching and teaching. The robust Oxford response to the judgements of the Council would have provided an environment in which the proWycliffite poem "Heu! quanta desolatio" could circulate as a libel that publicly defended named Wycliffites and denounced named opponents – an environment which would explain the cautious circumspection of "Vox in Rama."

"Heu! quanta desolatio" and "Sedens" circulated in Latin, among clerics, and were associated with a concern to defend academic privileges and freedoms. The continued interest in these texts in Oxford in the first decade

---

[67] See further on libels, Wendy Scase (*1084*).

[68] Rigg, *Anglo-Latin Literature*, 384 n.128 (but contrast 280). This poem has not been edited. I am indebted to Professor Rigg for supplying me with a copy of his unpublished edition and translation.

[69] Shirley (*139*, 292–3).

[70] A. G. Rigg, unpublished edition and translation. Rigg translates: "Yet I reprove the classes of individuals And not the individuals of those classes. From all the sects there's not one sect entire That doesn't spread its tares among the moral grain."

[71] Shirley (*139*, 306).

of the fifteenth century, witnessed by the book made by Peter Partriche, suggests that they continued to be of interest when academic freedoms were considered to be under threat.[72] But another development was the Lollard bill: a tradition of distribution of polemical bills and pamphlets, attested by surviving examples, such as the schedules circulated by John Aston in London and the "Twelve Conclusions of the Lollards," posted on the doors of parliament; as well as by the records of chroniclers about campaigns such as Pateshull's.[73] Arguably, as well as continuing to be of interest in academic circles, "Heu! quanta desolatio" and "Sedens" found another reflex in this tradition of Wycliffite bills. These libels replied to the pronouncement of heresy by asserting Wycliffite hegemony in the academy. However, with their dense intertextualities, their relation with the vernacular, with vernacular sermons, even, perhaps, with *Piers Plowman*, these verses were already pointing in the direction of new discursive spaces, beyond the academy, and beyond Oxford; pointing not towards London Blackfriars, but towards parliament and the streets.

---

[72] For the struggle over academic freedom at Oxford in the first decade of the fifteenth century see Catto (*378*, 238–53). However, the continental manuscripts of "Heu! quanta desolatio" show that interest in the poem extended far beyond Oxford: two manuscripts are of Bohemian origin and a third is probably French. See Hudson (*727*, 656).

[73] For John Aston's schedules see Shirley (*139*, 329–30). For the "Twelve Conclusions of the Lollards" see Scase (*1084*, 240–1) and references there. There is evidence that Hereford and Repingdon also distributed bills, though these do not survive (Anne Hudson, "Some Aspects of Lollard Book Production," in *67*, 183–4).

William Langland and the Invention of Lollardy

Andrew Cole

Since the 1980s, there has been a resurgence of interest in Wycliffism owing to the new editions and specialized research by Anne Hudson, Pamela Gradon, Margaret Aston, and others. Yet the relevance that this renaissance has on the study of Langland remains to be seen. For contemporary scholars usually describe the differences, not similarities, between the poet and his Wycliffite contemporaries, so as not to repeat the errors of Reformation readers who were "so enthusiastic about trying to show that Langland had Wycliffite sympathies."[1] Gradon, in fact, was the first scholar to stifle the centuries' old enthusiasm for a Wycliffite Langland by persuasively demonstrating that the apparent likenesses of thought between any version of *Piers Plowman* and Wycliffism are, rather, mutual expressions of common ideas held by many in the late Middle Ages.[2] She had, in other words, effectively disabused criticism of the notion that close proximity alone between Langland and these reformers should be reason enough to gloss *Piers Plowman* with Wycliffite texts, as Derek Pearsall had done in his 1978 edition of C, and as Skeat had done before him.[3] Indeed, with few exceptions, Langlandians, who work in one of the more lively and polemical quarters of late medieval English studies, are surprisingly at a consensus with Gradon.[4] Some even continue to widen the gulf between

My gratitude goes to the Bodleian Library of Oxford University and the British Library, London, for permission to cite from their manuscripts and for making my visit a pleasant one. This essay draws from my nearly completed book, *Heresy et al.* I thank David Aers, Katie Little, and Fiona Somerset for commenting on this piece.

[1] Christina von Nolcken (*1243*, 74).

[2] Pamela Gradon (*608*).

[3] *Piers Plowman by William Langland: An Edition of the C-text* (*170*). For comment, see Anne Hudson (*712*, 254).

[4] Here are the exceptions. David Aers has argued that Langland's wavering from orthodox ideology pushed him, by default, into a heterodox position characterized by Wycliffite dissent (*Chaucer, Langland, and the Creative Imagination* [London: Routledge and Kegan Paul, 1980], 59). In his more recent work, Aers has effectively shown that *Piers Plowman* and Wycliffite texts share a critical position toward dominant representations of Christ's suffering humanity while advocating alternative and resistant models to devotion and apostleship; see "The Humanity of Christ: Representations in Wycliffite Texts and *Piers Plowman*," in Aers and Lynn Staley (*263*, 43–76). James Simpson has, briefly, compared Langland's ecclesiology to Wyclif's (*Piers Plowman: An Introduction to the B-text* [London: Longman, 1990], 180, 227). Investigating the vernacular sources to the Tree of Charity, I have traced the similarities between Wycliffite (and reformist) uses of three estates theory and Langland's in "Trifunctionality and the Tree of Charity: Literary and Social Practice in *Piers Plowman*" (*399*, 4–5).

Langland and these heterodox contemporaries, arguing that the poet shows, in his revisions from B to C, an increased anxiety not only about heretical subjects but about retribution from censors on the look-out for offensive Wycliffite matter.[5]

Yet for Gradon and subsequent critics there's a devil in the details, namely the problem raised by a single but very important word in *Piers Plowman* – "lollare." If Langland distances himself from Wycliffite controversies, why is it that in the C-text he writes rather obsessively about "lollares," the same word used in orthodox circles to castigate the Wycliffites? Would it not seem likely that Langland's "lollares" are – there is no other way to put it – "lollares?"[6] Gradon answers in the negative, writing that it is "improbable that Langland's *lollers* [in the C-text] are Lollards, and the fact that the word *lollers* is used already in the B-text (Bxv.213) would support this contention."[7] She assumes that when Langland discusses "lollares" in C, he in essence expands his own, albeit brief, treatment in B: "Piers the Plowman – *Petrus, id est, Christus.* / For he nys noght in lolleris ne in londleperis heremytes" (15.212–13).[8] Thus Gradon finds that Langland so prefers his own sense of the term as to ignore the (anti)Wycliffite meaning that was purportedly circulating since 1382, when a Cistercian monk, Henry Crumpe, stepped out at Oxford and proclaimed the Wycliffites to be "Lollardos."[9] So what are "lollares" then? In answering, Gradon chooses a definition that comprehends virtually all the discourses of anti-vagrancy in England and on the continent: despicable "lollares" are *gyrovagi,* "wandering religious who had left their houses and joined the numerous wayfarers who infested fourteenth-century

---

[5] "It is as if the C reviser were trying to protect the poem from allegations of Lollardy levelled against the earlier versions" (David Lawton, "English Poetry and English Society, 1370–1400," in *The Radical Reader*, ed. Stephen Knight and Michael Wilding [Sydney: Wild and Woolley, 1977], 152; cf. his comment below); von Nolcken (*1243*, 78–82); John M. Bowers (*336*, 13). Kathryn Kerby-Fulton writes that "creeping political and ecclesiastical intimidation finally limited what [Langland] felt able to say on the subject of socio-political oppression and clerical abuse," leaving him to foreground his "latent social conservatism" in C ("*Piers Plowman,*" in Wallace *90*, 522). See also her "Langland and the Bibliographic Ego": "Langland made significant alterations in his final version [the C-text] so as to suppress the ideas most likely to offend" (*70*, 75). Yet if it can be shown that Langland's new "lollare" material responds directly to Wycliffite and anti-Wycliffite controversies, then these aforementioned opinions will have to be adjusted.

[6] In Middle English, "lollare" is a widely attested form of "lollard." Lawton, in the same essay cited above, made a challenging, though unfortunately unsubstantiated, claim: "I cannot accept the dictum that Langland means no reference to Lollards when he uses the word 'lollare,' although this is the usual scholarly view. It simply does not explain why 'lollare' suddenly becomes a favourite word in the C Text" ("English Poetry and English Society," 152). Lawrence Clopper, however, finds no Wycliffite significance to Langland's "lollares" (*70*, 158–59), a view that is consistent with his thesis that Langland is fascinated with earlier Franciscan heresies and totally unconcerned with the heresy that is Wycliffism (*70*, 164–65). Clopper elaborates upon these points in *"Songes of Rechelesenesse": Langland and the Franciscans* (*398*, 9, 33–34, 54, 66, 92, 103, 205, 208, 234, 320).

[7] Gradon (*608*, 197).

[8] *The Vision of Piers Plowman: A Complete Edition of the B-Text* (*169*), cited by passus and line.

[9] See Gradon (*608*, 196 n.1), referencing James Crompton, who recounts the received etymology of the term (*440*, 11). For the reference to Crumpe, see *Fasciculi Zizaniorum Magistri Johannis Wyclif cum Tritico* (hereafter *FZ*; *139*, 311–12).

England."[10] But the problem remains: do those notorious, wandering "lollards" belong to that infestation of "wayfarers?" Are they any different?

Scase addresses precisely this question and brings to bear a fascinating range of material to explain "lollare" discourse in the late fourteenth century. Her work has been rightly well-received and influential.[11] Scase builds on earlier research by Morton Bloomfield and Penn Szittya, showing that the longstanding satire about clerical duties, privileges, and negligence are refashioned into a new and more expansive critique in which friars, extra-regulars, the poor, and the laity are described with anti-monastic aspersions.[12] Yet despite her focus on the novelty of late fourteenth-century anticlericalism, Scase proposes a definition of "lollare" that, like Gradon's, preserves an older, pre-Wycliffite sense: Langland defines his "lollers" as gyrovagues:

> What we have described as the 'Piers Plowman sense' of 'loller' seems only briefly to have been viable. Usage in the poem, and in contemporary and later writings, suggest that it was only possible for a short time in late-fourteenth century England to use 'loller' as a satirical term for those who were defined by the law of Christ as the gyrovagues of the contemporary church. The evidence suggests that this definition was maintained despite (and most probably because of) the growing use of the near-homonym 'lollard' for the heretics who followed the teachings of Wyclif, but that the 'Piers Plowman sense' soon lost ground in competition with the other usage.[13]

Scase's definition, in so far as it underscores the difference between Langlandian and anti-Wycliffite senses of "loller," seems to rest on a premise that Langland's "lollers" in both B and C predate the anti-Wycliffite sense of the 1380s.[14] What of "lollares [lollards]" then?[15] Scase suggests that the '"Piers Plowman sense' of 'loller"' is unique, a hapax legomenon, "most probably because of the growing use of the near-homonym 'lollard' for the heretics who followed the teachings of Wyclif."[16] For a poet whom we know to be so attuned to local contro-

---

[10] Gradon (608, 196).

[11] Lawton predicted the importance of Scase's work for Langland studies; see his review in *Yearbook of Langland Studies* 4 (1990): 176–80.

[12] M.W. Bloomfield, *Piers Plowman as a Fourteenth-Century Apocalypse* (New Brunswick, NJ: Rutgers Univ. Press, 1962); Penn Szittya (1169).

[13] Wendy Scase (1081, 155; also see 150–51, 152).

[14] See Scase (1081, 151).

[15] Hudson says of the B-text "lolleris" that "[i]ts sense seems unlikely to be the technical one of 'follower of Wyclif', not only because of the date of the B version but also from its apparent rough equivalence with 'hermits' and 'anchorites'. In the C text the word is more common. At some occurrences it would appear to mean much the same as the one case in B, a 'religious eccentric' at the most specific" (713, 407). By deduction, so too, the C-text sense does not comprehend the anti-Wycliffite sense (ibid.). Kerby-Fulton builds on Hudson's and Scase's point, also understanding that "Langland provides his own definition of the word in this new passage (C9.213–218), a word which he used without defining in the B-text, and which in C he defends (at least apparently) on the basis of a traditionally English usage ('As by þe Engelisch of oure eldres, of olde mennes techynge,' 214) – a point which suggests he is *now* aware of an alternative use . . ." ("Langland and the Bibliographic Ego," 70, 102–03).

[16] I have removed Scase's parenthesis given in the block quotation.

versies, Langland surprisingly commits a "tactical error," as one critic believes, that would have modern readers puzzled over Langland's sense, wishing that the poet were indeed writing about familiar "lollards."[17] What is evident, to me at least, is that the divisions critics cast between Langland and Wycliffite contexts operate, sometimes perplexingly, on the level of a single word and that what always remains to be explained (or explained away) is the obvious homology between the poet's and other "lollares."[18]

1382: Not a Good Year for Lollards

I will suggest that Langland in his C-text registers and responds explicitly to the anti-Wycliffite sense of "lollare [lollard]." But before I argue this point, it seems necessary to spend this and the next two sections revisiting some of the textual and historical evidence on which contemporary critics have based their conclusions about "lollardy" and Langland. In this section, I want to re-calibrate the rule that measures the distance between *Piers Plowman* C and "lollare [lollard]" discourse – the rule being that the term "lollard" was first used in England in 1382, ever since Crumpe called the Wycliffites "Lollardos."[19] This episode has been pivotal for Langland scholarship, because it indicates that Langland had the opportunity to absorb about five years' worth of usages before writing C.[20] To some critics, Langland's use looks puzzlingly distinct because Langland seems to be writing *after* a touchstone sense had been advanced, deemed scandalous, and found "prominence in religious discourse" – "lollards" as "Wycliffite heretics."[21] A closer look at the episode and related texts seriously challenges this notion.

[17] Bowers (*336*, 15). Middleton adjusts Scase's account (*952*, 286), suggesting a "broad lay sense of the term" (282), meaning "an offender against the unwritten decorum that 'religion' is a marked discourse, appropriate for occasions so designated, and not at other times" (283; also 284–285).

[18] In other words, we can go farther than the suggestion that in "*Piers Plowman* the word 'loller' is used to denote the gyrovagues of the late fourteenth-century church in England. The choice of this word was appropriate to the tradition of naming this genus in antireligious satire. . . . [T]he commentary given on 'loller' in *Piers Plowman* evokes the essence of the genus . . . Such a word is appropriate to the essence of the false-hermit genus" (*1081*, 151–52). I will be studying the essence of Langland's "loller" as it attaches to contemporary uses of the same term. Relevant here is Pearsall's remark that "Langland is conscious . . . of the *gyrovagi* or wandering monks who violated the Benedictine rule of stability, though he may not be conscious of the historical context into which this attitude towards wandering needs to be set" (*1026*, 171). I take Pearsall to be referring to the earlier contexts discussed by Scase and others.

[19] "Whatever the origin of the term *Lollard*, its first recorded use in England to refer to a definable religious sect occurred in 1382 when Henry Crumpe was suspended from academic acts in the university for calling the 'heretics' *Lollardi*" (Hudson *713*, 2).

[20] I follow the consensus on the dates of Langland's versions, A (1367–70) and B (c.1377–79), established by J.A.W. Bennett, "The Date of the A-text of *Piers Plowman*," *PMLA* 58 (1943): 566–72; "The Date of the B-Text of *Piers Plowman*," *Medium Ævum* 12 (1943): 55–64. One could fairly question these dates, however.

[21] "Whatever work the word is doing here [in *Piers Plowman*], its prominence within religious discourse is datable from late Spring 1382, when an Oxford don was censured for insulting some of his fellows as Lollardi" (Ralph Hanna, "Emendation to a 1993 'Vita de Ne'erdowel,'" *Yearbook of Langland Studies* 14 [2000]: 190). See also Lorraine Kochanske Stock, "Parable, Allegory, History, and *Piers Plowman*," *Yearbook of Langland Studies* 5 (1991): 159.

Crumpe's story is told in the Carmelite *Fasciculi Zizaniorum*, a compilation of anti-Wycliffite documents recopied and strung together by a narrative detailing the rise and condemnation of Wycliffism. Crumpe had sat and determined on the Blackfriars Council, first held in May, which condemned twenty-four conclusions of Wyclif's (though Wyclif remained unnamed in the publications of the proceedings).[22] About a month later, after several of Wyclif's disciples had stood trial for holding these conclusions, Crumpe apparently celebrated the anti-Wycliffite cause by publicly condemning these Wycliffites as "Lollardos."[23] As a result of this extra-council proclamation, which was reported to have disturbed the peace, he was suspended from scholastic acts. The nature of this disturbance is difficult to know; Crumpe was eventually reinstated, only to be accused of heresy some years later.[24] Notwithstanding, this entry, which supposedly marks the advent of "lollard(y)," is not a primary document from 1382 (like the other episcopal and regal mandates compiled in this chronicle). Rather it is part of the *FZ*'s continuous narrative linking the primary documents themselves, a narrative written, as James Crompton believes, "sometime between 1393 and 1399."[25] Of course, to prove the existence of the term "lollard" in 1382, we need evidence other than accounts of 1382 written ten to fifteen years afterwards. Documents from 1382 designating "lollards" have yet to be produced.

One could, however, produce that notarial account from 1382 that documents a Wycliffite, Nicholas Hereford, preaching a scandalous Ascension Day sermon in English. The notary, who was commissioned by the Carmelite Peter Stokes (himself reporting to the archbishop on Wycliffite actiies in Oxford), records Hereford's English sermon in Latin. There are many polemic points, not the least of which is Hereford's accusation that "[fratres] non sunt / magistri theologie set magistri vanitatis, falsi praui, lurdici et loselli"[26] ("friars are not masters of theology but masters of vanity, false apostates, cripples, and reprobates"). Scase suggests that Hereford might have said "lollers and losels" (153), which was then Latinized by the notary as "lurdici et loselli." That reading would certainly put the term in 1382, but the reading of course emends the notarial account on the authority of a hypothesis about what the notary heard ("lollers") and what he wrote instead ("lurdici" [154]).[27] If, however, we leave the account as it is, we would have an easier case to argue and one perhaps more suited to the evidence as is. Rather than retro-fitting the account to satisfy the uncertain claim that the word "lollare" gained "prominence in religious discourse" by 1382, we could insist that the term in question was not available to the notary and that, moreover, the notary had before him the

---

[22] See *FZ* (*139*, 289).

[23] See *FZ* (*139*, 311–12; here, 312).

[24] Scase reflects upon this disturbance (*1081*, 154). For Crumpe's future difficulties, see *139*, 343–49, 356–58.

[25] James Crompton (*438*, 164).

[26] Forde (*151*, 240). In part, I follow Scase (*1081*, 152–53) on rendering the nouns of Hereford's sentence.

[27] See Scase (*1081*, 153–54), and her qualification: "Whether or not 'lurdici' was chosen to stand for the English 'loller,' its use by Frykes [the notary] certainly suggests that Hereford used the *loller* image with antifraternal implications" (153).

same set of semantic options available to his contemporaries, Wyclif and the Wycliffites. Wyclif never once mentioned the term "loller" in his writings, even in those works in which he advocates "poor, true, or faithful priests," who were later to be called "lollards" by the chroniclers. Nor does he mention it in his discussions of heresy involving linguistic puns that could comprehend the semantic and morphological relations between "lollia" and "lollard,"[28] as both the later canon lawyer William Lyndwood and the *FZ* compiler understood.[29] Obsessed with defending his version of Christianity by arguing every detail into the ground, Wyclif, during the last two years of his life (1382–84), his most strident phase, forgoes the opportunity to expose "lollard" as yet another orthodox mischaracterization of his assertions about apostleship and of his followers. Wyclif's oversight should seem strange in view of the current critical paradigms that have "lollards" afoot in his time. Yet what is more telling is that the Wycliffite sermonists, completing their work no earlier than 1386, omit the expression as well, even where they might readily use it in discussions about heresy.[30] (So, too, the vernacular prose texts edited by Frederic Matthew and Thomas Arnold omit reference to "lollards," preferring instead "lorelis."[31]) What do we make of these absences? If anti-Wycliffites were calling their adversaries "lollards" as early as 1382, the Wycliffites seem to have dropped the ball in not responding to the charges. We know, however, that the Wycliffites do respond to the term in defense against their opponents and, eventually, appropriate it as a sect nomination. It is not until the late 1380s, around 1389, that a Wycliffite author (Hereford?) in a commentary on the Apocalypse cites lamentingly the hostile sense of "lollard."[32] And probably not until at least the mid 1390s do Wycliffites

---

[28] Perhaps the best example would be *Sermones*, 4 vols., ed. J. Loserth (London: Wyclif Society, 1887–89), 1.94–97. Also see *Polemical Works*, 2 vols., ed. Rudolf Buddensieg (London: Wyclif Society, 1883), 2.432; *De Blasphemia*, ed. Michael Henry Dziewicki (London: Wyclif Society, 1893), 72; *De Eucharistia*, ed. Loserth (London: Wyclif Society, 1892), 155; *Trialogus* (*238*, 298–99). Wyclif plays on words, for instance, in showing how heresy turns an "apostle" into an "apostate" (*De Potestate Pape*, ed. Loserth [London: Wyclif Society, 1907], 214). His earlier discussion of heresy is in *De Veritate Sacrae Scripturae*, 3 vols., ed. Buddensieg (London: Wyclif Society, 1905), 3.274–310.

[29] See William Lyndwood's *Provinciale* (*181*, 1.300); and the final sections of the *FZ*, not edited by Shirley: Oxford, Bodleian Library, MS e Musaeo 86, f. 119, column b, where Wyclif's eucharistic heresies are called "lollardi," thus ending the chronicle where it begins, with a reference to the "lolli" of Wyclif (*139*, 1).

[30] See Hudson and Gradon (*158*, 1.336, 374–75, 481, 617–18; 2.17, 50, 163, 286, 377). These sermons, according to Hudson and Gradon, date to "the late 1380s or 1390s, after the Despenser crusade but before the enactment of the *De heretico comburendo* in 1401" (*158*, 4.19) – sometime after 1386, in other words. Oxford, Bodleian Library, MS Bodley 806, a partial redaction of the English Wycliffite Sermon cycle (see *158*, 1.110–15), inserts a commentary on "lollards" where there was none in the original; see ff. 47v, 70v. Also, London, British Library, MS Egerton 2820, a recension of a Wycliffite text published in Frederic D. Matthew (*182*), 362–93, inserts a new commentary on "lollardis" (f. 48), "lollers" (f. 48v).

[31] Matthew (*182*, 191–92; 212); Thomas Arnold (*100*).

[32] See the Apocalypse commentary, *Opus Arduum*, in Brno University Library MS Mk 28. Ff.136v, 157v refer to the persecutions of "Lolardi." The text is "firmly dated," as Hudson puts it, to 1389–90: see her "A Neglected Wycliffite Text" (*697*, 157). We can also note that the Carmelite Richard Maidstone, in his *Determinacio contra Johannem*, associated the views of his opponent, John Aswardby, "with those *qui sunt de secta lollardorum*" (qtd. in Hudson *713*, 96). Valerie

start to appropriate the term for themselves, in the *Epistola Sathanae* and in a series of texts compiled in CUL MS Ii 6 26.[33] Based on evidence involving Wyclif, the Wycliffites, Hereford's notary, and the reconsidered entry on Crumpe, it seems, then, that as late as 1386, there were no "lollards" in England, only Wycliffites; and that Langland was not hearing lots of "lollare [lollard]" furor between the writing of B and C. We can remove 1382 as a starting point for our critical "lollard" histories and, once and for all, relieve Langland of the burden of having to know about "lollardy" before it exists.

(Re)writing Lollard History

Having dealt with some of the critical constructs surrounding "lollard" history, we can now start to unpack some of the ways in which "lollardy" was invented by medieval chroniclers and bishops. Indeed by heeding the constant inventions and re-inventions of the term, we can begin to explain why the entry on Crumpe appears to be a reliable indicator of usage of "lollard" since 1382, and it is, importantly, an explanation that does not presuppose that the term was in use by then: not simply a blunt anti-Wycliffite aspersion, the term frequently appears as a back-formation in various legal, literary, and chronicle accounts concerning the events related to the Blackfriars Council of 1382. These accounts describe what is, in essence, the "lollardization" of Wyclif's disciples. For example, the continuator of the *Eulogium* writes of the year 1382: "Magistri tamen omnes in theologia regentes Oxoniæ determinabant contra hanc doctrinam, et præcipue regens Fratrum Minorum hanc doctrinam redarguit potenter et ipsos Lollardos esse probavit"[34] ("all the master regents in theology of Oxford determined against this doctrine and especially the regent of the Order of Friars Minor who powerfully refuted it and pronounced those preachers to be Lollards"). The *FZ* chronicler, in a similar vein, states:

> Unde, completo parliamento, Willelmus Cantuariensis, firma ecclesiæ columna, suos suffraganeos convocavit, cum aliis sacræ theologiæ doctoribus, et decretorum, et legum, et virorum valentium, ut deliberarent de certis

Edden dates Maidstone's text between 1384 and 1392 (*137*, 114–15). Based on the foregoing arguments, however, one could date Maidstone's text later; Crompton dated the work to around 1392 (*438*, 157).

[33] See "*Epistola Sathanae (or Luciferi) ad Cleros*," (*155*); Simon Hunt, "An edition of tracts in favour of scriptural translation and of some texts connected with lollard vernacular biblical scholarship" (Ph.D. diss., University of Oxford, 1994), 2.239.

[34] The entry is listed for 1381, confusing the condemnations of 1382 with those of 1381: see *Continuatio Eulogii*, *Eulogium Historiarum sive Temporis*, ed. Frank Scott Haydon (London: Longman et al., 1863), 3.351. Similarly, see Oxford, Bodleian Library, MS Bodley 703 (which contains texts by William Woodford): "Conclusiones Lollardorum dampnate Londonii anno Domini m ccc lxxxij regni regis Ricardi ii per dominum archiepiscopum Canteruarensis in suo generali consilio et pronunciatur in pleno parliamento" (f. 66) ("The conclusions of the Lollards condemned in London in the year of our Lord 1382 in the reign of Richard II by the archbishop of Canterbury in his general council and declared in full parliament").

conclusionibus hæreticis, *quas Wycclyff et illa secta quæ dicitur Lollardorum prædicaverunt.* Et damnaverunt certas conclusiones quæ inferius ponuntur, eodem anno, scilicet MCCLXXXII, in die S. Dunstani, post prandium, apud Prædicatores Londoniis.[35]

(Then, upon the completion of parliament, William of Canterbury, firm pillar of the church, called together his bishops, with other doctors of sacred theology, canonists, and lawyers, and valiant men, so as to deliberate on certain heretical conclusions, *which Wyclif, and that sect which is called Lollards, had preached.* And they condemned certain conclusions that were determined inferior, in the same year, 1382, on the day of St. Dunstan, after lunch, at the Preacher's house in London.)

Indeed, the *FZ* chronicler wrote his entry on Crumpe with a similar intent: Crumpe, so he says, "vocavit hæreticos Lollardos"[36] ("called the heretics Lollards"). This chronicler uses the expression as a short-hand to signify Crumpe's public condemnation against the Wycliffites. But it is not Crumpe who is doing the talking here, for the chronicler speaks through and for Crumpe to narrate with a degree of formulaic consistency the controversies, scandals, and persecutions at, and stemming from, Blackfriars. For chroniclers, these events of persecution are all linked by what ushers in, wittingly and unwittingly on the part of anti-Wycliffites, the heresiogenesis of "lollardy."

Episcopal documents effect a similar backformation, and in fact the earliest use of the term "lollard" in a written record, so far as we know, appears in such a document. In 1387 (10 August), Bishop Henry Wakefield of Worcester issued an anti-Wycliffite mandate,[37] declaring that persons belonging to the "Lollardorum confoederati" ("confederacy of Lollards") – Hereford, Aston, Purvey, Parker, and Swynderby "or any other of that prohibited sect" – are forbidden to preach in the diocese, in churchyards, cemeteries, or any of the profane places.[38] The names are familiar: Hereford and John Aston, infamous disciples of Wyclif. We know, however, that by the time of Wakefield's mandate, Hereford was already in prison, January 1387.[39] Aston and William Swynderby had already abjured.[40] Clearly, Wakefield is not castigating Aston and Swynderby as "lollards" still; nor was he suggesting that Hereford was an errant wandering "lollard" priest.[41] Rather, when he cites these names, he is both invoking the memory of the council of 1382 and is attempting to effect the arrest of others imagined to be persevering in Wycliffite activities ever since that time. For the sake of economy of expression, Wakefield compresses the legal processes of condemnation at Blackfriars, over several months, into a single term of

---

[35] *FZ (139,* 272), my emphasis.
[36] *FZ (139,* 312).
[37] David Wilkins (*228,* 3.202–03).
[38] Wilkins (*228,* 3.203). Wakefield draws from a continental motif, variously used to proscribe friars, "gyrovagi," and Beghards, to identify local Wycliffite problems. On the term's prehistory, see Dietrich Kurze (*816,* 53–58).
[39] See K.B. McFarlane's reading of this document, in *933,* 113.
[40] See Hudson (*713,* 73–76).
[41] Wilkins (*228,* 3.172).

condemnation, "lollard." As a result, the proceedings at Blackfriars come to be imagined as the event where Wycliffites were exposed as "lollards," with the unabjured remaining what they were always (already) known to be, "lollards."

Finally, the likenesses in back-formation and ideological work between the chronicles and the legal documents like Wakefield's are not accidental. For when chroniclers were writing their histories about the rise and condemnation of Wycliffism, they would copy, echo, and summarize legal documents (like this one) that supply the "lollard" typology. And they read this "lollard" backformation out of the later documents and incorporate it into narratives about the happenings of 1382.[42] By this process of incorporation, the term "lollard" became effectively coterminous – perhaps synonymous is a better word – with the year 1382.[43] More importantly, these likenesses between chronicle and legal documents evince a small part of a larger typological, semantic, legal, and historiographic phenomenon, which may best be described as "the invention of lollardy": from around 1387, there was a simultaneous emergence of a contentious term that preoccupied chroniclers, legislators, sermonists, vernacular and Latin poets, many Wycliffites, and, as I will soon show, Langland.

Reading 1387: The Invention of Lollardy

Orthodox and heterodox inventions of "lollardy" are similar in their differences, as Wycliffite examples would indicate. Sometime in the early 1390s, Wycliffites began to use the back-formation in a resistant fashion, punning on "lollare," expanding its lexical and grammatical range into verbs and adjectives, and reversing its sense.[44] Yet in these semantic expansions, the Wycliffites preserve some of the historiographic issues at stake with their orthodox contemporaries. The author of *Pierce the Ploughman's Crede*, for instance, views 1382 as a seminal event for "lollardy":

---

[42] For other uses of the term in primary documents that could affect the fashioning of historical narratives, see Wilkins (*228*, 3.208–09, 210, 211, 221) (in which embedded are the "Twelve Conclusions"). Some ecclesiastical documents show a rather extensive use of the word: see Wilkins (*228*, 3.225), and especially *The Metropolitan Visitations of William Courtenay* (*131*, 165–66). It is interesting that Wakefield's mandate about a "lollard confederacy" is corroborated by the *FZ*, which reports, through the supposed statements of John Ball, about Wycliffite preaching companies: "Qui etiam dixit quod erat certa comitiva de secta et doctrina Wyccliff, qui conspiraverant quandam confœderationem, et se ordinaverant circuire totam Angliam prædicando prædicti Wycclyf materias quas docuerat, ut sic simul tota Anglia consentiret suæ perversæ doctrinæ" (*139*, 274) ("He also said that there was a certain company among the sect and teaching of Wyclif, which had conspired as a confederacy, and which itself had arranged to travel about all of England in the preaching of the matters which the said Wyclif had taught, so that, at once, England entire would consent to his perverse teachings").

[43] Middleton's account about "the backformation loller" is different from, but congenial to, my own: see *952*, 282.

[44] See Helen Barr, *Signes and Sothe: Language in the Piers Plowman Tradition* (Cambridge: D.S. Brewer, 1994). See also David Lawton (*827*, 780–93).

Wytnesse on Wycliff that warned hem ["freers" (522)] with trewth;
For he in goodnesse of gost graythliche hem warned
To wayuen her wik[e]dnesse and werkes of synne.
Whou sone this sori men [seweden] his soule,
And oueral lollede him with heretykes werkes.   (528–32)[45]

By this poet's account, Wyclif was prophetically generous in warning the
friars about their wicked ways, but the friars took this unsolicited, sooth-
saying help as an insult and thus "lollede" him with "heretykes werkes" –
that is, charged him with heresy, "lollardized" him. The Wycliffite author of
Mum and the Sothsegger also returns to 1382 to speak of "lollards" and, like
his Wycliffite colleague, is clear about mendicant machinations against his
group:

For furst folowid freres Lollardz manieres,
And sith hath be shewed the same on thaym-self.
That thaire lesingz haue lad thaym to lolle by the necke;
At Tibourne for traison y-twyght vp thay were.   (417–20)

The Blackfriars Council is the imaginary backdrop here. According to this
Wycliffite, the friars persecuted "Lollardz" for their customs, their belief,
but now, irony of ironies, the friars themselves have been persecuted for the
"traison" of spreading rumors about Richard II's imminent return from
Ireland to reclaim his throne from the usurping King Henry.[46] This
Wycliffite takes the punitive energy stored up in "lollard" and directs it
back at the friars. He in effect argues that the friars are the real "Lollardz"
in so far as they "lolle by the necke."

What does this show? Looking at both texts, we can glimpse at the
Wycliffite historical imaginary that draws connections between the formation of "lollardy," the persecutions of 1382, and, perhaps most important of
all, mendicant conspiracies against Wyclif and his followers. Critics
frequently identify a systemic break between Wyclif, Wycliffism, and the
fraternal orders between 1381 and 1382 – all to the great chagrin of Wyclif –
and it is true that some evidence supports this narrative, especially where
the theologian runs afoul with his teaching on the eucharist.[47] But there is
also evidence suggesting that not all contemporaries comprehend this break
in their representations of heresy, apostasy, and lollardy. They prefer,
rather, to show the typological conflations between groups and to argue
that Wycliffism itself, "lollardy," gathers in other dissenters, such as friars
and unbeneficed priests. Such conflations, of course, are endemic to
representations of dissent and heresy involving regulars and extra-regulars,
as Gordon Leff and Ernest McDonnell show, and indeed, it is in this respect

---

[45] *The Piers Plowman Tradition* (*103*); cited by line.
[46] I follow Barr's reading of these lines: "'folowid' and 'shewed' (418) are used in their legal senses,
to prosecute a case at law . . . and to lodge a plea before the court" (*103*, 311 nn.416–22).
[47] For this view, see H.B. Workman (*1308*, 2.253); Aubrey Gwynn (*617*, 239); Szittya (*1169*, 152);
see, finally, Hudson's assessment in *Premature Reformation* (*713*, 348–49). I cannot deal here with
Wyclif's fraternalism, those aspects of his thought that are obviously influenced by fraternal
models, but see Michael Wilks (*92*, 73–74, 108–09, 183–87, 197–99).

that Scase's point rings true about the confusion of nomenclature owing to an expansion of "gyrovague" discourse about bad monks, friars, extraregulars, the poor, "all clerics."[48] Yet for us to derive a more specific sense about the expansion of "lollare" discourse in England, we have to heed how the term emerges as a fusion of Wycliffite and fraternal identities and practices: it is an anti-Wycliffite expression of the first order that is nonetheless laden with antifraternal sentiment.[49]

We can see these conflations at work in a variety of texts in a variety of ways, not the least of which is an account associated with a controversy in 1387. It regards Peter Patteshulle, an Austin friar who reportedly converted to "lollardy" and instigated with his sermons a riot at the Austin's House in London. The scandal involving Patteshulle was widely represented, both in major chronicles and in royal writs calling for the arrest of an apostate friar William Patteshulle, who is likely Peter.[50] (The writs list the names of other friars who converted to, or were perceived to have converted to, Wycliffism.[51]) From the perspective of the writ, Patteshulle (if in fact he is Peter) was an "apostate friar." From the perspective of the chroniclers, he was a "lollard." He was both, really, just one of the many radical mendicants who were imagined to be poised on the brink of conversion to Wycliffism in and after 1387. The anxieties about such an event are registered in a royal mandate issued on 13 October, 1388: "sheriffs, mayors, bailiffs, ministers and other the king's lieges [are] to arrest vagabond apostate friars of the Augustinian order."[52] In so far as Wycliffism was thought to draw in apostate friars, it is no wonder that the perceived sources of apostasy began to overlap: antifraternalism gets a new target – the Wycliffites. So thinks Austin Canon Henry Knighton, who believes that "lollards" embody what is so repugnant about friars:

[48] See Gordon Leff (*836*, 1.315–47); Ernest W. McDonnell, *The Beguines and Beghards in Medieval Culture, with a special emphasis on the Belgian scene* (New York: Octagon Books, 1969), 246, 266–67; Scase (*1081*, 138; see 132, 135, 138, 141–42, 145–47, 151–54).

[49] Scase supplies a rich account of antifraternalism in its continental contexts and understands that "lollard" has historically antifraternal implications. Her primary English evidence on this point, however, is the entry on Crumpe in *FZ* and Hereford's sermon (*1081*, 152–55). This evidence is meant to support a thesis that, in addition to Langland, others in the early 1380s embraced a non-Wycliffite sense of the word "loller," before consensus in the later 1380s suppressed that sense in favor of "follower of Wyclif." Yet as I show, both instances are dubious indicators about uses of "lollardy" in the early 1380s in England. Scase produces no other examples. We have no choice but to see Langland's "lollares" as responsive to contemporary "lollare [lollard]" issues.

[50] *Calendar of Patent Rolls* (hereafter, *CPR*) (London, 1901–), 3.386; *CPR*, 3.324. Walsingham (*221*, 2.157–59); *Historia Vitae et Regni Ricardi Secundi*, ed. George B. Stow (Philadelphia: Univ. of Pennsylvania Press, 1977), 102–104; *Polychronicon Ranulphi Higden Monachi Cestrensis*, 9 vols., ed. C. Babington and J.R. Lumby (Rolls Series, 1865–86), 8.479–80 (for Trevisa's rendering).

[51] *CPR*, 3.324, for writs dated 28 May and 18 July 1387, concerning the apostasy of Robert Stokulse. See F. Donald Logan (*875*, 74), regarding a citation for Thomas Beauchamp and John Lude, possibly Wycliffite sympathizers. Logan's claim that "only once does heresy or near-heresy appear connected with apostasy from the religious life" (74) is based on statistics and overlooks the figurations of apostasy and heresy in historical, literary, theological, and polemic writing, in which the sentiments and problems become greatly amplified and duly disseminated.

[52] *CPR*, 3.551. For related issues on fraternal apostasy, see Clopper (*398*, 44–46).

> Those things are there in the eighth chapter [of St-Amour's *De Periculis Novissimorum Temporum*] . . . with citations from Holy Scripture . . . which some have applied to the mendicant friars, but which better apply to those new people, the Lollards [lollardis].[53]

Two groups can be proscribed at the price of one set of terms. Knighton, of course, was not alone in classifying friars and Wycliffites together so as ultimately, but often contradictorily, to tell them apart. A Worcester sermonist, for instance, groups "lollards" with friars in a sermon against "ronners ouer contreys": "For we se now so much folk & specialiche þes lollardes, þay go barfot, þei gon openhed."[54] This sermonist views both groups as engaging in similar activities, while claiming that "lollares" in fact exacerbate what is so execrable about friars. Which is why he launches a patently antifraternal attack against the new heretics:[55]

> 'Take non hede,' abyt Crist, 'of false profites, ȝe, valse lollardes, þat cum to ȝow e cloþyng o mekenes & holi leuyng for to teche or to preche ȝow.' 'for hardeliche,' seith Crist, 'þei be with-in-forth mor cruwel þan any wlues, ȝe, & more cursedde þan any hondes. . . .'[56]

Yet despite all his vituperation about "lollares," how do you tell one from a friar? You cannot, if you go strictly by the stereotypes. "Lollards" dress like friars, like wolves in sheep's clothing, going about barefoot without a hood and wearing torn garments as a means to display a feigned fraternal piety. This sermonist does not even mention eucharistic controversies, that great mark of difference between Wycliffites and everyone else. He does, however, seem to refer to a Wycliffite so memorably irksome to Bishop Wakefield, Nicholas Hereford: "For þer was a lollard at Oxanfort but awhile agon þat forsuk al his errours & al his misleuyng & turnyd aȝen to þe leuyng of oþer good cristenmen, & tan a told certeyn rytes & doyng of hem, ȝe, so cursed & so oreble to her."[57] Yet the sermonist again eschews a discussion of these "certyen rytes" – "e good feyth, ich am greuyse for to telle hem" – for his aim is to cast the mendicant problem in a new light, showing now that Wycliffites infringe on the rights of parish priests: in short, "lollards" lower the standards of depravity first set by friars.

This sermonist is reduplicating a typological pattern on the question of friars and "lollares." We can see this pattern mimicked by the chroniclers whom we may regard as the best (hostile) witnesses to the movement. They are all, in one way or another, interested in demonstrating that Wyclif and his followers adopted fraternal postures and practices, or formed allegiances with friars, whenever it was rhetorically or politically expedient.

---

[53] *Knighton's Chronicle* (*165*, 249).

[54] *Three Middle English Sermons from the Worcester Chapter Manuscript F.10*, ed. D.M. Grisdale (Leeds School of English Language Texts and Monographs 5, 1939), 60.

[55] All are motifs discussed by Szittya (*1169*).

[56] *Three Middle English Sermons*, 66.

[57] Ibid., 65. Grisdale believes this is a reference to Hereford (xxiii); it could just as well be to Repingdon, however.

Purportedly, these heretics seduce to their ways the laity, who had already put their trust in friars. Knighton, who endorses a total recasting of anti-fraternalisms for "lollards," believes the "lollards" to comprise a "sect," a new but unauthorized religious order, which "wore clothes of plain russet, as though to show the simplicity of their hearts to the world, and so cunningly draw to themselves the minds of those who beheld them."[58] The St. Albans chronicler, Thomas Walsingham, follows suit. Certainly no friend of friars, he writes of Wyclif: "ut magis plebis mentes deluderet, ordinibus adhæsit Mendicantium, eorum paupertatem approbans, perfectionem extollens, ut magis falleret commune vulgus"("so that he might delude the people's minds all the more, so that he might better deceive the common people, he associated with the Mendicant orders, approving their poverty and extolling their perfection").[59] Walsingham, deploring in one breath Wyclif and the friars, goes on to call the Wycliffites "apostates": "[Wyclif] emisit viros apostatas, de fide Catholica pessime sentientes"[60] ("Wyclif sent out apostate men, disposed most evilly against the Catholic faith"). He readily applies, in other words, the terms of fraternal disobedience, apostasy, to the newer heretics.[61] Lastly, the Franciscan continuator of the *Eulogium* illustrates how Wycliffite missions took over the fraternal project of wandering preaching by collecting fraternal sermons: "Discipuli præfati Johannis studuerunt in compilationibus sermonum et sermones fratrum congregaverunt, euntes per totam Angliam doctrinam hujus sui magistri prædicabant"[62] ("The disciples of the said John Wyclif studied from compilations of sermons, and they gathered together the sermons of the friars; going throughout all of England, they preached the doctrine of their master"). When it came to typologies, witnesses could not keep friars and "lollards" apart, even when they were meant by some accounts to be clearly ideologically opposed.

Some of these representations of fraternal "lollares," no doubt, are generated by legal perceptions and problems. As we saw in the previous

---

[58] *Knighton's Chronicle* (*165*, 299). See Walsingham (*221*, 1.324–26). Clopper identifies russet as patently fraternal; see *398*, 195. As a fraternal narrator says:

> Than thei loken on my nabete,
> And sein, "Forsothe withoutton othes,
> Whether it be russet, blakk, or white,
> It is worthe alle oure werynge clothes." (21–24)

"Allas, What Schul We Freris Do" (*133*, 56–57).

[59] *Chronicon*, 116; for an aspersion against the fraternal orders, see 312, and *221*, 2.13.

[60] *221*, 2.53, see also 1.356. Unbeneficed priests are at issue, too. Walsingham mentions that "[i]nter quos" ("among them") there was a certain one (William Swynderby) who had the look and dress of a hermit (*221*, 2.53). McFarlane believed him to be an unbeneficed priest (*933*, 104).

[61] Whereas the Wycliffites, in numerous places, see apostasy as a sign that there may be friars sympathetic to their cause: "For ȝif a prest of her feyned ordre wole lyue poreli & iustly & goo freli aboute & teche frely goddis lawes, þei holden him apostata & prison hym, & holden hym cursed for þis prestis lif commaundid, ensaumplid of crist & his apostlis" (Matthew *182*, 127). Interestingly, Matthew references here Patteshulle and other fraternal Wycliffite sympathizers (see 507 n.127).

[62] *Eulogium*, 3.355. Some mendicants, after 1387, did have access to the networks of production and circulation enjoyed by Wycliffites, as Anne Hudson and Helen Spencer have shown: they adopted portions of the Wycliffite sermon cycle, expunging matters that would be offensive to friars. See Hudson (*689*, 206, 211–12); Spencer (*1133*, 318–20).

section, chroniclers join bishops and metropolitans in showing how forms of apostasy overlap. The *Eulogium* continuator thinks, for example, that Arundel's *Constitutions*, which were drafted in part to prohibit the itinerations of licenseless Wycliffites, were meant in broad terms to prevent the wanderings of an entire related group, "Lollardos et limitores illiteratos ac fratres vitiosos"[63] ("Lollards and illiterate limiters and corrupt friars"). Why did he think this? He is merely reporting a pervasive opinion about "Lollardos" and "fratres vitiosos" being equally impugnable. So pervasive was the opinion that the archbishop himself had to clarify the terms of his own anti-Wycliffite enactment and reassert the rights of friars to preach the word of God in the localities.[64] No one understood the problems of localities and preaching rights better than the now familiar Bishop Wakefield. When he issued his 1387 mandate against the Wycliffites, he was in some sense picking up where previous legal instruments, between 1382 and 1386, left off. His aim was also to control these "preachers of unsound doctrine" – the "plusours malurees Persones deinz le dit Roilame, alantz de Countee en Countee, & Ville a Ville, en certains habitz souz dissimulacion de grant Saintee, & sanz license de Seint Pere le Pape"[65] ("the many wicked persons within the said realm, wandering from county to county, town to town, in certain habits under simulation of great sanctity, and without license from the blessed father the Pope"). Wakefield perhaps felt, as did the Worcester sermonist, that Wycliffites were growing as numerous as their look-alikes, friars. Already out of favor in his diocese, friars were indeed some of the "plusours malurees Persones," who wear the habit ("habitz") and wander ("alanz") from place to place often without licenses ("sanz license"), to the chagrin of bishops and parish priests.[66] While, of course, this bishop knew that Wycliffites are different from friars, he also understood that the controversies of licensing and limitations traditionally surrounding the mendicants are re-appearing here in yet another form, "lollards."[67] For the sake of economizing a legal publication (twice over now), Wakefield, like the Worcester sermonist, does not bother to describe what makes "lollards" so different from friars. So is the name a good enough specification?

---

[63] *Eulogium*, 3.412.

[64] See Wilkins (*228*, 3.324).

[65] *CPR*, 3.200 (see also 3.145, 146); *Rotuli Parliamentorum*, 7 vols. (London, 1832), 3.124. In his assessment of the "lunatyk lollares," Clopper also broadens the interpretation of this statute; see *398*, 209–10. I read Langland's bad "lollares" in light of this and other enactments.

[66] Wakefield was among those bishops "not as well inclined towards friars" (Arnold Williams, "Relations between the Mendicant Friars and the Secular Clergy in England in the Later Fourteenth Century," *Annuale Medievale* 1 [1960]: 52, 53).

[67] See Benjamin Z. Kedar, "Canon Law and Local Practice: The Case of Mendicant Preaching in Late Medieval England," *Bulletin of Medieval Canon Law*, n.s. 2 (1972): 17–32; Szittya (*1169*, 63, 101–112, 123–51); Clopper (*398*, 44–45).

Piers Plowman *and the Lollard Tradition*

No, says Langland. In C9, he scrutinizes the name, "lollare," and studies its application to different groups who appear as friars or who are friars. We can now be clear about his place within (not without) contemporary "lollare" discourse. Sometime after 1387, Langland, writing from the same dialectal region as the Worcester sermonist, and perhaps once living in Wakefield's own diocese, eliminates the only reference to "lolleris" in B (15.212) to make way for a new use of "lollares" in C.[68] I want to detail two ways in which Langland conscientiously intervenes in a semantic field already inflected with the anti-Wycliffite, "lollare." First, I want to identify examples in which he shares "lollare" locutions with his contemporaries; and second, I want to offer a reading of several passages of *Piers Plowman* C in order to show that Langland's use of "lollare" is a function of the imagined confusions and distinctions between friars and Wycliffites. To begin with:

> Aȝen þe lawe he lyueth yf latyn be trewe:
> *Non licet uobis legem voluntati, set voluntat[em] coniungere legi.*
> Kyndeliche, by Crist, ben suche ycald lollares.
> As by þe engelisch of oure eldres of olde mennes techynge
> He þat lolleth is lame or his leg out of ioynte
> Or ymaymed in som membre, for to meschief hit souneth,
> Riht so, sothly, such manere Ermytes
> Lollen aȝen þe byleue and þe law of holy churche.   (9.213–19)[69]

This is the crescendo of "lollare" passages in *Piers Plowman*, where the poetry culminates in a definition of the term and its application to "such manere Ermytes." And in this definition, Langland thinks like his contemporaries. First, when he declares, "Kyndeliche, by Crist, ben suche ycald lollares" (214), he uses an expression, repeated time and again, by those writing within the Wycliffite and anti-Wycliffite polemic – "there are those called lollards." A Wycliffite preacher writes: "Ffor ȝit knewe I neuere prest þat goiþ aboute and freli prechiþ þe gospel as doen many of *þese þat been callid lollardis.*"[70] The *FZ* chronicler (and the *Eulogium* continuator and Walsingham) adapts the formula for his own purposes of representing

---

[68] Most critics understand C to be finished by 1387, when Thomas Usk, before his execution in 1388, referenced the C-version of the Tree of Charity in his *Testament of Love* (see Pearsall *170*, 9). However, in arguing that Langland takes the Statutes of 1388 as the "pre-text" for C5, Middleton dates C to after 1388 (see "Acts of Vagrancy" [*952*, 208–09]). On Langland's dialect, see M.L. Samuels, "Langland's Dialect," in *The English of Chaucer and his Contemporaries: Essays by M.L. Samuels and J.J. Smith*, ed. J.J. Smith (Aberdeen: Aberdeen Univ. Press, 1988), 70–85; and A.I. Doyle's and M.B. Parkes' remarks on the D-Scribe from Southwest Worcestershire in "The Production of Copies of the *Canterbury Tales* and the *Confessio Amantis* in the Early Fifteenth Century," in *Medieval Scribes, Manuscripts, & Libraries: Essays Presented to N.R. Ker*, ed. M.B. Parkes and Andrew G. Watson (London: Scolar Press, 1978), 174–82, 192–97.

[69] Cited by passus and line from *Piers Plowman: The C Version* (*171*).

[70] London, British Library MS Egerton 2820, f. 48v. See also Hudson (*155*, 19).

condemnation: Crumpe "vocavit" Wyclif's disciples "Lollardos."[71] A
medieval annotator of *Piers Plowman* (Cambridge University Library MS
Additional 4325) understands the salience of the formula, underlining line
214 in red.[72] These examples limn a mere formulaic correspondence, but
they are important, in so far as Langland understands (like his annotator)
that "lollare" discourse is about recognizable formulas. His formulaicism is
especially evident in the second point of agreement with his contemporaries:
he assesses "lollares" to be heretics. "Aȝen þe lawe he lyueth yf latyn be
trewe:/ *Non licet uobis legem voluntati, set voluntat[em] coniungere legi*"
(9.213–13a).[73] In this Latin – "It is not lawful for you to make the law
conform to your will, but rather for you to conform your will to the law"
(Pearsall, *C-Text*, 170n221a) – Langland goes to the heart of the word
"heresy," meaning a perversion of the will, the wrongful "choice" to depart
from the Church and skew its laws.[74] And in line 219, he strikes upon the
sense of "heresy" variously used by his contemporaries – "aȝen þe byleue
and þe law of holy churche" – only here he assimilates the activity of
"lollares" (the verb, "Lollen") with heretical practice itself.[75] While he thus
agrees with Wakefield in denoting "lollares" as heretics, he parts ways with
the bishop and the chroniclers on how one should reconstruct the past of
"lollardy."[76] He does not, that is, imagine the primary event of "calling"

---

[71] *FZ* (*139*, 312). See Walsingham (*221*, 2.157); *Continuatio Eulogii*, 351.

[72] As Scase notes, this practice "is usual only for the Latin quotations in this manuscript" (*1081*, 157).

[73] On this passage, cf. Scase (*1081*, 151); Middleton (*952*, 282).

[74] For Gratian's definition of heresy, see Decretum II Cxxiv Qiii cc. 27–31, in Emil Friedberg, ed., *Corpus iuris canonici*, 2 vols. (Leipzig, 1879–81), 1.997–98; another source is Isidore of Seville, *Etymologiarum sive originum libri xx*, ed. W.M. Lindsay, 2 vols. (Oxford, 1911, rpt. 1985), 8.3–8.5, no pagination. William Lyndwood provides a thorough catalogue of definitions of heresy drawn, of course, from various portions of canon law: see "De Hæreticis," *Provinciale seu Constitutiones Angliae*, 1.289–90, 292–93. English writers generally agree on the sense that heretics live and work against the laws of the church and scripture, which collectively comprise "the faith." An orthodox sermonist, for example, refers to "þe lawe canon . . . de hereticis": "But I prey þe, what is heresye? For-sothe, not else but for to preche and liff aȝeyns þe feyȝthe and good maner" (*Middle English Sermons*, ed. Woodburn O. Ross, Early English Text Society o.s. 209 [London: Oxford Univ. Press, 1940], 210). Langland thus generalizes in a similar fashion. His Latin lines approximate those of Tertullian: "haereses dictae graeca voce ex interpretatione electionis, qua quis maxime ad instituendas, sive ad suscipiendas eas utitur. Ideo et sibi damnatum [Paulus] dixit haereticum, quia in quo damnatur sibi elegit. Nobis vero nihil ex nostro arbitrio indulgere licet, sed nec eligere quod aliquis de arbitrio suo induxerit" ("They are called by the Greek word *haireseis* in the sense of choice . . . Therefore [Paul] has called the heretic damned [condemned] by himself because he has chosen for himself [something] for which he is damned. For us it is not lawful to introduce any doctrine of our own choosing, neither may we choose some doctrine which someone else has introduced by his own choice") (Tertullian, *De Praescriptione Haereticorum: Texte Latin, Traduction, Française, Introduction, et Index*, ed. Pierre de Labriolle [Paris: Librairie Alphonse Picard et Fils, 1907], 12–14).

[75] The Latin quotation is unidentified (John A. Alford, "Some Unidentified Quotations in *Piers Plowman*," *Modern Philology* 72 [1974]: 390–99; 398). But sources involving the violation of monastic rules have been suggested: see John A. Alford, *Piers Plowman: A Guide to the Quotations* (Medieval and Renaissance Texts and Studies: Binghamton, NY, 1992), 55–56. In proposing that in this Latin, Langland is defining heresy in a commonplace fashion, I suggest that there is no source but the accumulated commonplaces themselves. Langland is commenting on a social text – the text of heresy and its construction through "lollare" discourse.

[76] Gradon's view "that the *lollers* are not heretics" is untenable (*608*, 196).

heretics "lollares" to be Blackfriars 1382 but rather throws the "lollares" into a more distant English past – "As by þe engelisch of oure eldres of olde mennes techynge" (9.215).[77] The "*Piers Plowman* sense" thus draws in the contemporary anti-Wycliffite sense, even where Langland disagrees with some of his contemporaries: for his disagreement is about "lollare" commonplaces that he does not in any way occlude, obscure, or trivialize. After all, he gives so much new poetry to the "lollare" question.

Indeed, Langland's participation in the invention of "lollardy" is especially evident when we discern the narrative logic of some of that material new to C passus 9. There, Langland himself uses "lollare" as a term of wide classification (for hermits, friars, wasters) with respect to the spiritual rewards and punishments contained in the pardon. As we follow the unfolding of the pardon, however, we witness the disclosure, development, and particularization of the figure of the "lollare." In this disclosure, Langland at points clusters bad "lollares" with bad or "lewd" hermits (lines 193 and 241). Yet he always distinguishes good "lunatyk lollares" from "holy eremytes," giving each a separate passage of poetry (lines 105–39 and 196–203). That he isolates ideal "lollares" from despicable ones means that he, unlike Knighton and the Worcester sermonist, does not want to cluster all "Lollardes" together, nor does he want to predicate every sense of "lollare" with antifraternal terms. He is recuperating and appropriating the term "lollare" for an ideal form of apostleship (105–39), which indicates, yet again, that Langland is participating in the appropriate, but alternative "lollare [lollard]" motifs concerning lay, theoretical poverty.[78] There is, however, only space for me to deal here with "lollares and lewede Eremytes."[79] I want to show that with these figures, Langland goes to the letter of anti-Wycliffite "lollare" discourse and restricts its sense to antifraternal terms. To him the bad "lollare" heretic is a friar who shuns work – not a Wycliffite.[80]

At the start of passus 9, Langland establishes criteria to determine who warrants inclusion in Truth's pardon. In lines 58–69, he speaks of labor and begging, and it is from here that the additions to C9 proceed in two major portions, lines 70–161 and 188–280. In the first portion, he adds some new criteria – impoverished worthiness – against which other groups will be checked: these worthies are the "poor folk in cotes," who despite being hungry (77) and too ashamed to beg (86), rise every morning to work (79–97). Not the voluntary poor praised by Patience in C15 but rather the "chronic urban poor," as Pearsall calls them, these "coterelles and crokede men and blynde" should be comforted by all with alms.[81] Langland contrasts other groups in the pardon in light of this one:

---

[77] Cf. Kerby-Fulton, "Langland and the Bibliographic Ego" in *70*, 102–03.

[78] See my "William Langland's Lollardy," *Yearbook of Langland Studies* 16 (2003).

[79] I do not have space here to deal with Will in C5, "yclothed as a lollare" (2).

[80] Clopper would agree with my conclusions about fraternal "lollares" (*398*, 204–08) but not with my understanding of the historical background against which they should be read – that of "lollare" discourse and Wycliffite and anti-Wycliffite controversies.

[81] Derek Pearsall (*1026*, 166).

> Ac beggares with bagges þe whiche brewhous[es] ben here churches,
> But they be blynde or tobroke or elles be syke,
> Thouh he falle for defaute þat fayteth for his lyflode
> Reche ȝe neuere, ȝe riche, Thouh such lo[rell]es sterue.
> For alle þat haen here hele and here yesyhte
> And lymes to labory with and lollares lyf vsen,
> Lyuen aȝen goddes lawe and þe lore of holi churche.   (9.98–104)[82]

Langland insists that those who (mis)*use* the "lollarne lyf" (103; 140), live falsely "lyke a lollare" (158), and beg with bags (154), are distinct from the worthy "cotterelles" and from the "lunatyk lollares" who beg "Withoute bagge" (120; 139–40).[83] What's wrong with these beggars is not only that they feign worthiness but that, in so doing, they live against the "law" and "lore" of "holi churche" (104). In thus damning these figures, Langland anticipates his declaration of heresy in the crescendo – "sothly such manere eremtyes / Lollen aȝen þe byleue and þe law of holy churche" (9.218–19). Aptly, Piers ejects these "lollare" hermits from the pardon: "Forthy lollares þat lyuen in sleuthe and ouer land strikares / Buth nat in this bulle,' quod [Peres], 'til they ben amended . . .'" (159–60).

This first section of new material establishes the basic difference between bad and ideal "lollares"; the second section (188–280), to which I now turn, resumes the meditation on social distinctions, this time between kinds of hermits – holy and unholy.

> Ac Ermytes þat inhabiten by the heye weye
> And in borwes among brewesteres and beggen in churches –
> Al þat holy Ermytes hatede and despisede,
> As rychesses and reuerences and ryche menne Almesse,
> Thise lollares, lachedraweres, lewede Ermytes
> Coueyten þe contrarye for as cotterelles they libbeth.   (9.189–94)

Langland puts the "Ermytes þat inhabiten by the heye weye" within a larger group of " lollares, lachedraweres, [and] lewede Ermytes," and shows them all to be despicable for not only failing to measure up to the criteria established at the outset of passus 9 but for proving themselves to be anti-types to holy hermits who practice desert asceticism, embrace poverty (196–203), and earn a place in the pardon (186–88). Having thus clustered "lewede Ermytes" with bad "lollares," Langland is ready, in the remainder of the material new to C9, to explore the fusions between these two groups, dropping the "lachedraweres." He begins by explaining the malpractices of "lewede ermytes":

> Ac thise Ermytes þat edifien thus by the heye weye
> Whilen were werkmen, webbes and taylours
> And carteres knaues and Clerkes withouten grace,
> H[e]lden ful hungry hous and hadde muche defaute,

---

[82] As Russell and Kane report, an alternative reading for "lo[rell]es" in line 101 is "lollares."
[83] Clopper perceptively points to these distinctions regarding the issue of imitation ("Langland's Persona," in *70*, 158; *398*, 204).

> Long labour and litte wynnynge and at the laste they aspyde
> That faytede in frere clothinge hadde fatte chekes.
> Forthy lefte they here labour, thise lewede knaues,
> And clothed hem in copes, clerkes as it were
> Or oen of som ordre or elles a profete.
> Aʒen þe lawe he lyueth yf latyn be trewe:
> *Non licet uobis legem voluntati, set voluntat[em] coniungere legi.*
> Kyndeliche, by Crist, ben suche ycald lollares.
> As by þe engelisch of oure eldres of olde mennes techynge
> He þat lolleth is lame or his leg out of ioynte
> Or ymaymed in som membre, for to meschief hit souneth,
> Riht so, sothly, such manere Ermytes
> Lollen aʒen þe byleue and þe law of holy churche. (9.204–19)

Langland rationalizes as to why "lollares" and "lewede Ermytes" should be clustered by detailing the evolution of a social type, from "lewede Ermytes" to "lollares." Those "Ermytes" by the highway were once tradespersons, knaves, and unbeneficed clerks, but feeling the pinch and the hunger pangs, they discover that whoever begs in friar's clothing lives large without having to lift a finger. So, opportunistically, they "clothed hem in copes, clerkes as it were." "Kyndeliche, by Crist, ben suche ycald lollares."[84] In other words, "lollares" look like friars. Langland presents the "lollares" of contemporary discourse, predicated as they are with antifraternalisms and labeled in key passages with anti-Wycliffite expressions that a medieval reader could not but recognize.[85] Langland reduces the valence of "lollare" to its antifraternal kernel.

This means that Langland's commentary and criticism here is not about Wycliffites but about the terms circulating about them, terms that appear on the semantic scene after Wycliffism was condemned. Understanding that "Eremyte" can mean "friar,"[86] and implying that corrupt friars prostitute out their own habit to wasters,[87] Langland offers a new explanation as to

---

[84] Interestingly enough, a contemporary poem makes a somewhat similar point:
> When beggers mow nether bake ne brewe,
> Ne have wherwith to borrow ne bie,
> Than mot riot robbe or reve,
> Under the colour of Lollardie. (61–64)
"Lo, He That Can Be Cristes Clerc" (*133*, 92–96).

[85] See Huntington Library MS HM 143, f. 41, with the annotation to line 9.140, "propure lollares" – as transcribed by Scase (*1081*, 157).

[86] See Hanna, "'Meddling with Makings' and Will's Work," in *75*, 86 n.5; Edwin Jones, "Langland and Hermits," *Yearbook of Langland Studies* 11 (1997): 79–80; Clopper (*398*, 205–206). Also see Malcolm Godden, "Plowmen and Hermits in Langland's *Piers Plowman*," *Review of English Studies* 35 (1984): 129–6, especially, 137–39. On Austin hermits, Francis Roth, O.S.A (*1069*); F. A. Mathes, *The Poverty Movement and the Augustinian Hermits, Analecta Augustiniana* 31 (1968): 5–154 and 32 (1969): 5–116.

[87] He expands the common criticism of the laity adopting fraternal garb (for, among other things, burial), a practice for which friars are to blame as much as lay persons. See Wyclif, *Polemical Works*, 1.35, 143, 306, 381; *De Blasphemia*, 209; *Opera Minora*, ed. Loserth (London: Wyclif Society, 1892), 322; *Jack Upland* (*159*, 63, lines 204–08); Williams, "Relations," 64. Wycliffites, with extreme frequency, criticize the fraternal habit; see Matthew (*182*, 316); and: "Fferþermor we shal suppose þat bodyliche abyte, or wantyng þerof, makiþ not men religiose neyþer apostataes, al ʒif þey semen siche bi jugement of men; for oonliche charite þat sewiþ it makiþ men religiose, or of Cristis ordre" (Arnold [*100*, 3.431]).

why friars shun work: under the covers, they are all wasters, bereft of grace, and "Clerkes" by title alone.[88] In this fusion between wasters and fraternal "lollares," he is looking back to passus 8 where to a passage already present in B, he adds a new "lollare" gloss (emphasized below) to some lines about friars and workers:

> Y shal fynde hem fode þat fayfulleche libbeth,
> Saue Iacke þe iogelour and ionet of þe stuyues
> And danyel þe dees playere and denote þe baude
> And frere faytour and folk of þat ordre,
> *That lollares and loseles lele men holdeth*
> And Robyn þe rybauder for his rousty wordes.   (C.8.70–75).

Piers, speaking here, realizes that the faithful know that "folk of þat ordre" are "lollares and loseles," and that they all can be excluded from provisions along with the wasters.

After lines 204–19, the crescendo "lollare" passage, Langland can go no higher. So he starts over. He addresses all persons – "For holy churche hoteth alle manere peple / Vnder obedience to be and buxum to þe lawe" (220–21) – and offers positive prescriptions for the religious, lewd, and lords:[89] "Furste, Religious of religioun a reule to holde / And vnder obedience be by dayes and by nyhtes" (222–23).[90] After detailing the duties of "Lewede men" and "lordes" with clichés drawn from three estates theory, Langland's narrator points out the faults of the first group, the religious:

> Loke now where this lollares and lewede Ermites
> Breke þis obedience þat beth so fer fram chirche.
> Where se we hem on sonendayes the seruise to here,
> As matynes by þe morwe til masse bygynne,
> Or sonendayes at euensong? se we wel fewe!
> Or labory for here lyflode as þe lawe wolde?   (9.241–46)

These "lollares and lewede Ermites" exceed their limits (their obedience), do not show up at the service, and do not "labory for her lyflode" as the law requires. Who are these people? The narrator answers:

> Ac aboute mydday at mele tyme y mette with hem ofte,
> [C]o[m]e in his cope as he a Clerk were;
> A bacheler [o]r a be[au]pere beste hym bysemede
> And fo[r] þe cloth þat keuereth hym ykald he is a frere,
> Wascheth and wypeth and with þe furste sitteth.
> Ac while a wrouhte in þe world and wan his mete with treuthe

---

[88] See Matthew (*182*, 51). On Langland's wasters, see Aers, *Chaucer, Langland*, 9–20, and *Community, Gender, and Individual Identity: English Writing 1360–1430* (London: Routledge, 1988), 20–72.

[89] Lyndwood identifies regular disobedience ("inobedientiae") as one of three forms of apostasy (*181*, 1.306). See also the Wycliffite comment on "obedience," Arnold (*100*, 3.449).

[90] On "lewd hermits" and labor, see Hanna (*75*, 86 n.5), and Edwin Jones, "Langland and Hermits," *Yearbook of Langland Studies* 11 (1997): 78–79.

> He sat at þe syde benche and at þe seconde table;
> Cam no wyn in his wombe thorw þe woke longe
> Ne no blanke[t] on his bed ne whyte bred byfore hym   (9.247–55)

For that cloth, he is "ykald" a friar, but for these depravities he is a "lollare," a "lewede Ermite," a friar who engages in the same bad, stereotypically fraternal, activities deplored in passus 15, where the "maystre, a man lyk a frere," dines with Will, Reason, Conscience, Clergy, and Patience, the delegate for Piers (15.25–175).[91] The parallel is meant to be seen: whereas Will wants no company with the friar with "two grete chekes" (15.85), wasters strive to emulate those "in frere clothinge" with "fatte chekes" (9.209).

Conclusion

Langland, by writing the C-text "lollare" passages, produces what is the longest and most thorough meditation in the vernacular on the "lollare" question, unrivaled until some early fifteenth-century material, such as a sermon in Oxford, Bodleian Library, MS Bodley 649 (especially ff. 102–105), and another in London, British Library, MS Harley 2268 (ff. 190v, 191v, 194v–95v). He directs his work toward that contemporary context rife with anti-Wycliffite usages and takes a side, seeing "lollare" heresy as a fault of friars, *not* Wycliffites. In short, he makes distinctions between groups where others would see none. He thus neutralizes the anti-Wycliffite term. In so far as this new C-text material comprises a substantial addition to B, it is evident that *Piers Plowman* C does not evince a move away from controversies, much less Wycliffite and anti-Wycliffite controversies, discourses, and typologies.[92] How could Langland be worried about offending anti-Wycliffite readers with all these "lollares" prominently featured in C? He is not worried. I submit the foregoing as evidence against the near consensus among critics regarding the poet's general conservatism in this latest version.[93] By maintaining a nuanced, and not reductive, sense of

---

[91] In my view, Langland refers to "hermits" so as to produce an (anti)fraternal discourse about failed pristine aspirations. He sees friars as the progenitors of eremitic practices, according to the legends of the Austin friars:

> Paul *primus heremita* hadde yparroked hymsulue
> That no man myhte se hym for moes and for leues.
> Foules hym fedde yf frere Austynes be trewe
> For he ordeyned þat ordre or elles þey gabben.   (C.17.13–16)

The entire passage (17.6–36) featuring desert eremeticism ends with a lesson about those desiring, or having, property: "For wolde neuere faythfull god þat freres and monkes / Toke lyflode of luyther wynnynges in all her lyf tyme" (17.35–36). These passages can be paired with 9.196–203, where I believe holy "hermits" forefront a fraternal ideal that then goes wrong in the figure of the "lewede Eremite," a friar himself, a "lollare." For a defense of the fraternal life using similar hermetic ideals, see *Friar Daw's Reply* (*159*, lines 282–321).

[92] Most recently, Kathryn Kerby-Fulton, "Langland and the Bibliographic Ego," in *70*, 70, 75.

[93] After Hudson (*713*, 408), David Aers and Ralph Hanna have recently urged for such a reconsideration. See Aers, "Review of Steven Justice and Kathryn Kerby-Fulton, eds. *Written Work: Langland, Labor, and Authorship*. Philadelphia: Univ. of Pennsylvania Press, 1997," *Yearbook of Langland Studies* 12 (1998): 212; and Hanna (*66*, 239–40).

"lollare," we will not miss Langland engaging his own context on this particular but very important issue. For he makes choices in C9 that confound both medieval and contemporary expectations that there is, or should be, a predictable Wycliffite creed behind these odious figures.[94] This does not mean Langland is a Wycliffite, only that he is not seeing "lollardy" through the eyes of orthodoxy.

---

[94] Hudson rightly writes that "loller for [Langland] was not to be associated with any specific creed," yet continues to say that "analysis of his use of the word does not advance our understanding of Langland's relationship to Wycliffism" (*713*, 407). See also Hanna (*70*, 60 n.59). It seems, however, that an analysis of Langland's use can advance our understanding of the poet's sense about the social-symbolic significance of Wycliffism.

Are All Lollards Lollards?

Andrew E. Larsen

Ralph de Tremur was a heretic with a long career as a troublemaker. Having studied for a few years at Oxford, he resigned his living at Warleggan as a rector, but subsequently returned to Warleggan, despoiled the new rector of his goods and burned down the man's house. Some years later, Tremur began teaching in the diocese of Exeter that the bread and wine of the sacraments were not transmuted into the body and blood of Christ, a teaching popular enough to attract a secret following, according to a letter written by John Grandisson, the bishop of Exeter. According to witnesses, Tremur ridiculed both St. Peter and St. John and said of the Eucharist "You foolishly adore the work of your hands. For what else does the priest do but gape over a piece of bread and breathe on it?" Motivated apparently by this attitude, he broke into a church, stole a pyx and burned the host it contained. He escaped capture by the bishop of Exeter by going to London, where he vanishes from the records.[1]

Ralph de Tremur appears, on the surface, to fit the profile of a typical Lollard, offering a good example of the anticlericalism and rejection of transubstantiation that are often seen as the chief characteristics of Wyclif's followers. The only problem with identifying Tremur as a Lollard is that these events took place in the 1330s and 50s, at least two decades before John Wyclif's teaching attracted notice.[2] Tremur's case highlights several important issues in the historiography of English heresy which, while individually of minor importance, combine to offer a serious challenge to the current interpretation of the Lollards. Heresy was somewhat more widespread in thirteenth- and fourteenth-century England than has often been acknowledged, and the lack of attention to this fact has encouraged scholars to lump non-Lollard heretics in with genuine Lollards.

The first of the issues illustrated by Tremur's case is quite simply the fact that heresy existed in England long before the advent of the Lollards. In the

My thanks go to the editors of this volume, who offered many invaluable suggestions for this essay.

[1] Tremur's actions can be traced in *The Register of John de Grandisson*, ed. F.C. Hingeston-Randolph (London: Bell, 1894), 2.621–2, 627, 660, 715, 1147–9, 1180, 1303, and 3.1285. See also Margaret Aston (*283*, 34 n.20).

[2] However, as Aston points out, Tremur's uncle held the living of Lifton, Devonshire, from which later came the Lollard preacher Lawrence Bedeman. There is no known direct connect between Tremur and Bedeman, but the coincidence is intriguing; Aston (*283*, 35 n.20).

period from 1160 to 1377, there are at least forty-five recorded cases of an individual or a group accused of, investigated for, or punished for heresy or actions or ideas indicative of heterodox belief. Part of the reason for the scarcity of cases has to do with issues of documentation rather than a real absence of heresy.[3] Another factor seems to be a general lack of interest in or unwillingness on the part of English bishops to pursue heresy aggressively. There is a great deal that can be said about these cases, but this paper is chiefly concerned with the historiography of pre-Lollard heresy, so I will make only occasional reference to these cases as the need arises.

The earliest historian to consider the question of heresy in England was Bishop Stubbs, back in 1833, and his opinion was that before the time of Wyclif heresy was rare and unimportant, and this has been the standard statement on the question ever since.[4] Scholars such as Felix Makower, F.W. Maitland, H.G. Richardson, and Malcolm Lambert have all discussed the subject in passing, and all have been of essentially the same opinion as Bishop Stubbs, that pre-Lollard heresy is historically unimportant and that its study has little to offer the study of either the English church or Lollardy.[5] Thus, even in relatively recent works, one can easily learn that England was "remarkably free of this problem" and that "England produced no significant heresy before the late fourteenth century," and that what little heresy there was centered around academics "carried away by their ideas."[6] The only work to examine cases of pre-Lollard heresy in any detail is a doctoral dissertation in 1942 by John Rea Bacher, who aimed to dispel the notion that heresy was an unknown phenomenon in pre-Lollard England.[7] Regrettably, his work has been almost entirely overlooked by later scholars.

This assumption that there was no heresy in pre-Lollard England has discouraged historians from closely examining evidence related to this issue. For example, in her essay on the statute *De Heretico Comburendo*, A.K. McHardy makes the statement that "The only real precedent for the measures taken against the Lollards was the campaign waged against the Templars early in the reign of Edward II."[8] But she seems to have

---

[3] For a brief discussion of the issue of documentation of heresy in late fourteenth- and fifteenth-century ecclesiastical records, see Anne Hudson (*713*, 32–5), and Aston (*286*). Both Hudson and Aston point out that episcopal registers clearly omit the majority of heresy cases which were overseen by bishops. The argument can, and I think should, be extended to early- and mid-fourteenth-century episcopal records. See also J.A.F. Thomson (*1189*, 3), and R.I. Moore, *The Formation of a Persecuting Society* (Oxford: Blackwell, 1987), 66–8.

[4] *Report of the Ecclesiastical Courts Commission* (British Parliamentary Papers, 1833), 24, Historical Appendix 2, 52, and William Stubbs, *The Constitutional History of England in its Origin and Development* (Oxford: Clarendon, 1874–78), 3.365.

[5] See Felix Makower, *The Constitutional History and Constitution of the Church of England* (London, 1895), 183–5; Sir Frederick Pollock and Frederick William Maitland, *The History of English Law before the Time of Edward I* (Cambridge: Cambridge Univ. Press, 1895), 2.544–52; H.G. Richardson (*1062*); Malcolm Lambert (*821*, 225).

[6] Adrian Morey and C.N.L. Brooke, *Gilbert Foliot and his Letters* (Cambridge: Cambridge Univ. Press, 1965), 241; Lambert (*821*, 225); R.N. Swanson (*1165*, 309).

[7] John Rea Bacher (*290*). Given that World War II was happening when Bacher's work was published, and also that it seems to have enjoyed a quite limited print run, it is hardly surprising that it quickly fell into obscurity.

[8] A.K. McHardy (*941*, 112).

overlooked the fact that there is reliable evidence that the Council of Oxford in 1222 condemned a deacon to burning for having converted to Judaism, the sentence being carried out by the sheriff of Oxford.[9] An Albigensian was burned in London in 1210 by officials of either the Crown or the City of London.[10] There is also evidence that a group of Spiritual Franciscans were burned in England in 1330.[11] All three of these cases surely qualify to some extent as "precedent for the measures taken against the Lollards" in 1401, and a closer look at them and at other early heresy cases may help us better understand the legal mechanisms employed against the Lollards.

This brings us to my second issue, namely that the myth that there was no heresy in pre-Lollard England has resulted in distortions of the record of pre-Lollard heretics, as scholars sought to connect them to Wyclif and the Lollards somehow. In dealing with the case of Marion Rye, a nun of Romsey accused of rejecting the sacraments and consorting with itinerant preachers, T.F. Lirby speculated that Marion was a follower of Wyclif, despite the fact that the events which led to the accusations occurred in 1369, at least eight years before she could plausibly have learned about Wyclif's teachings on the sacraments.[12] Over the years, several historians have attempted to link the notorious priest John Ball to Wyclif.[13] This overlooks the fact that Ball was already going "from country to country" preaching articles contrary to the faith of the church" as early as 1364.[14] At some point a scholar who had access to the *Liber cancellari* at Oxford suggested in a marginal note that an unspecified Friar John who was removed from regency in 1358 because of his teachings on dominion was actually John Wyclif, even through Wyclif was not a friar and couldn't have been a regent master that early.[15] Most startlingly, the editors of the *Victoria History of the County of Huntingdon* discussed the case of Maud de Algekirk, a recluse who was examined for suspect beliefs, and commented that 1346 seemed early for Lollard teaching.[16]

---

[9] Ralph of Coggeshall, *Chronicon*, 190–1; Walter of Coventry, *Memoriale Fratris* (RS 58), 2.251–2; *Annales de Dunstaplia* in *Annales Monastici* (RS 36), 3.76. There are also unreliable and confused reports of this council and its legal proceedings in other sources. See also Bacher (*290*, 10–11). The best analysis of these events is provided by F.W. Maitland, "The Deacon and the Jewess," in *Roman Canon Law in the Church of England* (London: Methuen, 1898), 158–79.

[10] *De Antiquis Legibus Liber* (Camden Society: 1846), 34.3; Ranulf Higden, *Polychronicon* (RS 41), 8.190; Ralph of Coggeshall, *Chronicon* (MGH Scriptores 27), 357 (this passage was not included in the Rolls Series edition); *Chronicle of London from 1089 to 1483*, ed. Nicholas Harris Nicolas and Edward Tyrell (London: Longman, 1827), 7. See also Peter Biller, *William of Newburgh and the Cathar Mission to England* (in *94*, 27).

[11] Thomas de Burton, *Chronica Monasterii de Melsa* (RS 43), 2.323. This same event is also recorded in the Beguin Martyrology; see Louisa Burnham, "So Great a Light, So Great a Smoke: The Heresy and Resistance of the Beguins of Languedoc (1314–1330)" (Ph.D. diss., North-western University, 2000), 315–20.

[12] *Register of William of Wykeham*, ed. T.F. Lirby (London: Simpkim, 1899), 77–9.

[13] Thus, for example, Philip Lindsay and Reg Groves reject the connection between Ball and Wyclif, but then argue that Ball *was* probably influenced by Wyclif (*864*, 70–1).

[14] *The Patent Rolls of Edward III*, 12.476. This document seems to have been largely overlooked by those studying Ball.

[15] *Munimenta Academica*, ed. H. Anstey (RS 50), 1.208–11; see also Andrew E. Larsen (*824*).

[16] *Victoria History of the County of Huntingdon*, ed. William Page and Glanville Proby (London: St. Catherine, 1926), 1.46 n.2.

In all of these cases, the myth that there was no heresy in England before John Wyclif and the Lollards has led scholars to attempt to read them as if they were somehow Lollards, overlooking in all cases the fact that they are simply too early to have any connection to Wyclif or Lollardy. That normally reliable scholars could overlook something so basic as simple chronology is a testament to the strength of this myth in English historiography. The point here is not to pick nits in these scholars' work; in most cases these are small mistakes. But they demonstrate the myth's power to distort the historiography on pre-Lollard heresy.

However, some of these cases do share a common feature with Lollardy, namely the heretical doctrines which attracted attention. Ralph de Tremur's denial of transubstantiation and desecration of the host are certainly things which look Lollard. Friar John's position on dominion does have something in common with Wyclif's stance on the issue. Marion Rye's disinterest in the sacrament and preference for itinerant preachers would be plausibly Lollard had the charges been brought twenty years later than they were.

Nor are these the only cases of pre-Lollard heresy that share common points with the Lollards. In 1240, a renegade Carthusian was apprehended in Cambridge because he refused to enter churches, claiming instead that the pope was a heretic who had polluted the church.[17] In 1319, Margaret Syward was discovered to have averted her face from the elevation of the host in an apparent denial of transubstantiation and the Incarnation, for which she was excommunicated.[18] In 1334, Friar Henry de Staunton developed a following in York for his unspecified teachings against the faith, from which "a certain sect of men arose under the guise of piety, distrust and schism increased between clergy and people, [and] insults, scandals, fighting, quarrels, conspiracies and assemblies illicitly occurred."[19] In 1336, an apostate Franciscan named Ranulf proposed "many things against the Catholic faith and the sacraments of the church."[20]

The list could be continued, but the point here is that heresy was not unknown in England before the Lollards, and some of that heresy could easily be associated with Lollardy, were it not for the fact that it occurred too early. The Lollards were not the first people in England to deny transubstantiation, reject the sacramental power of the clergy, and engage in anti-clerical activity.[21]

This brings us to my third point and the central issue of this essay. If there were cases of heresy which resemble Lollardy in the period before 1377 but which can have no direct connection to Lollardy, it follows as probable that

---

[17] Matthew Paris, *Chronica Majora* (RS 57), 4.32–4.

[18] Irene J. Churchill, *Canterbury Administration* (London: Church Historical Society, 1933), 1.313–14.

[19] "secta quedam hominum sub pietatis specie insurrexit, diffidium et schisma inter clerum et populum excrevit, convicia, opprobria, contentiones, rixe, conspirationes, conventiculeque illicite fiebant et fiunt, ac datur conjugibus audacia et occasio et econtra suos perperam dimittendi maritos." *Register of William Melton* (London: Canterbury and York Society, 1988), 76.131–2.

[20] "Hic multa contra fidem catholicam et sacramenta ecclesiae superstitiose ac pertinaciter proponebat coram magistris Theologiae tam religiosis quam saecularibus, et similiter coram episcopo Stephano." *Annales Paulini de Tempore Edwardi Tertii* (RS 76), 1.365.

[21] Hudson (*694*, 125).

there were similar cases in England after 1377, which, like the cases of Marion Rye and John Ball, have been mistaken for cases of Lollardy by scholars. The corollary to the myth that there was no heresy in England before 1377 is that all heresy occurring in England after 1377 must be associated with Wyclif and Lollardy. And thus, I ask the question, "Are all Lollards Lollards?"

The answer, I believe, must be "No." Not every heretic currently identified as a Lollard had a meaningful connection to that heresy. A prime example is the butcher of Standon, who was accused in 1452 of maintaining that there was no god save the sun and the moon. But, to quote K.B. MacFarlane on this case, "the fact that he was opposed to baptism and the veneration of images proves that, drunk or sober, he was a Lollard."[22] The holes in this statement become obvious once it is examined. If the man was drunk enough that we should ignore his statement about the sun and the moon, can his position on baptism and the veneration of images be considered any more reliable? On the other hand, if he was sober enough for us to consider his statement as broadly representative of his actual beliefs, we cannot reasonably consider this man a Lollard, since no Lollard would have denied Christ's divinity and the existence of God. The fact that the man held two ideas which are in harmony with Lollardy makes him no more a Lollard than it makes Ralph de Tremur a Lollard. At best, we may suspect that he was influenced by Lollardy, but even that assumption is unnecessary.

It is commonly remarked that the Lollards held a wide variety of beliefs, due in large part to their lower-class origins and lack of mental refinement. J.A.F. Thomson sees Lollardy as "a series of attitudes from which beliefs evolved rather than as a set of doctrines."[23] Other scholars, like Shannon McSheffrey, have preferred to emphasize social factors over doctrinal ones.[24] R.N. Swanson has challenged the movement's existence as anything more than an historian's construct.[25] It has sometimes been acknowledged that the heterogeneous nature of Lollard beliefs makes it difficult to assess their relationship to John Wyclif, but it has less often been admitted that it also problematizes talking about the Lollards as a group. If the Lollards held few common doctrines or practices, then there is little point in discussing them as a sect, since the thing which unites a religious sect is its common beliefs and practices.[26]

But this eclecticism of belief is itself to some extent an assumption. In his study of the Norwich heresy trials of 1428–31, Norman Tanner found that

---

[22] K.B. McFarlane (*933*, 185). See also Thomson (*1189*, 67, 241). Thomson suggests that his worship of the sun and the moon was sign of a pagan survival, but such a conjecture is unnecessary. An interesting parallel to the Butcher of Standon is the case of Giovanni Freyria, a fourteenth-century heretic from the Italian Alps, who rejected the Holy Spirit and adored the sun and the moon, but still recited the Pater Noster and the Ave. See Malcolm Lambert, *The Cathars* (Oxford: Blackwell, 1998), 291.

[23] Thomson (*1189*, 244).

[24] Shannon McSheffrey (*949*).

[25] Swanson (*1165*, 335, 343).

[26] Aston (*288*) contains a detailed look at the medieval usage of the term "sect," especially in reference to the Lollards.

the accused Lollards had a considerable degree of uniformity to their beliefs, even allowing for standardization imposed on the records by the questionnaire being used.[27] He noted that those investigated had a core set of beliefs, focused around

> denying the value of the sacraments as they were then administered by the Church, and [around] a positive alternative to them. The heart of the alternative was the belief that man could reach God directly and that he might therefore bypass intermediary things and persons, particularly priests.[28]

He goes on to note that they generally wished to dispose of baptism and the Eucharist completely, but wished to retain matrimony as a sacrament.

How is it that Tanner could find such close agreement in a sect noted for its eclectic beliefs? In part, the answer lies in the fact that many scholars who have studied the Lollards have made the assumption that heretics in England after 1377 must be Lollards, and the resulting plethora of beliefs has forced them to conclude that the Lollards were heterogeneous in their beliefs. If we allow for the possibility that there were non-Lollard heretics in late medieval England, some of this heterogeneity vanishes, and it becomes possible to recognize non-Lollards among the Lollards.

The presence of non-Lollard heretics in such proceedings should not be a surprise. Once English authorities became concerned about heresy, it was only to be expected that they would begin to look closely at individuals who a few generations earlier might have been ignored by bishops less concerned with the problem of heresy. Thus those with a wide variety of heterodox beliefs were bound to be swept up with the Lollards.

The assumption that all heretics after 1377 are Lollards also has another flaw in it, namely that it suggests that all people who became Lollards either remained Lollards or returned to Catholic orthodoxy. In fact, it is also possible that a man or woman might become a Lollard and then drift out of that sect without returning to Catholic orthodoxy, following instead an idiosyncratic mixture of orthodox, Lollard, and personal beliefs not part of Lollardy. The butcher of Standon might well have followed such a path.

Another example of a probable non-Lollard is the case of Lawrence of St. Martin, a Wiltshire knight who desecrated the host in 1381 by taking it home after the Mass and eating it with oysters, onions, and wine.[29] Although Thomas Walsingham does not explicitly say Lawrence was a Lollard, he clearly wants his readers to make the association, and H.B. Workman accepts this, saying that the incident affected Bishop Erghum of Salisbury, who had to deal with Lawrence's action, by "incensing him" against all Lollards. With some surprisingly lenient prodding by Erghum, Lawrence eventually acknowledged his error and submitted to penance.

---

[27] Norman F. Tanner (*208*, 10–22).

[28] Tanner (*208*, 20).

[29] Thomas Walsingham (*221*, 450–1); Herbert B. Workman (*1308*, 2.255). See also Aston (*287*, 34–5) and (*283*, 39–40). Workman argues that this is the same Lawrence of St. Martin who is referred to in other documents as a converted Jew, which, if correct, might shed additional light on his rejection of transubstantiation. Aston, however, rejects this identification.

Although Lawrence could have been a Lollard, there is nothing in the recorded events to connect him to the sect except for his denial of transubstantiation, and 1381 is a few years too early for Lollardy in Salisbury. Even Walsingham seems reluctant to make the association between Lawrence and Lollardy (although he does incorrectly associate Lawrence with the household of Sir John Montagu). More likely, Lawrence had simply arrived at his rejection of transubstantiation independently.

But the best example of this whole historiographic problem is William Colyn, who appears in the Norwich heresy records.[30] In addition to saying that images ought not be honored and that he would rather pay for the burning than the painting of images, Colyn also said that he would rather travel to see the king of England than go to his cottage door to see the sacrament, that he would rather touch the secret member of a woman than the sacrament of the altar, that marriage ought to be completely eliminated, that mankind is bound to Christ rather than to the Father because it was Christ who redeemed man while the Father damned man, and that no souls had entered Heaven since Christ's time (although Colyn denied having made this last statement). When Colyn is compared to the other heretics in the Norwich trial records, he stands out. His dislike of images and disregard for the Eucharist seem typical of the others accused, but his views on the Trinity and the fate of souls stand in sharp contrast, since no other accused person in the Norwich trial records makes any statement like these. His rejection of marriage is also atypical, and makes his rejection of the sacrament seem like a bawdy joke.[31] Clearly Colyn had moved away from orthodoxy, and he must have been familiar with Lollard teachings, but it is equally clear that he disagreed with both orthodox Catholics and Lollards in his views on the Trinity and marriage. Thus we must classify Colyn as a non-Lollard heretic, since he departed from what was evidently the core beliefs of Lollards in the vicinity of Norwich at his time.[32]

William Colyn is not alone in standing out among Lollards for the peculiarity of his beliefs. Thomas Semer rejected the Virgin Birth, the existence of Heaven and Hell, the immortality of the soul, the Trinity, the supremacy of God over the Devil, the universality of Christ's atonement, and the divine origin of the Scriptures, a range of beliefs that make it unclear that he should be considered a Christian, let alone a Lollard.[33] Another heretic denied the immortality of the soul, and a third rejected the Son and the Holy Ghost, as well as the resurrection, images, and priests.[34] Thomson prefers to label these men, and others like them, as "extremists," but the term is a misleading one. Such beliefs are not extreme in the sense of

---

[30] Tanner (*208*, 89–92).

[31] It is also worth noting that Colyn appears to have been socially anomalous for the Norwich Lollards as well. He came from South Creake, and to judge from the distribution map of the defendants in Tanner (*208*, 27) this was some distance from the home towns of any of the other accused heretics.

[32] Aston calls him "more of a crank than a Lollard," (*287*, 43 n.100).

[33] Thomson (*1189*, 36–7, 248).

[34] Thomson (*1189*, 82, 248–9).

being intensely Lollard, since they ran against some of the basic notions of Lollardy. They are only extreme in the sense of being further removed from orthodoxy than normal Lollard belief.

One final case will serve as a good point of comparison. Under the year 1391, Henry Knighton describes an incident in which a woman in London taught her daughter to dress as a priest (complete with a tonsure) and celebrate the mass secretly.[35] This continued for some time, until it was reported to Bishop Braybrooke, who put a stop to it and imposed penance on them. Knighton's account makes no mention of Lollardy in this case, nor does he connect it in any way with other instances of Lollardy. Indeed, nothing in his narrative for 1391 points toward Lollardy at all. Thus it seems possible that these two women were independent heretics. But in this case, there are reasons to believe that they probably were Lollards. Margaret Aston has pointed out several striking parallels between this case and that of William Ramsbury, a Lollard who secretly received a tonsure and performed the sacraments illicitly.[36] The events occurred in London at a time when Lollardy was circulating in the city and therefore the women could easily have had Lollard contacts. On the balance, it seems likely that these women were Lollards, although it is wise to remember that Lollardy was not the only possibility.

In order to make distinctions between Lollards and other heretics, it is necessary to establish more closely what constitutes a Lollard. If there were no heretics in England before the Lollards, then it is reasonable to assume that those heretics that we can find in England after 1377 or so must be Lollards. But, as has been shown, that assumption is groundless. There were heretics in England before 1377 and there were heretics in England after 1377 who had no connection with Lollardy. If we are to gain the clearest possible picture of Lollardy, we must establish some definition for the term "Lollard", or at least impose a set of boundaries, to help us distinguish between Lollards and non-Lollard heretics.

However, before we can attempt to define "Lollard," it will be necessary to establish the scholarly criteria for identifying any heretic, and here we need to be more precise than many scholars have so far been. Until scholars have determined what guidelines to use for identifying and classifying heretics, it will remain difficult to discuss the Lollards with any precision. We could, for example, define a medieval heretic as anyone who was formally found guilty of heresy as it was technically defined by canon law. This definition has the advantage that it is very clear and specific and offers us a solid guideline. But it is also extremely restrictive. It requires us to consider as heretics only those who passed through church courts, were found guilty, and left a surviving record. It leaves us no room for opinion, because it entirely removes us from process of classification. It also makes it difficult to speak of "heretical writings," because in many

---

[35] Henry Knighton (*164*, 2.316–17). See also Aston (*274*, 454–5).

[36] Aston (*274*, 461). She seems to feel that these women were Lollards, but that there is not enough evidence to assume that there was any coordinated effort of Lollard women to act as priests.

cases (particularly with Lollard writings) a work is anonymous, and therefore almost inherently outside this criterion.[37] By this criterion, Ralph de Tremur was not a heretic, since he never underwent a formal trial, so far as we know.

A second approach would be to identify as a heretic anyone who was considered to be a heretic by the Church. Essentially, this is a less strict version of the previous approach. It is a more flexible approach, because it does not require solid evidence that a person was condemned by the Church, only that Church authorities thought that the person held erroneous ideas at some point. By this criterion, Ralph de Tremur was a heretic, since Bishop Grandisson labeled him one. But, as the first option does, it excludes us from considering anonymous works as heretical unless we can prove that the work in question was considered to be heretical. Furthermore, it leaves the process of identification and classification entirely in the hands of the medieval clergy, who often lumped unrelated groups together. In the eleventh and twelfth centuries, Church authorities tended to call any heretic a Manichean, and in fifteenth-century England, they tended to call any heretic a Lollard. Scholars often see the need to correct the classification applied by Church authorities, but doing this counters much of the point of using the opinion of Church authorities as the guideline.

These first two options also repeat a problem of the earlier historiography on pre-Lollard heresy. The majority of those scholars who have examined the question of heresy in pre-Lollard England have for the most part approached it as a legal question; in other words, they studied the *crime* of heresy. Such an approach carries with it the unspoken assumption that individuals consciously set out to commit heresy the way one might set out to commit murder or arson. Because of this, these scholars were generally uncritical of the intellectual dimensions of the heresy records they studied, and generally took the charges at face value. Thus, for example, Maitland began his discussion of heresy by saying, "It remains for us to speak of an offense of which few Englishmen were guilty, and about which therefore our courts seldom spoke."[38]

But individuals who actively set out to commit heresy must have been rare. Had John de Hamslap literally "preached against the faith" ("pre-d[i]cavit contra fidem") as government documents from 1233 claim, he would have been a shocking deviant.[39] Those labeled as heretics generally believed that their religious ideas were correct, and that it was the mainstream Church which had somehow deviated from the truth. Instead, charges of heresy arise from a disjunction between the beliefs of an individual or a group and the beliefs of a higher authority which had the power to label people as heretics. Therefore, heresy is as much a barometer of the mindset of the authorities who "make heretics" as it is to the mindset

---

[37] Hudson (*694*, 125).
[38] Pollock and Maitland, *English Law*, 2.544.
[39] For the case of John de Hamslap, see the *Liberate Rolls*, 1226–40, 207, and the *Curia Regis Rolls*, 15.57.

of those who are "made heretics."[40] These first two options essentially
concentrate on Lollardy as it was constructed by English authorities, and if
it is consciously studied that way, they can reveal a great deal about the
mindset of English authorities at the time. However this approach will
necessarily paper over many variations of belief.

A third option is to label as a heretic anyone who consciously saw
themselves as deviating from the established Church and its doctrines. It
approaches Lollardy from the documents of those who considered themselves Lollards, to see how they constructed Lollardy for themselves. Much
of the recent work done on Lollards has employed this approach and has
opened up new questions about Lollard ideas and writings. But this option
requires us to be able to clearly demonstrate that an individual thought of
him or herself as a Lollard, when in many cases we cannot definitely prove
this. Explicit self-identification is rare, which limits the value of this
approach.[41]

The final option is to label as a heretic anyone whom modern scholarship
can demonstrate to have held beliefs or taken actions that are sufficiently
outside the mainstream of medieval orthodox teaching. In practice, this is
the option employed by most scholars, who adhere to the second or third
option until they find some error in classification, find a person or piece of
writing that escaped the attention or commentary of Church authorities, or
find a document that appears outside the mainstream without a clear self-
designation as Lollard. It has the benefit of being a more flexible approach
than the other two, and it focuses directly on what a person evidently
believed, said, and did, rather than simply on what the Church thought
about what a person believed, said, and did. It enables us to see into the
assumption of church authorities in a much clearer way than the other two
options. It also allows us to incorporate into our discussion written works
that were anonymous or which escaped evaluation by the Church. It does,
however, have the drawback that it requires us to pass judgment on people
and writings and on the opinions of clergy who may well have had more
information about a given case than we do today. It requires that scholars
get into the business of heretication, evaluating people and writings and
determining to what degree they were heretical according to the standards
of the time.

While some may be uncomfortable with the idea of hereticating, in
practice scholars do this all the time. Margery Kempe is a good example.
She aroused suspicions of being a heretic and was interrogated by church
authorities on more than one occasion. In the course of her interview with
Archbishop Bowet, she demonstrated several heterodox qualities, including
an insistence on wearing white, refusal to swear an oath, an ability to quote
Scripture directly, a tendency to preach, and attitudes bordering on anticlericalism. The clergy present openly accused her of heresy, and while she
managed to satisfy Archbishop Bowet with her answers to questions of

[40] Moore, *Formation*, 68–72.
[41] Swanson (*1165*, 336).

doctrine, he was evidently sufficiently uncomfortable with her that he ordered her to leave his diocese and paid someone to escort her, apparently in an effort to make sure she actually left the area.[42] Yet most recent scholars have chosen not to classify her as a heretic and prefer to call her a "religious enthusiast" or something similar. Thus, for instance, Karma Lochrie accepts Margery's orthodoxy, although she acknowledges close points of similarity between Margery's defense of herself and Lollard arguments, and R.N. Swanson asserts that she was not a Lollard, while David Lawton is concerned to defend Margery from the charge of blasphemy and heresy.[43] But not all scholars agree with this position. To take only one example, Lynn Staley sees Margery as being highly sympathetic to Lollardy but refuses to call her a Lollard.[44] But regardless of their respective positions, these scholars have made decisions about Margery's orthodoxy by evaluating what we know of her thoughts and actions.

This fourth option is the most logical approach, and it accords most closely with what modern scholars generally do. But it does require some degree of precision in the way we use terms and how we classify people. In particular, there must be some degree of consensus about how "Lollard" is defined in modern scholarly usage. The term could be given a broad definition of "any heretic in England after 1377." Given that it took some time for the term "Lollard" to assume a fixed meaning in the sources, this definition has some value.[45] But such a definition is unsatisfying and awkward. If the term has no fixed doctrinal or ideological meaning, then 1377 is a meaningless starting date, and we would need to extend the term to cover any heretic in England at any point. But to do that robs the term of any value as a historical label, and, I suspect, offends the sensibilities of those who wish to study Lollards as they are more generally understood. Even if we arbitrarily limit Lollardy to the period after 1377 and simply apply the term to all heretics regardless of their beliefs, it becomes meaningless to discuss Lollards as a whole, since they share no other characteristics than being English heretics.

The other option is to give the term "Lollard" a much narrower meaning, based on a set of agreed-upon criteria. A Lollard, I propose, is someone in the period after 1377 who shares a significant number of beliefs associated with John Wyclif and his identifiable followers. Unlike the first definition, this one has much to recommend it. Firstly, it accords roughly with the common scholarly usage of the term. And it is clear that at least by 1400, English authorities conceived of Lollardy as rooted in Wyclif's teachings,

---

[42] *The Book of Margery Kempe*, trans. Barry Windeatt (New York: Penguin, 1985), 161–7.
[43] Karma Lochrie (*871*, 108–112); David Lawton (*829*); Swanson (*1165*, 337).
[44] Lynn Staley, *Margery Kempe's Dissenting Fictions* (University Park: Pennsylvania State, 1994), 127.
[45] It is also important to note that in the late fourteenth and fifteenth centuries, the term's meaning was never completely fixed. In addition to the way trained theologians used it, it was also a term of abuse that was not always synonymous with "heretic," as when Chaucer's Shipman uses it in the famous "I smelle a loller in the wind" passage. So even in the fifteenth century, not every Lollard was a Lollard. See Thomson (*1190*, 42–3).

so it accords roughly with the term's usage by theologians in the fifteenth century.[46] Secondly, it offers a relatively clear set of guidelines for identifying a Lollard. A Lollard is someone who can be shown to have held a specific set of doctrinal ideas based originally on the teachings of Wyclif, or, failing that, someone who can be shown to have adhered to some of those doctrinal ideas and who can be shown to have had significant social contacts with Wyclif or with someone who can be shown to be a Lollard.[47] The female priest of London is a good example of this. Her actions demonstrated a number of parallels to Lollard belief and she lived in a community where Lollardy was comparatively common. Possession of Lollard writings is another useful criterion, especially given how prominently it features in the records of heresy investigations. Thirdly, it enables us to exclude those who may have held heretical ideas but who cannot be considered Lollards because of other beliefs, such as William Colyn and the butcher of Standon. Finally, it allows us to talk in a meaningful way about Lollardy as a specific set of ideas, instead of as a vaguely defined system of anticlericalism and opposition to the sacraments and the veneration of images.

To define Lollardy based on the teachings of John Wyclif may seem problematic, since it is unclear how well many Lollards understood those teachings.[48] Yet it is also clear that there were many who understood Wyclif's ideas quite well, both in Oxford and elsewhere, and since in many cases these were the men responsible to transmitting Wyclif's teachings, it is reasonable to make those teachings the basis for Lollardy. Much of the body of Lollard writing shows an awareness of Wyclif's main ideas, and Tanner was able to identify parallels between many of the ideas of the Norwich heretics and Wyclif's writings. To define Lollardy more broadly, without basing it in Wyclif's teachings, is to cast the net so as to include many who were not Lollards and thus to continue the problems identified in this paper.

The final question then is which ideas form the core of the "Lollard Creed." In Tanner's examination of the Norwich heresy trial records, he classified the beliefs mentioned according to broad categories.[49] Of the 60 cases, 45 of them contained specific charges about various categories. Of these 45, 29 contain unorthodox statements on baptism, 37 on confession, 35 on the Eucharist, and 23 on confirmation. 23 cases involved the rejection of veneration of images, 37 the rejection of veneration of saints, and 34 the rejection of pilgrimages. 22 cases involved the rejection of swearing oaths, 32 the rejection of fasting and abstinence, 25 the rejection of special days, and 32 the rejection of tithes or similar dues to the clergy. Thus, these ideas occurred in one half to three quarters of all cases in which specific charges were levied, and Tanner was able to find parallels for most of these

---

[46] Swanson (*1165*, 334–5); J.A.F. Thomson (*1190*, 40–42).
[47] Since there has been a lot of attention paid in recent decades to Lollard society and social networks, this task may be easier than it sounds.
[48] Thomson (*1190*, 54–55); Thomson (*1189*, 239).
[49] Tanner (*208*, 11).

positions in the works of Wyclif, although in some cases Wyclif's position was more moderate than those expressed in the Norwich records. Thus the person in question must hold more than one of these ideas and ideally should hold several of them. Anticlerical statements occur frequently in these records, but are so common in orthodox works of the period that they cannot themselves be considered a definitive indicator of Lollardy. This list provides a good starting point for defining the core Lollard beliefs.

It is also worth noting that the absence of a standard Lollard belief, such as the rejection of transubstantiation, from a recorded confession or abjuration is not necessarily proof that the person in question did not hold that belief. If those asking the questions did not ask about transubstantiation or were unable to draw out a clearly heretical response to the question, the record would not indicate any statement about transubstantiation.[50] Thus, while only 35 of 45 Norwich Lollards are recorded as holding heretical views about the Eucharist, the actual number of people who held such views may have been higher. So it is possible that the degree of uniformity of belief may be slightly underrepresented in the evidence.

On the negative side, the person in question must not hold any beliefs significantly at odds with any of the core beliefs of Lollardy. He or she must not advocate radical notions about the nature of God or the possibility of salvation, for example. They must accept the basic authority of the Bible and must not reject Lollard practices, such as marriage or preaching. Obviously, it would be awkward to try and compose an exhaustive list of ideas outside of Lollardy, but this "negative principle" is important, because it is often the point at which the identification of a Lollard falters, as the butcher of Standon and William Colyn demonstrate.

However, the Norwich records are at best an imperfect record of what the accused actually believed. The records reflect the interests and assumptions of the ecclesiastical authorities, and may easily have omitted or misunderstood issues which were important to the accused themselves. In working with documents related to heresy, it is important to remember that the reasons documents were produced were numerous and complex, and their relationship to heresy cases can vary widely. Thus some documents were produced by church authorities investigating heresy, while others were produced by those accused of heresy or by others in their defense. Some documents were the cause of an investigation, while others were unrelated to any formal proceedings. These varying pressures shape the form and content of the document, and an uncritical reading of them will miss important nuances.

Using the Norwich records as the basis for a "Lollard Creed" has another problem. While these records are broadly indicative of what Lollardy in East Anglia was like in the early fifteenth century, we cannot assume that they are normative for Lollardy as a whole. Any effort to define a "Lollard Creed" must take into account the variations in Lollard belief both over time and across various regions of England, as well as the degree to which

---

[50] Hudson (*694*, 131–2).

Lollardy evolved beyond Wyclif's original ideas. Thus a complete picture of Lollard belief must base itself on a wider study of various records than simply a single set of heresy trials.

To argue that the Lollards had a core set of beliefs is not to say that they were homogenous in their beliefs or that they anticipated sixteenth century confessionalism. Far from it. It is clear from a look at the Norwich heretics that there was considerable diversity of opinion even within that group. Thomson's approach of seeing Lollardy as a set of attitudes which drove belief has much to recommend it. But that range of opinion had limits.

I do not pretend that my proposed criteria comprise a definitive list, but rather one which needs development. The concept of a "Lollard creed" is a contentious one, and many scholars will undoubtedly feel that it goes too far. At a minimum, there needs to be a greater sense of the boundaries of the term "Lollard," an awareness that in some cases modern scholars have cast the net too wide and that our usage of the term must be more cautious. Individuals such as William Colyn and Thomas Semer stand as a clear demonstration of this. Such an awareness will be rewarded by a clearer picture of who the Lollards were and what they believed, and by a greater understanding of the complexities of religious life in late medieval England.

Lollardy in Oxfordshire and Northamptonshire: The Two Thomas Compworths

Maureen Jurkowski

To Thomas Compworth, an esquire of Thrupp (in Kidlington), Oxford-shire, belongs the dubious distinction of being the first layman convicted of heresy in late medieval England. As an early member of the gentry converted to Wycliffite doctrine, and as a link between the gentry and Wyclif's disciples in the Oxford colleges, he is an important figure in Lollard history. Although the role of the gentry as sponsors of Lollard book production and itinerant preachers in the later fourteenth and early fifteenth centuries is now widely accepted,[1] much remains to be discovered about the extent of gentry support, and the nature of their interaction with each other and with the Oxford academics who carried on Wyclif's work. An examination of Compworth's life and career could potentially shed light on these questions, and he has understandably attracted the attention of a number of historians of the Lollard heresy.[2] No biographical study has yet appeared, however, and he remains still a shadowy figure. Found all too rarely in extant records, he is, moreover, difficult to distinguish from his son of the same name, a successful Northamptonshire lawyer.[3]

Exploiting new archival findings, this essay will attempt to disentangle the activities of the father from those of his son and ascertain the place of both Thomas Compworths in the history of the Lollard heresy in their counties of residence: Oxfordshire and Northamptonshire. Wycliffitism was particularly strong in these counties, which, together with neighbouring

I am grateful to Dr. Simon Payling for several of the references cited below, and to Dr. Hannes Kleineke for his assistance with the map.

[1] See, for example, Anne Hudson (*691*, 181–91); K.B. McFarlane (*934*, 139–232); C. Kightly, "The Early Lollards, 1382–1428" (D.Phil. thesis, Univ. of York, 1975); Maureen Jurkowski, "John Fynderne of Findern, Derbyshire: an Exchequer official of the early fifteenth century, his circle and Lollard connections" (Ph.D. thesis, Keele Univ., 1998), 301–43; Aston and Richmond (*45*).

[2] Kightly, thesis, 107–8; A.K. McHardy (*941*, 119–20); Maureen Jurkowski (*761*, 163–4).

[3] My own recent work on Thomas Compworth senior has done little to clarify this issue: see Jurkowski (*761*, 163–4). K.B. McFarlane seems to have confused the two Thomas Compworths further with the Lincolnshire knight Sir Thomas Cumberworth, perhaps because of the spelling "*Compereworth*" adopted by the chroniclers, and the unusual will left by Cumberworth: McFarlane (*933*, 126–8, 161); and see n. 4 below. For Cumberworth, see C. Rawcliffe, "Thomas Cumberworth (d.1451), of Somerby and Stain, Lincs. and Argam, Yorks.," in *The History of Parliament: House of Commons, 1386–1421*, ed. J.S. Roskell, L. Clark and C. Rawcliffe, 4 vols. (Stroud: Sutton, 1992), 713–15.

Buckinghamshire, supplied a number of insurgents for the Lollard revolt of 1414, and it is surely no accident that all three counties were near to the heresy's academic centre. Tracing the associations of the Compworths with known and suspected Lollard sympathisers in these counties will help to reconstruct the networks of association vital to tracking the heresy's spread and to assessing its character and extent. As we shall see, however, the extreme mobility of the late medieval gentry meant that locality was not always paramount, and our protagonists' ties to gentry sympathetic to the heresy outside these counties are easier to demonstrate. That such ties are here revealed is nonetheless a testament to the benefits of prosopography as a methodology for the study of the Lollard heresy. This essay seeks to prove above all that prosopographical study is one of the most promising lines of enquiry for understanding the nature of the heresy and its spread.

We must first establish the nature of Thomas Compworth senior's unorthodoxy itself. What were the grounds upon which he was convicted of heresy and what do we know of his religious opinions? Unfortunately, for our knowledge of the circumstances of his arrest, trial and conviction we are wholly dependent upon hostile sources. The story of Compworth's heresy is reported in a chronicle known as the *Vita Ricardi Secundi*, written by a monk of Evesham Abbey, probably the prior Nicholas Herford (d.1390), and often found in manuscripts as a continuation of Ranulf Higden's *Polychronicon*. The episode appears also in an English version of the *Polychronicon*, although the *Vita Ricardi* contains a fuller account.[4] Both chronicles state that the bishop of Lincoln was informed by the abbot of Oseney that Compworth had refused to pay tithes to him, would not be confessed by his curate and had travelled about England preaching heresy for many years. After pursuing him without success, the bishop then procured the king's letters patent authorising secular officials to arrest Compworth and secure him in the nearest castle.

All of this is confirmed by entries in Bishop Buckingham's register, which record the bishop's appointment of two successive commissions in August 1385. The first authorised three members of the bishop's household[5] to make enquiries and proceed against Compworth by reason of both his heresies and his withholding of tithes. The second commission was ordered to arrest Compworth and imprison him in Banbury castle, citing as its authority powers granted by the crown to the bishops to effect the arrest of heretics in 1382.[6] The bishop's emissaries failed, however, to take Compworth into custody, and on 18 October 1385 he was excommunicated.[7]

[4] *Historia Vitae et Regni Ricardi Secundi*, ed. G.B. Stow (Philadelphia: Univ. of Pennsylvania Press, 1977), 93–4; R. Higden, *Polychronicon*, ed. C. Babington and J.R. Lumby, 9 vols. (London: Rolls Series, 1865–86), 8.473–4. For the *Vita* and its relation to the *Polychronicon* tradition, see J. Taylor, *English Historical Literature in the Fourteenth Century* (Oxford, 1987), 74, 102–3.

[5] John Belvoir was official of Lincoln, and Thomas Brandon was the bishop's chancellor: *BRUO* (6, 164, 2155).

[6] *Royal Writs Addressed to John Buckingham, Bishop of Lincoln 1363–1398*, Lincoln Record Society 86 (Woodbridge: Boydell, 1997), 140–3; McHardy (*938*, 133–4). On the conferral of secular powers to arrest heretics, see H.G. Richardson (*1062*).

[7] PRO, Chancery, Significations of Excommunication, C85/108, no. 13.

According to the chronicles, it was the abbot of Oseney himself who arrested Compworth at his estate in Thrupp. After a period of imprisonment in Banbury castle and consultation between the archbishop of Canterbury and bishop of Lincoln, Compworth was handed over to the chancellor of the university for examination before a committee of theologians in Oxford, just before Christmas. The *Vita Ricardi Secundi* reports that when Compworth was asked about the Wycliffite errors taught to him, he answered "quod reus inventus est,"[8] but was nonetheless convicted of heresy by the testimony of witnesses and "ex confessione propria" ("by his own confession"). He is then alleged to have said that he was willing to hold fast unto death his heresies, if those who had taught him his heretical doctrine would stand by him, as they had promised. When his teachers were questioned on their views, however, "they were dombe and durste not speke, and departede. The esqwyer perceyvynge that, thoughte veryly that thei hade inducede [him] into a wronge way," and he therefore abjured his heresy.[9] He was then adjudged to pay the abbot of Oseney £40 in tithes, £10 of which were pardoned by the abbot, perhaps in exchange for a promise of immediate payment, since he reportedly paid the rest to the abbot within two days of his release. By way of penance, he was ordered to "go afore the generalle procession in the ende of the terme with a cerge or taper of wexe in his honde," although the penance was never performed, because, according to the English version, he died long before that time, rather implausibly, of "infirmite causede by sorowe and what for schame."[10]

The chronicles make clear that he was a disciple of Wyclif, but only two articles of his heretical doctrine are cited: he would neither confess his sins nor pay tithes to his parish priest. The reason for his refusal is not given, but much can be inferred from the common Lollard positions on these issues. The Lollards' denial of the necessity of confession stemmed from Wyclif's premise that the intermediacy of the priest was irrelevant to the process of obtaining God's absolution from sin, which could come only from God himself; he alone knew the sinner's state of contrition. Wyclif objected further to the decree of the Lateran Council of 1215 which imposed oral confession as an annual obligation, and to the link between absolution and the performance of penance, which often required the payment of money by the penitent. Confession had no value unless it was voluntary and the purchase of absolution was tantamount to simony. The putative efficacy of the sacrament was further diminished, moreover, by the corrupt state of the clergy who administered it. All of these ideas were expressed in contemporary Wycliffite texts, and Compworth's neglect of the confessional was probably founded upon some combination of these beliefs.[11]

Considering that the other known article of heresy against him was the withholding of tithes, it seems likely that a belief in the unworthiness of his

---

[8] Probably to be translated as "guilt has to be proven."

[9] *Polychronicon*, 8.473–4; *Vita Ricardi Secundi*, 93–4.

[10] This premature report of his death does not appear in the *Vita*: *Polychronicon*, 474. Compworth was still alive in 1398, as we shall see.

[11] Anne Hudson (*713*, 294–301).

parish priest was uppermost in his mind. His refusal to pay tithes was probably for the same reason, the Wycliffite position being that it was legitimate to withhold tithes on such grounds, although there were variant views on what made a priest unworthy and indeed on whether priests should receive a regular salary or merely alms. Many Lollards texts express hostility also to the obligatory nature of tithes and charges such as mortuaries, and the use of sanctions such as excommunication to obtain them; they put forward the view that it should be left to the judgment of the individual layman, who ought to be entitled to give his alms instead to the deserving poor, if he so chose.[12]

Compworth's objections on this score would have been exacerbated by the particular circumstances of his situation. The parish church of Kidlington had been granted to Oseney Abbey by its founder Robert d'Oilly and by 1226 had been appropriated to that Augustinian house. The abbey thus took the tithes due to the rector for itself, the endowment of the vicarage in the thirteenth century assigning little to the vicar, who was an appointee of the abbey. The vicar's paltry endowment had become a problem by the early fifteenth century, if not earlier. In 1446 the vicarage was re-endowed and a more equitable division of the tithes was made by the bishop after complaints from the parishioners that services were neglected by the vicar, an Oxford graduate who was often absent from the parish and claimed to be unable to afford an assistant chaplain.[13] This vicar was just the latest in a series of graduates instituted at Kidlington, and there is every possibility that the parish of Kidlington was similarly ill-served by its vicar at the time of Compworth's refusal to pay tithes.[14]

In any event, Compworth probably objected to the abbey's appropriation of the church in principle. The Wycliffites were fundamentally opposed to the concept of the monastic orders, whose members shut themselves away from the people to whom it was their solemn duty to preach Christ's gospel.[15] They roundly condemned monastic appropriation of churches, effected for the sole purpose of augmenting the monks' income, complaining that the latter "techen not þe parischenes goddis lawe ne mynystre hem sacramentis ne releven pore men wiþ residue of tiþes and offrynges. But setten þer a viker or a parische prest for litel cost, þou3 he be unable boþe of kunnynge and lif to reule his owene soule, and for povert of benefis he may not go to scole."[16]

On the other hand, it may have been with the abbot, rather than the parish priest, that the problem lay, since there was evidently bad feeling between Compworth and John Bokeland, abbot of Oseney from 1373 to 1404. Bokeland had clearly made the Compworth case something of a

---

[12] Hudson (*713*, 341–6).

[13] *VCH*, Oxon., 12.206–7. The bishop's re-endowment ordination exists only in a sixteenth-century copy, now among the muniments of Exeter College, Oxford (M.III.5).

[14] Unfortunately the identity of Kidlington's vicar at the time of the tithe dispute is unknown. For lists of the known incumbents, see Bodleian Library, MS Top. Oxon. d.460, 172; B. Stapleton, *Three Oxfordshire Parishes*, Oxon. Hist. Soc. 24 (Oxford: Clarendon, 1893), 40–1.

[15] Hudson (*713*, 347–51).

[16] Matthew (*182*, 116; see also 223, 427).

personal crusade, informing the bishop of Lincoln that Compworth was a Lollard and personally bringing about his capture. In addition to their quarrel over tithes, Compworth and Bokeland seem to have been in dispute over boundaries and/or property rights in Kidlington. On 6 July 1384, Compworth had come before the court of the Honour of Wallingford, overlord of his manor of Thrupp, and asked for licence to come to a formal agreement with the abbot, who had brought proceedings against him for detaining his livestock, and had also amerced him in his manorial court for emparking pigs on the abbey's common.[17] Compworth was not, moreover, the only Lollard to fall foul of the truculent Bokeland. In 1401, the same abbot was in dispute over unpaid tithes from the manor of Wharton (in Leominster, Herefs.) with John Croft, an esquire of Croft, Herefordshire.[18] Croft held other heretical views, and had been excommunicated for earlier refusing tithes to the abbot of Leominster.[19]

A further guide to Compworth's views might be found among those of a group of Lollards with whom he associated in Northampton in 1393. Compworth's presence within this circle of Wycliffites is revealed in a petition sent to the king and his council by Richard Stormsworth, a wool merchant of Northampton. Stormsworth complained that, among other Lollards, the town's mayor John Fox was sheltering "un Thomas Compworth del countee doxenford qe fut convictz devant le chanceller [de] la universitee doxenford des plusours errours et heresies."[20] Under an investigation instituted in the same year by Bishop Buckingham, several of the town's alleged Lollard sympathisers (though not Compworth, against whom no proceedings were brought) were found to subscribe to fifteen articles of heresy.[21] These included the denunciation of the worship of images and a lack of faith in the efficacy of either pilgrimages or papal indulgences. The group's contention that anyone hearing mass in a state of mortal sin was damned suggests that they believed in the value of confession, but they did express radical views on the church and the office of the priesthood. Not only did they maintain that the church should hold no property, they also disclaimed the need for either a material church or an order of priests, and held further that it was unlawful for

---

[17] *Cartulary of Oseney Abbey*, ed. H.E. Salter, 6 vols., Oxon. Hist. Soc. 84–91, 97–8 (Oxford: Clarendon, 1929–31, 1934–6), 4.141.

[18] Kightly, thesis, 180–2; O.G.S. Croft, *The House of Croft of Croft Castle* (Hereford: E.J. Thurston, 1949), 3, 5, 10–14, 28.

[19] This dispute was over the tithes of his land in Newton (in Leominster): Kightly, thesis, 181; W. Dugdale, *Monasticon Anglicanum*, ed. J. Caley et al., 6 vols. (London, 1817–30), 4.52. Imprisoned by the king in Windsor Castle in September 1394, he was released only after swearing an oath that neither he nor his family would hold any Lollard opinions: *CPR 1392–6*, 314; John Trefnant (*213*, 147–50).

[20] "A Thomas Compworth of the county of Oxford who was convicted before the chancellor of the university of Oxford of many errors and heresies." PRO, Special Collections, Ancient Petitions, SC8/142/7099. An English translation, in a seventeenth-century hand, is in BL, Cotton MS Cleo. E.II, pt. ii, ff. 213–17, and printed in E. Powell (*197*, 45–9). A petition written in response to it by Fox's supporters is printed in H.G. Richardson (*1062*, 27).

[21] For what follows, see *Royal Writs to Buckingham*, 140–3; A.K. McHardy (*938*, 138–45). The group was later imprisoned in Northampton castle. For a petition submitted by their wives to the chancellor, pleading for their release, see PRO, Chancery, Early Proceedings, C1/68/46.

priests to receive payment for celebrating divine services, objecting in particular to mortuaries and marriage oblations.

Even if we cannot be certain that Compworth shared all, or indeed any, of these opinions, he clearly held views which were perceived to be heretical by both the abbot of Oseney and the committee of university theologians before whom he was examined, and his case was important enough to come to the attention of the monk chronicler of Evesham. The extent of his involvement in an organised movement is open to question, but the author of the *Vita Ricardi Secundi* portrays him definitively as a member of a sect led by disciples of Wyclif in the Oxford colleges. The penance imposed upon him, moreover, of leading the university procession at the end of term with a candle in his hand, must have been intended to associate his supporters among the university community with the shamed man publicly. Compworth's residence at Thrupp was only some four miles north of the town, and it is significant that the bishop had ordered that he be imprisoned in Banbury rather than Oxford castle. Probably a member of the legal profession, as I shall argue below, he would have had ample opportunity to interact with these scholars, and in all likelihood, had learned his heretical doctrine through such interaction.

Who, then, was Thomas Compworth? The *Vita Ricardi Secundi* refers to him as "domicellus" and "armiger," translated in the English version as "gentylle man" and "esqwyer," but information about his birth, parentage and place of origin, is wholly lacking. He acquired his manor of Thrupp by marriage, and no Compworths are known to have held land in Oxfordshire before him. The surname "Compworth," occasionally spelled "Cumpworth," probably derives from the place-name "Cumberworth," which occurs in both Lincolnshire and Yorkshire, but there is nothing to suggest that he came from either county, and I have been able to trace only a few other Compworths in the whole of England – in London, Surrey and Essex.[22] He was a landowner in Oxfordshire by March 1361, when he gave that county as the location of his collateral for a mainprise undertaken in Chancery on behalf of John Noble, clerk. Under bonds of £10, Compworth and William Langshurst of Kent personally appeared in Chancery and promised that they would have Noble before the court to answer a debt suit in London on an appointed day, in exchange for a stay of the outlawry writ against him.[23] Compworth's role as a mainpernor suggests that he was either a practising common lawyer, who earned some of his income from acting as a professional mainpernor,[24] or a friend of the obscure John Noble, and there is sufficient other evidence to surmise the former.

[22] An "Agnes, daughter of Thomas de Compeworthe" and her husband Adam de Bassieshaw, a London tailor, were tenants of Holy Trinity Priory, London in 1275–6, and a "William de Cumpewurth" was joint owner of a tenement in Walkingstead (in Godstone), Surrey in 1243–4: PRO, Exchequer, Treasury of Receipt, Ancient Deeds, Series A, E40/2060; *Curia Regis Rolls, 1243–45*, 18, no. 731. In 1412, Exchequer officials confused Thomas Compworth the younger with another man of the same name from Colchester, who had acted as a bail bondsman for a man delivered from Cambridge gaol: PRO, Exchequer, King's Remembrancer, Memoranda Rolls, E159/189, Mich. *communia*, rot. 19.

[23] *CCR 1360–4*, 253.

[24] For this form of employment by common lawyers, see Jurkowski (*761*, 156, 162, 164–5).

By 1362 Compworth had married Agnes, widow of John Dounhall of Hanborough, and daughter and heiress of Roger Sprotton of Spratton, Northamptonshire,[25] whose ancestors had acquired the manor of Thrupp in 1298.[26] Thereafter, the Sprottons' tenure was intermittent; in 1316, John de Mymmes and his wife Joan held this estate, but Roger's father, William Sprotton, had recovered it by 1346.[27] Based upon a settlement in tail male made by his grandfather John de Mymmes, Sonette Mymmes established the title to Thrupp of her underage son Nicholas in 1360 before the council of the Black Prince, to whom the wardship of Nicholas and his lands belonged as overlord of Thrupp.[28] In Michaelmas term 1362, probably soon after their marriage, Thomas Compworth and his wife set about recovering the manor from Nicholas Mymmes and Margery, widow of his uncle William Mymmes, in the court of Common Pleas, and won the case by default in Michaelmas 1363.[29] A counter action brought by a relation of young Nicholas was soon abandoned, and the Compworths remained in possession of Thrupp for several years.[30]

Within a few years of the manor's recovery, a son, Thomas, was born to Agnes and Thomas Compworth. By Hilary term 1376, however, Agnes was dead and Nicholas Mymmes, now of age, had begun what was to prove a prolonged legal challenge to Compworth's tenure. Because he and Agnes had had issue, Thomas the elder was entitled to a life interest in the manor of Thrupp after her death.[31] The estate would then revert to Elias Dounhall, her heir and eldest son by her first marriage to John Dounhall, whom she had wed in c.1355.[32] Elias was still a minor in 1376, but his tenure of the reversion meant that Compworth could "pray his aid" in his defence of the plea of land brought against him by Nicholas Mymmes. This manoeuvre enabled him to seek an adjournment of the case until Elias had attained his majority. Mymmes opposed this adjournment, and the court ordered that jurors try the issue of whether or not it should be granted to Compworth.[33] The latter appeared at the pleading stage of this case on his own behalf, not by attorney, which was the usual practice. His ability to represent himself in this complicated suit and his employment of the strategy of invoking his stepson's aid reveal his knowledge of common law writs and procedure and suggest, moreover, that he was a man of some education and legal training. This impression is strengthened by his appointment to the commission

[25] Agnes' father probably held the manor in Spratton known as "Downhall" by the sixteenth century: *VCH, Northants.*, 4.102; and see below.

[26] *VCH, Oxon.*, 12.191–2; PRO, Court of Common Pleas, Feet of Fines, CP25/1/188/12, no. 50.

[27] *Inquisitions and Assessments Relating to Feudal Aids, 1284–1431*, 6 vols. (London: Mackie, 1899–1920), 4.163, 177.

[28] *CPR 1313–17*, 478; *Register of Edward the Black Prince*, 4 vols. (London: H.M. Stationery Office, 1930–33), 4.366.

[29] Margery held a dower interest: PRO, Court of Common Pleas, Plea Rolls, CP40/461, rot. 33; CP40/416, rot. 210; *Black Prince's Register*, 4.521.

[30] PRO, Justices Itinerant, Assize Rolls, JUST1/1458, rot. 68d.

[31] W. Holdsworth, *A History of English Law*, 5th edn., 12 vols. (London: Methuen, 1942), 3.185–8.

[32] The Dounhalls' manor in Hanborough was settled on the couple in March of that year: Corpus Christi College Archives, Oxford (hereafter CCCA), A3.ca12(1), 11, 14, 20, 21, 23.

[33] PRO, CP40/461, rot. 33.

charged with assessing the poll tax in Oxfordshire in December 1380. He was the third-named member of the commission; the first two, John Baldyngton and Edmund Stonor, were both lawyers, as were many other poll tax commissioners.[34] As I have argued elsewhere, common lawyers were particularly attracted to Wycliffite doctrine.[35]

Although Mymmes abandoned the suit in Michaelmas term 1377,[36] he initiated a new plea of land in February 1380, probably soon after Compworth's stepson Elias had attained his majority.[37] The legality of Compworth's tenure was ordered to be tried by a jury, but the case was put into respite from term to term, due to lack of jurors, for the next nine years. Compworth had meanwhile begun to be harassed by a number of local men, perhaps acting as allies of Mymmes (or possibly the abbot of Oseney), whom he sued for trespass.[38] After the trial of the Mymmes case failed to take place before assize justices at Oxford in the summer of 1387, a similar trial was scheduled for January 1388.[39] In the meantime, on 28 December 1387, in the highly charged atmosphere of the Appellant crisis, a fracas occurred at Thrupp between a party of men led by Thomas Compworth, senior, and his son Thomas, during which Roger Foliot of Tackley was slain by the younger Compworth. At an inquest held a few days later before the coroner, Compworth junior was indicted, together with his accomplices as accessories, of ambushing and killing Foliot. The indictment was called into King's Bench in March 1388, but no further action was taken for the time being. The death of the unfortunate Roger Foliot was clearly linked to the impending trial; a "Nicholas Mymmes, junior" was one of the inquest jurors.[40] What led the professional soldier Roger Foliot to make common cause with Mymmes is not altogether certain, but it may have been a by-product of his property dispute with William Shareshull, grandson of the former chief of the King's Bench Sir William Shareshull.[41] The latter had been a close associate of the Dounhall family, and Foliot may have been on poor terms with Compworth senior's stepson Elias Dounhall, as a result. Dounhall's lawsuit in 1395 against a William Foliot and others for dispossessing him of his estate in Hanborough would seem to support

[34] *CFR 1377–83*, 226. Baldyngton and Stonor were appointed *quorum* justices of gaol delivery in Oxford in 1379 and 1380, respectively: PRO, Chancery, Patent Rolls, C66/304, m. 9d; C66/305, m. 46d; C66/307, m. 22d.
[35] Jurkowski (*761*, 155–82).
[36] The last jury respite is recorded in Trin. 1377: PRO, CP40/466, rot. 2d.
[37] PRO, CP40/480, rot. 507. Elias was certainly of age by July 1382: CCCA, A3.ca12(1), 28.
[38] In one suit he claimed that William Cook of Kidlington and three others had abducted one of his bondmen and carried away property worth 100s. A second plea alleged that Cook and six others had raided his estate in August 1379, damaging crops: PRO, CP40/478, rot. 99; CP40/480, rot. 560d.
[39] PRO, CP40/505, rot. 423; CP40/507, rot. 179.
[40] PRO, Chancery, *Certiorari corpus cum causa* files, C258/24, no. 22A.
[41] PRO, CP40/468, rot. 2d enrolled bills; *CChR 1372–1441*, 310; "Final Concords or *Pedes Finium*, Staffordshire, 1327–1547," ed. G. Wrottesley, *Collections for a History of Staffordshire, ed. by William Salt Archaeological Society* 11 (1890): 187; PRO, Chancery, Inquisitions *Post Mortem*, C139/145, no. 10; Chancery, Inquisitions *Ad Quod Damnum*, C143/299, no. 22; PRO, CP40/468, rot. 260; CP40/492, rot. 21; CP40/498, rot. 294; CP40/499, rots. 151, 300; CP40/502, rots. 52d, 199d.

this hypothesis.[42] Violent property disputes were endemic among the late medieval gentry, and Lollard sympathisers within this class were not immune; the lives of Thomas Tykhill and Henry Bothe, both Lollards from Derbyshire, provide examples of similarly violent behaviour.[43]

At last, in April 1389 jurors were procured to try the Mymmes case in Oxford, but Compworth failed to appear and judgment was given against him by default. Mymmes formally recovered possession of Thrupp in Hilary term 1390, and soon after sold the estate to the influential knight Sir Richard Abberbury.[44] Having lost his Oxfordshire residence, Compworth then moved to the town of Northampton, where he was given shelter by the town's Lollard mayor, John Fox, together with a runaway mercer's apprentice from London and three clerics. Among the latter was the notorious Master William Northwold, who was alleged to have stirred up trouble at a number of religious houses; one of them, notably, was Oseney Abbey.[45] Of Compworth's four companions, only the chaplain Richard Bullocke was investigated by Bishop Buckingham, but the bishop's enquiries brought to light the group of Lollards in Northampton whose heretical beliefs were discussed above. At least one member of this group, a mercer named Thomas Peyntour, was of some local prominence: he was a burgess of the town and had held office as bailiff in 1380–81.[46] He probably operated as a middleman in the wool trade between the Cotwolds and London; in 1384 Henry Coteler of Burford, Oxfordshire sued him and the London mercer Hugh Curteys for a debt of £22.[47] The Lollard mayor John Fox was also a man with interests beyond the confines of the town. In addition to messuages and shops in Northampton, he owned property in Bozeat, held jointly with Richard Pyel, perhaps a member of the Pyel family of Irthlingborough,[48] and may also have acquired land in Hanslope, just over the border of Buckinghamshire.[49]

Fox had connections with at least one influential figure outside the town: the Lollard knight Sir Richard Sturry. In 1398, a few years after Sturry's death, his widow Alice and co-executors sued Fox for a debt of £10, indicating that the two men had been business associates and perhaps also friends.[50] Lord of the Northamptonshire manor of Barnwell (in Barnwell All Saints), it was probably no coincidence that Sturry had headed the county justices of the peace who indicted Fox's enemy, Richard Stormsworth, for a

---

[42] CCCA, A3.ca12(1), 20, 21, 23, 30; *CPR 1361–4*, 516–17.

[43] Maureen Jurkowski (759); idem, thesis, 75–82, 303–43, 361–75.

[44] PRO, CP40/513, rot. 132; C. Rawcliffe and L.S. Woodger, "Sir Richard Adderbury I (c. 1331–1399), of Donnington, Berks. and Steeple Aston, Oxon.," in *Hist. Parl.*, 12–15.

[45] More recently, Northwold had been living at St. Andrew's Priory, Northampton: PRO, SC8/142/7099.

[46] M.A. Cullen, "The Lollards of Northamptonshire, 1382–1414" (Oxford, M.Litt. thesis, 1989), 66.

[47] PRO, CP40/492, rot. 121d.

[48] Cullen, thesis, 67–8. For this prominent family, see *A Calendar of the Cartularies of John Pyel and Adam Fraunceys*, ed. S.J. O'Connor, Camden Soc., 5th ser. (London: Royal Historical Society, 1993), 22–36.

[49] PRO, CP40/560, rot. 245d; *VCH, Bucks.*, 4.353.

[50] PRO, CP40/548, rot. 374. Alice is not believed to have shared her husband's religious views: J.A.F. Thomson (*1191*, 101).

series of offences in 1393.[51] It was this indictment that prompted Stormsworth to petition the chancellor about Fox's sponsorship of Lollards.[52]
There are also some grounds to suppose that there had been contact between
the Northampton Lollards and another of the so-called "Lollard knights,"
Sir Thomas Latimer of Braybrooke.[53] William Northwold was probably the
same man as "William Northwode, parson of Anderby" (in Lincolnshire),
who served as Latimer's feoffee of the manor of Braybrooke in 1371, and
might even have been the chaplain of that name first presented to Braybrooke by Latimer's father in 1349.[54] Sir Thomas Latimer himself, moreover, owned property in the town of Northampton and on its outskirts.[55] It
is likely, therefore, that these wealthy gentry sponsors played some part in
the spread of the heresy to this town in the 1390s.

How long Compworth continued to reside in Northampton is not
altogether certain; perhaps he lay low there until his son was able to
procure the king's pardon for the slaying of Roger Foliot in July 1395.[56]
In December 1396 Thomas Compworth "of Oxfordshire" mainprised in
Chancery for the release of Henry Senkere, if taken at the suit of the
Northamptonshire lawyer Thomas Beeston for leaving his service without
licence.[57] This mainpernor was probably Compworth senior, who, in
Michaelmas term 1397 brought a writ of error against the recovery made
by Nicholas Mymmes of the manor of Thrupp.[58] Although Mymmes
appointed an attorney to defend the action in Hilary 1398, Compworth's
writ progressed no further, perhaps because he had died.[59] Certainly, there
is no later mention in the records of Compworth senior; all subsequent
references to Thomas Compworth would appear to denote the activities of
Compworth junior.

In Easter term 1398, the King's Bench held sessions in Oxford and the
county coroners were required to show their records for several years past
to the justices, which resulted in a writ compelling the appearance before
them of Thomas Compworth junior. On 15 May he thus surrendered to the
court to answer the charge of the felonious killing of Roger Foliot and was
released to the custody of mainpernors until the following term. He was
then acquitted by proffering a general pardon of all treasons and felonies
dated 12 June 1398, putting an end to the matter.[60] By this time, if not
earlier, he had begun to receive legal training in London. His residence there

---

[51] *VCH, Northants.*, 3.174; PRO, C258/48, no. 18. For Sturry's appointment to the peace
commission, see *CPR 1391–6*, 292.

[52] The contents of this petition and the surrounding circumstances are discussed at length in Cullen,
thesis, 54–64, and briefly in Hudson (*713*, 79–80), and McFarlane (*933*, 126–9).

[53] For Sturry and Latimer, see McFarlane (*934*, 148–96).

[54] *CCR 1369–71*, 547; Cullen, thesis, 41–2.

[55] *CIPM*, 18, no. 439; PRO, CP40/556, rot. 97d; BL, Additional Charter 8131.

[56] *CPR 1391–6*, 600.

[57] *CCR 1396–9*, 68.

[58] PRO, CP40/513, rot. 132.

[59] PRO, King's Bench, *Coram Rege* Rolls, KB27/547, rot. 1 attorneys.

[60] PRO, KB27/548, rot. 8d rex; Chancery, Pardon Rolls, C67/30, m. 23. In Easter term 1398, he also
acted as bail bondsman for an Oxon. man indicted for manslaughter in Banbury: KB27/548, rot.
13 rex.

is signalled by a lawsuit that he initiated in Michaelmas 1398 against a man of Bedminster (in Bristol) for detinue of chattels in London worth 100s.,[61] and his frequent presence in the law courts at Westminster is similarly indicated by his regular employment henceforth as a professional bail bondsman and financial guarantor.[62] In the first of these mainprises, in October 1398, he (or possibly his father) gave surety in Chancery for a writ of *supersedeas* for John Welles, a chaplain, in the event that he was arrested for travelling abroad (i.e. to the Roman *curia*) to prosecute lawsuits.[63] A fellow of New College, Oxford, Welles was presented to the vicarage of Kidlington in 1428, and, at this time was obviously seeking preferment to a disputed benefice.[64]

Thomas Compworth junior clearly enjoyed the patronage of the aristocratic Holand family from early in his legal career, and it must have been this debt of loyalty which led him to become involved in the revolt of the earls against Henry IV in January 1400.[65] On 20 March 1400 he purchased a general pardon of all treasons, insurrections and felonies committed before 2 February of the same year. Among his mainpernors were William Sawtry, chaplain, and John Newton, clerk. Sawtry was, of course, the same Lollard chaplain burnt at the stake in March 1401, and as Alison McHardy, discoverer of this pardon, has pointed out, Newton was rector of the church of St. Benet Sherehog in London, where Sawtry was parochial chaplain.[66] Sawtry had also purchased a general pardon of "divers treasons and felonies" on 6 February 1400,[67] and this was clearly because of his participation in the revolt.

On 12 January, some seventy-five rebels who had followed the Holands – John, duke of Exeter and earl of Huntingdon, and his nephew Thomas, duke of Surrey and earl of Kent – had been indicted in the presence of the king before the court of the steward and marshal of his household in Oxford castle, and a "William Sawtre, clerk" was among them. All but one were convicted of having risen in Bampton, Wantage, Faringdon or Cirencester and proclaimed themselves for Richard II, and the four ringleaders were executed immediately. Although also condemned to death, Sawtry and his co-conspirators were instead committed to prison while the king deliberated on their fate,[68] and like Sawtry, many, if not all,

[61] He represented himself in this suit: PRO, CP40/551, rots. 407, 554.
[62] For mainprises not cited below, see: *CCR 1399–1402*, 318, 503; PRO, Chancery, Special Bail Pardons, C237/26, m. 27; KB27/570, rot. 1d fines; *CCR 1409–13*, 297; *CFR 1413–22*, 64, 260–1; *CFR 1422–30*, 190; *CFR 1430–7*, 111; PRO, KB27/698, rot. 33.
[63] *CCR 1396–9*, 405.
[64] Stapleton, *Three Oxon. Parishes*, 41; Emden, *BRUO*, 2011.
[65] For the revolt generally, see J.H. Wylie, *History of England under Henry IV*, 4 vols. (London, 1884–98), 1.91–111; A. Rogers, "Henry IV and the Revolt of the Earls, 1400," *History Today* 16 (1968): 277–83; D. Crook, "Central England and the Revolt of the Earls, January 1400," *BIHR* 64 (1991): 403–10; McNiven, "The Cheshire Rising of 1400," *BJRL* 52 (1969–70): 375–96; *Chronicles of the Revolution 1397–1400*, ed. C. Given-Wilson (Manchester: Manchester Univ. Press, 1993), 48–51, 224–39.
[66] PRO, C237/24/2, no. 144; McHardy (*941*, 119–20).
[67] *CPR 1399–1401*, 190.
[68] PRO, Exchequer, Court of the Marshalsea and Court of the Verge, E37/28; Paul Strohm (*1159*, 59).

were pardoned in February.[69] The only man acquitted at the trial in Oxford castle was Sir Alan Buxhill the younger, stepson of the rebel earl of Salisbury, John Montague.[70] In October 1399 Buxhill had acted as a mainpernor with Thomas Compworth, both men posting bonds of £20 to guarantee that William Hyham would keep the peace towards Walter Byston.[71] These circumstances, together with the evidence for the young Compworth's employment by the Holand family that will be presented below, strongly suggest that Compworth played some part in the revolt as a servant of the Holands. Whether Sawtry's involvement came about through the same connection, or possibly through an association with John Montague, earl of Salisbury, cannot now be determined, but it certainly provides an additional reason why his execution was so anxiously sought by the crown in 1401.[72]

The identification of a Lollard sympathiser with the cause of the dissident earls seeking to restore Richard II to the throne is difficult to fathom, but Montague was, of course, the poet and soldier Sir John Montague named by the St. Albans chronicler Thomas Walsingham as one of the Lollard knights.[73] He was alleged to have protected Lollard preachers at his home in Shenley, Hertfordshire – most famously Master Nicholas Hereford, upon his return from Rome in 1385.[74] By then he had stripped his chapel at Shenley of images, and at his death in 1400 reportedly refused to confess his sins to a priest.[75] The lawyer William Stourton of Stourton, Dorset, a man of many Lollard associations, who left a will containing Lollard phrases and had borrowed a book of gospels in English, had evidently been a supporter of Montague.[76] A tenant of the earl at Othery, Somerset,[77] he successfully petitioned the Exchequer for a grant of the earl's forfeited manor of Knowle (in Shepton Montague), Somerset.[78] In Hilary 1402, moreover, he was summoned before the Exchequer barons to answer the charge that in 1400 one of Montague's servants had delivered to him a coffer filled with gold, worth about £1,000, for concealment from the king's officers. Although acquitted before the assize justices in Salisbury in February 1403, he had clearly aroused suspicion.[79]

No further Lollard support for the earls' uprising has come to light, but the Ricardian cause was soon after taken up by Benedict Wolman (or Wilman), former under-marshal of Richard II's household, who was later

[69] *CPR 1399–1401*, 190, 228–9.

[70] Buxhill's acquittal is discussed in detail in J.L. Leland, "The Oxford Trial of 1400: Royal Politics and the County Gentry," in *The Age of Richard II*, ed. J.L. Gillespie (New York: St Martins, 1997), 165–89.

[71] PRO, KB27/555, rot. 19d. Alison McHardy believed that this mainpernor was Thomas Compworth senior, but he is not identified as such in the document: (*941*, 120).

[72] This new finding supports the view of McHardy in (*941*, 114–22).

[73] McFarlane (*934*, 148, 162–3, 167–8, 174–6, 178–82); W.T. Waugh (*1268*, 55–6, 73–4).

[74] Anne Hudson (*697*, 58–9).

[75] Margaret Aston (*277*, 169); Waugh (*1268*, 74).

[76] Thomson (*1191*, 100–1); Jurkowski (*761*, 169).

[77] McFarlane (*934*, 215n.).

[78] PRO, Exchequer, Lord Treasurer's Remembrancer, *Bille et Petitiones*, E207/11/2; *CFR 1399–1405*, 53.

[79] PRO, E159/178, Hil. *communia*, rot. 6.

associated with Lollardy. Wolman was arrested by the mayor of London early in 1405, after he was implicated by the king's knight Sir Thomas Pickworth of conspiring with Constance, Lady Despenser to kidnap the two Mortimer heirs from Windsor Castle and spirit them away to Wales in February of the same year.[80] In May 1407 Wolman and three others publicly affirmed their support for the Ricardian impostor in the town of Westminster, where they were living in sanctuary, and were alleged to have supplied money, arms and horses to the rebel lords Percy and Bardolf.[81] Still operating from Westminster in October 1409, Wolman and others were accused of sending letters abroad promising that Richard II would return from Scotland before Christmas and urging the king's enemies to invade.[82] He took part in the Oldcastle revolt of 1414, and was executed in 1416 for plotting with the former Merton fellow Thomas Lucas to overthrow the king. One chronicler named Wolman as a Lollard, and among his possessions in 1416 was a book described as "unum parcell psalterii glosed cum Anglic" ("part of a psalter glossed in English").[83] A statute passed in the parliament of 1406 sanctioning the arrest of Lollard preachers and Ricardian plotters alike clearly sought to associate the two groups of dissidents, as Peter McNiven has pointed out – and perhaps with some justification.[84]

Through his involvement with his patrons, the Holand family, Thomas Compworth junior was on the fringes, at the very least, of the continuing opposition to the rule of Henry IV. He was clearly acting on their behalf in May 1400, when he procured from the king custody of the manor of Langton in Yorkshire, which had been forfeited to the crown by the treason of John Holand, duke of Exeter.[85] In November 1401 the Exchequer barons were ordered to refrain from making demands upon Compworth for the annual farm of Langton while a suit brought against the king by Warin Waldegrave for title to the manor was decided in Chancery.[86] Waldegrave had been one of the mainpernors for the grant to Compworth and was previously a servant of the duke of Exeter; he had been receiving the duke's profits at Langton at the time of the manor's forfeiture.[87] An inquest found that Waldegrave and others had been enfeoffed with the manor of Langton by the duke (then earl of Huntingdon) in 1385, well before his forfeiture,

---

[80] The mayor was ordered to bring Wolman before Chancery on 30 April 1405: PRO, Chancery, Recognisance Files, C259/36, m. 30. For the kidnap plot, see J.L. Kirby, *Henry IV of England* (London: Constable, 1970) 182–3. Wolman had been under suspicion since January 1404: S.J. Walker, "Rumour, Sedition and Popular Protest in the Reign of Henry IV," *Past & Present* 166 (2000), 61.

[81] He also reportedly declared that the Mortimer heir should succeed the pseudo-Richard as king: PRO, KB9/196/1.

[82] Henry Porter, a member of the king's household, was indicted for having sheltered them in Westminster since 9 May 1407: PRO, KB27/595, rot. 3d rex; Aston (*269*, 28n.).

[83] PRO, Exchequer, King's Remembrancer, Escheators' Accounts, E136/108/13; Jurkowski (*762*, 675–6).

[84] Peter McNiven (*945*, 101–2).

[85] *CFR 1399–1405*, 58.

[86] *CCR 1399–1402*, 480.

[87] *Cal. Inq. Misc.*, 7, nos. 21–2, 54.

and Compworth's collusion in failing to appear in Chancery to answer Waldegrave's plea ensured its success. The Holands' feoffees were again in possession of the estate in June 1402.[88]

Compworth was by then a servant of Constance, daughter of John Holand, the rebel duke. In the summer of 1400 she had married Thomas Mowbray, Earl Marshal, the 14-year-old son and heir of Thomas, duke of Norfolk (d.1399), and the manor of Langton was one of the Holand estates which had been settled in jointure upon the couple by the duke of Exeter's feoffees.[89] The marriage brought Compworth into the affinity of the Mowbray family; the Mowbray estates were in the king's hands during the young Mowbray's minority, and in July 1402 Compworth was a mainpernor for the grant of custody of two of their manors to a group of five men, all Mowbray servants, to be held at farm until the heir came of age.[90] It seems likely that the young Thomas Mowbray gave some support to the Percies at the battle of Shrewsbury in July 1403, since his retainer Robert Butvillan of Cottesbrook, Northamptonshire, had to purchase a pardon in the following November exonerating him of all treasons and insurrections committed before 7 September, with Compworth acting as one of his mainpernors.[91] Another of Mowbray's retainers, John Kingsley, had also fought with the Percies.[92] In the aftermath of Lady Despenser's plot to kidnap the Mortimer heirs in February 1405, Mowbray admitted to prior knowledge of the plan, and is known to have met and drunk wine with her a year earlier, but he denied any involvement and was pardoned. In May 1405, however, he joined the rebellion of Archbishop Scrope and was beheaded with him, after their betrayal by the earl of Westmorland.[93] Robert Butvillan, who had accompanied Mowbray, was again pardoned, and maintained a close relationship with Constance, the Earl Marshal's widow, throughout his life.[94]

Compworth similarly continued to serve the Countess Marshal and the Mowbrays. In November 1407, together with the duchess of Norfolk's receiver-general John Lounde, he mainprised for the grant to Sir Gerard Braybrooke and three others (at least two of whom were Mowbray servants) of the Northamptonshire manor of Crick, which was in the king's hands during the minority of John Mowbray, brother of the late Earl Marshal and next heir of the duke of Norfolk.[95] A year later, Compworth was again a financial guarantor for the award of custody of another Mowbray manor (Weston in Warwickshire) to three Mowbray

---

[88] CPR 1401–5, 110–11, 172.
[89] L.E. Moye, "The Estates and Finances of the Mowbray Family, Earls Marshal and Dukes of Norfolk, 1401–1476" (Ph.D. thesis, Duke Univ., 1985), 3; PRO, Exchequer, Treasury of Receipt, Ancient Deeds, Series AA, E41/202; CPR 1401–5, 110–11.
[90] CFR 1399–1405, 162; BL, Additional Rolls 16,556 and 17,209.
[91] PRO, C237/27, m. 408. For his retention by Mowbray: CPR 1401–5, 335.
[92] Walker, "Rumour, Sedition," 32; PRO, Chancery and Exchequer, King's Remembrancer, Parliamentary and Council Proceedings, C49/48, no. 6.
[93] Moye, thesis, 4–6.
[94] CPR 1405–8, 68, 80. He made her executrix of his will and bequeathed valuable objects to her: PRO, Prerogative Court of Canterbury Wills, PROB11/2B, f. 197v.
[95] CFR 1405–13, 84; BL, Additional Roll 16,556.

retainers.[96] In February 1409, Compworth gave a recognisance for 110 marks with (and probably on behalf of) Sir John Grey of Ruthin, the Countess Marshal's second husband, to a group of creditors.[97] Her remarriage seems to have ended Compworth's connection with both the Mowbrays and high political intrigue.

Compworth was now reaping the benefits of a blossoming legal career. He had acquired property in Northamptonshire by 1400,[98] and had married Elizabeth, daughter of William Hondsacre, heiress to lands in Warwickshire[99] and Northamptonshire, by the autumn of 1406. In Northamptonshire, Compworth held an estate in Helmdon by 1412, where the couple made their residence,[100] and they recovered at law joint tenure of the manor of Newbold (in Clipston) in 1428.[101] Further lands in the county had been acquired in Marston St. Lawrence by 1436 and Greatworth in 1439,[102] as well as an estate in Foxton, Leicestershire by 1433.[103] Compworth was representing clients as an attorney in the Common Pleas by Trinity term 1410, and he mainprised on occasion for defendants before both this court and the King's Bench.[104] He provided legal counsel to John Malory of Welton, Northamptonshire, a relation of his by marriage,[105] and to William Daventre of Hardwick, Oxfordshire.[106] He continued still to serve the Holand family; by 1415, and probably much earlier, he was employed by Maud, widow of John, Lord Lovell (d.1408) and daughter of Sir Robert Holand, a cousin of the late duke of Exeter, who had taken a vow of chastity after her husband's death.[107]

In May 1415 he mainprised for the grant to Lady Lovell of custody of the manor of Titchmarsh, Northamptonshire after the death of her son John, Lord Lovell in 1414.[108] When a royal commission contradicted the verdict given at the inquisition *post mortem* that tenure of Lord Lovell's lands had

---

[96] *CFR 1405–13*, 132. His co-mainpernor, John Verdon, was another Mowbray servant: BL, Additional Rolls 16,556 and 17,209.

[97] *CCR 1405–9*, 492; *Complete Peerage*, 9.605. Grey had earlier appointed him his attorney while in Wales: *CPR 1405–8*, 437.

[98] *CFR 1399–1405*, 73; *CCR 1399–1402*, 318, 503.

[99] PRO, CP40/583, rot. 1d enrolled bills; CP40/590, rot. 53; *Warwickshire Feet of Fines, iii, 1345–1509*, ed. L. Drucker, Dugdale Soc. 18 (London: Oxford Univ. Press, 1943), no. 2433; *CCR 1422–29*, 34; *VCH, Warwicks.* 4.259.

[100] PRO, E159/189, Mich. *communia*, rot. 19; KB27/617, rots. 12, 78; CP40/726, rot. 286. He acquired the farm of further lands in Helmdon in 1420, when he obtained joint custody of the wardship of the heir of Ralph Parles: *CPR 1416–22*, 308; PRO, Chancery, Inquisitions *Post Mortem*, C138/53, no. 107.

[101] PRO, JUST1/1537, rots. 41–41d. They probably sold their interest to Elizabeth's cousin Joan, daughter of Edward Raleigh, and her husband Thomas Brounfleet: PRO, Chancery, Inquisitions *Post Mortem*, C140/1, no. 5.

[102] PRO, CP40/700, rot. 34d; CP25/1/179/94, no. 87.

[103] PRO, KB27/689, rot. 13; KB27/691, rot. 28d.

[104] PRO, CP40/598, rot. 158d; CP40/595, rot. 262; KB27/608, rots. 27–29d.

[105] *CCR 1409–13*, 404; PRO, CP40/618, rot. 66. Malory's aunt, Agnes, had married a Compworth: PRO, Exchequer, Treasury of Receipt, Ancient Deeds, Series A, E40/14829.

[106] PRO, KB27/617, rot. 12; KB27/618, rot. 47; KB27/624, rot. 29.

[107] *Complete Peerage*, 5.195–200; 6.528–32; Lambeth Palace Library, Register of Thomas Arundel, Archbishop of Canterbury, ii, f. 111.

[108] *CFR 1413–22*, 107–8.

been vested in feoffees in trust for his underage son and heir William, by maintaining that they ought to have escheated to the king,[109] Compworth represented Lady Lovell in Chancery to traverse the commission's findings and judgment was given in her favour in 1417.[110] He was also employed by Lady Lovell's cousin, John, earl of Huntingdon (d.1447), brother of the Countess Marshal. In a petition to the chancellor in 1416, the earl asked that Compworth and five others be named to a commission of enquiry into the value of the lands of William, Lord Zouche, of which the earl had obtained custody.[111] In an inquest held before Compworth and a fellow commissioner at Shrewsbury in 1417, it was discovered that the Zouche estate in Shropshire had been significantly undervalued at Lord Zouche's inquisition *post mortem*.[112] It was undoubtedly in recognition of his long service to the Holand family that Lady Lovell directed her executors in 1419 to pay Compworth a life annuity of 5 marks.[113]

Compworth's legal talent, together with his employment by the Holands, inevitably enhanced his political standing in Northamptonshire, and by 1412 he had begun to play a part in county administration. In February of that year he was named to the *quorum* of the peace commission, and although absent from the ensuing commission, was re-appointed in November 1413.[114] In the 1420s he served three times as escheator of Northamptonshire and Rutland, and in 1427 was elected to parliament to represent the town of Northampton, where he had owned property since at least 1410.[115] From 1422 to 1432 he was a regular attestor of parliamentary elections in Northamptonshire,[116] and, until his death in c.1440, associated frequently with leading members of the county gentry as a feoffee and mainpernor.[117]

Is there any evidence that Thomas Compworth junior was sympathetic to the Lollard heresy? He was never accused of having given support to Sir John Oldcastle or his followers, but there are some suggestions that he played a part behind the scenes. Firstly, there seem to have been suspicions about his loyalty to the king; he was removed from the Northamptonshire peace commission in February 1414 and never restored, which is surprising, given his heavy involvement in county politics and administration.[118] A second point is that several participants in the 1414 uprising came from

[109] *CIPM*, 20, nos. 196–203; *Cal. Inq. Misc.*, 7, no. 518.
[110] PRO, Chancery, *Recorda* Files, C260/130, m. 32; KB27/621, rots. 1d attorneys, 13, 14 rex.
[111] PRO, Chancery, Warrants for the Great Seal, C81/1423, no. 18.
[112] *CPR 1416–22*, 80; *CIPM*, 20, nos. 408–39.
[113] *CCR 1419–22*, 125.
[114] *CPR 1408–13*, 483; PRO, Exchequer, Lord Treasurer's Remembrancer, *Originalia* Rolls, E371/177, rot. 8; E371/178, rot. 50.
[115] *List of Escheators for England and Wales*, List & Index Society 22 (1971), 95; PRO, Chancery, Writs and Returns of Members to Parliament, C219/13/5, pt. 2; *CCR 1409–13*, 171; Northants. Record Office, Knightley charter 166.
[116] PRO, C219/13/1; C219/13/2, pt. 2; C219/13/4; C219/14/1, pt. 2; C219/14/2, pt. 2; C219/14/3, pt. 3.
[117] *CFR 1413–22*, 260–1; *CPR 1416–22*, 308; *CPR 1422–9*, 300; PRO, CP25/1/179/93, no. 32; CP40/666, rots. 75, 78; Exchequer, Inquisitions *Post Mortem*, E149/164, no. 3; *CPR 1436–41*, 227; *CCR 1435–41*, 198; PRO, E40/10894; E40/8384.
[118] *CPR 1413–16*, 421.

areas where the Compworths possessed, or had possessed, influence (see Map). A similar coincidence has been perceived in other studies of Lollard sympathisers among the gentry – most notably, in those of Thomas Tykhill and Sir Thomas Latimer.[119] Four of the Oxfordshire insurgents were from the town of Oxford, one was a Banbury carpenter,[120] and another was an esquire from nearby Swalcliffe,[121] but all the others lived in Kidlington and neighbouring towns and villages in the lower Cherwell valley. Two men of Kidlington (John Webbe, junior, a weaver, and Robert Couper, a cooper) indicted for taking part in the revolt were probably among those Oxfordshire Lollards imprisoned in Banbury castle by the bishop of Lincoln in 1415.[122] In their company were three men from villages just north of Kidlington: William, son of John Bygge, a labourer, and William Taillour, a tailor, both of Kirtlington, and John Rook, a fuller of Upper Heyford.[123] A Richard Fuller of Kidlington was also later accused of having given shelter in January 1417 to two Lollards from Northamptonshire – Laurence Fuller and Robert Taillour, a tailor.[124]

It is by no means certain that Thomas Compworth maintained any links with his home village after his father's loss of Thrupp manor, but he did continue to have contacts in the area. In June 1403 he had acted as bail bondsman, together with Thomas Coventre (then bailiff of Oxford), for the release from Oxford gaol of John Milton, who had been committed to the custody of the mayor and bailiff by the chancellor of the university for unknown reasons. Under bonds of £100, Compworth and Coventre undertook to produce him in Chancery in early July.[125] It is possible, however, that the more recent Lollard activity in the Kidlington area was fostered by association with sympathisers among the London tailors. By 1410, when he sued John Rewele of Kidlington for abducting Thomas Rewele, his apprentice there, the London tailor Thomas Shragger must have had a workshop in Kidlington.[126] Shragger was among the mainpernors for the release from the Marshalsea in July 1418 of another London tailor, John

[119] Jurkowski (*759*, 37–40); McFarlane (*934*, 192–6).
[120] Namely, John Mybbe, principal of St. Cuthbert's Hall, John Garthorpe, "scolar," Thomas Gray, clerk, of both Oxford and Northants., John Wynforlong, an Oxford weaver, and John Chacombe, *alias* William de Banbury: PRO, KB9/205/1, mm. 55, 57; KB27/615, rots. 6–6d, 32d rex; C237/37, m. 11; E153/1483, mm. 2, 4; Exchequer, Escheators' Files, E153/1278, mm. 14–15; Exchequer, Sheriffs' Accounts, E199/26/30; *CCR 1413–19*, 148; *CPR 1413–16*, 271. For Mybbe, see also Maureen Jurkowski (*762*, 677n.).
[121] Captured and convicted of treason at St. Giles's Field, John Wykeham of Swalcliffe later successfully petitioned for a pardon and the return of his confiscated goods: PRO, C81/1422, mm. 21–2; *CPR 1413–16*, 250.
[122] PRO, KB9/205/1, m. 55; *The Register of Bishop Philip Repingdon, 1405–19*, ed. M. Archer, Lincoln Record Society 74 (Hereford: Hereford Times Ltd, 1982), 3.120.
[123] PRO, KB9/205/1, m. 55; Exchequer, Lord Treasurer's Remembrancer, Memoranda Rolls, E368/187, rot. 300.
[124] PRO, KB9/209, mm. 57, 62; KB27/630, rot. 3 rex; KB27/669, rot. 15 rex.
[125] PRO, C259/5, m. 23. Milton may have been the same man as the John Milton, draper of Oxford, who petitioned the chancellor over a debt owed to him by Thomas Yonge of Bristol, in c.1422: PRO, C1/5/70. For Coventre, parliamentary burgess for Oxford in 1404, see C. Kightly, "Thomas Coventre I, of Oxford," in *Hist. Parl.*, 675–7.
[126] PRO, CP40/598, rot. 82; CP40/600, rot. 24.

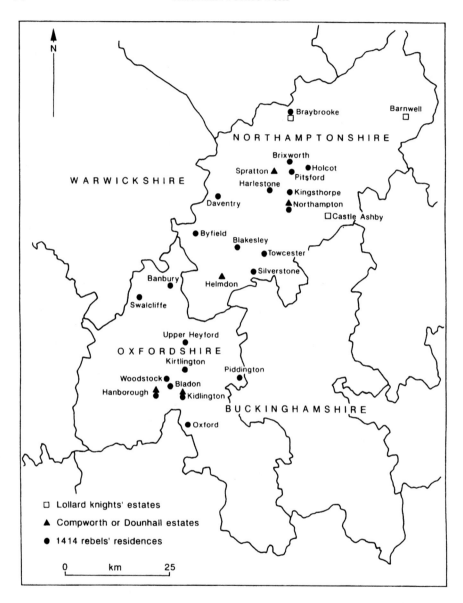

Compworth and Lollard locations in Oxfordshire and Northamptonshire

Clement, who had been held in custody on suspicion of heresy until after the capture of the fugitive Sir John Oldcastle.[127]

Another of the neighbouring towns which contributed insurgents in 1414 was Hanborough. Joining forces at Woodstock with the Kidlington men

---

[127] PRO, KB27/629, rot. 17d rex. Clement and another of the mainpernors, the London tailor William Kyrkeby, were associates of the Lollard priest Richard Wyche: *CCR 1419–22*, 82. Another London tailor, John Reynald, was also later arrested as a supporter of Oldcastle: PRO, Chancery Files: Tower Series, *Habeas Corpus Cum Causa*, C250/12, no. 40.

were John Parchemyner and Henry Melleward, a millward, of Hanborough,[128] quite possibly tenants of Compworth's step-brother Elias Dounhall, who owned a manor in Hanborough. An obscure figure, Dounhall is nonetheless known to have lived at Hanborough until at least 1416.[129] As a young man left in the care of his step-father, it would have been unusual had he not been influenced by the religious views of the elder Compworth. William Broun *alias* William Davy *alias* William Redehed, a glover from the town of Woodstock, also turned out in 1414 for Oldcastle,[130] as did John Geffray, a mason from the village of Bladon, which lay between Hanborough and Woodstock.[131] Sir John Oldcastle, moreover, took refuge in Piddington, Oxfordshire in October 1416, where he was sheltered by the chaplain John Whitby.[132]

In Northamptonshire, there was persistent support for Oldcastle at both the time of the revolt and in its aftermath, centred primarily in Daventry and Northampton. At least five rebels were from Daventry in 1414 – three of whom were also said to be Lollards – and one woman, Eleanor Warde, was also accused of Lollardy. They were perhaps led by the parchment-maker John Asser; he expressed views against the efficacy of pilgrimages and the worship of images.[133] Another Daventry man involved was the yeoman Simon Horn; he gave succour to the fugitive Lollard Philip Turnour in 1416.[134] Three of the 1414 rebels (John Preest, Thomas Maydeford, weaver, and John Billyng) were resident in the town of Northampton and jurors there presented three others as Lollards.[135] The nearby villages of Kingsthorpe, Harlestone, Pitsford and Brixworth provided one each,[136] and, although William Tebaud of Holcot did not take part in the revolt, he was accused of Lollardy in 1414.[137] The Northampton group seems to have been led by John Preest, who instructed his fellow

---

[128] PRO, KB9/205/1, m. 55; E199/26/30; C237/37, m. 11; *CCR 1413–19*, 148; *CPR 1413–16*, 271.

[129] CCCA, A3.ca12(1), 27–8, 30, 32, 34–6. Another of Dounhall's estates was in Spratton, which lay close by the villages just north of Northampton from which Oldcastle's insurgents were drawn: n. 25 and see below.

[130] PRO, KB9/205/1, m. 55; KB9/991, m.4. Broun may also be the William Brown, priest, who was later a companion of Richard Wyche: Jurkowski (762, 680).

[131] PRO, KB9/205/1, m. 55; KB27/617, rot. 6d rex; *CPR 1413–16*, 261.

[132] Whitby, who was later hanged for this crime, was probably the same man summoned with Richard Wyche before the bishop of Durham in c.1402 for preaching heresy: PRO, KB9/209, mm. 62–62d; Jurkowski (762, 679–80).

[133] Philip Turnour, a hostiller, and Roger Swan were alleged to hold the same opinions. The other rebels were Edmund Clerk and John Heywode, a husbandman; Thomas Robyns of Grandborough, a few miles west across the Warwicks. border, rose with them: PRO, KB9/204/1, mm. 104–5; KB9/994, m. 41; KB27/616, rots. 5–5d rex; KB27/630, rot. 17d rex.

[134] Allegedly sheltered also by John Heywode, Turnour died of the plague in the Marshalsea prison in July 1417: PRO, KB9/83, m. 51; KB9/210, m. 39; KB9/994, m. 41; KB27/630, rots. 17d, 18d rex; KB27/632, rot. 11d rex. Asser, Heywode and Horn were all friends: Northants. Record Office, Knightley charters 144, 146–7.

[135] Namely, Thomas Seyton *alias* Rayenere, a hosier, John Clerk, a fuller, and John Tukley: PRO, KB9/204/1, mm. 93, 99–100; KB27/616, rot. 1 rex; *CCR 1413–19*, 262.

[136] John Turnour, William Asshe, Thomas Spencer, vicar of Pitsford, and Thomas Gylour, chapman *alias* mercer, respectively: PRO, KB9/204/1, mm. 85, 93, 99–100; KB27/616, rots. 1, 5d rex; *CPR 1413–16*, 262. A general pardon purchased by Gylour in 1409 indicates that he also used the surnames Fauconberge, Bryklesworth and Burton: PRO, C237/32, m. 180.

[137] PRO, KB9/204/1, m. 111; KB27/619, rot. 2d rex.

insurgent John Billyng to deliver letters to Oldcastle in London just prior to the revolt.[138] One of Thomas Compworth's associates, the draper Thomas Spryggy, was empanelled as a juror to make presentments before the Lollard commissioners in Northampton, but he declined at first to serve and had to be fined for contempt before he would comply. His brother John Spryggy was also amerced for refusing to open the door of Thomas' house to the mayor.[139] Lollards continued to be active in the area; handbills advocating a new uprising reportedly appeared in Northampton in late 1416 and in the following year the bishop made enquiries into reports of heresy there.[140]

There were Lollards in other parts of the county as well, although none from Castle Ashby or its vicinity, where Oldcastle's two Northampton-shire manors were located.[141] William Emayn of Byfield, which lay on the road between Daventry and Banbury, was probably preaching heretical doctrine there at the time of the revolt. Imprisoned for heresy by Bishop Repingdon for two years, he later moved to Buckingham. He appeared before the bishop three more times, and by 1429, when he was tried as a heretic by the bishop of Bath and Wells, was living in Bristol.[142] Another man of Byfield, William atte Well, probably the same William, son of John atte Well of Stanbridge, Bedfordshire, who was pardoned for rising in 1414, was indicted, together with his wife Beatrice, for sheltering Oldcastle at Byfield in 1417.[143] Thomas Ile *alias* Scot, a scrivener of Braybrooke, a well-known centre of Lollard activity, was another insurgent in 1414,[144] and there were a few other participants from towns close to where Thomas Compworth's estates lay. John Wykyn, a honeymonger of Towcester, and Robert Aleyn of Blakesley, just a few miles north of Helmdon, were both pardoned for their role in the uprising.[145] Perhaps more significantly, in July 1417, Oldcastle was given shelter by Hugh Frayn and his wife Joan in Silverstone, about five miles east of Helmdon, and apparently narrowly missed capture, since some of his goods were

---

[138] PRO, KB9/204/1, mm. 99–100. He was possibly the same John Prest *alias* John Clerk, vicar of Chesterton, Warwicks., who was indicted for sheltering Oldcastle in 1417: Cullen, thesis, 93; PRO, KB9/209, mm. 45, 50.

[139] PRO, KB9/204/1, m. 103. Compworth and Thomas Spryggy were co-mainpernors in 1410 for a writ of *supersedeas* for Robert (or Richard) Couper of Northampton: *CCR 1409–13*, 171 (surely not the Robert Couper of Kidlington indicted as an insurgent in 1414?: see above).

[140] PRO, KB9/209, mm. 6, 27; J.A.F. Thomson (*1189*, 98).

[141] *VCH, Northants.*, 4.233.

[142] Hudson (*713*, 35, 140); Thomson (*1189*, 28–30).

[143] *CPR 1413–16*, 262; PRO, KB9/209, mm. 6, 12, 20, 27; E153/1281, m. 4. Together with his father and brother John, William had also been indicted in 1415 for holding conventicles in Tilsworth, Beds.: PRO, Justices Itinerant, Gaol Delivery Rolls, JUST3/2/7, m. 1.

[144] PRO, KB9/204/1, m. 111; KB27/616, rot. 5d rex; PRO, C237/37, m. 66. For Braybrooke, see McFarlane (*934*, 193–6).

[145] *CPR 1413–16*, 262. Aleyn was a substantial tenant of Luffield Priory: *Luffield Priory Charters*, ed. G.R. Elvey, 2 vols., Bucks. Record Society, 15, 18 (1968, 1975), I, nos. 136, 144; II, no. 313. He is probably also the Robert Aleyn (d. by 1447) who served as a county coroner from 1407 to 1444 and, as such, attested several parliamentary elections: PRO, C219/10/4; C219/10/5; C219/10/6, *etc.*; KB27/679, rot 16d rex; KB27/733, rot. 17 rex; KB27/745, rot. 17 rex. For his links to leading members of the county gentry, see: Devon Record Office, Simcoe MSS, 1038M/T13/58.

found at Frayn's house when the latter was taken into custody.[146] Old-castle had also been in Silverstone two months earlier in the company of his fellow insurgents Sir Thomas Talbot of Yorkshire and John Walmesley of Lancashire.[147]

Although it is difficult to link Compworth firmly with any of these Northamptonshire insurgents, he did have connections with other suspected sympathisers with the Lollard heresy outside the county. He is similar in this respect to the lawyer Thomas Lucas, who was evidently in contact with Lollards from many parts of England.[148] In December 1424 Compworth and Thomas Belwode of Lincolnshire each posted bonds of £100 in Chancery guaranteeing that William Hert of Lincoln would commit no breaches of the peace nor hold any unlawful assemblies. Together with William Ardern of Oxfordshire and the London tailor John Clement, Compworth and Belwode promised under a second recognisance in February 1425 that they would personally escort Hert to the next assizes in Lincolnshire, when he would be required, by mandate of the chancellor, to post a further bond of 200 marks, backed by other mainpernors at £100 each. Compworth and his co-mainpernors duly delivered Hert to the assize justices sitting at Lincoln in April, where Hert produced further main-pernors who again guaranteed his behaviour.[149]

Hert had only recently moved to Lincoln, perhaps after his marriage by 1421 to Agnes.[150] Previously of Syresham, Northamptonshire, he was a mainpernor with Thomas Compworth in the Common Pleas in 1409,[151] and clerk to the escheator of Warwickshire before February 1415, when he was pardoned for failing to answer the debt plea of Thomas Spryggy, the Northampton draper.[152] Probably a lawyer, Hert was named as a Lollard sympathiser in a Chancery petition written in c.1432 by Robert Burton, precentor of Lincoln cathedral, in which the latter accused Hert of having assaulted him because he was a member of the commission appointed by Richard Fleming, bishop of Lincoln (1419–31), before which Robert Sutton, clerk, had been convicted of heresy.[153] It is possible that Comp-worth's undertaking on behalf of Hert, and the involvement of his co-mainpernor John Clement – the same associate of Richard Wyche who had earlier been imprisoned for heresy himself[154] – was purely professional, although the terms of the bond requiring them to travel to Lincoln with Hert imposed a heavier burden than was usual in a professional mainprise.

In 1430 Compworth acted as a feoffee for John Cheyne, an esquire of Isenhampstead Chenies in Buckinghamshire, for the conveyance of two of

---

[146] PRO, KB9/209, mm. 6, 12, 20; E153/1281, m. 3.

[147] PRO, KB9/215/1, m. 27; KB9/994, m. 42; KB27/630, rot. 13d rex.

[148] Jurkowski (762, 675–80).

[149] CCR 1422–29, 186–7; PRO, JUST1/1537, rot. 10d.

[150] CFR 1413–22, 409; PRO, C1/207/35; A. Rogers, "Parliamentary Electors in Lincolnshire in the Fifteenth Century," Lincolnshire History and Archaeology 3 (1968): 71.

[151] PRO, CP40/595, rot. 262.

[152] CPR 1413–16, 217.

[153] Hert was said to have refused to confess his sins; Sutton had been found in possession of a Wycliffite sermon cycle: Jurkowski, thesis, 323–5, 334–5.

[154] See n. 127.

his estates. In May he demised the manor of Ellesborough to Cheyne, which the latter was forced to mortgage to a group of London merchants two years later,[155] and in June Compworth received a quitclaim from Cheyne of the manor of Upper Dean (in Dean), Bedfordshire, and lands in Huntingdonshire.[156] Compworth later passed this estate on to the secular college of Higham Ferrers in Northamptonshire on behalf of the college's founder Robert Chichele, archbishop of Canterbury.[157] Although Cheyne's sympathy for the Lollard heresy is not as well known as that of his cousin Sir John Cheyne of Drayton Beauchamp, Buckinghamshire,[158] to whom he eventually sold his manor of Ellesborough, he too sponsored a heretical preacher at the the time of the Oldcastle revolt. When John Angret, parson of Isenhampstead Chenies (or Latimer), was arrested for rising with Oldcastle in 1414 and his goods were confiscated by the county escheator, they were found to be in the possession of Cheyne, Angret's patron.[159]

Finally, another associate of Compworth's with Lollard connections was Sir Gerard Braybrooke (d.1429), to whom his wife Elizabeth was related by marriage.[160] As mentioned above, Compworth was a financial guarantor for the grant to Braybrooke and others of the Mowbray manor of Crick in 1407, and in 1427 he was again involved with Braybrooke, as a feoffee for the latter's sale of the manor of Chesterton in Huntingdonshire to Archbishop Chichele.[161] Braybrooke left a will strongly Lollard in tone and had been at one time a close associate of the Welsh Lollard Walter Brut (d.1403),[162] but he remained loyal to the king at the time of the Oldcastle revolt and apparently also held many orthodox views.[163] It is perhaps also worth mentioning that Compworth was probably at one time employed by Sir Hugh Lutterell of Dunster, Somerset; in February 1404 he witnessed a quitclaim to Lutterell of his family estates in Suffolk and Norfolk.[164] Lutterell has not come under any suspicion as a Lollard sympathiser, but he was evidently on good enough terms with Oldcastle to act as feoffee of his manors in Norfolk, Suffolk and Wiltshire, and the king wrote to him in February 1414, questioning him about the rebel leader's escape.[165]

---

[155] PRO, E326/1452, 1456–8; *VCH, Bucks.*, 2.332.

[156] *CCR 1429–35*, 59.

[157] *CPR 1429–36*, 334–5; *VCH, Beds.*, 3.133.

[158] L.S. Woodger, "Sir John Cheyne II of Drayton Beauchamp, Buckinghamshire," in *Hist. Parl.*, 552–4.

[159] PRO, KB27/611, rots. 13–13d rex; E153/483, m. 3; Exchequer of Receipt, Receipt Rolls, E401/675 (18 Jan.).

[160] Braybrooke's son and heir Gerard (d.1422) was the first husband of Elizabeth's cousin Joan, daughter of Thomas Raleigh: L.S. Woodger, "Sir Gerard Braybrooke II (bef. 1354–1429), of Colmworth, Beds., Horsenden, Bucks. and Danbury, Essex," in *Hist. Parl.*, 346–9; *CFR 1413–22*, 338, 426; and see above.

[161] See n. 95; *CCR 1422–29*, 391. The manor was used to endow the college of Higham Ferrers: *VCH, Hunts.*, 3.140–1.

[162] He was a feoffee of the Herefs. estate which Brut forfeited to the king for his part in the Welsh revolt: *Cal. Inq. Misc.*, 7, no. 263. For Brut, see: Hudson (*722*, 222–30).

[163] Jurkowski, thesis, 331–3; J.A.F. Thomson (*1191*, 104, 108–9).

[164] *CCR 1402–5*, 285.

[165] PRO, E368/187, rots. 80–80d; *Cal. Inq. Misc.*, 7.558; F. Devon, *Issues of the Exchequer* (London: John Murray, 1837), 31.

Compworth's network of associates is suggestive, but, in the absence of any knowledge of his religious opinions, it is inadequate as evidence of heretical leanings. We are left to ponder the implications of his acquaintances with known sympathisers, apparent coincidences in the geographical distribution of Lollard support and the effect of his exposure to the views of both his father and William Sawtry. What can clearly be perceived from the pattern of his career and his long association with the Holands is that he was not the pillar of the Lancastrian regime that Sir Gerard Braybrooke was. Yet the upheavals of his youth, the misfortunes of his father, and the disasters that befell his noble patrons probably made him wary of political intrigue and far more cautious than his father had been. If he did give active support to Lollard preachers, he did so with considerable discretion.

Another conclusion that can be drawn from this examination of the lives of the two Compworths is that religious heresy and political subversion began to converge well before the failure of the 1414 uprising. It was this convergence that ultimately drew the attention of both the secular and ecclesiastical authorities to heresy in Northamptonshire, and their combined efforts appear to have brought about its virtual eradication there.[166] Of undoubted consequence also was the falling away of support of members of the gentry like the two Compworths, whose contribution to the spread of heretical doctrine may have been considerable. More archive-based studies of both influential individuals and geographical regions need to be undertaken before significant conclusions can be drawn about the depth of gentry support and the extent of the heresy's appeal generally, but the findings presented here make some progress towards that eventual goal.[167]

---

[166] After 1425, only one subsequent accusation of heresy (in c 1452) is known to have been made in the county: *The Register of Henry Chichele, Archbishop of Canterbury, 1414–1443*, ed. E.F. Jacob, 4 vols. (Oxford: Clarendon, 1938–47), 3.105–12; Thomson (*1189*, 104).

[167] Other comparable studies are Jurkowski, thesis, 301–43, and (*759*, 33–52); both deal with Lollardy in Derbyshire. The thesis of Charles Kightly offers a starting point for other county studies. Also helpful are some of the biographies in *Hist. Parl.*.

Part II

LOLLARD THOUGHT

Lollards and the Cross

Margaret Aston

Ymagines crucifixi et salutifera crux Christi
adoracione latrie a Christi fidelibus sunt adorande.[1]
Roger Dymmok, 1395–6

Crux Christi super qua mortuus est non est adoranda.[2]
Richard Wyche (d.1440)

Cross and crucifix were always at the heart of image controversy. Representations of the instrument of Christ's death and of the crucifixion itself were problematical for early Christians, and in later centuries difficult questions were attached to what became the central symbol and image of the Christian faith. What material creation could show this meeting point of divinity and humanity? And if such were made, what degree of veneration did it call for? Issues that had vexed the early church and the Byzantine iconoclastic controversy were present in Lollard disputes over church imagery, and these show how Wycliffites had grasped the nettle that stung most in the contest over image worship. The theology that had grown up round this matter was something they knowingly questioned.

In late fourteenth-century England the ubiquity of cross and crucifix affected life and worship in many ways and places. From wayside crucifix to the rood dominating the parish church, visual encounters with this image were a daily experience. The liturgy honoured the Holy Cross on appointed days, and the faithful rendered their respect by creeping to the cross on Good Friday and Easter Sunday. Relics of the true cross were treasured (even carried about) by the privileged, and visited by pilgrims who took their way to Broomholm in Norfolk; while at Boxley in Kent there was a rood whose ability to move and respond to prayer corresponded with miracle stories that might be heard from preachers. To be Christian was to be marked with the sign of the cross from baptism to grave and, as Julian of

---

[1] *Rogeri Dymmok Liber contra XII errors et hereses Lollardorum*, ed. H.S. Cronin (*136*, 181). ("Images of the crucifix and the saving cross of Christ are to be worshipped by Christ's faithful with the worship of *latria*.")
[2] *Fasciculi Zizaniorum* (*139*, 503). ("The cross of Christ on which he died is not to be worshipped.")

Norwich tells us, the image of the saviour on the cross was the final comfort set before the eyes of the dying.[3]

Lollards challenged this accepted presence in several ways, and even if this questioning, and some actions that went with it, only affected a minority, they made a scar on contemporary consciousness. Small though this may have been, its effect on the church – measurable through words more than ascertainable actions – formed part of the "premature reformation." It anticipated the logic of later charges and changes, and shows a certain solidity in the intellectual core of the early Wycliffite movement, and a certain continuous consistency thereafter.

As with the case against church imagery as a whole, attacks on the worship of the cross developed after Wyclif's death, and went well beyond his stated views.[4] The case against cross worship had become programmatic for Wycliffites before the end of the fourteenth century, in so far as it was incorporated in the Twelve Conclusions advertised to parliament and convocation in 1395. Among the points lumped together in the eighth conclusion as necessary for enlightening "the puple begylid," several related to the cross. Pilgrimage, prayers and offerings to "blynde rodys" amounted to idolatry ("ben ner of kin to" was the phrase used). Since the highest worship (*latria*) belonged to the godhead alone, the service done twice a year to the rood (creeping to the cross) was an idolatrous performance. Added to this was the polemical corollary that if holiness was attributed to the wood of the cross, the nails, spear and crown of the crucified Christ, then it was equally in order to make a relic of Judas's lips (as comparable instruments of the Passion).[5] The "pore men, tresoreris of Cryst and his apostlis" in whose name the conclusions as a whole were issued seem to speak here with a superior educated clerical voice, enjoying familiarity in the Latin terminology of *latria*, *dulia* and the theology of image worship, by which the people at large were deluded. They spoke as missionaries to a misguided world, which was known to a later generation as the "blind devotion" of the people.

Yet already well before 1395 some of the "puple begylid" were beginning to see things differently, thanks to the inculcation of new teaching. In 1383 Bishop Brinton of Rochester remarked in an Easter sermon on heretics'

[3] Jeremy Catto (*372*, 48–9); P.W. Fleming, "Charity, Faith, and the Gentry of Kent 1422–1529," in *Property and Politics: Essays in Later Medieval History*, ed. Tony Pollard (Gloucester: Sutton, 1984), 43; Eamon Duffy, "Devotion to the Crucifix and Related Images in England on the Eve of the Reformation," in *Bilder und Bildersturm im Spätmittelalter und in der frühen Neuzeit*, ed. B. Scribner and M. Warnke (Wolfenbüttel: Herzog August Bibliothek, 1990), 21–36.

[4] See John Wyclif, *Tractatus de Potestate Pape*, ed. J. Loserth (London: Wyclif Society, 1907), 290 for an attack (in a list of corrupted episcopal insignia) on the use of a gold cross as being more indicative of sumptuous service of the world than of following Christ in pastoral office. For the Lollard case against images as a whole see M. Aston, *England's Iconoclasts* (*284*, 96–159).

[5] Anne Hudson (*155*, 27, 153). The idea of making a relic of Judas's lips was a challenge to the Thomist endorsement of the principle of contact with Christ's body as a reason for reverencing instruments of the Passion (nails, crown of thorns and lance) as well as the cross ("quantum ad rationem contactus membrorum Christi, adoramus non solum crucem, sed etiam omnia quae sunt Christi" "as for the question of the contact of Christ's limbs, we worship not only the cross, but everything of Christ's"). St. Thomas Aquinas, *Summa Theologiae*, ed. P. Caramello, 3 vols. (Turin-Rome: Marietti, 1952–62), 3.147–8; pt. III, qu. xxv, art. 4.

preaching that the cross of Christ and images were not to be worshipped.[6] Six years later, when Lollard critics were attacking pilgrimage to the famous rood at the north door of St. Paul's cathedral in London,[7] two Leicester heretics, Roger and Alice Dexter, were prescribed the penance of walking in procession carrying crucifixes in their hands to which they had to kneel thrice and kiss devoutly; a punishment designed to fit the offence of maintaining that no cross ought to be worshipped.[8] And a few years later some Northampton suspects were charged with believing there to be "as much merit kissing stones lying in the field as the feet of the crucifix in church."[9] Incumbents who sympathized with views like those expressed in the "manifesto" might instruct their parishioners to reject the perceived idolatry of traditional forms of worship. One man who ran into trouble on this score was Robert Hook, rector of Braybooke in Northamptonshire. In 1406 he was sentenced to public penance both in his own church and in Lincoln Cathedral, for having prevented his parishioners from performing the customary worship of the cross on Good Friday. He kept them sitting in their seats instead of creeping to the cross and worshipping it in the usual way. It is a unique incident, most suggestive of the kind of indoctrination open to a convinced Wycliffite in command of a parish.[10]

Through some of the verbal jousting in reports of Lollard trials we can detect a kind of counterpoint between examining judges, clerical suspects and parochial learners that ranged over the critical issues of worshipping the cross. The filtered exchanges of such accounts catch allusions to the theology of the schools. William Thorpe's account of his interview with the archbishop in 1407 describes his answers to the charge that he had preached at Shrewsbury that images ought not to be worshipped. Thorpe expatiated on the point that it was wrong to worship the matter or form of an image, which of course the archbishop readily granted. "But," he said, at once going to the heart of the matter, "a crucifix owith to be worschipid for the passioun of Crist that is peyntid thereinne, and is brought therethorugh into manus mynde." Thorpe countered tangentially, by citing Old Testament sources against image worship. Arundel kept to his point. The New Testament superseded the Old and "now sith Crist bi cam man it is leful to have ymagis to schewe his manhood." Again Thorpe digressed via the Old Testament, this time into a lecture on the power of word over image,

[6] Aston (284, 105).
[7] Thomas Walsingham (221, 2.188). The St. Paul's pilgrimage rood, which was dismantled in August 1538, must be distinguished from the cathedral's great rood, demolished in 1547 (cf. Two Wycliffite Texts (156, 121); W. Sparrow Simpson, St. Paul's Cathedral and Old City Life (London: Eliot Stock, 1894), 246–7; Wriothesley's Chronicle, ed. W.D. Hamilton (London: Camden Society, n.s. 11, 20, 1875–77), 1, 84; Ben Nilson, Cathedral Shrines of Medieval England (Woodbridge: Boydell, 1998), 139.
[8] J.H. Dahmus (131, 50, 170–2); Knighton's Chronicle, 1337–1396, ed. G.H. Martin (165, 533n., 534–5).
[9] A.K. McHardy (938, 139–40, 144).
[10] Register of Henry Chichele, ed. E.F. Jacob (Oxford: Clarendon, 1938–47), 3, 106; K.B. McFarlane (934, 195–6, 217–18). Hook, who owed his tenure of Braybrooke from 1401 to 1425 to Sir Thomas Latimer, one of the suspect Lollard knights, pleaded guilty to the charge before Bishop Repingdon (in the first year of the latter's episcopate). He failed to perform the penance, but remained in situ.

which rendered the latter needless, imagery of Christ as much as any other supposedly instructive depiction. His extremism and his refusal to come to the point angered the archbishop. And however we judge the way in which Thorpe represents himself getting the better of the argument, it is quite clear that this was a contest over authorities in which both sides were well informed, and in which the centrality of the crucifix was edged to one side.[11]

A similar vivid exchange on the same topic is described as taking place between Archbishop Arundel and Sir John Oldcastle, Lord Cobham in 1413. The text surviving in the 1530 imprint fleshes out the bare bones of the official record, which also includes images as one of the matters of the examination.

"Why Sir," said one of the clerkis, "will ye not worship ymagis?"
"What worship?" saide the lorde.
Than said frier Palmer,[12] "Sir, ye will worship the crosse of Christe that he died on?"
"Where is it?" said the lorde.
The frier said, "I put case Sir that it wer here before you."
The lorde said, "This is a redy man to put to me a question of a thing, that they wote never where it is. And yet I aske you, what worship?"
A clerke said, "Soche worship as Paul spekith of, that is this. God forbid me to ioye but in the crosse of our lorde Jesu Christe."[13]
Than said the lorde, and spred his armes abrode, "This is a very crosse."
Than said the bisshop of London, "Sir, ye wote well that he died on a materiall crosse."
Than said the lorde, "Our salvacion cam in onely by hym that died on the crosse and by the materiall crosse. And well I wote that this was the crosse that Paul ioyed on, that is, in the passion of our lord Jesu Christe."
The Archebisshop said, "Sir John, ye must submit you to the ordinaunce of the chirche."
The lorde said, "I wote not wherto."[14]

It is evident from the examinations of Thorpe and Oldcastle that worship of the cross was central to image-worship in general. We can see also that it involved several aspects. There was the matter of relics of the true cross on

[11] *Two Wycliffite Texts* (*156*, 56–9/1082–4, 1105–6). See Introduction xlv–xlviii for the editor's helpful discussion of the character of this record. On Thorpe's evasions see Fiona Somerset (*1129*, 202–4).

[12] For the team of university theologians present at Oldcastle's trial on 25 September 1413 see *Fasciculi Zizaniorum* (*139*, 442–3); D. Wilkins (*228*, 3.355–6, 357). The Dominican Thomas Palmer had contributed to academic debates with Wycliffites, including at Oxford, over Bible translation and in London at St. Paul's, where his defence of images cited the miraculous rood at the north door (above, n. 7) and seems to have taken account of the Conclusions recently posted there. Anne Hudson (*67*, 67–84); Anne Hudson (*713*, 50n., 58, 93, 99); A.B. Emden (*6*, 3.1421–2); BL, MS Harley 31, f. 192.

[13] Gal. 6.14. "But God forbid that I should glory, save in the cross of our Lord Jesus Christ, by whom the world is crucified unto me, and I unto the world."

[14] *The examinacion of Master William Thorpe . . . The examinacion of the honorable knight syr John Oldcastell Lorde Cobham* (STC 24045; BL, G 12012), sigs. I.3v–4. I have modernized the punctuation. On this book see *Two Wycliffite Texts* (*156*, xxx–xlv). A modern English version was printed by Alfred W. Pollard in *Fifteenth Century Prose and Verse* (Westminster: Constable, 1903), where this passage appears 187–8.

which Christ died; critical questions were raised over the kind of worship owed to cross and crucifix, and there was the fundamental issue of whether painted or sculpted representations of the crucifixion could be regarded as true representations of Christ and his passion. Or was man the only true image of God?

On both these occasions Archbishop Arundel was faced by individuals who in their different ways contested the accepted scholastic theology of image worship. The well-educated and experienced Thorpe seems to have carefully sidestepped direct confrontation on the topic of roods. Oldcastle, the partially instructed, perhaps partly Latinate layman,[15] seemingly bluff and confident in his theological investment, was ready to parry clerkly subtleties in his own direct way. In order to understand what was going on in these conversations, it is necessary to look at the theology that was under appraisal.

Worship of the cross was of course ancient; its place in the liturgy well established in the office for Good Friday, and in the feast days celebrating the Invention of the Holy Cross and the Exaltation of the Holy Cross. But the development of scholastic theology affected relics and images, just as it affected the sacrament of the altar, by producing subtleties in a pro and contra intellectual world that was designed to foster thought through disputation. Worship (*adoratio*) was a divisible concept, and its very divisions were to prove divisive.

The church's adoption and endorsement of imagery evolved over the centuries. Its justification was based on a well-known letter of Pope Gregory the Great, involving the concept of *pictura* and *scriptura* as comparable modes of understanding and remembering Christian stories. It was in the thirteenth century that the theory built on this text reached its full development, stated authoritatively and influentially by both Aquinas and Bonaventure. The value of imagery was now seen as threefold: to instruct the simple or unlettered; to fix the mysteries of the incarnation and examples of saints in the memory; and to increase devotion, which was moved more by seeing than hearing.[16] By now (in contrast to Gregory's day, when images of all kinds were fewer, including those of Christ) lay uses of Christian depictions could not be considered without thinking about worship, and that, as Oldcastle's question ("what worship?") indicated, meant more than one kind of respect. The question "whether the cult of *latria* ought to be shown to the image of Christ" had become an essential element in considerations of holy images.

The nature of worship was indeed the context in which the role of church imagery was now discussed. As such it entered the schools in commentaries on the Sentences of Peter Lombard, and it was in the course of questions teasing out the differences between *latria* and the lesser service of *dulia* that

[15] See Wilkins (*228*, 3.355) for the points on which Oldcastle was to reply being given to him "in scriptis terminis Latinis pro leviori intellectu ejusdem, in Anglicum translatis . . ." ("in writing with the Latin terms translated into English for his easier understanding. . . .").

[16] For a recent critical and fully annotated survey of this theory see Lawrence G. Duggan, "Was art really the 'book of the illiterate'?," *Word and Image* 5 (1989): 227–51.

the influential pronouncements of thirteenth-century doctors were made. St. Thomas and St. Bonaventure both considered fully the nature of the worship owed to Christ and his imagery. Both lent the full weight of their opinion to the view that *latria* belonged to Christ, and to imagery of Christ, including cross as well as crucifix.[17]

In the *Summa Theologiae* Aquinas stated unequivocally that the highest worship of *latria* was owed to both the image and cross of Christ. His six-part discussion of the worship of Christ took as its starting-point the question of whether Christ's divinity and humanity were owed the same *adoratio*. Having settled that the hypostatic union of the divine and human nature in Christ called for one adoration and honour from the worshipper, it followed that Christ's humanity was worshipped with *latria*, not for itself, but by reason of the divinity to which it was united. Against the Old Testament's commandment of Exodus 20 ("Non facies tibi sculptile" "Thou shalt not make unto thee any graven image") stood the New Testament in which God became man, making possible worship of his corporeal image. And since, as St. Basil had put it, the honour rendered to the image returned to its prototype, the proper worship for imagery of Christ was the worship of *latria*. "We worship the image of Christ who is truly God with the worship of *latria*, not for the sake of the image, but for that which the image represents." How could Christ's cross similarly be given *latria*, given the extreme opprobrium of his death, which might seem to argue for aborrence of the wood on which it occurred, and given the inapplicability of the previous argument for worshipping images of Christ? Aquinas returned an equally firm answer here. The shame of the cross represented triumph in the eyes of the faithful, the means of salvation, celebrated in the church's hymn (*O crux, ave, spes unica*). The honour owed to the cross was comparable to that given to the image of Christ, and indeed the two were assimilated. The cross both represented the body of Christ that had been extended on it, and was physically linked with that body through receiving the blood shed by his limbs. As a representation of Christ's passion the highest honour was therefore due to the cross. "So when we speak of the representation [*effigies*] of the cross of Christ in any material, whether of stone, wood, silver or gold, we venerate it as the image of Christ, which we venerate with the worship of *latria*, as said above."[18] This passage may seem rather to gloss over the distinctions between image, symbol and relic, but nevertheless provided a secure base for those who accepted the

---

[17] *Sancti Thomae Aquinatis Opera Omnia*, 25 vols. (Parma: Petrus Fiaccadorus, 1852–72), 7.107, *Commentum in quatuor libros sententiarum Magistri Petri Lombardi*, Lib. III, dist. ix, qu. 1, art. 2; S. Bonaventura, *Opera Omni*, 10 vols. (Quaracchi, 1882–1902), 3.202–5, *Commentaria in quatuor libros sententiarum Magistri Petri Lombardi*, Lib. III, dist. ix, art. 1, qu. 2.

[18] Aquinas, *Summa Theologiae*, ed. Caramello, 3.144–8; pt. III, qu. xxv, arts. 1–4, citing arts. 3 and 4, p. 147; "quia in novo Testamento Deus factus est homo, potest in sua imagine corporali adorari" ("Because in the New Testament God is made man, he can be worshipped in his corporeal image"); "nos autem adoramus adoratione latriae imaginem Christi qui est verus Deus, non propter ipsam imaginem, sed propter rem cujus imago est, sicut dictum est"; "si vero loquamur de effigie crucis Christi in quacumque alia material, puta lapidis vel ligni, argenti vel auri, sic veneramur crucem, tantum ut imaginem Christi: quam veneramur adoratione latriae, ut supra dictum est."

various forms of worshipping cross and crucifix embedded in church liturgy and practice. Not everyone, however, was happy with these dicta, as became plain in the university of Oxford.

It was therefore a relatively recent development in the theology of the cross that was subjected to close scrutiny in the fourteenth century, and Wycliffites were not the first to be worried. Robert Holcot had given a lead in the university of Oxford, and his influential commentary on the book of Wisdom shows how, two generations after the death of the *Doctor angelicus*, doubts about the latter's pronouncements on rendering *latria* to Christ's image were being voiced in university circles. It seems that the theology of *latria* was being mulled over at Oxford in the 1370s, and the prominence given to the issue by Wyclif's academic followers produced a number of learned replies, written to defend the church's position in the 1390s, including Roger Dymmok's.[19] What is of particular interest is the way in which so inherently abstruse and academic an issue was taken out of learned circles and Latin terminology, into a wider world. It was not easy, given the need for phrases like "reverence dew to God alone," or "that worship that longith to him [Christ], eithir bi title of his godheed or ellis bi title of his manheed."[20]

Holcot's discussion of "whether it is lawful for Christians to worship images" suggested distinct qualifications about the worship that could be rendered to imagery of Christ. The idea that *adoratio* could be given to such an image was unacceptable since this highest form of spiritual devotion and love ought never to be given to any creature. There was inherent contradiction in saying that *latria* was the honour owed to God alone and that it was also owed to the image of Christ. Even if it was possible to say, speaking loosely, that we worship the image, what was intended was not worship of Christ's image of wood or stone, but rather "I worship Christ before the image of Christ because it is the image of Christ and incites me to worship Christ." The words of St. Thomas and St. Basil and the rites of the church ought to be understood in this way. Holcot did not mince his own words. "It doesn't seem good to me at this time to say that the image is honoured with the same honour as God who is imaged."[21] This can only be read as putting a serious caveat over the pronouncement of the Angelical Doctor. It was evidently taken to heart in some quarters.

An unfinished *Postilla super Matthaeum* by Wyclif's opponent William Woodford, which has been dated 1372-3, shows Holcot being brought to bear on the question of whether *latria* was owed to the humanity of Christ. This formed part of a wider discussion of idols and idolatry, which bore on imagery in churches and specifically on worship of the cross. Christ's flesh was part of his humanity, and his humanity was united with his divinity, but

---

[19] Dymmok's *Liber* (*136*, 180–91), gave a full rebuttal to the eighth conclusion on this question, with due reference to St. Thomas. On the emergence of the counter-polemic against Wycliffites at Oxford see J.I. Catto (*378*, 227–31).

[20] *Two Wycliffite Texts* (*156*, 120, 134).

[21] Robert Holcot, *Super librum Sapientiae* (Basel, 1489), cap. xiii, lectio 157; Aston (*284*, 120–4, and 119 n.79) for the argument that no words of Christ sanctioned honouring him through his image.

was it licit to worship it with *latria*? Arguably this worship should not be given either to Christ's humanity or to the cross of Christ, and here Holcot's words in his Wisdom commentary were cited. It was not the cross that was worshipped with *latria*, but Christ himself: worship was *before* not *to* the image. Woodford fully endorsed the traditional threefold justification of the church's multiplying images. But he was concerned about the question of *latria*, and looked hard at the implications of Holcot's words.[22]

In the 1390s an impressive number of replies were written by university men to counter Wycliffite denial of image worship. The full scale of this academic riposte remains to be measured, and it would be well worth investigation since it promises to be of interest for image debates in general, as well as the heretics' stance in particular. At the heart of the matter stood cross and crucifix and the rites and observances surrounding them in ecclesiastical worship. It had become critical to consider the precise nature of worship in order to defend current orthodoxy. "What is honour?" "What is worship?" occupied minds in the schools. The problem of whether, as Nicholas Radcliffe put it, it was permissible for the faithful and devout to render *latria* mediately and indirectly to the image of the crucifix, perhaps shows that the debate was moving on, as well as going round in circles.[23] What happened to this ongoing discussion in the schools? Did this battery of answers mark the end of open argument over what might seem like a theological can of worms? If the Lollard case against worship of the cross stemmed from academic questioning, free talking in the schools was certainly not helped by extramural airing. In mid-fifteenth-century Oxford, theology still called for the study of Peter Lombard's Sentences, and the defence of holy statues and images was still a topic for academic exercise.[24] But intellectual barricades were no longer being built against Wycliffites, and Archbishop Arundel had actively discouraged debate about ecclesiastical definitions, "particularly concerning the worship of the glorious cross" and the veneration of images.[25] Maybe, as in the matter of vernacular scripture, the fearful censors closed what might otherwise have been rather healthy developments.

The reservations about cross worship expressed by Holcot found their way into the vernacular and so took the issue into circles beyond the university worlds in which the whole issue was bred. The author of *Dives*

---

[22] Cambridge University Library, Add. MS 3571, ff. 117–122; Catto (*378*, 179, 196–8); also Catto, "William Woodford, O.F.M. (c.1339–c.1397)" (D.Phil. diss. University of Oxford, 1969), 98, 150–55 for reference to a longer (not extant) work in which Woodford distinguished exterior acts of kneeling etc. from the act of will which constituted the essence of *latria*. This indicates a refinement of the distinction between worshipping before an image and rendering *latria* to it.

[23] See Hudson (*713*, 92–94), for the manuscript treatises, including the discussion of Radcliffe, an Oxford Benedictine, that "lictum est fidelibus et devotis mediate et indirecte ymagini crucifixi cultum latrie exhibere" ("it is permissible for the faithful to render the worship of *latria* to the image of the crucifix mediately and indirectly") which appears in both BL Royal 6 D X, ff. 274–77v (at f. 276) and Royal 10 D X, ff. 308v–12 (at f. 310v). Thomas Palmer's defence of images in BL MS Harley 31, ff. 182–94v includes a chapter on "quid sit honor" (ff. 190–92).

[24] Catto (*379*, 267–8, and on the change from engagement in theological controversy and Wycliffite refutation, 264, 275).

[25] Wilkins (*228*, 3.317–18).

and Pauper (whose book came under suspicion) expressed views on this matter that were on the iffy side of contemporary orthodoxy. Crucifixes were placed on a par with other images in the argument that believers should kneel, pray and worship *before* not *to* imagery. When men crept to the cross on Good Friday they were reverencing Christ and "that heye wurshepe that day" was done "nought to the cros that the preist heldyght in his hond but to hym that deyidde that day for us alle upon the cros." The shift of emphasis was narrow, but decisive. To say that "the lykenesse of a thing owyght nought been in as mechil reverence ne in wurshepe as the thyng on theself" was certainly not current correctness where the crucifix was concerned. There is also a curious uncertainty in what may read like Pauper's last word on this subject. "Also to the cros that Crist deyid on, yf meen haddyn it, as clerkys seyn, longyght *yperdulia*, for of alle thyngys that wantyn lyf the cros of Crist howyt most to been wurshepyd and been in most veneracioun and reverence. But that veneracioun is clepyd *yperdulia* unpropyrly."[26]

A crucifix, as Arundel told Thorpe, ought to be worshipped for the Passion of Christ that is painted therein.[27] It was just at this time that the archbishop was formulating the Constitutions in which this doctrine was publicly defended. No one should presume to dispute the teaching of the church's decretals and constitutions concerning the worship (*adoratio*) of the glorious cross and the veneration (*veneratio*) of images, or about pilgrimages to special places and their relics. "From henceforth let it be taught commonly and preached by all that the cross, crucifix, images of saints" and other holy places and relics, ought to be venerated in the accustomed ways with processions, kneeling, bowing, censing, kissing, offerings, lights, and pilgrimages.[28]

The veneration of the cross so widely endorsed by the church was about much more than the representations of art. It was also about relics, and Wycliffites long contested the very idea that worship of the true cross was either possible or proper. Not long after the appearance of the Twelve Conclusions, a list of points on which the Wycliffites expected they might face examination instructed Lollards how to answer the charge of denying cross and image worship; the assertion that "though a man saughe before him the same crosse wereon Crist suffered deth, he schulde not worshipe it, for, as it is seid, all that worschipen the crosse or ymages ben cursed and done mawmentri." The correct response was a firm denial of *latria* – in layman's language, "neither the crosse that Crist was don upon, neither any other roode or ymage maad of mannys hand schulde be worschipid as God."[29] William Sawtry was certainly quizzed on just these lines, and seems to have been well prepared to make clear that he would not worship the wood of the cross ("gross matter"), and would not waver from this even were the true cross right before him. The view that "the cross on which

[26] *Dives and Pauper* (*134*, 1.86–91, cited at 88, 108); B.L. Manning (*915*, 97–101).
[27] Above, 101.
[28] Wilkins (*228*, 3.317–18).
[29] Hudson (*155*, 19, 23).

Christ died is not to be worshipped" was also one to which Richard Wyche subscribed.[30] Lollard opposition to any kind of veneration of relics of the true cross was long-lasting, and perhaps came to loom larger than concerns about *latria* and academic distinctions of worship.

How long did Wycliffites continue to be troubled about the worship of the cross? Did the nature of their opposition change as time went on? Thirty years into the fifteenth century misbelief of this kind was anticipated and found. In 1428, a comprehensive list of errors produced for ecclesiastical examiners included "whether the holy cross and images of Christ ought to be venerated" and (interestingly), "whether it is permissible for anyone to bless themselves with the sign of the cross."[31] Had Wyclif's followers taken a step down the road that was subsequently to be so well trodden by puritans? We cannot answer that question as there seems to be no evidence of Lollards objecting to the sign of the cross, but proceedings in the diocese of Norwich at this time reveal individuals who were committed to denying the worship of cross and crucifix.

The story of the didactic housewife, Margery Baxter of Martham, gives a vivid picture of what such convictions could amount to. Joan Clifland told the bishop of Norwich about the instruction Margery had given her one Friday at the end of January 1429. The conversation is presented as a cross-examination in more than one sense. What do you do every day in church? Joan's reply that her first action on entering church was to kneel before the cross and say five Paternosters and Aves in honour of the crucifix and the Virgin was the opening for Margery's censure. Such kneeling, worship and prayer were ill done, and images of the crucifix no more worthy of honour than a gallows on which your brother was hung. If you want to see the true cross of Christ, Margery told Joan Clifland in January 1429, "I'll show it to you here, in your own house." Joan declared that she would be very pleased to see the true cross of Christ. "Look," said Margery, stretching her arms out wide, "this is the true cross of Christ, and you can and ought to see and worship this cross every day here in your own home, and you're labouring in vain when you go to church to worship or pray to other images and dead crosses." That was Oldcastle's message – that man was the true image of God.[32] The ancient figure of the *orans*, the priest standing *in modum crucis*, was the only true representation of the crucifixion (Fig. 1). Vernacular learners clung to this tenet. "Fy! fy! fy!"; Reginald Pecock berated Lollards of the next generation, for their obstinacy in maintaining it was "greet heresie . . . for to holde that a stok or a stoon graved is a fuller and a perfiter ymage of Crist than is a Cristen man."[33]

If that claim was ultimately scriptural, opposition to worship of the true

[30] *Fasciculi Zizaniorum* (*139*, 408–9, 503).
[31] Hudson (*67*, 134–4). On Lollards and the aerial sign of the cross see Thomas Netter's remark in his *Doctrinale Antiquitatum Fidei Catholicae Ecclesiae* (*188*, 3, col. 964).
[32] *Heresy Trials in the Diocese of Norwich, 1428–31* (*208*, 44); 1 Cor. 11.7 "For a man indeed ought not to cover his head, forasmuch as he is the image and glory of God."
[33] Reginald Pecock (*190*, 1.221–2); Moshe Barasch, *Giotto and the Language of Gesture* (Cambridge: Cambridge Univ. Press, 1987), 8–9, 57–9, for the "depicting gesture" of the priest's *orans* posture.

Fig. 1. *Orans* in fourth-century fresco, SS Giovanni e Paolo, Rome.
(Photo: Warburg Library, London)

cross had special resonance for Norfolk Lollards. On the continent in the south of France, the heretical Peter of Bruis had taught his twelfth-century followers that the cross should rather be disgraced than honoured, with the result that some of them took to cross-burning and breaking.[34] A few Lollards did likewise. The seeming illogicality of worshipping the instruments of Christ's death – an argument rebutted by Aquinas – expressed by Margery Baxter's words about the gallows, was echoed by Thomas Moon of Loddon, and denial of worship to the dead wood of the cross may here have owed something to the teaching of William White, who had compared the dead wood of images with the vitality of growing trees.[35] On rare occasions Lollards, like Petrobrusians before them, translated rejection of cross-worship into direct action against crosses. On the evening of Saturday 10 July 1428, John Burell was making his way home to Loddon with Edmund Archer, who the following year was to be charged with denying image worship, especially to any image of Christ's cross, "for every such crosse is the signe and the tokene of Antecrist." As the two friends passed the gate of Loddon Hall, Burrell, who was carrying a faggot-hook, struck out with it and hit an old cross lying there. "What did you do that for?" he was asked by another villager. "I replied," reported Burell, when under examination the following April, "that 'even if I were to strike that cross

[34] Malcolm Lambert (*821*, 47–9).
[35] Aston (*284*, 115–16; and *43*, 90).

harder and sharper with a sharper tool, that cross would never bleed.' "[36] Dead images were dead teachers; beyond miracle, beyond respect. There was no comparability between the wood of the cross and the living/dying figure of Christ.

Physical attacks on crosses, for all the critical talk, feature rarely among the Lollards. But another example is linked with this Norfolk village of Loddon, which might almost be described as a Lollard cell, doubtless thanks to the teaching of Hugh Pye who was chaplain there before he went to the stake in 1428. According to a record that only survives in Foxe's Book of Martyrs, Hugh Pye was charged in 1424 with having "cast the crosse of Bromholde into the fire to be burned, which hee tooke from one John Welgate" of Loddon. The Cluniac priory of Broomholm, situated (as the crow flies) twenty odd miles due north of Loddon near Bacton and the coast, would have been an obvious target for Norfolk cross critics. It was one of the few English pilgrimage centers that claimed possession of a relic of the true cross, acquired in 1220 having been stolen from Constantinople at the time of the fourth crusade in 1204. This relic attracted many pilgrims, and was celebrated by an annual fair on the feast of the Exaltation of the Holy Cross. Surviving pilgrim badges show that the relic was in the form of a patriarchal cross, and it was most likely a pilgrim souvenir of some kind representing this that Pye destroyed in his demonstrative burning.[37] (Figs. 2 and 3)

The fact that Lollard opposition to worship of the cross included objections to liturgical celebrations might be taken as an indication of their church attendance.[38] John Seynon of "Dounton," who appeared before Archbishop Arundel in 1400, was charged (along with heretical views of the mass) with maintaining that the office of the Holy Cross contained idolatry, and that it was idolatry to worship crucifixes.[39] Half a century later Bishop Pecock went to some lengths to justify the ceremonies of Palm Sunday and Good Friday because "the adversaries" held the deeds done on those days "to be greet and cursed wickidnes."[40] We can be sure that Margery Baxter, for one, would never have dreamt of going to Broomholm. But what did she do on Palm Sunday, or Good Friday and Easter Sunday – let alone Holy Rood day? Adherence to this clause of the 1395 conclusions seems to have lasted for a good two generations or more, and we can place alongside fidelity to this part of the manifesto, the fact that

---

[36] Tanner (208, 72–8, at 76, 166).

[37] John Foxe, Actes and Monuments (142), 660; Frances Wormald, "The Rood of Bromholm," Journal of the Warburg Institute 1 (1937): 31–45; Brian Spencer, Pilgrim Souvenirs and Secular Badges (London: Stationery Office, 1998), 161–5; Aston (284, 138). The burning could have been a lesson for John Welgate, or someone in the parish who had gone to Broomholm.

[38] Of course there are examples of non-attendance but there is plenty of evidence pointing the other way; see Richard Davies (460, 206).

[39] Reg. Arundel (Lambeth), 1, f. 411; Wilkins (228, 3.248–9); Hudson (713, 160). Seynon was in London (accused of more heresies) in 1402, and was handed over to the bishop of London; the outcome is unknown. His case is considered by Charles Kightly, "The Early Lollards: A Survey of Popular Lollard Activity in England, 1382–1428" (D.Phil. diss., University of York, 1975), 113, 455.

[40] Repressor (190, 1.269–73, at 273). On the cross and crucifix in the ceremonies of Holy Week see Eamon Duffy (512, 22–37).

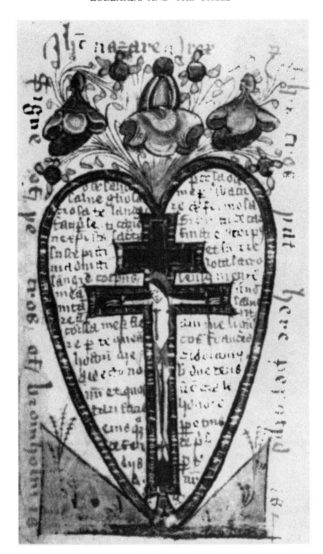

Fig. 2. Devotional picture of the Cross of Broomholm in a fifteenth-century Book of Hours. (Lambeth Palace Library, London, MS 545, f. 186)

the Lollard sermon-cycle included no address for the Invention of the Holy Cross (3 May), though there was a sermon for the Exaltation (14 September).[41]

[41] *English Wycliffite Sermons* (*158*, 2.302–4, 5.252–3). According to Netter (*188*, 3, col. 959) "haeretici sileant, qui cum diabolo crucis inventione tristantur" ("Let the heretics keep silence, who grieve with the devil at the invention of the Cross"). The homilies in *Mirk's Festial* (*186*) for the feasts on which worship of the cross was salient, show the kind of instruction and allusion which the Wycliffite addresses studiously eschewed: "ryght soo we worschip this day the cros yn our procescyon, thrys knelying to the cros yn worschip and yn mynd of hym that was for us don on the crosse" (115, Palm Sunday): "I counsell that we do reverence and worschyp to the cros" (146, Invention); "ye schull come to the chirche, and worschip the holy rode yn worschip of the crosse that Cryst deyet on" (249, Exaltation); see also 118, 124, 146.

Fig. 3. Mid thirteenth-century tin ampulla of Broomholm, from waterfront of
Billingsgate, Lower Thames Street, London.
(Museum of London, 83. 367)

But there were different forms of the Lollard gospel. All along we have to
allow for reticence, for the wariness of the unsaid, as well as the dangers of
explicit denial. The entry on "Adoracio" in the *Floretum* complemented its
scriptural illustrations of worship with a general explication of *dulia*,
hyperdulia and *latria*, that steered clear of their application to images.[42]
The long Good Friday sermon in the Wycliffite cycle predictably recounted
in full the scriptural record of that day without the least inkling of the
accepted idea that "when we worschipp the tokenys and schap of the crosse,
then we reduce to mynde what he suffred for us."[43] "Reducing to mind" was
a process of gospel grounding. Likewise the entry on "Crosse" in the
Rosarium Theologie expands at large on scriptural parallels in the Old
Testament, as well as the Passion in the New. It allowed that the cross was
holy – but there is nothing about worship here either, though this authority

[42] BL MS Harley 401, ff. 15–16. The vernacular *Rosarium* proved capable of serving a more radical
position: Christina von Nolcken (*220*, 96–101, 124–7); Hudson (*713*, 304).
[43] *English Wycliffite Sermons* (*158*, 3.172–87); *Speculum Sacerdotale*, ed. E.H. Weatherly, EETS o.s.
200 (London: Oxford Univ. Press, 1936), 110–11 (Good Friday).

goes so far as to accept that the cross was more than a sign, it was a true instrument of salvation. "The crosse is takene for the signe or tokone of the crusified, and so was the tre in wiche criste hong the holy crosse. For it was the holy signe, and not only a signe, but a very instrument in wich criste bought man kynde."[44]

In the early sixteenth century heretical suspects were still being accused of refusing cross worship and in the 1520s and 30s, when new currents of reform were percolating the English scene, there were several incidents of crosses and roods being broken and burned. The old strains of Lollard opinion are still detectable, in phrases like those of Henry Phip of Hughenden, calling the rood the "block almighty," or John Edmunds of Burford, saying the image of God was the poor people, or in behaviour like that of Agnes Frank, who turned away from the resurrected crucifix as it was carried round the church on Easter morning.[45] In Kent, William Baker of Cranbrook, who had been "mynded to goo and offer to the roode of grace" at Boxley, described in 1511 how shared criticism of pilgrimage had decided him instead to give his offering to a poor man.[46] Talk and action went on. But things had changed. The theological niceties that had informed and vexed Thorpe and Oldcastle seem to have faded from the scene. It was now not so much a question of "what worship?" was owed to cross and crucifix, as the wrongfulness of all church imagery (cross included). The doctrine formulated by St. Thomas had not left English controversy for good, but for Wyclif's followers it sank from view with the loss of learned input. Scholastic theology was no longer in the forefront of Lollard debates, for there were fewer learned debaters, fewer questioning theologians. But there were still readers and learners, and of course the strength of credal certainty is not dependent on subtleties.

---

[44] Gonville and Caius College, MS 354/581, f. 26.

[45] Foxe, *Actes and Monuments* (1583), 823, 834–5. George Brown (799) opposed worship of the cross on the grounds that if a friend of his had been hanged, he would thereafter "have loved that gallowes .. rather worse for that, then better." The "book of William Thorpe" was circulating in these circles.

[46] *Kent Heresy Proceedings 1511–12* (209, 53).

Walter Brut's Theology of the
Sacrament of the Altar

David Aers

"Amen, amen I say unto you: He that believeth in me, hath everlasting
life. I am the bread of life." (John 6.47–48)[1]

Walter Brut is an early Wycliffite whose extraordinarily rich testimony
has received surprisingly little attention.[2] This latinate layman and Herefordshire farmer (278, 284) had been accused of heresy in the 1380s by both
the Archbishop of Canterbury and Bishop John Gilbert of Hereford, cited
to answer articles allegedly against the Catholic faith which he had been
maintaining in public (279). The testimony we have is written in Latin at the
command of Bishop John Trefnant, the successor of John Gilbert who
accused Brut of erring in many matters of the faith (285). Anne Hudson has
described the "seriousness" with which Trefnant addressed Brut's views and
the ways in which "interest in the trial spread far beyond the bounds of
Hereford or its diocese."[3] Her study of his learning and latinity, his identity
as "laycus litteratus," shows the academic sources of Lollardy and corrects
K.B. McFarlane's condescending and inaccurate account of Brut's work
and its significance.[4] But while Hudson gives us important contexts in which
to study Brut, she acknowledges that, "The views of Brut are not my

---

[1] John 6.47–48: for English translation of the vulgate I use *The Holy Bible translated from the Latin
Vulgate*, Douay-Rheims revised Richard Challoner (Rockford: Tan Books, 1989).

[2] Text in *Registrum Johannes Trefnant* (*213*): his text at 285–356: 278–394 for trial documents with
judges' responses. The main commentary on Brut is by Anne Hudson (*722*) and by Curtis Bostick
(*335*, 147–154). The passage of Brut's testimony most noted concerns women and their ability to
consecrate the host: see *Woman Defamed and Woman Defended*, ed. Alcuin Blamires (Oxford:
Clarendon, 1992), 250–60; Margaret Aston (*274*, 52–59), and Fiona Somerset, "*Eciam Mulier*:
Women in Lollardy and the Problem of Sources," in Kathryn Kerby-Fulton and Linda Olson,
eds., *Reading Women: New Approaches to Female Literacy in Late Antiquity and the Middle Ages*
(Univ. of Notre Dame Press, forthcoming). Also relevant here is A. Blamires and C.W. Marx
(*119*).

[3] Hudson (*722*, 224).

[4] See K.B. McFarlane (*933*, 135–38). McFarlane's condescending dismissal of Brut's use of the
Apocalypse simply overlooks its importance in the claims it makes for "Britones" as an elect
people (Brut, 293–96), its attempts to distinguish medieval fables of Antichrist from scriptural
prophecies and its application of the latter to Church history, with its carefully institutionalizing
reading of Antichrist (296–303): see Bostick (*335*, 147–54) and Penn Szittya, "Domesday Bokes:
The Apocalypse in Medieval English Culture," ch. 16 in *The Apocalypse in the Middle Ages*, ed.
R.K. Emmerson and B. McGinn (Ithaca: Cornell Univ. Press, 1992), see 396–97 (though it seems
odd to call Brut's Latin text "popular rather than learned," 396: cf., Hudson, *722*).

primary concern."[5] It is one central aspect of these views that concerns the present chapter: namely, Brut's reflections on the sacrament of the altar. The more carefully we study Walter Brut, the more we will be encouraged to unpack the ways in which the linguistic, theological and political homogeneity of Wycliffites has been seriously exaggerated, by enemies and friends, past and present. Perhaps this essay will encourage further study of individual Wycliffites and further study of their treatment of particular topics. The documents around Brut are rather unusual in giving us an extensive statement of a Wycliffite's self-description *alongside* the ecclesiastic judges' construals of that statement and their responses to what they so construed. Exploring the clash in representation here would illuminate the well-known problems presented to Wycliffite studies by the fact that so many Wycliffites are known only through their judges' construals. Brut's trial enables readers to see how the authorities went about the business of composing a version of this Wycliffite, what they included, what they excluded, and it invites us to think about the role of different genres in producing different versions of teaching. Such invitations cannot be pursued in the present essay but they are certainly in its margins and calling for attention.

The testimony as a whole is a remarkably wide-ranging and often extremely shrewd work of theological inquiry by a very searching Christian. It certainly deserves far more complete analysis than I can offer here. Brut attempts to subject the Church's practices and doctrines, together with his own reflections on these, to the authority of sacred Scripture, especially the New Testament, and to the authority of probable reasoning grounded in Scripture (285–286).[6] Yet he never advocates anything remotely like the vulgar materialism or the abstract rationalism with which contemporary orthodoxy habitually charged Wycliffites. Such charges are illustrated in Nicholas Love's *Mirror of the Blessed Life of Christ*.[7] Love asserts that Wycliffites are worse than Judas because of the trust they place in "bodily felyng, as in siht, tast & touching" (153). They refuse to set aside "manus reson" in the face of divine activity (153–154), "presumptuously leuyng vpon hir owne bodily wittes & kyndely reson" (227). How wide of the mark is this characteristic generalization will emerge below. Nor is Brut's exegesis shaped by the kind of scriptural fundamentalism with which Wyclif and his followers are so often associated.[8] His approach here is thoroughly Christocentric. While he allows for the activities of reasoning and imaginative speculation in reading Scripture, he tries to prevent these from becoming totally autonomous of what he, like his orthodox opponents, understood to be the revealed word of God. The language of his inquiries into the

---

[5] Hudson (*722*, 224).

[6] On Wycliffite hermeneutics see these differing accounts: M. Hurley (*738*); Paul de Vooght (*484*, 168–200); Kantik Ghosh (*598*).

[7] Nicholas Love (*179*): references to Love in my text are to this edition. On Love see: Ghosh (*598*, ch. 5); Sarah Beckwith (*300*, 63–70); Katherine C. Little, "Interpretation and Instruction in Late Medieval England" (Ph.D. dissertation, Duke University, 1998), ch. 3.

[8] The most recent example I have encountered is by Marcia Colish, *Medieval Foundations of the Western Intellectual Tradition, 400–1400* (New Haven: Yale Univ. Press, 1997), 255–256.

contemporary Church and its ways of constituting authority is more
theologically careful and tentative than McFarlane's terms ("cloudy
grandiloquence") register.[9]

When Brut comes to the sacrament of the altar he notes something the
Church was increasingly invested in denying: that over the centuries diverse
authorities had produced diverse accounts of the mystery (336).[10] In this
complex situation his own commitment, he says, is to what Christ taught
explicitly or implicitly. For Christ is ("I believe and I know") the true bread
of God who descended from heaven and gives life to the world (336). He
sets out from the words of Christ in John's gospel, citing John 6.32–35,
words that represent Christ as the life-giving bread from heaven. The mode
of exposition here seems so unpolemical that a reader not immersed in late
medieval discourses of the eucharist and their conflicts might well overlook
the force of Brut's decision here. To grasp this one needs to recollect that for
the vast majority of late medieval Christians the sacrament which brought
them Christ's body was a spectacle performed by a priest, often behind
increasingly elaborate screens, in a language very few would have understood even if they had been able to hear the words. For most of the service
the priest had his back turned to the people who were not called on to make
any responses. Indeed, as vernacular texts such as the *Lay Folks' Mass Book*
show, the laity were encouraged to make prayers and readings which might
often bear little relation to what was being enacted at the east end of their
church. The mass thus embodied and fostered the clearest division between
clergy and laity. The consecration bell would tell the people that the
elements had been transubstantiated and as the priest turned to face them
they could adore the actual body of Christ, elevated between the priest's
hands.[11] As the Franciscan historian Paul Lachance observes, "One went to
Mass, however, not so much to receive the body of Christ as to see it."[12] The
late medieval mass was for the vast majority of Christians a spectacle where
pious attendance at the display of Christ's body guaranteed a range of
benefits endlessly reiterated. For example, Bishop Brinton of Rochester, a
contemporary and opponent of Wyclif, taught that these benefits included

---

[9] McFarlane (*933*, 136).

[10] The literature here is immense, but the following are especially relevant to my concerns: Miri
Rubin (*1071*); Beckwith (*300*); John Bossy, "The Mass as Social Institution, 1200–1700," *Past
and Present*, 100 (1983): 29–61; Henri de Lubac, *Corpus Mysticum: L'euchariste et l'église au
moyen-âge* (Paris: Aubier, 1949); Gary Macy, "The Dogma of Transubstantiation in the Middle
Ages," *Journal of Ecclesiastical History* 45 (1994): 11–41.

[11] *The Lay Folks' Mass Book*, ed. Thomas F. Simmons, EETS o.s. 71 (1879), 38–41, 280–88. For my
description of the medieval mass see Bossy, "The Mass," esp. 33; Beckwith (*300*, 33–37, 140);
Eamon Duffy (*512*, ch. 3, esp. 91); V.L. Kennedy, "The Moment of Consecration and the
Elevation of the Host," *Medieval Studies* 6 (1994): 121–50 with P. Browe, "Die Elevation in der
Messe," *Jahrbuch für Liturgiewissenschaft* 9 (1929): 20–66. On the "undifferentiated dorsality" of
the mass before Vatican II, see P.J. Fitzpatrick, *In Breaking of Bread: Church Eucharist and
Ritual* (Cambridge: Cambridge Univ. Press, 1993), 209–17. Also relevant here is Edouard
Dumoutet, *Le désir de voir l'hostie at les origin de la dévotion au saint-sacrament* (Paris:
Beauchesne, 1926).

[12] *Angela of Foligno: Complete Works*, tr. and intr. Paul Lachance (New York: Paulist Press, 1993),
27; for an example of the host as spectacle, see Angela's account at 146–147. See too Suzanne
Lewis, *Reading Images: Narrative Discourse and Reception in the Thirteenth Century Illuminated
Apocalypse* (Cambridge: Cambridge Univ. Press, 1995), 260, and 263–65.

the necessary material food for the day, forgiveness of light speech and oaths, one's eyesight not diminishing, freedom from sudden death that day, freedom from aging during mass and the privilege of having one's steps to and from mass counted by angels.[13] Even members of the Franciscan Third Order would receive communion only three times a year, and Eamon Duffy has rightly observed that to communicate monthly was viewed as "something of a prodigy."[14] This is the context that so frustrated the Wycliffite priest William Thorpe in Shrewsbury, soon after Brut composed his testimony. In a well-known scene Thorpe recounts how he was "in þe pulpitte, bisiinge me to teche þe heestes of God," when a "sacringe belle" was rung from an altar in the church. Immediately "myche peple turned awei fersli and wiþ greet noyse runnen fromwardis me" to behold the body of Christ being elevated for adoration.[15] And this is the context assumed and implicitly challenged in the way Brut decides to approach the sacrament of the altar, through John 6.

Christ the bread of life is to be *eaten* and those who do eat will live eternally ("ex quo pane qui manducat vivet in eternum, ut patet in eodem capitulo" [John 6], 336). Without direct polemic, there is simply not the slightest suggestion in Brut's text that devoutly *watching* the bread of life could be an appropriate response, nor that presence at the display of the consecrated host would bring the benefits described in Brinton's standard list. Brut's strategy foregrounds reception of the bread of life, communion, before he engages with the consecration of the elements, the issue that obsessed late medieval defenses of current orthodoxy.[16]

He then considers what is entailed by eating Christ, the bread of life. This consideration turns to faith in Christ's redemption of humanity which, by grace, justifies those who have been immersed in sinful lives unable to fulfill the teachings of the divinely given law (336–37: he quotes from Galatians 2.16, 3.11–12, 21–24; Romans 5.20–21). In this move Brut is following connections made in the chapter of John's gospel from which he began: "Jesus said to them: I am the bread of life. He that cometh to me shall not hunger: and he that believeth in me shall never thirst" (John 6.35). Jesus warns that seeing is *not* the same as believing (John 6.36). Responding to this, Brut emphasizes the role of faith in communion with the flesh and blood of Christ. Whoever eats the flesh of Christ and drinks his blood dwells in Christ and Christ in that person (he cites John 6.57) but it is faith alone that enables this reception (337).[17] By unfolding the connection of reception

[13] *The Sermons of Thomas Brinton, Bishop of Rochester (1373–1389)*, ed. Mary Aquinas Devlin (London: Royal Historical Society, 1954), 2 vols.: see sermon 69 (320); similarly sermon 48 (215–216). For other examples and references see David Aers and Lynn Staley (*263*, 26–27).

[14] Respectively, Lachance, *Angela of Foligno*, 34 and Duffy (*512*, 93).

[15] Thorpe's text is published in *Two Wycliffite Texts* (*156*, 52).

[16] See Strohm (*1159*, ch. 2).

[17] St. Thomas Aquinas's teaching that faithful desire for the sacrament *constitutes reception* involves a similar emphasis on faith but it separates faith from reception in a way not implied by Brut. See *Summa Theologiae*, III.79.1, ad 1 (using parallel text edition, London: Blackfriars, 1964–73, 60 vols.). For Brut's teacher on the eucharist, see John Wyclif, *De Eucharistia*, ed. J. Loserth (London: Wyclif Society, 1892), and for discussion of Wyclif and Wycliffite theology of the eucharist, see: Hudson (*713*, 281–90); Catto (*373*); Maurice Keen (*775*, 1–16, esp. 6–16).

and faith through reading John 6, Brut introduces his understanding of what is entailed by eating Christ's flesh and by Christ's real presence in sacramental communion. He does so *before* he engages with current arguments over what exactly happens to the elements at their consecration, arguments that were a mixture of physics, metaphysics, and theology.[18]

He decides to open out another important dimension of the eucharist before addressing these issues, one that seems to get obscured in the apologetic writings of those responsible for formulating orthodoxy against Wycliffite Christians. The dimension I have in mind here is the eschatological. As St. Thomas wrote of the sacrament, it looks to the past (Christ's passion and sacrifice), the present (the unity of the Church) and the future: "It prefigures that enjoyment of God which will be ours in heaven. That is why it is called a '*viaticum*,' because it keeps us on the way to heaven . . .[and] called 'eucharist,' that is 'desirable gift or grace [*bona gratia*],' because *the free gift of God is eternal life* [Romans 6.23]" (*ST* III.73.4, resp.). Brut argues that as the wayfaring Christian is fed spiritually through the body and blood of Christ, so in the future the faithful will be eternally fed and utterly fulfilled in all their potentials by Christ in his humanity and his divinity (337). So Jesus gave the sacrament of his body and blood, in bread and wine, as a memorial of a double feast: the last supper *and* the future banquet of eternal beatitude (337). In this eschatological perspective Brut quotes Jesus's words at the last supper (Matthew 26.26–28, Luke 22.19–20: 337–38). Only now, only in the carefully articulated context I have described, does Brut take up the issues around consecration and, in particular, the currently orthodox version of transubstantiation.[19]

To appreciate what Brut is doing, and the way he is doing what he does, one needs to recall that the late medieval Church had made the reception of the bread and wine, the body and blood, a *supplementary* adjunct to the eucharist whose essence, for lay observers, was now defined as the act of consecration. While this is certainly implicit in the liturgical practices outlined above, the position had been explicated and defended. For example, in the *Summa Theologiae* St. Thomas had argued that the eucharist "is fully established when the matter is consecrated," unlike the other sacraments which demand the faithful's participatory use of them. He emphasized "the use by the faithful of this sacrament is not required for validity, but is something that takes place afterwards [usus autem fidelium non est de necessitate sacramenti, sed est aliquid consequens ad sacramentum]." And again, "in this sacrament use is not an essential part [usus materiae consecratae qui non est de necessitate hujus sacramenti]."[20] Not

---

[18] For examples of this mixture see Ockham's approaches to the eucharist in *Quodlibetal Questions*, tr. Alfred J. Freddoso and Francis E. Kelley (New York: Yale Univ. Press, 1991), 2 vols. 298–310, 369–75, 497–99; and *De Sacramento Altaris*, tr. T.B. Birch (Burlington: Lutheran Literary Board, 1930): for a critical edition of the relevant text here see *De Corpore Christi*, ed. Carolus A. Grassi, with *De Quantitate*, in William of Ockham, *Opera Theologica*, volume 9 (New York, St Bonaventure: St Bonaventure University, 1986), 87–234.

[19] Love's treatment of the last supper offers an illuminating contrast to Brut's approach: (*179*, 146–56); as do the responses of Brut's judges: Brut, 380–81.

[20] *Seriatim, ST* III.73.1, ad 3; III.74.7, resp; III. 78.1, ad 2.

only was this theology embodied in contemporary liturgical practices, it also informed the processions of the consecrated host on Palm Sunday and Corpus Christi, the latter a procession around the town in a form which sacralized current distributions of political power.[21] It is also evident in eucharistic miracles such as the one Margery Kempe reports in Lynn: "an hydows fyer and grevows" destroyed the Guild Hall and seemed about to burn down St. Margaret's, the parish church.[22] Her confessor asked her whether "it wer best to beryn the sacrament to the fyr er not," and Margery replies that this should be done. So the priest "toke the precyows sacrament and went beforn the fyer," returning to the church around which sparks were flying. This combined with Margery's own prayers, brings a "myra-cle:" God sends snow to quench the fire and preserve the church. Indeed, the essential role of the priest in orthodox accounts was that he consecrated the eucharist.[23] But Brut's very approach to the sacrament sets all this aside. His emphasis on reception in faith, on communion with Christ, negates the habitual foregrounding of consecration as the *essence* of the sacrament with its corollary that the "use" of the sacrament by the faithful is a supplement-ary aspect. He builds on this decision when he later argues that current doctrine misleads the people into only eating the body of Christ at Easter and on the verge of death, something for which he notes that he can find no precedents in the New Testament and early Church (339).

When he does address the issue of consecration directly, Brut affirms that Christ's words, "hoc est corpus meum" ("this is my body") and "hic est sanguis meus novi testamenti" ("this is my blood of the new testament"), were spoken over the bread and the cup of wine (337–38). How do these words relate to the current version of transubstantiation affirmed in the English Church and the controversies around it? Brut emphasizes that the bread is indeed Christ's body *in whatever mode* Christ determined ("credo illud fuisse corpus eius illo modo quo illud voluit esse corpus eius quoniam cum sit omnipotens cuncta que voluit fecit" [338]). He acknowledges that if the omnipotent Christ wanted to convert the bread into his body so that after the conversion no bread remained, as current orthodoxy insisted, then he certainly could do so. He certainly does not hold a realist metaphysics in which such transubstantiation would demand that God enact a self-contra-diction, like making a game of cricket be at the same time a game of basketball, or making a square be a triangular circle (338).[24] Nor does he hold to a dogmatic empiricism or materialism. His ground for rejecting the doctrine of transubstantiation as a necessary component of Catholic

---

[21] See Rubin (*1071*, 243–71); and M. James, "Ritual, drama and social body in the late medieval town," *Past and Present*, 98 (1983): 3–29.

[22] *The Book of Margery Kempe* (*121*, 157–58).

[23] *ST* III.67.2, resp.

[24] On Wyclif's realist metaphysics see *On Universals* (*250*) with Gordon Leff (*836*, 2.500–510, 512, 515). However, Leff seriously exaggerates the role of realist metaphysics in Wyclif's eucharistic theology: a reading of *De Eucharistia*, ed. J. Loserth (London: Wyclif Society, 1892), makes clear how driven by his response to the narratives of the New Testament is Wyclif's approach to contemporary theology and ritual around the sacrament of the altar. On this issue see Anthony Kenny (*784*, 87) and Maurice Keen (*775*, 11–12).

Christianity is that he cannot find any such insistence in the Gospels (338). There he sees no denial that the bread remains substantial bread after consecration. And if the revealed word of God does not insist on this teaching, then Brut thinks the modern Church has no authority to do so. He confesses that as God was able to assume human nature while remaining God, so Christ could have made the bread become his own body while the bread remained substantial bread (338). Yet here too Brut finds nothing in the New Testament expressly maintaining that this possibility was actually willed by Christ.

What then does Scripture suggest? Brut argues that by using the words "this is my body" Christ could have intended the disciples to understand that the bread he was giving them remained bread while it became his body sacramentally or memorially (338). For him, as noted earlier, memory included the eucharist's eschatological dimension, joining past and future. This is the interpretation of Christ's words that he finds most congruent with the command, "Do this for a commemoration of me" (Luke 22.19). As Christ gave his disciples actual bread to eat so he gave them himself whom they were to eat in faith as redeeming food for their souls (338–39). The substantial bread chewed in the disciples' mouths passed into the stomach and thence into the "privy," as Jesus said in Matthew 15.17. But the true bread of the soul, Christ himself, was eaten through faith, in spirit, informing their minds and remaining with them in love (339). Such is the form of Christ's real presence in the sacrament he gives to his disciples. Brut finds this reading congruent with St. Paul's statement to the Corinthians: "the bread, which we break, is it not the partaking [*participatio*] of the body of the Lord?" (1 Cor. 10.16). He considers Paul's text to be congruent with the view that the consecrated bread remains substantial bread but becomes sacramentally the body of Christ (339).

Brut then aligns Christ's language at the last supper with earlier identifications of Christ in the gospel: "I am the vine; you the branches: he that abideth in me and I in him, the same beareth much fruit" (John 15.5); "Destroy this temple, and in three days I will raise it up. The Jews then said: Six and forty years was this temple a building; and wilt thou raise it up in three days? But he spoke of the temple of his body" (John 2.19–21). Throughout John's gospel Christ's disciples and interrogators are continually misreading such figural language and Brut is suggesting that his Church's teaching on the sacrament reproduces errors exposed and corrected in the Gospels. If this is how a sacramental sign works in the language of the Gospels, if this is the mode of figuration within which Christ chose to disclose his identity, if this is the language in which Christ ordered priests to consecrate the sacrament of the altar in his memory, and if he wishes to be sacramentally present rather than present in his Galilean body, then priests who ask him to convert the bread into the Galilean body err grievously. They substitute their own version of Christ's presence in the Church for the gift he has actually given. This gift is to be eaten *spiritually and really* ("spiritualiter et realiter") by those who believe (340).

But *whatever* the mode of presence Christ himself has chosen, Brut is sure that contemporary Christians are seriously misled when they believe that in the mass they are looking at the Galilean body of Christ elevated between the priest's hands. So pervasive is this view that it has generated the conventional oath, "through him whom I saw today in the hands of the priest" (339: see too 341). Brut's account of conventional attitudes matches that of the Catholic historian Eamon Duffy.[25] Not surprisingly, for the Church was committed to propagating the belief that the Galilean body of Christ was present in the priest's hands, "not only the flesh, but the whole body of Christ, that is, the bones and nerves and all the rest," as St. Thomas maintained (*ST*, III.76.1, ad 2). In propagating this belief, the Church generated a collection of eucharist miracle stories to illustrate it, ones widely recited in Brut's England. These stories are replete with examples to demonstrate that any questioning of current teaching on the mode of Christ's presence is unbelief, heresy or Judaism.[26] But for Brut, Christ's sacramental presence, real as it is, includes forms of absence, forms of lack, of waiting for a plenitude that is eschatological.[27] As St. Paul reminds the Corinthian Christians, the sacrament includes a memorialization of Christ's promise, "until he come" (1 Corinthians 11.26). That is, the form of Christ's presence amongst those receiving the sacrament is simultaneously an acknowledgement that this feast also involves a lack, a prefiguration of a future plenitude. These forms of absence include the absence of Christ's Galilean body, resurrected and ascended as it is. With such recognition of absence in the present gifts of Christ goes a refusal of the extraordinary confidence with which orthodox formulations of transubstantiation were being deployed as markers determining whether a Christian was orthodox or heretical, a member of Christ's body or a rotten branch fit for burning.[28]

Brut's reflections on the sacrament of the altar includes a consideration of its orthodox representations as the sacrifice of Christ, immolated on the altar by the priest and presented to God for the sins of the world.[29] His approach is to juxtapose the New Testament with the practices and

[25] Duffy (*512*, 91; see ch. 3).

[26] For examples of late fourteenth- and early fifteenth-century propagation of eucharistic miracle stories in England see the following: John Bromyard, *Summa Praedicantium* (Antwerp, 1614), 251–52, 254–55; Brinton, *Sermons*, sermon 40, 179, sermon 55, 251, sermon 67, 306, sermon 83, 446 (see sermon 40, 179); Roger Dymmok (*136*, 99–100); *John Mirk, Festial* (*186*, 170–75) (on this Corpus Christi sermon, see Rubin [*1071*, 222–24]).

[27] For these terms, thoroughly Augustinian in their import, see Denys Turner, "The Darkness of God and the Light of Christ: Negative Theology and Eucharistic Presence," *Modern Theology* 15 (1999): 143–159; this would be fruitfully accompanied by the author's earlier study, *The Darkness of God* (Cambridge: Cambridge Univ. Press, 1995). I have explored these issues in relation to *Piers Plowman* in "The Sacrament of the Altar in *Piers Plowman* and the Late Medieval Church in England" (*262*).

[28] On the long process in which the English Church's leadership sought to impose the death penalty on those judged to be "heretics," see H.G. Richardson (*1062*), together with Strohm (*1159*, ch. 2).

[29] On the mass as involving the sacrifice of Christ on the altar see *The Sarum Missal*, ed. J. Wickham Legg (Oxford: Clarendon, 1969), 227 ("immolamus tibi patri filium . . ."), with 223 and 221; see too *ST* III.73.4, resp and ad 3, III.79.5, resp. Trent formulated and confirmed medieval views on this: see Session 22 (17 September 1562), ch. 1–2 and canons 1, 3, 4: parallel texts in *Decrees of the Ecumenical Councils*, ed. Norman P. Tanner, 2 vols. (London: Sheed and Ward, 1990), 1.732–34, 735.

theology of the modern Church, concentrating on Hebrews 8–10 (342–43). What fascinates Brut is the canonical text's insistent contrast between *often* (*saepe*) and *once* (*semel*), between the high priest who had to sacrifice often for the people's sins, with the blood of oxen and goats, and Jesus who sacrificed once only, and with his own life, not another's. The epistle to the Hebrews emphasizes that the priest's daily sacrifices could never remove sins, whereas Christ's sacrifice, once offered, achieved forgiveness and sanctification of those reconciled to God. Now Christ intercedes for his people in the presence of God (343). Musing on priestly sacrifice, Brut observes that Christ says little to distinguish priests from others and apparently did not use the term "priest" to describe his followers, preferring to call them "disciples" and "apostles" (343). Where the New Testament does refer to priests (as in 1 Timothy 3 and 5 and Titus 1) it seems, according to Brut, the distinction between priests and others lies in knowledge and good works, not in any consecrational or sacrificial functions (343–44). This contrasts with the Roman Church, where priests are ordained to sacrifice, pray and bless, only priests being able to offer Christ's body day by day, at the altar, for the sins of the people. With this understanding of priesthood goes a very sharp and very hierarchical distinction between clergy and most Christians (344), one that was, as observed earlier, embodied in the mass.

Brut expresses amazement at the relations between his Church and the views of the early Church (presented in Hebrews 9–10) on sacrifice. He wonders why contemporary priests claim to offer sacrifice for our sins every day (contrasting Hebrews 10.10–14). He observes that he can find no warrant in the New Testament for this understanding of the sacrament as a continually reenacted sacrifice of Christ. Instead he finds that the body of Christ is a sacrament and memorial of his unique sacrifice of himself for our sins. It is not fitting, he argues, that Christians should claim that Christ is now sacrificed on their altars, a claim which has priests crucifying Christ. In insisting that no Christian should believe this ("quod non est a cristianis credendum") Brut goes against conventional iconography and the wide-spread miracle stories of the bleeding Christ appearing in the consecrated host to confirm the Church's current doctrine on the sacrifice of Christ in the mass.[30] So central was this sacrificial economy and its enactments to the late medieval Church that Brut's judges had no hesitation in classifying as *heresy* Brut's denial that Christ is sacrificed for the sins of the world in the sacrament of the altar (items 28–29, 364 and 382).

Having made clear how he sees no support in the New Testament for his Church's teaching on Christ's immolation in the eucharist, Brut retraces scriptural narratives of the last supper and the practices of the early Church in the breaking of bread (especially Acts 2.42, 46). Here too he reads nothing about disciples *sacrificing* the body of Christ. The disciples are remembering Christ's love and self-sacrifice for the remission

---

[30] See Aers and Staley (*263*, 24 with references in nn. 25–27), together with n. 26 above. Also relevant here is Thomas H. Bestul, *Texts of the Passion* (Philadelphia: Univ. of Pennsylvania Press, 1996), ch. 2 and ch. 5.

of sins, remembering in such a way that they lovingly offer *themselves* to God, prepared to sustain death for their faith and the welfare of the Christian community (344). This indicates how Brut envisages sacramental memory as an active power, individual and collective. The memory of Christ's sacrifice shapes and enables the believers' commitment to the faith and community, a faith that knows nothing of priestly immolation of Christ. Such discipleship, Brut remarks, fulfilled Christ's commands that his followers should love one another as he had loved them (344: John 15.12).

With this Brut could have concluded his remarks on sacrifice. But he added a brief speculation on the path by which the practice and doctrine of the early Church could be transformed into the present situation. He suggests that the pressures of persecution gradually led to the transformation in question. At some stage of persecution priests began to flee from death, in a variety of ways. This was a flight from the loving self-sacrifice practiced by early disciples. During this failure of charity, Christians reconstituted the sacrament of the altar. From an eschatological memorial of Christ's unique sacrifice, calling disciples to absolute self-sacrifice, they turned the sacrament into the supposedly actual sacrifice of Christ. The modern Church's sacrificial economy is thus represented as an ideological legitimization of what had been the consequences of lack of faith and charity (344–45).[31]

Brut's analysis of sacrifice and the ecclesiastic history he imagines dovetails with Wyclif's insistence that were Christ to visit the contemporary Church as an unknown Christian to preach and practice as he had done, with the same tenacity, he would be persecuted and burned as a heretic.[32] Just as Caiaphas thought it "expedient" that Jesus should be sacrificed "for the people and that the whole nation perish not" (John 11.50) so the modern Church sacrifices Christ both on its altar and in its members. These sacrifices are bound together as the Church becomes a persecuting and a sacrificing community perpetuating the very violence its founder's self-sacrifice and forgiveness was designed to end, forever.[33] Brut's brief but resonant reflections on sacrifice and persecution are closely related to his earlier demonstration that Christ was committed to the path of non-violence, essential to the kingdom of God he proclaimed, a path whose hallmark was the love and forgiveness of enemies (he quotes Matthew 5.21–22, 38–48: see 308–321). There he had turned his irony on the modern Church that approved and even organized contemporary wars, inventing fables and justifications to set aside Christ's own unequivocal commands to

---

[31] Brut's preoccupation with persecution and its place in sanctification represents both a response to his own situation and an important component of Wyclif's own theology, well analyzed by Michael Wilks (*1292*).

[32] See John Wyclif, *Tractatus de Blasphemia*, ed. M.H. Dziewicki (London: Wyclif Society, 1893), 62; see too 72; and *Dialogus sive Speculum Ecclesie Militantis*, ed. A.W. Pollard (London: Wyclif Society, 1876), 22: see Wilks (*1292*).

[33] For fascinating reflections on the issue raised by Brut, see René Girard, *Things Hidden since the Foundation of the World* (London: Athlone, 1977) and *The Scapegoat* (Baltimore: Johns Hopkins Univ. Press, 1986).

those who would be his disciples (309–10, 313–17).[34] The abandonment of these commands is bound up with the cultivation of a sacrificial economy legitimizing war. So the sacrament, its theology and liturgical forms, is inextricably bound up with ecclesiology, politics and conflicts between very different models of authority. This was well appreciated by both orthodox apologists and Wycliffites, and remains as true in the contemporary world as in the fourteenth century.[35]

Brut's attempts to reform sacramental practices include the question as to whether women can confect and administer the body of Christ (341, 345–47).[36] Given the way in which the sacrament of the altar, *Corpus Christi*, had become a central symbol in late medieval culture, one intrinsic to the formation of identities, any radical challenge to its current forms would have implications for a diversity of practices.[37] Brut acknowledges that his theology of the sacrament and his related understanding of priesthood have consequences that go against the deeply rooted misogyny of his culture and Church.[38] His affirmative answers to the questions about women's power and authority in the ministry of the sacrament flow from a number of his positions: his rejection of transubstantiation; his rejection of the view that priests immolate Christ on the altar; his high valuation of preaching (which he says women have certainly done, converting many when priests did not dare speak the word[39]); his analysis of the fact that the Church allows women to administer the sacrament of baptism (in emergencies), the gateway to all the other sacraments and, according to the Church's teaching, the only one necessary to salvation (345–46). Brut characteristically emphasizes the tendency of the Roman Church to exaggerate its own authority in relation to the revealed word of God and to God's sovereignty. Given that lay people can licitly enact the sacrament of marriage without a priest (346), given that God's power can work through women in baptism and given that God's power works through even the most sinful priest consecrating the bread (as the Church taught), Brut feels unable to say that Christ cannot or will not consecrate through holy women. To maintain such a position one would have to say that Christ could not consecrate unless he

---

[34] Brut explains inconsistencies in the Church's use of the Old Testament to justify its participation in violence as well as arguing that Christ's "New Commandment" (John 13.34) supersedes any previous justifications for war (313–18, esp. 318–19). For Wyclif's arguments on the irrelevance of Old Testament wars for Christians, see *De Officio Regis*, ed. A.W. Pollard and C. Sayle (London: Wyclif Society, 1887), 270; see too 277–79.

[35] See the profound account of Pinochet's regime of torture in Chile and the relevant history of the Catholic Church by W.T. Cavanaugh, *Torture and Eucharist* (Oxford: Blackwell, 1998).

[36] See references in note 2 to Blamires, Aston, and Somerset.

[37] On the symbolic centrality of the eucharist in medieval culture see: Miri Rubin, "The Eucharist and the Construction of Medieval Identities" and Sarah Beckwith, "Ritual, Church and Theatre: Medieval Drama of the Sacramental Body," both in *Culture and History: 1350–1600*, ed. Aers (Hemel Hempstead: Harvester Wheatsheaf, 1992), ch. 2 and ch. 3; Rubin (*1071*); Strohm (*1159*, ch. 2).

[38] The literature on this is vast, but see Judith M. Bennett, "Medieval Women: Across the Great Divide," in *Culture and History*, ed. Aers, ch. 5 and the very different approach of H.R. Bloch, *Medieval Misogyny and the Invention of Western Romantic Love* (Chicago: Chicago Univ. Press, 1991).

[39] Compare Chaucer's *Second Nun's Tale* and the discussion in Aers (*261*, ch. 2).

did so in conformity to the current ordinances of the Roman pope. Restrictions of this kind on Christ's powers seem unthinkable to Brut. So he sees no grounds for denying that Christ could be willing to consecrate in response to the prayers of holy women speaking the sacramental words (346–47). Discipleship of Christ, once more, is shown to have potentials unacknowledged by the Church. Its hierarchy is too hasty in its willingness to sacrifice others for its own conformity with the world. Brut's discussion of women's authority to administer the sacrament follows the logic of his theology and ecclesiology. In doing so it crosses immense cultural barriers.

Yet Brut is not particularly concerned with women's discipleship and current restrictions on its practice. Time and again he limits the force of his arguments about women's ability to perform priestly offices, asserting that women should only do so when those ordained "in the church" are absent (345–47). He does this although the only warrant for such a restriction in his own testimony seems to be that the Roman Church restricts the adminis- tration of the sacrament of baptism by lay people to emergencies, when no priest is available. Why this should have a binding force for Brut is not clear for he continually undermined the authority of determinations made by the Roman Church which seem to have no compelling sources in the New Testament. So why back off here? Because, it seems to me, he wished to draw back from the version of the priesthood of all believers which was to be articulated by Wycliffites such as Hawisia Mone, one that finally dissolved boundaries between male and female, and between priest and lay person in Christian discipleship:

> Every man and woman beyng in good lyf oute of synne is good prest and hath as muche poar of God in al thynges as ony prest ordred be þe pope or bisshop.[40]

Brut's refusal to pursue this line suggests his position on priesthood is very close to Wyclif's.[41] But it must be acknowledged that while the confession we have tells us a great deal about what Brut took to be the betrayal of Christ's gospel by the modern Roman Church, it does not construct a coherent ecclesiology. One might think that this absence was purely contingent on the genre and the work's relative brevity. In my view, however, the absence represents unresolved and corrosive problems in Wyclif's own theology, an absence that Wycliffism may not have had the resources to address coherently. But that is another, though closely related story.[42]

---

[40] *Heresy Trials in the Diocese of Norwich, 1428–31 (208,* 142): this position was widespread among these East Anglian Wycliffites: see Margery Baxter, 49; John Skylly, 52, 57; John Godesell, 61; Sibil Godspell [sic], 67; John Skylaw, 147; Edmund Archer, 166; Thomas Mone, 179.
[41] On John Wyclif, his followers and the priesthood see: Hudson (*713,* 325–27, 351–58); *English Wycliffite Sermons (158,* 4.111–20); Leff (*836,* 2.520–27, 549–57, 579–80).
[42] See Aers (*261,* ch. 6).

Here, There, and Everywhere?
Wycliffite Conceptions of the Eucharist and
Chaucer's "Other" Lollard Joke

Fiona Somerset

The debate over the Eucharist in the *Upland Series* has long been demanding proper explanation and reappraisal.[1] Working on his own, before the explosion in the study of Wycliffite texts that began soon after he finished, Heyworth could make little of the exchange, as he readily admits:

> . . . it is difficult not to side with [the antiWycliffite friar] Daw against his interlocutors. Upland (390–3) ascribes to the friars the Wyclifian heresy that after consecration the bread remains both in accidents and substance. As Daw complains (841) *þou drawist a þorn out of þin hele & puttist it in oure*; he goes on to restate the orthodox doctrine (844–62). Of [*Upland's Rejoinder*]'s reply I can make nothing; but I feel safe in assuming confusion of thought rather than corruption of the text. (Heyworth, 171)

Still, although opaque to the uninitiated in their allusiveness, the Upland arguments are anything but confused. By now it has become much easier to investigate the Eucharistic debate hotly contested in both Latin and English, in Oxford and beyond, from the early 1380s onward. We can arrive at a much clearer idea of what various Wycliffites argued, what various antiWycliffite contenders argued back, and what each claimed about the other.[2] Rather than ascribing Wycliffite ideas to the Friar, as I will show, the Wycliffite writers of Upland and Upland's Rejoinder allude

---

[1] The Middle English parts of the *Upland Series* (for a full list of its components, see below, 128) were first published together as P.L. Heyworth (*159*); this edition predates most of the work on vernacular Wycliffite texts that has been produced since the late sixties, and is therefore unable to draw upon its new discoveries and insights. A subsequent edition for students (in Dean [*132*, 115–226]) intelligently restores some of Heyworth's unnecessary emendations, but does not substantially improve on his notes, while for reasons of space it omits some of Heyworth's justifications for omissions. I will use Heyworth's edition, citing each work in the *Upland Series* by title and line number and Heyworth's notes by page number.

[2] The views I will attribute to Wycliffites here represent one dominant strand of argument in the movement, found (with some small variations) in Wyclif's Latin works and in a variety of Latin and Middle English works by Wycliffites, and refuted in antiWycliffite works. I do not mean to suggest, however, that this argument represents the sum of Wycliffite thinking on the Eucharist: David Aers's article in the present volume shows how one Wycliffite's Eucharistic views avoid this dominant strand of argument, for example.

to just the arguments Wycliffites typically claim the friars give. And despite his attempts at obfuscation, Friar Daw clearly does hold this position, and counters the Wycliffites much as friars and others usually did.

Yet a better acquaintance with the precise terms of this Eucharistic debate also allows us to see that another, far better-known vernacular writer alludes to it as well, in one of his best-known works. In *The Summoner's Tale*, Chaucer uses the same set of Eucharistic arguments the *Upland Series* does, as part of what I am now calling, after Paul Strohm's paper on *The Pardoner's Tale*, Chaucer's "Other" Lollard joke.[3] Obviously, though, Chaucer's allusion does not participate in the Eucharistic debate in anything like the same way as the *Upland Series*. It would be silly to attempt to subsume Chaucer, or even the Summoner, to the Wycliffite controversy. But it is interesting that Chaucer knew about this debate, and even more interesting that he refers to it without fear of somehow being drawn into the controversy. These contrasting examples, and the quantity and variety of the Latin and English writings on the Eucharist that explain them, help to show that it was by no means as "dangerous" even to allude to matters of religious controversy in the 1380s and 90s as some scholars have suggested.[4] Nor was there yet a single, dogmatically asserted "true doctrine" of the Eucharist, but rather a variety of beliefs and propositions, only a few so far subject to censure.[5]

Let us begin with the less familiar example, the controversy at issue within the *Upland Series*. The *Upland Series* consists of replies and counter-replies to a set of antifraternal questions in prose posed by the Wycliffite lay persona Jack Upland: it includes a Latin response in prose to those questions by the antiWycliffite Franciscan William Woodford, *Friar Daw's Reply* to the questions in English verse, and one or perhaps two further English verse rejoinders to Friar Daw, written in the margins of the single manuscript copy of his reply, by another Upland persona.[6] Since the

---

[3] Paul Strohm (*1157*). It has been common knowledge since Levy's and Levitan's researches in the late sixties that *The Summoner's Tale* refers to Pentecost. (See Bernard Levy, "Biblical Parody in the *Summoner's Tale*," *Tennessee Studies in Literature* 11 (1966): 45–60, and Alan Levitan, "The Parody of Pentecost in Chaucer's *Summoner's Tale*," *University of Toronto Quarterly* 40 (1970–71): 236–46.) For a recent in-depth investigation of the late fourteenth-century cultural meaning of Pentecost and its celebration, see Glending Olson, "The End of *The Summoner's Tale* and the Uses of Pentecost," *Studies in the Age of Chaucer* 21 (1999): 209–45. Glending Olson is the only other person, to my knowledge, who has noticed that *The Summoner's Tale* refers to the Eucharist as well as Pentecost: I thank him for generously sharing his ideas with me when we discovered our mutual interest.

[4] This tendency to evoke a pervasive sense of danger can be seen, for example, in Kathryn Kerby-Fulton (*789*); Nicholas Watson (*1265*); Anne Middleton (*952*); and in James Simpson, "The Constraints of Satire in *Piers Plowman* and *Mum and the Sothsegger*," in *Langland, the Mystics, and the Medieval English Religious Tradition*, ed. Helen Phillips (Cambridge: D.S. Brewer, 1990), 11–30. I argue against this view in "Professionalizing Translation at the Turn of the Fifteenth Century: Ullerston's *Determinacio*, Arundel's *Constitutiones*," forthcoming in *The Vulgar Tongue: Medieval and Postmedieval Vernacularity*, ed. Fiona Somerset and Nicholas Watson (Penn State Univ. Press).

[5] For a useful assessment of these, see Anthony Kenny, "The Body of Christ" in *784*.

[6] For a full account of the manuscripts and all previous editions, see Fiona Somerset (*1129*, 136 n.2).

series is not well known, I will quote extensively from the relevant passages. Here is Jack's faux-naive question, which opens the debate:

> Frere, whi sclaundre ȝe trewe preestis & oþere trewe meke men of þe sacrament of Goddis bodi, for þei seien þat þe holi breed duli sacrid is Goddis bodi in foorme of breed, & ȝe seien þat it is an accident wiþ outen subiect, & not Goddis bodi. Frere, who ben eritikis here & fer fro Cristis wordis, þat took þe breed & blissid it & brak it & seide, þis is my bodi[.]
>
> (*JU* 390–95)

True men, that is, Lollards,[7] say that consecrated bread is God's body in the form of bread; friars say it is an accident without a subject, and not God's body. But Christ in the Bible said "this is my body" ("hoc est corpus meum"), and other venerable doctors agree – so why do friars slander true men for saying this? Just who are the real heretics? Friar Daw in his reply claims that Jack has mischaracterized the friars' position:

> þou drawist a þorn out of þin hele & puttist it in oure,
> þou berist vs on honde þat we seien *þer is not Cristis bodye*,
> But roundnesse & whitenesse, and accident wiþouten suget.
> Iak, we seie with Holy Chirche þat *þer is Cristis bodi*
> & not material breed with Wiclyf ȝour maistir,
> þe whiche put þer but as a signe & not verre Cristis bodi[.]
>
> (*FDR* 841–6, my emphases)

Heyworth, as we saw in his note on this passage, believes Daw's claim. But Heyworth misses the key change in the demonstrative from "this" (or "that") to "there" (or "here"): in Friar Daw's formulation the *hoc* in "hoc est corpus meum" ("this is my body"), becomes *hic*, "there is my body." The most detailed extant vernacular Wycliffite treatise on the Eucharist, the *Tractatus de Oblacione Iugis Sacrificii*, explains the position fully:

> Sum seien þat what tyme Crist seide þus "Take þe and ete ȝe alle of þis; þis is my bodi", the raþur worde *þis* þat answereþ to þe raþur *hoc* in Laten schewiþ brede; but, as þei seien, so doþ not þe secunde worde *þis*, for þat answeriþ to þis aduerbe *hic* in Laten, þat is as meche to seie as "here" in Englische. So þat aftur þis witt Cristis wordis in Laten ben þus meche to seie in Englische "Take ȝe and ete ȝe alle of þis; here is my bodi", schewing bi þat worde *here* þe place of þe accidentis.[8]

According to some, this tract suggests, the second "hoc" should when the passage is translated be replaced by "hic," or "here" – a solution that neatly avoids the problem of explaining what Christ means by "this is my body."

To show what is at stake in this seemingly very minor grammatical point, here is the antiWycliffite Cistercian William Rymington's version of an

---

[7] On this terminology and other key terms used as self-descriptions by Wycliffites, see Anne Hudson (*698*).

[8] The tract is edited in Anne Hudson (*157*). This passage appears on pp. 207–8, ll. 1989–96. I am grateful to Anne Hudson for allowing me to read her transcription in its entirety at an earlier stage in my research, as well as for allowing me to use this passage before her edition was published.

assertion very similar to Friar Daw's, from his c.1385 dialogue between Catholic Truth and Heretical Depravity.[9] Rymington, of course, is not a friar, but a monk; and he is anything but a sophisticated philosopher (as will be apparent when Catholic Truth neatly kicks one of his opening premises out from under himself by denying the copresence from which he began).[10] Yet the *Dialogue*, as its prologue and overall contents make clear, is Rymington's attempt at a sort of "official" reply to Wyclif designed to contain his heresy after his death. It provides, I think, a sort of compendium of arguments against Wyclif's ideas that had been made by university men. Its inclusion of the argument on "hoc" and "hic" in its material on the Eucharist shows that this argument was current in Oxford; the way it is presented also helps to show why the argument upset people. At issue, at this point in the *Dialogue*, is whether Christ is corporeally present in the church on earth as a comfort to men until the end of time. The argument then segues neatly to disputing the nature of Christ's presence in the Eucharist – a telling conceptual linkage that helps to reveal how the Eucharist's emotional and social significance within this culture became bound up with this seemingly trivial semantic debate.[11] Catholic Truth begins by insisting that the Wycliffite doctrine of copresence, where both material bread and Christ's body are present in the Eucharist, necessarily implies Christ's corporeal presence:

> Confirmatur sic: hoc demonstrando, panem materialem in altari est hic corporaliter et dimensionaliter, et hoc eodem demonstrato est corpus Christi, ergo *corpus Christi est hic* corporaliter et dimensionaliter.
>
> (f. 191v /21–3, my emphasis)

> (This is the proof: material bread in the altar is here corporeally and dimensionally, and that same bread is the body of Christ, therefore *the body of Christ is here* corporeally and dimensionally.)

If the bread is *here* corporeally, then the body of Christ is *here* corporeally: *corpus Christi est hic*. Of course the difficulty then is to explain *how* either of the two is *hic*, and whether they are here in the same way. If Christ's body has a size, Catholic Truth goes on to say; that is, if it is present *dimensionaliter*, then absurdities follow:

> . . . quelibet pars istius panis est corpus Christi, ergo infinita sunt hic corpora Christi integra. Vel sequitur quod idem corpus Christi est quelibet pars istius panis, et per consequens quelibet pars istius panis est equalis isti pani.

[9] William Rymington, *Dialogus inter catholica veritas et heretica depravitas*; the dialogue, which is unpublished, is extant in a single copy in Oxford, Bodleian Library, MS Bodl. 158 ff. 188–97. I thank the Bodleian Library for giving permission to reproduce the passages that follow. My transcription employs modern punctuation and word division; all translations are my own.

[10] See below, 131.

[11] Historians in recent years have paid increasing attention to the insights into culture provided by psychology and anthropology, and as a result, these aspects of the late medieval Eucharist's significance have received increasing attention. On the emotional temperature of Eucharistic debates in the period surrounding Wyclif, see J.I. Catto (*373*). On the cultural significance of Eucharistic rituals, see among others Miri Rubin (*1071*).

Similiter sequitur . . . quod quantumcumque modica pars istius panis est
corpus septipedale, quia est ipsum corpus Christi dimensionatum in celo.

(f. 191v /24–9)

(. . . every part of this bread is the body of Christ, therefore there is an infinite
number of whole bodies of Christ here. Or it would follow that the same body
of Christ is every part of this bread, and so every part of the bread is equal to
the whole. Likewise . . . every part of this bread, however small, is a seven-foot
body, because it is one and the same as the body of Christ, having the size that
that body has in heaven.)

There is no fixed proportion between bread and Christ-content: every part
of the bread would be a Christ if he were present *dimensionaliter*, so there
would be an infinite number of *septipedali* Christs, seven feet long just like
Christ's body in heaven, and every part would be equal to the whole. This
reductio is the basis for Catholic Truth's insistence that although the body
of Christ obviously cannot be present *dimensionaliter* (and Heretical
Depravity agrees, as it turns out), it must be present in substance,
substantialiter: "Licet corpus Christi non sit sub specie panis dimensionaliter, est tamen sub ea vere corporaliter et substantialiter" ("Although the
body of Christ is not under the appearance of bread dimensionally, it is
nonetheless truly under it corporeally and substantially") (f. 191v /32–3).
What is more, to avoid the proportion problem, after consecration its
substance must *replace* that of the bread and wine through transubstantiation: "Post consecracionem non remanet in sacramento substancia panis vel
vini sed virtute verborum subito transubstanciatur in corpus vel sanguinem
Christi" ("After consecration there remains in the sacrament no substance
of bread or wine, but by the power of the words it is suddenly transubstantiated into the body or blood of Christ") (f. 192 /10–12). The only
intelligible solution to the problem of explaining how Christ is *hic*,
corporeally present in the Church in the Eucharist until the end of time,
is that his substance, yet not his size, replaces that of the bread and wine in
the consecrated Host.

For Wyclif, and many Wycliffites, the claim that the substance of the
bread is annihilated and replaced with the substance of Christ's body
inhering in the accidents of bread is tantamount to saying that Christ's
body is not-this, or nothing: for they assert that an accident without a
subject is impossible, an absurdity, a nothing or worse than nothing: in that
case, anything in God's creation would be better than the Host, as these
Wycliffite tracts object while taking issue with what they see as the friars'
attempt at misdirection: "beter þing þan Cristis bodi is everywhere," or in
the second, "in iche knotte of a stree is better þing þen Gods body."

And it is not ynow3 to seie þat þer is Goddis bodi, for beter þing þan Cristis
bodi is everywhere for þe godhede; and men axen not what is þere, but what is
þat þat men worshipen so. (Arnold [*100*, 3.353/1–3])

þes folis leeven þo letter of þo gospel, and seyn þat we schulde not aske what
þing þat is, bot trowe þat þere is verey Gods body. Bot þo gospel telles not

what þing is þere, but seis þat þis brede is Cristis owne body. For wil we
witten þat in iche knotte of a stree is better þing þen Gods body, for þo holy
Trinyte.   (Arnold [*100*, 3.428/12–17])

For these writers, the friars' claim that "Christ's body is there" is a way to
fudge the issue: the friars insist on Christ's presence but refuse to explain,
when "men axen not what is þere, but what is þat" what happens to the *hoc*
in "hoc est corpus meum," the "this bread" that Christ himself said was his
body. Friars, say the Wycliffites, are changing Christ's words; in their book,
misquoting Christ and misrepresenting the witness to his words found in the
Bible seems to be as bad as making him worse than straw, multiplying him,
or splitting him into bits. Instead, Christ's words support the Wycliffite
theory of copresence, as the writer of the second tract insists:

> For þo gospel seis, þat Crist toke bred in his hondes, blessid hit, and brake hit,
> and gaf his disciplis, and bad hom ich one, Eete ȝe of þis; for, as he seide, þis is
> my body . . . as everiche gode mon by resoun con se, þat as þo wisdome of
> Crist shulde first schewe bread, so schulde he aftir shewe þo same bred; ffor
> elles þis were a causel wiþouten any witte, Eetis alle of þis, for þis is my body.
> (Arnold [*100*, 3.406/12–20])

Rather than altering Christ's words or making him a liar, friars should
instead admit that their theory is impossible.

It is now easier to see why it matters that Friar Daw substitutes "there"
for "this" in the lines I emphasized. He is *changing* Jack's claim before
denying it: you say we say that Christ's body is not there, but in fact we say
"there is Christ's body." Friar Daw next counterattacks, then follows up by
stating the friars' belief. Although Heyworth notices extensive quotation
here of Aquinas's Eucharistic hymn *Laude Sion Salvatoris*, in fact Aquinas
did not accept that substance is annihilated in transubstantiation,[12] and
Friar Daw adds to the hymn the lines I italicize in order to emphasize his
own difference from Jack Upland:[13]

> And now I wil þee telle þe freris confiteor
> Touching to þis sacrament how þat þei bileuen.
> þei seie breed is turned in to fleish, & wyne in to blood,
> þourȝ þe myȝt of oure God & vertue of his wordis:

---

[12] Aquinas lays out his views in *ST* III.75: see especially articles 2 and 3. Note that article 2's reply
agrees with the Lollard position that a change in the biblical words that accompany the
sacrament's enactment would be an absurdity – though for different reasons. Misprision
(deliberate or accidental) of the last phrase in Aquinas's brief foray into analysis of the words
of consecration here may be the original source of the Lollard claim that friars want to substitute
"here is my body" for "this is my body": "[H]aec positio contrariatur formae hujus sacramenti,
in qua dicitur, 'Hoc est corpus meum.' Quod non esset verum si substantia panis ibi remaneret:
numquam enim substantia est corpus Christi. Sed potius esset dicendum, 'Hic est corpus
meum.'" ("This suggestion [that the substance of bread and wine remains after consecration]
is contrary to the words of this sacrament, in which one states 'This is my body.' This would not
be true if the substance of bread were to remain there, for at no point is that substance the body
of Christ. Rather, one would need to say, 'Here is my body.'") (Text quoted from the Blackfriars'
edition and translation of St. Thomas Aquinas, *Summa Theologiae* III.73–78, vol. 58 [New York:
McGraw Hill, 1963], 62. Translation my own.)

[13] For more detail, see Somerset (*1129*, 161 n.43).

þe fleish is mete, þe blood is drynke, & Crist dwelliþ,
No þing rasyd, no þing diuidid, but oonli broken in signe,
& as moche is in oo partie as is al þe hole.
þer leeueþ not of þe breed but oonli þe licnesse,
Which þat abidiþ þerinne noon substeyned substans;
It is deþ to yuel, lyf to good, encresing of oure grace. (*FDR* 853–62)

There is nothing of the bread remaining there after consecration: "Christ is there" in every part, but in such a way that he can be neither multiplied (for example by repetition of the sacrament) nor divided (for example through the bread's fragmentation and consumption). What Friar Daw has added to Aquinas's hymn is, in the end, the claim Jack Upland imputed to the friars, and that Daw dodged affirming, while he also dodged admitting that he is changing the words of the Bible: "Christ's body is 'not this,'" if "this" stands for bread.

Both parts of *Upland's Rejoinder* use terms similar to those of the Wycliffite arguments we have already examined to pick up on Friar Daw's substitution of "hic" for "hoc." The first rejoinder makes the contrast twice in twelve lines:

þou saist, Dawe, as þou felist, þat þere is Cristis body;
Bot I afferme faiþfully þat þat is Cristis body.

. . .

For 3e sayen þer is Cristis body & nou3t þat sacred host.
Commutauerunt veritatem Dei in mendacium. (*UR1* 380–93)

And the second rejoinder both restates the contrast yet more explicitly, as I emphasize here, and reveals rather clearly why Wycliffites consider this point worth belabouring:

. . . we sey alle þe sacrid oste þat is sene with eye
Is verey Cristes body; but þy sette seyþ not soo.
But 3e sey þer is Cristes body, but 3e tel not where;
But Crist seyþ þis is my body & not þer is my body.
Whi, 3e templers messe sellers, grante 3e not Cristes wordes,
Syþ 3e chafyr þus þerwith, by gylyng þe pupil.
Lete 3oure sette write 3oure byleue of þis sacrid osste,
& preche it as 3e write it, & sette þerto 3oure sele,
& J am sikir of my feyþ 3e schul be stonde to deþe.
(Heyworth 172; *UR2* 5–13. Punctuation modified.)

If friars were to state their belief straightforwardly and precisely, they would be revealed as beguilers of the people, removed from their pastoral duties, even "stonde to deþe." As in Rymington's direct linkage of Eucharistic doctrine with the basis of the Church's earthly mission, as in the Wycliffite tracts on the Church's members and on blasphemy, here too the precise ways "hoc est corpus meum" may be explained turn out to be closely tied with the question of the proper constitution of the Church on earth: Who are its members? Who may rightly teach them? Who are the blasphemers who should be silenced and violently excluded from membership?

Now, I am not so sure that friars really *do* go around affirming "hic est corpus meum" and changing the words of the Bible: William Rymington does, but he is a monk, and is reproducing argumentative positions he had heard without perhaps fully understanding or believing them; Friar Daw does, but the Daw persona may be nothing more than a Wycliffite straw man. In any case, Upland's claim that friars will not even *try* to explain "hoc est corpus meum" is unfair – though I will delay my example of one argument where friars use "hoc est corpus meum" for their own purposes until the point where it will be most useful, in my discussion of *The Summoner's Tale*.

Rather than exhibiting "confusion of thought," then, clearly the participants in the *Upland Series* are aware of all the nuances in a complex and highly sensitive debate that was articulated in both Latin and the vernacular. The theories of the Eucharist in question are coherent and easily distinguished: while the participants may certainly aim to confuse onlookers and even their opponents through equivocations of various kinds, they are not confused themselves. Yet at the same time, it is easy to see why confusion over this issue among onlookers has been common. Heyworth is not the first scholar to get the wrong end of the stick: famously, the chronicle writer Henry Knighton, a contemporary of Wyclif's, included in his chronicle Wyclif's confession on the Eucharist, a summary argument for his heretical views, thinking it was the opposite, a recantation of those views.[14] But even if it is not the case that the Lollard texts here attribute a Wycliffite position to the friars, what Heyworth says is importantly true in another way, and David Lawton in his recent book *Blasphemy* draws this out in citing Heyworth's note: "In the *Jack Upland* texts, exchange transactions become so circular that the Lollard texts attribute to the friars the Wycliffite position and attack them accordingly; it seems as if the exchange is more important than the substance of it."[15] Although it is not correct that a Wycliffite position is attributed to the friars, it is still true that the exchanges here are circular, and use the same coin. What is traded back and forth here emphasizes divisive invective far more than doctrinal content: that is why its allusions to debates laid out far more clearly elsewhere can become so obscure. Rather than explaining their own position in full, each side is far more interested in insisting that their opponents are evasive, that they distort authority, that they attempt to mislead those with less education, and that their statements about the Eucharist are, specifically, blasphemous.

In this atmosphere of heightened concern over the division and multiplication of Christ's body and over lay interpretation of the doctrine of the Eucharist; amidst greater and wider propagation of argumentation on the subject in Latin and the vernacular, by Wycliffites and antiWycliffites alike, Chaucer writes *The Pardoner's Tale* – which contains a Lollard joke about transubstantiation, as Paul Strohm and David Lawton have already noticed

---

[14] For an edition of Wyclif's confession with commentary, see "Wyclif's Confessions on the Eucharist," in Anne Hudson (*155*, 17–18, 141–4).

[15] David Lawton, *Blasphemy* (Hemel Hempstead: Harvester Wheatsheaf, 1993), 93.

and discussed – but he also writes *The Summoner's Tale*, in which there is *another* Lollard joke, closely linked to the terms of debate from the *Upland Series* that we have been examining.[16] In this case, too, blasphemy is the substance of the accusation. Although certainly Friar John is angry in part simply because Thomas's retort against his sermon takes the form of farting at him, the reason for his incandescent rage that he actually articulates in the Lord's court is the blasphemy implied in what Thomas has made him promise:

> "This false blasphemour that charged me
> To parte that wol nat departed be
> To every man yliche, with meschaunce!"   (2213–15)

It is *blasphemy* to require the division of what cannot be divided: the Eucharistic reference is clear.

Chaucer's allusion to the specific Eucharistic debate we have already been examining is even clearer earlier on, when the Friar enters the sick man Thomas's house – circumstances in which he might possibly be carrying the Eucharist, ready to administer it to the sick man.[17] The Friar does not use the standard Franciscan greeting and blessing *Pax huic domui*, peace to this house; instead, he announces "Deus hic" – God is *here* – a strange variation for which no one has been able to find a good explanation.[18] God is "hic" for this friar, but not "hoc" – although this reference is even more elliptic than the ones in the *Upland Series*, it is clear to those of us "in the know" that this is a joke on the friars' explanation of "hoc est corpus meum". Of course the joke works even without that recognition – but the full implications of what the Friar is saying in this remarkably presumptuous greeting make his implied hiccup, "Deus ⟨hic⟩," all the more funny: here, as later with Thomas's Eucharistic fart, God becomes expelled air.

Thus humour, as well as offense, in this tale centres round the location and potential division of mysteriously intangible bodies. But who is to adjudicate their presence, or the accusation of blasphemy involving them? The friar resorts to the secular arm, perhaps because what he wants is monetary compensation for the insult. But in so doing he also opens his blasphemy charge to lay judgment – just what writers like Rymington tried so strenuously to avoid through their insistence that the discussion of all such matters should be restricted to the "congregatio cleri" ("assembly of clerics").[19] Although the Lord dismisses the blasphemy case out of hand, the

---

[16] All citations from Chaucer's *The Summoner's Tale* will be drawn from L.D. Benson (*127*) and cited by line number from the tale. Notes in the same volume will be cited by page number.

[17] On the common practice of bringing the Eucharist to the sick, see Rubin (*1071*, 77–82, 235–6). Within *The Summoner's Tale* this implication of course remains only a possibility that intensifies the joke: the narrator nowhere states that the Friar might intend to administer the Eucharist.

[18] Janette Richardson's notes in Benson (*127*) gloss line 1770 as "God be here" but make no attempt to explain the substitution: "The prescribed Franciscan blessing when entering a home was *pax huic domui* (peace to this house), Matt. 10.12" (877).

[19] I quote Rymington's attempted restrictions (192–3), and discuss other examples of writers concerned about lay judgment of clerical affairs (188–93), in Somerset (*1130*). The passage appears in Rymington's dialogue on f. 188.

problem of dividing something intangible – a problem belonging to the
"congregatio cleri" in that it resembles a scholastic *insolubile* – is the focus
of his interest in the Friar's petition:

> Who evere herde of swich a thyng er now?
> To every man ylike? Tel me how.
> It is an inpossible; it may nat be.   (2229–31)

And when the Squire, whose courtesy contrasts with the Friar's angry
abruptness, provides an elegant solution to the problem, he too (as I have
already shown elsewhere) stages a lay appropriation of clerical privilege.[20]

But the Squire's joke also delicately implies a third Eucharistic allusion.
His cartwheel distributes the undivided fart to *twelve* friars, just as Christ
gave his undivided body to twelve apostles. Friars too refer to Christ's
indivisible distribution at the Last Supper – and his precise wording, "hoc
est corpus meum" – to reinforce their claim that Christ's body is "hic,"
here, in the Eucharist, and potentially "hic" in several places at once, yet
not such that it can be divided or multiplied. Here is the friar Roger
Dymmok's version of that argument, as it appears in an antiWycliffite
refutation of 1395:

> Tercium miraculum est quod "corpus Christi multiplicatur ita quod simul et
> semel est hic et in celo et ubique in terra; ubi est uerum sacramentum corporis
> Christi, idem corpus numero." Et hoc sequitur ex dictis Christi, quando sedit
> in cena et dedit discipulis suis corpus suum sub specie panis, et omnibus
> discipulis idem corpus dicens: *Comedite ex hoc omnes*, et *non dixit: "Hec sunt
> corpora mea" set "Hoc est corpus meum," ut ostenderet omnes idem corpus
> sumere.*[21]

> (The third miracle is that "the body of Christ is multiplied in such a way that
> at one and the same time it is here and in heaven and everywhere on earth;
> where the true sacrament of the body of Christ is, there is the same body
> identical in number." And this follows from Christ's words, when he sat at
> supper and gave his disciples his body under the appearance of bread, and
> gave all the disciples the same body, saying "*All eat this*," and *he did not say
> "These are my bodies," but "This is my body" so that he could show that all ate
> the same body.*)

Even at the Last Supper, Christ was eaten by all the apostles; yet he said
"this is my body," not "these are my bodies," so division without multiplication was part of the sacrament from the first: the same Christ who is in
heaven is everywhere on earth, "hic et in celo et ubique in terra," yet
remains one and the same. Similarly, the Squire's cartwheel allows the fart,
and the insult, to be received by all twelve friars – here, there, and
everywhere – without any division or multiplication being necessary.

Thus the secular court refuses even to countenance the friar's charge of

---

[20] On the Squire's lay appropriation of ecclesiastical privilege, see Somerset (*1130*, 204–7).
[21] For more on Dymmok's refutation of the *Twelve Conclusions*, see chapter 4 in Somerset (*1129*,
103–34). For this quotation, see Dymmok (*136*, 96, ll. 27ff.). My emphasis.

blasphemy. Public laughter acclaims the Squire's joke, and the Friar's appeal is forgotten. Lay judgment insists on a noncombatant position, reducing the Friar's insistence on remuneration to laughter, and to other kinds of *efflatus*. Chaucer carefully does not imply that the Squire is equivalent to himself: instead, as usual, he distances himself from anything like a direct political opinion through layer upon layer of literary voicing. This is the story of one corrupt friar, not a statement about friars in general; it is a squire within the story, not the narrator and certainly not Chaucer, who pronounces the solution; the story's delightfully outrageous blasphemy is allusive and clearly parodic, so that it does not need to be taken seriously, and in any case the story itself is told by a Summoner. Nonetheless, the Squire does stand in as Chaucer's textual analogue: he engages in something very much like Chaucer's typical mode of political allusion, courteously flattering secular power and reinforcing its policies and decisions while entertaining it through a parody of an issue on which he remains delicately nonpartisan.

The first question that normally arises in response to a paper like this, though, is not how Chaucer can allude to this Eucharistic debate without at the same time allying himself with Wycliffites or their opponents, but how he can possibly allude to it at all. How could Chaucer (and similar questions might arise for Langland, or the Pearl-poet) possibly have known this much about the Eucharistic debate? Do I mean to suggest that Chaucer went to Oxford? If not, how could he have had the same sort of extensive exposure to the university debate over the Eucharist that the writers in the *Upland Series*, as well as of the other vernacular tracts we examined, have clearly had? Here, I think, remnants of an isolationist attitude to Chaucer studies reassert themselves. While scholars are usually happy to acknowledge Chaucer's Latin, French, and Italian literary influences, they can remain reluctant to admit that Chaucer could have read or been influenced by English writings – much less by highly charged controversies that were going on around him in England at the time.

My answer would be that neither Chaucer, nor the audience he expects to understand his allusions, need have had anything like the sort of extensive exposure to the Eucharistic debate that the Upland writers have had – or even that readers of this article have now had. Chaucer's reference to the debate helps to show that it was being discussed, and that it could be mentioned – by some, at least, and in some circumstances – with impunity. It must have been widely known among the laity, particularly in the privileged circles of influence in which Chaucer moved, that there was an ongoing controversy over the Eucharist. The circumstances in which John of Gaunt intervened in the Earthquake Council of 1382 (during which three of Wyclif's Eucharistic propositions were condemned) must have been fairly common currency, for example. Part of the controversy centred on the words "hic" and "hoc" in relation to "hoc est corpus meum" – surely one of the most widely recognized Latin tags of its time – and the problem had to do with the dimensions and location of Christ's intangible body: this is just the sort of knowledge we would expect to circulate freely among

those with any leisure for gossip in London and Oxford and beyond, and
this is all Chaucer need have known. Yet his *Tale*'s humour, unlike that of
the *Upland Series*, is also readily accessible to a wider audience unac-
quainted with even these basics of the debate. It is certainly not necessary to
recognize Chaucer's allusions in order to participate in his audience's
laughter, as the critical history of this Tale attests. Still, *The Summoner's
Tale* can also contribute, through this analysis, to the history of Wycliffism.
I mean here to further a revisionist critical view according to which
Wycliffite ideas are not isolated by their dangerous unsayability from
everything else going on in England at the time – except in cases where a
particular writer, persona, or character should be aligned with some
position in the partisan debate and newly annexed to Wycliffite studies –
but instead everywhere enmeshed with mainstream literary and cultural
history.

Part III

LOLLARDS AND THEIR BOOKS

English Biblical Texts before Lollardy
and their Fate

Ralph Hanna

The following pages are excerpts from a book in progress, tentatively entitled *London Literature, c.1310–c.1380*. In this project, I examine works, primarily English ones, composed, disseminated, and read in the capital in the years immediately preceding the formation of a national literary tradition. The study (and this particular rendition) is always engaged in enacting analytical modes necessary to reformulate the literary history of late medieval England. And this current form of my fascination with Middle English as a literature of the locality, not the nation, allows me one considerable rhetorical frisson, the paradox that the metropole is, for much of the Middle Ages, just another locality.

The beginning of my study is constrained by the documentary record: until just the end of Edward I's reign, there's no surviving vernacular literature from London. I conclude at the temporal confluence of three widely acknowledged revolutions. Primary is, of course, the appearance of new "Chaucerian" literature, *The Parliament of Fowls* in 1381, *Troilus* in 1386. These productions are contemporary with the fairly abrupt demise of an older variety of written London English (M.L. Samuels's "Type II") and the appearance of a new sort (his "Type III," Chaucerian English); "Type III" is first recorded in the writings of Thomas Usk c.1384–88 and in the London guild returns of 1389.[1] Finally, the very writing system changed at this moment: just after 1375, a new variety of book-hand, "Secretary," was introduced into England. This presumably occurred at Lambeth, since Secretary first appears in documents produced in the Chancery of the Archbishops of Canterbury (the wills recorded by the Prerogative Court from 1383 begin in the script).[2]

---

[1] The identification of Type II, and most of the MSS providing evidence for it, is dependent on the research of M.L. Samuels, particularly "Some Applications of Middle English Dialectology," *English Studies* 44 (1963): 81–94 at 87–88 and 87 n.7; *Linguistic Evolution with Special Reference to English* (Cambridge: Cambridge Univ. Press, 1972) at 166. The first examples of Type III are the initial selections in R.W. Chambers and Marjorie Daunt, *A Book of London English, 1384–1425* (Oxford: Clarendon, 1931).

[2] See M.B. Parkes, *English Cursive Book Hands 1250–1500* (Oxford: Clarendon, 1969), xx and plate 9; for the first of the Prerogative Court of Canterbury volumes, see Public Record Office, MS Prob. 11/1 (formerly PCC Rous).

Until this moment "London literature" exhibited two distinct foci. One, obviously not germane here, is romance, well known from "the Auchinleck MS" (National Library of Scotland, MS Advocates 19.2.1). Considerably less familiar is an extensive body of prose texts which, the surviving remains indicate, comprised another basic stock of the London vernacular book-trade at mid-century, and through its third quarter, but thereafter is rather seldom recorded. Considering these, and their fate in the period after c.1380, will show some important, if not surprising, aspects of the relationship between Lollard and orthodox biblical culture.

The centre of this canon of prose texts is a book very nearly as large as the Auchinleck MS and just as culturally central, Cambridge, Magdalene College, MS Pepys 2498. Placing the Pepys MS in some historical continuum has been a matter of some concern and controversy. The only protracted discussion of the book identifies it as a Lollard effort, but Neil Ker dated the volume at a point too early for this to be an accurate assessment, "the middle of second half of the fourteenth century."[3] That statement looks to me as if a bit of compromise, although I suspect a wise one. The script, remarkably consistent throughout a very large book, shows features one would not have been surprised to find in a book written c.1340 and others which would seem fairly consistent with books of c.1400.[4]

The features of the hand which seem to me most telling include:

(a) Generally, a perception of the hand as relatively heavy. This sense is created by a number of relatively broad strokes, and is especially evident in the occasional heavy transverse stroke of anglicana *d* ("goddes" b/19), an inelegant technique (so most palaeographers) going back to the 1290s.[5]

(b) Of comparable antiquity and perceived inelegance are occasional hooked ascenders, here residual features on *litterae notabiliores*, see a/12 "Lorde" and a/14 "Hij" (this spelling is the standard early London for "they").

(c) Exclusive use of an undotted "sidesaddle" *y* with box-shaped top and a relatively flat concave left curve (as opposed to the triangular top and relatively vertical lower portion with a left "pigtail" loop or sweeping right curve usual in late fourteenth-century hands (b/8 "souryng of a lytel"). Compare the universal use of the form in Dan Michael of Northgate's dated autograph of *Aȝenbite of Inwit*, British Library, MS Arundel 57.

[3] See Eric Colledge (*403*). Ker offered his dating to A. Zettersten, who reports it in *96*, xix n.1; ix–xxi have an extensive description of the book.

[4] I will cite parallels from the standard troves of dated manuscripts: Andrew G. Watson, *Catalogue of Dated and Datable Manuscripts c.700–1600 in the Department of Manuscripts, the British Library*, 2 vols. (London: The British Library, 1979) (hereafter DMBL); Watson, *Catalogue of Dated and Datable Manuscripts c.435–1600 in Oxford Libraries*, 2 vols. (Oxford: Clarendon, 1984) (hereafter DMO); and P.R. Robinson, *Catalogue of Dated and Datable Manuscripts c.737–1600 in Cambridge Libraries*, 2 vols. (Cambridge: D.S. Brewer, 1988) (hereafter DMC). For Michael of Northgate, see DMBL plate 222 and the descriptive entry 435 (1:88), with references to other published samples. For Harley 2253, see N.R. Ker, ed., *Facsimile of British Museum MS. Harley 2253*, EETS o.s. 255 (London: Oxford Univ. Press, 1965). With all the examples I cite, one could well contrast DMC 177 (Peterhouse MS 75(I), the supposed Chaucer autograph of 1393).

[5] In this palaeographic discussion, I refer to columns and lines of the plate included in EETS 274 as a frontispiece.

(d) What appears as an approach stroke, but probably represents a cursive glide from the foot of the descender to x-height, on the *littera notabilior P* ("Poule," b/6; and "Psalmista," a/29). Compare Harley 2253 endemically, the stroke there appearing as part of the scribe's normal rendition of initial *p*, *f*, and *s* as well).

(e) Perhaps not so telling is a relatively unbalanced *g*, with lower lobe smaller and less round than upper, "gret" (b/8), "gobett" (b/8), "god" (b/12). This form here replaces the textura derivatives for the graph in the two earlier manuscripts I have mentioned.

(f) Perhaps similarly advanced is the system of otiose strokes, finish on the right horizontal extenders of final *t*, *g*, *k*, and *f* ("est" a/8, "hert" a/21, "wakyng fastyng" b/27, "of" a/16; *k* is not represented).

I have compared these forms against samples of anglicana datable 1340–1400 in the three published catalogues of English dated manuscripts. Although I would want to offer some qualifications – the details I examine appear features more normal in "informal" writing, especially in legal documents, than in bookhands, and may have had a longer life there – the evidence suggests that Ker's judgment is correct. The features I single out in the Pepys scribe's bookhand would make most sense in the decade 1365–75, and although those dates could well be extended somewhat, the manuscript cannot likely represent a late fourteenth-century hand. The texts written in it certainly, given normal patterns of manuscript dissemination, should well predate Lollardy.[6]

One particular qualification to this view might be indicated by my use of Michael of Northgate as a writer of 1340. For Michael was probably the man of that name ordained priest in 1296, and he thus may have been nearly seventy when he copied Arundel 57.[7] In other words, his scribal habits could

---

[6] For the features I here analyse, I would cite the following analogues in plates from the Catalogues of Dated Manuscripts (I star examples from legal, rather than literary, texts): for (a), DMO 202 (1369), residual examples only in DMO 211 (1377); for (b), *DMO 207 (a hooked H; 1373, Dover); *DMBL 278 (a slight hook on H; 1387, Saffron Walden); for (d), DMC 159 (1367), *DMC 169 (a touch of the stroke at f. 39/2 "Priori," but not on its repetition 39/8; 1382 × 1391); for (e), DMO 197 (1361 × 1376), DMO 213 (1380), DMC 162 (1376 × 1400), DMC 167 (1381); for (f), only isolated examples, DMBL 225 (1342, not localisable as English), DMO 196 (1353, inconsistently), DMBL 271 (1381).

For feature (c), there is quite a lot of evidence, suggesting that anglicana *y* was transformed in two stages during the period – first in the 1370s by the loss of the right-angle turn in and gradual decline of the lower stroke toward the vertical; then from some point, perhaps in the early 1380s, by the development of the top of the letter to the triangular shape customary from the last years of the fourteenth century. For this sequence of changes (only the last two examples show developed anglicana *y*), cf. *DMC 156 (1359 × 1380, Romsey); *DMO 207 (the *y* dotted; 1373, Dover); DMC 163 ("Caym" in a/9 and 13, one in each style; 1377 × 1396); *DMC 166 (cf. "Talyngton" a/6 with "Bradewey" b/15; St. Albans donors' book, 1380 × 1396).

One should note DMO 207, dated 1373, which appears twice above. Although not in a bookhand but a legal script, this book, Bodleian Library, MS Rawlinson B.355, may provide the closest dated analogies to the Pepys scribe.

[7] See A.B. Emden, *Donors of Books to S. Augustine's Abbey Canterbury*, Oxford Bibliographical Society, occasional publication 4 (Oxford, 1968), 14; and Pamela Gradon's discussion, *Dan Michel's Ayenbite of Inwit* Volume II, EETS o.s. 278 (Oxford: Oxford Univ. Press, 1979), 7, 12 (connections Gradon makes with Bodleian Library, MS Ashmole 43, a *South English Legendary* MS copied no later than 1325, indicate the possibly retardetaire nature of the hand).

have been antique, the conservative work of an old man. And that, I suppose, might equally be argued of Pepys 2498.

If one might place the Pepys MS slightly before 1375, the age of the Middle English texts there communicated can be estimated only very roughly. Here perhaps the best information is provided by British Library, MS Additional 17376. This book has two independent portions in two different languages, although copied by a single scribe and the parts further linked by common decorative features. Part 1, which includes an English prose Psalter which also appears in Pepys, is written in comparable London language; part 2, devoted to the poems of William of Shoreham, vicar of Chart iuxta Leeds (Kent) in the 1320s, retains Kentish forms, presumptively those of the scribe's archetype. Ian Doyle long ago under ultraviolet read an ownership inscription of one "William Pelka," who signed himself as "civis Londoniensis."[8]

Palaeographically, Additional could date from any time between about 1330 and 1370, but one rubric in the Shoreham portion probably fixes copying in the first half of this period. The colophon to one of the poems (f. 198r–v) reads, "Oretis pro anima domini Willielmi de Schorham quondam vicar' de Chart iuxta Ledes Qui composuit istam compilationem de septem mortalibus peccatis Et omnibus dicentibus oracionem dominicam cum salutacione Angelica xl[a]. dies uenie a domino Symone Archiepiscopo Cantuarie conceduntur" ("You should pray for the soul of don William of Shoreham, formerly vicar of Chart near Leeds, who put together this compilation about the seven deadly sins; and Lord Simon, archbishop of Canterbury, has granted forty days of pardon to all those saying the Pater noster and Ave Maria [for his soul]"). This is Simon Mepham, archbishop at the time of Shoreham's death, around 1330 (Mepham's register, which would show appointment of Shoreham's successor, does not survive). But he could be referred to by his unqualified Christian name only so late as 1349, when a new Archbishop Simon (Islip, followed by Simon Lanham) was appointed.

This dating may be confirmed by the earliest London will to mention an English book. In 1349, Robert de Felstede, a vintner, bequeathed "a psalter written in Latin and English."[9] At this date, there is no possibility whatsoever that Felstede was bequeathing a copy of Rolle, and the other possible candidate, the verse "Surtees Psalter," usually presented with Latin versals as sidenotes, circulated only in Yorkshire (specifically a limited part of the West Riding).[10] Thus, at least this Pepys text is apt to be a full

---

[8] See also R.W. Hunt, "A Dismembered Manuscript: Bodleian MS. Lat. th. e.32 and British Museum Add. MS. 17376," *Bodleian Library Record* 7 (1966): 271–75. The Latin contents of MS Lat. th. e.32 (mainly Grosseteste) may well indicate that this is another priest's book.

[9] See Reginald R. Sharpe, *Calendar of Wills Proved and Enrolled in the Court of Husting, London . . .*, 2 vols. (London: John C. Francis, 1889–90), 1.636.

[10] *IMEV* 3103, ed. Horstmann (*154*) 2.130–273. For the geographical dispersal of the text, see the analysis of such copies as British Library, MSS Harley 1770, Cotton Vespasian D.vii, and Egerton 614; Bodleian Library, MS Bodley 425, L(inguistic) P(rofile)s 191, 364, 603, and 601, respectively, in Angus McIntosh et al., *A Linguistic Atlas of Late Mediaeval English*, 4 vols. (Aberdeen: Aberdeen Univ. Press, 1986).

generation younger than the Auchinleck romances and probably dates from the second quarter of the fourteenth century.

A quick survey of contents will show very quickly that Pepys 2498 is, in some ways, the utter contrast to Auchinleck. The latter is entirely poetic, the former entirely prose.

1. Pages 1a–43a: a unique harmony of the gospels.[11]
2. Pages 45a–212b: the unpublished Middle English prose *Mirror*, in Pepys's presentation, the original set of fifty-nine sermons.[12]
3. Pages 212b–26b: "good techinges of wise men wiþ þe ten hestes afterward distinctelich expouned," unpublished, but also in the Vernon MS (Bodleian Library, MS Eng. poet. a.1), ff. 392rb–93rb; and Bodleian Library, MS Bodley 938, ff. 13–16.
4. Pages 226b–63b: the prose Apocalypse with commentary.[13]
5. Pages 263b–370a: "The Early English Prose Psalter," including the canticles and Athanasian creed.[14]
6. Pages 371a–449a: "þis good book Recluse," i.e. *Ancrene Riwle* (the title shared with the Vernon MS contents table).[15]
7. Pages 449a–59b: "The Complaint of Our Lady."[16]
8. Pages 459b–63b: a translation of the Gospel of Nicodemus.
9. Pages 463b–64b: a sequence of five prayers.

Moreover, excepting items 3 and 9, all the prose in Pepys is comprised of biblical translation. This description extends to this MS's unique recension of *Ancrene Riwle* ("The Recluse"). Among its many other distinctive features, the Pepys *Riwle* has been rewritten (and reformatted) as if it were a biblical commentary, paragraphed so that each section appears as analysis of a Latin Vulgate citation quoted by the author.

The producer of the Pepys MS sought to present a grouped genre-based canon, "vernacular Bible" with commentary. From the large manuscript,

---

[11] Margery Goates, ed., *The Pepysian Gospel Harmony*, EETS o.s. 157 (London: Oxford Univ. Press, 1922); see R.E. Lewis (*18*, 530).

[12] Ed. in part, Thomas G. Duncan, "A Transcription and Linguistic Study of the Introduction and First Twelve Sermons of the Hunterian MS. Version of the 'Mirror'" (Oxford B.Litt. diss., 1965); and Kathleen Marie Blumreich Moore, "The Middle English 'Mirror': An Edition Based on Bodleian Library, MS. Holkham misc. 40 . . ." (Michigan State University Ph.D. diss., 1992), described *Dissertation Abstracts International* 53 (1992): 3598A. See further Duncan, "The Middle English Mirror and its Manuscripts," in *Middle English Studies Presented to Norman Davis*, ed. Douglas Gray and E.G. Stanley (Oxford: Clarendon, 1983), 115–26.

[13] Elis Fridner, ed., *An English Fourteenth Century Apocalypse Version* (Lund: C.W.K. Gleerup, 1961); R.E. Lewis (*18*, 584).

[14] Karl D. Bülbring, ed., *The Earliest Complete English Prose Psalter*, EETS o.s. 97 (London: Trübner, 1891); R.E. Lewis (*18*, 114); a new edition, which will compensate for Bülbring's failure to print the important glosses to the text, is in preparation by Robert Black and Raymond St-Jacques.

[15] See note 3; earlier ed. Joel Påhlsson, ed., *The Recluse* (Lund: H. Ohlson, 1911); R.E. Lewis (*18*, 559).

[16] With the next item, ed. C. William Marx and Jeanne F. Drennan, *The Middle English Complaint of Our Lady and Gospel of Nicodemus*, Middle English Texts 19 (Heidelberg: C. Winter, 1987), published subsequent to and not included in R.E. Lewis (*18*). This pair of texts had a modest later circulation and was still loose in the London booktrade at the end of the fifteenth century, when it was copied into Huntington Library MS HM 144. Yet equally, in its Anglo-Norman source, it was an early London book, for example in the splash "Neville of Hornby Hours," British Library, MS Egerton 2781 (1330s), analogous to some Anglo-Norman books I will mention below.

an interested reader could assemble a substantial, if incomplete – there would be no Acts or epistles of either set, Pauline or catholic – New Testament with authoritative commentary, together with a commented Psalter and the most influential of the apocryphal gospels. The generic centering of the text is unusual but important; what will appear as learned impulses of Pepys canon, not just "Bible," but "Bible authoritatively expounded," reflect a sophisticated interest in clerical Latinate forms of discourse but at a social remove from customary Latinate culture.[17]

These texts, in their various repetitions, provided one core of London literary circulation in the period under discussion. In addition to Auchinleck and Pepys, I know eight other manuscripts conveying texts written in Type II London English. Three of these books are irrelevant to the current discussion, two of them that to some extent belong in the ambit of Auchinleck: Bodleian Library, MS Laud misc. 622, in the same hand as Pepys, and the later English additions to a fine *Somme le roi* illuminated in London in the 1320s, Cambridge, St. John's College, MS S.30 (256), pp. 233–70.[18] The third, Cambridge, University Library, MS Gg.4.32 (part 1), with minimal English, was compiled by a London parish priest c.1315–20.

But the other five survivors all demonstrate the repeated production in London of Pepys texts. Of the six copies of the Pepys *Mirror*, four are in Type II London; the other three are:

Cambridge, Corpus Christi College MS 282

Glasgow, University Library, MS Hunterian U.4.8 (250)

London, British Library, MS Harley 5085

In addition, yet a third book in the hand of the Pepys scribe (on this basis, he was certainly a professional), London, British Library, MS Harley 874, contains only Pepys's prose Apocalypse. And the second of the four surviving copies of the prose Psalter, Additional 17376, as I have already mentioned, is also a Type II book.

Considering the matter in another way, this is specifically a London literary canon. With a single exception from the end of the century, these works are only known before 1400 from copies written in Type II London English. The exceptional example, two books that count as one, Trinity College, Dublin MS 69 and Princeton University, Scheide deposit MS 143, are in the same hand, by a scribe from the Arundel (Sussex) area. But the evidence suggests that the Arundel scribe was either copying from an imported London exemplar or was a country boy plying his trade in the metropolis.[19] In the Trinity MS, he copied not only the Psalter, as he also

---

[17] Contrast "Miscellaneity and Vernacularity: Conditions of Literary Production in Late Medieval England," in *76*, 37–51.

[18] Laud misc. 622 shows the scribe accessing materials of an early fourteenth-century stripe, the unique copy of Adam Davy's dreams (from the London suburb, Stratford-at-Bow, perhaps composed so early as 1310) and the London romance *Alisaunder* (before 1330, when a version, now only fragmentarily extant, was copied into the Auchinleck MS). St. John's S.30 also includes one Auchinleck text, the "Speculum Guy de Warwick" (*IMEV* 1101).

[19] The association of the Trinity MS with a "John Hyde" does not help unravel these options, since it could equally refer to the place outside Winchester or to a London family recorded c.1400.

did in the Scheide MS, but two other Type II London texts as well, the prose Apocalypse and a sermon from the *Mirror*.[20]

The Pepys texts also are unified by the type of translation they exemplify: all are "second-hand." In every case, their authors have Englished an Anglo-Norman text which is itself a vernacularisation of Latin scripture; one might see here a particularly textbooky (and simplified) model of language contact and transition in later medieval England.

Thus, for example, the prose Apocalypse began as Berengaud of Ferriere's Latin commentary;[21] translated into Anglo-Norman, the text commonly circulated in thirteenth-century England in an almost captional form accompanying elaborate cycles of illumination.

Apocalypses were the thirteenth-century splash devotional book for lay-people, and preceded the craze for elaborate ("East Anglian") Psalters of the early fourteenth century. Frequently, Apocalypses circulated among people who could certainly have read the Latin, apparently as decorative objects. For example, British Library, MS Additional 42555, probably of the third quarter of the thirteenth century, has Berengaud's Latin with a French gloss. This would not be exceptional, were it not that this book was supposedly produced for Giles de Bridport, bishop of Salisbury (d.1262), and bequeathed by him to the Benedictine house at Abingdon.[22] And it had a more distinguished later history: in 1362 it was loaned to Joan, queen of Scotland, daughter of Edward II.

The only item in Pepys which may call for particular comment has a similar history. The prose *Mirror*, a lengthy text, usually fifty-nine sermons, has been derived from Robert of Gretham's Anglo-Norman verse *Miroir*, a poetic rendition of Gregory the Great's homilies on the gospels, with other materials. Again this was an Anglo-Norman text with a large circulation for such a long work, more than twenty surviving copies. In origins, the *Mirror* was certainly an expression of magnatial power; Robert translated Gregory into verse for Aline de Zouche, daughter of Robert de Quincy. And while not a hyper-illustrated text, a heady number of the surviving copies lack their opening leaves, probably excised for their decoration.[23]

Such background may suggest some social placements for the texts communicated in English by Pepys 2498 and related books (but without

---

[20] Inclusion of "the standard decalogue tract" in Trinity Dublin 69 (as well as in the post-1400 Oxford, University College MS 97, which also includes London records), may imply that this is an early London text. For an edition, see W. Nelson Francis, ed., *The Book of Vices and Virtues*, EETS o.s. 217 (London: Oxford Univ. Press, 1942), 316–33; R.E. Lewis (*18*, 48). In Trinity 69, this text is juxtaposed with the "Tale of Charity," the sermon from the *Mirror*, now retitled; the MS thus presents the two laws, old and new, together.

[21] Ed. *PL* 17:765–970.

[22] For provenance and discussions, see N.R. Ker, *Medieval Libraries of Great Britain*, 2nd edn. (London: Royal Historical Society, 1964), 266; Nigel Morgan, *Early Gothic Manuscripts [I] 1190–1250; [II] 1250–1280*, A Survey of Manuscripts Illuminated in the British Isles 4.1–2 (London: H. Miller, 1982–88) number 127; and Suzanne Lewis, "Giles of Bridport and the Abingdon Apocalypse," in *England in the Thirteenth Century*, ed. W.M. Ormrod, 2nd edn. (Woodbridge: Boydell Press, 1986), 107–19, and, more generally, *Reading Images* (Cambridge: Cambridge Univ. Press, 1995).

[23] On the patronage, see K.V. Sinclair, "The Anglo-Norman Patrons of Robert the Chaplain and Robert of Greatham," *Forum for Modern Language Studies* 28 (1992): 193–208 at 200–3.

the decorative cycles which distinguish their Anglo-Norman predecessors). We might recall William Pelka (who signed himself "civis") or Robert de Felstede, vintner. To sell wine involved membership in a major company of victualers, and consequently, being a City aristocrat. Felstede was certainly such a figure: he was surely an associate of Chaucer's father; he was also connected by marriage to a major City player of the 1380s – who lost his head for it – Nicholas Brembre. So far as one can localise Pepys prose texts, they seem to belong in the ambit of leading City figures. One standard view would identify mercantile culture as non-innovative but rather centered in acquisitive appropriation from – and emulation of – other cultural sites.[24] Great London merchants, in such an account, assimilate aristocratic materials as a mode of self-aggrandisement (just as Anglo-Norman literate magnates may have done with Latin monastic texts a century or so earlier). In the case of Pepys texts, we may be viewing the emulation/ appropriation of aristocratic materials, but with a telling difference – the appropriators are not aristocrats of blood, and their texts are anglophonic.

Here I want to consider the fate of the textual community created by these texts. What happened, at the very end of the fourteenth century and in the early years of the fifteenth, to mid-century London biblical translation? Where did it go? And what happened to the literary community, the readers, which had supported it? The most useful information may be derived from later copies of the London texts.

Four of the six copies of the Englished version of Gretham's *Miroir* were produced by Type II London scribes and constitute one focus of this local literary community. One can get some explicit clues to its fate by looking at the fifth manuscript of Gretham in English, Bodleian Library, MS Holkham misc. 40. The sermon collection here forms what one may consider an "expanded version," typical of the two later copies. The Holkham manuscript includes fourteen more sermons than does Pepys; the first of these occurs in some early *Miroir* MSS and is found in the Arundel scribe's Trinity 69 as an independent tract on charity.

Four scribes collaborated on the *Miroir* in Holkham 40, probably sometime in the first twenty years of the fifteenth century. But the fourth ("D") wrote more than 70% of the text, in what appears Chaucerian Type III London, but with some Type II relicts, e.g. occasional "hij" they and "-and(e)" pres.p., probably inherited from his exemplar. The MS has no medieval provenance, but in 1552 belonged to an Essex rector.

The extra sermons are not the only expansion in Holkham 40. For the producers of the MS display canonising procedures like those already noted in Pepys 2498 – in their case, an effort at providing a full English New Testament. In Pepys, the compilers emphasised narrative completeness – the gospel pericopes provided by the *Mirror* were supplemented by a unique diatesseron. In contrast, the Holkham team sought textual inclusiveness: after completing the *Mirror*, scribe "D" provided, at ff. 133–62va, the

---

[24] Cf. Lee Patterson's formulation, in his chapter "Chaucerian Commerce," in *Chaucer and the Subject of History* (Madison: Univ. of Wisconsin Press, 1991), for example the argument at 330–31 and its application to "The Merchant's Tale" at 333–44.

general and Pauline epistles (ignored in the collection procedures under-lying Pepys). These the scribe (or his director) acquired from that congeries of originally separate texts known as "The Paues Version." This biblical translation in its fullest form, exemplified by Cambridge, Selwyn College MS 108.L.19, joins chunks from at least three different, and each partial, New Testament translations, one of them Wycliffite (but not The Wyclif-fite).[25]

But the Holkham team's efforts at inclusiveness were not yet completed. After the procedures I have described, a fifth scribe ("E") worked on the MS and wrote into it a huge "appendix," ff. 162va–257rb: his contribution is a full text of the gospels, in the Wycliffite later version. The Holkham manuscript enacts a subsumption of the Type II London canon into that of organised Wycliffism.

One can multiply book biographies like this in some profusion. They are endemic in a small but persistent class of volumes which present parts of Wycliffite scripture. As one further example of the handling of an early London text in a fifteenth-century book, consider the second MS (ff. 17–127) of what is now bound as Cambridge, St. John's College MS G.25 (193). This originally separate volume begins in a predictably scriptural fashion – its first text is the Pepys prose Apocalypse, one of the nine later copies not written in Type II London English; it is succeeded, in a fashion which should now be familiar, by gospel – in this instance a Passion narrative, extracted from *Oon of Foure*, the possibly Lollard translation of Clement of Lanthony's diatesseron.[26]

The St. John's Apocalypse resembles other post-Type II copies in having been redacted. The recensions, of which two are typically recognised, share one feature: the biblical text, which originally had been translated from the Anglo-Norman source, has been replaced by that of the later Wycliffite translation. Unlike Holkham, Lollardised by accretion, here the earlier text has actually been infiltrated. But the revisions of the prose commentary (which distinguish the two recensions) do not reflect Wycliffism, or at least no strong or discernible variety of it.[27]

Or so one would say of the Apocalypse in the St. John's MS, viewed as an isolated text. But although two-thirds of the MS appears comparable to earlier books in being squarely biblical, the remainder isn't. The MS again shows progressive expansion of contents; its concluding three texts were added, the last two as a separate booklet each. But all these added materials are emphatically Lollard, and of a particularly strident variety.

The first booklet of the MS, which contains the biblical texts, ends (ff. 85–93) with an unpublished tract "how [in] þe sacrament of þe auter crist is [to] be resceyued worþili and deuotly"; this text addresses what is always taken as the defining heretical tenet of the movement and is neither overtly Lollard nor overtly orthodox but accommodating of any view. The work

---

[25] Anna C. Paues (*107*); R.E. Lewis (*18*, 263).
[26] Unedited, but see Richard Sharpe (*34*, 87–88).
[27] See Anne Hudson's comments (*713*, 267).

may be construed as a bit of filler, since it occupies the blank end of the quire concluding the *Oon of Foure* excerpt. But it was important filler, since the scribe did not scruple to add an additional full quire to accommodate the end of the text, and this he only half-filled (the leaves at the end are blank, but bounded and ruled for writing).

But subsequent decisions about the production indicate that this is far from a random choice: the final two booklets (one for each text) present those most virulent appendages to the Lollard sermon cycle, the antifraternal "Vae octuplex" and the antipapal "Of ministers in the church."[28] As nearly unique loose copies of these works, their inclusion bespeaks deliberate religious provocateurism. In the St. John's MS, the London prose Apocalypse has been recuperated for Lollard use, amid other biblical texts, themselves perhaps Lollard, and in the company of aggressive Lollard appropriations of scripture for the purposes of ecclesiology.

One may advance this account into the fifteenth century by examining yet a further book. Manchester, John Rylands University Library, MS Eng. 77, a Wycliffite New Testament, contains the note "This booke . . . was overseyn And redd by doctor Thomas Ebbrall and Doctor Yve or þᵗ my moder bought it," a unique instance of an examined copy of Lollard scripture.[29] The names in the note place the event sometime in the 1460s and in London: Thomas Eborall and William Ive had Oxford degrees, Doctors of Theology both, and were in succession masters of Whittington College, London (1444–64 and 1464–70, respectively). Moreover, neither could be construed tepidly orthodox: both were among those who confuted Reginald Pecock. And Ive appears an outspoken vehicle of strict doctrine, committed to pulpit chastisement of royalty (even rejecting limitations on such chastisement proposed by the Dean of St. Paul's) and to confuting the heresy of Christ's absolute poverty, which was bruited by contemporary London Carmelites.[30]

Yet simultaneously, Mother (and her son), who were careful not to write an explicit note of ownership in the book, may have selected their examiners with a certain wary foreknowledge. Ive, who bequeathed books to various Oxford colleges, owned Oxford, Magdalen College, MS lat. 98, which includes Wyclif on the decalogue.[31] Eborall, more provocatively still, was willed in 1465 two volumes of Latin and English New Testament (gospels and epistles); and he owned Lambeth Palace MS 541 (*The Pore Caitif*), as well as a more predictably clerical volume in Latin (British Library, MS Royal 5 C.iii). At this latish date, lines between orthodoxy and other endeavours would seem considerably blurred.

---

[28] Pamela Gradon (*158*, 2.328–78); see also the discussion of the manuscript transmission by Hudson (*158*, 1.49–50).

[29] N.R. Ker, *Medieval Manuscripts in British Libraries*, 4 vols. (Oxford: Clarendon, 1969–92), 3.404; Ker reports the note as having been added on a flyleaf somewhat later, "s. xv/xvi."

[30] See A.B. Emden (*6*, 622–23, 1008); and cf. the interesting materials unearthed by Wendy Scase (*1083*, a reference to Eborall at 273 n.38).

[31] Although what one may read as Ive's guilt of ownership is enshrined in the binding of the book. At some point in the mid fifteenth century, the two texts in the volume were reversed, rendering the Wyclif not so incriminatingly visible at the front.

One might consider Mother a bit as well. She looks like the sort of person who, had she lived a century earlier, would have been reading at the archetypes behind Pepys 2498. She was quite clearly wealthy and pious. She was literate, wanted access to Scripture in English, and yet knew Archbishop Thomas Arundel's 1409 Constitutions (which banned the Lollard Bible) well enough to be at least fastidious about the source of her textual access. Moreover, she was prepared to pay handsomely for her reading: her book although compact (190mm × 130mm) was thick, 266 folios worth, as well as expensive, priced in the note at £3 1m. Further, she had been able to find this large bible for open sale (although again, the note carefully does not say where), and, if the note is not just conspiratorial smokescreen (which seems unlikely – why name your examiners, if you've invented them?), in circumstances which allowed inspection by persons alleged impeccably orthodox.

In this account, Mother, Eborall, and Ive testify to a situation thoroughly removed from the crusades of extirpation by which Lollardy is often known to us. Here we witness a transaction involving all the trappings at least of orthodoxy, with Lollard scripture at its centre. Although the text may be potentially dangerous, that possibility can be defused and the John Rylands volume declared safe pious reading matter. Rather than heresy, it has become the only game in town. This seems to me the most plausible reading of English biblical dissemination during the fifteenth century: the Lollard Bible was a huge success. For a time, it progressively infiltrated earlier, orthodox biblical versions, perhaps as a form of camouflaged circulation, for Arundel's constitutions only ban translations made since Wyclif's time.[32] But ultimately the banned text became a full substitute and drove out, destroyed the circulation of, competing biblical versions.

Whatever its ultimate source and mechanics of generation, Lollard scripture worked. While a tool that might foster heresy, the very fidelity to the Latin text and the absence of sectarian additions, both integral to sustaining literal Lollard biblical reading, also made the book useful to a general interested audience. Moreover, Lollard scripture had enormous advantages over any competitor: it was textually complete and an accurate rendition of its source,[33] relatively compact, and (in the Later Version) readily legible. The translation, in fact, turned out to be so good an idea that, whatever official pronouncements said, it could be re-appropriated to orthodoxy and used, without particular anxiety, as a convenient consultation text.

In this view, the Cultural Revolution of the 1380s, as I defined it at the opening of my paper, may be too narrowly conceived. (I reserve for other

---

[32] "nemo deinceps aliquem textum sacrae scripturae auctoritate sua in linguam Anglicanam vel aliam transferat . . . nec legatur aliquis huiusmodi liber . . . jam noviter tempore dicti Johannis Wycliff sive citra compositus . . ." ("No one henceforth should translate of his own authority any text of Holy Scripture into the English language or any other, nor should any book of this sort be read which has been composed more recently than the time of the said John Wycliffe or later" – the redundancy is the insistence of the Latin) from David Wilkins (*228*, 3.317).

[33] Indeed, more accurate than the clerical Latin, according to the author of the prologue to the historical books; see Anne Hudson (*155*, 67/26–31, 69/72–78).

occasions, specifically ones which would address the position of *Piers Plowman*, the meta-question, that of the transition from Edward III to Richard II.) But is there not a fourth revolution one might add to those I have mentioned: the appearance of "public Wycliffism," certainly marked, but by no means contained, in the Blackfriars condemnations of May 1382?

This condemnation, like Arundel's later one, was surely abortive, and failed to stem the composition and the later encroachment into nonheterodox circles of Lollard vernacular scripture. Such a view – which denatures the provocateurism of the Wycliffite biblical book – would suggest that the persistent interest in Wycliffism as oppositional and revolutionary may occlude much of the historical dynamic at work.[34] Further, efforts to set Lollardy to one side of Middle English literary endeavours, as a religious extremism, may misrepresent as well. The *grand récit* of Middle English privileges as "canon," of course, the development of "the Chaucerian tradition." And at its generative moment, for example with Hoccleve's stridency in the 'teens, this narrative requires the marginalisation of Wycliffism. From this perspective, the Lancastrians fostered one literary endeavour, courtly poetry, and tried to root out the other, Bible in English.

My account would suggest that "canonisation" was a considerably more fractured and less programmed process than this retrospective teleology might imply. For example, the current view of Lancastrian suppressive behaviour (Hoccleve yes, Lollards no) must ignore some thought-provoking information. First of all, Henry IV's dad, John of Gaunt, was until mid-1382 one of Wyclif's (and other named vernacular dissenters') protectors, certainly the most influential one and perhaps the only one powerful enough to insure Wyclif's personal safety. Second, Henry's uncle and fellow Appellant, Thomas of Woodstock, owned at least four Lollard books (two of which survive) and organised at least one Lollard-friar debate on theological issues. Henry IV's son Thomas owned another surviving Lollard Bible, and although it doesn't survive, Henry himself appears to have had one, too.[35] Third, chroniclers generally describe Henry himself as strenuously anticlerical (most notably with regard to the "illiterate parliament" of 1404), in contrast to either his predecessor or successor. One might notice, shortly after his usurpation, his order to reinstate in the University of Oxford Lollard troublemakers expelled by Richard II.[36] Fourth, one "commoner" member of his council, until removed in the putsch of 1410, Sir John Cheyne of Beckford (Gloucs.), was one of McFarlane's "Lollard knights" and probably complicit in a Lollard library and book-production centre in nearby Kemerton

---

[34] I am particularly interested in confronting such partial presentations as John Bowers (*336*); or Paul Strohm (*1159*), passim.

[35] For Woodstock's books and the debate, see Hudson (*713*, 12 n.29); A.I. Doyle notes his bibles and John's in (*505*, 163–81, 168–69). For Henry's own bible, see Henry Summerson (*1164*, 109–15, esp. at 112).

[36] See Hudson (*713*, 89).

(Gloucs.).[37] Finally, on our way toward Mother, Eborall, and Ive, one could note two figures of unimpeachable orthodox piety who transmitted Lollard scripture: John Lacy, Dominican recluse of Newcastle, book-active c.1420–34, who probably insured that Bodleian Library, MS Rawlinson C.258 was passed on, as was his homemade, but most professional, Book of Hours (now Oxford, St. John's College MS 94), to a local parish church; or King Henry VI, who donated his personal copy, now Bodleian Library, MS Bodley 277, to the London Carthusians.[38]

In fact, one might consider that the development of an English literary canon in the early fifteenth-century shows inconsistencies and divergent motivations. In my account, for example, the literary revolution of Type III London English could be construed as an irrelevance. Chaucerianism might well be disaggregated from other literary efforts; it transforms into the literarily innocuous, the courtly game, the more politically querulous inflections of Langlandian poetic. As one later Langlandian poet sees, modern courtliness is the literary mechanism for silencing older and plural discourses of counsel, the "sothsegger" with his composite medley of voices, literally a "satyra," a grab-bag.[39]

In contrast to the Chaucerian mode, a vernacular bible has, since the tenth century, always been central to English literary production. And the Wycliffite effort proved an enormously successful consolidation of this interest – to the extent that it progressively supplanted, and then thoroughly extinguished, pre-existing indigenous efforts. Rather than an oppositional force, one might find in the Lollard translators and their efforts at propagating Scripture an example of the movement toward (and the recuperation of) a central English literary tradition.

[37] For Cheyne, see J.S. Roskell, "Sir John Cheyne of Beckford, Knight of the Shire . . . ," *Transactions of the Bristol and Gloucestershire Archaeological Society* 75 (1956): 43–72; and K.B. McFarlane's famous discussion in *934*, 162–76 etc.; on Kemerton as a copying centre, see Hudson (*713*, 90–91).

[38] For brief notices of these books, see Ker, *Medieval Libraries*, 134, 222, and 284; 122 and 277, respectively.

[39] Cf. Helen Barr (*103*, 186–88, 194–202, *Mum* 1343–1412, 1565–1752); and see also Frank Grady, "Chaucer Reading Langland: *The House of Fame*," *Studies in the Age of Chaucer* 18 (1996): 3–23.

Lollardy and the Legal Document

Emily Steiner

And yet forto by man out of þe deueles þraldam, [God] sende [Christ] into þis world, and wyth his owne hert-blod wrot [man] a chartur of fredome, and made hym fre for euer, but hit so be þat he forfet hys chartur. So whyle þat he loued God, he kepeth his chartur, for God asket no more of a man but loue.[1]

If one poem alone could stand for the traditional ideologies and pieties of late medieval English literature, it would seem to be what modern editors call the *Long Charter of Christ*, a well-attested and intriguingly versatile Passion lyric appearing around 1350 in Oxford, Bodleian Library, MS Rawlinson poetry 175. The poem is essentially an apocryphal retelling of Christ's life, as might be found in any number of late medieval cycle plays or didactic poems. Christ as speaker recounts his life (the Incarnation, Temptation and Last Supper) and concludes with a brief description of post-Crucifixion events (the Resurrection, Harrowing of Hell, and the Celebration of the Mass). All these events are allegorized as the production of a land-grant: the Incarnation is the initial "sesyng" or formal occupation of heaven, the Crucifixion is the bloody inscription of the charter on Christ's body, the Harrowing of Hell is the re-negotiation of the contract, and the Eucharist is the indentured copy of the charter (for security and remembrance). The charter itself, the centerpiece of the poem, grants heavenly bliss to all readers and listeners in exchange for a "rent" of sincere and absolute penance. The *Long Charter*, which survives in at least twenty manuscripts, was copied continuously until the end of the fifteenth century, usually in collections of vernacular lyrics and pastoral miscellanies. Its popular appeal was such that, by the end of the fourteenth century, it had already generated an abridged version which modern editors call the *Short Charter* (surviving in at least twenty-five manuscripts), as well as a vernacular prose tract called the "Charter of Heaven" which circulated with the pious compilation called *Pore Caitif* (extant in forty-seven out of fifty-six manuscripts containing extracts from *Pore Caitif*).[2] Enthusiastic antiquarians called the *Charters of Christ* "curiosities," a term that rarely reveals much more about medieval texts than their unforgivable ordinariness.

[1] John Mirk (*186*, 172 ll. 15–19).
[2] For a manuscript list, see Valerie Lagorio and Michael Sargent, "Bibliography: English Mystical Writings," in (*33*, 9.3470–71).

Sometime after 1400, however, the *Long Charter* was twice revised and expanded. The two revisers together contributed over four hundred lines to the original, most conspicuously a new introduction. This essay takes these revisions as its focus, arguing that they point in one way to the peculiar censorship strategies of early fifteenth-century readers and writers, but in a much more striking way to the fierce competition for the language and symbolism of vernacular piety that characterized that particular moment of religious controversy. Despite the fact that the *Charters* originate in mainstream preaching texts and promote strictly orthodox doctrine on controversial issues, the image of Christ as a legal document posited a relationship between author and audience that by the 1410s and 20s served orthodox and heterodox agendas alike. Lollard sermon-writers and polemicists seized upon the image of Christ's charter to express radical theories about official texts (indulgences, letters of fraternity, royal charters, Scripture) and the spiritual and political communities that official texts claimed to represent. As I will argue, such Lollard appropriations of Christ's charter motivated fifteenth-century scribes of the *Long Charter* to re-affiliate the poem with an unambiguously orthodox polemic, and, in the process, to redefine the textual community (Brian Stock's influential term for "a group that arises somewhere in the interstices between the imposition of the written word and the articulation of a social organization") that a legal document might be seen to produce.[3] The first section of the essay traces the early reception of the *Charters of Christ* and the significance of that literature to Lollard theories of textual authority and spiritual community. The second section discusses three fourteenth- and early fifteenth-century texts which use Christ's charter for anti-pardon polemic. The third and final section investigates the revisions to the *Long Charter* and argues that they respond directly to the threat of Lollard appropriation as well as to more general concerns about mediation and translation that charters had come to represent.

I. Fifteenth-Century Censorship and the Reception of *the* Long Charter

The fifteenth-century anti-Lollard initiative, spearheaded by the Archbishop of Canterbury Thomas Arundel at the turn of that century, identified Lollards in part by their books and book-learning. As a result, much of vernacular literary production was affected in some way by anti-Lollard legislation.[4] Fifteenth-century censorship accordingly took on a number of shapes and guises. The most conspicuous form, external censorship, ranged from the confiscation and burning of heretical books to the expurgation of offensive material (as in the case of the Lollard sermon cycle discussed by Anne Hudson), to the excision of particular words (as in San Marino,

---

[3] Brian Stock, *Listening for the Text* (Baltimore: Johns Hopkins Univ. Press, 1990), 150.
[4] See Anne Hudson (*722*); and Peter McNiven (*945*).

Huntington Library, MS HM 143, a *Piers Plowman* manuscript in which a scribe systematically crossed out in red ink every occurrence of "Piers" and "Plowman," suggesting, perhaps, some kind of "police action").[5] External censorship supposes, of course, that forces outside a given text – legislation, critics, errant readers, or unorthodox texts – may call attention to the presence of heterodox material within that text, and, consequently, will identify both the text and its transmitters as disciplinary sites. By contrast, internal or self-censorship supposes a deliberate authorial act to fashion a text which will successfully escape correction, discourage errant readings, or counter heterodox texts. For example, new authors or translators such as Nicholas Love, might offer up their work to official scrutiny, or, like Thomas Hoccleve, actively collaborate with the Lancastrian "counter-offensive."[6] But late medieval internal censorship also involved more cunning strategies. A careful writer might, for example, conceal heterodox material in ambiguous or codified language (e.g. the author of *Mum and the Sothsegger*), or, like the author of *Jack Upland*, transfer potential conflict to fictionalized interlocutors, unreliable or naïve characters who debate with institutional authorities.

Of course external and internal censorship are artificial categories insofar as they work together to shape a given text – a writer modifies a text to address the expertise or inclinations of a particular readership or the temper of a literary climate. But, as the *Long Charter* makes clear, revision might embody a peculiar relation of text to readership, and of what I am calling internal and external censorship, namely that the reviser, who simultaneously plays the roles of external and internal censor, recognizes the original text to be at once doctrinally exemplary and hermeneutically fraught. And that is not simply to say that the reviser fears the text will be misread by errant readers, but rather that he or she understands that the tropes and vocabularies by which that particular text is supposed to convey doctrine – in this case Christ's charter – have become common property, and, as such, they elide distinctions not only between heterodox and orthodox doctrine, but, more insidiously, between heterodox and orthodox reading practices. The first four lines of the revised *Long Charter*, for example, seem to be responding to a heterodox threat emanating from outside the text. The original text begins quite conventionally with Christ's voice urging readers and listeners to take note of his suffering:

> Jhesu, kyng of heuene and helle,
> Mon and wommon, I wol þe telle
> What loue I haue i-don to þe;
> Loke what þou hast don to me! (A. 1–4)[7]

---

[5] Hudson (*689*); John Bowers (*336*). Russell and Kane suggest the possibility that the erasures were done to prepare for the rubricator to replace these words in red ink. See Russell and Kane (*171*).

[6] In the *Regement of Princes*, for example, Hoccleve goes so far as to define his whole writerly enterprise against the Lollard threat, arguing that good counsel counters heresy and deserves remuneration. See Thomas Hoccleve (*152*, 11–15 ll. 281–374ff.).

[7] The three versions of the *Long Charter* are edited in *The Minor Poems of the Vernon Manuscript*, ed. Frederick J. Furnivall and Carl Horstmann, 2 vols., EETS o.s. 117 (London: K. Paul, Trench, Trübner & Co., 1892–1901), 2.637–57. The Vernon Manuscript contains the earliest version of the

The revised texts, by contrast, are introduced by a new speaker, who warns his audience that heretical "schools" will not save them from the devil,[8] and proposes the *Long Charter* as a preventive to their teachings:

> Wo-so wil ouer-rede this boke,
> and with gostly eyen ther-on loke,
> to other scole dare he not wende,
> to saue his soule fro þe fende. (B. 1–4)

If we take its "self-declarations" (Paul Strohm's phrase) at face value, this new introduction suggests that the threat of heresy lies comfortably outside the text; the reviser is merely advertising the fitness of this older vernacular religious poem. But if the original *Long Charter* was such a model of orthodoxy, why did it need this strange new introduction? In their capacity as external censors the revisers of the *Long Charter* found little material to excise. Their labors include several noteworthy deletions but consist mainly of seemingly unmotivated insertions which bloat the slender original into a nearly unrecognizable form. They include, as we will see below, a garrulous clerical narrator (a fastidiously orthodox version of the fictionalized interlocutor) and long asides on the sacraments. Nor are these additions gratuitous exercises in *amplificatio*; they seem, rather, to be a coherent program to point readers in the right interpretative direction and divert their attention from heretical misreadings. Why did the poem require such extensive revision throughout, and what obstacles did the original text present?

The subversive implications of the *Long Charter* are hardly obvious. The original *Long Charter* contains no overtly heretical material or evidence of Lollard tampering. It offers no criticism of possessioners, friars, pardoners, or popes. It acknowledges, if briefly, the necessity of auricular confession ("soþfast schrifte"), and it promulgates the orthodox position on transubstantiation in the image of the Host as an indentured copy of Christ's charter-body: "On endenture I lafte wiþ þe,/ þat euer þou schuldest siker be:/ In preostes hondes my flesh and blode,/ þat for þe dyede on the Rode"

Long Charter (the A-text), but Furnivall and Horstmann have also included revised versions of the *Long Charter* for comparison (the B- and C-texts) edited from British Library MS Harley 2382 and British Library MS Royal 17 C xvii respectively. Subsequent citations will be to this edition and will follow the quotation in the text with line numbers.

[8] It is by no means certain whether the *Long Charter* reviser is referring here to a doctrine or a school, or whether the doctrine or school is supposed to be Lollard or merely an oppositional group or behavior (e.g. "the devil's school"). That this "scole" might refer to a coherent set of heterodox beliefs or educational program becomes more apparent after working through the revisions. Official statutes and confessions of prosecuted heretics indicate that Lollards did form underground schools in which the vernacular Bible and other texts were discussed in intimate groups. The statute *De Heretico Comburendo* asserts, for example, that the Lollards "make unlawful coventicles and confederacies, they hold and exercise schools (*scholas*)" (quoted in *713*, 175), and in 1430 Thomas Moon confessed to having "kept, holde, and continued scoles of heresie yn prive chambres and places of myne, yn the which scoles Y have herd, conceyved, lerned and reported the errours and heresies wiche be writen contened in these indentures" (Norman P. Tanner [*208*, 179]). See also Anne Hudson's comments on Lollard schools in (*713*, 176–80). For a terrific account of Lollard schools (and pedagogy), see Rita Copeland's introduction to *422*, 8–19.

(A. 205–208). Further, the image of Christ's body as a bleeding charter nailed to the cross comes from an iconographical tradition antithetical to Lollard sensibilities. Early Lollards were ambivalent about religious images, regarding them as necessary if faulty teaching aids, but later Lollards were notorious iconoclasts who denounced crucifixes as vain and distracting images.[9] The "Charter of Heaven" from *Pore Caitif* makes Christ's charter more vivid to its readers by reminding them of these familiar images of the crucifix: "þe printe of þis seel is þe shap of oure lord ihesu crist hanginge for oure synne on þe cros as we moun se bi þe ymage of þe crucifix."[10] Notably, several Lollard versions of *Pore Caitif* omit the phrase "as we moun se bi þe ymage of þe crucifix," one scribe substituting, "as the gospel þat is our believe techiþ us" (in British Library MS Harley 2322).[11] In short, the charter of Christ motif belonged to a literary and artistic tradition that Lollards should and did find in extremely bad taste.

The reception of the *Long* and *Short Charters* also suggests that they appealed to squarely orthodox readers who identified them with practices of the institutional church. Some readers, for example, associated the *Charters* with indulgences and relic worship, practices especially repugnant to committed Lollards. One fifteenth-century reader doctored his *Short Charter* into a pardon granting an indulgence of 26,030 years and 11 days (a crucial addendum since both the *Short* and *Long Charter* insist on the strictest terms for salvation: true love of God and neighbor). Another *Short Charter* was carved on a gravestone in Kent (c.1400), a practice usually reserved for indulgences, which were sometimes carved into the tomb of dignitaries (passersby who prayed for the souls of the dead earned a specified number of days off purgatory).[12] The image of Christ as a crucified charter also reminded readers of illustrations of the *arma christi* and of Christ as the Man of Sorrows. Both these images were used to decorate indulgences and often served as substitutes for relic-worship.[13] The fifteenth-century illustrator of British Library MS Additional 37049, for example, depicts the charter of Christ as a juxtaposition of the Man of Sorrows and the *arma christi*. In this graphic illustration, Christ gazes down sorrowfully at his midsection, which has been expanded into an unfurled parchment nailed to the cross. On the parchment are written the verses of the *Short Charter*, floating around

---

[9] Sawtre, the first Lollard martyr, protested the idea of worshipping a dead image of Christ on the cross when he could very well worship the "quicke ymage of God" among the poor and sick (Hudson [713, 304–5]). Likewise, the *Twelve Conclusions of the Lollards* (1395) decry the homage paid to images of "tre and of ston," especially during the twice-yearly services of the cross in which "þe rode tre, naylis, and þe spere . . . ben so holiche worschipid" (Conclusion no. 8 in Hudson [155, 27]).

[10] Printed by M.C. Spalding in *The Middle English Charters of Christ* (Bryn Mawr: Bryn Mawr College, 1914), 102.

[11] See M. Teresa Brady (*345*, 188).

[12] Nicholas Orme, "Indulgences in the Diocese of Exeter 1100–1536," *Transactions of the Devonshire Association for the Advancement of Science, Literature, and Art* 120 (1988): 21.

[13] Flora Lewis, "Rewarding Devotion: Indulgences and the Promotion of Images," in *The Church and the Arts*, ed. Diana Wood (Oxford: Blackwell, 1992), 179–94. See also the illustrated York indulgence recorded in the *Lay Folks' Catechism* (*176*, 159, n. B.13).

the cross are the instruments of Christ's torture, and affixed to the stem of the cross is a pierced and bleeding heart which does double duty as the charter's seal.

For many medieval readers, then, Christ's charter resembled a number of ostentatious pardons already in circulation, textual relics that could be displayed and adored. It would surely follow that this connection between the *Charters*, indulgences, and relic-worship would repulse Lollard preachers, who notoriously campaigned against relic-worship and who denounced pardons as the insidious workings of the Roman antichrist.[14] More to the point, the "mainstream" reception of the *Charters* should suggest that the *Long Charter* revisers attached an anti-Lollard introduction to advertise the poem's orthodoxy, but, as will become clearer, both the introduction and other revisions indicate that the poem needed major rehabilitation to serve that purpose. One readership may have treated Christ's charter as an exaggerated pardon, but another, clearly heterodox, readership could just as well recruit it *against* indulgences and letters of fraternity. The problem with the *Long Charter*, then, concerned not so much the doctrine it espoused as its potential for radical interpretive and literary transformations. And as we shall see, the indeterminacy of Christ's charter was produced not so much by the extended metaphor of Christ as charter but by the controversial relationship between reader, text, and author that such a metaphor might imply. As a result, Lollard writers were able to adapt Christ's charter to heterodox notions of textual authority and spiritual community. And by doing so they challenged not just institutional beliefs and practices, but the very affiliations of vernacular pious discourse.

II. Lollard Polemic and Christ's Charter

Lollard writers were notoriously hostile to legal documents, particularly to indulgences but also to preaching commissions, certifications, and trial depositions, all of which would bring no end of grief to Lollards on trial. Consequently, to understand how Lollards could have transformed Christ's charter into an "anti-pardon" and a symbol of Lollard textual community, it is useful to review briefly some objections to indulgences and to other documents of the institutional church. One of the most common objections to pardons and to letters of fraternity was that they were simoniacal and hence uncharitable: by selling spiritual benefits for material gain, the clergy excluded the poor and meritorious. The Lollard speaker in *Jack Upland*, for example, upbraids Friar Daw for withholding letters of fraternity from poor men:

---

[14] See, for example, the confessions of John Skylly and Robert Cavell in Tanner (*208*, 53, 58, 95).

Frere, whi axe ȝe not lettris of briþered of oþer pore mennes preieris, good & cristen leuers, ne of preestis, ne of monkis, ne of bischopis, as ȝe desire þat oþer rich men axen ȝou letteris for a certeyne summe bi ȝeer?[15]

Indulgences were also considered uncharitable because they were doled out without respect for the common profit. The pope, who claims to be the "tresorer of holi chirche," is really a "tresourer most banisschid out of charite," both because he exchanges pardon for money and because he does so "at his owne wil."[16] An early Lollard writer likewise explains that "þese pardouns bene not grauntid generally for fulfillyng of Goddis hestis and werkis of mercy to most nedy men, as Crist biddis, but for syngulere cause and syngulere place."[17] According to the *Sixteen Points* of Lollard belief, popes and bishops may issue pardons as long as they do so according to Scripture, to release those who have entered into foolish bonds or forgive those who have personally trespassed against them.[18] But pardons that release the sinner from divine punishment in return for money or service are damning both because they exchange spiritual for material goods – an oft-repeated Lollard objection – and because the grantor assumes an exclusive power belonging to Christ alone.[19] Finally, indulgences and letters of fraternity were criticized as newfangled documents lacking confirmation in Scripture and authorized by sinful men who, according to one Lollard preacher, deceive the common people with "here nouelerie of massis . . . & newe pardons & pilgrimages."[20]

These objections to ecclesiastical documents were derived from two basic tenets of early Wycliffism. The first concerns the predestined community of the faithful, an idea of spiritual brotherhood that necessarily invalidates the works of the institutional Church, the prayers of religious associations, and the intercession of the saints. According to this tenet, indulgences and letters of fraternity, which draw from the works of others and are authorized by the clergy, are at best ineffectual and at worst deceptive because they pretend to influence or even override divine judgment.[21] Additionally, these documents, when exchanged for money, create privatized, worldly communities of the rich, as opposed to the

[15] P.L. Heyworth (*159*, 187–90).
[16] Conclusion no. 9. Hudson (*155*, 27).
[17] From "Octo In Quibus Seducuntur Simplices Christiani," in Arnold (*100*, 3.460).
[18] Hudson (*155*, 21–22).
[19] This last reason points to a more theologically significant objection to spiritual letters, namely, that they are not only uncharitable and singular but superfluous and distracting. They purport to draw from the merits of saints or of the fraternal orders, which have no bearing on salvation of the individual Christian. As one sermon-writer comments about fraternal letters, "ȝif men schewen þanne þese lettres oþur to God or his lawe, þei profiȝte nothing to hem, ne defenden hem aȝen God. And so þese lettres ben superflew, as ben þese ordres þat maken hem" (Hudson [*158*, 1.329]).
[20] F.D. Matthew (*182*, 102).
[21] Technically, of course, indulgences were only intended to reduce purgatorial punishment, but predestinarianism has little room for purgatory, and indulgences were often misunderstood by Lollards and others to release sinners from both *poena* and *culpa*. There were, however, notorious cases of extravagant pardons issued *a poena et a culpa* in the fourteenth century. One Lollard sermon-writer rails against a particular papal pardon that offered release from "peyne and blame" and granted 2000 years off purgatory – probably the plenary indulgence issued by

"open" and inclusive spiritual community of the meritorious. The second tenet concerns the authority and antiquity of Scripture. As one early Wycliffite writer argued, the authority of Scripture (the gospels and Pauline Epistles) is based on its antiquity, and therefore other more recent scriptures, commentaries, and man-made documents are inherently false.[22] Consequently, charters, indulgences, and all "new" texts should be upheld only if they are supported by the gospels. For example, according to a debate recorded in the *Fasciculi Zizaniorum*, Wyclif argued that even if the Magna Carta itself promises to maintain the temporalities of the Church, this ordinance can be properly interpreted only in light of the gospels, which advocate clerical poverty.[23] Both Wycliffite tenets, then, the predestined community and the primacy of Scripture, posit an inclusive spiritual community constituted by Christ at the originary moment on the cross and authorized by Scripture alone.

Contempt for ecclesiastical documents generated a wealth of anti-materialist rhetoric ridiculing their worthlessness and frailty. One Lollard writer, for example, infuriated by the sale of pardons, complains that they were made up of a "litel leed not weiynge a pound, hengid with an hempryn thrid at a litil gobet of a calfskyn, peyntid with a fewe blake draugtis of enke."[24] Yet if some Lollards vilified the written record in order to discredit indulgences and emphasize the authority of Scripture, others seized upon Christ's charter to point up the weaknesses of indulgences and to describe heterodox ideas of spiritual and political community. It is not surprising that even Lollard writers would choose to portray Christ as a charter in a period when justice was increasingly centered upon the written record (conveyances of property, bonds of debt, manumissions, and wills).[25] It's true that medievalists, and especially literary critics, have long regarded legal documents as sites of literate corruption and as instruments of oppression and insurrection; important studies by Susan Crane, Steven Justice, and Richard Firth Green have done much to delineate the contentious political and juridical space that documents occupied in late medieval England.[26] But, as the *Charters of Christ* literature shows, medieval legal culture was also subject to a larger cultural appropriation in which its official ideologies and instruments were converted to serve vernacular modes of piety, social critique, and authorship. Or to put it another way, documentary culture, when translated into the vernacular, provided a framework that could be stretched to accommodate a variety of religious and political agendas.

Boniface VIII at the request of Philip IV (Hudson [*158*, 4.49]). Another sermon-writer complains that "hyt were ydel to traueylon for any pardoun, siþ a man myȝte at home geton hym fowrty thowsande ȝeer by noon!" (Hudson [*158*, 1.436]).

[22] Matthew (*182*, 287).

[23] This is John Kenningham reporting Wyclif in his own determination. See W.W. Shirley (*139*, 4–5, 18–19).

[24] Quoted in Hudson (*713*, 300).

[25] See Michael Clanchy, *From Memory to Written Record: England 1066–1307*, 2nd edn. (Cambridge: Blackwell, 1993), 49–52, 200; and Richard Firth Green (*611*, 38–39 and throughout).

[26] Susan Crane (*436*); Steven Justice (*765*); Green (*611*).

More specifically, Christ's charter appealed to both orthodox and heterodox readers because it had come to signify a public and open letter available to all Christians and a foundational grant coequal with Christ's crucified body and with Scripture. I have argued in other places that charters and patents were used to represent Christ's body and message because they were inherently public texts directly addressed to a universal audience of readers and listeners.[27] Fourteenth-century writers also imagined certain kinds of legal documents to be transhistorical and performative: they seemed to transmit the original voice of the author/legal actor to future generations and continually put into effect his or her wishes. We can see this desire for documentary authenticity and agency in official Latin formulas (as in the typical land-grant salutation: "*Sciant presentes et futuri quod ego Johannes . . .dedi et concessi et hac presenti carta mea confirmaui . . .*" ["Let all present and future know that I John have given and granted and with my present charter have confirmed"]), but even more so in their vernacular transformations (as in the salutation to the *Charter of the Abbey of the Holy Ghost*: "*Sciant presentes & futuri &c.* Wetiþ ye þat ben now here, & þei þat schulen comen after you, þat almighti god in trinite, fader & sone & holy gost, haþ gouen & graunted & wiþ his owne word confermed . . . etc."[28]). In pious contexts, then, legal documents came to signify the original, continuous, and public proclamation of crucial spiritual legislation (i.e. the contract of the Redemption). But whereas for mid fourteenth-century writers, Christ's charter was largely a penitential strategy of making Christ's Word and Passion significant and immediate, for later writers with Lollard sympathies, it came to represent a relationship between text and community diametrically opposed to that represented by ecclesiastical letters. If ecclesiastical letters constituted private and privileged communities organized by the pope and fraternal orders, Christ's charter might serve as the foundational text for a spiritual brotherhood inclusive of all (saved) Christians, unmediated by institutional authorities and texts, and authorized by the crucifixion and the gospels.

We see this kind of drastic appropriation of Christ's charter, for example, in an interpolation of *The Lay Folks' Catechism* (appearing in London, Lambeth Palace Library MS 408 and Oxford, Bodleian Library, MS Douce 274), in which Christ's heavenly grant is opposed to indulgences and equated with the gospels.[29] What we take to be a copy of the original vernacular text, written down in Archbishop Thoresby's register in 1357 and attributed to the archbishop's reforming efforts, was intended for the sacerdotal instruction of the laity and includes a lengthy exposition on the Ten Commandments. But whereas Thoresby's copy merely extols the

---

[27] Emily Steiner, *Documentary Culture and the Making of Medieval English Literature* (Cambridge: Cambridge University Press, 2003).

[28] Edited in Carl Horstman (*154*, 1.338.340).

[29] For a discussion of the manuscript tradition of *The Lay Folks' Catechism* and its interpolations, see Hudson (*706*). As Hudson shows, the Lollard-sympathetic views of the Lambeth interpolator are often riddled with contradictions (for example, he does not omit Thoresby's injunction that any lay person who learns their catechism will enjoy an indulgence of forty days), and, moreover, no interpolated manuscript of the wildly variant *LFC* corpus is the same.

virtues of the Ten Commandments, the Lollard-sympathetic interpolator finds an occasion to denounce pardons and temporalities. If you break the Ten Commandments and do not amend, he says, you will be "dampnyd in helle in body and sowle withouten ende," despite your impressive collection of a "þowsand bullys of pardoun, lettris of fraternite, and chauntres."[30] Conversely, if you fulfill the Ten Commandments, you will enjoy perpetual bliss in heaven, whether or not you have ever purchased a pardon. In short, concludes the interpolator, pardons and fraternal letters have no legal bearing on salvation. Heaven is a grant issued in the gospels and authorized by Christ's crucified body: "þe erytage of heuyn ys þyn be graunt of cristys gospel, aselyd with his precious blod þat may neuer be fals: for no creature in erthe ne in heuyn."[31]

Although the interpolation of the *Lay Folks' Catechism* does not use the word "charter" to describe Christ's land-grant of heaven, it clearly refers to a written document and to the *Charters of Christ* literature. The *Short Charter*, for example, also imagines Christ's charter to be sealed with his own blood: "To this chartre trewe and good/ I have set my seal, myn herthe blood."[32] The passage from the *Lay Folks' Catechism* has distinct verbal echoes, moreover, in the "Charter of Heaven" from *Pore Caitif*. The *Lay Folks' Catechism* insists that Christ's charter is sealed with his blood and therefore is both legally incontestable and physically indestructible: it "may neuer be fals: for no creature in erthe ne in heuyn." Likewise, the "Charter of Heaven" confirms that Christ's charter is imperishable because it is inscribed upon Christ's body: "þis scripture is oure lord Ihesu crist: chartre & bulle of oure eritage of heuene . . .þis chartre may not fiyr brenne ne watir drenche: neiþir þeef robbe neiþir ony creature distroie," and a few lines later, "alle þe creatures in heuene neiþir in erþe neiþir in helle moun not robbe it neiþir bireue it fro þe."[33] As in the "Charter of Heaven," then, the interpolator demonstrates the superiority of Christ's charter (i.e. the gospels) by identifying Christ's charter with his crucified body. Notably, by doing so, he has also adapted the mainstream rhetoric of Christ's charter to articulate what would become distinctly Lollard concerns.

A second more explicitly Lollard sermon also evokes Christ's charter to discredit other spiritual letters and to posit a predestined community of believers. In this sermon for Quinquagesima Sunday, compiled in an early fifteenth-century manuscript (Rawlinson C. 751) with the "Charter of Heaven," the sermon-writer has provocatively sandwiched a description of Christ's charter between condemnations of letters of fraternity and indulgences.[34] He admonishes those who think that, by becoming lay brothers of a fraternal order "bi lettre and bi seel," they will partake of the good deeds performed by the brothers. Rather, they should believe that those who will be saved are free partners of all good deeds performed from

---

[30] Hudson (*706*, 57, ll. 879–83).
[31] Hudson (*706*, ll. 888–91).
[32] Spalding, *Middle English Charters*, 98, ll. 27–28.
[33] Ibid., 102.
[34] For a description, see Jeremy Griffith's introduction to *Lollard Sermons* (*128*, xxiv–xxv).

prelapsarian Eden to the day of Judgment through the mercy of God and according to their deserts. They should steadfastly believe, moreover, in a universal brotherhood of the predestined constituted by Christ's charter, rather than in the elitist brotherhood of fraternities founded by profane letters:

> Alle we beþ breþeren of oo Fadir in heuene, and breþeren to oure Lord Jesus Crist, and into his broþerhede we beþ receyued bi þe worshipeful chartre of þe hooli Trinyte: Fadir, and Sone, and Hooli Goost. The chartre of þis breþerhede is þe blessid bodi þat hynge on a cros; writen wiþ þe worþi blood þat ran doun fro his herte, seelid wiþ þe precyous sacramente of þe auter in perpetuel mynde þerof. And þis blesside bretherhede schal abiden foreuere in blisse (whanne alle false faitouris schullen fare) wiþhire Fadir.[35]

The sermon-writer goes on in the same vein to denounce another deceptive document, the "bulle purchasid of a fals pardener," which further distracts the sinner from the true righteousness and severity of God. As in the case of the interpolated *Lay Folks' Catechism*, this passage links Christ's body on the cross to a divine charter and, by doing so, quite deliberately evokes the *Charters of Christ* tradition. As in the passage from the *Lay Folks' Catechism*, moreover, this one borrows Christ's charter to formulate a spiritual fellowship authorized by Scripture and by the liberating terms of the Passion. Conversely, it uses Christ's charter to prove that the documents of the institutional church, pardons and letters of fraternity, represent new practices and exclusive communities lacking proper authorization. Finally, this passage reveals once again how heterodox concerns may sharpen even specific borrowings into pointed polemic. As in the *Charters of Christ* literature, here Christ's charter is written with his own blood, but uniquely its seal is the Eucharist ("seelid wiþ þe precyous sacramente of þe auter"), which is described as a reminder ("in perpetual mynde therof"), rather than an extension or reenactment of Christ's body on the cross. By contrast, the author of the *Long Charter* describes the Eucharist as an indentured copy – a duplicate and binding copy of Christ's charter-body – continually issued to priests at their altars: "On endenture I lafte wiþ þe,/ þat euer þou schuldest siker be:/ In preostes hondes my flesh and blode,/ þat for þe dyede on the Rode" (A. 205–208).

In short, both passages suggest that heterodox writers were critical readers of the charter of Christ literature and deliberately adapted it to polemical ends. We may speculate, too, that the "Charter of Heaven" served as a kind of "bridge" text, relaying the rhetoric of Christ's charter to heterodox readers. As mentioned above, this tract was the most frequently copied of the fourteen tracts in *Pore Caitif*: it survives in forty-seven out of fifty-six manuscripts containing the full text of or extracts from *Pore Caitif*, and it was circulated independently of the rest of its compilation in five manuscripts, all of which, interestingly enough, contain the Lollard or

---

[35] *Lollard Sermons* (*128*, 113, ll. 266–84).

"variant" version of the text. Additionally, several non-interpolated versions of the "Charter of Heaven" were published in fourteenth- and fifteenth-century manuscripts with a fervent "Lollard-style" treatise, further attesting to its heterodox readership.[36] At least one medieval reader, moreover, directly identified this text with a Lollard program. The "Charter of Heaven" warns that Christ's charter is too precious to be locked in a chest but should be inscribed on the hearts of those who hope to receive their heavenly inheritance: "þis scripture is oure lord Ihesu crist: chartre & bulle of oure eritage of heuene! Locke not þis chartre in þi coffre: but sette it eiþir write it in þin herte."[37] In the margin of one non-interpolated "Charter of Heaven" (Cambridge University Library MS Ff.6.34), a fifteenth-century reader wrote "letters of fraternite" next to the line, "locke not þis chartre in þi coffre," implying that the kind of charters that *are* locked away in chests are the fraternal letters decried in the sermons discussed above.[38]

The marginal gloss in the "Charter of Heaven" suggests ways in which Christ's charter might be used to formulate radical ideas of political as well as spiritual community. Although Lollard writers borrowed the image of Christ's charter to argue for the absolute legal authority of Scripture (i.e. *lex Christi*), by depicting Scripture as a charter rather than the more ambiguous "law," they might allude not just to the nature of the Church but to more politically charged notions of dominion (in particular, the subordination of clerical to royal authority). The "coffre" in the "Charter of Heaven" ("locke not þis chartre in þi coffre") is doubtlessly meta-phorical; it shows the superiority of open to closed forms of spirituality, and of the spiritual to the material – Christ's charter is no pricey object to be stowed in a chest (as of course charters were). Rather, it is a message of salvation at once personally relevant and publicly inscribed. Yet its language of archives and locks recalls more explicitly seditious texts such as the 1381 rebel broadsides, one of which famously warns that "Trewþe" is "under a lokke." In a different context, Nicholas Watson agrees that the line, "locke not þis chartre in þi coffre," points to the inclusiveness of (in his opinion, vernacular) spirituality, but he argues that it is antithetical to the actions of 1381: "The images of charter and coffer, both connected with the secular world of wealth, are used not to exclude all but the privileged from ownership – in the rebellion of 1381 it was this identifica-tion of the charter with privilege which led to systematic burning of charters – but to confer the status of freeman on all."[39] Granted, some rebels were bent on destroying the middlemen of justice and their written

---

[36] Oxford, Bodleian Library, MS Rawlinson C. 209 and MS Douce 13. Some Lollard concerns of this treatise include the integrity of the "felawschip of perfite men," the imitation of the first church, the ability of each man to determine the moral character of his own works, the necessity of "trewe compuncioun of herte," and the conspicuous absence of the clergy or of oral confession (Douce 13, ff. 7v–14).

[37] Spalding, *Middle English Charters*, 101.

[38] F. 74. The same reader may have had Lollard sympaties generally. Most of his *notae*, consisting of "be war" and "tak good heede," mark passages on the evils of swearing, a favorite Lollard issue.

[39] Nicholas Watson (*1266*, 109).

instruments, but the chroniclers were impressed more by the rebels' demands that ancient charters be liberated from monastic archives, or royal confirmations of privileges be issued from the long-obsolete Domesday Book, or that a new charter of manumission be issued by King Richard himself, than they were by acts of destruction. (Even when the Abbot of St. Alban's offered the rebels a new charter of privileges they continued to agitate for King Offa's eighth-century "original."[40]) The rebels claimed that these liberated documents would reveal the truth about their privileges, and in doing so, restore a commonwealth in which service was owed directly to the king, and in which the king was the sole and unmediated dispenser of justice.[41] Indeed, the rebels' desire for authentic royal documents closely resembles the Lollard "free" brotherhood founded by Christ's charter and opposed to ecclesiastical letters which withhold spiritual privileges from the meritorious poor. This is not to suggest that Lollard writers, by appropriating Christ's charter, were advocating revolt.[42] Rather, the radical political implications of Christ's charter are brought into focus by Lollard adaptations and annotations; when taken to its logical extreme, Christ's charter represents theories of textual authority and of political and spiritual organization that informed Lollard and rebel ideologies alike.

The capacity of a divine charter to embody heterodox ideas of political and spiritual community can be seen even more clearly in a third tract, "The Grete Sentence of Curs Expouned" (dated by Arnold to c.1383), which invokes Christ's charter to accuse the orthodox clergy of treason and to demonstrate royal sovereignty over the temporal possessions of the Church. We have already seen that Lollards condemned pardons and fraternal letters as "singular," selfish or self-ruled acts. "The Grete Sentence" turns singularity into sedition by creating an analogy between Christ's charter (Scripture) and the king's charter (the Magna Carta). It begins by arguing that worldly clerks, "bi fals prechynge . . . bi sikernesse of letteris of fraternyte and synguler preieris," teach all men to be "rebel aȝenis þe kyng and lordis" and to destroy the "pees of þe kyng and his rewme."[43] It then compares the king's charter to Scripture and contrasts both to the "singular" and unauthorized claims of canon law. According to the Magna Carta, the king donates temporal goods to the Church as alms, but some clerks deceive the king and malign his charter by styling themselves sovereign lords. They are subsequently cursed every time the Magna Carta is

---

[40] *Gesta Abbatam Monasterii Sancti Albans*, ed. Henry Thomas Riley, Rolls Series (London: Longman, 1863–4), 308, 317–322.

[41] For the rebels' use of the Domesday Book, see Rosamund Faith, "The 'Great Rumor' of 1377 and Peasant Ideology," in *The English Rising of 1381*, 43–73; and Barbara Harvey, "Draft Letters Patent of Manumission and Pardon for the Men of Somerset in 1381," *English Historical Review* 80 (1965): 89–91.

[42] Medieval chroniclers easily lumped together "Lollards, traitors, and rebels," but modern scholars have discredited any confabulation between Wyclif's early followers and the 1381 leaders. See Margaret Aston (*269*).

[43] Arnold (*100*, 3.298). Subsequent citations to this tract will appear in the text.

proclaimed: "alle þe þat falsen þe kyngis chartre and assented þerto ben cursed solempnely of God and man, puppliched foure tymes in þe ȝeer." By analogy, they are even more cursed by "þe *chartre of alle kyngis, þat is holy writt,*" in which God commands all priests to live "in honest povert and forsake seculer lordischip . . . as crist and his apostlis diden" (306, emphasis added). By impugning the Magna Carta, that is, the clergy necessarily impugn Christ's charter as well; the two documents together attest to royal sovereignty, but also to the intrinsic authenticity and primacy of royal documents, as contrasted with the treasonous, newfangled, and self-interested texts of the institutional Church. In light of the analogy between Christ's charter and the king's charter, it may be significant too that scribes of the *Charters of Christ* frequently gave them titles that deliberately evoked the Magna Carta, such as *magna carta saluatoris* and *magna carta liberationis et remissionis.*[44]

III. *Reclaiming the* Long Charter

The Lollard appropriations of Christ's charter place us in a better position to understand the peculiar revisions of the *Long Charter* because they clarify the issues at stake in the idea of a divine charter. To my knowledge, only one Lollard manuscript (Rawlinson C. 751), mentioned above, actually contains the early version of the *Long Charter* (A), along with a collection of Lollard sermons and an interpolated "Charter of Heaven." Few fifteenth-century writers, however, could have been ignorant of some form of Christ's charter, and, as we have just seen, Lollard polemicists freely adapted it to fit their own ideological agendas. The revisers would have had sufficient cause for alarm. The *Long Charter* was revised in two stages. The first revision (B) survives in nine manuscripts, the earliest of which was copied around 1400 (Harvard University, Houghton Library, MS W.K. Richardson 22). The second revision (C) survives in a unique manuscript (British Library MS Royal 17. C.xvii) probably compiled by a parish priest before 1425, to judge from the other items in the manuscript. Both revisers attempted to prevent possible misreadings of the poem by showing that the terms of Christ's charter can not be grasped without clerical mediation, nor can they be met without fulfilling the sacraments of the church. Not that all the revisions of the *Long Charter* should be attributed solely to an anti-Lollard agenda. The C-reviser, for example, who added over three hundred lines to the B-text, seems to have wanted to make the poem more informative, and many of his additions merely flesh out the gospel narrative which is presented only schematically in the original. On the whole, though, most of the revisions to the *Long Charter* – the fictive narrator, rambling digressions on orthodox doctrine, and attempts to re-historicize Christ's charter –

---

[44] "Magna Carta" or "gret chartre" nearly always refers in Middle English texts to the 1215 document, usually in contradistinction to the Charter of the Forest (*MED*, s.v. "chartre").

seem tailored to discourage the kinds of readings found in the Lollard sermons discussed above.[45]

As discussed above, the implicit challenge of Lollardy was the reorganization of a spiritual community around an original text to the exclusion of other texts and the devaluation of other practices and mediators.[46] Lollard appropriations of Christ's charter thematize this vexed question of textual authority by usurping mainstream pious discourse and documentary culture. The fifteenth-century revisers of the *Long Charter*, like their Lollard counterparts, recognized the general claims of Christ's charter, namely that the making of textual community is the making of spiritual community, and reshaped the poem accordingly. Most significantly, they inserted a new narrator and commentator, a peevish and bossy preacher whose voice frames the poem and frequently interrupts to comment on the narrative. This clerical persona is inconsistent and by no means suggests that the poem was reworked simply for oral delivery. Rather, the overall effect of the fictive preacher is to control access to Christ's voice and charter; neither reader nor listener can receive Christ's voice without taking into account the preacher's distinctive interjections. We already saw that the speaker of the first four lines of the revised introduction warns his readers not to stray to that "other scole." This admonitory voice goes on to present Christ as if He were a guest speaker: "Now ye shal here anon-righte,/ your sauyour speke to yow as-tyte/ wordes of a chartour þat he hath wroght," and, a few lines later, "Now y wil begynne to rede þeron;/ his pes he yeue [give] vs euery-chon!" (B.13–15, 23–24). The C-text narrator likewise soberly introduces his text, "Now sal ȝe here with-outyn delyte/ ȝoure sawyour [savior] spek to ȝou als-tyte [just so]" (C.13–14). In the original poem, Christ is the only speaker, but as the revised version progresses it becomes increasingly difficult to distinguish between Christ's voice and that of the fictive preacher. By intervening, the fictive preacher immediately reestablishes the clergy as scriptural interpreters and spiritual policemen, and by doing so he diminishes the agency of Christ's document by reading it aloud and subjecting it to commentary. Or to put it another way, the fictive preacher effectively assumes the power to effect the linguistic performance of the divine charter, replacing Christ not only as the primary speaker but as the enactor of spiritual legislation.

The revisers further reshaped the textual community of the *Long Charter* by turning Christ's universal charter into a private conversation between Christ and preacher. Whereas in the A-text Christ explains the significance of the Last Supper directly to the reader – "And þis I made for Monkynde,/ Mi loue-dedes to haue in mynde: *Hoc facite in meam commemoracionem*" (A. 61–62) – in the B-text Christ addresses the narrator as a sermon-writer

---

[45] The difficulties of dating vernacular Wycliffite texts make it impossible to establish a direct causal relationship between these heterodox appropriations of Christ's charter and the *Long Charter* revisions that reassert its orthodoxy. I will suggest, however, that the *Long Charter* revisers were responding to this kind of interpretation, if not to my particular examples.

[46] Lollards did have spiritual leaders who disseminated information aurally to a group that valued lay literacy but probably remained at least ocularly illiterate. On Lollard literacy, see Hudson (*722*) and Margaret Aston (*278*, 198–204).

might address a practicing preacher: "Here wol y foure wordes *yow* teche/ and to þe peple loke *ye* hem preche: *Hoc facite in meam commemoracionem/* that *they* heue hem euer in mynde" (B. 111–13, emphases added). Just as the preacher replaces Christ as primary speaker, so he replaces the reader as Christ's primary interlocutor. As such, he transforms the audience from active participants to passive receivers of doctrine. The fictive preacher acknowledges that textual dissemination is in some sense beyond his control; it might be perused silently or communicated aurally by any reader. "Wo-so wil ouer-rede this boke and with gostly eyen ther-on loke" (B. 1–2), he begins, and a few lines later adds, "who this boke can vnderstonde,/ teche it forth thurgh al the londe" (B. 17–18). At the same time, he repeatedly insists upon his role as preacher expounding a text to an audience that must be exhorted, cajoled, and quieted. "Herken now to my word hende!" exclaims the narrator several times, as if addressing a noisy, bustling crowd (B. 92, C. 130).[47] The C-reviser goes to greater lengths to portray his audience as an unruly mob. In every B-text manuscript the fictive preacher blesses his imaginary audience with the conventional phrase, "his pes he yeue vs euery-chon!" (B. 24–25). By contrast, the C-text narrator demands silence: "Ald youre pese now euer-ilkon!" (C. 29–30). Thus if aural reading forges communal bonds between speaker and audience, as Joyce Coleman has recently argued about Chaucer, the revised *Long Charter* drastically reconfigures these bonds.[48] Rather than binding Christ and "alle folk" or Christ and the individual, unchaperoned reader, Christ's charter has become the text that binds preacher and congregation.[49]

By creating this fictive preacher, moreover, the revisers of the *Long Charter* brought the poem in line with some of the concerns expressed by the Oxford debates on Bible translation that took place during the first decade of the fifteenth-century, the same period in which the *Long Charter* B-reviser probably set to work. As Watson has so influentially argued, vernacular English literature before 1350 enjoyed the "relatively uncomplicated position . . . of being able to express a concrete relationship between a defined author and a defined audience." After 1350, however, vernacular

---

[47] Sally Poor has suggested to me that what I am calling a pastoral exhortation may actually be drawn from romance formulas.

[48] *Public Reading and the Reading Public in Late Medieval England and France* (Cambridge: Cambridge Univ. Press), 108.

[49] Instructively, the *Long Charter* A-text is the only example of a supernatural charter in which Christ appeals directly to the individual reader without an authoritative intermediary. There is, in fact, a conspicuous absence in the original *Long Charter* of the kind of mediating voices that usually accompany fictive documents. In Guillaume de Deguileville's *Pèlerinage de la vie humaine* and its English adaptations, for example, Charity reads aloud Christ's last will and testament to a parliament of pilgrims, and in the sequel, the *Pèlerinage de l'âme*, Mercy recites Christ's charter of pardon to the Archangel Michael and his heavenly court (the pilgrim-narrator hanging upon her every word). Langland, perhaps following Deguileville, also assigns an official intermediary to every one of his documents: Christ's charter of pardon is successively if contentiously disseminated by the priest (*Piers Plowman* B. VII), Moses (B. XVII), and Peace (B. XVIII). If, in these examples from other fictive documents, reading a charter aloud could be interpreted as charitable or instructive (it relays crucial information to people who are not able or have not had the chance to read the document), in the context of the *Long Charter* it could also be read as a safety measure in the guise of pastoral beneficence.

authors were increasingly aware of "presenting an ever wider array of theological concerns to an ever larger and less clearly defined group of readers."[50] Although English writers had been translating parts of the Bible into vernacular literature for centuries (from apocryphal narratives to contemplative treatises), the nebulous and variable character of vernacular reception was thrown into relief by the Wycliffite Bible and by the corresponding backlash of the orthodox clergy. And those opposing translation in the Oxford debate fully recognized the interpretative dislocations of translation and deemed it to be spiritually and politically destabilizing. It could, argued one opponent, enable any fool or woman to usurp the role of preacher and lead himself and their followers to heretical or seditious conclusions.[51] Another debater, William Butler, recommended that the laity should gain biblical knowledge through hearing rather than reading, the former being less dangerous since it involves the testimony of preachers who function as "living holy books."[52]

During the fifty or so years, then, in which the *Long Charter* was composed, disseminated, and revised, scriptural translation changed dramatically from a pastoral imperative to a site of major ideological conflict. Conversely, the legal document was becoming linguistically and socially accessible, an accessibility bitterly contested in the 1381 revolt, but evident in the Englishing and expansion of the royal bureaucracy, the wider circulation of documentary culture (especially in wills), and the literary appropriation of documentary forms. To be sure, documentary Latin retained its monumentality and conventionality beyond the Middle Ages, but it also became subject to discursive and linguistic experimentation and could be re-contextualized to serve a variety of literary and ideological agendas. The fact that Scripture could be depicted as a vernacular charter publicly proclaimed and openly displayed on the cross entailed a heady juxtaposition of two official discourses. The analogy between charter and Scripture still worked, in other words, but it had come to represent an increasingly problematic relationship between official texts and their readers that Lollard readers were eager to exploit. In the *Charters of Christ* literature, moreover, Christ's charter represents spiritual agency as well as textual authority (it depicts Christ as both the authenticating agent and written contract of salvation), in short, the effective performance of the Word that Lollards refused to limit to the institutional priesthood.[53] The fictive preacher of the *Long Charter* thus served not only as a means of reasserting clerical authority, but as the vessel through which Christ's charter might be both legitimately transmitted and ritually performed.

To return briefly to some of the other *Long Charter* revisions, it should be added that just as the fictive preacher can be understood as a legitimate way of transmitting official texts, whether legal or scriptural, so he can also be understood as a way of marking the text: his very presence discourages

---

[50] Nicholas Watson (*1265*, 838).
[51] Watson (*1265*, 843).
[52] Watson (*1265*, 842).
[53] See Hudson (*713*, 324–27).

heterodox readers. The revisers further mark the *Long Charter* as an orthodox text by making it overtly polemical. For example, the metaphor of Christ's charter-body is implicitly eucharistic, but the revisers dwell upon transubstantiation at every conceivable opportunity. The A-text records that Christ made a supper for friends and fed them with "holi word [his] flesch and blode" so that humankind might remember his "loue-dedes" (A. 57ff.). The B-reviser takes this opportunity to remind readers that this story refers to the Eucharist ("thes wordes twocheth þe sacrament/ that men receueth, verrament") and offers his readers a catchy mnemonic on transubstantiation: "it semeth many, & is but one;/ it semeth bred, & it is none;/ it is quyk, & semeth ded:/ it is my body in fourme of bred" (B. 117–20). It is true that catechism does not necessarily imply censorship, but in the case, I would argue it serves as a kind of rhetorical "padding" of a poem much more affective than catechistic in its pieties. The C-reviser omits the Last Supper passage altogether, embarking instead on a tedious speech about the dangers of believing that the Host is not Christ's body (C. 135–66). First Christ (or the preacher-narrator) hastily explains that he is discussing this subject in English only to reinforce the faith of the laity ("þis wordys are þus to vnderfong/ to lewed men in ynglys tong" [133–34]); he then warns his readers that transubstantiation is the best lesson one can learn, and the best defense against the devil:

> It es þe best leson þat þou may lere
> þi gostly enmy aw [always]to fere;
> for þe grettest temptacyon,
> wyt þis þou may lay all don.
> Af [have]it in mynde stedfastly,
> And þou sall af [shall have]þi purpos, trewly.   (C. 159–64)

This move illustrates C-reviser's general method to seize upon opportunities for didacticism and direct them toward Lollard-sensitive issues. Such excessive commentary also has the effect of creating a structurally orthodox text. Where the sparer *Long Charter* A-text threats to take biblical (and legal) quotations dangerously out of context, the revised versions encase Christ's charter in more traditional biblical narrative and buffer it with expositions on the sacraments.[54]

Finally, if the original *Long Charter* seemed to promise unmediated

---

[54] A similarly proactive revision occurs in the metaphor of the indenture discussed several times above. The A-text compares the Eucharist to an indentured copy of Christ's crucified charter-body, a duplicate copy of the same substance. The B-reviser considered this indenture metaphor to be a sufficient explanation of transubstantiation and saw fit only to add the warning that "who-so-euer be-leveth ther-on,/ endeles payn shal he fynde non" (B. 357–58). This clever indenture metaphor proved too abstruse, however, for the C-reviser, who apparently judged it safer to compare the Eucharist to the original charter than to an indentured copy (an indentured copy might undermine the sacramental nature of the Eucharist or suggest that there are multiple available copies). Christ says, "þis charter þus celyd [sealed] leve I wyll þe,/ ware-by þu sall ay sekyr [secure] be/: My precyus body, of þe preste hande" (C. 557–59), and he insists that his body is the sacrament performed simultaneously by different priests at different altars: "My precyus body es þe sacrament/, þat [at] many a autyre verament/ þe prestes sakyre [consecrate]at þer messe" (C. 561–63).

access to divine revelation, as suggested above, this problem was further exacerbated by its peculiar transhistoricity. As suggested above, the appeal of Christ's charter stemmed, in part, from its fiction of authorial presence – it purports to be continually issued by Christ at an originary moment on the cross. This fiction appealed to Lollard fundamentalist historicism – it illustrated the "contrast between the modern corrupt church and the apostolic church" – and convinced more mainstream readers that Christ's charter was a talisman imbued with divine presence (both approaches eliminating the need for human intermediaries or textual glosses).[55] Correspondingly, the *Long Charter* revisers (particularly the C-reviser) attempted to mediate the effects of the charter by restoring the boundaries of temporality and textuality. The A- and B-texts, for example, make no distinction between Christ as narrator and Christ as charter, moving seamlessly through literary, biblical and documentary modes. Beginning with Christ's first-person narration ("To shewen on alle my loue-dede,/ Miself I wole this chartre rede" [A. 91–92]), the poem swiftly moves to Christ's scriptural lament from the cross (*"O [v]os omnes qui transitis per viam attendite & vidite, etc./* Ye Men that gon bi this weye,/ A-bydeth a luytel [little], I ow preye,/ And redeth alle on this parchemyn,/ Yif eny serwe beo lyk to myn" [A. 93–96]); and finally to the alternating first-third person voice of his charter (*"Sciant presentes et futuri,/* Wite ye that are and schal be-tyde,/ that Jhesu crist with blodi side . . . Made a sesyng whon I was born . . ." [A. 98–105]). As a result, Christ's charter-voice seems to be perpetually present, forever regenerating itself and its terms to new readers and listeners. In the C-text, however, the narrator interrupts at this pivotal place to explain that Christ issued his charter at a historical moment on the cross, not to the present readers and listeners:

> Goddis son of heuen, þe sothe to say,
> þis wordy[s] spake on gode fryday,
> pyned on þe mounte of calwery,
> to þe pepull þat passyd hym by.   (C. 253–56)

The charter, in other words, is not a timeless communiqué from Christ to a modern-day audience. It merely reports Christ's speech on the cross to a historical "pepull," and consequently it must be glossed by the ordained clergy as represented by the preacher-narrator. The audience should not think to draw directly upon an original document, however open and immediate it may claim to be, because both its text and authorizing body have been consigned to a sacred past.

Conclusion

Whereas his opponents in the Oxford Bible debate disparaged the laity as an unruly and unpredictable mob, one debater named Richard Ullerston

---

[55] Gordon Leff (*836*, 2.526).

praised them as the "people of God to whom Christ preached in the mother tongue and who both need and are fit to receive God's law translated into that tongue."[56] For Ullerston, then, the vernacular forged a revelatory link between Christ's historical audience and the present lay audience. And, as mentioned above, it was exactly this nostalgic link between past and present audiences that was advertised by the conventional salutations of Latin charters and their fictive English counterparts. Ullerston's position may seem socially progressive, but by the early fifteenth century it was untenable and politically naïve. Both he and the charters of Christ belonged to an earlier period in which a documentary fiction could be drafted incontestably into the service of vernacular piety. But starting in the 1380s or 90s, Lollard writers began to appropriate this fiction for their own ends: to devalue the "new" documents of the institutional church and to fashion an "open" spiritual community based on scriptural authority and vernacular translation. The original *Long Charter* was thus doubly implicated: first, by its inherent claims to immediacy and authenticity; and second, by Lollard appropriations of orthodox imagery for heterodox polemic.

Clearly, the *Long Charter* revisers were not concerned simply to delete or conceal heterodox positions but also to insulate the poem from misreadings and appropriations. But what this strategy reveals ultimately is a more nuanced picture of late medieval censorship than is often drawn. Censorship is often conceived of as the influence of legislation or social mores on literary production, which results in the adding and subtracting of material. But it can also be understood as a creative impulse, and as the competition for language and symbols at a time when the written vernacular was at once expanding and newly circumscribed. The charter, which embodied all the expectations and fears of vernacular literary production, became such a symbol.

---

[56] Watson (*1265*, 846).

Part IV

HERESY, DISSIDENCE, AND REFORM

Franciscans, Lollards, and Reform

Lawrence M. Clopper

Historians of the English Franciscans have in the past expressed puzzlement at the apparent absence of dissent among the English brothers. Where are the Ubertino da Casales? the Peter John Olivis? the Ockhams? Where is the evidence that the English friars were involved in or engaged with the disputes within the order that were so rancorous and divisive – and at times deadly – such as those that took place in the south of France and Italy? Although we know that some writings of Olivi and Ubertino and some pseudo-Joachist texts were circulating in England, we have no direct evidence that there were Spirituals like those in southern France and Italy.[1] Nevertheless, I believe there is more evidence of Franciscan and mendicant dissent in England than has been recognized in the past. I also think that some of this evidence has not been recognized as such because the texts in which it appears have been labeled Lollard.

Recent scholars who have turned to the study of English Lollard writers have become increasingly aware of the wide diversity of thought in these texts; they have also begun to map out the Lollard indebtedness to the larger pool of reformist rhetorics prior to Wyclif's.[2] I wish to enlarge the latter discussion by making the claim that some texts that have been ascribed to the Lollards may attest to Franciscan rigorist rhetoric in England; indeed, whether they were written by English authors or simply brought into England and translated, they may bespeak an English interest in the rigorist position. A second possibility that I will explore is that friars who objected to the papal limitations on preaching may have moved to a position reminiscent of the rigorist one when they found themselves pursued as apostates to their orders. The ways the critiques of Franciscan practice are framed within the "Wycliffite" translation of the *Rule* and *Testament*, "Of the Leaven of Pharisees," and "Fifty Heresies and Errors of the Friars" suggest to me that these texts were written by Franciscan rigorists or

---

[1] Morton Bloomfield, *"Piers Plowman" as a Fourteenth-Century Apocalypse* (New Brunswick, NJ: Rutgers Univ. Press, 1961), 227 n.13; Wendy Scase (*1081*, 115, 209 n.131); and Kathryn Kerby-Fulton, *Reformist Apocalypticism and "Piers Plowman"* (Cambridge: Cambridge Univ. Press, 1990), 172–200.

[2] I am referring here in particular to papers and discussions in the Lollard Society sessions at Kalamazoo and Leeds over the last several years, but also to the work of Anne Hudson, Margaret Aston, Wendy Scase, Fiona Somerset and others, including contributors to this volume.

dissidents or derive from such texts and were incorporated into Lollard collections because the charges in the texts coincided with Lollard anti-mendicant interests.

Before proceeding further, I wish to clarify some terms. I will use "rigorist" to refer to that small group of people, Ubertino da Casale and others, who vociferously opposed themselves to the majority of the Franciscan order whom we call the Conventuals. I shall largely avoid using the term "Spiritual" because often it has been used casually to refer to persons such as William of Ockham who do not belong in this group.[3] By "dissenters" or "dissidents" I mean those Franciscans who were displeased with the papal rulings on Christ's poverty or those among all four mendicant orders who objected to the practice of licensing friars and acted in violation of the papal bulls. My primary focus, however, will be on Franciscan dissidents. My argument is that the existence of polemical texts containing the rigorist position allows that at one time there were rigorists in England like those in southern France and Italy, though it might be safer to say that there were Franciscan dissenters to whom the rigorist polemic was appealing.

English Mendicant Dissent

The evidence for English mendicant dissent is fragmentary but we can discern two major areas of focus not unlike those elsewhere: opposition to John XXII's rulings on the Franciscan position on the utter poverty of Christ and his disciples; and infringement of the papal bulls regarding mendicant preaching with the subsequent pursuit of those friars who preached but were neither authorized by their orders nor the local ordinaries. On the surface the English response to John's bulls on Christ's poverty seems largely politic. Decima Douie has published two defenses of Franciscan poverty written during or shortly after John's papacy in which the writers attempt to preserve the Franciscan understanding of poverty without using the condemned phrase that Christ did not have possession of anything either personally or in common.[4] However, some other bits of evidence suggest less tempered response. In the aftermath of the burning of the friars who refused obedience in 1318 and of John's rulings on poverty, there were four Cambridge friars who preached against the papal bulls, of whom John complained that one "burst forth into such madness as to have publicly preached certain damnable and wicked errors and

---

[3] I make this point because Workman includes Ockham among the Spirituals in his brief discussion of the relations between their positions and those of the Lollards: see Workman (*1308*, 2.98–101). William of Ockham was a Michaelist, and along with Michael of Cesena and others was opposed to the rigorists.

[4] Conyngton's and Chatton's in "Three Treatises on Evangelical Poverty by Fr. Richard Conyngton, Fr. Walter Chatton and an Anonymous from MS. V III 18 in Bishop Cosin's Library, Durham," *Archivum Franciscanum Historicum* 24 (1931): 341–69; 25 (1932): 36–58, 210–40. By contrast, Ockham reargued the Franciscan position to claim that John's views were heretical.

heresies."[5] The pope demanded they be brought to Avignon but to quash their dissent, he ordered the distribution of his own book against the heresies of Michael Cesena, the Franciscan Minister General who had fled with Ockham to Bavaria.

There was trouble again at mid-century. In 1354 two Fraticelli were burned at Avignon for heresy, an event that was sufficiently noteworthy that it was entered into a number of English chronicles.[6] Among other things, these two men taught the condemned theses on Christ's poverty and accused John XXII of having been a heretic.[7] D.A. Whitfield has published a MS fragment from Bedford that states the charges they admitted: that they did not believe that John could alter the rule, especially in the matter of poverty and possessions.[8] The existence of the fragment shows there was interest in the position in England. Richard FitzRalph's actions against the friars, by contrast, exhibit more obvious concern about the teaching of false doctrine. In the 1350s FitzRalph, Archbishop of Armagh, had used mendicants in his diocese but turned against the friars, especially the Franciscans in later years.[9] In 1356 he preached in London against the Franciscan theses on Christ's absolute poverty and other fraternal abuses. In 1357 in his *Defensio Curatorum* he attacked abuses within all four mendicant orders, but about halfway through the tract he turns to the Franciscans to blame them in particular for their disruptions and laxities. He puts most of the blame on the condemned Franciscan theses on Christ's poverty and the use of this doctrine to justify importunate begging. He says that not long before he had heard that a friar had preached a sermon on Christ's poverty in which the friar claimed that Christ and the apostles had no *dominium* or possession of things either personally or in common.[10] That phrase – *nihil in mundo habere proprium aut commune* – tips us off to the source of FitzRalph's concern and provides a rationale for his attack. This was the Franciscan doctrine condemned by John XXII.

Some dissent seems to have originated in objections to the restrictions upon mendicant preaching by *Super cathedram* (1300) and *Dudum* (1312;

---

[5] *Calendar of Entries in the Papal Registers Relating to Great Britain and Ireland: Papal Letters 1305–42*, ed. W.H. Bliss and J.A. Twemlow, 14 vols. (London: HMSO, 1893–1960), 2.492–93; and see further the items on 453, 485, 489, 497.

[6] E.g. Adam Murimuth, *Chronicon: continuatio (ad M.CCC.LXXX) a quodam anonymo*, ed. Thomas Hog (London: English Historical Society, 1846), 184; *Polychronicon Ranulphi Higden*, ed. Churchill Babington and Joseph Rawson Lumby, 9 vols. (London: Rolls Series, 1882), 8.357; Henry Knighton (*164*, 2.82–83); and Thomas Walsingham (*221*, 1.278).

[7] Knighton (*164*, 2.82–83).

[8] "A Bedford Fragment and the Burning of Two Fraticelli at Avignon in 1354," *Publications of the Bedfordshire Historical Record Society* 38 (1958, for 1957): 1–11.

[9] Katherine Walsh (*1254*, 349–451); and Lawrence M. Clopper (*398*, 58–63).

[10] "Loquor contra Fratres Minores diffusus super isto: quia ipsi Londoniis incoarunt negotium, occasionem aliis Ordinibus ministrantes. Et quia ipsi prae ceteris de perfectione Euangelica disputantes eam spontaneae mendicitati ascribunt in tantum, quod vnus de ipso Ordine praedicando in Festo omnium Sanctorum, vt mihi fuerat reportatum, descriptis quatuor gradibus paupertatis, quartum perfectionis maioris, imo summae perfectionis Euangelicae affirmabat: scilicet nihil in mundo habere proprium aut commune, sed mendicare cum Christo." *Defensio curatorum*, in Melchior Goldast, *Monarchia s. romani imperii* (Graz 1960; rpt. of Hanover: Conrad Bierman, 1614), 1402. This statement occurs at the point that FitzRalph says that he will turn to peculiarly Franciscan issues and abuses.

promulgated, 1317), but since the latter was enacted by John XXII, who also ruled against the theses on Christ's poverty, some dissenters may have associated both issues and thus created a rigorist-like platform without being directly indebted to Ubertino and others.[11] If FitzRalph's charge that Franciscans legitimize their begging by appeal to the condemned theses on Christ's poverty is not simply rhetorical extravagance, then it would appear that FitzRalph is making two claims: that some friars are still teaching the condemned theses and thus are heretics (and thus for our purposes, dissenters); and that the legitimacy of begging is justified on the basis of the condemned theses even if most Franciscans no longer explicitly teach those theses.

As for the regulation of preaching, there had been legislation within the Franciscan and Dominican orders regarding the examination and naming of preachers, but they were slow to insist on adherence to the earlier papal decrees on licensing. Not until 1316–after Vienne–did the Franciscans explicitly require members to obey the papal statute; and it was not until 1318 that the Dominicans entered a similar order into their constitutions.[12] However, not all members of the orders were so docile. In a writ, dated 2 October 1314, to the sheriff of Oxford, the king, acting on information from the archbishop of Canterbury, says that it is understood that certain apostates, who are Dominicans, defame their order by false suggestions and produce defamatory writings which they read and recite in public thereby defaming not only their own order but all orders. All persons aiding them are to be arrested.[13] From other extant royal writs we know that friars from all four mendicant orders engaged in unauthorized preaching activities some of which involved attacks on the laxities of their orders and other clergy.[14] The writs order the arrest of apostate friars who, abandoning their discipline, have become vagabonds and go about in secular habit, or their

---

[11] Although *Dudum* was one of the decrees from the Council of Vienne (1311–1312), Clement V wanted it debated in the schools before issuing it. He died in 1314 and the bull was not promulgated until 1317 when John XXII issued the constitutions under the title of the Clementines (see Jean Dunbabin, *A Hound of God: Pierre de Palud and the Fourteenth-Century Church* [Oxford: Clarendon, 1991], 58–59).

[12] Respectively, Constitutions of 1316, 282 (cap. 3.2; in Dr. Armandus Carlini, "Constitutiones generales ordinis fratrum minorum anno 1316 Assisii conditae," *Archivum Franciscanum Historicum* 4 [1911]: 269–302, 508–26); and *Acta capitulorum generalium ordinis Praedicatorum*, ed. Benedictus Maria Reichert, O.P., 2 vols., in *Monumenta ordinis fratrum Praedicatorum historica*, 3–4 (Rome, 1899), 4.107.

[13] PRO C.66.142/17: ". . . intelliximus quod quidam fratres de ordine predicatorum qui in ordine illo professi sunt spreta professione sua et [. .] religionis proiecto vagantur et discurrunt in balliam tuam in habitu seculari et quidam aliij portantes habitum supradictum set obedienciam deserentes extram domum ipsorum fratrem in v[. . .]moram faciunt. . . Et quia intelleximus quod predicti apostate . . . falsis suggestionibus diffamare scripturas diffamatorias ediderunt et eas in locis publicis . . . legi et recitari fecerunt vt sic eiusdem ordinem amplius diffamarent et derogacionem fidelium ab eodem ordine retraherent et adhuc de die in diem consimilia et pecora versus eiusdem ordinem facere non desistunt et quod plures hominess assistunt eisdem apostates in primissis eis prebendo auxilium et fauorem" (the brackets indicate illegible readings run off the margin). In the same year there is a writ to the mayor and sheriffs of London for the arrest of vagabond friars and the prohibition of their defamatory writings (*Calendar of the Patent Rolls 1313–17* [London: HMSO, 1898], 176).

[14] F. Donald Logan (*875*).

own habits, to the peril of their souls, the scandal of their orders, and the harm of honest ecclesiastics. Though apostates did not always abandon their habits, the adoption of secular habit–a detail frequently cited in the writs–suggests that they sometimes dressed themselves as members of the secular clergy so that they could preach with less risk of interference.[15] These friars are to be returned to their houses where they were to be disciplined.

At mid-century, therefore, about the same time that we find commissions for mendicant preaching in bishops' registers according to *Dudum*, we also find directives to the bishops' administrators that there are persons going about the countryside preaching and granting pardon without authority. Grandisson complained in 1358–59 that there were "quaestores," false hermits, "gyrovagi," and confessors going about his diocese seducing the people.[16] Because he uses the scriptural language recalling that of William of St. Amour and the text from one of FitzRalph's London sermons, it has been argued that he is complaining about unlicensed itinerant friars. Indeed, as Arnold Williams and Penn Szittya point out, Grandisson had been carrying on a running battle with unlicensed, itinerant friars since 1330.[17] But we should also note that Grandisson used mendicants for pastoral work; consequently, his appropriation of antimendicant language should not be read as a demonstration of antagonism to all friars but only to those who preach without his license. The latter are the ones who are "quaestores" and "gyrovagi." In 1354 bishops Grandisson and Trillek revoked the licenses for friars to hear confession in their dioceses, suggesting that they thought the trouble was widespread.[18] Grandisson complained there were persons going about *in habitu religiosi* of the mendicants of his diocese acting as plenipotentiaries without licenses (*Register*, 2.1128). In 1351 Grandisson (2.1108–09) appointed several rectors to inquire into and put an end to the "disciples of Antichrist" who live in the mode of "gyrovagi" in an illicit conventicle at Tounstale. He says they are religious who falsely call themselves Austin Friars and who hold services and hear confessions without episcopal permission. In 1367 Archbishop Simon Langham complained that several Franciscans and Dominicans asserted

[15] See the writ (in 1373) for the arrest of a Dominican who is now a vagabond in secular habit and calls himself Nicholas Corf that he may better deceive the innocent (*Calendar of the Patent Rolls: 1370-74*, 392).

[16] *The Register of John de Grandisson, Bishop of Exeter (1327–69)*, ed. F.C. Hingeston-Randolph, 3 vols. (London: Geo. Bell, 1894–99), 2.1197–98.

[17] Williams, "Relations between the Mendicant Friars and the Secular Clergy in England in the Later Fourteenth Century," *Annuale Mediaevalia* 1 (1960): 55–57; and Szittya (*1169*, 62–63). It also should be stressed that throughout the period Grandisson continued to license mendicants (*Register*, 1.557-58). His objections are not to the fraternal orders (see the bequests in his will, *Register*, 3.1517-19), but to those members who have no license from him or who exceed the limits of their license (see the grant to some Dominicans, February 1341-42, to hear confessions according to *Super cathedram* in which he spells out the limits of the license [2.954]).

[18] Grandisson, *Register*, 2.1134-35 (the new lists of confessors [2.1143-47] name only rectors and vicars); similarly, Bishop Trillek of Hereford, *Registrum Johannis de Trillek, Episcopi Herefordensis, A.D. 1344-1360*, ed. Joseph Henry Parry, Canterbury and York Society 8 (London, 1912), 232.

the canonical right to preach and hear confessions without the license of the rector or the archbishop.[19]

I think the writs and the episcopal complaints provide considerable contrast to the antifraternal tracts. In the latter there are accusations that bishops license friars who are incompetent or who come to recite fables and chronicles (the second point occurs in rigorist complaints as well); or there is the charge that friars are licensed but not by the local bishop. In contrast, the apostate friars are arrested at the urging of their own orders because they are not authorized by them. Some of these surely are those who go about in the habit of friars without the bishop's license, as Grandisson charged. Similarly, FitzRalph's complaint that the mendicants intrude themselves into the affairs of secular clerics by preaching without authorization is an assertion that there are friars from all four orders who do not observe the provisions of *Super cathedram* and *Dudum*, whereas the evidence otherwise suggests that the orders normally observed the restrictions.[20]

Since the mendicant orders had been lax about enforcing earlier rulings on preaching, some mendicants may have regarded *Super cathedram* and *Dudum* as novelties and continued their earlier practice because they believed their vow entailed preaching. But officials governing the orders now acted in accord with the bulls. Mendicant legislation divided the countryside into local areas (or limits) and provinces, established houses, and effectively settled the brothers in specific areas; as a consequence, mendicants were *not* to be itinerant unless they were licensed or sent on a mission, and, when they were itinerant, they were expected to carry letters or testimonials authorizing them.

The situation within the Franciscan order was complicated by the disputes between the rigorists and Conventuals over the practice of poverty, and between the papacy and its supporters and the Franciscans of all positions over the matter of Christ's poverty.[21] During the debates over poverty, which coincided with attempts to reach an acceptable compromise in the matter of papal privileges to preach, hear confession, and bury the dead, there was increased legislation within both the Franciscan and Dominican orders to control public debate and to apprehend and discipline

---

[19] *Registrum Simonis Langham, Cantuariensis Archiepiscopi (1366–68)*, ed. A.C. Wood, Canterbury and York Society 53 (Oxford, 1956), 148–49.

[20] Arnold Williams, "Relations," 22–95; and B.Z. Kedar, "Canon Law and Local Practice: The Case of Mendicant Preaching in Late Medieval England," *Bulletin of Medieval Canon Law* 2 (1972): 17–32.

[21] The bull *Cum inter nonnullos* (November 1323) ruled that the persistent claim that Christ and the apostles did not possess anything either privately or in common shall be deemed heretical and erroneous (Malcolm D. Lambert, *Franciscan Poverty: The Doctrine of the Absolute Poverty of Christ and the Apostles in the Franciscan Order, 1210–1323* [London: SPCK, 1961], 235–36); and see Clopper (*398*, 53–55). We should keep in mind that before their condemnation, the theses on Christ's poverty constituted the theoretical position held by all members of the Franciscan order whether from the left, right or middle. The argument between the rigorists and the Conventuals was about practice, not the theses concerning Christ's poverty per se. On the other hand, the espousal of the theses after their condemnation would mark one as a dissident, though not necessarily a rigorist in the strictest sense of the term.

apostate friars. In the Franciscan legislation of 1354 brothers are prohibited from conveying in words or writing anything that would assert scandal about anyone (106) or to sow seeds of discord among secular clergy, great princes and magnates (108).[22] Friars who blaspheme the pope or the apostolic constitutions are to be incarcerated (182);[23] brothers are strictly forbidden to make internal dissensions public (184).[24] According to papal ruling, apostates are excommunicated and can be chained and placed in prison (193). The last thirteen articles of this chapter, *De correctione delinquentium*, arts. 64–76, concern the apprehension and imprisonment of apostate friars.[25] It is clear that the order was prepared to act against those internal critics who publicized debate within the order or internal criticisms of it.

An apostate friar, therefore, is anyone who preaches without a license or who is itinerant without authorization.[26] Such a friar, who initially may have acted merely in defiance of the bulls, would soon find himself at odds with his order and might very quickly become critical of other practices of his order. It may be significant then that the writs seem to be particularly numerous in 1312–18, after *Dudum*, in the 1350s, when the bishops took action (but also perhaps as a consequence of the tightening of the Franciscan and Dominican legislation in these matters in 1354), and in the 1380s (the Statute against Itinerant Preachers was enacted in 1382).

The ME Translation of the Franciscan Rule and Testament

Scholars have expressed puzzlement why a Lollard should translate the *Rule* and *Testament* of St. Francis, but F.D. Matthew, its editor, ascribed the text and its commentary to Wyclif because he believed another tract assigned to Wyclif, "The Fifty Heresies and Errors of Friars," to be an

---

[22] Similarly, Dominican preachers are warned to be careful not to upset religious or clergy by their preaching but should try to correct them privately ("Les Constitutions des Frères Prêcheurs dans la redaction de s. Raymond de Peñafort [1241]," ed. Raymond Creytens, O.P., *Archivum Fratrum Praedicatorum* 18 [1948]: 5–68: Dist. II, cap. 12).

[23] The "apostolic constitutions" are the papal decrees on the *Rule* and Christ's poverty. The pope is John XXII. The injunction derives from the Constitutions of Lyons (1325) at the height of the crisis. Michael Cesena circulated a letter at the time requiring the same (see Moorman, *A History*, 318).

[24] Some of these concerns are evident in the Constitutions of Narbonne (1260), 5.12, 7.12–13 (64, 84–85), but become more specific, and the admonitions more vehement, as the conflict between the rigorists and Conventuals intensifies. P. Michael Bihl, "Statuta generalia ordinis edita in capitulis generalibus celebratis Narbonae an. 1260, Assisii an. 1279 atque Parisiis an. 1292," *Archivum Franciscanum Historicum* 34 (1941): 13–94, 284–337.

[25] These concerns are also expressed in general terms in the Constitutions of Narbonne 7.17–19 (85), but again the legislation becomes lengthier and more vehement – and more defensive – in later redactions of the constitutions.

[26] Essentially the definition provided by the Franciscan Constitutions of Lyons (1325), 7.3 (appendix to Assisi 1316; and see Assisi 1316, 534). Dominican legislation, as far as I have determined, does not define "apostate" so specifically; nevertheless, there are numerous *acta* that restrict brothers. The 1354 constitutions have a number of reform orders (*Acta* 4.358–59) including one that forbids the assumption of the habit of a clerk (360).

amplification of the commentary at the end of the translation.[27] Matthew acknowledged that the translation is longer than the commentary but remained unperturbed; the translation, he said, was made so that readers would know "just how completely that rule was disregarded or evaded" (39). What he does not tell us is that the translation is accompanied by a copy of the *Rule* and *Testament* in Latin; moreover, the ME text is a faithful, literal translation of the Latin, not a paraphrase. The English and Latin *Rules* take up three times the space that the commentary does (roughly 21 sides vs. 7). We must wonder why someone who was simply opposed to mendicants would expend the effort to copy the *Rule* and *Testament* in two languages. The effort suggests to me that the writer may have had a vested interest in the *Rule* and *Testament*.

If we look at the text as it is preserved in the Lollard compilation Bodl. 647, the earliest copy, we might come to the conclusion that the text was appropriated from another source.[28] The English translation and commentary and the Latin text are contained within a single quire and fill folios 71 through part of 83 of the compilation. The remaining folios in the quire, 83 and all of 83v, 84 and 85, were originally left blank.[29] Moreover, the text does not start on the first folio of the quire (70) but the second (71). The first folio acts as a cover for the text. We know that the Lollards used the booklet system for compiling and transmitting texts, but if that were the original purpose of this quire, they would not have wasted the first folio.[30] The physical make-up of the quire, and the fact that much of it was left blank at the end, suggests to me that the quire was a personal copy of the *Rule* and *Testament* in English and Latin with an English commentary.

The English commentary contains many of the antimendicant accusations that we find in works ascribed to the Lollards. The *Rule* forbids them to receive property but they do; they live in rich dwellings; they take money in many ways; they are called masters of divinity; they preach for their profit; they come telling tales rather than preaching the gospel; they do not work but live in idleness. But there are also a number of differences. First, the practices to which the commenter objects are to be found among those charged by external critics and internal reformers alike. Bonaventure's first letter to the community as the General Minister of the order contains many

---

[27] *A Manual of the Writings in Middle English 1050–1500* (*33*, 2.63); and F.D. Matthew (*182*, 39). "Fifty Heresies" is in Arnold (*100*, 3.366–401). Wyclif is no longer thought to be the writer of any of the English tracts (Anne Hudson [*705*, 249]).

[28] My remarks are based on Bodl. 647 (Matthew used Corpus Christi College Cambridge 296 collated with Trinity College Dublin 244 and Bodl.). The assumption has been that since the compilation, Bodley 647, and those related to it contain texts that are evidently Lollard, then the compilation was made by Lollards, and that all the texts were authored by Lollards, but the latter conclusion does not necessarily follow from the first two premises: the Lollard compilers may have collected texts of interest to them but authored by persons who were not Lollards.

[29] Subsequently, two scribes entered other material into the quire, but their scripts differ from that of the main scribe.

[30] Ralph Hanna (*66*, 21–59); and Anne Hudson (*691* and *713*, 200–05).

of the same charges.[31] Secondly, it is not critical of the four orders but only the Franciscans. Although Wycliffite tracts and other external critiques usually focus on the Franciscan form of mendicancy, they then deploy their arguments against all four orders. The English commentator does not. He attacks many of the practices of the order–desire for riches, books, excessive houses, and the like–that are in internal critiques, but he does not concern himself with cure of souls or right of sepulture. He does not focus on clamorous begging, and, except for the reference to Iscariot, seems little interested in *bursarii* and the use of *custodes* and friends. He does not use the terminology of William of St. Amour, nor, particularly, that with which we associate Wyclif and his followers. The single focus, indeed the frame of his argument, is that the *Testament* and *Rule* are one, and that these are the words of God as given to Francis and as written in the gospel. The frame of the argument is important because the writer understands that it was only by setting aside the *Testament* that the *Rule* could be glossed as it had been. The accusatory tone in the ME commentary points to the polemical voice of someone like Ubertino da Casale, who represented the rigorists against the Conventuals before Pope Clement V.

I do not claim that the ME commentary derives from Ubertino's statements in his dispute with the community before Pope Clement; nevertheless, the two have a similar framework and Ubertino is representative of the rigorist position.[32] The foundation for Ubertino's condemnation of the community is that their desire for papal privileges and papal clarifications of the *Rule* undermine the "altissima paupertas" that Francis intended when he wrote the *Rule* and *Testament*. Ubertino's "Responsio" and "Religio viri" are then filled with a catalogue of abuses of the *Rule*. The abuses that Ubertino cites are ones that the order had struggled with in the past, as is evidenced in commentaries on the *Rule*, papal legislation, and legislation within the order itself – as well as in external critiques of mendicant practice. Although there are some criticisms that may be peculiarly rigorist, most are not. What makes Ubertino's position rigorist is the framework: the charge that setting aside the *Testament* and glossing the *Rule*, which is specifically disallowed by Francis in the *Testament*, are responsible for the debilitation of the order.

[31] Epistle 1, *Epistolae officiales*, in *Opera omnia*, ed. College of St. Bonaventure, 10 vols. (Quaracchi, 1882–1902), 8:468–69; Michael Cesena sent a similar letter with his reformed constitutions, Assisi 1316 (270). I give a succinct discussion of the internal debates in '"*Songes of Rechelesnesse*,"' (*398*, 39–55).

[32] Ubertino's *Rotulus* is not extant in its entirety; however, there are two versions that survive: the one quoted by the community in their "Religiosi viri" and the version edited by Franz Ehrle (*Archiv für Literatur- und Kirchengeschichte des Mittelalters*, 3 (1887): 93–130) in which the responses of the community are inserted into Ubertino's text. Citations from the former are noted as "Relig. Viri"; those from the latter as *Rotulus*. The *Rotulus* gives a more devastating account of the failures of the order than does Ubertino's earlier *Responsio* to questions posed by Clement V (text in Ehrle, 3:51–89). For discussion of Ubertino, see Decima Douie, *The Nature and Effect of the Heresy of the Fraticelli* (Manchester: Manchester Univ. Press, 1932), 120–52, and Charles T. Davis, "Le pape Jean XXII et les spirituals: Ubertin de Casale," in *Franciscans d'Oc: Les Spirituels ca. 1280–1324*, ed. Edouard Privat, Cahiers de Fanjeaux, no. 10 (Toulouse: Centre d'Études historiques de Fanjeaux, 1975), 263–83.

In this respect the ME commentary on the *Rule* and *Testament* is much like Ubertino's.

The ME commentary is framed as a complaint of a rigorist or dissenting friar against the laxities of the order; he is so opposed to the Johannine rulings that he has allied himself with those persecuted by the pope and the order itself. The comment opens with the statement that the minors, by which he means the majority whom we call Conventuals, say that the pope has discharged them from the *Testament*, but this cannot be, he continues, because Francis said that God showed him this way of life and not any other man: "And after þat þe lord hadde ȝouen to me of freris no man schewid to me what I schulde do, but he þat is hiȝest shewid to me þat I schulde lyue after þe forme of þe gospel: & I in fewe wordis & sympliche maade to write it, & þe lord pope confermyd it to me" (46). Also Francis says that the *Testament* is not another rule but the same rule as the first, which may account for the fact the ME translator numbers the *Testament* as chapter 13 of the *Rule*. These are the rigorist positions, as can be seen from the opening of the *Speculum perfectionis*, Ubertino's briefs and other texts.[33] The commentator charges that the friars do more according to the false commandment of a "synful idiot," and in this case, a "dampnyd deuyl," than after the commandment of almighty God. The context suggests he is talking about the papal rulings and their effect (48–49).

Space does not permit a detailed analysis of the charges in the text, but in any event, they are mostly commonplace. There are some, however, that suggest the rigorist position. After listing a number of abuses of appropriation and of rich living, the commenter says that "o strong beggere or flaterere haþ a chaumber for a lord, erl or duk wiþ many preciouse iuellis, & anoþer frere haþ nakid sidis & many other myscheues þouȝ he be worþ siche a þousand bifore god." Note the construction – "o" has such while "anoþer frere" has nothing – which suggests that the "o" is a friar, not just some poor, disabled person. Ubertino had charged that, in violation of chapter 4, ministers and custodians did not take care of the infirm and the abjectly poor brothers ("Relig. Viri," art. 11 [61–62]); that ill and dying brothers – simple brothers – are not cared for as required (art. 17 [73–74]). And he went on to argue that much is taken away from the infirm in order to build edifices and to lavish alms on food and drink for brothers higher in the order (see also art. 15 [69–70]).[34]

Towards the end of the ME commentary, the writer says that at Rome "frere menours bi false name pursuen trewe pore freris to deþ" because they would keep Francis's *Rule* to the letter (and therefore without the papal glosses). Again echoing the rigorists, he concludes: "Also, ȝif fraunseis take

---

[33] *Speculum*, ed. Paul Sabatier (Paris: Librairie Fischbacher, 1989); see the Prologue where a voice from heaven tells Francis, "Francis, nothing in this *Rule* is yours; for all is Mine. I wish the *Rule* to be obeyed to the letter, to the letter, without a gloss, without a gloss" (trans. in *St. Francis of Assisi: Writings and Early Biographies*, ed. Marion A. Habig, 4th rev. ed. [Chicago: Franciscan Herald Press, 1983], 1125–26). The admonition recalls Francis's words at the end of the *Testament* that the *Rule* not be glossed. And see Ubertino, "Responsio," 52 et passim.

[34] The Constitutions of Lyon (1325) 4.5 (see "Assisi 1316," 530) seem to respond to Ubertino when they require brothers to care for infirm and indigent brothers.

only þe gospel and no þing addiþ of his owne þer-to [which is what the rigorists claimed], it schulde not be clepid frau*n*seis reule but reule of c*r*ist or of þe gospel" (51). He goes on to say: and if Francis only used what he found in the Gospel, why should he make thereof a new order, a statement that might sound as if the writer was objecting to the Franciscan order as a new order, a position that we associate with Lollard antimendicancy. However, it is clear that the writer understands the "new order" to be the one legislated by the popes when they glossed the *Rule* and denied the *Testament*, for, he says, "þe pope haþ no power to dispense aȝenst frau*n*seis testament & his reule, siþ þei ben al on" (51). The rigorists insisted that the *Rule* was the rule of Christ and the gospels because that was what Francis had said it was.[35] In his summation, Ubertino said that reformation was sought by those who wished to adhere to the intention of St. Francis who rejected all glosses and privileges [*repulit omnem glosam et omne privilegium*] ("Responsio," 87). The rule comes from Christ and cannot be amended; the brothers took a vow to observe the rule, not saying "secundum declaracionem," but simply to the *Rule* of the Friars Minor confirmed by Lord Honorius (the cardinal protector of the order who had overseen the writing of the *Rule of 1223*).

I think this text was collected by the Lollard compilers because it echoed their antagonism towards the friars. However, we should see that the meaning was shifted when the text passed to the Lollard compilers from the hands of the rigorist author or the dissenter who appropriated the rigorist position. The rigorist objects to the practice of the Conventuals for the purpose of recalling them to their rule or for justifying why he continues to live "afte*r* þe forme of þe gospel," as laid down by Francis. The Lollard collectors of the tract may have read it as a condemnation of all friars.

The Matter of the "Pore Prestis"

In his classic 1899 essay, "The Poor Priests: A Study in the Rise of English Lollardy," H.L. Cannon made two principal claims that shall be of concern here: that Wyclif was responsible for sending out poor preachers, some as early as 1376 or 1377; and that their activities and manner can be delineated because Wycliffite tracts contain a kind of sect vocabulary that identifies them.[36] In the Latin texts, he said, Wyclif's followers were called "sacerdotes simplices" or "sacerdotes fideles" and "viri evagelici" or "viri apostolici" and in the English ones "pore prestis" (463–64).[37] "Pore prestis"

---

[35] Angelo Clareno, *Expositio regulae fratrum minorum*, 15, 33, argued that the *Rule* is inviolate because it is a summary of the counsels in the gospels (ed. P. Livarius Oliger, O.F.M. [Quaracchi: College of St. Bonaventure, 1912]). Bonagratia of Bergamo asserted that both Olivi and Ubertino had maintained that the *Rule* was the same as the gospel and that to vow the former was to vow the latter (Charles T. Davis, "Ubertino da Casale and his Conception of 'altissima paupertas,'" *Studi Medievali*, ser. 3 22 [1981]: 1–56; see 5).

[36] H.L. Cannon (*366*).

[37] Cannon does not refer to "trewe prestis" in this analysis, though the term was also thought to refer to the "pore prestis."

by definition and assumption were persons sent out by or influenced by Wyclif, persons who adopted an itinerant life in order to evangelize. Astonishingly, later in his essay Cannon acknowledged that the tract "Why Poor Priests Should Have no Benefice" indicated that not all "pore prestis" were itinerant (468–70).[38] He did not appear to realize that this concession wreaked havoc with his thesis: that "pore prestis" always referred in Lollard texts to Wycliffite itinerant preachers who are unauthorized by the establishment.

We shall not be concerned with most of the other details of Cannon's analysis though I should like to note that even though he acknowledged that Wyclif was at times indifferent to, or at other times attacked special garments, Cannon argued that the "pore prestis" went barefoot and dressed in a recognizable garment of russet wool; consequently, references to preachers in russet were subsequently assumed to be Wycliffites.[39]

Some scholars questioned Cannon's conclusions, but the subsequent discussion centered on whether Wyclif himself sent out poor priests, not whether the term "pore prestis" referred to Lollard itinerant preachers.[40] Similarly, when Anne Hudson addressed the matter in *Premature Reformation*, she did not focus on whether the terms denote Lollard preachers but whether these references provided evidence for a connection between Wyclif and the Lollards (62–63). She argued that early skepticism about Cannon's conclusions was reversed by the work of Michael Wilks: "The tide has fully turned in the writings of Michael Wilks, who has reinstated much of Cannon's evidence, though he has moved the emphasis away from the insignificance implied in the term 'poor preachers' to the aristocratic world of the Lollard gentry" (63). In an early article, indeed, Wilks had said of Cannon: "Although outdated in some respects, the best survey of the material [on Poor Priests] is still H.L. Cannon."[41] In her essay on sect vocabulary Hudson appeared to accept the commonplace that "pore prest" and related vocabulary often specified Wycliffite preachers. She pointed out that Knighton had asserted the Lollards used a sect vocabulary that included phrases such as "Trewe Prechoures" to refer to those who propound Wycliffite doctrine and "False Prechours" to refer to those who controvert these teachings or who preach orthodox beliefs rejected by the Lollards.[42] Although she later acknowledged that phrases such as "pore prest" are "lexically commonplace, occurring frequently in neutral contexts," she argued that the usage is often particularized. Her examples on this point are: "and herfore þei pursuen wiþoute merci pore prestis þat in lyuyng and word techen þe pouert of pore Crist and hise apostlis to be kept

---

[38] The tract is in Matthew (*182*, 244–53).

[39] H.L. Cannon (*366*, 472–73).

[40] K.B. McFarlane (*933*, 100–01); May McKisack (*942*, 519–20); Margaret Aston (*271*, 49–50); Gordon Leff (*836*, 2.524 n.5); and M.D. Lambert (*821*, 241). W.R. Thomson expressed doubt at times that the language we will examine necessarily refers to itinerant priests sent out by Wyclif; see *The Latin Writings of John Wyclyf* (*39*, 281, but also 93).

[41] "Predestination, Property, and Power" (*1285*, 220–36). It remains unclear to me how an investigation using inaccurate data can come to an accurate, historical picture.

[42] "A Lollard Sect Vocabulary?" (*698*, 165–66).

in al þe staat of þe clergie"; and, if a "trewe prest or pore man spekiþ openly aȝenst þis cursed marchaundise, he shal be sumoned, suspendid fro prechyng and trueþe-seyng, or cursed, prisoned, or exilid."[43] She said such terms as "trewe prest" have a "strongly approbatory sense" and that the persecution described is that which the Lollards were suffering. She concluded that the terms are often "obliquely self-naming," a point with which I would agree in general but the question remains of who is being named.[44]

Cannon's admission that "pore prestis" does not always refer to itinerant Wycliffite preachers and Hudson's more cautious remarks require the examination of each usage in its context. And we must begin with an empty slate; we must not assume that these texts are written by Wyclif or a Lollard lest we prejudice our examination of the evidence. In many cases it is impossible to determine whether a given writer is referring to an itinerant preacher, a parish priest who lives modestly (like Chaucer's Parson), or some other kind of cleric. In other cases, however, the context is sufficiently detailed that one can identify the kind of cleric the author seems to be talking about. My argument is that "pore prestis" and related terms do not constitute a Lollard sect vocabulary but are part of a larger reformist vocabulary and that this language has content – more specific or less so – depending upon the user and his purposes. Although many of these tracts are too unspecific to allow identification of the status or position of the author, we should approach each tract with the assumption that its author could be a Lollard, as we have traditionally understood such a person, or a reformist secular cleric who wishes to reform the hierarchy of secular clerics but who is little interested in the mendicant question, or a reformist secular cleric who sees the mendicants as a major disrupter of or impediment to the reform of the secular clergy, or a reformist or dissident friar, or a rigorist Franciscan friar, or some other type I have not thought of.

My immediate interest is to distinguish the reformist agendas of secular clerics and canons from those of the Franciscans on the matter of itinerancy. In some of the Latin treatises – and here I am unconcerned with author-position – "viri evangelici" are distinguished from "sacerdotes simplices" on the ground that the former are – and ought to be – itinerant whereas the latter are settled.[45] The foundation for this distinction, which is

---

[43] 170–71. The first passage is cited from BL Egerton 2820, f. 47, an ampler version of "Of Clerks Possessioners" (see Matthew *182*, 114–40); the second from "The Grete Setence of Curs Expouned" (Arnold, *100*, 3.332/1).

[44] Matti Peikola has done a systematic search and analysis of "trewe men" and words related to it, including "pore prestis," "trewe prestis," and others. Impressive as Peikola's analysis is, he presupposes that most of the texts identified in the nineteenth century as Lollard are Lollard whereas my discussion questions whether the three texts under review are Lollard or whether they appropriate large patches of Franciscan reformist rhetoric. In either case, the presupposition that these three texts are Lollard would prejudice any examination that there is a larger arena of reformist rhetoric prior to the Lollards that used such terminology. See Peikola (*1031*).

[45] Neither Wyclif nor the Lollards invented the term "sacerdos simplex." It is used, for example, in canon law to distinguish the lower clergy from the "sacerdos" or bishop (*Decretum*, Gregory IX, Lib. III, tit. XI, c. ix; *Corpus iuris canonici*, ed. Emil Friedberg, 2 vols. [Leipzig: Bernhard

preserved in canon law, is the description of the early church in the book of Acts: the apostles were to go from church to church to preach on matters of the faith, especially to clarify doctrinal issues, while the priests and deacons were to remain stable in order to see to the more ordinary spiritual and material needs of the faithful. This simple model is a reformist ideal for a range of people concerned with the proliferation of offices within the church. In itself, it has no interest in monks or mendicants and questions of their relation to the hierarchy. The most basic reformist agenda of a secular cleric or a canon might simply be to return the secular clergy to the church of Acts (as the Canons Regular believed themselves to be doing, for example). Of course, some secular clerics and canons may have felt that monks and mendicants were an impediment to reform because both monks and mendicants claimed to be heirs of the apostles just as did bishops in the secular ecclesiastical hierarchy.[46] But my point is that a secular reformist ideology need not move beyond the desire to simplify the secular ecclesiastical hierarchy, to return it to an apostolic model. I might add that Langland endorses this reform – though from different motives – when he says that bishops are obligated to walk through their provinces while parish clergy are expected to remain in their parishes.[47]

The mendicant orders – specifically the Franciscans and Dominicans – claimed that they renewed the apostolic orders by their itinerancy and preaching. It is difficult for us, perhaps, to imagine the shock that the notion of itinerancy caused. In monastic culture itinerant monks constituted the two bad categories of monks: the gyrovagues and sarabites (*Rule of St. Benedict*, chapter 1). Itinerancy, however, was fundamental to the work and life that Francis and Dominic envisaged for their brothers. For Dominic itinerancy was necessary because the brothers had to move from place to place to preach so that they might rescue those fallen into heresy or those neglected by institutional structures. Since Francis did not establish his order specifically as a preaching order – indeed, the first brothers were mostly laymen and not authorized to preach – he tended to make itinerancy visual in order to spiritualize it: it was to remind people that everyone was without a permanent home in this world; it was to remind people that

---

Tauchnitz, 1879–81], 2.635). Wyclif often uses the term in this sense when he refers to curates or the lesser clergy. See *Responses to 44 Conclusions* where "sacerdotes simplices et fideles" are to be given cures in parishes and *De daemonio meridiano* where "sacerdotes fideles" are said to be deprived of clerical office and hence must have held parish charges (*Op. Min.*, 201; *Pol. Wks.*, 2.424–25). English texts make the same point: see Matthew (*182*, 79, 236–37). Wyclif also uses the terms in those discussions when he talks about the descendants of the apostles and the seventy-two (*Sermones*, 2.234, 3.373–74). The English sermon 58 (Arnold *100*, 1.175) distinguishes "lesse prestis," the parochial clergy, from "grete apostlis," who figure the apostles. "Viri evangelici" and "viri apostolici" are fairly common in Wyclif's works; the usages distinguish apostolic men – who are often described as being itinerant – from "sacerdotes simplices." See, for example, *Sermones*, 1.179, 281, 289; 2.204, 205, 229–31, and 282 (ed. Johann Loserth, 4 vols. [London: Wyclif Society, 1887–90]).

[46] M.-H. Vicaire, *L'Imitation des apostres: moines, chanoines et mendiants, IVe–XIIIe siècles*, Tradition et spiritualité, vol. 2 (Paris: Éditions du Cerf, 1963).

[47] B.15.570–76 and C.17.283–86 (bishops); and B.11.283–95 and C.13.100–07 et passim (parish clergy). The editions cited are George Kane and E. Talbot Donaldson's B-text (*168*) and George Russell and George Kane's C-text (*171*).

Christ had no place to rest his head.[48] As the Franciscan order developed and as more and more brothers were or became priests, itinerancy became the practical necessity that it was in the Dominican order. But institutionalization of the mendicant orders had its price: not all friars were literally to be itinerant, only those authorized by their ministers and by the local ordinary. This was the compromise worked out among the papacy, the bishops and the mendicants in *Super cathedram* and *Dudum*. As a consequence of this agreement, someone who joined the order of Francis might be told that he must remain in his friary. The only itinerancy permitted him would be *non pedibus*, a spiritual itinerancy but not of the kind practiced by Francis.

The texts that we have assigned to the Lollards and Wyclif are filled with references to the pursuit of "pore prestis." In many cases who these "pore" or "trewe prestis" are is not made clear, but in some they are specified as those who would be faithful to Francis. Thus, some "pore prestis" are Franciscan apostates as that term was used in the order's legislation, or dissidents who have become itinerant because that was the calling to which they believed themselves to have been called. It is possible that some of these references indicate Lollard sympathy for dissident friars because "lollers" suffered the same kind of persecution, but we must also allow that such sympathy may indicate influence of the Franciscans on the Lollards and that some of these tracts may not be Lollard at all but the writings of dissident friars. I have suggested that the Middle English translation of the *Rule* and *Testament* is the work of a dissenting friar, but there are other texts that represent this position as well.

"Of the Leaven of Pharisees," and perhaps more obviously, "Fifty Heresies and Errors of the Friars," attacks the laxity of the friars who no longer hold to their rule but the one "founden of synful men."[49] Scholars have read the "Fifty Heresies" as an attack by the secular clergy, specifically the Lollards, on the mendicant orders not just because of the charges made in the tract but because they misunderstand the first sentence: "FIRST, freris seyn þat hor religioun, founden of synful men, is more perfite þen þat religion or ordir þo whiche Crist hymself made." It has been assumed, I believe, that the "religioun, founden of synful men" is the rule of a mendicant order, specifically the Franciscan order, and that the "sinful man," therefore, is Francis. But this is not the logic of the text; indeed, at the end of the first paragraph and the beginning of the second the "synful men" are identified as the pope and others. The friars claim that this "newe religion of freris," if they keep it, makes them better than Christ's apostles; those who do not keep it are apostates. Since the "ordir of Crist" is most perfect, our writer claims, those who leave it are apostates; thus, the friars who follow their "newe religion," "founden of synful men," are apostates.

---

[48] Although Innocent III had tonsured the lay brothers in the Fransciscan order and allowed them to testify, the Constitutions of Narbonne (1260) and subsequent legislation allowed only the learned to preach: Narbonne 6.9–11 (71); for licensing of confessors see 6.3 (70). Ubertino argued that all brothers were to preach and did not need to be licensed ("Rotulus," 122).

[49] "Fifty Heresies," in Arnold (*100*, 3.367).

The use of the term "apostate" and the argument about apostasy is crucial, I believe, in locating the subject position of the writer; it identifies him as a friar, not a Lollard.[50]

Within the dissident and possibly rigorist circles for whom this tract may have been written, it would be clear that the "newe religion" is not the *Rule* and *Testament* of St. Francis since those texts were not created by Francis but were given to him by God; they are the "religioun of Crist." The "newe religion" is the rule as it had been interpreted by the papacy and legislated by the order. Those who do not submit to this "newe religion" are declared apostates whereas the writer complains that those who follow this accommodated rule are the apostates.

Although the opening chapter might be – and has been – misread, the second chapter cannot be, for it is quite explicit:

> Also freris seyn prively þat hit is apostasie and heresie for a prest to lyve as Crist ordeyned a prest to lyve, *by forme of þo gospel*. Ffor if þer be any frere þat is a prest, cunnynge in Gods lawe, and able to travel to sowe Gods wordis amonge þo puple, if he do þis offis frely, goynge from cuntre to cuntre where he may most profite, and ceesse not for prioure ne any oþir satrap, and *charge not singuler habite*, and begge not, but be payed with comyne mete and drinke, as Crist and his apostils were, þei wil poursue hym as apostata, and drawe hym to prisoun, and sey þat he is cursed for þis dede. Ffor þis fre goynge aboute and fre prechinge is leeveful to suche a frere, sith hit is ensaumplid and comaundid of Crist, and not to be cloosid in a cloyster, as hit were Caymes Castel. (3.368; emphases added)[51]

The writer's point is that once a person is made a priest, he is charged with preaching, but the friars say, he argues, that their members may not preach freely and generally the gospel of Christ without a license. The friars pursue "treue prestis, and letten hom to preche þo gospel" (3.375); sometimes they pursue "trewe prechoures, for þei wil not glose myghty men, and counfort hom in hor synnes, but wil scharply telle hom þo sothe" (3.377); and they "pursue trew men to þo deth, for þei techen þo comaundementis of God, and crien to þo puple þo foule synnes of fals freris" (3.384). The implication of the last sentence is that friars who are false pursue those who are true and who publicly denounce the failings of false friars.

Similarly, "Of the Leaven of Pharisees" says that false friars "beren on pore prestis þat techen þe trewþe of þe gospel and þe goodenesse of cristis ordynaunce . . . þei pursuen to þe deþ pore freris serabitis, þat kepen fraunseis reule and testament to þe riȝte vndyrstondynge and wille of fraunceis wiþ outen glose of antecristis clerkis; þei beren false wyttenesse

---

[50] Fiona Somerset has suggested to me that the argument makes sense as a Lollard one. I think it could come to be read that way, which may account for why the compilers of the codex collected the text.

[51] The notion of the friars as descendants of Cain appears not to have originated with Wyclif or the Lollards. Prior to his departure from Oxford in 1367, Uthred of Boldon charged that false friars were *caymitis* because they "murder" fraternity (Szittya *1169*, 110–11). Bradwardine called those who said restitution is necessary for absolution *cainistae* (Bloomfield, *Fourteenth-Century Apocalypse*, 131, 219 n.20).

aȝeyns here patron and ben caynis breþren þat killyd his broþer for his goode lyuynge" (11–12). Normally, we understand "sarabites" to be a pejorative term, but "Leaven" uses the term "serabitis" in a positive sense. "Freris serabitis" are those who wander about to teach a simple understanding of God's law and of Christ's poverty. They imitate the life of Christ and the apostles as it is described in Francis' *Rule* and *Testament*.[52]

Since the mendicant orders defended the practice of begging, it might seem that the sections on begging in "Fifty Heresies" argue against my postulation that the tract represents something like the rigorist position; however, the appropriateness and manner of begging was debated within the Franciscan order in part because the *Rule of 1223* contains some obscurities about these matters.[53] The *Rule*, chapter 5, says that those who have a trade should continue to practice it – an admonition that would not only seem to sanction labor but to encourage it. Similarly, in the *Testament* Francis says that he labored and wishes that the brothers do as well. However, in chapter 6 of the *Rule*, the chapter in which Francis says the brothers are to appropriate nothing, Francis encourages the brothers to go out to beg with confidence; indeed, in a number of stories Francis suggests that begging is desirable, among other things, because it is humiliating (chapter 6 of the *Rule* says that there is no reason the brothers should be ashamed to beg because God made himself poor in this world). The irresolution in the matter of laboring and begging can be seen in rigorist writings as well. Ubertino da Casale, like the later Lollards, offers Peter and Paul as examples of those who labor for their needs as opposed to depending on others; nevertheless, Ubertino does not take the position that friars are never to beg.[54] Instead, he complains that they beg too importunately or that they *seek* or *quest for* rather than *receive* alms.[55] Begging can be seen as a charitable and virtuous act, but it also is a spiritually endangering activity, especially if one seeks more than one needs or if one takes what may more appropriately belong to someone who is in greater need. My point is that there is not a simple divorcement between friars who make the argument for begging and Lollards who deny it; there is not a simple division between those who promote begging over labor and those who require that people labor for their needs.

With these guidelines in mind, let us look at the passages on begging in

---

[52] See Angelo Clareno's rule commentary where he cites John Cassian's favorable view of the original Sarabites who, like the Franciscans, were without solicitude for the morrow (*Expositio regulae fratrum minorum*, ed. P. Livarius Oliger, O.F.M. [Quaracchi: College of St. Bonaventure, 1912], 160–61).

[53] I have discussed Franciscan reformist attacks on inappropriate and improper begging in *"Songes of Rechelesnesse": Langland and the Franciscans* (398, 59–60, 82–85, 96, 202–08). The rigorist Ubertino da Casale was as appalled by clamorous begging as were, among others, Peter John Olivi, Bonaventure, and John Pecham.

[54] Ubertino in his *Rotulus* had argued that labor is a precept. P. Anicetus Chiappini, "Communitatis Responsio 'Religiosi Viri' ad Rotulum Fr. Ubertini de Casali," *Archivum Franciscanum Historicum* 8 (1915): 62–3 (art. 12). Ubertino's charges are embedded in the community's response to them. See also the *Rotulus*, ed. Franz Ehrle, *Archiv für Litteratur-und Kirchengeschichte des Mittelalters* 3 (1887), 109–10.

[55] "Communitatis Responsio," 59; "Rotulus," 114–15.

"Fifty Heresies". The discussion in chapter 5 (370–72) might seem the argument typical of the Lollards or of secular clerics opposed to the friars. The writer begins with the flat-out claim that friars say that begging is "leveful" even though it is damned by God in both the Old and New Testaments. The statement seems unequivocal and absolute.[56] He continues by citing the passage from Prov. 30.8 in which Solomon asks to be given neither poverty nor riches. This passage is cited routinely by the opponents of the mendicants; indeed, it is often the first biblical passage cited.[57] But it is usually taken simply to mean that clerics should seek a medial position between the two extremes whereas the writer of this text continues with the verse: "bot gif onelich þinges þat ben nedeful for my lyvelode in avauntre, lest I, fulfilled, be drawen to renaye, and sey, Who is Lord? As who sey, I know no Lord; and lest I be compellid or made of force by nedynesse to stele, and to forswere þo name of my God." The latter part of the verse is crucial here since it reduces the state which the speaker desires to necessities, a position in keeping with all mendicant thinking; it does not suggest a medial position. The passage is followed by a recitation of the Apostolic Counsels, which provide the foundation of Francis's *Rule* and life. The writer then argues that Paul and Peter labored with their hands. Although this statement might seem to be in opposition to the practice of living off the provision of others as allowed by the Apostolic Counsels, we should note the way the statement about labor is entered into the argument. The writer has just given the Apostolic Counsel which enjoins those who preach to eat and drink whatever is given by those who hear them. "*Also*," he says, Peter and Paul labored (my emphasis). Laboring is not required, but is an activity in which an apostolic man engages when he is not provisioned otherwise. The chapter concludes with a long list of saints who admonish men to labor. Some of these saints one might expect to see in a Lollard tract, but I am skeptical about some of the others. The writer appeals to "Seynt" Clement, Augustine, Benedict, Bernard, Francis and Jerome. Perhaps more important, he says that "Seynt Clement" ordained that men should not beg "opunly." And at the end when he denies that Christ was a beggar, he says that such a claim is an error because Christ did not engage in "open beggynge." The issue here, it seems to me, is not whether one is allowed to beg or whether Christ was a "beggar" but how one receives alms. Surely Christ would not have clamorously cried out for alms, but just as surely there are instances in the scriptures when Christ is shown to receive his daily necessities from those who listen to his words.

Later in the tract the writer condemns mendicant begging on the grounds that it deprives the legitimate poor. Chapter 6 focuses primarily on the moral dilemma that arises from receiving alms when there might be others who are in great need. The writer rejects the friars' argument that alms

---

[56] The analysis in this passage about the legitimacy of begging is much like that in *Piers Plowman* in the Hunger and Pardon scenes. In both cases an apparently unequivocal statement damning begging is followed by a series of qualifications that distinquish unacceptable from acceptable begging.

[57] Clopper (*398*, 59).

should be given to them rather than to crooked, blind and bedridden men. But if we read this within the larger concerns of the tract, it seems to me that he is not just arguing that friars should not take alms, but that they take more than they need and thereby deprive the legitimate poor. This point is made more explicit in chapter twenty-one when the writer complains that "freris beggen wiþouten need for hor owne riche secte . . . And herfore charite is outelawed amonge hom, and so is God . . . For þei desseyven men in hor almes, to make costily houses, not to herberow pore men" (383). This point is much like the one that Ubertino made: the friars were called to poverty and a life of neediness, yet they go about questing alms in order to build great houses and in the meantime do not concern themselves with the needs of those who are poor.

Many of the accusations of "Fifty Heresies and Errors" are the commonplaces of both antimendicant and reformist Franciscan writing. However, one charge that suggests to me that the tract at the least incorporates rigorist rhetoric. In a chapter that begins, "Also freris chargen more brekyng of hor owne tradiciouns þen brekyng of þo comaundementis of God," the writer complains, "And so þei chargen more hor bodily habite þen charite and oþer vertues. Ffor if a frere leefe his bodily habite, to þo whiche he is not bounden by Gods lawe, he is holden apostata and scharply pursued, sumtyme to prisoun, and sumtyme to þo deth."[58] The friars "chargen" (require), as he says elsewhere, "a rotten habite"; they "chargen singular habit." Although this complaint may signify the superstitious reverence said to be held by the Franciscans for their habit – an accusation made in a number of antimendicant tracts and referred to in "Fifty Heresies" (3.382) – the word "singular" and the context of some of these complaints suggest to me legislation against the habit that had been allowed by Francis in the *Rule*. The ME translation phrases the allowance thus: "And be alle freris cloþid wiþ foule cloþis, & þei may pese hem aȝen or cloute hem of sacchis & oþere pecis" (41). The fact is that while most Franciscans wore a recognizable habit of gray wool – russet wool – with a knotted rope around the waist, the order had never legislated a garment and some friars wore garments in accord with that allowed in the *Rule*, that is, a foul garment with patches. John XXII, the same pope who denied the Franciscan theses on Christ's poverty, admonished the order to adopt a regular habit, which it did. At the same time the order forbade the irregular dress of the rigorists and others.[59] The writer of "Fifty Heresies and Errors" charges that, in effect, the regularized habit no longer suggests poverty but is a means of gaining greater proceeds. The concern about regularity in dress fetishizes the garment, placing more value on outward appearance

---

[58] "Fifty Heresies," in Arnold (*100*, 3.372–73, and see 389): the complaint is that the regular habit is required by the order's legislation, not by God's law and thus not by the *Rule*.

[59] *Quorundam exigit* (1317); see Moorman, *A History*, 311. Interestingly, the Conventuals claimed that they legislated against the irregular habit of Ubertino and others because *they* held it in superstitious reverence, a claim which may account for the phrasing of the countercharge in "Fifty Heresies."

than inward sanctity. That some friars abandoned the regular, the "singular" garment of their order is attested by the writs for the apprehension of apostate friars and by the legislation labeling as apostates those who abandon the habit and dress in some other garb.

These passages in this and other texts like them make clear that some writers distinguish on the one side between the rigorist or dissenting friars who follow Christ's law "after þe forme of þe gospel" and the accommodated friars of the order who live according to the Franciscan rule as it was interpreted by the popes and legislated by the order. The references to the imprisonment of brothers is to legislation that allowed it and to prelatical and royal pursuit of apostates. These statements also echo Ubertino da Casale's denunciations before Pope Clement V of the persecutions of the poorer brothers by the Conventuals. The assertion that the friars pursue their brothers to the death and murder them cannot be to any situation in England since there was no apparatus for the execution of heretics before 1401.[60] Rather, as in the commentary on the ME translation of the *Rule* and *Testament*, the references are to the friars who refused to submit to papal authority in 1318 and were burned and to those who would not recant in 1354 and were burned. But the more general accusation that true friars are chased and imprisoned may simply refer to the pursuit of apostates in England and elsewhere.

I am suggesting that in some texts we have ascribed to the Lollards, "pore prestis" are Franciscans who have left their order – but not Francis's *Rule* and *Testament* – to preach Christ's poverty. They are itinerant; they are unauthorized and therefore liable to pursuit by their own brothers, the prelates and the king's officers. My analysis of these texts argues that the evidence of a rigorist or dissident Franciscan presence in England has been lacking because we have misascribed their texts to the Lollards or have not seen that some appropriate Franciscan rhetoric.[61] In making the argument that some of our "Lollard" texts are dissident Franciscan ones, I am also arguing that rigorist and dissident Franciscans – and Dominicans – had an impact on the reformist rhetorics of the later Middle Ages in England and elsewhere.[62]

---

[60] *De heretico comburendo*; see H.G. Richardson (*1062*).

[61] Towards the end of the century Richard II issued a patent letter, 4 November 1384, to defend the friars against attacks on their privileges and their manner of living (*Calendar of Patent Rolls, 1381–84*, 527, 599). Although this writ has been understood to have been issued against the Wycliffite tract writers, it need not have been confined to them.

[62] Space does not permit further discussion of how dissident Franciscan discourses anticipated and were received by Wyclif and the Lollards. I intend to address these issues in another paper.

Wycliffite Representations of the Third Estate

Helen Barr

According to Adam Usk, Wyclif's followers "most wickedly did sow the seed of murder, snares, strife, variance, and discords, which last unto this day, and which, I fear, will last even to the undoing of the kingdom."[1] Usk was not alone in associating Wycliffites with civil dissent and unrest. Walsingham stated that the failure of the late Archbishop Sudbury to suppress the heresy of Wyclif and his followers was the primary cause of the revolt in 1381.[2] Both Walsingham and Knighton frame John Ball as an associate of Wyclif; the latter terming him "Wycliffe's John the Baptist."[3] While modern criticism is generally sceptical of the notion that Wyclif and/ or his followers were the *cause* of the uprisings in 1381, it is hard to ignore the considerable body of contemporary opinion which apparently believed that there was a very strong connection between Lollardy and insurrection.[4] When one turns to what the Wycliffites actually wrote themselves, however, rather than what was written about them, it is clear that Lollard texts are unanimous and univocal in their declaration of obedience to secular authority. The king must be obeyed, even if he be a tyrant, and members of civic society must be ordered according to the normative tripartite division into lords, clergy and labourers.[5] How is such a polarity of view possible? If the stated opinions of the Lollards on civil society were so declaredly orthodox, and even quietist, how could contemporary commentators associate them with a series of uprisings for which the third estate – the peasants, or "rustics," as the commentators term them – were held to be chiefly responsible?[6] This investigation of Wycliffite representations of the third estate is, in part, an attempt to answer that question.

[1] Adam Usk, *Chronicon Adae de Usk, 1377–1421*, 2nd ed., ed. E.M. Thompson (London: Henry Frowde, 1904), 3–4.

[2] Thomas Walsingham (*223*, 310–11).

[3] Walsingham (*223*, 320–21); Henry Knighton (*164*, 2.151).

[4] For discussion of the connection, see Margaret Aston (*269*); Anne Hudson (*723*, 85–106), and Steven Justice (*765*, 67–101). Hudson notes that the furthest that Wyclif went in condemning the commons in *De Blasphemia* was to say that "they acted rather outside the law" (98); while Justice argues that Wyclif's programme of disendowment put into circulation a vocabulary that could be put to insurgent use, even if Wyclif himself stressed secular obedience to the king (89–101).

[5] See Anne Hudson (*713*, 362 and 366–67), and *English Wycliffite Sermons* (*158*, 4.152–60).

[6] Although modern historians have established that the majority of the rebels were artisans rather than peasants, together with some priests in minor orders (e.g. John Ball) and a spattering of lesser gentry, see Rodney Hilton, *Bondmen Made Free: Medieval Peasants and the English Rising*

Apart from the tract titled by Matthew *Of Servants and Lords* there is no sustained discussion of the third estate in Wycliffite prose texts.[7] From collation of localised comments in other tracts about the place and function of the third estate, however, a coherent and consistent Wycliffite view of this social group does emerge, especially in the discussion of labourers. While they strenuously maintain the place of labourers within overt support for a three estate structure of civil society, Wycliffite texts are much less vitriolic in their views of the commons and far less condemnatory of labourers than is the norm. As I shall argue, much of the reason for this stems from how the commons are viewed within Wycliffite ecclesiology. For all the declared support for a traditional three estate structure, Wycliffite representations of the third estate can be seen to have a radical potential and to harbour dissident energy. Wycliffite texts can be seen to re-write the contemporary, normative language of social description in the ways that they re-figure social relationships between the commons and the lords, but even more profoundly, in how they re-fashion social relationships between the commons and the material church.[8] The most radical attention to the position of labourers is seen in the distinctive Wycliffite treatment of the figure of the ploughman. The fullest representation of this figure occurs in *Pierce the Ploughman's Crede*; a depiction which is entirely consonant with localised discussion in the prose texts, but which is distinctively different from the treatment in *Piers Plowman*.

Overwhelmingly, Wycliffite prose texts represent the third estate through the figure of the peasant labourer.[9] The artisan class is scarcely visible and the peasants depicted are the rural poor rather than labourers with their own plot of land.[10] That Lollard tracts should focus their treatment of the third estate on the rural poor peasant is itself significant. As Paul Freedman has recently shown, there is a tension in medieval images of the peasant. There are two intertwined traditions: on the one hand, the peasant was held to be a figure of utter contempt and ridicule, and on the other, seen to be much closer to God than members of the other two estates because of his poverty and simple way of life. As Freedman illustrates, both these discourses are held in tension and reinforce one another,[11] and are often

---

of 1381 (London: Temple Smith, 1973), 176–185. The chroniclers are insistent in disparaging the social status of the insurgents by characterising them as "rustici": e.g. Thomas Walsingham (*221*, 1.454, 459, 477) and the chronicler of Bury St. Edmunds, *Memorials of Bury St. Edmunds*, 3.125.

[7] F.D. Matthew (*182*, 226–243). This tract appears to attempt to distance Wycliffite thought from the riots of 1381 and is discussed further below.

[8] On the language of social description and the changes it underwent in the late fourteenth century, see Paul Strohm (*1156*, 2–10).

[9] There is some localised attention to merchants and lawyers which I discuss below.

[10] For the distinction between peasants with no land or less than a full holding, and those who could support themselves from their tenements, see R. Hilton, "Reasons for Inequality among Medieval Peasants," in *Class Conflict and the Crisis of Feudalism: Essays in Medieval Social History* (London: Hambledon, 1985), 139–51, and W. Rösener, *Peasants in the Middle Ages*, trans. Alexander Stürtzer (Cambridge: Polity, 1992), 191–207.

[11] Paul Freedman, *Images of the Medieval Peasant* (Stanford: Stanford Univ. Press, 1999), 31–33. One reason for this duality is the existence of contradictory legacies on the value of labour: either that all labour was the result of sin, and toil was Adam's punishment for the Fall, or that it was

found inter-related in medieval commentaries on the value of labour.[12] Both of these traditions employ distinctive tropes which appear time and again in medieval texts. While the "contempt" branch of peasant discourse was the more voluminous in the Middle Ages, as Freedman has so amply demonstrated, the tradition of peasant representation is fissured. The peasant is both the virtuous, spiritually blessed bedrock of Christian society, *and*, more frequently, the seditious "other"; a greedy, filthy, lying, ignorant, bestial and deformed body.

What is most striking in Wycliffite texts is how this dual legacy of peasant representation is split. Overwhelmingly, the third estate, as represented by the rural poor labourer, is invested with the characteristics of the ameliorative strain of peasant discourse. The virulent tradition of peasant contempt is not obliterated, however. It is highly visible, but instead of being used of the peasant labourer, its features are used to describe friars, monks, and prelates. In Wycliffite texts, it is members of the second estate who are demonised, accompanied by an idealization of the place and worth of those belonging to the third.

At the root of the favourable view of peasant labourers in Wycliffite texts is that they live in praiseworthy poverty. Their discussion of this topic is entirely consonant with Wyclif's own views, expounded most fully in *De Civili Dominio*, II, chapters 7–10. Wyclif believed that the apostolic poverty of the early church should form the true model for later Christian behaviour. While not condemning riches as such, he asserts that the evangelical poor should renounce all civil possession; the endowment of the church was intended, not for the enrichment of the clergy, but for the care of the poor in the world. To avoid revolt, a king should dispense goods wisely, rule prudently, and avoid collusion in the appropriation of goods into the dead hand of the church. The temporalities of the church would be better dispensed if they were in the hands of the laymen.[13]

Discussion of this issue by his followers runs along similar lines. Wycliffite texts show a passionate concern with poverty.[14] Christ is the holy exemplar of praiseworthy indigence. *The Rosarium Theologie*, for example, states that he was "moste pore, als wele as vnto mekenes of spirite

---

not toil *as such* that was a consequence of the Fall, but the difficulty and hardship of labour that was enjoined on Adam for his transgression. God laboured over his Creation, and even before the Fall, Adam worked happily to maintain the garden in Paradise, see Freedman, 28–29. As Freedman has documented examples of the tradition so fully, I have here summarised characteristics of the traditions, and detail them more individually in my treatment of their altered appearance in Wycliffite texts in the discussion which follows.

[12] For example, the sermon by Jacques de Vitry, taking as his text Zachariah 13.5 ("homo agricola sum" – "I am a husbandman"), quoted in Freedman, *Images of the Medieval Peasant*, 33, from Jacques de Vitry, "Sermo ad agricolas et vinitores et alios operarios" in J.-Th. Welter, *L'exemplum dans la littérature religieuse et didactique du Moyen Âge* (Paris: E.H. Guitard, 1927), 458.

[13] Discussion drawn from Anne Hudson (*729*, 41–53, 47–49). I am grateful to Professor Hudson for an off-print of this article. Wyclif's views on poverty are also discussed by Justice (*765*, 75–101); M. Aston (*281*, 95–131).

[14] As noted in *English Wycliffite Sermons* (*158*, 4.159).

as vnto renoncyng of ciuile lordeschepe."[15] Lollard texts are not alone in using Christ's humble birth as an example of praiseworthy rural poverty; Griselda's father in *The Clerk's Tale* is the poorest of the poor folk in the village, but as the narrator states, "hye God somtyme senden kan/His grace into a litle oxes stalle."[16] What is distinctive about Wycliffite texts, however, is the use of this image as an argument against the temporal endowment of the church. The fourteenth point of *The Twenty-Five Articles* explicitly contrasts the apostolic poverty of Christ and his disciples with the "possessioun" enjoyed by the contemporary church: "Jesus Crist hade not by worldly lordschipe whereupon he schuld bowe his heved." The first apostles could not become disciples of Christ until they had renounced their nets and boats, and even their family. On what basis then, can contemporary priests claim the status of apostles, and yet be greater worldly lords than earls, dukes, kings' uncles, and princes?[17]

An integral part of the praise of virtuous poverty in contrast to temporal possession, is the Wycliffite stress on the necessity of the labourer. Far from being outside civil society, alien and deformed, his toil is essential to the health of the realm, and in contrast to associating labourers with filth and dirt because they work on the land, the Lollard sermon for Septuagesima Sunday, based on the parable of the vineyard, exalts the "grobbyng aboute þe erþe" of "þe comyne peple," their "erynge, and dungynge, and sowynge, and harwynge." The commons are the root of the three types of workers in the spiritual vineyard. With their "trwe labour," they "bere vp and susteyne þe oþere tweie parties of þe chirche, þat is: kny3tes and clerkis."[18] This privileging of the work of the third estate is a common strain in Wycliffite texts. Allegiance is declared to the normative, tripartite division of society into lords, clerics and labourers.[19] Transgression against this tripartite ordering of civil society or the church is hotly condemned. An expansion to a sermon written for the first Sunday in Lent criticises the sin of pride and upward mobility in all three estates, but the poor are seen to less blameworthy

---

[15] *The Middle English Translation of the Rosarium Theologie* (*220*, 94/11–13); cf. *Lollard Sermons* (*128*, 61/316–319).

[16] "The Clerk's Tale," in *The Riverside Chaucer* (*127*, E.206–7).

[17] *Select English Works of John Wyclif* (*100*, 3.475); cf. similar views in Arnold (*100*, 3.415) and Matthew (*182*, 425.8).

[18] Cigman (*128*, 86/206–214); cf. Arnold (*100*, 3.207). In *Jack Upland*, the office of the commons is to "truli laboure for þe sustinaunce of hem silf, & for prestis and for lordis doynge wel her office" (*159*, 54/17–18). In *Super Cantica Sacra* labouring the earth is seen, not as a sign of filth, but as a spiritual necessity, Arnold (*100*, 3.30–31). Thomas Wimbledon also uses the parable of the vineyard to model the three estates of society, stating that it is the duty of the labourers to "trauayle bodily and wiþ here sore swet geten out of þe erþe bodily liflode for hem and for oþer parties" (*225*, 63/44–46); cf. *The Lanterne of Li3t* (*174*, 33/11–13).

[19] See *English Wycliffite Sermons* (*158*, 4.15). The tract *Tractatus de Regibus* states briefly and simply that society is composed of these three estates, *Four English Political Tracts of the Later Middle Ages* (*145*, 6, 14), cf. *Upland* (*159*, 54/4–10). *The Clergy May Not Hold Property* likewise compares each of the three estates to the respective figures of the Trinity. This formulation figures God's church. The commons correspond to the true love or good will which the Holy Spirit owes to the Father and to the Son. Consequently, the commons "owiþ true loue & obedyente wille to þe statis of lordis & prestis" (Matthew [*182*, 363]).

than the lords and clergy.[20] Indeed, the conclusion offers a remedy against social strife by enjoining the hearer to bestow generous almes on the truly poor. This will be pleasing to God, "help of alle seyntis, and þe endles blisse of heuene." The saints, who can help to bring the congregation to the "blisse of heuene" are said to have been "pore men."[21] While the sermon is anxious to support the three estate structure and criticise any estate that usurps its allotted role, the poor are seen to be potentially less blameworthy, and closer to the promise of eternal life, than the other two estates.

Often, in criticisms of the third estate, it is lawyers and merchants who are singled out rather than the poor labourer, as in William Taylor's sermon, where merchants are condemned for enhancing their wealth and worldly station "bi vnleeful meenes."[22] *Of Servants and Lords* criticises the guile of merchants and lawyers alongside the deceitfulness of servants: the latter "traueilen faste" in the presence of their master but in his absence are idle; and mess about unproductively, claiming that they are unable to work harder and more honestly than they do. Gower might have written this, but not, perhaps the sentence that comes after: "& ʒit generaly in clerkis regniþ most gile, for þei disceyuen men bi here veyn preieris & pardons & indulgencis."[23] While there is nothing exclusively Wycliffite in this particular criticism, the tract as a whole is much more lenient towards the vices of the first and third estates than it is to the second. Of all the estates, it is the clerics who are the most vicious.

The exculpation of the third estate from the grievous sins committed by the second pervades *þe Ten Comaundementis*. Their faults are attributed to the neglect of the clergy. Surprisingly, there is no criticism of peasant idleness. Instead: "pore men of þo comyne, for hor bisye travel, synnen lesse in envye and in oþer synnes þen done men above hom þat traveilen not þus."[24] In texts such as *De Blasphemia, Contra Fratres*, support for the labourer against the vices of the clergy is given a radical twist. The "foundement" of the church is said to be "comyners and laboreres." However, more "ordiris and sectis" have been "clotirde on hem." This is seen to be contrary to God's ordinance because these new sects do not labour for the profit of the church and are instead "raveyners" who rob the

[20] Cigman (*128*, 137/207–211). This sermon contains a rare example of more economically tuned criticism of the labourers than is common in Wycliffite texts. They are wretched knaves who plough and cart, who, nonetheless desire costly apparel, and whereas they used to serve for ten or twelve shillings in a year, now demand twenty or thirty, plus a livery to boot (137–39).

[21] Ibid., 147–48.

[22] *The Sermon of William Taylor* in *Two Wycliffite Texts* (*156*, 15/439–42); cf. Matthew (*182*, 185–6), where merchants are criticised for maintaining the great houses of the friars; and 182 and 234 (on lawyers), and 237–8 (on both).

[23] Matthew (*182*, 238). Cf. *The Order of Priesthood*, where priests are said to be "more worldly & vicious þan þe comune peple, þat bi hem þe peple takiþ ensaumple & boldnesse in synne," Matthew (*182*, 167), and *Of Prelates*, where prelates are blamed for the wickedness of the lords, clerics and commons, and said to lead them to hell for breaking of God's commandments, Matthew (*182*, 88).

[24] Arnold (*100*, 3.133). Cf. Cigman (*128*, 240/1145) where clerics are said to prevent literacy in the third estate, and actively to lead labourers astray; cf. Matthew (*182*, 94); *Lanterne* states that they oppress the commons by magnifying their sermons above the law of God (*174*, 120/10–11).

people. Since the new orders have come in, the church has been "payred in everiche membre."[25] Friars, monks and false prelates are seen in Wycliffite texts to be superfluous to the three estate structure; to be outside society in ways reminiscent of how the discourse of contempt figured the labourer as "other" and the antithesis of civilisation. In contrast to the necessary work of the labourers who are the foundation of the church, new orders are an idle superfluity. In a sermon on the parable of the vineyard for Septuagesima Sunday, the labourers are the "trewe men" to whom God has given the wit to cultivate good fruit. The labourers delve around the roots in case evil herbs grow and "bastard braunchis wiþowten byleue." These branches must be cut away because they represent the superfluity in the church; the prelates whom God has not ordained and who contravene His ordering of the estates.[26]

This superfluous estate is seen to compromise obedience to secular and civil rule.[27] The writer of *Of Servants and Lords* urges all people to be content with their allotted role, and counsels obedience to earthly lords with fear, quaking and trembling. Yet, he says, the devil moves some men to say that Christian men need not be servants to heathen lords – nor to Christian – because they are brethren in blood and Christ redeemed Christian men on the cross with his blood.[28] Far from being in cahoots with seditious rebels, as Walsingham, Usk and Knighton accused, this follower of Wyclif deplores the civil disobedience which stems from mis-placed belief in commonality of all things. It is also important that the formulation of this statement removes the blame from members of the third estate, and attributes such notions of equality to the "fend," the father of the church of Antichrist.

While Wycliffite texts portray the commons performing their duty meekly and truly;[29] worldly priests and feigned religious trumpet their "newe feyned obedience founden of synful men" which was never taught or commanded by Christ.[30] In this splitting of the dual legacy of peasant discourse, the poor labourer is shown to be a model of civil obedience while the friars strive against secular and civil authority. Jack Upland states that the various sects brought in by Antichrist are not obedient to bishops, liegemen, or kings because they neither till or sow, weed or reap. They are without place.[31] In contrast to the labourer, they perform no necessary work and cannot be accommodated within the structure of

---

[25] Arnold (*100*, 3.418).
[26] *English Wycliffite Sermons* (*158*, 1.380–81/53–68); cf. 512/75–85 where the three estates established according to God's law are contrasted to the new sects, and Arnold (*100*, 3.239) where the friars are again called bastard branches, crept in by the devil. By contrast, Wimbledon likens the branches of the vineyard to sins which priests must cut away with the sword of their tongue (63/39–41); cf. Matthew (*182*, 364) and Arnold (*100*, 3.184).
[27] On Wyclif's theory of dominion and discussion by his followers, see Hudson (*713*, 46, 362, 366–67).
[28] Matthew (*182*, 227–43).
[29] Matthew (*182*, 276).
[30] Matthew (*182*, 279–80); cf. Matthew (*182*, 38) where prelates are asked to cease slandering "pore men" by saying that they will not obey their lords.
[31] *Jack Upland* (*159*, 57/69–78).

human society. It is not peasants who make the land lawless, but the friars.[32]

Instead of perceiving the commons to be threat to social order, they are seen to be the victims of the lawlessness of the sects and prelates who have no place. Through building, the sects destroy the pasture that ought to be in common to produce food;[33] they live in rich houses while the labourers are condemned to poverty,[34] and the privileges of the sects rob the poor.[35] In contrast to the pomp and luxury of these new orders, workmen are forced to beg even if their work beasts are distressed, and their wife and children hungry and naked;[36] poor men labour, but new sects waste their goods, both through wicked pomp and self-indulgence, and drinking at taverns.[37] The bread of poor men is turned into masonry: sects have fine buildings and the poor hollow bodies and shrunken flesh.[38] Friars are seen to deceive the lords and commons through their false teaching, such as holidays for saints, and articles of belief which deny poor men's rights.[39] The poor labourer is exonerated while traits of traditional anti-peasant discourse: lying; greed; luxury; ignorance, and sloth, are transferred to the new orders and prelates.

Further, it is the superfluous estate rather than the peasantry who are keen to usurp social rank. They behave like kings and lords, merchants and reeves, and prefer to ape secular lordship rather than engage in "wilful traueil and povert."[40] The commons bear the burden of this social climbing, being oppressed by the taxes necessary to support this superfluous estate.[41] The Grete Sentence of Curs accuses worldly prelates of slander for claiming that they live as Christ and his disciples did in apostolic poverty. This is seen to camouflage "here owene raveyne, bi whiche þei stelen fro lordis and comyns here temperal lordischip and goodis. . . . ȝif it be resonable þat a man shal be hangid for stelyng of fourtene pens, moche more schulden þes blasphemeris of God, þat stelen so many lordischipis and temperal goodis from comynte of seculeris, and wasten hem in synne."[42] The writer argues that prelates would rather: "rere baner aȝenst þe kyng and his lordis and comyns, þan temperal lordischipis schulden turne to þe kyng and lordis, and þei on spiritualte, as God ordeyned."[43] In contrast to the humble

---

[32] Arnold (100, 3.384). In a re-registering of 1381 anti-peasant discourse, The Grete Sentence of Curs Expouned states: "alle þe newe lawis þat clerkis han maad ben sutilly conjectid by ypocrisie, to brynge doun power and regalie of lordis and kyngis þat God ordeynede, and to make hem self lordis, and alle at here dom" (Arnold [100, 3.298]).

[33] English Wycliffite Sermons (158, 1.266/53–55).

[34] Anne Hudson (155, 85/72); Matthew (182, 186).

[35] Matthew (182, 97, 118, 128–29).

[36] Matthew (182, 214).

[37] Matthew (182, 149); Arnold (100, 3.474); Matthew (182, 152).

[38] Lanterne (174, 38/3–14); Rosarium (220, 70/24–31).

[39] Arnold (100, 3.233, 490, 455).

[40] Matthew (182, 139); Cigman (128, 137); Matthew (182, 366, 172, 265 and 376).

[41] E.g. Matthew (182, 22, 233, 279).

[42] Arnold (100, 3.292).

[43] Arnold (100, 3.276). In repeating the charge, the writer refers to "oure" king, lords and commons, to invoke a discourse of solidarity against the prelates (276). To raise a banner ("rere baner") against the king is seen to be a sign of treason which deserves death in Wynnere and Wastoure, ed. Stephanie Trigg, EETS o.s. 297 (Oxford: Oxford Univ. Press, 1990), ll. 131–33.

obedience of the poor labourer, Wycliffite texts figure the estate without order as treacherous thieves, and agents of civil dissent.

The insistence of prelates to collect tithes is also seen as a sign of their usurpation of social rank and their oppression of the poor. Nicholas Hereford, in his Ascension Day sermon, argued that if the king were to remove the possessions and riches of these orders as he should, then he would not have to tax the poor commons.[44] Writers on this subject are at pains to make a distinction between the withdrawing of tithes from worldly prelates, and the withholding of rents from secular lords: "summe men þat ben out of charite sclaundren pore prestis wiþ þis errour, þat seruantis or tenauntis may lawefully wiþholde rentis & seruyce fro here lordis whanne lordis ben opynly wickid in here lyuynge."[45] The agents of civil disobedience are seen to be members, not of the third estate, but the second. The idealized view of the rural poor labourer that emerges in Wycliffite texts serves as a foil against which to contrast the superfluity and corruption of the material church. The commons, through their honest toil and true obligation to secular authority, are seen to be more worthy and meritorious than the grasping superfluity and luxury of the material church.

In reversing the orthodox relationship between the third and second estates, Wycliffite texts maintain that the "lewed," or labourers, are better priests than the temporal clergy of the new orders. The discourse of bestial animal imagery is frequently mobilized in this re-configuration: the superfluous estate are characterised as wolves of hell,[46] bears,[47] dogs,[48] hounds returning to their vomit,[49] vipers,[50] and swine.[51] They are given over to drunkenness and gluttony; bodily excesses of all kinds,[52] and associated with muck, dirt and stink.[53] The trope of the bizarre appearance of the peasant is re-registered to frame comments on the irregular clothing of the new orders,[54] and the description of dissident peasants as a rebellious multitude, threatening the order of civilization, appears as the multitude of new orders without number which cause strife and dissension within the realm.[55]

And, while traditionally it was the peasant who was ridiculed for his ignorance, in Wycliffite texts this accolade goes to the superfluity of clergy. Ignorant of the bible, prelates blabber all day like magpies and jays from costly books of "mannus ordynaunce."[56] They are more worldly and vicious than the common people, and people laugh them to scorn for their ignorant

[44] See the edition by Simon Forde (*151*, 205–41), and discussion in Hudson (*729*, 50–51).
[45] Matthew, *Of Servants and Lords* (*182*, 229).
[46] E.g. *English Wycliffite Sermons* (*158*, 1.439/37); Matthew (*182*, 149 and 151).
[47] E.g. *English Wycliffite Sermons* (*158*, 1.439/38).
[48] E.g. Matthew (*182*, 104, 110, 319); Arnold (*100*, 3.440).
[49] E.g. Matthew (*182*, 253).
[50] E.g. Matthew (*182*, 161); *Lanterne* (*174*, 111/12).
[51] E.g. Matthew (*182*, 156, 165–66, 243).
[52] E.g. Matthew (*182*, 152, 165–66, 182, 267–8).
[53] E.g. Matthew (*182*, 134, 182).
[54] E.g. *Jack Upland* (*159*, 59–60/130–43).
[55] E.g. Matthew (*182*, 162, 212, 236, 222).
[56] Matthew (*182*, 194).

leading of services and their reading of the gospel and epistle, and yet: "ignoraunce of good lif & goddis hestis is werse þan ignoraunce of latyn or of ony oþer langage."[57] The superfluous estate is seen to be ignorant not only of clerical knowledge, but more importantly, also of the simple good works, and true faith of honest Christians. Members of the third estate are, in this respect, better priests than the temporal clergy. Lollards claimed: "þat þer schulde be bot oo degre aloone of þe prestehod in þe chirche of God, and euery good man is a prest and haþ power to preche þe word of God."[58]

With the espousal of such beliefs, the second estate does not simply become superfluous, it disappears altogether. The sacerdotal duties of the temporal priesthood are better performed by the third estate; absolution, for example, according to the writer of *Of Confesssion* might be performed better by good "lewed men" than wicked priests.[59] While worldly prelates despoil the poor, simple priests help them and bestow alms,[60] and true, honest, priests advise the commons how to preserve charity and reason.[61] Together with the denial of transubstantiation in the sacrament of the Eucharist, and the belief that auricular confession is unnecessary since contrition alone is necessary to wipe out sin, sacerdotal authority is eliminated and the dividing line between clerical and lay removed.[62] The Wycliffite investment in the honest simplicity of the poor third estate re-draws the map of social relations. Overt support for the normative tripartite estate structure is predicated on the existence of a fourth, superfluous estate, represented by the new orders and false prelates. Even more radical is the logical extension of the argument for the temporal disendowment of the clergy, the re-definition of the church as the predestined congregation of the church in heaven,[63] and the belief in the priesthood of all believers. All these produce a model of civic society predicated on a two estate structure: the lords and the commons.

Such is the Wycliffite investment in the "sanctitas" of the "lewed" that writers adopt the role and voice of members of the third estate as a narrative position from which to preach their views. *The Twelve Conclusions of the Lollards* affixed to the doors of Westminster hall during the parliament of 1395, demanding the reformation of the Church, are presented by "we pore

---

[57] Matthew (*182*, 167).

[58] *Selections from English Wycliffite Writings* (*155*, 19/16–18). The quotation is from the accusations made against the Lollards by the bishops. *Lanterne of Liȝt* notes that Christ's disciples were not graduate men in schools, but "symple ydiotis" inspired in heavenly teaching by the grace of the Holy Spirit (*174*, 5/16–19).

[59] Matthew (*182*, 333).

[60] Arnold (*100*, 3.293).

[61] Arnold (*100*, 3.359).

[62] For further discussion on these points and views of Wyclif and his adherents, see Hudson (*713*, 325–27).

[63] See *Selections from English Wycliffite Writings* (*155*, 116/21–6): "but howeuere we speken in diuerse names or licknessis of þis holi chirche, þei techen nouȝt ellis but oo name, þat is to seie, 'þe congregacioun, or gedering-togidir of feiþful soulis þat lastingli kepen feiþ and trouþe, in word and in dede, to God and to man, and reisen her lijf in siker hope of mercy and grace and blisse at her ende, and ouercoueren, or hillen, þis bilding in perfite charite þat schal not faile in wele ne in woo.'"

men, tresoreris of Cryst and his apostlis."[64] Lollard preachers appropriated for themselves the epithets "true," "pore," and "simple" as terms of approbation in opposition to the temporal possessions of the Church. In contrast to the deceit, corruption and false preaching of the material church the words of the humble Lollard preacher are true.[65] Friars persecute those who speak the truth,[66] while the author of *The Twenty Five Articles*, states that "pore men" answer accusations made against them honestly, and: "þat if þei erren in ony poynt of þeire onswerynge, þei submytten hem to be correctid openly to þo kynge and his chivalrye and þo clergye and comyns, ȝe, by deþe, if hit be justly demed lawefulle." The voice of the poor and the honest is subject to temporal correction and castigation in a way that the members of the superfluous estate, through their contravention of obedience to secular authority, refuse.[67] As Justice observes of the 1395 bill, in claiming to issue from the hands of "pore men" Wycliffite texts speak as if they embody "the collective voice of England's poor."[68] This is diametrically opposed to Gower's narrative strategy in *Vox Clamantis*. So alarmed is Gower by the challenge to civil order posed by the greedy, exploitative members of the third estate, that in Book V he mobilizes "the people's voice" against them; a voice which, in the words of David Aers, calls for the law to launch against them an "unspecified but terrorizing preemptive strike."[69]

For Gower, the figure of the ploughman is the source of the "evil disposition widespread among the common people."[70] This remark is representative of a sub-strain of anti-peasant discourse which figures those who work at the plough as the very worst representatives of the peasant class. Just as peasant discourse as whole is fractured into an ameliorative and a pejorative strain, however, so too is the tradition of the representation of the ploughman.[71] There is biblical warrant for the plough itself as a sigh of fruitful labour, and by extension, a metaphor for good preaching,[72] and a sermon attributed to Berthold speaks of Christ willingly plowing the field of Christianity himself; with the wood and iron of

---

[64] *Selections from English Wycliffite Writings* (*155*, 24/1). In his written defence of the charges against him Walter Brut terms himself an "agricola" – a husbandman – despite his academic education, see *Registrum Johannis Trefnant* (*213*, 257–8).

[65] See Gloria Cigman (*391*). See also *Selections from English Wycliffite Writings* (*155*, 146 n.50), and the Lollard use of the term "true men" or "true cristen men" to refer to themselves. Hudson notes that Wyclif often refers to himself as "quidam fideles" which accords with the claim that Wyclif and his followers were alone in the true line of descent from Christ and the primitive church. See also Anne Hudson (*698*).

[66] E.g. Arnold (*100*, 3.231).

[67] Arnold (*100*, 3.457). Cf. Matthew (*182*, 225), where the lords and commons are called upon to correct the clergy.

[68] Steven Justice (*766*, 662–689, 672–73).

[69] David Aers (*259*, 432–453, 440).

[70] Gower (*147*, 4:5.574).

[71] See Freedman, 223–35.

[72] See Proverbs 12.11 and 20.4; Isaiah 28.24 and 1 Corinthians 9.10. For ploughing and preaching see Stephen A Barney, "The Ploughshare of the Tongue: The Progress of a Symbol from the Bible to *Piers Plowman*," *Mediaeval Studies* 35 (1973): 261–93. This metaphor was used in Gregory's *Moralia*, and was thus widely disseminated through the Middle Ages, see Freedman, 34.

the plough symbolizing the wood and iron of the Cross.[73] Before the late fourteenth century, possibly the most well-known favourable depiction of a ploughman, rather than a symbolic plough, was in the poem *De Duello Militis et Aratoris*, which, as Edward Wheatley has shown, was part of the *Liber Catonianus*, a standard compilation of schooltexts used in the Middle Ages.[74]

Until the appearance of the figures of the ploughman in Chaucer's *General Prologue* and *Piers Plowman*, however, the tradition of representing the plougher rather than the plough was overwhelmingly negative.[75] The progenitor of the husbandman was seen to be Cain, the first to till the land, while the spiritual ancestor of shepherds, and by extension, priests, was Abel. Tillers were thus associated with disobedience, murder, fratricide and outcasts. Further, it was shepherds, not ploughmen, who were the first to receive word of the birth of Christ.[76] Artistic representations of Cain as ploughman are wholly pejorative: for instance, the portrait in the Holkham Bible which shows him ploughing furiously, but pointlessly.[77]

Wycliffite texts continue the tradition of the negative representation of Cain, but instead of representing the peasant labourer, he represents the superfluous fourth estate. In counterpoint, shepherds, represented by Abel, are the *true* priests. A sermon for the birth of Christ says that angels led the shepherds to the nativity because they lived a simple and holy life: "for God louede Abel betture þan Caym þat was his broþur. And þe furst was an herde, and þe toþur a tylinge man; and tylynge men han more of craft þan þe herdus in þer dedis."[78] This is as unflattering a view of tilling men as exists in Wycliffite texts. Here, while Abel is associated with an honest simple, life, the symbolic force of Cain receives no mention. Elsewhere, the progeny of Cain are the damned, while Abel's children are persecuted true

---

[73] Berthold von Regensburg, *Vollständige Ausgabe seiner Predigten* (Vienna: W. Braumueller, 1862) 1.14, quoted in Freedman, 380 n.77. Freedman also notes the existence of a Byzantine hymn in which Mary is described as the nourisher of the "loving ploughman" (224).

[74] Edward Wheatley, "A Selfless Ploughman and the Christ/Piers Conjunction in Langland's *Piers Plowman*," *Notes and Queries* n.s. 40, 238 (1993): 135–42.

[75] See Elizabeth D. Kirk, "Langland's Plowman and the Recreation of Fourteenth Century Religious Metaphor," *Yearbook of Langland Studies* 2 (1988): 1–21. The case of Chaucer and Langland is discussed below. In Iolo Goch's *Cwydd y Llafurwr* the figure of the ploughman is praised as both a literal and figurative lynchpin of a stable, ordered society, see Morgan Thomas Davies, "Plowmen, Patrons and Poets: Iolo Goch's *Cwydd y Llafurwr* and Some Matters of Wales in the Fourteenth Century," *Medievalia et Humanistica* 24 (1997): 51–74. Davies argues that the figure of the ploughman also validates Iolo's profession as a minstrel. Andrew Breeze has argued that *Piers Plowman* was an influence on Iolo Goch's poem, "A Welsh Addition to the *Piers Plowman* Group?," *Notes and Queries* n.s. 40, 238 (1993): 142–51. Camille notes the depiction of a foolish ploughman trying to work an illogical assemblage, a nonsense plough, which does not touch the soil, in the margins of the East Anglian Gorleston Psalter, see Michael Camille, *Mirror in Parchment: The Luttrell Psalter and the Making of Medieval England* (London: Reaktion Books,1998), 188.

[76] See Freedman, 34.

[77] See Edmund Reiss, "The Symbolic Plow and Plowman and the Wakefield *Mactatio Abel*," *Studies in Iconography* 5 (1979): 3–30, 11. See also Kirk, 3.

[78] *English Wycliffite Sermons* (*158*, 2.209–10/88–100). In other sermons, there is the standard equation between Christ and the shepherd, *English Wycliffite Sermons* (*158*, 1.439/18–19).

priests.[79] *The Clergy May Not Hold Property* states that Abel, the true shepherd is dead, and Cain, as possession, usurps the care of souls.[80] The true church is Abel's while the fiend's church belongs to Cain.[81] Wycliffite writers were not slow to catch onto the acrostic potential of the Middle English spelling of Cain as "Caim" and to spell out the initial letters of the four orders of friars from his name.[82] The friars are linked with Cain in a variety of texts, and their friaries referred to as Cain's castles. The writer of *De Officio Pastorali* states that true priests should not belong to a false order, but live in poverty as Christ did: "not in hye castels of caym & lustful fode as boris in sty."[83]

The corollary of the Wycliffite alignment of friars and false prelates with Cain is that the figure of the ploughman is freed from all negative characteristics. Instead, Christ himself is seen as an earth-tiller;[84] there is praise for the labour that Christ and the apostles performed with their hands, in contrast to criticism of hypocrites who disdain so to travail.[85] When contrasting the true Christian life of the third estate to the vicious living of the prelacy, the distinction between the merit of shepherd and ploughman is collapsed. They, and their prayers are seen to be equally meritorious in the sight of God if they live well and love God well.[86] Most crucially, the good ploughman is oppositional to the evil prelate or friar:[87]

> Cristen men shulden wel wite þat good lif of a plouman is as myche wrþ to þe soule as preyer of þis frere, al ȝif it profite sumwhat.[88]

> A symple pater noster of a plouȝman þat his in charite is betre þan a þousand massis of coueitouse prelatis & veyn religious ful of coueitise & pride & fals flaterynge & norishynge of synne.[89]

In Wycliffite texts, the figure of the ploughman is an exemplar of poverty, simplicity, honesty and *necessary* social labour in contrast to the idle cunning and superfluity of ungrounded members of the second estate.

[79] *English Wycliffite Sermons* (*158*, 2.106/6–15); cf. Cigman (*128*, 30/699–703).

[80] Matthew (*182*, 374).

[81] *Lanterne* (*174*, 133/14–15).

[82] Wyclif had used the acrostic in *Trialogus* (*238*, 4.33, 362). Apart from Fitzralph who used the acrostic in one of his London sermons in 1357, see P.R. Szittya (*1169*, 129); there appear to be no instances of the use of this acrostic outside medieval texts, see further, Helen Barr, *Signes and Sothe: Language in the 'Piers Plowman' Tradition* (Cambridge: D.S. Brewer, 1994), 126–7. Szittya comments, 229–30, that the friars are linked with Cain because he is the archetype of all those who wander without place or number within a divine order, governed by the principles laid down in Wisdom 2.21. Friars are also invested with the characteristics of Cain even when he is not named, for instance, as the cursed of God (Matthew [*182*, 91]), and as aliens, like Jews, murderers and other enemies to the realm such as Frenchmen (Arnold [*100*, 3.492–3, 516]).

[83] Matthew (*182*, 425); cf. 12. *Jack Upland* (*159*, 56/86); *Upland's Rejoinder* (*159*, 108/223); *Mum and the Sothsegger*, in *The Piers Plowman Tradition* (*103*, ll. 501–4); *Pierce the Ploughman's Crede*, line 486 (see further on this below), and for discussion, see Aston (*281*).

[84] Christ is depicted elsewhere as a tiller, drawing on John 15.1 and 20.15, and Christ is shown with a spade in a fifteenth century alabaster, see Freedman, 224.

[85] Matthew (*182*, 236).

[86] Matthew (*182*, 173 and 321).

[87] *Upland's Rejoinder* accuses friars of stealing ploughmen from the true life (*159*, 109/261).

[88] *English Wycliffite Sermons* (*158*, 3.313/20–21).

[89] Matthew (*182*, 274).

These latter, like Cain, are treacherous villains, and like Cain, are outcasts both from earthly civil society, and from heaven.

Of course, it cannot be claimed that the re-valorization of the negative image of the ploughman is exclusively Wycliffite. There remain the instances of Chaucer's plowman in the *Prologue*, and the figure of Piers in *Piers Plowman*.[90] Yet, when these are compared to what is the fullest exposition of the ploughman in Wycliffite texts, namely Peres in *Pierce the Ploughman's Crede*, the distinctiveness of the Lollard appropriation of the ploughman figure is apparent. While the undoubtedly Wycliffite *Plowman's Tale* was fathered onto the Ploughman from *The General Prologue*, Chaucer's figure is exemplary, but lacking in the distinctively Wycliffite conception of the figure.[91] To be sure, he lives in peace and perfect charity, loves God and his neighbour best, is an honest labourer,[92] and works for the poor without payment; none of which would be out of place in a Wycliffite text (though a Lollard reader might have frowned on his prompt payment of tithes).[93] That he is cast as the brother of the virtuous Parson is suggestive of the Wycliffite link between the sanctity of ploughmen and poor priests,[94] but there is a crucial dimension lacking: this ploughman is not explicitly contrasted with figures from the superfluous fourth estate.[95] Further, in Chaucer's portrait, as Christina von Nolcken observes of the difference between *Piers Plowman* and Wycliffite texts, "the perspective is bounded by the temporal, whereas Wycliffites seek to superimpose the archetypal on the temporal."[96] And what else is the Wycliffite splitting of the ploughman tradition, in order to *impe* Cain onto the friars, but one such superimposition?

[90] The ideal of kingship in *Richard the Redeles* is said to be to labour on the law "as lewde men on plowes" in *The Piers Plowman Tradition* (*103*, 3.267).

[91] For reasons of space (and of date) I have excluded *The Plowman's Tale* from this study. While the frame of the tale juxtaposes the virtuous toil of the ploughman against the vices of the clergy, and has the ploughman consoling the griffin at the conclusion, it is likely that this is a sixteenth-century addition to fourteenth-century material, see Andrew Wawn (*1269*), and (*1271*), and Anne Hudson (*712*, 251–66, 257). Some original lines do preserve the typical Wycliffite opposition between the virtuous ploughman and Antichrist's church, however: "What knoweth a tyllour at the plowe/ The Popes name and what he hate?/ His Crede suffyseth to hym ynowe" (453–5), and 1041–43, of the monks: "had they ben out of religion,/ They must have honged at the plowe,/ Threshynge and dykynge fro towne towne,/ With sory mete, and not halfe ynowe," quoted from *Six Ecclesiastical Satires* (*132*).

[92] Jill Mann notes that this, and the other positive qualities of the ploughman might be seen as an inversion of the usual derogatory remarks about peasants (*914*, 69–71).

[93] See Anne Hudson (*713*, 342–5) for the range of Wycliffite views on the granting of tithes. At the moderate end of the spectrum, Lollard writers were content with the granting of tithes even if they criticised draconian methods of obtaining them irrespective of the circumstances of the payer. More radical was the view that the individual was due to pay his tithes so long as the recipient had earned them, and the most extreme: that, in keeping with apostolic poverty, priests should not be paid tithes at all.

[94] Hudson (*713*, 391) notes the closeness of the portrait of the Parson to Wyclif's ideal of apostolic priesthood, and further that there is, significantly, no mention of the Parson's celebration of the Mass or his role as a confessor. Mann observes that the link between the Parson and Ploughman illustrates the close union inspired by two ideals of Christian virtue (*914*, 68). Through the series of negatives in his portrait, the Parson is implicitly contrasted to corrupt contemporary priests, see Mann (*914*, 55–67).

[95] Mann notes his absence of suffering in contrast to ploughmen in *Piers Plowman* (*914*, 72–73); a contrast which is applicable also to the depiction of ploughmen in Wycliffite texts.

[96] Christina von Nolcken (*1243*, 88).

The treatment of ploughmen in *Piers Plowman* is much more complex.[97] In addition to his appropriation by the 1381 rebels,[98] the figure of Piers was also the inspiration for the unequivocally Lollard *Pierce the Ploughman's Crede.*[99] It is not hard to see how a reader with Wycliffite sympathies might warm to the presentation of ploughmen in *Piers*.[100] In the *Prologue* ploughmen are "ordeyned" for the profit of the whole community and fulfil their obligations, garnering what wasters, those who "putten hem to pride" will consume.[101] While this does not reproduce exactly the dynamic in Wycliffite texts whereby the ploughman is seen to be necessary and the fourth estate superfluous, a Lollard reader might "concretize" it to yield up this very sense.[102] Piers is Truth's "pilgrym atte plow for pouere mennes sake" (B 6.102),[103] and displays admirable social husbandry in his organisation of the ploughing of the half acre, which, in its substitution for the pilgrimage, might have pleased the sensibilities of a Lollard reader.[104] Although a labourer, Piers also appears as a priestly figure; he opposes the priest in the tearing of the pardon scene in the B text (B 6.105–48),[105] explains the significance of the tree of Charity to Will (B 16.21ff.)[106] and is at the apex of the apostolic ploughing at the conclusion of the poem (B 19.214–337). Most particularly, while it is Piers who establishes the Barn of Unity, it is the friars, part of Antichrist's army, who cause its destruction by selling penance (B 20.53–64; 313–71). Conscience sets off at the end of the poem seeking to *haue* Piers the Plowman in a quest that has been seen as moving outside the institutional church.[107]

---

[97] Mann suggests that Chaucer's Ploughman was influenced by *Piers* (*914*, 68–73), and Helen Cooper examines the relationship between the two prologues in "Langland's and Chaucer's Prologues," *Yearbook of Langland Studies* 1 (1987): 71–81.

[98] For discussion of the rebels' letters which refer to *Piers Plowman*, see Hudson (*713*) and "*Piers Plowman* and the Peasants' Revolt"; Richard Firth Green (*610*); Justice (*765*), and John M. Bowers (*336*).

[99] *Pierce the Ploughman's Crede* (*103*). There is clear support for Wyclif (528–30) and Walter Brut (657–70).

[100] For the relationship between *Piers* and Wycliffite beliefs see Pamela Gradon (*608*); Hudson (*713, 398–408*); David Lawton (*827*). Lawton concludes that Lollards had Langlandian sympathies, 793; Justice (*765*), von Nolcken (*1243*), and Barr, *Signes and Sothe*, 122–25. On ploughmen, see Malcolm Godden, "Plowmen and Hermits in Langland's *Piers Plowman*," *Review of English Studies* n.s. 35 (1984): 129–63.

[101] William Langland (*173*, B Prol. 119–20 and 20–22). All further citations will be to this edition in the main text. See discussion of these lines by Cooper, 78–79.

[102] "Concretization" is the term used by Wolfgang Iser to describe the way that the reader realizes the schematic aspects of a text by filling in the gaps of indeterminacy it inevitably contains, *The Act of Reading: A Theory of Aesthetic Response* (London: Routledge, 1978), 171–79. Szittya notes that Piers is the true labourer, while the friars are the false beggars who do not work (*1169*, 284).

[103] The line is the same in A, but in C, altered to "to pore and ryche" (8.111).

[104] Lollard texts are generally, though not universally, hostile to physical acts of pilgrimage, see Hudson (*713*, 307–09).

[105] The quarrel is substantially abbreviated in C and the tearing of the pardon cut. Aers notes how readers could have found in *Piers* congenial materials for dissent, with Piers Plowman as the opposer of official priests, and finally the absent leader of what has finally become a thoroughly corrupt Catholic Church (*259*, 438–89).

[106] In the C text, Liberum Arbitrium replaces Piers, Passus 18.

[107] Kirk notes how Conscience seeks to "haue," not to "know" Piers Plowman – "to have him means infinitely more than becoming a labourer," 19. On leaving behind the institutional

Nothing in *Piers Plowman*, however, is straightforward. Criticism of the contemporary church shares many issues with Wycliffite polemic, including the prophetic disendowment of the religious and their return to the pristine apostolic state (B 10.316–329; cf. B 15.563: "Takeþ hire landes, ye lordes, and let hem lyue by dymes;/ If possession be poison, and inparfite hem make"), but when it comes to the friars in Passus 20 , Conscience, in a rather enigmatic line, wishes that they had a "fyndyng" rather than oppose him and flatter out of need (B 20.384–5). Clearly, the friars are figured as corrupt in the poem (and useless as guides to Will in Passus 8), but there is no suggestion of the typical Wycliffite complaint that they are "ungrounded."[108] Nor are the friars associated with Cain. Wit's long disquisition on the progeny of Cain in B 9.119–60 reproduces all the negative characteristics with which he was invested, but to characterise illegitimacy, not to vilify unnecessary mendicants.[109]

As in Wycliffite texts, there is passionate concern with the poor, most movingly in two additions to the C text (9.70–158; 13.1–96),[110] while the A text finishes with the lines:

> þanne pore peple as plouȝmen, and pastours of bestis,
> Souteris and seweris – suche lewide iottis
> Percen wiþ a *Paternoster* þe paleis of heuene
> Wiþoute penaunce at here partyng, into þe heiȝe blisse.
> (A 11.310–13)

The similarity to the elevation of the "paternoster" of a ploughman over the masses of a priest in *How Satan and his Priests* (Matthew, 274) is striking. And while in the B and C texts, the dramatic force of these lines is attenuated since they do not form a conclusion, the revisions bring the sentiment closer in line to Wycliffite representations of the third estate. There is a progressive elimination of the artisan class. "Souteres" remain in B (10.461) but "pouere commune laborers" are added (460). C runs:

> Ne none sonnere ysaued ne saddere in bileue
> Then ploughmen and pastours and pore comune peple.
> Lewed lele laboreres and land-tulyng peple
> Persen with a *Paternoster* paradys oþer heuene
> And passen purgatorie penaunceles for here parfit bileue.
> (11.296–300)

Shepherds are still present, but the presence of tillers is amplified at the expense of the artisan class, which produces a profile of the third estate very

---

church, see David Aers, *Chaucer, Langland and the Creative Imagination* (London: Routledge, 1980), 61. See also James Simpson, *Piers Plowman: An Introduction to the B-Text* (London: Longman, 1990), 234–43.

[108] Szittya notes that they are the only religious group whose institution poses a danger to the church (*1169*, 284).

[109] The characteristics listed are exactly those that are grafted onto Cain in Wycliffite texts but there is no explicit association with the friars in *Piers*. Clergy prophesies that before the king comes to reform the clergy, Cain shall awake, but "Dowel shal dyngen hym adoun and destruye his myȝte" (B 10.329, not in C). There is no explicit association between Cain and superfluous orders.

[110] See Derek Pearsall (*1026*).

much in keeping with Wycliffite representation. "Parfit bileue" ("pure" in B 10.464) is also added in both texts, which suggests that the faith of husbandmen is truer than that of the clever clerics with all their book learning.

Once again, however, as with the oppositional depiction of fraternal corruption and Piers's apostolic ploughing, the crucial dimension lacking is that the clergy are unneccessary. The relationship between the clergy and labourers is comparative ("sonner"; "saddere"). In Wycliffite texts, the comparative is deployed to assert that husbandmen are necessary to society while the material church is harmful and otiose.[111] There is a further important difference between the Wycliffite representation of the plough-man and that in *Piers*. In keeping with von Nolcken's distinction between archetypal and temporal representation, the figure of Piers, for all his typological transformations, is still recognisably an actual fourteenth century ploughman.[112] For all the concern with the poor, and the amelioration of the ploughman figure, Langland does not idealize the third estate. As Christopher Dyer has shown, Piers is not a tenant labourer; he owns both his plough and his plot of land. He is a small landowner, and in Passus 6, he is shown to be pitted against the poorest of the rural poor. Piers's confrontation with the wastrel labourers foregrounds contemporary economic concerns and reproduces the kinds of tensions experienced in actual local villages.[113] Individual lines and passages of *Piers Plowman* can be adduced to show compatibility with Wycliffite ideas, but taken as a whole, the poem does not reproduce the particular delineation of the third estate common in Wycliffite texts. Lacking is the sustained idealization of the rural poor as a foil against which to argue for the superfluity of monks, friars and prelates.

Nor, despite the contemporary elevation of the authority of the figure of Piers over the author of the poem, does Piers emerge as the spokesman for the whole poem.[114] In *Pierce the Ploughman's Crede*, by contrast, the ultimate speaker of truth in the poem *is* the ploughman, whose voice at the conclusion merges with that of the narrator and the poet in his insistence on the truth of what he has told.

> . . . all that euer I haue seyd soth it me semeth
> And all that euer I haue writen is soth, as I trowe,
> And for amending of thise men is most that write.   (836–8)

Entirely consonant with representations of the third estate in Wycliffite texts as "pore" men and "simple," endowed with a corrective voice fit to

---

[111] Hilton, "Reasons for Inequality among Medieval Peasants," 250, notes briefly that Wycliffite poems contrast the idle clergy, especially the friars, with the ploughman at work.

[112] Kirk explores this in detail. On the figural interpretation of Piers, see Elizabeth Salter, *Piers Plowman: An Introduction*, 2nd ed. (Oxford: Blackwell, 1969), 83–105.

[113] Christopher Dyer, "*Piers Plowman* and Plowmen: A Historical Perspective," *Yearbook of Langland Studies* 8 (1995): 155–76. On Langland's treatment of labour issues, see Anne Middleton (*952*).

[114] See Anne Middleton (*951*) and Barr, *Signes and Sothe*, 5–7.

speak as reformers for the whole of civic society, this ploughman/narrator/ poet is bearer of the truth against the calumny of "thise men" the friars. The satiric strategy of the whole poem is based on the contrast between the virtuous ploughman and the corrupt friars.[115] The singularity of the friars: "neyther in order ne out" (45), and their contravention of secular and ecclesiastical regulation is ingeniously exposed by having a representative of each of the four orders expose the illegitimacy of the others. All that Peres does when he condemns them is to confirm their very own words. While at lines 511–13 and line 75, Peres draws back from a full-blooded condemnation of the existence of the friars per se by praising the founding ideals of St. Francis, in lines 482–7, he says that fraternal orders were instituted by the devil.[116] Satan sent them into the Church to destroy it:

> Of the kynrede of Caym he caste the freres;
> And founded hem on Farysens feyned for gode.   (486–7)[117]

As in other Wycliffite texts, the friars are the progeny of Cain, and additional to the church; they are "put in" by the devil (505–06). They are invested with all the traits of anti-peasant discourse which Wycliffites transfer to the friars: covetous ignorance (336–7; 357; 497; 591–2; 820); physical grotesqueness (244; 459); bodiliness (44–51; 55; 73; 92; 221–25; 339–40; 594); resemblance to animals (225; 357; 375; 644; 648; 663) dirt (226; 644; 752); lying (359; 379); stealing (68–70); usurpation of social rank (204–5; 499); bizarre clothing (550–4; 608), and sloth (726). They also oppress the poor (216–18; 721–29).

Peres, with his honest toil, is a perfect example of labouring charity, offering to "lene" the narrator "lijflode" as soon as he meets him (445). Probably the most graphic example of the re-registration of peasant muck to symbolise the harsh virtue of true husbandry is the description of Peres wading ankle-deep through the fen, toes poking out of his tattered shoes, as he drives the plough. His four heifers are so painfully thin that you could count their ribs (symbolic presumably of the scarcity of preaching based on the four gospels). The painful poverty of his wife and children is further laid on with a trowel (421–442). In contrast to Piers, this ploughman is an idealized representative of the poorest rural labourer: "Peres . . . the pore man, the plowe-man" (473). There is no suggestion that he owns the land he tills, nor even that the land is good; it seems to consist of sticky mire and ice.[118] The figure is socially deracinated: as in Wycliffite prose texts, there is no attempt to frame the peasant labourer within contemporary economic

---

[115] David Lampe, "The Satiric Strategy of *Pierce the Ploughman's Crede*," in *The Alliterative Tradition in the Fourteenth Century*, ed. B.S. Levy and P. Szarmach (Kent, OH: Kent State Univ. Press, 1981), 69–80.

[116] This is in line with Wyclif's initial admiration of the friars because of their apostolic founding ideals. After the friars' denunciation of his views on the Eucharist, he turned against them, and between 1382 and 1384, denounced them in pamphlets and sermons, see A. Kenny (*784*, 93–94), and A. Gwynn (*617*, 211–79).

[117] Cf. the comparison of a friary to a "heyghe helle-hous of Kaymes kynde" (559).

[118] Though, as Camille points out, ploughing was an activity which chiefly took place in winter (183).

conditions.[119] The ploughman is a non-institutionalised true preacher who is able, and willing, to teach the "lewed" narrator his creed, an act which the friars, too much concerned with conning money from him and slandering each other, were distressingly unable to perform. Peres is a true priest in contrast to the idle superfluity of the mendicant orders:

> Thei vsen russet also somme of thise freres,
> That bitokneth trauaile and trewthe opon erthe.
> Bote loke whou this lorels labouren the erthe,
> But freten the frute that the folk full lellich biswynketh.
> With trauail of trewe men thei tymbren her houses, . . .
> . . . And ryght as dranes doth nought but drynketh vp the huny,
> Whan been withe her bysynesse han brought it to hepe,
> Right so, fareth freres with folke opon erthe;
> They freten vp the furste-froyt and falsliche lybbeth.   (719–29)

The collectively responsible, true labour of the husbandman is contrasted with the false greed of the friars.[120] That which should belong to the ploughman (2 Timothy 2.6: "The husbandman that laboureth must first partake of the fruits"), is gobbled up by the fraternal orders to nourish vain building and parasitic gluttony. Figuring the friars as drones places them outside the hard-working community of bees, and thus, outside civil society.[121] This passage encapsulates in miniature the textual dynamic of Lollard representations of the third estate. *Crede* is a straightforward verse depiction of the relationship between the second and third estates seen in Wycliffite prose texts.[122] While greatly amplified from the local vignettes in the prose, the presentation of the ploughman is much closer in spirit to these texts, than it is to *Piers Plowman*, however much the figure of Peres was inspired by Langland's poem.

Were Usk, Walsingham and Knighton correct, then, in attributing civil sedition to Wyclif and his followers? The answer must be both yes and no. Wyclif condemned the murder of Archbishop Sudbury,[123] and there is no call in Wycliffite texts for all goods to be in common, or for any subversion of secular authority. And yet, the logical outcome of Wycliffite representations of the third estate is to re-write the language of social description and

---

[119] The exception is the criticism of the labourers demand for higher wages and livery, see n. 21 above.

[120] Camille observes that the plough was an absolute essential in the life and prosperity of all levels of society (180).

[121] This, as Lawton has observed (*827*, 791), is very similar to the exemplum of the community of bees in *Mum and the Sothsegger*, 966–1090. I argue elsewhere that the bee exemplum in *Mum* figures a Lollard utopia (*296*, 164–70).

[122] There is a long passage (744–69) which condemns the upward mobility of artisans and beggars, which has been seen as a vicious satire of labourers with economic aspirations, Kathryn Kerby-Fulton, "*Piers Plowman*," in *Cambridge History of Medieval English Literature* (*90*, 513–38, 537). I think that the invective is directed primarily at how the fraternal orders subvert secular hierarchy by making the sons of shoemakers and beggars members of their orders, from which they can go on to be made bishops, and force the nobility to kneel to them (748–756).

[123] *De Blasphemia*, 190/20; see further, Hudson (*729*, 44–46).

to re-draw the map of civil society in a fashion which resonates with the claims of the rebels. To uphold the sanctity of the third estate while arguing for the superfluity of the second, or indeed its eradication, brings Wycliffite polemic close to the insurgents' re-figuring of the political community encapsulated in their apparent watchword: "with Kyng Richarde and the trew commons."[124] The sentiments are not identical, to be sure: Wycliffite texts do not call for the abolition of the lords, but the rebels' watchword claims no explicit place for the clerical estate.

In celebrating the virtuous worth of the poor labourer, Wycliffite texts can also be seen to voice support for exactly the social group who were blamed for revolt (even if the demographic composition of the rebels was rather different). And in promoting the "commune vois" of the "pore" and "simple" as necessary and astringent correction of the corruptions in the civic community, Wycliffte texts nourish the potential of vernacular literacy as an agent of sedition.[125] The distinctiveness of this representation is foregrounded when compared with a text such as *The Pore Caitif*. While this is a work which (dubiously) has been seen to have Wycliffite affiliations, its treatment of the third estate is very different from the characteristic depiction in Lollard texts.[126] MS Bodley 938, which preserves the fourteen chapters of the *Caitif*, interleaved with some Wycliffite additions, brings out the contrast very tellingly.[127] There is stalwart support for the plight of the poor. To eat the bread of poor men is considered to be an act of manslaughter, for anyone to misappropriate their property is to kill the child in the sight of the father, and anyone who withdraws sustenance from a poor man deprives him of his very blood (ff. 135r–v). Significantly, however, there is no accusation against the second estate for such oppression. And while Wycliffite texts praise acts of charity towards the poor, in the section *The Loue of Jesu*, the writer states that even if you "ȝiue alle þingis þat ȝe han to pore men, but if ȝe schulen loue þis name iesu, ȝe traueile in ydel for whi oonli siche schulen be gladdid of iesu" (f. 185v). This is a hierarchy of devotional obligation not likely to have issued from a Lollard quill.[128] Further, while the interests of the poor are championed,

---

[124] The watchword is reported in *The Anonimalle Chronicle, 1333–1381* (*98*, 139): "Et les ditz comunes avoient entre eux une wache worde en Engleys, 'With whom haldes yow?' et le respouns fuist, 'Wyth kynge Richarde and wyth the trew communes.'"

[125] Cf. Aston (*269*, 215).

[126] See Sr. M. Teresa Brady (*342*, 543–8).

[127] Brady (*342*) discusses these insertions on 533; cf. Hudson (*713*, 425, and n.154), where printed versions of some of these additions are noted. See also, Brady (*345*). MS Bodley 938 is not one of the manuscripts discussed. This manuscript is said to contain six such tracts interleaved between two parts of the *Caitif*, between f. 50 and f. 117v. There is also Wycliffite material prior to f. 50, most notably in "The Pater Noster," f. 24, which calls for the Gospel to be declared in English, and states that it is Antichrist who prevents this help to the "lewed." Cf. Arnold, 3.98. I propose to examine the contents of MS Bodley 938 in more detail in a separate study.

[128] We might compare the Wycliffite sermon on the text of 1 Corinthians 13. The writer uses the text to expound sixteen conditions of "charite." The four orders of friars are consistently exempted from these exemplary conditions, leading to the conclusion that, if this epistle of Paul were fully executed as it ought to be, then, "þe rewme of Englond schulde be discharged of þes foure sectis þat ben spokon of," *English Wycliffite Sermons* (*158*, 1.545/146–7). The sermon ends with a call for kings to cast out the four "sectis" from the realm in order to fulfil the office which God has enjoined on them.

there is no attendant idealization of the labourer. Glossing the third precept of the ten commandments, for example, the writer states that it is better to plough on the sabbath than to attend dances and taverns, which is how labourers would spend their time, selling their souls to the devil, if not engaged in work. They are also warned against performing their labour by deceit or trickery (f. 141). Most crucially, at no point is the labourer, or ploughman, held up as essential and uncorrupted, to form a contrast with the superfluity of friars or prelates. *The Pore Caitif* is demonstrably orthodox in its representation of the third estate.

But to free, as Wycliffite texts do, the husbandman from the curse of Cain, and ban the "fourth estate" instead, is to call for a total re-alignment of what is considered "inside" and "outside" both the civic community, and the Church triumphant. Well might writers belonging to the second estate be offended and alarmed by their Wycliffite adoption into the family of Cain. After all, who would wish to be part of a family from hell? Even the self-assured Cain in *The Wakefield Pageant* hardly has a free choice in the matter:

> Now fayre well, felows all, for I must nedys weynd,
> And to the dwill be thrall, warld withoutten end:
> Ordand is my stall, with Sathanas the feynd.[129]

---

[129] *Mactatio Abel*, 463–5, *The Wakefield Pageants in the Townley Cycle*, ed. A.C. Cawley (Manchester: Manchester Univ. Press, 1958).

Reginald Pecock's Vernacular Voice

Mishtooni Bose

Certis, thou3 Crist and his Apostlis weren now lyuyng at Londoun, and wolden bringe . . . braunchis fro Bischopis wode and flouris fro the feeld into Londoun, and wolden delyuere to men that thei make there with her housis gay, into remembraunce of Seint Iohun Baptist . . . 3it tho men receyuyng so tho braunchis and flouris ou3ten not seie and feele that tho braunchis and flouris grewen out of Cristis hondis, and out of the Apostlis hondis. Forwhi in this dede Crist and the Apostlis diden noon other wise than as othere men mi3ten and couthen do. But the seid receyuers ou3ten seie and holde that tho braunchis grewen out of the bowis upon whiche thei in Bischopis wode stoden . . . and in lijk maner the feld is the fundament of tho flouris, and not the hondis of the gaderers, neither tho bringers . . .

What if Crist and hise Apostlis wolden fische with bootis in the see, and wolden aftirward carie tho fischis in paniers upon horsis to London, schulde men seie for reuerence or loue to Crist and hise Apostlis that tho fischis grewen out of the panyeris or dossers, or out of the hondis of Crist and of hise Apostlis . . . ? . . . Certis treuthis of lawe of kind which Crist and hise Apostlis schewiden forth to peple were bifore in the greet see of lawe of kinde in mannis soule eer Crist or his Apostlis were born into this lijf . . .[1]

As this extract from the *The Repressor of Over Much Blaming of the Clergy* illustrates, Reginald Pecock's experiment in annexing vernacular territory for orthodox theology occasionally involved complementary, albeit figurative excursions into the urban territory with which, as Master of Whittington College from 1431 to 1444, he would have been very familiar. The passage is meticulous in its discrimination between ultimate and proximate sources of authority, while the presence of Christ and his apostles in the illustrative hypotheses, far from sacralising their urban setting, do not overwhelm the concreteness of the rituals and quotidian practices of the city.[2] The vernacular voice that Pecock adopts here is that of

---

[1] *The Repressor of Over Much Blaming of the Clergy* (*190*, 1.28–29, 30). I am grateful to the Master and Fellows of Trinity College, Cambridge, the Syndics of Cambridge University Library, and the British Library for permission to quote from manuscripts in their possession during the course of this article. I am also grateful to the editors of the present volume, to two anonymous readers, and to James Simpson for their helpful criticism of an earlier draft of this paper. I have expanded manuscript abbreviations throughout.

[2] Pecock's associate, John Carpenter, common clerk of the City of London, had produced a compilation of documents relating to London customs and rituals, the *Liber Albus* (1417–1419), and the *Repressor* exhibits a similar self-consciousness about city rituals. For further discussion of

his readers' London contemporary, who shows that the principles for understanding the authority of an unwritten "lawe of kinde" can be established from the fruits of their own social observation.[3] In tribute to this particular conception of the natural capacities of the lay intellect, he continuously freights the arguments of the *Repressor* with vignettes of London life, inviting his readers to participate in the fusion of intellectual and imaginative work that the understanding of such examples requires. Thus, when explaining the force of figurative speech, he imagines himself in his reader's "halle or chaumbir." confronted by the "storie" of King Arthur, Caesar or Hector, whether "peintid or wovun."[4] Likewise, when acknowledging the value of images and pilgrimages in the processes of "remembraunce," he draws a parallel with the commemoration of Bishop Gravesend at St. Paul's.[5]

Originality of this kind, as both Pecock and his critic Thomas Gascoigne were aware, can be dismissed as mere idiosyncrasy. In the prologue to his earliest surviving work, the unfinished vernacular *summa* entitled *The Reule of Crysten Religioun*, he concedes that a book similar to his in concerns and argumentative disposition might exist, but that "oon eny book bi hym silf or with his purtenauncis y haue not ʒit seen."[6] In a characteristic rhetorical manoeuvre from the prologue to *The Folewer to the Donet*, he ventriloquises his opponents' view that his teaching originated "al of him silf and of his own heed, fforwhi he alleggith not for him alwey holi scripture or summe doctoures."[7] This hostile view was to receive terse corroboration in Gascoigne's effortless discrediting of Pecock's arguments concerning the preaching obligations of bishops, on the grounds that they were not drawn from the sayings of the sacred doctors, "sed de suis propriis glosis" ("from his own interpretations").[8] Recent developments both within and beyond the field of Wycliffite studies, however, have suggested ways in which Pecock might be liberated from the historical and critical cul-de-sac to which the singularity both of his extant writings and of his eventual arraignment for heresy were in danger of banishing him.[9] His "eccentric

---

this dimension of Pecock's work, see Sheila Lindenbaum, "London Texts and Literate Practice," in *The Cambridge History of Medieval English Literature* (*90*, 298); and, on Carpenter, William Kellaway, "John Carpenter's Liber Albus," *Guildhall Studies in London History* 3 (1978): 67–84.

[3] For further treatment of this literary territory, see Ruth Kennedy, "A Bird in Bishopswood: Some Newly-Discovered Lines of Alliterative Verse from the Late Fourteenth Century," in *Medieval Literature and Antiquities: Studies in Honour of Basil Cottle*, ed. Myra Stokes and T.L. Burton (Cambridge: D.S. Brewer, 1987), 71–87. I am grateful to Julia Boffey for this reference. Kennedy points out the similarities between the "secularised and demystified" city depicted in the anonymous poem that she edits and discusses here, and that of Hoccleve (82). The comparison could be extended to include Pecock.

[4] *Repressor* (*190*, 1.150).

[5] *Repressor* (*190*, 1.215–16). For further discussion of Pecock's investment in "the observation of things as they are" and the historical criticism that often results from this, see Arthur B. Ferguson, "Reginald Pecock and the Renaissance Sense of History," *Studies in the Renaissance* 13 (1966): 150.

[6] *The Reule of Crysten Religioun* (*194*, 13).

[7] *The Folewer to the Donet* (henceforth *Folewer*; *193*, 8).

[8] Gascoigne, *Loci e Libro Veritatum* (*144*, 15).

[9] On Pecock's posthumous career as a proto-Protestant, a piece of historiographical misprision resulting from his arraignment for heresy, see C.W. Brockwell, Jr., "The Historical Career of

corpus of simplified theology" has been sympathetically reinterpreted as an extreme example of the diversification of the discipline during this period, and his intellectual individuality constructively viewed as a quality shared by his critic Gascoigne and later English theologians.[10] There have been further successful attempts to establish his place within new critical narratives of the mid-fifteenth century, including assessments of his role in the complex milieux of its vernacular and religious cultures, and his original contributions to contemporary developments in legal theory.[11]

Of most relevance for the present discussion is the growing attention to the complexities of Pecock's vernacular voice, which have recently provoked contrasting critical assessments of his authorial persona. When E.F. Jacob described Pecock as "a literary figure, pure and simple," it was in order to emphasise his belief in the superiority of the *littera* of the written text over the sermon as vehicles of polemic and religious doctrine.[12] A much later study has usefully shown that at least three different levels of style can be discerned in Pecock's vernacular prose and that he was clearly aware of the proprieties of literary decorum.[13] However, the critical investigation of "literariness" now provokes further consideration of the rhetoricity of a text, its possible performative aspirations and its place in cultural politics more broadly conceived, and Pecock's writing has also begun to receive analysis in these terms. On one hand, it has been argued that he and Richard Rolle "were the [Middle English writers] closest to the Latin tradition and its notions of authorization."[14] It is at least plausible, for example, that the voice of the aspiring *auctor* can be heard in Pecock's concern to control the way in which his imagined readership might gain access to the canon of his works.[15] However, Pecock's most recent biographer makes clear the possibility that the authorised circulation of vernacular works by individuals during this period could be associated with heretical practices: "Pecock . . . had borrowed from the modes of discourse current among the anticlericals and heretics, in that in his attempt to refute [them], he had adopted their habit of circulating theological and polemical writings."[16] The possibility that Pecock's literate practices may have been

---

Bishop Reginald Pecock, D.D.: The Poore Scholeris Myrrour or a case study in famous obscurity," *Harvard Theological Review* 74 (1981): 177–207.

[10] Jeremy Catto (*378*) and (*379*, 175–280, 265, 278); see also (*53*, 772–3, 782).

[11] Wendy Scase (*1082*) and (*1083*); R.M. Ball, "The Opponents of Bishop Pecock," *Journal of Ecclesiastical History* 48 (1997): 230–262; Norman Doe, *Fundamental Authority in Late Medieval English Law* (Cambridge: Cambridge Univ. Press, 1990); James H. Landman, "'The Doom of resoun': Accommodating Lay Interpretation in Late Medieval England," in *Medieval Crime and Social Control*, ed. Barbara A. Hanawalt and David Wallace (Minneapolis and London: Univ. of Minnesota Press, 1999) 90–123.

[12] *The Fifteenth Century, 1399–1485* (*744*, 682–3). For Pecock's comments concerning the respective merits of preaching and texts, see for example *Folewer* (*193*, 102–106).

[13] Joseph F. Patrouch, Jr. (*1016*, 47–72).

[14] Tim William Machan, *Textual Criticism and Middle English Texts* (Charlottesville and London: Univ. Press of Virginia, 1994), 112.

[15] Nicholas Watson has described the ways in which Rolle could be viewed as a late medieval *auctor* (*1264*, 257–270), and it is clear that Pecock wanted to achieve comparable status through the authorised circulation of his works: see for example the prologue to the *Reule* (*194*, 17–22).

[16] Scase (*1082*, 117).

contaminated by those of the heretics is taken further in a second critical approach to his work. Steven Justice suggests that his voice could be mistaken for that of a Lollard, since "[i]n the absence of a clear and technical English vocabulary of *orthodox* theology, anyone trying to persuade or refute the heretics had to use a language identified as theirs." In such a climate, it has been argued, Pecock "discovered the dangers of sounding like them: his attempts to answer the Lollards on their own terms . . . earned him formal condemnation by the English episcopacy."[17] The emergence of this critical dichotomy provides the most immediate context for the concerns of the present discussion.

As models of further enquiry into the nature of Pecock's literary voice, each of these contrasting views is as problematic as it is suggestive. Neither can be easily dismissed, because each reflects some of the dimensions of his writing. Clearly, some of Pecock's stylistic choices were made specifically to distance his vernacular voice from that of his opponents. His concern to infuse his writing with the Latinate idioms of legal and academic prose are easily recognisable in his often curial style (one of his characteristic idioms, and clearly distinguishable from those of Wycliffite writings).[18] Moreover, notwithstanding Gascoigne's jibe at his originality, he makes frequent and explicit recourse to the authorities of the schools and, as is well known, abandons the vernacular entirely when moving dialectical questions concerning the relationship between the persons of the Trinity.[19] On the other hand, given that "it was part of the crusade of Wycliffism to take learning and learned ways of thought out from the university to the rural and urban populace,"[20] it is also possible that the notion that Pecock "sounded like" a Lollard is one, albeit very impressionistic, way of accounting for the fact that his translation of some academic terms and techniques into English appears to continue what Wycliffite experimentation in this area had pioneered. Certainly, the intellectual ambition shared by Pecock's writings and certain of the Wycliffite texts makes them equally transgressive by the standards of Archbishop Arundel's notably anti-intellectual eighth Constitution, with its prohibition against "conclusions or propositions that sound as if they are contrary to the catholic faith or good morals" and the use of elaborate technical terms. Furthermore, its warning that a "prefatory protestation" (*protestatio praemissa*) could not excuse the errant teacher casts a dark shadow over Pecock's habit of using the vernacular

---

[17] Steven Justice (*764*, 304). Sheila Lindenbaum concurs with this approach, asserting that Pecock's English, which lacks the aureation favoured by Lydgate, for example, could be "confused with [that of] Lollard writing" ("London Texts," *90*, 298).

[18] The characteristic lexis and syntax of curial prose, "a style with a public and legal function," are assessed in J.D. Burnley, "Curial Prose in England," *Speculum* 61 (1986): 593–614 (the quotation appears on 596). Pecock's experiments with this register are unusual: Burnley points out that much late fourteenth- and early fifteenth-century English prose (including that which he ascribes to "Wiclif") "shows no evidence at all of curial influence" (611). On the ideological implications of Wycliffite prose style, see Christina von Nolcken (*1248*). Further assessment of Pecock's style is given in Janel Mueller (*973*, 132–47).

[19] On Pecock's scholarship, see V.H.H. Green (*614*, 76–88). Pecock's excursion into Latin occurs in *Reule* (*194*, 88–89).

[20] Anne Hudson (*716*, 50).

prologue for variations on precisely this kind of academic *captatio benevolentiae*.[21] Writing decades after the promulgation of the Constitutions, Pecock is self-conscious about the possibilities of transgression in his own texts, although his attitudes veer between anxious compliance and an evident yearning for more freedom of discussion in the world beyond the schools.[22] The above-mentioned recourse to Latin in his discussion of the Trinity, for example, hardly constitutes a simple retreat behind the façade of academic discourse. He robustly frames this passage with an energetic discussion of the proprieties of theological discussion in the vernacular that keeps in play the radical possibilities of his experiment.[23] Later, however, he accepts that his work will be "diligently ouer seen and examyned," and that if, as a result, this portion of his discussion "be not to be leernyd of lay men in her modir langage, y wole al redy suffre and obeie þat þilk porcioun be left out of þis book whanne þis book is to be writun in þe comoun peplis langage . . ."[24]

By aligning him either with a "Latin tradition" or with the idioms and ambitions of the vernacular Wycliffite texts, the incipient critical disagreement concerning the nature of Pecock's authorial persona threatens to perpetuate among his modern readers interpretative constraints similar to those of the period in which he was attempting to establish an independent voice. In particular, the apparently compelling but ultimately misleading notion that Pecock's vernacular voice might be easily confused with that of Wycliffite discourse not only leaves uncontested the notion that Wycliffite discourse is itself univocal, but also threatens a regression from the important assessment of Pecock in the most comprehensive account to date of Wycliffite literature and culture. In *The Premature Reformation*, Anne Hudson concluded that "to a contemporary Lollard, the differences [between Pecock's writings and those of the Wycliffites] must have been more striking than the similarities."[25] The present discussion, likewise, will maintain that it is not at all clear that Pecock ever argued with Lollards on terms that they had established. However, to conclude that Pecock did not "sound like" a Lollard is not to deny that Wycliffite discourses, among others, "marked" his extant works in a number of ways other than at the level of explicit citation. Further exploration of these markings provides but one way of delineating more sharply the relatively unmapped contours of the complex literary and intellectual culture of mid-fifteenth-century

---

[21] *Concilia Magnae Britanniae et Hiberniae* (*228*, 3.317): "statuimus, et . . . inhibemus, ne quis, vel qui . . . conclusiones aut propositiones in fide catholica seu bonis moribus adverse sonantes . . . protestatione praemissa vel non praemissa, asserat vel proponat, etiamsi quadam verborum aut terminorum curiositate defendi possint." In his *Book of Faith*, Pecock referred to "protestaciouns bi me made, in prologgis of myn othere bokis" (*191*, 121).

[22] For a classic statement of the constraints within which Pecock was writing, see Nicholas Watson (*1265*). Watson acknowledges, however, that there are certain respects in which Pecock resists easy incorporation within this narrative of the period (833). See further R.M. Haines (*622*).

[23] *Reule* (*194*, 85–8, 90).

[24] *Reule* (*194*, 99). Pecock's remarks here also shed interesting light on the possible "draft" status of this, the only extant version of the *Reule*.

[25] Anne Hudson (*713*, 442).

England, a period in which original Lollard writings had largely ceased to appear.[26]

To date, Pecock's characteristic place in Wycliffite studies has been that of an imaginative and resourceful but ultimately problematic witness to fifteenth-century Lollard culture.[27] The most recent biography of Pecock makes clearer the way in which a shift of critical focus, involving concentration on the cultural politics of his particular authorial project, can suggest new directions in this field. Recommending "further research on [Pecock's] surviving books, in particular textual criticism and investigation of their relations with contemporary heretical and polemical material," it thereby attempts to instigate a more subtle appreciation both of Pecock's relationship with Wycliffite textual practices, and of those practices in themselves.[28] Isolated chronologically from the earlier Wycliffite controversies, Pecock's work nevertheless aspires in part to forge discursive continuities with them, and even, on occasion, explicitly fashions itself from their materials. He is therefore obliged to negotiate between the competing stances of hostility and hospitality, rejecting Wycliffite conclusions while drawing some rhetorical sustenance from the kinds of polemical and generic experimentation promoted by participants in the earlier controversies. The present discussion, therefore, will define more precisely the nature of Pecock's compromise between the demands of experimentation and repression.

I

Pecock's writing has a strongly rhetorical dimension that arises from his fundamental awareness that the history of confrontation with heresy, no less than the history of pedagogy in general, was also to some extent inextricable from the history of method. This sensibility has its scholastic precedents. Aquinas had addressed the rhetorical purposes of scholastic discourse in a quodlibetal question discussing the validity of the use of authorities in disputations. He concluded by acknowledging the extent to which techniques of disputation depend for their success on a disputant's willingness to adapt material and argumentative grounds according to the expectations and assumptions of his interlocutor.[29] In the *Book of Faith*, Pecock "translates" this rhetorical imperative into the vernacular, making it clear that he was prepared to give some ground to a sceptical laity in general, rather than specifically to avowed Wycliffites, by allowing the genre of some of his works to be dictated by their perceived needs. Rather than using the established methods of the clergy, therefore, he chose to proceed by "an other wey, and in another maner, and bi meene which the lay

[26] Anne Hudson (*713*, 451).
[27] Anne Hudson (*713*, 55–57).
[28] Scase (*1082*, 118).
[29] Quodlibet 4, q.9, a.3, in *Quaestiones Quodlibetales*, ed. R. Spiazzi (Turin and Rome: Marietti, 1949), 83.

persoonys wole admitte and graunte . . . that we owen to bileeve and stonde to sum seier or techer which may faile, while it is not knowe that thilk seier or techer theryn failith."[30] The basis for his authority, therefore, was to be a calculated but clearly risky investment in the acknowledged vulnerability of the individual "seier or techer," a stance that emphasised Pecock's separateness not only from his potential lay audience but also, and more controversially, from his fellow-clergy.

However, by exposing the complexity of this role, he was abandoning the clerical inscrutability that the academic and polemical idioms (rather than simply the Latin) favoured by his predecessors, Woodford, Dymmok and Netter, could have afforded him. Increasing attention is being given to the way in which Pecock eagerly exploited the rhetorical opportunities afforded by the vernacular prologue to articulate the opportunities and burdens of authorship.[31] Pecock's particular inflection of the literary vernacular included a rhetoric of self-disclosure which would on occasion leave him precariously poised between authority and vulnerability.[32] He could not resist drawing attention to the fact that his works had emanated from a frequently embattled individual.[33] Moreover, in crafting such a literary persona – in crafting a distinctive persona at all, in fact – he rendered himself more transparently vulnerable than did any of the Lollard writers, the most notable point of contrast being the assiduously exemplary authorial voice of *The Testimony of William Thorpe*.[34] In the prologue to his theological primer, *The Donet*, Pecock probed the inseparability of vulnerability and authority in the literary personae of the church fathers, who are here characterised as the victims of misinterpretation and misprision. In Pecock's version of the patristic canon, to be great is certainly to be misunderstood. Thus, St. Gregory "founde . . . moche mys disposid men forto lette and diffame and distroie his bokis," to the extent that he would not allow any of his works to be disseminated before his death. Likewise, St. Jerome "had manye detractouris and inpugners of hise writingis."[35] In this prologue, however, Pecock parts company with these patristic precedents, claiming a different authorial role, "forto be a profitable procutoure to lay men."[36] In carving such a position for himself, he was, however unwittingly, recycling a term which had featured in the polemical register of Lollard writings. "Anticristis procatour" had been condemned in *The Lanterne of Liȝt*, and "worldly prelatis" had been characterised elsewhere as "procuratours of þe fend" because they substituted "lesyngis" and "fablis" for

[30] *Book of Faith* (*191*, 113).
[31] For references to recent criticism, see Mishtooni Bose, "The Annunciation to Pecock: Clerical *Imitatio* in the Fifteenth Century," *Notes and Queries* 47 (2000): 172–6, at 172.
[32] For further consideration of this medieval *topos*, see A.J. Minnis (*958*).
[33] G.M. Trevelyan's comments regarding the *Repressor* are still very pertinent, although their rhetorical and ideological implications deserve to be unravelled further: "[Pecock] adopts the tone, not of a pope speaking 'ex cathedra,' but of a man taking his readers into his confidence" (*1219*, 345).
[34] On William Thorpe's persona and his command of academic techniques, see Fiona Somerset (*1129*, 179–215); Rita Copeland (*418*).
[35] *The Donet . . . Collated with The Poore Mennis Myrrour* (*192*, 7).
[36] (*192*, 8).

"goddis word."[37] Admittedly, the term *procutoure*, or *proctour* is a mobile, contested term in such texts: sometimes it is used pejoratively, as in these examples, but it is also subject to prescriptive use when Wycliffite writers are attempting to imagine a mediating social role for the clergy. On such occasions, *procutoures* are viewed as good stewards, capable of husbanding both spiritual and material resources with humility.[38] The stubborn semantic instability of the word chosen by Pecock to encapsulate his mediating role neatly illustrates the problems attendant on his experimentation with the vernacular. His success would depend on the extent to which he could appropriate and extend its argumentative resources, while staking out rhetorical territory clearly distinguishable from that of the earlier Wycliffite controversies.

Nowhere does Pecock's self-imposed role as "procutoure," mediating between clergy and laity but set apart from both, lead to more complex consequences in his work than in the "entre, or the introductorie or inleding" that followed the prologue to the *Reule*. Here, Pecock uses the conventions of a popular medieval genre, the literary vision, to rhetoricise and authorise his unique position. He depicts himself as having been visited by the "treuthis of philosophie," personified here as the daughters of God, who choose him to redress a cultural grievance, namely their abandonment by the clergy and, by implication, from theological texts. The daughters authorise Pecock to write an approved theological text composed of truths which are "enbrethid" into him by each woman as she embraces him.[39]

It is possible to situate the "entre" to the *Reule* in a more precise literary context than has hitherto been recognised. I have argued elsewhere that, despite its obvious Boethian resonances, this passage has a much closer analogue (if not, indeed, a source) in the visionary opening to Christine de Pizan's *Le Livre de la Cité des Dames* (1405).[40] Here, Christine depicts herself as having been visited by three women, "Raison," "Droiture" and "Justice," who authorise her to redress their cultural grievance, namely the presence of misogynist attitudes among certain of the *auctoritates*. If the relationship between Pecock's "entre" and Christine's "annunciation" is accepted as plausible, it becomes possible to view their strategies as complementary, Christine appropriating the learned discourse of *clergie* for the valorising of women and Pecock fashioning a new body of vernacular *clergie* for the valorisation of orthodoxy. Nevertheless, it is not necessary to impute a single authorial intention behind Pecock's "entre," since this richly connotative passage evokes several disparate literary contexts.[41] As the urban rituals scattered throughout the *Repressor*

---

[37] For the range of uses, see *MED*, *proctour* (n) 1 (b). *The Lanterne of Liȝt* (*174*, 117); "Of prelates," in Matthew (*182*, 60; see also 70).

[38] For examples of this latter use, see Matthew (*182*, 91, 139, 279).

[39] *Reule* (*194*, 30–6).

[40] Bose, "The Annunciation to Pecock."

[41] Pecock's account bears comparison with the osculatory vision that occurs in the "autobiographical apologia" written by Robert of Liège (also known as Rupert of Deutz) to accompany his commentary on St. Matthew's gospel. Robert discloses that he had experienced a vision in which Christ, suspended on a crucifix above a high altar, kissed him deeply, thereby authorising his

show, Pecock could be aggressively contemporary, and the lexical precision of this visionary interlude likewise tethers it more firmly to its historical moment than might at first be supposed. The cultural grievance aired by the daughters of God has a precise focus in their complaints against the clergy's use of unsound teaching materials, "oolde rehercellis, strange stories, fablis of poetis, newe invenciouns," which have been "gaili aparailid" with "curiose divisyngis" and "new langage forgyng."[42] Use of these materials, the daughters complain, has become a prerequisite for clerical authority: "no man is holde a clerke but if he can of hem be a talker," and no man is considered worthy or acceptable to preach unless "he be of his sermoun bi hem a florischer."[43] The abandonment of philosophically-informed theology has resulted in "manye untrewe opynyouns feyned and forged bi enviosite" without "ground of sufficient resoun or holy scripture."[44]

The daughters' terms, which are evidently endorsed by Pecock, invoke controversies concerning the appropriateness of different preaching styles and materials that preceded and outlasted the most vigorous phase of Wycliffite attention to this matter.[45] Nevertheless, one particular image cements a connection between the discourse manipulated by Pecock here and Wycliffite anticlerical polemic. Pecock's concern with the legitimation of his theological project finds its correlative in the daughters' promise that, should he reject the degenerate example of his fellow-clergy, he will be able to produce work of true legitimacy, "stuf enouȝ of our delyveraunce," without "additamentis or to settyngis of eny bastard braunchis."[46] The final phrase recurs when the daughters make yet more explicit the nature of the spiritual congress which Pecock is to enjoy with them, a consummation of the relationship between theology and philosophy complicated by the fact that they will permit him to pay court to the "daughters of men," but that the latter may only serve as his concubines, to engender books which the daughters of God will adopt as "children of purchace legal and leful and no bastard braunchis."[47] Pecock's meaning is clear: only a philosophically-informed theology has the authority to sanction the exempla and other "additamentis" (accretions) associated with pastoral theology, and with the homiletic tradition in particular. The repetition of the phrase "bastard braunchis," however, which anchors the general assumption throughout the "entre" that religious discourse can be divided into legitimate essences and

worthiness for ordination and his further understanding of Christian mysteries. For discussion of Robert and other male visionaries, see Robert Lerner, "Ecstatic Dissent," *Speculum* 67 (1992): 33–57. I am grateful to Nicholas Watson for this reference and for further discussion of the medieval tradition of male visionaries.

[42] *Reule* (*194*, 32–3).

[43] *Reule* (*194*, 33).

[44] *Reule* (*194*, 33).

[45] H.L. Spencer (*1133*, 78–133, 228–247). Pecock's involvement in a 1447 preaching controversy is described by Scase (*1082*, 95–99). Although much work remains to be done in this area, the homiletic and pastoral commitments of Pecock's contemporaries are the subject of thorough and illuminating discussion in Ball, "The Opponents of Bishop Pecock." See further Ball (*293*) and Jeremy Catto (*378*, 257–259).

[46] *Reule* (*194*, 34).

[47] *Reule* (*194*, 35–6).

illegitimate accretions, brings the *Reule* more directly into the hinterlands of the Wycliffite controversies, and makes more urgent the question as to what extent Pecock was familiar with the vernacular literature that they had produced. "Bastard" alone was used both nominally and adjectivally in the antifraternal literature produced by Lollards: thus, one writer describes "freris" as "bastardis to goddis lawe" because they "tellen iapes and lesyngis" and abandon the gospel.[48] The collocation with "braunchis" appears in a Wycliffite sermon in which the preacher emphasises the need to uproot "evyl herbis . . . and bastard braunchis wiþowten byleve."[49] More systematically, anxieties about the illegitimate forms and uses of theology that resound throughout the *Upland* series are partly articulated through accusations and counter-accusations of bastardy. Jack Upland demands an explanation for the friars' alleged persecution of secular priests: "whi ben ȝe so unkynde as bastard braunchis to pursue prestis to prisonynge & to fire for prechinge of Cristis law freli?"[50] Friar Daw appropriates the phrase in his response, arguing that the real "bastard braunches" in this case are the heretics that "launchen from oure bileue," abandon the teaching of the church and "beren yuel fruyte & soure to atasten."[51]

The use of this distinctive phrase has only been recorded for Wycliffite and related literature. Although it may have survived independently in oral contexts, there remains a strong possibility that its appearance in the *Reule* may indicate Pecock's familiarity with terms used in the vernacular literature of the earlier controversies. The problem with Pecock's use of the phrase, however, is precisely that it occurs outside this context. The close correspondence between the arguments of Daw and Upland makes it a simple matter to register the changing value of the phrase in their debate, whereas in the *Reule* it has broken loose from the previous controversy, and is consequently a less stable form of argumentative currency. By using a contested phrase, and one strongly associated with the idiom of Wycliffite writings, Pecock was running the risk of appearing to collude with the rhetoric of his natural opponents, rather than appropriating it and turning it against them in the manner of a latter-day Daw. He clearly intended, through this melding of visionary and polemical discourses, to distinguish his distinctive conception of religious teaching from that of his contemporaries. In seeking to distance himself from his fellow-clergy, however, he failed on this occasion to guard himself against the merging of his idiom with that of their common antagonists. In later works, written in different genres, Pecock would take care to use literary techniques intended to achieve separateness and clarity for the vernacular voice of a *procutoure*.

---

[48] "Of faith, hope and charity," in Matthew (*182*, 347).
[49] MED *bastard*, n. as adj., 2 (b); *English Wycliffite Sermons* (*158*, 1.380).
[50] *Jack Upland, Friar Daw's Reply and Upland's Rejoinder* (*159*, 64–5).
[51] *Jack Upland* (*159*, 92).

II

In the prologue to *The Book of Faith*, Pecock deals with a similar issue to that tackled in the "entre" to the *Reule*, namely lay disenchantment with the clergy's defence of its authority. In this text, however, lay dissatisfaction is viewed as a response to the attitudes and assumptions of the clergy rather than to the dearth of philosophy in their teaching materials. Pecock acknowledges the laity's ability to recognise that "the clergie may faile and erre as weel as thei . . . sith, as thei seien, the clergie is not worthi be visited by eny special inspiracioun or revelacioun fro God more than thei hem silf ben worthi."[52] As has been seen, this openly admitted fallibility was a vital aspect of his bid for a new kind of clerical authority.

Pecock's brief experiment with the polemical dialogue, a genre comparable to similar examples in Netter and some Lollard writers, further illustrates the way in which the argument from personal "freelte" could be extended in ways that would not compromise the integrity of his authorial voice.[53] In the fifth part of *The Repressor*, he considers the challenges that have been posed to the mendicant orders. Lay people, he points out, have not only objected to the religious practices of these orders, but also object even to their distinctive forms of dress, to their maintenance of stately buildings for the reception of aristocrats, and large churches that are grand enough to bear comparison with cathedrals. Lastly, they criticise the mendicant rule that permits neither the touching nor the conveying of money while allowing it to be amassed in coffers and counted with the end of a stick and, furthermore, allowing the handling of jewels and expensive plate.[54]

Pecock proceeds to answer each of these arguments in turn, but confutation of the final argument provokes a significant modulation in style. Instead of answering in his own voice, he stages a debate between a "frere of Seint Francessis ordre" and his hostile interlocutor, resuscitating a prominent literary genre of vernacular Wycliffism in order to ventriloquise a response on the imaginary friar's behalf.[55] "Frere," says the imaginary layman, "thou louest money as myche as othere men louen, and more than othere men louen; for ellis thou woldist not so bisili begge for to haue it; whi wolt not thou thanne handle money as othere men handlen?" The embattled friar, Pecock suggests, "myȝte weel answer thus, 'sir, if y loue money more than othere men louen, and more than y schulde loue; ȝit if ne were this forbering fro touche of money, y schulde loue money more than y loue now; and therfore this forbering fro touche is not in vein.'"[56] Clearly,

---

[52] *Book of Faith* (*191*, 110).
[53] Netter stages a "Dialogus religiosi & clerici curati": *Doctrinale Antiquitatum Fidei Catholicae Ecclesiae* (*188*, 3.512B–544D). This is both an elaborate and self-consciously exemplary dialogue in which "Clericus" and "Regulus" each argue for the superiority of the other's vocation. For one Lollard example, see below.
[54] *Repressor* (*190*, 2.543).
[55] *Repressor* (*190*, 2.558–560).
[56] *Repressor* (*190*, 2.558–9).

Pecock is here appropriating contentious material and attempting to
"launder" it, and once again his rhetorical exercise raises the question of
his familiarity with vernacular literature of this kind. Although the idiom
that he constructs here for the antifraternal interlocutor is once again
strongly reminiscent of that of *Jack Upland*, the specific arguments that he
confronts occur not in that text but in, for example, the Wycliffite
commentary on the testament of St. Francis.[57]

By modelling one possible response to an anticlerical argument, Pecock's
brief experiment deliberately recalls, and possibly attempts to revive, the
controversial atmosphere of the anti- and profraternal dialogues of the late
fourteenth century. The antifraternal dialogue between "Jon and Richerd,"
for example, had concluded with the robust recommendation that
"comouns," "seculer lordes" and "parsons and pristis" should be mobi-
lised to further the dialogue's achievements by conducting their own
interrogation of the mendicant orders, and it supported this aim by
suggesting a brief list of the kinds of questions that they might use.[58]
The suggested questions concerned the long-established topics of antifraternal literature: the dubious spiritual benefits of alms-giving; the scriptural
inauthenticity of assertions in favour of the poverty of Christ, and the
ontology of the consecrated host. The dialogue had concluded, therefore,
by scripting the possible ways in which its ideas might be replicated and
appropriated among the different estates. Pecock's own dialogue shows his
alertness to the rhetorical efficacy of the exemplary text, and reveals that he
shared with both Netter and the writers of the Lollard dialogues an
imaginative awareness of the potential, and even the necessity, of the
form as an active means of intervention in social, ecclesiastical and
doctrinal disputes. In this particular instance, the friar's description of
himself as a "man freel bi kinde and not hardi for to feele of my silf that y
am in the fulnes of perfeccioun" furthers Pecock's pragmatic investment in
the admission of clerical frailty. This is a realistically-conceived friar for
whom compromise – "an other wey," in fact – is a route, not an obstacle,
to perfection.[59] The voice adopted in this polemical dialogue, therefore,
distances Pecock's position from his opponents while allowing him to
plunder the rhetorical resources of the earlier controversies.

---

[57] Although Jack asks a friar why mendicants will not touch silver (*159*, 68), the commentary on the
testament is even closer: "þei wolen telle gold and money & touche it wiþ a sticke or wiþ gloues &
a grete cuppe of gold or pece of siluer worþ many markis to drynke noble wyn of . . ." (Matthew
[*182*, 49]). Lawrence Clopper has shown that this kind of critique originated not with the
Wycliffites but with "rigorists" such as Ubertino da Casale, who criticised the order from within
(*398*, 31–33). Clopper draws an explicit comparison between the Wycliffite commentary and
Ubertino's criticisms (*398*, 44). On the Latin antifraternal tradition, see Penn R. Szittya (*1169*);
Wendy Scase (*1081*); Somerset (*1129*, 135–178) and Somerset (*1130*).

[58] Cambridge, Trinity College B.14.50, f. 55v. For further discussion of this dialogue, see Somerset
(*1129*, 208); for the context, see Anne Hudson (*687*).

[59] *Repressor* (*190*, 2.560). There is some precedent for Pecock's use of the topos: in "Jon and
Richerd," Richerd accuses himself of having "synned in ypocrisie" and admits that friars
"synnen more here, for þei oblychyn hem more to mekenes and to poverte" (37v).

III

As may be seen from this example, Pecock's alertness to the proprieties of literary genre made it possible to for him disengage himself from the more problematic aspects of experimentation with vernacular idioms that had left him exposed in the ambitious "entre" to the *Reule*. Although in the more narrowly polemical *Repressor* he discusses scriptural texts favoured by Lollards, his most devastating critique of Lollard *literature*, as opposed to Lollard *culture* more broadly understood, is his habitual refusal to acknowledge its existence, let alone to evaluate its command of disputational tactics: in effect, his version of vernacular argumentation is installed to displace the Wycliffite versions, if not actually to efface them. In this, he differs greatly even from Netter, whose *Doctrinale* incorporates a lively assessment of the rhetorical efficacy or otherwise of the Wycliffites' tactics of argumentation. A vigorous example of this is provided by Netter's blistering treatment of the Wycliffites' defence of their master on the grounds that he was not making assertions, but asking questions ("non omnia asserit . . . quia *inquisitive* [inquiunt] aut *arguitive* multa dicit, quae asserere non proponit").[60] Netter is unimpressed: when Wyclif corroborates his heretical assumptions with reason, and defends them by twisting scriptural and patristic passages, he asks, does he seem to be proceeding by argument or by tentative inquisition? Such a method of proceeding, he argues, is similar to the tactics of Pilate, whose habit of making statements under the guise of questions was exposed by Christ: when Pilate asked "Are you the King of the Jews?" Christ responded, "You have said that I am a king."[61] Netter goes on to lay out the criteria that a faithful disputant should observe, drawing on Augustine's treatise *Contra Cresconium*, which explicates and defends the use of dialectical procedures in theological discourse.[62] The passage from chapter fifteen quoted by Netter describes how the true disputant is able to distinguish truth from falsehood, and contrasts such clarity and humility with the procedures of the heretics, who capture the assent of their reckless audience with insidious "questions."[63] Netter goes on to expose another argumentative tactic that he deems characteristic of heretical discourse: the habit of expressing contentious views in the third person, "as if others were saying this and not they" ("quasi alii hoc dixissent, & non ipsi"). Once again, Netter draws on Augustine's confrontations with heresy, this time using his description of Pelagius's habit of introducing arguments by attributing them to others. This engagement with Wycliffite thought combines a critical appreciation of the resources of rhetoric with a historically-informed sense of its own context. Consequently, although he stalwartly opposes them, there is a

[60] Netter (*188*, 2.16A).
[61] Netter (*188*, 2.16D).
[62] The full text is *Contra Cresconium Grammaticum Donatistam libri IV*: *PL* 43, 446–594.
[63] Netter (*188*, 2.17B, 17D) (cf. *PL* 43, 457). Netter gives the passage added weight through repetition.

sense in which Netter is nevertheless doing some justice to the intellectual aspirations and achievements of the Wycliffites.

Pecock, by contrast, gives little sense of how familiar he was with the more academically ambitious of the Wycliffite texts. One striking example of the way in which he was able to limit the intellectual impact of Lollard arguments (pitting himself against a rather unsophisticated text, admittedly) occurs in the *Repressor*, in a passage which constitutes the most tangible evidence of Pecock's links with a lively, complex textual community. Here, he cites and responds to the arguments of a short Lollard tract which occurs in a common-profit book made from the goods of John Colop, a member of Pecock's London circle.[64] The tract in question expounds an essential aspect of Lollard hermeneutics, namely the insistence that the words of scripture must neither be added to nor abridged in any way.

Awareness of the complexities of contemporary manuscript culture provokes sharper understanding of the level of repression on Pecock's part here. Together with Richard Lavenham's treatise on the seven deadly sins, the common-profit manuscript contains other Lollard texts: the comparatively well-known "The holi prophete Dauid seith," concerning the literal interpretation of scripture; a much longer tract (ff. 27v–35v) on the "seiyngis of dyvers doctoris" concerning the Eucharist; short tracts (ff. 36r–40r) expounding Matthew 21.43–6; and a declaration of "foure errours which letten þe verrey knowyng of holy writ" (ff. 98v–99v).[65] Orthodox and heretical materials are openly juxtaposed here, although the particular network of literate practices that fostered the compiling of this enigmatic codex remains largely inscrutable.[66] Pecock's writing makes close contact here with a heterogeneous literary culture, characterised by a spectrum of relationships between orthodox and heterodox texts, and of which identifiably Wycliffite writings formed only a part.[67] In this case, however, Pecock's response was to maintain clear boundaries between his literary experimentation and the kinds of activity that surrounded him. He does not explicitly identify this tract as his source, but accurately summarises its arguments: "to Holi Writt men schulde not sett eny exposiciouns, declaracions, or glosis, no more than that men ouȝten take awei fro Holi Writt eny proces or parti writen in Holi Writt."[68] The tract tersely asserts that if any man adds to the words of prophecy contained in the book of Revelation, God will inflict "plagis" on him, and "if any man do it awey fro the wordis

---

[64] The book is Cambridge University Library Ff.vi.31. Pecock's response to the Lollard tract has been noted by Wendy Scase (*1082*, 267).

[65] "The holi prophete Dauid seith" is printed in Margaret Deanesly (*475*, 445–56).

[66] A.I. Doyle notes that "the contents are remarkable for combining moderate Lollard tracts . . . with the rare epistles of spiritual counsel connected with the *Cloud of Unknowing*" (*506*, 133). He has speculated that the manuscript "may have been made up from parts written at different dates": "A Survey of the Origins and Circulation of Theological Writings in English in the 14th, 15th, and Early 16th Centuries with special consideration of the part of the clergy therein" (Ph.D. diss., University of Cambridge, 1954): 2.211.

[67] On the mingling of orthodox and heterodox materials in the fifteenth-century theological miscellany, see for example Ralph Hanna (*628*); Hudson (*713*, 423–430).

[68] The tract occupies f. 61r–v. Pecock summarises its argument in *Repressor* (*190*, 1.55), and discusses it at greater length on 64–5.

of tho book god schal do away his part fro the book of lif." In his discussion, Pecock correctly reports the opinion of the writer, saying that he uses the phrase "book of prophecie" in the widest sense, applying it to "the hool Bible or the Newe Testament"; the writer emphasises this point at the conclusion of his tract, arguing that "it spekiþ nat of þis book but of all þe wordis of holi writ in the bible." Pecock dispatches this argument swiftly, asserting that the "book of prophecie" in this case can only be "the Apocalips," and arguing that only someone who actually adds to or shortens the text itself is interfering with its integrity in the manner prohibited by the scriptural curse, whereas an expositor or interpreter is not actually tampering with the text itself. He concludes rather tartly by pointing out that, whenever the "Bible men" use portions of scripture with which to defend themselves, "thei muste needis graunt hem silf to be cursid" according to their own arguments. Whatever the complexity of the culture that produced it, the sense, fostered by Colop's common-profit book and other fifteenth-century codices, that orthodox and heterodox texts may have been "promiscuously read" during this period (to borrow Milton's phrase from *Areopagitica*), is utterly repressed in the *Repressor*.

IV

In Pecock's experiments with the translation of academic discourse into the vernacular, the urge to contain is matched by a similar urge to reinvent. Given the extent of Wycliffite experimentation in this area, it might be expected that Pecock's voice would be at its most contaminated in passages addressing this subject. In fact, what distinguishes Pecock's work from the earlier phases of experimentation is the systematic nature of his approach and the comparatively simplistic level at which he deals with formal argumentation. Pecock did not underestimate the intellectual capacities of the lay people. In the prologue to the *Book of Faith*, he acknowledged "the witte and conceite of the riȝt wittid lay men" who "han colour of doctouris writing." He also recorded, more specifically, that "the lay peple whiche ben clepid lollardis . . . alleggen witnessing of Seynt Austyn in his book of Baptym aȝens Donatistis."[69] Nevertheless, he seemed to have expected this discerning readership to suppress any natural curiosity about the alternative and sometimes more sophisticated models of argumentation that Wycliffite and other literature had already pioneered.

Pecock's experiment with the polemical dialogue has already been noted, but his exploitation of the discursive possibilities of the vernacular dialogue went much further than this. His desire to be a profitable mediator between clergy and laity and his concern to cultivate a discriminating readership both found literary expression in his decision "forto make summe of [his] bokis in foorme of a dialog, bi togider talking bitwixe the sone and the fadir." In this way, he hoped that these books would receive "the favour

[69] *Book of Faith* (*191*, 111–112, 114–115).

which such dialogazacioun or togider talking and clatering ou3te have and may have."[70] In choosing this form, he was inviting the alignment of his work with, among other texts, a "canon" of English prose dialogues that had already marked out an arena, somewhere on the boundaries between "heterodoxy" and "orthodoxy," for imagined, experimental versions of relationships between clergy and laity, or between differing levels of the clergy.[71] These dialogues have shared features beyond their controversial airing of theological topics in the vernacular. One way of writing a history of this genre would be to treat it as an event in the history of theological style, tracing the development of the dialogues' common recourse to metadiscursive observations, since their interlocutors frequently criticise the quality of their own theological discourse. This in turn is frequently seen to be dependent on the willingness of the teacher or other authority-figure in the dialogues to use effective "skiles," that is, persuasive arguments.[72] In these dialogues, the lay interlocutor turns critic. It is not enough for the teacher to be a repository of *auctoritates*, the raw materials of *inventio*; skill in the technique of *dispositio* is also essential. In *Dives and Pauper*, written between 1405 and 1410, the text becomes an arena of discovery in which Pauper's skilful arrangement of arguments is decisive in absorbing and "assoiling" Dives's doubts. Dives explicitly recognises this: "þyn skyllis arn so gret and þyn speche so opyn þat ignoraunce my3t nout excusyn me ne ony wy3t ellys þat can resoun."[73] He is eager for a well-argued exposition rather than a merely declarative one ("Tel me som oþir sckyl") and commends Pauper when he satisfies this desire ("þin answer is skilfol").[74] Pauper willingly exposes the provisional nature of much academic discourse, thereby informally initiating his lay interlocutor in established clerical practices: "Clerkys spekyn oftyn be opynyoun in þis materie & oþir materyys also & nout alwey affermyn þat þey seyn [to þe utterest] but puttyn it in þe doom of oþir clerkis 3if þey connyn seyn betere, and so do Y as þis tyme, 3if ony clerk conne [seyn] more skylfolyche."[75] At its most engaging, the text is much more than a compilation of citations from the scriptures and canon law: by permitting its interlocutors to assess the quality of their own discourse, it achieves the further dimension of reflexivity. Likewise, in the contemporaneous *Lyfe of Soule* (c.1400), the "sone" is not a mere stooge but a shrewd interrogator of the "fader."[76]

---

[70] *Book of Faith* (*191*, 122). *The Donet*, *The Folewer* and *The Book of Faith* could be regarded as increasingly sophisticated variations on the catechetical dialogue.

[71] On literary treatment of these relationships in the late fourteenth century, see Somerset (*1129*, especially 22–61). On the problematic classification of *Dives and Pauper* and other vernacular texts, see Hudson (*713*, 411–430).

[72] *MED*, *skil* (n), 5.

[73] *Dives and Pauper* (*134*, 1.220).

[74] *Dives and Pauper* (*134*, 1.38, 2.332).

[75] *Dives and Pauper* (*134*, 2.129).

[76] *The Lyfe of Soule* is extant in three manuscripts, and the characters of the interlocutors vary between the surviving versions. I have chosen to use the only unedited version (London, British Library, Arundel 286, ff. 115r–129r), on the grounds that its characterisation of the interlocutors as "fader" and "sone" makes transparent the extent to which it is part of the same tradition as Pecock's "dialogazacioun."

After requesting that the father teach him the way to the "abiding city" to which St. Paul refers, the son listens to the father's response and then argues back spiritedly, "sum þinges ȝe say ful soþe, but it is not al soþe þat ȝe hopen in ȝoure seyinge," before advancing his own arguments concerning the vicissitudes of temptation.[77] Although the son ends his interventions by accepting that "þer is none oþer wey to heuene but lyfe of soule & forsakynge of synne in doynge goode dedis," his request for further clarification takes the form of a respectful but firm reproach for the terms in which the father has expressed himself: "þe answer þat þou ȝeuest to myn askynge is ful schort & derke to me & þerfore I prey ȝou ȝeue ȝe me a more opun answere & my hope is whan I knowe cristis techynge I wole lyfe þer after."[78] It is clear that the quality of the son's moral commitment is strongly dependent on the communicative skills of his "father," and the dialogue thus acknowledges that the success of this transaction depends on the teacher's acceptance of responsibility for the rhetorical quality, as well as the content, of his discourse.

Within this genre of self-consciously "skillful" texts, the relationship between *skiles*, broadly conceived, and specific forms of academic argumentation such as the syllogism, was often very flexible. The elasticity of the genre in this respect can be most notably seen from the prologue to *A Fourteenth-Century English Biblical Version* (the printed title given to the vernacular translation of a selection of scriptural books). This prologue takes the form of a conversation between a monk, a nun and their "brother superior." Here, the two unlearned participants are not only able to ask searching questions about the content of the scriptures but are also able to negotiate the terms of their relationship with their superior, making it clear that his value as a teacher is dependent on his willingness to embrace the obligation to explain the truths of faith to them. The monk makes this clear in such uncompromising and resourceful terms that the superior is overwhelmed: "Broþer, þou hast a-gast me sumwhat wiþ þyn argumentys. For þouȝ þou ne hafe noȝt y-ben a-mong clerkes at scole, þi skelis þat þou makest beþ y-founded in loue þat is a-bofe resoun þat clerkis useþ in scole: & þerfore it is hard for me to aȝenstonde þyn skelys & þyn axynges . . . For þy loue haþ ouercome my resoun."[79]

Although it is not easy to establish the extent of Pecock's familiarity with this tradition, it furnishes precedents and analogues, if not actually sources, for his experiments with vernacular argumentation. Like the writers of these earlier dialogues, Pecock explores the potential of the vernacular treatise to offer paradigms of learning, and emphasises the importance of argumentation in exchanges between clergy and laity. In the prologue to *The Folewer*, he ventures much further than does the author of *Dives and Pauper* in acknowledging the rhetorical purpose of some scholastic idioms:

[77] *Lyfe of Soule*, f. 116v.
[78] Ibid., ff. 120r, 121r.
[79] Anna Paues, ed., *A Fourteenth-Century English Biblical Version* (*107*, 8, 9).

[I]f [his conclusions] be founde trewe . . . thei be bi so mych the redier araied
and foormyd to be acceptid, holden and grauntid of the reder and of the
heerer for trewe; And, if thei ben founde untrewe . . . the reder or the heerer
may knowe the bettir of what conclusions he schale be ware . . . y take and
schal take ech argument of mocioun maad, or to be maad, bi me in eny of my
writyngis . . . as for argument and mocioun oonli, and not as for a proof
uttirli, thouჳ for more cleer foorm and forto the more enclyne men into the
conclusions of tho argumentis . . . y seie ofte thus . . . "y proue," or "y schal
proue," "y schewe," or "y schal shewe . . ."[80]

The willingness to expose the persuasive intentions behind his vernacular
terminology, to draw a careful distinction between provisional "argument"
and conclusive "proof," and even to countenance the idea that his
conclusions might be "founde untrewe," all show the extent to which
Pecock was prepared to present his works as the currency of discussion
between clergy and laity, rather than simply as repositories of undisputed
fact. Indeed, in one sense, Pecock goes much further than both the
Wycliffites and the authors of the other vernacular dialogues in explicitly
recommending the use of a "schort compendiose logik" in English that
would enable laymen already skilled in mercantile and other worldly
business to evaluate the form and content of their arguments and those
of others.[81] Nevertheless, where the Wycliffite texts, in particular, offer a
variety of examples of experimentation with academic techniques, Pecock's
chosen model of argumentation is monolithic and constrained, encapsulated in what he acknowledged to be the necessarily crude form of syllogistic
reasoning outlined in the *Repressor*. His acknowledgement in the *Folewer*
that lay people "han in her undirstondyng naturali þe same logik whiche
clerkis han craftili or doctrinali," is not contradicted by his assertion in the
Repressor that the "comon peple" are "blunt and . . . ruyde and unformal
and boistose in resonyng."[82] In each case, Pecock is emphasising the gulf
between uninstructed "resoun" and academic logic. There is, therefore, a
sense in which he was writing in denial (if not actually in ignorance) of the
experimentation with academic strategies of argumentation that the Wycliffite controversies had released into the vernacular. In fact, he appears to be
attempting to "seal up" that particular line of experimentation by imposing
upon it a markedly conservative character.[83] In this way, he attempted to
safeguard a fundamental role for orthodox clergy in assisting and directing

---

[80] *Folewer* (*193*, 6).
[81] *Repressor* (*190*, 1.9).
[82] *Folewer* (*193*, 38), and *Repressor* (*190*, 1.9). Pecock does not describe the different moods of the
syllogism, and admits that he is omitting consideration of "[w]hat propirtees and condiciouns ben
requirid to an argument, that he be ful and formal and good" (*190*, 1.9). It is clear that the
projected vernacular logic would have been far more ambitious. On the variety of Wycliffite
achievements in this area, which range far beyond the simple syllogistic that Pecock recommends,
see Somerset (*1129*) (particularly chapter six, "Vernacular Argumentation in *The Testimony of
William Thorpe*," 179–215); Hudson (*713*, 217–227).
[83] It could be argued that in this respect, at least, Pecock seems to be colluding with the climate of
repression that has been said to characterise this period: Watson argues that Arundel's
Constitutions may have helped to create "a canon of theological writing by simply sealing it
up, making it . . . hard for later writers to contribute further to this literature" (*1265*, 835).

the lay response to difficult texts and abstract arguments. For this reason, his work may be seen as partly furthering the experimentation with lay and clerical roles at work in the earlier prose dialogues, while seeking more aggressively than they to control the consequences of such an experiment. Rather than continue a process that the Wycliffites and their contemporaries had initiated, Pecock appropriated the translation of academic techniques by re-launching it entirely on his own terms, offering the lay intellect something at once more systematic and less ambitious. Clearly, the combined study of Pecock's writings and Wycliffite texts furthers our understanding of cultural practices to which they both contributed, in this case the development of vernacular argumentation in late-medieval England. When it is taken into account that Thomas More's own "skilful" texts, most notably *A Dialogue Concerning Heresies* (1529), appear in their turn to efface what Pecock had achieved in this area, it seems even more reasonable to claim that this particular history must be described in terms of rupture rather than continuity.

Pecock's attitude towards Wycliffite argumentation is ultimately of a piece with his more general intentions. Despite its controversial and destabilising hospitality to the rhetoric of earlier controversies, the "entre" to the *Reule* gives the strong impression of having been designed not only to express conventional deference to the "treuthis of philosophie," but also to install Pecock himself as a source, the pioneer of a new theological vernacular that might efface Wycliffite achievements in this area. Thus the critical dichotomy regarding Pecock, which this discussion began by considering, adumbrates what on closer inspection reveals itself to be an ambivalence in his writings, which fluctuate in their commitment to a self-regulating culture of constructive disputation between clergy and laity.[84] In laying claim to a vernacular territory of his own, Pecock produced work whose expressive resources continually probe the precarious literary and linguistic territory between the literary idioms of "orthodoxy" and "heterodoxy." Despite his strenuous attempt to fashion the original vernacular voice of a *procutoure*, his *translatio studii* continuously invites measured comparison (as opposed to conflation) with that of the Wycliffites. His use of the phrase "bastard braunchis" illustrates the dangers of using pejorative terms outside their original polemical context, but this is only one example of the way in which his language constantly bristles with the effort of continuous negotiation between dissent and reform. It is never wholly defined by these discourses, but is heavily marked by moments of hospitality and resistance to both of them.

Despite his denial of the Wycliffites' literary achievements, there is no doubt that subsequent Wycliffite scholarship has gradually rendered Pecock more intelligible to modern readers, providing new critical contexts in which to assess the aims and limitations of his own vernacular experimentation. As this essay has sought to show, he has distinctive claims on the

---

[84] James Landman likewise identifies "a central tension in Pecock's work," namely between the desire to increase lay access to vernacular materials and to preserve the authority of the clergy "to judge the validity of lay interpretations" ("Doom of resoun," 107–8).

attention of those engaged in the future development of Wycliffite studies in general; and in particular, his works remain a unique and valuable resource for those interested in the impact of the Wycliffite controversies on later attempts to formulate new and separate discourses of reform, and to imagine new possibilities for relations between laity and clergy. There are other reasons why Pecock deserves further study in his own terms. Despite his own representation of his works as constituting a self-sufficient literary monument, "oon seemly, beuteful, esiful, and confortable habitacioun," shorn of its murky affiliations with previous controversies, his writings have mixed, shifting literary and linguistic textures, which still await critical analysis.[85] Whatever his stated intentions, his writing demonstrably fluctuates between an absorption in the intellectual adventure of vernacularisation for its own sake, and a clerkly desire to control the outcomes of his experiments. Writing in the vernacular obliged him to confront the less calculable consequences of textuality, most notably the near-paradox that in seeking authorship through engagement in literate practices that were not defined or controlled exclusively by the clergy, he risked compromising his authority. His works provide us with a unique English resource for the exploration of cultural "translations" and their consequences, and are all the more valuable for his own remarkable candour about the process and pressures of such an activity. Pecock's resourceful evocation of Bishopswood at midsummer, a fusion of intellectual and imaginative work, is only one of the more flamboyant reasons for which he may still be regarded as, to use E.F. Jacob's phrase, "a literary figure, pure and simple." Indeed, if a revision of Jacob's perceptive observation may be permitted in the interests of Pecock's future readers, it must also be insisted that he is a supremely textual figure, impure and complex.

---

[85] The phrase comes from *Reule* (*194*, 22).

Wyclif, Lollards, and Historians, 1384–1984

Geoffrey Martin

John Wyclif is probably the most famous academic figure in the English-speaking world. There may be other academics who are as widely or even more celebrated, but they have had some other calling besides. An academic reputation is by its nature established in and then largely or wholly confined to academic circles. Academics whose names are familiar in the wider world have, like Aristotle, or St. Thomas Aquinas, or Woodrow Wilson, had to cut some other figure in it. Wyclif attained and then sustained fame, the kind of fame that has inspired Wyclif colleges and institutes, and street-names and statues as well as biographies and icons and college songs, through nothing more than a lifetime of study and argument and exposition. He discharged some priestly duties, though not as many as he might have performed, he had some limited administrative experience, and he undertook several commissions for the crown, but his contemporary reputation and his enduring authority rested simply upon the force of his personality and his academic prowess, and the impression which they made upon his colleagues, friends and enemies alike, and his pupils.

The great volume of commentary on Wyclif's life spans more than six centuries of posthumous fame, but for much of that time it has been only incidentally historical. The reasons for that are complex. In the first place we know almost nothing, in any ordinary sense, of his life. His death is documented, but not his age nor, thereby, the date of his birth. The conventional markers of his early academic career – matriculation, baccalaureate, even his mastership – can only be inferred. Wyclif had exceptional qualities, but there were many less influential men amongst his contemporaries who happen to be better documented.[1] The archival sources of the day, though abundant, touch the great majority of individuals only tangentially. Even the universities then lacked systematic administrative records, a deprivation for which they have since been amply compensated.

Wyclif's acknowledged writings are voluminous, but in the nature of things they contain little personal matter, and that not precise. In his own time both his friends and his enemies recognized him as an outstanding master of his profession, but their recorded concern with him was,

---

[1] As a random glance at A.B. Emden's magisterial *Biographical Register of the University of Oxford to A.D. 1500* (6) will show.

appropriately, literally and strictly academic. Ever since his death he has been much discussed, but for most of the time as a symbol rather than as an individual, and that most often in the course of vituperative contention. The slender facts of his career have been used to a variety of ends, but they are considerably, even painfully, stretched when they are arrayed for bio-graphy.[2]

If Wyclif's followers had not been so promptly dispersed from the university more might have been written about his life as historians seek to reconstruct and contemplate it. Much the same could be said about the followers themselves, for most of them are also fleeting figures. It may even be that there were some hagiographical writings which have not survived, and for which posterity might have been grateful, if posterity is ever grateful for such benisons. As it happens, however, the paucity of material has not greatly inhibited the uses to which it has been put.

To his contemporaries and immediate successors Wyclif lived and lived on in the tradition of his teaching and his writings. To friend and foe alike he was a fact, and what everyone knew about him was enough for everyone's purposes. There is thus no biography nor historical commentary in *Fasciculi zizaniorum*, though that mountainous denunciation of Wyclif and all his works is a valuable source of Wycliffite material. If we set aside for the moment the near-contemporary chroniclers, the first recorded historical comment on Wyclif is a note amongst the archives of Merton College, Oxford. About 1410 Thomas Robert, then one of the bursars, began to compile a list of the fellows of the college since its foundation a century-and-a-half earlier.[3] Down to his own time he arranged the names alphabetically, but thereafter the list was continued, as it is maintained today, in order of election. Wyclif appears in the bursars' rolls as a steward of hall in 1356, when he accounted for money spent on the entertainment of the college's guests. Having entered Wyclif's name, Robert or some contemporary glossed it with two notes, one to say that Wyclif was a doctor of divinity who trusted too readily in his own judgement, and the other that he was in truth not a fellow of the college because he did not complete his probationary year.

There are accordingly three layers to be distinguished in what appears to be quite a simple text. In the first place Wyclif had emerged, in the middle years of Edward III's reign, as a junior member of what was then the best-endowed college in either of the English universities, a promising start to a conventionally promising career. In the second, he had continued that career to its summit, and success appeared to have gone to his head. That was arguable, though anyone who knew him would acknowledge that Wyclif was an unpromising interlocutor with whom to start, or rather to try to conclude, an argument. The third was that within a few decades of his death, and in the aftermath of Archbishop Arundel's efforts to purge the university, Wyclif's association with the college, in all ordinary expectation

---

[2] Most notably in H.B. Workman (*1308*).
[3] See further G.H. Martin and J.R.L. Highfield (*925*, 99–100, 116–17).

a source of pride, had become a deep embarrassment. So deep, in fact, that some conscientious keeper of the archives thought it better to deny the evidence of the record than to invite further and unwholesome speculation. It would be a long time before anyone else in the learned world would be able to take so uncomplicated a view of all the issues involved.

At the time the risks of controversy and recrimination must have seemed quite high. It is clear enough in retrospect that Archbishop Courtenay's sweeping action in 1382 had sapped the academic roots of Lollardy, and that Arundel had since been wrestling rather with donnish intransigence than with a vigorous intellectual movement.[4] However, not all the recantations that had been offered were sincere, and Merton had inevitably been more deeply riven by Wycliffism and its contingent loyalties than it could afford to admit.[5] The college needed to keep itself at a distance from a destructive force that might have proved, might yet prove, a scandal throughout Christendom.

As with Wyclif, so with the Wycliffites, or Lollards as they came both to be called and to call themselves. The fact that the term Lollard was first used abusively in Oxford marks an attempt to dismiss the highly technical opinions of Wyclif and his first disciples by associating them with unsophisticated popular dissent.[6] In the event, the suppression of Wyclif's doctrines in the university ensured that what survived would be clandestine and populist, but that brief association of the learned and the self-instructed worlds had an enduring effect upon both the practices of piety and historiography.

Of the chroniclers closest in time to Wyclif the Franciscan contributor (or contributors) to the continuation of the *Eulogium historiarum* noticed Wyclif's commendation of the mendicant orders, without animadversion, before describing the development of his heretical views, whilst Walsingham's account of Wyclif, Lollardy, and Lollards is comprehensive and *ex post facto*.[7] The most interesting and informative commentator is Henry Knighton, of St. Mary's abbey, Leicester, who was writing in the 1380s and died in 1396 or soon after. Knighton shows us, reluctantly enough, the process by which popular dissent as it existed before Wyclif in the Midlands, and no doubt elsewhere, was mixed with the pure milk of academic heresy from Oxford. He deeply disapproved of the process and its consequences, and he was an uncomfortably close observer of them because they clearly implicated his own house. His abbot, Philip Repingdon (d.1424), was perhaps the most talented of all Wyclif's first disciples, and William Swinderby, the most adroit and capable of Leicester's indigenous dissenters, had been lodged in the abbey. There he had not improbably been instructed by Repingdon, who had also

---

[4] See the account in H. Rashdall, *The Universities of Europe in the Later Middle Ages*, ed. F.M. Powicke and A.B. Emden (1936), 3.130–35 and nn.

[5] See M. Jurkowski (*762*).

[6] A point well taken by James Crompton (*440*, 11).

[7] See *Eulogium historiarum siue temporis*, ed. F.S. Haydon (RS, 1863), 3.345, 347–9, 350–51; *Thome Walsingham historia Anglicana* (*221*, 1.345–64).

brought home like-minded colleagues from Oxford, and set them loose in the neighbourhood.

Knighton's testimony has been undervalued in the past, chiefly because of confusion over his identity and chronology, but he is a first-class and painfully truthful witness, more abashed by his abbot's indiscretions than was Repingdon himself.[8] Most of the cruces of Lollard studies: the pervasiveness of indigenous dissent, the springs of lay literacy, the inter-mingling of academic and populist themes, even the nature of Wyclif's own contributions to the movement are prefigured in Knighton's narrative. Though he was disposed to overestimate their numbers, fearing them to amount to half the population, perhaps Knighton's most useful observation on the Lollards is that they declared themselves unmistakably by comport-ing themselves like Lollards.

The subsequent persistence of Lollardy under persecution, largely divorced from any kind of political or social protection, is now a cause of wonder, but in the fifteenth century was a lesser fact of life. The church had to remain vigilant, as Bishop Pecock discovered to his cost, but it was not a matter that called for continuing comment. The Hussite movement, explicitly close to Wycliffite thought in its earliest phases, took its own course, though its followers were probably better informed of Wyclif's intellectual contribution to their tradition than were the third or fourth generations of Lollards in England. In Oxford and Cambridge intellectual vitality was by that time manifested in the stirrings of humanism rather than in the exercises of convalescent scholasticism.

When protestantism finally erupted, again as a movement of intellectual dissent, Wyclif emerged once more as a theologian. Though we have a snap-shot of Robert Barnes OESA urging earnest Lollards to replace their treasured but obsolete Wycliffite texts with new works from the Continent, the *Trialogus* was printed at Basle in 1525 and William Tyndale acclaimed Wyclif as a luminary.[9] It was, however, eventually John Foxe (1516–87) who reinstated Wyclif at the head of English dissent, and so in a measure of the Reformation. As the Marian reaction set in Foxe left England and arrived in Strasbourg in the spring of 1554. He had with him a preliminary draft of his martyrology which celebrated Wyclif and Hus as the fathers of reform, and for which he found a publisher that year.[10] That text was reprinted as the proem to *Rerum in ecclesia gestarum* at Basle in 1569, and Wyclif maintained his primacy in *Actes and Monuments of these latter and perilous days* (1563), which established him as the well-spring of the Reformation. Foxe's work was, next after the Bible itself, the most powerful engine of protestant piety in England, and those whom it honoured or denounced stayed for centuries in the public mind. European scholars of the

---

[8] See Knighton (*165*, xlii–xlvi).

[9] On Barnes, see T.M. Parker, *The English Reformation to 1588* (Oxford, 1950), 28–30; and on Wyclif's reputation see M. Aston (*271*).

[10] *Commentarii rerum in ecclesia gestarum maximarumque per totam Europam persecutionem a VVicleui temporibus ad hanc usque ætatem descriptio, Liber primus* (1564). Printed by Wendelelin Richelius.

Counter-Reformation also distinguished Wyclif as a harbinger of protestant reform, though Luther himself saw Hus as the conduit of the apostolic
tradition.[11]

In a sense the price of Wyclif's reinstatement was the further suppression
of Lollardy. The English reformation was a parliamentary process, and
although passions could run high in parliament they were not the passions
which the Word inspired in conventicles. The survival of Lollardy into the
sixteenth century is a fact, though arguments continue, apparently inex-
haustibly, about the extent to which it then informed protestant opinion. It
is also a fact that the manner in which *ecclesia Anglicana* embraced
protestantism was far removed from any settlement which Lollards might
have propounded for themselves, and the radicalism at the heart of their
doctrines was driven underground again for another century.

Although humanism had triumphed on either side of the ecclesiastical
divide, both the early protestant writers and their opponents understood
scholasticism well enough, and eventually could have agreed, if they had
chosen to agree about anything, that it had had its day. By the end of the
sixteenth century, despite the institutional conservatism of the Church of
England, deeply abrasive to the puritan conscience, the intellectual and
cultural traditions of the Middle Ages had been decisively interrupted.
Antiquarians began, about that time, to explore the medieval centuries as a
lost and forgotten country, and it is evident both from their approach and
from the cast of their discoveries that a sympathetic view of medieval
thought was likely to be a long time in emerging.[12]

In the meantime puritans and high churchmen alike were free to invoke
Wyclif as they pleased. His scripturalism was unassailable, but his radical
thinking was certainly alien to Laudians, and Peter Heylyn (1600–62), to
whom controversy was second nature, said roundly that the authority of the
church came from the Roman tradition, and not from any medieval
disturber of the peace. Fuller, on the other hand, whom few but Heylyn
might have thought an entrenched puritan, saw Wyclif as the "firm
restorer" of religion after the excesses of the papal monarchy had ravaged
the church. Daniel Neal (1678–1743), grounded in nonconformity, had no
doubt about Wyclif's affinities, and hailed him as "the morning star of the
Reformation" in his *History of the Puritans* (1732–8).

In the 1660s the emergent nonconformist congregations were closer
than any other bodies to historic Lollardy, but Wyclif rather than his
followers remained the focus of debate. The restored Anglican church
found its own way between extremes of fervour, but the Non-jurors saw
Wyclif as a disruptive force, rather than as a spiritual ancestor. He
seemed to them more likely to measure divine right against the uncomfortable doctrine of grace than to sympathize with those who having
wilfully taken one oath then scrupled to take another. Jeremy Collier

---

[11] Antoine Varillas (1624–96) distinguished Wyclif in *Histoire du Wicklefianisme . . . avec cells des guerres de Bohème* (1682). See Workman (*1308*, 1.12–16).
[12] See, e.g., M. McKisack, *Medieval History in the Tudor Age* (Oxford, 1971), particularly 155–69.

(1650–1726), in his *Ecclesiastical History of Great Britain* (1708–14) took so temperate a view of Wyclif's merits that he was ranked by John Lewis (1675–1747) with Antoine Varillas, the leading post-Tridentine historian of heresy.[13]

Lewis, vicar of Margate and master of Eastbridge Hospital at Canterbury, was a low-churchman, a Whig, and a prolific writer. The *Dictionary of National Biography* ranks his topographical studies well above his theological and biographical works, but his lives of Wyclif, Pecock, Caxton, and Fisher were carefully documented, and he sought to trace the intellectual history of protestantism from its beginnings. He understood the importance of Wyclif's works, and made a serious attempt to trace and list the manuscripts. He also has a place in the history of biblical scholarship as the editor of the first printed text of the Wycliffite New Testament (1731). His introduction to the volume included an historical survey of the translations of the Bible, which he later expanded and published as a separate work. It appeared in a third edition as late as 1818.

Wyclif's next champion was another topographer, of broader interests than Lewis but of less scholarly bent. William Gilpin (1724–1804), like Lewis, was a conscientious parish priest, but he was also an innovative schoolmaster and a painter. Before he began the topographical studies for which he is chiefly celebrated he came to historical biography as a means of discharging his debts. He wrote a life of his own distinguished kinsman Bernard Gilpin (1517–83), known as the apostle of the north, and encouraged by its reception went on to a biography of the martyr Hugh Latimer (1755), and ten years later to *The Lives of John Wicliff and of the most eminent of his disciples: Lord Cobham, John Huss, Jerome of Prague, and Zisca*. Gilpin's tone is resolute. His epigraph is from Acts 24.14: "After the way which they call heresy, so worship we the God of our fathers," and his first chapter begins: "About the thirteenth and fourteenth centuries the usurpations of the church of Rome had arisen to their greatest height." He acclaims Wyclif as "the first person of any eminence who espoused the cause of liberty," and sees his path to enlightenment as his discovery of the authority and sufficiency of the scriptures when he turned from the fashionable toils of scholastic philosophy to study theology. Gilpin supposed cheerfully that at that juncture Wyclif rejected "without much difficulty" the methodology of his day.

The Lives is prefaced by a poem by Thomas Denton (1724–77), "The house of superstition: a vision," which effectively sets out the theme of the book though it was first published three years earlier, in 1762. It is a composition in the graveyard style, and it makes an interesting use of current imagery of ruin by attributing the decay of the gothic fane in which Superstition broods to the corruption of "distorted fancy's wayward freaks," in other words to the growth of irrational devotions in the medieval church. However, the lovely maiden Truth comes, at the head

---

[13] See above, n. 11.

of a distinguished company, to confront Superstition and to free the Scriptures from her deadening grasp.

> Marching in goodly row, with steady feet,
> Some reverend worthies followed in her train,
> With love of truth whose kindred bosoms beat,
> To free the fettered mind from error's chain,
> Wicliff the first appeared and led the croud
> And in his hand a lighted torch he bore,
> To drive the gloom of Superstition's cloud,
> And all corruption's mazes to explore.
> Next noble Cobham, on whose honoured brow
> The martyr's crown is placed, wreathed with the laurel bough.

Hus, Jerome of Prague, and others follow. Superstition's acolytes include, besides Ignorance, Error, Prejudice and Penance, Indulgence, who (or which) is sternly glossed as celibacy: an interesting reflection.

Denton was himself a biographer, but neither he nor Gilpin had any particular knowledge of the Middle Ages. Nor was there very much to be had. Gilpin confused Sir John Oldcastle, known as Lord Cobham, with Oldcastle's wife's grandfather, John, third Lord Cobham, but in doing so he was only following Bale, a generally well-informed writer who happened on that occasion to be wrong. There were no reliable general histories available, and certainly no helpful studies of medieval philosophy. Wyclif was trebly insulated from historical inquiry, by the obscurity of the age and society in which he lived, by the protracted acerbities of theological dispute, and by the repugnant technicality of speculative thought in the Middle Ages. It would take the best part of another century for historical scholarship to look sympathetically at any aspect of medieval society, and rather longer for it to come to terms with its mentality.

The change began with the systematic study of archival sources. The report of a parliamentary committee on the public records in 1799 produced a series of royal commissions between 1800 and 1837, and then in 1838 an act establishing a public record office. The annual reports of the deputy keeper began to demonstrate the astonishing range of the documents which were brought by the cartload from Westminster and elsewhere and assembled on the site in Chancery Lane. Over the same years another long-discussed proposal to publish medieval sources issued in the *Chronicles and Memorials of Great Britain*, more widely known as the Rolls Series, because they were published under the supervision of the master of the rolls, the senior chancery judge who was the titular keeper of the public records.[14]

Like all enterprises of its kind the Rolls Series included such volumes as were ready and available at any particular moment, but the time was one of some religious irritability and of the first five volumes, all published in 1858,

---

[14] See further G.H. Martin, "Narrative Sources for the Reign of Richard II," *The Age of Richard II*, ed. J.L. Gillespie (Stroud, 1997), 52–55.

the *Fasciculi zizaniorum* made one. The *Fasciculi*, which the author would have been pained to think of as a protestant text, was edited sympathetically by W.W. Shirley (1828–66), an Arnoldian liberal who was then moving towards an accommodation of dogmatic Christianity, and had become deeply interested in medieval thought. Shirley planned a life of Wyclif, but accomplished only a list of his works (1865) and a paper on scholasticism (1866) before his own early death.

In 1869–71 Thomas Arnold (1823–1900), Arnold of Rugby's second son, published *Select English Works of John Wyclif*, which was followed by an important biography, Gotthard Victor Lechler's *Johann von Wiclif und die Vorgeschichte der Reformation* (1873). Lechler had already edited Wyclif's *Trialogus* (1862), and his work was the first authoritative study of its kind, matching modern German scholarship with the new stirrings in England. It was translated in 1874 by Peter Lorimer, principal of the English Presbyterian College, as *John Wiclif and his English Precursors*, and led a growing interest both in medieval theology and in the beginnings of dissent.

An early and substantial consequence was the foundation of the Wyclif Society in 1882. Like the Ballad Society, the Chaucer Society, the New Shakespeare Society, the Hammersmith Sculling Club (for men and women), and the project which in time became the Oxford English Dictionary, it was the brainchild of Frederick James Furnivall (1825–1910). Furnivall had already launched the other great instrument of research which has sustained Lollard studies, the Early English Text Society, now flourishing in its second century. The Wyclif Society survived only until 1922. Its momentum had been checked by Furnivall's death in 1910, though Furnivall's remarkable energies were not always evenly applied, and by the impact of the First World War. It had nevertheless published some thirty-six volumes of Wyclif's Latin works from a standing start. Shirley's *Catalogue of the Original Works of John Wyclif* was refined by the Austrian scholar Johann Loserth (1846–1936), who drew on the society's work, to which he had himself contributed more than thirty-six texts, in *Shirley's Catalogue of the Extant Works of John Wyclif* (1924). The latest authoritative survey is that by W.R. Thomson, *The Latin Writings of John Wyclif* (1983).

The establishment of a canon of Wyclif's works and their elucidation was in the first place in the hands of theologians and philosophers. They made their own assessments of his contribution to their fields of study, and did so, inevitably, in a context of their own devising. In the meantime, in the aftermath of the rapid development of historical techniques, the attention of medieval historians, themselves a new species, began to turn in England from the the development of royal power and the business of government in the early and high Middle Ages to their developing forms and the stirrings of national sentiment. In one sense the Middle Ages were familiar ground, but the familiarity was emotional rather than intellectual. The revival of the styles of Gothic as a predominant artistic idiom, and the independent but associated appeal of romanticism meant that popular perceptions had for a time outrun scholarly expertise.

The new methodology focused first and intensely on institutions, and then more slowly upon the nature of the society that they served, but studies of all kinds were greatly enriched by the accessibility of the public records. In 1899 the young George Macaulay Trevelyan (1876–1962) published the dissertation which he had presented for his fellowship at Trinity College, Cambridge, as *England in the Age of Wyclif*. Trevelyan was not a medievalist, and indeed was impatient of the cast of mind that made such specialists. He was a liberal and an anti-clerical, but a romantic of warm sympathies, and he knew a cause when he saw one. His apprehension of Wyclif, the outspoken guardian of liberty and the individual conscience, as an icon of his time prefigured the manner and style of his *English Social History* (1944), the work which made Trevelyan's books the most-widely read of any English historian's before the age of television.[15] From the first he brought Wyclif to a wider audience than ever before, and he saw Lollardy as a popular response to Wyclif's evangelical fervour. Shortly afterwards, John Neville Figgis (1866–1919) contributed a more specialized essay on Wyclif to the Church Historical Society's *Typical English Churchmen* (1909). That was an interesting categorization, but hardly a formidable challenge to an author who had made his own way from the Countess of Huntingdon's connection to the Community of the Resurrection. Meanwhile Wyclif's Lollards stood centre stage.

Of Wyclif's next biographers, respectively a Congregationalist and a Methodist, Bernard Lord Manning (1892–1941) was still at school when Figgis's essay was published, whilst Herbert Brook Workman (1862–1951), an experienced minister, was the established and innovative principal of Westminster College. Manning's *The People's Faith in the Time of Wyclif*, a university prize essay, appeared in 1919. It was an interesting sequel to and development of Trevelyan's study, and made Manning a natural choice to contribute a chapter on Wyclif to the *Cambridge Medieval History of Europe* (8 vols, 1911–36), which was then in progress. The bibliography which accompanied it is still a useful conspectus. However, Manning did not pursue the subject, partly no doubt because he knew that Workman had a life of Wyclif in hand. In the meantime the publication of Margaret Deanesly's *The Lollard Bible* (1920) marked a great advance in the scholarly perception of Lollardy, and provided a new foundation for the discussion not only of Wyclif's teachings but of religious practice and popular beliefs in the fourteenth and fifteenth centuries.

Workman's *John Wyclif: A Study of the Medieval English Church*, published in 1926, is still a landmark. It is in many, even in most, respects superseded, but it nevertheless claims attention. It was in preparation from 1914, and ranges over Wyclif's life and his influence in England in the decades following his death, including the political activities of the Lollards to 1395, events in Oxford down to Arundel's visitation in 1411,

---

[15] *English Social History* was conceived as a companion volume to Trevelyan's popular *History of England*, but war-time restrictions on publishing confined it to the period since Chaucer (and Wyclif). Social history has since taken other directions, but Trevelyan's sense of it and his learning alike are probably best displayed in his *Trinity College: An Historical Sketch* (1943).

and an account of the ultimate condemnation of Wyclif's works and his exhumation.

Workman's object was to treat Wyclif in context. The scale of the book is ample. The first volume ends with the murder of Robert Haulay in Westminster Abbey in 1378, and Wyclif's consequent arguments on the usage of sanctuary. The second, which is subtitled "The Reformer," covers the development of Wyclif's views on the church, the effects of the schism, and the impact of Lollardy on the university. The opening chapter of the first volume is business-like and effective. It reviews the general significance of Wyclif's career, his influence at home and abroad, and the work of his biographers, and ends with the distribution of the manuscripts of his works. The impression given is one of a writer who has a firm grasp of a complex subject.

That impression is quickly dispelled by the succeeding chapters, which cover the early years of Wyclif's life. Workman apparently realised that questions about the number of Wyclifs present in fourteenth-century Oxford, and which of them may have been which, were mainly products of variant spellings and a rich variety of misconceptions. Even so, he took care to turn every stone. Having debated the uncertainties of Wyclif's birth and family background, he was drawn into the feudal geography of north-east England, and even beguiled by the fact that coal was already being mined there in Richard II's reign and would be of much greater importance in later centuries.

Wyclif's removal to Oxford, at an uncertain date, calls out more anxious detail. If his first sight of Oxford was from Shotover, he may have heard (or might have heard, because for all we know he may have travelled by some other route) that some students had recently been poaching in the woods there. If he entered the city by the north gate he may or may not have noticed that although the rest of the defences had been neglected, the gatehouse had recently been restored. All such assertions and observations are scrupulously documented; in the later chapters they are not less frequent, though generally more cogent. In the early stages they sap the vitality of the narrative and of the reader alike.

The weakness lies in the author's desire to cast an historical treatise in the form of a biography, when what is known of its central figure is, despite his prolific writings, remarkably exiguous. Workman made a brave effort to make the man fill his rôle, but the task was beyond him, and not improbably beyond anyone else. His labour was not all in vain. The book is not, as the conventional phrase goes, a quarry or mine of material, but rather a warehouse. The material has been painstakingly brought together, and arranged systematically, though not always enticingly, upon its many floors.

Workman had projected a third volume, on the origins of nonconformity. That work never appeared, and the challenge was not taken up for a quarter of a century. A study on the scale of Workman's *Wyclif* is apt to arrest other inquiries, and as it manifestly contained most of if not all the material that could be used to its ends, it was unlikely to be matched for some time. There were, however, other things to do. The work of the Wyclif Society was continued by individual editors. The medieval church as a whole was increasingly well documented by the publications of national and local record societies, and the work of Dom David Knowles on the monastic and the religious orders.[16] A notable advance in Wycliffite studies, however, came with the publication in 1940 of Aubrey Gwynn's *The English Austin Friars in the Time of Wycliffe*. Gwynn discussed, with delicate scholarship, the whole range of the friars' activities in and outside the universities in the late fourteenth century. His review of their early accord with, and subsequent hostility to Wyclif established that part of the story in an authoritative fashion.

In 1952 Kenneth Bruce McFarlane (1903–66), a fellow of Magdalen College, Oxford, and a formidable figure in medieval studies, published *John Wycliffe and the Beginnings of English Nonconformity*, arguably the most influential work of the century. Its origins were unusual. At the end of the Second World War McFarlane's friend Alfred Leslie Rowse (1903–98) had taken on the editorship of the history volumes in the popular Teach Yourself series run by the English Universities Press. Rowse believed that the most effective way to inculcate history upon minds uninstructed but willing to learn was to introduce themes and periods through biography: the lives of those "whose actions have been so much part of history, and whose careers in turn have been so moulded and formed by events." It is not clear that McFarlane believed anything of the kind, but he showed willing. The prologue to *John Wycliffe* begins austerely but justly: "If you wish to teach yourself medieval history you must learn first that the sources, though often abundant, are patchy, voluminous on some topics, entirely absent for others." That is by way of explaining that we have no means of judging the perceptions and motives, "the springs of action" in medieval minds, and that in that sense a biography of Wyclif, or indeed of any of his contemporaries is beyond us. Nevertheless the historian could at least clear the ground, which McFarlane proceeded to do.

The most important feature of *John Wycliffe* is its elucidation of Wyclif's career in Oxford. The history of the university, and especially of the medieval university, has been so intensively studied over the past half-century that it is difficult now to appreciate the perspicacity with which McFarlane approached the subject.[17] He explained the original rôle of the colleges, which came so to dominate the university in later centuries as to distort much of its history. He expounded the medieval university and its workings, and Wyclif's part in it, and he incisively reduced the multiple Wyclifs to one.

In the process, McFarlane sought to present Wyclif as his own time had known him. He identified him as a don, and as a don of exceptional

---

[16] *The Monastic Order in England* appeared in 1940. *The Religious Orders* was complete in 1958 (*801*).

[17] A.B. Emden's *Biographical Register of the University of Oxford to 1500* (6), the foundation of most subsequent studies, was only published between 1957 and 1959, although its content was available to inquirers from its inception.

influence. In assessing that influence, however, he came to perceive Wyclif rather as Archbishop Courtenay saw him, not as a spiritual leader but as a menace to the church, which had come to rely on the universities for the administrative talent and expertise which the monasteries had once provided.[18] A radical heresy amongst graduates would rapidly permeate and subvert the entire hierarchy and its executive.

The difference between McFarlane and Courtenay was that although they might have agreed in their assessment of Wyclif, McFarlane saw no need for a church at all, let alone for archbishops or poor preachers. His scholarly detachment betrayed no overt opinion of that kind, but it is plain that his real measure of Wyclif was that he would have been a difficult and almost certainly a troublesome colleague. His acerbity was fired, McFarlane thought, by frustrated ambition, and his testiness may have been attributable to high blood pressure. A man's colleagues, and a well-conducted common room, can only absorb so much of that kind of thing.

At the same time, however, McFarlane had discovered that although the failure of academic Lollardy circumscribed and even nullified Wyclif's academic consequence, there was much to be learned from archival sources about those who revered him outside the university. That part of *John Wycliffe* which dealt with the beginnings of English nonconformity was not the study which Workman would have written, but it was not the less valuable an enlargement of the literature.

Like Workman, McFarlane imposed a pause on biographical studies of Wyclif, but there was already a growing interest in late medieval thought which encouraged technical studies of its metaphysics and theology. John Robson's *Wyclif and the Oxford Schools*, published in 1961, examined the relationship between Wyclif's *Summa de ente* and the work of the masters of the preceding generations. It appeared at a time when scholasticism was no longer regarded as intrinsically absurd, and theology had lost some, at least a modicum, of its earlier rancour. Robson observed that Dom Paul de Vooght's *Les sources de la doctrine chrétienne* (1954) had given such measured attention to Wyclif's use of scriptural authority as to make him "almost . . . the hero of the work."

Lollardy, on the other hand, was now studied as much as a social and a literary as a religious phenomenon, and though there was continuing disagreement about its affinity with the protestantism of the Reformation, there was no questioning its persistence and its importance as a key to the social structures and intellectual history of fifteenth-century England. James Crompton's papers, "*Fasciculi zizaniorum*" (1961), "John Wyclif: A Study in Mythology" (1966), and "Leicestershire Lollards" (1968) were in part an attempt to reconnect Wyclif and Lollardy with the central tradition of the English church.[19] A learned and devout high Anglican, Crompton was at odds with most of the tenets of popular Lollardy, but he could understand its driving force, and Wyclif's own, more readily than McFarlane could. He

---

[18] McFarlane (*933*, 100–01).
[19] "John Wyclif" (*439*) and "Leicestershire Lollards" (*440*); *Fasciculi* (*438*).

had no doubt of Wyclif's commanding role, nor of the spiritual affinities of Lollardy, Anglican piety, and developed nonconformity. Crompton remarked on the resurgence of interest in Wyclif's thought, and planned further studies. He did not live to complete them, nor to see the reconstruction of the scholar, teacher, and evangelist which has been effected by those, most notably Anne Hudson, who have recently approached Wyclif through the study of vernacular texts.

That reconstruction has been both helped and hindered by McFarlane's work. His rescue of Wyclif himself from the entanglements of piety and anachronism was a substantial benefit, as was his exploration of the record sources, also innovative in its day, in search of Wyclif's Lollards. He had also observed that popular Lollardy had a strong foundation of its own, though his mistrust of Knighton, which also informed his later studies of the Lollard knights, led him to underestimate the interplay of scholastic and popular thought, and the wide diffusion of the free-ranging piety which resulted from it. In the same fashion, the recklessness and unsurprising failure of Oldcastle's rebellion strengthened McFarlane's perception of Lollardy as ultimately futile. With the disappearance of Wyclif's poor preachers from the canon and the implausibility of any connection between Lollardy and the rebels of 1381, the age of Wyclif might seem like an evening gone, were it not for the vigour of Middle English dissent. That could be, as it has been, intensively studied on its own terms, but in the shadow of McFarlane's dismissive judgement.[20]

The sexcentenary of Wyclif's death, however, offered a useful occasion to take account of the new shape of Wycliffite studies. It was commemorated by a series of lectures in the hall of Balliol College in Michaelmas term, 1984, which were published in 1986 as *Wyclif in his Times*, under the editorship of Sir Anthony Kenny. The portrait of Wyclif from Balliol was allowed a place on the dust-jacket, though not in the volume, as a reminder that even the antiquarian mist has its own place in the historical process. The papers themselves, including contributions on behalf of the faculties of Theology, History, and English, and the sub-faculty of Philosophy, were models of lucidity. What was most striking about them was a new accord in the historical and literary perceptions of Wyclif and the Lollards. They were a fitting climax to a century of study in which Wyclif had maintained his place through formidable ideological and other convulsions. Having survived every kind of attention from adulation to vilification, and taking clinical diagnoses in his stride, he remains, as Sir Anthony Kenny observes, "a genius . . . a metaphysical thinker of compelling power, and a historical figure of far-reaching influence." His poor preachers may have succumbed to critical scrutiny, the Lollard Bible is now recognized, and justly, as a corporate academic endeavour, but his own stature has been enhanced rather than diminished. He seems likely to remain even in the twenty-first century, and perhaps beyond, "the subject of more biographies than

---

[20] Although it did not revise his doubts about Knighton, McFarlane's posthumously published *Lollard Knights* (934) does help to modify and overturn other earlier dismissals.

probably any other medieval Englishman."[21] Yet beside him, his followers, and not least those of the great extra-mural class, with the writings to which they clung so tenaciously, also invite our scrutiny and understanding. At present there is every reason to believe that they will continue to receive, perhaps even to enjoy, that attention.

[21] K.B. McFarlane (*933*, xii).

A Selected Bibliography for Lollard Studies

Derrick G. Pitard

This is a Selected Bibliography of texts and studies for the study of Lollardy. While it is not exhaustive, this attempts to be a full record of significant contributions to the study of Wyclif and Lollardy over approximately the last century, with some reference to earlier work. Earlier Bibliographies on this topic have been more limited (see 4, 33).

Part A contains alphabetical lists of primary and secondary texts, forgoing disciplinary distinctions. This functions as a Works Cited list for the volume, and will be helpful as a reference work and quarry for sources. Yet, this format is admittedly difficult for a scholar who might want to discover work by topic. To enable this, Part B indexes current work on a variety of topics related to Lollardy. Hopefully, this arrangement will allow for access as well as interdisciplinary discoveries.

Several sorts of texts are not included. First, no dissertations or other unpublished work appear. Second, it excludes manuscript sources. For an index of manuscripts, see Severs and Hartung (33), along with emendations and additions by Hudson (13). Finally, no primary texts appear which are not directly related to Lollardy, even though they might provide context for its study; this includes, for instance, many ecclesiastical and state records, and orthodox religious texts.

Anthologies are listed under the editor's name. Any volume cited just by author or editor is listed in Section 2, "Collections of Articles." Brief introductory notes are prefixed to each section where relevant:

Part A: The Bibliography

1. Bibliographies and Indices
2. Collections of Articles
3. Primary Texts and Documents
4. Secondary Sources

Part B: Introductions to Selected Topics

1. General Introductions
2. Biographies of Wyclif
3. Biographies of Other Figures
4. History
5. Philosophy and Theology
6. The Bible
7. Sermon Studies
8. Langland and Chaucer
9. Drama
10. Other Literary Texts
11. Manuscript Studies, Book Production, and Book History
12. Philology and Linguistics
13. Lollardy and Images
14. Lollardy and Literacy
15. Lollardy and Women
16. Lollardy and Central Europe

Part A: The Bibliography

1. Bibliographies and Indices

1. Baker, Derek, ed. *The Bibliography of the Reform 1450–1648 Relating to the United Kingdom for the Years 1955–1970.* Oxford: Basil Blackwell, 1975.
2. Bale, John. *Scriptorum Illustrium Maioris Brytanniae . . . Catalogus.* Basle, 1557–59. Facs. Westmead: Gregg, 1971.
3. ——. *Index Britanniae Scriptorum.* Ed. Reginald L. Poole and Mary Bateson. Oxford: Clarendon, 1902. Rpt. Cambridge: D.S. Brewer, 1990.
4. Berkhout, Carl T., and Jeffrey B. Russell. *Medieval Heresies: A Bibliography 1960–1979.* Toronto: Pontifical Institute, 1981.
5. Edwards, A.S.G., gen. ed. *Index of Middle English Prose.* Handlists 1–17. Cambridge: D.S. Brewer, 1984–2001.
6. Emden, A.B. *A Biographical Register of the University of Oxford to A.D. 1500.* 3 vols. Oxford: Clarendon, 1957–59.
7. Erben, W., and A. Kern. "Johann Loserth als Geschichtsforscher: Eine Übersicht seiner wissenschaftliche Werke." *Zeitschrift des historischen Veriens für Steiermark* 22 (1926): 3–28.
8. Guth, DeLloyd J. *Late-Medieval England, 1377–1485.* Cambridge: Cambridge Univ. Press, 1976.
9. ——. "Fifteenth-Century England: Recent Scholarship and Future Directions." *British Studies Monitor* 7 (1977): 3–50.
10. Graves, Edgar. *A Bibliography of English History to 1485.* Oxford: Clarendon, 1975.
11. Gecheva, Krastina. *Bogomilism: A Bibliography.* Sofia: Editions Académiques, 1997. [In Bulgarian, though references are given in the language of origin.]
12. Haring, Nicholas, S.A.C. "Commentaries on the Pseudo-Athanasian Creed." *Mediaeval Studies* 34 (1972): 208–252.
13. Hudson, Anne. "Additions and Modifications to a Bibliography of English Wycliffite Writings." Hudson, *Lollards and their Books* 249–252.
14. Jolliffe, P.S. *A Checklist of Middle English Prose Writings of Spiritual Guidance.* Toronto: Pontifical Institute, 1974.
15. Kennedy, Arthur G. *A Bibliography of Writings on the English Language, from the Beginning of Printing to the end of 1922.* New York: Hafner, 1961.
16. Kühn-Steinhausen, H. [I.H. Stein]. "Wyclif-Handschriften in Deutschland." *Zentralblatt für Bibliothekswesen* 47 (Dec. 1930): 625–28.
17. Lester, G.A. "Unedited English Prose in Rylands Manuscripts." *Bulletin of the John Rylands Library* 68.1 (1985): 135–60.
18. Lewis, R.E. et al. *Index of Printed Middle English Prose.* New York: Garland, 1985.
19. Lewis, R.E., and A. McIntosh. *A Descriptive Guide to the Manuscripts of the Prick of Conscience.* Medium Aevum Monographs 12 (1985).
20. Loserth, J. "Bietrage zur Geschichte der hussitichen Bewegung." *Archiv fur österreichische Akademie Wissenschaften* 55 (1877): 265–400; 57 (1879): 203–276; 60 (1880): 343–561; 75 (1889): 287–413; 82 (1895): 327–418.

21. ——. "Neuere Erscheinungen der Wiclif-Literatur." *Historische Zeitschrift* 53.1 (1885): 43–62; 62.1 (1889): 266–78.

22. ——. *Studien zur Kirchenpolitik Englands im 14. Jahrhunderts.* 2 vols. *Sitzungsberichte der kaiserlichen Akademie Wissenschaften in Wien, Philosophisch-historische Klasse* 136 (1897); 156 (1908).

23. ——. "Neue Erscheinungen der Wiclif-Literatur." *Historische Zeitschrift* 95 (1905): 269–77.

24. ——. "Neuere Erscheinungen der Wiclif- und Huss-Literatur." *Historische Zeitschrift* 116 (1916): 271–82.

25. ——. "Neuere Erscheinungen der Wiclif- und Huss-Literatur." *Zeitschrift des Vereins für Geschichte Mährens und Schlesiens* 20 (1916): 258–71.

26. ——. *Shirley's Catalogue of the Extant Latin Works of John Wyclif.* London: Wyclif Society, 1924.

27. Molnár, Amadeo. "Recent Literature on Wyclif's Theology." *Communio Viatorum* 7 (1964): 186–92.

28. Morey, James H. *Book and Verse: A Guide To Middle English Biblical Literature.* Illinois Medieval Studies. Chicago: Univ. of Illinois Press, 2000.

29. Revell, Peter. *Fifteenth Century English Prayers and Meditations: A Descriptive List of Manuscripts in the British Library.* London: Garland, 1975.

30. Rosenthal, Joel T. *Late Medieval England (1377–1485): A Bibliography of Historical Scholarship, 1975–1989.* Kalamazoo: Medieval Institute, 1994.

31. ——. "Bibliography of English Scholarship: 1970–82: Part II – 1307–1509." *Medieval Prosopography* 4.2 (1983): 47–61.

32. Royal Historical Society. *Writings on British History 1901–1933.* Volume 2: The Middle Ages, 450–1485. New York: Barnes and Noble, 1968.

33. Severs, J. Burke, and Albert Hartung, gen. eds. *A Manual of the Writings in Middle English 1050–1500.* 9 vols. Connecticut: Archon Books, 1967–1993.

34. Sharpe, Richard. *Index of Latin Writers of Great Britain and Ireland before 1540.* Brepols: *Journal of Medieval Latin*, 1997.

35. Shirley, W.W. *A Catalogue of the Original Works of John Wyclif.* Oxford, 1865.

36. Smeeton, D.D. *English Religion 1500–1540: A Bibliography.* Macon, GA: Mercer Univ. Press, 1988.

37. Smith, David M. *Guide to Bishop's Registers of England and Wales.* London: Royal Historical Society, 1981.

38. Tajima, Matsuji. *Old and Middle English Language Studies: A Classified Bibliography 1923–1985.* Amsterdam: John Benjamins, 1988.

39. Thomson, Williell R. *The Latin Writings of John Wyclif.* Subsidia Medievalia 14. Toronto: Pontifical Institute, 1983.

40. Vermaseren, B.A. "Nieuwe Studies over Wyclif en Huss." *Tijdschrift voor Geschiedenis* 76 (1963): 190–212.

41. Zeman, Jarold K. *The Hussite Movement and the Reformation in Bohemia, Moravia, and Slovakia (1350–1650): A Bibliographical Study Guide.* Ann Arbor: Michigan Slavic Publications, c. 1977.

2. Collections of Articles

The books listed in this section contain more than one article listed elsewhere by a shortened reference (given in the first place by name, and then title as well if necessary).

42. Alford, John, ed. *A Companion to Piers Plowman*. Berkeley: Univ. of California Press, 1988.
43. Aston, Margaret. *Lollards and Reformers: Images and Literacy in Late Medieval Religion*. London: Hambledon, 1984.
44. ———. *Faith and Fire: Popular and Unpopular Religion, 1350–1600*. London: Hambledon, 1993.
45. Aston, M. and Colin Richmond, eds. *Lollardy and the Gentry in the Later Middle Ages*. New York: St. Martin's, 1997.
46. Baker, Derek, ed. *Schism, Heresy, and Religious Protest*. Studies in Church History 9. Cambridge: Cambridge Univ. Press, 1972.
47. ———, ed. *The Materials, Sources, and Methods of Ecclesiastical History*. Studies in Church History 11. London: Barnes and Noble, 1975.
48. Beer, Jeanette. *Translation Theory and Practice in the Middle Ages*. Kalamazoo: Western Michigan Univ. Press, 1997.
49. Benskin, M., and M.L. Samuels, eds. *So Meny People, Longages, and Tonges: Philological Essays in Scots and Mediaeval English Presented to Angus McIntosh*. Edinburgh: Middle English Dialect Project, 1981.
50. Biller, Peter, and Anne Hudson, eds. *Heresy and Literacy, 1000–1530*. Cambridge Studies in Medieval Literature 23. Cambridge: Cambridge Univ. Press, 1994.
51. Biller, Peter, and Barrie Dobson, eds. *The Medieval Church: Universities, Heresy, and the Religious Life*. Studies in Church History, Subsidia 11. Woodbridge: Boydell and Brewer, 1999.
52. Boffey, J., and V.J. Scattergood, eds. *Texts and their Contexts: Papers from the Early Book Society*. Dublin: Four Courts Press, 1998.
53. Catto, J.I., and Ralph Evans, eds. *The History of the University of Oxford*. Vol. 2, Late Medieval Oxford. Oxford: Oxford Univ. Press, 1992.
54. Copeland, Rita, ed. *Criticism and Dissent in the Middle Ages*. Cambridge: Cambridge Univ. Press, 1996.
55. Copeland, Rita, David Lawton, and Wendy Scase, eds. *New Medieval Literatures II*. Oxford: Clarendon, 1998.
56. Cuming, G.J., ed. *The Church and Academic Learning*. Studies in Church History 5. Leiden: E.J. Brill, 1969.
57. Dimmick, Jeremy, James Simpson, and Nicolette Zeeman, eds. *Images, Idolatry, and Iconoclasm in Medieval England: Textuality and the Visual Image*. Oxford: Oxford Univ. Press, 2002.
58. Dobson, Barrie, ed. *Church, Politics and Patronage in the Fifteenth Century*. Gloucester: Alan Sutton, 1984.
59. Edwards, A.S.G., ed. *Middle English Prose: A Critical Guide to Major Authors and Genres*. New Brunswick: Rutgers Univ. Press, 1984.
60. Edwards, A.S.G., and Derek Pearsall, eds. *Middle English Prose: Essays on Bibliographical Problems*. New York: Garland, 1981.
61. Fletcher, Alan J. *Preaching and Politics in Late Medieval England*. Dublin: Four Courts Press, 1998.

62. Given-Wilson, Christopher, ed. *Fourteenth Century England II.* Woodbridge: Boydell and Brewer, 2002.
63. Griffiths, Jeremy, and Derek Pearsall, eds. *Book Production and Publishing in Britain 1375–1475.* Cambridge: Cambridge Univ. Press, 1989.
64. Hanawalt, Barbara, ed. *Chaucer's England: Literature in Historical Context.* Minneapolis: Univ. of Minnesota Press, 1992.
65. Hanawalt, B., and David Wallace, eds. *Bodies and Disciplines: Intersections of Literature and History in Fifteenth Century England.* Minneapolis: Univ. of Minnesota Press, 1996.
66. Hanna, Ralph III. *Pursuing History: Middle English Manuscripts and Their Texts.* Stanford: Stanford Univ. Press, 1996.
67. Hudson, Anne. *Lollards and Their Books.* London: Hambledon, 1985.
68. Hudson, Anne, and M. Wilks, eds. *From Ockham to Wyclif.* Studies in Church History, Subsidia 5. Oxford: Basil Blackwell, 1987.
69. *John Wyclif e la tradizione degli studi biblici in Inghilterra.* [No editor given.] Genova: Il Melangolo, 1987.
70. Justice, S., and K. Kerby-Fulton, eds. *Written Work: Langland, Labor and Authorship.* Philadelphia: Univ. of Pennsylvania Press, 1997.
71. Lášek, Jan Blâhoslav. *Jan Hus mezi epochami, národy a konfesemi.* Praha: Ceská krestanská akademie: Husitská teologická fakulta Univerzity Karlovy, 1995.
72. Lawton, David, Rita Copeland, and Wendy Scase, eds. *New Medieval Literatures III.* Oxford: Clarendon, 1999.
73. Kenny, Anthony, ed. *Wyclif in His Times.* Oxford: Clarendon, 1986.
74. Minnis, A.J., ed. *Crux and Controversy in Middle English Textual Criticism.* Cambridge: D.S. Brewer, 1992.
75. ——, ed. *Late Medieval Religious Texts and Their Transmission: Essays in Honour of A.I. Doyle.* Cambridge: D.S. Brewer, 1994.
76. Nichols, Stephen, and Siegfried Wenzel, eds. *The Whole Book: Cultural Perspectives on the Medieval Miscellany.* Ann Arbor: Univ. of Michigan Press, 1996.
77. Pánek, Jaroslav, Miloslav Polívka, and Noemi Rejchrtová, eds. *Husitství – Reformace – Renesance. Sborník k 60. narozeninám Františka Šmahela [Hussitisim – Reformation – Renaissance. Festschrift for František Šmahel on his Sixtieth Birthday].* Praha: Historicý ústav, 1994.
78. Patschovsky, A., and F. Šmahel, eds. *Eschatologie und Hussitismus.* Prague: Historisches Institüt, 1996.
79. Pearsall, Derek, ed. *Studies in the Vernon Manuscript.* Cambridge: D.S. Brewer, 1990.
80. Scase, Wendy, Rita Copeland, and David Lawton, eds. *New Medieval Literatures I.* Oxford: Clarendon, 1997.
81. Seibt, Ferdinand et al., eds. *Jan Hus: Zwischen Zeiten, Volkern, Konfessionen.* Veroffentlichungen des Collegium Carolinum, 85. Munich: R. Oldenbourg, 1997.
82. Sheils, W.J., and Diana Wood, eds. *Voluntary Religion.* Studies in Church History 23. Oxford: Basil Blackwell, 1986.
83. Sheils, W.J., and Diana Wood, eds. *The Church and Wealth.* Studies in Church History 24. Oxford, Basil Blackwell, 1987.
84. Šmahel, František, and Elizabeth Müller-Luckner, eds. *Häresie und vorzeitige Reformation im Spätmittelalter.* München: Oldenburg, 1998.

85. Southern, R.W., ed. *Oxford Studies Presented to Daniel Callus.* Oxford: Oxford Univ. Press, 1964.

86. Spinka, M. *Advocates of Reform from Wyclif to Erasmus.* Library of Christian Classics, vol. 14. Philadelphia: Westminster, 1953.

87. Spufford, Margaret, ed. *The World of Rural Dissenters, 1520–1725.* New York: Cambridge Univ. Press, 1995.

88. Stanley, Eric G., and Douglas Gray, eds. *Five Hundred Years of Words and Sounds: A Festschrift for Eric Dobson.* Cambridge: D.S. Brewer, 1983.

89. Riche, Pierre, and Guy Lobrichon, eds. *Le Moyen Âge et la Bible.* Paris: Editions Beauchesne, 1984.

90. Wallace, David, ed. *The Cambridge History of Medieval English Literature.* Cambridge: Cambridge Univ. Press, 1998.

91. Walsh, Katherine, and Diana Wood, eds. *The Bible in the Medieval World: Essays in Memory of Beryl Smalley.* Studies in Church History, Subsidia 4. Oxford: Basil Blackwell, 1985.

92. Wilks, Michael. *Wyclif: Political Ideas and Practice.* Intro. by Anne Hudson. Oxford: Oxbow Books, 2000.

93. Wood, Diana, ed. *The Church and Sovereignity c. 590–1918: Essays in Honour of Michael Wilks.* Studies in Church History, Subsidia 9. Oxford: Basil Blackwell, 1991.

94. ——. *Life and Thought in the Northern Church, c. 1100-c. 1700: Essays in Honour of Claire Cross.* Studies in Church History, Subsidia 12. Woodbridge: Boydell and Brewer, 1999.

95. Zimmermann, Albert, ed. *Antiqui und Moderni: Traditionbewusstsein und Fortschrittsbewusstsein im späten Mittelalter.* Miscellanea Mediaevalia, Vol. 9. Berlin: de Gruyter, 1974.

3. Primary Texts and Documents

While opinions have differed, this Bibliography assumes the predominant view that virtually no known vernacular Lollard writings can be with certainty ascribed to a specific author or translator; on this anonymity, see Hudson (699, and 713, ch. 1; an exception would be the two texts in 156). Without this traditional method of distinguishing texts, most modern distinctions between "Lollard" and "orthodox" works rely on analyses of their content. Yet this causes significant problems, since "Lollardy" is, in Anne Hudson's term, a "variable creed" which includes a wide range of beliefs ranging from mild reformist sympathy to unregenerate heresy. Many religious manuscripts and individual texts are "mixed," advocating Lollard beliefs next to ideas which other Lollards often condemned. Rather than compiling a list of "Lollard texts," therefore, this section contains texts (and anthologies which contain at least some texts) "concerned with Lollardy": not just those written by Lollards, but those which directly address (perhaps oppose) Lollardy. Relevant chronicles and ecclesiastical records also appear. This section is inevitably, and indeed deliberately, a vague category, and a listing here does not imply that a text was written by a Lollard, however defined. It should be noted that many texts are not included here since they have been edited in dissertations and theses.

Where an author is known the work is listed under the author's name. Anonymous works are listed in the first instance by title, and then by editor. Multiple works by individual authors are listed by date of modern publication.

96. [*Ancrene Riwle*]. *The English Text of the Ancrene Riwle, Edited from Magdalene College, Cambridge MS. Pepys 2498*. Ed. A. Zettersten. EETS o.s. 274. London: Oxford Univ. Press, 1976.

97. *Annales Monasterii Sancti Albani a Johanne Amundesham*. Ed. H.T. Riley. 2 vols. Rolls Series 28. London, 1870.

98. *The Anonimalle Chronicle, 1333–1381*. Ed. V.H. Galbraith. Manchester: Manchester Univ. Press, 1970.

99. *An Apology for Lollard Doctrines Attributed to Wicliffe*. Ed. James Henthorn Todd. Camden Society o.s. 20. London, 1842.

100. Arnold, T., ed. *Select English Works of John Wyclif*. 3 vols. Oxford, 1868–71.

101. Banning, Jozef H.A. "Two Uncontroversial Fragments of Wyclif in an Oxford Manuscript." *Journal of Theological Studies* 36.2 (1985) 338–49.

102. Barlow, Jerome, and William Roye. *Rede Me and Be Nott Wrothe*. Ed. Douglas Parker. Toronto: Univ. of Toronto Press, 1992.

103. Barr, Helen, ed. *The Piers Plowman Tradition*. London: J.M. Dent, 1993.

104. [Bible]. *The New Testament, Translated from the Latin in the year 1380, by John Wyclif, D.D., to Which are prefixed memoirs of the life, opinions, and writings of Dr. Wiclif . . . by Henry Harvey Baber*. London: Richard Edwards, 1810.

105. [Bible]. *The New Testament . . . now first printed from a contemporary manuscript formerly in the monastery of Sion, Middlesex . . ..* Oxford: C. Whittingham for W. Pickering, 1848.

106. [Bible]. *The Holy Bible, Containing the Old and New Testaments, with the Apocryphal Books, in the Earliest English Versions, made from the Latin Vulgate by John Wycliffe and his Followers*. 4 vols. Ed. J. Forshall and F. Madden. Oxford, 1850. Rpt. New York: AMS, 1982.

107. [Bible]. *A Fourteenth Century English Biblical Version Consisting of a Prologue and Parts of the New Testament edited from the Manuscripts*. Ed. A.C. Paues. Cambridge: Cambridge Univ. Press, 1902.

108. [Bible]. *The Later Version of the Wycliffite Epistle to the Romans: Compared with the Latin Original*. Ed. Emma C. Tucker. Yale Studies in English 49 (1914). New York: Henry Holt, 1914.

109. [Bible]. *MS. Bodley 959: Genesis-Baruch 3:20 in the Earlier Version of the Wycliffite Bible*. Ed. Conrad Lindberg. Stockholm Studies in English 6, 8, 10, 13, 20. Stockholm: Almqvist and Wiksell, 1959–68.

110. [Bible]. *The Earlier Version of the Wycliffite Bible . . . Edited from MS Christ Church 145*. Ed. Conrad Lindberg. Stockholm Studies in English 29, 81, 87. Stockholm: Almqvist and Wiksell, 1973–95.

111. [Bible]. *The Middle English Bible: Prefatory Epistles of St. Jerome*. Ed. Conrad Lindberg. Oslo: Norwegian Univ. Press, 1978.

112. [Bible]. *The Middle English Bible: The Book of Baruch*. Ed. Conrad Lindberg. Oslo: Norwegian Univ. Press, 1985.

113. [Bible]. *The New Testament in English*. Portland, Oregon: International Bible Publications, 1986. [A facsimile of Bodleian, Rawlinson 259.]

114. [Bible]. *The Middle English Bible: The Book of Judges*. Ed. Conrad Lindberg. Oslo: Norwegian Univ. Press, 1989.

115. [Bible]. *Wycliffite Manuscript: The New Testament*. CD-ROM. Oakland: Octavo Corporation, 1999. [A fascimile of Southern Methodist University, Bridwell Library Prothro B-01.]

116. [Bible]. *King Henry's Bible: MS Bodley 277 The Revised Version of the Wyclif Bible*. Ed. Conrad Lindberg. Stockholm Studies in English 89, 94.

Stockholm: Almqvist and Wiksell, 1999, 2001. [Vol. 1: Genesis-Ruth; Vol. 2, 1 Kings-Psalms.]

117. [Bible]. *The Wycliffe New Testament, 1388, an Edition in Modern Spelling with an Introduction, the Original Prologues, and the Epistle to the Laodiceans.* Ed. William Cooper. Toronto: Univ. of Toronto Press, 2002.

118. Blake, Norman, ed. *Middle English Religious Prose.* York Medieval Texts. Evanston, IL: Northwestern Univ. Press, 1972.

119. Blamires, Alcuin and C.W. Marx. "Women Not to Preach: A Disputation in British Library MS Harley 31." *Journal of Medieval Latin* 3 (1993): 34-63.

120. *The Book of Margery Kempe.* Ed. S.B. Meech, with prefatory note by H.E. Allen. EETS o.s. 210. London: Oxford Univ. Press, 1940.

121. *The Book of Margery Kempe.* Ed. Lynn Staley. TEAMS Middle English Texts Series. Kalamazoo: Medieval Institute, 1996.

122. *Book for a Simple and Devout Woman: A Late Middle English Adaptation of Peraldus' Summa de Vitiis et Virtutibus and Friar Laurent's Somme le Roi.* Ed. F.A.M. Diekstra. Medievalia Groningana, vol. 24. Groningen: Egbert Forsten, 1998.

123. Bowers, John, ed. *The Canterbury Tales: Fifteenth-Century Continuations and Additions.* TEAMS Middle English Texts Series. Kalamazoo: Medieval Institute, 1992.

124. Bremmer, Rolf H. *The Fyve Wyttes . . . Edited from BL MS Harley 2398.* Amsterdam: Rodopi, 1987.

125. Brown, Edward, ed. *Fasciculus Rerum Expetendarum et Fugiendarum.* 2 vols. London, 1690.

126. Bühler, Curt, ed. "A Lollard Tract: On Translating the Bible Into English." *Medium Aevum* 7.3 (1938): 167-183.

127. Chaucer, Geoffrey. *The Riverside Chaucer.* 3rd ed. Gen. ed. Larry Benson. Boston: Houghton Mifflin, 1987.

128. Cigman, Gloria, ed. *Lollard Sermons.* EETS o.s. 294. Oxford: Oxford Univ. Press, 1989.

129. Clanvowe, John. *The Works of Sir John Clanvowe.* Ed. John Scattergood. Cambridge: D.S. Brewer, 1975.

130. Crowder, C.M.D., ed. and trans. *Unity, Heresy, and Reform, 1378-1460: The Conciliar Response to the Great Schism.* New York: St. Martin's, 1977.

131. Dahmus, Joseph. *The Metropolitan Visitations of William Courtenay, Archbishop of Canterbury, 1381-1396: Documents Transcribed from the Original Manuscripts of Courtenay's Register.* Urbana: Univ. of Illinois Press, 1950.

132. Dean, James M., ed. *Six Ecclesiastical Satires.* TEAMS Middle English Texts Series. Kalamazoo: Medieval Institute, 1991.

133. ——. *Medieval English Political Writings.* TEAMS Middle English Texts Series. Kalamazoo: Medieval Institute, 1996.

134. *Dives and Pauper.* Ed. Priscilla Barnum. EETS o.s. 275, 80. Oxford: Oxford Univ. Press, 1976, 80.

135. Dobson, R. B., ed. *The Peasant's Revolt of 1381.* 2nd ed. London: Macmillan, 1983..

136. Dymmok, Roger. *Liber Contra Duodecim Errores et Hereses Lollardorum.* Ed. H.S. Cronin. London: Wyclif Society, 1922.

137. Edden, Valerie, ed. "The Debate between Richard Maidstone and the Lollard Ashwardby (ca. 1390)." *Carmelus* 34 (1987): 113-134.

138. Embree, Dan, ed. *The Chronicles of Rome*: An Edition of the Middle English

'*The Chronicles of Popes and Emperors and the Lollard Chronicle*'. Woodbridge: The Boydell Press, 1998.

139. *Fasciculi Zizaniorum Magistri Johannis Wyclif cum Tritico*. Ed. W.W. Shirley. Rolls Series 5. London, 1858.

140. Forshall, J., ed. *Remonstrance Against Romish Corruptions in the Church Addressed to the People and Parliament of England in 1395*. London, 1851.

141. Foxe, John. *Acts and Monuments. Popularly known as The Book of Martyrs*. London, 1563. Rpt. ed. S.R. Cattley and G. Townsend. 8 vols. London, 1843.

142. ——. *Facsimile of Foxe's Book of Martyrs, 1583: Actes and Monuments of Matters most Speciall and Memorable*. Ed. David G. Newcombe and Michael Pidd. CD-ROM. Version 1.0. Oxford: Oxford Univ. Press, 2001.

143. Gage, John, ed. "Letters from King Henry VI to the Abbot of St. Edmundsbury, and to the Alderman and Bailiffs of the Town, for the Suppression of the Lollards." *Archaeologia* 23 (1831): 339–43.

144. Gascoigne, Thomas. *Loci et Libri Veritatum*. Ed. J.E. Thorold Rogers. Oxford, 1881.

145. Genet, Jean-Phillippe, ed. *Four English Political Tracts of the Later Middle Ages*. Camden Society, fourth ser., vol. 18. London: Royal Historical Society, 1977.

146. *Gesta Henrici Quinti: The Deeds of Henry V*. Ed. Frank Taylor and John. S. Raskell. Oxford: Clarendon, 1975.

147. Gower, John. *The Complete Works of John Gower*. 4 vols. London: Oxford Univ. Press, 1899–1902.

148. ——. *Confessio Amantis*. 2 vols. Ed. G.C. Macaulay. EETS e.s. 81, 82. London: Oxford Univ. Press, 1900.

149. ——. *The Major Latin Works of John Gower*. Trans. Eric W. Stockton. Seattle: Univ. of Washington Press, 1962.

150. Halliwell, J.O. "A Sermon against Miracle Plays." *Reliquiae Antiquae* 2 (1841–43): 42–57.

151. [Hereford, Nicholas]. Forde, Simon, ed. "Nicholas Hereford's Ascension Day Sermon, 1382." *Mediaeval Studies* 51 (1989): 205–41.

152. Hoccleve, Thomas. *Hoccleve's Works: The Regement of Princes and Fourteen Minor Poems*. Ed. F. Furnivall. EETS e.s. 72. London: Kegan, Paul, 1897.

153. ——. *Selections from Hoccleve*. Ed. M.C. Seymour. Oxford: Clarendon, 1981.

154. Horstman, Carl, ed. *Yorkshire Writers: Richard Rolle of Hampole, An English Follower of the Church and his Followers*. 2 vols. New York, 1895. Repub. with an Intro. by Anne Clark Bartlett. Woodbridge: Boydell and Brewer, 1999.

155. Hudson, Anne, ed. *Selections from English Wycliffite Writings*. Cambridge: Cambridge Univ. Press, 1978.

156. ——, ed. *Two Wycliffite Texts*. EETS o.s. 301. Oxford: Oxford Univ. Press, 1993.

157. ——, ed. *The Works of a Lollard Preacher*. EETS o.s. 317. Oxford: Oxford Univ. Press, 2001.

158. Hudson, Anne, and Pamela Gradon, eds. *English Wycliffite Sermons*. 5 vols. Oxford: Clarendon, 1983–1996.

159. *Jack Upland, Friar Daw's Reply, and Upland's Rejoiner*. Ed. P.L. Heyworth. London: Oxford Univ. Press, 1968.

160. Jeffrey, David Lyle, ed. *The Law of Love: English Spirituality in the Age of Wyclif.* Grand Rapids: William B. Eerdmans, 1988.

161. Ker, Neil. "A Middle English Summary of the Bible." *Medium Aevum* 29 (1960): 115–18.

162. Kingsford, C.L., ed. *Chronicles of London.* Oxford: Clarendon, 1905.

163. Klawitter, George. "The Wycliffite Tract 'Pryde Wrathe and Envie' of HM 502." *Medievalia* 14 (1988): 143–155.

164. Knighton, Henry. *Chronicon Henrici Knighton.* Ed. J.R. Lumby. Rolls Series 92. 2 vols. London, 1889–95.

165. ——. *Knighton's Chronicle 1337–1396.* Ed. G.H. Martin. Oxford Medieval Texts. Oxford: Clarendon, 1995.

166. Kuhn, S.M., ed. "The Preface to a Fifteenth-century Concordance." *Speculum* 43 (1968): 258–73.

167. Langland, William. *Piers Plowman: The A Version.* Ed. George Kane. London: Athlone, 1960.

168. ——. *Piers Plowman: The B Version.* Ed. George Kane and E. Talbot Donaldson. London: Athlone, 1975.

169. ——. *The Vision of Piers Plowman: A Complete Edition of the B-Text.* Ed. A.V.C. Schmidt. London: Dent, 1978.

170. ——. *Piers Plowman by William Langland: An Edition of the C-Text.* Ed. D. Pearsall. York: York Medieval Texts, 1981.

171. ——. *Piers Plowman: The C Version.* Ed. George Kane and George Russell. London: Athlone, 1997.

172. ——. *Piers Plowman: The Z Version.* Ed. A.G. Rigg and Charlotte Brewer. Studies and Texts 59. Toronto: Pontifical Institute, 1983.

173. ——. *Piers Plowman: A Parallel-Text Edition of the A, B, C, and Z Versions.* Ed. A.V.C. Schmidt. London: Longman, 1995.

174. *The Lanterne of Liȝt.* Ed. L.M. Swinburn. EETS o.s. 151. London: K. Paul, 1917.

175. *The Last Age of the Church.* Ed. James Henthorn Todd. Dublin: Univ. Press, 1840.

176. *The Lay Folk's Catechism.* Ed. T.F. Simmons and H.E. Nolloth. EETS o.s. 118. London: K. Paul, Trench, and Trübner, 1901.

177. Lindberg, Conrad, ed. *English Wyclif Tracts 1–3.* Studia Anglistica Norvegica 5. Oslo: Novus Forlag, 1991.

178. ——. *English Wyclif Tracts 4–6.* Studia Anglistica Norvegica 11. Oslo: Novus Forlag, 2000.

179. Love, Nicholas. *Nicholas Love's Mirror of the Blessed Life of Jesus Christ.* Ed. Michael G. Sargent. New York: Garland, 1992.

180. [Lychlade, Robert]. "Robert Lychlade's Oxford Sermon of 1395." Ed. Siegfried Wenzel. *Traditio* 53 (1998): 203–230.

181. Lyndwood, William. *Provinciale (seu Constitutiones Angliae) Continens Constitutiones Provinciales Quatordecim Archiepiscoporum Cantuariensium.* Oxford, 1679.

182. Matthew, F.D., ed. *The English Works of Wyclif.* 2nd ed. EETS o.s. 74. London: Oxford Univ. Press, 1902.

183. McHardy, Alison K., ed. *The Church in London, 1375–1392.* London: London Record Society, 1977.

184. McIntosh, A., ed. "Some Linguistic Reflections of a Wycliffite." *Franciplegius: Medieval and Linguistic Studies in Honor of F.P. Magoun.* Ed. J.B. Bessinger and R.P. Creed. New York: New York Univ. Press, 1965. 290–93.

185. Mirk, John. *John Myrc: Instructions for Parish Priests*. Ed. E. Peacock. EETS o.s. 31. London, 1868.

186. ——. *Mirk's Festial*. Ed. T. Erbe. EETS e.s. 96. London: Oxford Univ. Press, 1905.

187. More, St. Thomas. "The Affairs of Richard Hunne and Friar Standish." Ed. J.D.M. Derrett. *The Complete Works of St. Thomas More*. Vol. 9. Gen. Ed. L.L. Martz. New Haven: Yale Univ. Press, 1979. 215–46.

188. Netter, Thomas. *Thomae Waldensis Doctrinale Antiquitatum Fidei Ecclesiae Catholicae Ecclesiae*. Ed. B. Blanciotti. Venice, 1757–9. Rpt. Farnborough: Gregg, 1967.

189. Parkes, M.B. "Manuscript Fragments of English Sermons Attributed to John Wyclif." *Medium Aevum* 24.2 (1955): 97–100.

190. Pecock, Reginald. *Repressor of Over Much Blaming of the Clergy*. Ed. C. Babington. London, 1860.

191. ——. *The Book of Faith*. Ed. J.L. Morison. Glasgow, 1909.

192. ——. *The Donet of Reginald Pecock*. Ed. E.V. Hitchcock. EETS o.s. 156. London: Oxford Univ. Press, 1921.

193. ——. *Folewer to the Donet by Reginald Pecock*. Ed. E.V. Hitchcock. EETS o.s. 164. London: Oxford Univ. Press, 1924.

194. ——. *Reule of Cristen Religioun*. Ed. W.C. Greet. EETS o.s. 171. Oxford: Oxford Univ. Press, 1927.

195. Peters, Edward. *Heresy and Authority in Medieval Europe: Documents in Translation*. Philadelphia: Univ. of Pennsylvania Press, 1980.

196. *The Plowman's Tale: The c. 1532 and 1606 Editions of a Spurious Canterbury Tale*. Ed. M.R. McCarl. New York: Garland, 1997.

197. Powell, E., and G.M. Trevelyan, eds. *The Peasants' Rising and the Lollards: A Collection of Unpublished Documents forming an Appendix to "England in the Age of Wycliffe."* London: Longman, Green, 1899.

198. *The Praier and Complaynte of the Ploweman vnto Christe*. Ed. Douglas H. Parker. Toronto: Univ. of Toronto Press, 1997.

199. *A Proper Dyalogue betwene a Gentillman and a Husbandman*. Ed. Douglas H. Parker. Toronto: Univ. of Toronto Press, 1996.

200. Rolle, Richard. *The Psalter or Psalms of David and Certain Canticles With a Translation and Exposition in English by Richard Rolle of Hampole*. Ed. H.R. Bramley. Oxford, 1884.

201. Salter, Herbert E., and V.H. Galbraith, eds. *Snappe's Formulary and Other Records*. Oxford Historical Society 80. Oxford: Clarendon, 1924.

202. Shinners, John, ed. *Medieval Popular Religion 1100–1500: A Reader*. Medieval Studies Series, vol. 2. Peterborough, ON: Broadview, 1997.

203. Shinners, John, and William J. Dohar, eds. *Pastors and the Care of Souls in Medieval England*. Notre Dame: Univ. of Notre Dame Press, 1998.

204. Skelton, John. *John Skelton: The Complete Poems*. Ed. John Scattergood. New Haven: Yale Univ. Press, 1983.

205. Strype, John. *Memorials of the Most Reverend Father in God, Thomas Cranmer sometime Lord Archbishop of Canterbury*. London, 1694. New ed. Oxford: Ecclesiastical History Society, 1848–54.

206. Swanson, R.N., ed. and trans. *Catholic England: Faith, Religion, and Observance before the Reformation*. Manchester: Manchester Univ. Press, 1993.

207. Talbert, Ernst W., ed. "A Lollard Chronicle of the Papacy." *Journal of English and Germanic Philology* 41 (1942): 163–93.

208. Tanner, Norman P., S.J., ed. *Heresy Trials in the Diocese of Norwich, 1428–31*. Camden Society Fourth Series, vol. 20. London: Royal Historical Society, 1977.

209. ——, ed. *Kent Heresy Proceedings 1511–12*. Kent Records, vol. 26, gen. ed. A.P. Detsicas. Maidstone, Kent: Kent Archaeological Society, 1997.

210. "The Thirty-Seven Conclusions of the Lollards." Ed. H.F.B. Compston. *English Historical Review* 26 (1911): 738–749.

211. Thomson, S. Harrison. "Four Unpublished *Questiones* of John Hus." *Medievalia et Humanistica* o.s. 7 (1952): 71–88.

212. Todd, James Henthorn, ed. *Three Treatises by John Wycklyffe, now first printed from a manuscript in the library of Trinity College, Dublin*. Dublin, 1851.

213. [Trefnant, John]. *Registrum Johannis Trefnant, Episcopi Herefordensis*. Ed. W.W. Capes. Canterbury and York Society 20 (1916).

214. *A Tretise of Miraclis Pleyinge*. Ed. Clifford Davidson. Early Drama, Art, and Music Monograph Series 19. Kalamazoo: Medieval Institute, 1993.

215. "The Twelve Conclusions of the Lollards." Ed. H.S. Cronin. *English Historical Review* 22 (1907): 292–304.

216. Trevisa, John. *Dialogus Inter Militem et Clericum*. Ed. A.J. Perry. EETS o.s. 167. London: Oxford Univ. Press, 1925.

217. [–]. Waldron, Ronald, ed. "Trevisa's Original Prefaces on Translation: A Critical Edition." *Medieval English Studies Presented to George Kane*. Ed. Edward D. Kennedy, R. Waldron, and Joseph S. Wittig. Cambridge: D.S. Brewer, 1988. 285–97.

218. Tyndale, William, ed. "The Examinations of the Constant Servant of God, William Thorpe, before Archbishop Arundel, Written by Himself, A.D. 1407." *Religious Tract Society* (1831): 39–102.

219. Usk, Adam. *Chronicle of Adam of Usk 1377–1421*. Ed. and trans. Chris Given-Wilson. Oxford Medieval Texts. Oxford: Oxford Univ. Press, 1997.

220. von Nolcken, Christina, ed. *The Middle English Translation of the Rosarium Theologie*. Heidelberg: Carl Winter, 1979.

221. Walsingham, Thomas. *Historia Anglicana*. 2 vols. Ed. H.T. Riley. Rolls Series. London, 1863–4.

222. ——. *Annales Ricardi Secundi*. Ed. H.T. Riley. London, 1866.

223. ——. *Chronicon Angliae*. Ed. E.M. Thompson. Rolls Series. London, 1869.

224. ——. *Ypogdima Neustriae*. Ed. H.T. Riley. Rolls Series. London, 1876.

225. Wimbledon, Thomas. *Wimbledon's Sermon Redde Rationem Villicationis Tue: A Middle English Sermon of the Fourteenth Century*. Ed. Ione Kemp Knight. Pittsburgh: Duquesne Univ. Press, 1967.

226. Winn, Herbert E., ed. *Select English Writings*. With a preface by H.B. Workman. London: Oxford Univ. Press, 1929.

227. *The Westminster Chronicle: 1381–1384*. Ed. and trans. L.C. Hector and B.F. Harvey. Oxford Medieval Texts. Oxford: Oxford Univ. Press, 1982.

228. Wilkins, D. *Concilia Magnae Britanniae et Hiberniae, A.D. 466–1718*. 4 vols. London, 1737.

229. [Wyche, Richard]. "The Trial of Richard Wyche." Ed. F.D. Matthew. *English Historical Review* 5 (1890): 530–44.

230. *Wycklyffe's Wycket*. Nuremburg, 1546. Rpt., ed. T.P. Pantin. Oxford, 1828.

231. [Woodford, William]. Doyle, Eric. "William Woodford's *De Dominio Civili Clericorum* against John Wyclif." *Archivum Franciscanum Historicum* 66 (1973): 49–109.

232. ——. "Bibliographical List by William Woodford O.F.M." *Franciscan Studies* 35 (1975): 93–106.

233. ——. "William Woodford O.F.M. (c. 1330–c.1400): His Life and Works, together with a Study and Edition of His *Responsiones contra Wyclevum et Lollardos.*" *Franciscan Studies* 43 (1983): 17–187.

234. Wogan-Browne, Jocelyn et al., eds. *The Idea of the Vernacular: An Anthology of Middle English Literary Theory, 1280–1520.* University Park: Penn State Univ. Press, 1998.

235. Wright, T., ed. *Political Songs and Poems Relating to English History.* 2 vols. Rolls Series. London, 1859–61.

Wyclif, John. Works Edited in Latin:

236. ——. *Dialogorum Libri Quatuor.* Francofurti: Impensis Io. Gott. Vierlingii, 1753.

237. ——. *De Officio Pastorali.* Ed. G.V. Lechler. Leipzig, 1863.

238. ——. *Trialogus, cum Supplemento Trialogi.* Ed. G.V. Lechler. Oxford, 1869.

239. ——. *Wyclif's Latin Works.* 36 vols. Ed. R. Beer et al. London: Wyclif Society, 1883–1922. Rpt. New York: Johnson Reprint, 1966.

240. ——. "A 'Lost' Chapter of Wyclif's *Summa de Ente.*" Ed. S. Harrison Thomson. *Speculum* 4 (1929): 339–346.

241. ——. *Johannis Wyclif Summa de Ente.* Ed. S. Harrison Thomson. Oxford, 1930.

242. ——. [Complaint]. "The Latin Text of Wyclif's *Complaint.*" Ed. I.H. Stein. *Speculum* 7 (1932): 87–94.

243. ——. [Confessio]. "An Unpublished Fragment of Wyclif's *Confessio.*" Ed. I.H. Stein. *Speculum* 8 (1933): 503–10.

244. ——. *Tractatus de Trinitate.* Ed. Allen duPont Breck. Boulder: Univ. of Colorado Press, 1962.

245. ——. *Tractatus de Universalibus.* Ed. Ivan J. Mueller. Oxford: Clarendon, 1985.

246. ——. *Johannis Wyclif Summa Insolubilium.* Ed. P.V. Spade and G.A. Wilson. Binghamton: Center for Medieval and Renaissance Texts and Studies, 1986.

247. ——. *De Civili Dominio, chs. 1–10.* Ed. John Kilcullen. August, 1999. Available from http://www.humanities.mq.edu.au/Ockham/wlatcor.html. Accessed July 2002.

Wyclif, John. Modern English Translations:

248. ——. *On the Eucharist.* Ed. and trans. F.L. Battles. Spinka 61–88.

249. ——. *On the Pastoral Office.* Ed. and trans. F.L. Battles. Spinka 32–60.

250. ——. *On Universals.* Trans. A. Kenny; Intro. by P.V. Spade. Oxford: Clarendon, 1985.

251. ——. *On Simony.* Trans. Terrence A. McVeigh. New York: Fordham, 1992.

252. ——. *On the Duty of the King.* Trans. Cary Nederman. *Medieval Political Theory–A Reader.* Ed. Cary Nederman and Kate L. Forhan. London: Routledge, 1993. 221–230.

253. *On Civil Dominion. The Cambridge Translations of Medieval Philosophical Texts, vol. 2: Ethics and Political Philosophy.* Ed. and trans. A.S. Mcgrade,

J. Kilcullen, and M. Kempshall. Cambridge: Cambridge Univ. Press, 2001. 587–654.

254. ——. *John Wyclif: On the Truth of Holy Scripture.* Trans. with Intro. and notes by I. C. Levy. Kalamazoo: Medieval Institute, 2001.

4. *Secondary Sources*

Multiple studies by individual authors are listed in order of publication.

255. Adams, Robert. "Piers' Pardon and Langland's Semi-Pelagianism." *Traditio* 39 (1983): 367–418.

256. ——. "Langland's Theology." Alford 87–116.

257. Alford, John. "The Design of the Poem." Alford 29–66.

258. Aers, David. "Christ's Humanity and Piers Plowman: Contexts and Political Implications." *The Yearbook of Langland Studies* 8 (1995): 107–25.

259. ——. "Vox Populi and the Literature of 1381." Wallace 432–53.

260. ——. "Christ's Humanity and Piers Plowman: Contexts and Political Implications." *The Yearbook of Langland Studies* 8 (1995): 107–25.

261. ——. *Faith, Ethics, and Church: Writing in England, 1360–1409.* Woodbridge: Boydell and Brewer, 2000.

262. ——. "The Sacrament of the Altar in Piers Plowman and the Late Medieval Church in England." Dimmick, Simpson, and Zeeman, 63–80.

263. Aers, David, and Lynn Staley. *The Powers of the Holy: Religion, Politics, and Gender in Late Medieval English Culture.* University Park: Penn State Univ. Press, 1996. Portions Rptd. in "The Humanity of Christ." *Chaucer to Spenser: a Critical Reader.* Ed. Derek Pearsall. Oxford: Blackwell, 1999. 1–41.

264. Aita, Shuichi. "Negation in the Wycliffite Sermons." *Arthurian and Other Studies Presented to Shunichi Noguchi.* Ed. T. Suzuki and T. Mukai. Woodbridge: Boydell and Brewer, 1993. 241–45.

265. Allen, Hope Emily. *Writings Ascribed to Richard Rolle, Hermit of Hampole, and Materials for His Biography.* New York: D.C. Heath, 1927.

266. Ames, Ruth M. "Corn and Shrimps: Chaucer's Mockery of Religious Controversy." *The Late Middle Ages.* Ed. P. Cocozzella. Binghamton: Center for Medieval and Renaissance Studies, 1984. 71–88.

267. Archer, Margaret. "Philip Repingdon, Bishop of Lincoln, and his Cathedral Chapter [1405–19]." *University of Birmingham Historical Journal* 4 (1953–54): 81–97.

268. Arnold, John. "Lollard Trials and Inquisitorial Discourse." Given-Wilson 81–94.

269. Aston, Margaret. "Lollardy and Sedition, 1381–1431." *Past and Present* 17 (1960): 1–44. Rpt. in Aston, *Lollards and Reformers* 1–47.

270. ——. "Lollardy and the Reformation: Survival or Revival?" *History* 49 (1964): 149–70. Rpt. in Aston, *Lollards and Reformers* 219–242.

271. ——. "John Wycliffe's Reformation Reputation." *Past and Present* 30 (1965): 23–51. Rpt. in Aston, *Lollards and Reformers* 243–72.

272. ——. "The Impeachment of Bishop Despenser." *Bulletin of the Institute of Historical Research* 38 (1965): 127–48.

273. ——. *Thomas Arundel: A Study of Church Life in the Reign of Richard II.* Oxford: Clarendon, 1967.

274. ———. "Lollard Women Priests?" *Journal of Ecclesiastical History* 31 (1980): 441–62. Rpt. in Aston, *Lollards and Reformers* 49–70.

275. ———. "William White's Lollard Followers." *Catholic History Review* 48 (1982): 469–97. Rpt. in Aston, *Lollards and Reformers* 71–100.

276. ———. "Devotional Literacy." Aston, *Lollards and Reformers* 101–133.

277. ———. "Lollards and Images." Aston, *Lollards and Reformers* 135–192.

278. ———. "Lollardy and Literacy." *History* 62 (1977): 347–71. Rpt. in Aston, *Lollards and Reformers* 193–217.

279. ———. "Richard II and the Wars of the Roses." *The Reign of Richard II: Essays in Honour of May McKisack.* Ed. F.R.H. Du Boulay and Caroline M. Barron. London: Athlone, 1971. 280–317. Rpt. in Aston, *Lollards and Reformers* 273–311.

280. ———. "Popular Religious Movements in the Later Middle Ages." *The Christian World: A Social and Cultural History of Christianity.* Ed. Geoffrey Barraclough. London: Thames and Hudson, 1981. 157–70. Rpt. in Aston, *Faith and Fire* 1–26.

281. ———. "'Caim's Castles': Poverty, Politics, and Disendowment." Dobson 45–81. Rpt. in Aston, *Faith and Fire* 95–132.

282. ———. "Works of Religious Instruction." Edwards 413–432.

283. ———. "Wyclif and the Vernacular." Hudson and Wilks 281–330. Rpt. in Aston, *Faith and Fire* 27–72.

284. ———. *England's Iconoclasts.* Oxford: Clarendon, 1988.

285. ———. "Iconoclasm at Rickmansworth, 1522: Troubles of Churchwardens." *Journal of Ecclesiastical History* 40 (1989): 524–52. Rpt. in Aston, *Faith and Fire* 231–260.

286. ———. "Bishops and Heresy: The Defence of the Faith." Aston, *Faith and Fire* 73–94.

287. ———. "Corpus Christi and Corpus Regni: Heresy and the Peasant's Revolt." *Past and Present* 143 (1994): 3–47.

288. ———. "Were the Lollards a Sect?" Biller and Dobson 163–92.

289. Auksi, P. "Wyclif's Sermons and the Plain Style." *Archiv für Reformationsgeschichte* 66 (1975): 5–23.

290. Bacher, John Rea. *The Prosecution of Heretics in Medieval England.* Philadelphia: Univ. of Pennsylvania Press, 1942.

291. Baker, James. *A Forgotten Great Englishman, or, The Life and Work of Peter Payne, The Wycliffite.* London: Religious Tract Society, 1894.

292. Baldwin, Anna. "The Historical Context." Alford 67–86.

293. Ball, R.M. "Thomas Cyrcetur, a Fifteenth-Century Theologian and Preacher." *Journal of Ecclesiastical History* 37 (1986): 205–39.

294. Barish, Jonas. *The Antitheatrical Prejudice.* Berkeley: Univ. of California Press, 1981.

295. Barisone, Ermanno. "Wyclif and his Followers and the Method of Translation." *John Wyclif* 143–53.

296. Barr, Helen. *Socioliterary Practice in Medieval England.* Oxford: Oxford Univ. Press, 2001.

297. Bartoš, František Michálek. "Hus a Viklef." *Husitsví a cizina.* Prague: Cin, 1931. 20–58.

298. ———. "Hus, Lollardism, and Devotio Moderna in the Fight for a National Bible." *Communio Viatorum* 3 (1960): 247–54.

299. Baudry, L. "A propos de G. d'Ockham et de Wyclef." *Archives d'Histoire Doctrinale et Littéraire du Moyen Âge* 12 (1939): 231–51.

300. Beckwith, Sarah. *Christ's Body: Identity, Culture and Society in Late Medieval Writings*. London: Routledge, 1993.

301. ——. "*Sacrum Signum*: Sacramentality and Dissent in York's Theatre of Corpus Christi." Copeland 264–288.

302. ——. *Signifying God: Social Relation and Symbolic Act in York's Play of Corpus Christi*. Chicago: Univ. of Chicago Press, 2001.

303. Bennett, H.S. "The Production and Dissemination of Vernacular Manuscripts in the Fifteenth Century." *The Library: A Quarterly Journal*. Fifth Series, vol. 1 (1946/7): 167–78.

304. Bennett, J.A.W. *Chaucer at Oxford and at Cambridge*. Oxford: Oxford Univ. Press, 1974.

305. Bennett, Michael. *Richard II and the Revolution of 1399*. Phoenix Mill, UK: Alan Sutton, 1999.

306. Bennett, W.F. "Communication and Excommunication in the N-Town Conception of Mary." *Assays* 8 (1995): 119–40.

307. Benrath, Gustav A. "Wyclif und Hus." *Zeitschrift für Theologie und Kirche* 62 (1965): 196–216.

308. ——. *Wyclif's Bibelkommentar*. Berlin: De Gruyter, 1966.

309. ——. "Stand und Aufgaben der Wyclif-Forschung." *Theologische-Literaturezeitung* 92 (Apr. 1967): 261–64.

310. ——. "Traditionsbewusstsein, Scriftverständnis und Schriftprinzip bei Wyclif." Zimmermann 359–83.

311. ——. *John Wyclif*. Gestalten der Kirchengeschichte 4. Stuttgart: W. Kohlhammer, 1983.

312. Beonio-Brocchieri Fumigalli, M.T. *Wyclif: il Comunismo dei Predestinati*. Florence: Sansoni, 1975.

313. ——. "Il pensiero di J. Wyclif nel quadro della filosofia del suo secolo." *John Wyclif* 45–60.

314. Beonio-Brocchieri Fumigalli, M.T., and M. Parodi. *Storia della Filosophia Medievale: Da Boezio a Wyclif*. Rome: Editori Laterza, 1988.

315. Bergs, Alexander. "Social Networks in pre-1500 Britain: Problems, Prospects, Examples." *European Journal of English Studies* 4 (2000): 239–51.

316. Bernard, P.P. "Heresy in 14th Century Austria." *Medievalia et Humanistica* 10 (1956): 50–67.

317. ——. "Jerome of Prague, Austria and the Hussites." *Church History* 27 (1958): 3–22.

318. Bertelloni, Francisco. "Implicaciones políticos de la eclesologia de Wyclif." *Patristica et Mediaevalia* 15 (1994): 45–58.

319. Bertoldi, Lenoci. *Il cristianesimo di John Wyclif*. Bari: Milella, 1979.

320. Besserman, Lawrence. *Chaucer's Biblical Poetics*. Norman: Univ. of Oklahoma Press, 1998.

321. Betts, R.R. "English and Czech Influence in the Hussite Movement." *Transactions of the Royal Historical Society* 4th series, 21 (1939): 74–102. Rpt. in Betts, ed. *Essays in Czech History* (London: Athlone, 1969) 132–59.

322. ——. "Jan Hus." *History* 24 (1939): 97–112.

323. Bisson, Lillian M. *Chaucer and the Late Medieval World*. London: Palgrave, 1998.

324. Black, Antony. *Political Thought in Europe 1250–1450*. Cambridge: Cambridge Univ. Press, 1992.

325. Black, Merja [Merja Stenroos]. "Lollardy, Language Contact, and the Great

Vowel Shift: Spellings in the Defence Papers of William Swinderby."
Neuphilologische Mitteilungen 99 (1998): 53–69.

326. Blake, Norman. "Varieties of Middle English Religious Prose." *Chaucer and Middle English Studies in Honour of Rossell Hope Robbins.* Ed. Beryl Rowland. Ohio: Kent State Univ. Press, 1974. 348–356.

327. Blamires, Alcuin. "The Wife of Bath and Lollardy." *Medium Aevum* 58.2 (1989): 224–242.

328. Block, Edward A. *John Wyclif: Radical Dissenter.* Humanities Monograph Series 1:1. San Diego: San Diego State College Press, 1962.

329. Blythe, James. *Ideal Government and the Mixed Constitution in the Middle Ages.* Princeton: Princeton Univ. Press, 1992.

330. Bobrick, Benson. *Wide as the Waters: The Story of the English Bible and the Revolution It Inspired.* New York: Penguin, 2001.

331. Boffey, J., and John J. Thompson. "Anthologies and Miscellanies: Production and Choice of Texts." Griffiths and Pearsall 279–315.

332. Böhringer, Friedrich. *Die Vorreformatoren des vierzehnten und fünfzehnten Jahrunderts, Erste Hälfte: Johannes von Wycliffe.* Zurich, Meyer & Zeller, 1856.

333. Boitani, Piero. *English Medieval Narrative in the 13th and 14th Centuries.* Trans. J.K. Hall. Cambridge: Cambridge Univ. Press, 1982.

334. Borinski, Ludwig. *Wyclif, Erasmus, und Luther: vorgelegt in der Sitzung vom 1. Juli 1988.* Joachim Jungius-Gesellschaft der Wissenschaften e.V., Hamburg. Jg. 6, H.2. Göttingen: Vandehoeck & Ruprecht, 1988.

335. Bostick, Curtis V. *The Anti-Christ and the Lollards: Apocalypticism in Late Medieval and Reformation Thought.* Studies in Medieval and Reformation Thought, vol. 70. Leiden: E.J. Brill, 1998.

336. Bowers, John. "*Piers Plowman* and the Police: Notes toward a History of the Wycliffite Langland." *Yearbook of Langland Studies* 6 (1992): 1–50.

337. ———. "The Politics of *Pearl.*" *Exemplaria* 7 (1995): 419–41.

338. ———. *The Politics of Pearl: Court Poetry in the Age of Richard II.* Cambridge: D.S. Brewer, 2000.

339. Bowman, Glen. "William Tyndale's Eucharistic Theology: Lollard and Zwinglian Influences." *Anglican and Episcopalian History* 66 (1997): 422–34.

340. Boyd, Beverly. "Wyclif, Joan of Arc, and Margery Kempe." *Mystics Quarterly* 12.3 (Sept. 1986): 112–118.

341. Boyle, L.E. "Innocent III and Vernacular Versions of Scripture." Walsh and Wood 97–107.

342. Brady, Sr. M. Teresa. "*The Pore Caitif:* an Introductory Study." *Traditio* 10 (1954): 529–48.

343. ———. "The Apostles and the Creed in Manuscripts of *The Pore Caitif.*" *Speculum* 32 (1957): 323–325.

344. ———. "Lollard Sources of the *Pore Caitif.*" *Traditio* 44 (1988): 389–418.

345. ———. "Lollard Interpolations and Omissions in Manuscripts of the *Pore Caitif.*" *De Cella in Saeculum: Religious and Secular Life and Devotion in Late Medieval England.* Ed. Michael G. Sargent. Cambridge: D.S. Brewer, 1989. 183–203.

346. Brandt, Miroslav. *Wyclifova hereza i socijalni pokreti u Splitu krajem XIV. st.* Zagreb: Kultura, 1955.

347. ———. "Wyclifitisim in Dalmatia in 1383." *Slavonic and East European Review* 36 (1957–58): 58–68.

348. Brandt, W.J. "Church and Society in the Late Fourteenth Century." *Medievalia et Humanistica* 13 (1960): 56–67.

349. ——. *London and the Reformation*. Oxford: Clarendon, 1989.

350. Breck, Allen duPont. "The Manuscripts of Wyclif's *De Trinitate*." *Medievalia et Humanistica* o.s. 7 (1952): 56–70.

351. ——. "John Wyclyf on Time." *Cosmology, History, and Theology*. Ed. W. Yourgrau and Allen d. Breck. New York: Plenum Press, 1977. 211–18.

352. Breeze, A. "The Wycliffite Bible Prologue on the Scriptures in Welsh." *Notes and Queries* 46.1 (1999): 16–17.

353. Brewer, Thomas. *Memoir of the Life and Times of John Carpenter*. London, 1856.

354. Brockwell, Charles W., Jr. *Bishop Reginald Pecock and the Lancastrian Church: Securing the Foundations of Cultural Authority*. Texts and Studies in Religion 25. Lewiston, NY: Edwin Mellon, 1985.

355. Brooks, Douglas A. "Sir John Oldcastle and the Construction of Shakespeare's Authorship." *Studies in English Literature 1500–1900* 38 (1998): 333–361.

356. Brown, Andrew. *Popular Piety in Late Medieval England: The Diocese of Salisbury, 1250–1550*. Oxford: Clarendon, 1995.

357. Brown, David. "Wiclif and Hus." *British and Foreign Evangelical Review* 33 (1884): 572–8.

358. Bruce, Frederick F. "John Wycliffe and the English Bible." *Churchman* 98.4 (1984): 294–306.

359. Buddensieg, R. *Johann Wiclif und seine Zeit*. Schriften des Vereins für Reformationsgeschichte, 8–9. Halle: Verein für Reformationsgeschichte, 1885.

360. Burrows, Montagu. *Wiclif's place in history: Three Lectures Delivered before the University of Oxford in 1881*. London: W. Isbister, 1882.

361. Bushill, T. *John Wycliffe, Patriot and Reformer*. Coventry, 1885.

362. Butterworth, Charles C. *The Literary Lineage of the King James Bible, 1340–1611*. Philadelphia: Univ. of Pennsylvania Press, 1941.

363. Butterworth, Charles C., and A.G. Chester. *George Joye 1495 (?)–1553*. Philadelphia: Univ. of Pennsylvania Press, 1962.

364. Cadman, S. Parkes. *The Three Religious Leaders of Oxford and their Movements*. New York: Macmillan, 1916.

365. Cammack, Melvin M. *John Wyclif and the English Bible*. New York: American Tract Society, 1938.

366. Cannon, H.L. "The Poor Priests: A Study in the Rise of English Lollardy." *Annual Report of the American Historical Association for 1899* 1 (1900): 451–82.

367. Cannon, W.R. "John Wyclif and John Hus." *Emory Univeristy Quarterly* 15 (1959): 80–87.

368. Capes, W.W. *The English Church in the Fourteenth and Fifteenth Centuries*. A History of the English Church, vol. 3. London, 1900.

369. Carr, J.W. *Über das Verhältnis der Wiclifitschen und der Purvey'schen Bibelübersetzung zur Vulgata*. Leipzig, 1902.

370. Carre, Meyrick H. *Realists and Nominalists*. Oxford: Oxford Univ. Press, 1946.

371. Carrick, J.C. *Wycliffe and the Lollards*. New York: Scribners, 1908.

372. Catto, J.I. "Religion and the English Nobility in the Later Fourteenth

Century." *History and Imagination: Essays in Honour of H.R. Trevor-Roper.* Ed. H. Lloyd-Jones et al. London: Duckworth, 1981. 43–55.

373. ——. "John Wyclif and the Cult of the Eucharist." Walsh and Wood 269–86.

374. ——. "Religious Change under Henry V." *Henry V: The Practice of Kingship.* Ed. G.L. Harriss. Oxford: Oxford Univ. Press, 1985. 97–115.

375. ——. "Wyclif and the Lollards: Dissidents in an Age of Faith." *History Today* 37 (November 1987): 46–52.

376. ——. "Some English Manuscripts of Wyclif's Latin Works." Hudson and Wilks 353–359.

377. ——. "Sir William Beauchamp between Chivalry and Lollardy." *The Ideals and Practice of Medieval Knighthood III: Papers from the Fourth Strawberry Hill Conference 1988.* Ed. C. Harper-Bill and R. Harvey. Cambridge: D.S. Brewer, 1990. 39–48.

378. ——. "Wyclif and Wycliffism at Oxford 1356–1430." Catto and Evans 175–261.

379. ——. "Theology After Wycliffism." Catto and Evans 263–280.

380. ——. "Fellows and Helpers: The Religious Identity of the Followers of Wyclif." Biller and Dobson 141–62.

381. ——. "The King's Government and the Fall of Pecock, 1457–58." *Rulers and Ruled in Late Medieval England: Essays Presented to Gerald Harriss.* Ed. R. Archer and S. Walker (London: Hambledon, 1995) 201–22.

382. ——. "A Radical Preacher's Handbook." *English Historical Review* 115 (Sept. 2000): 893–905.

383. Catto, Jeremy, Pamela Gradon, and Anne Hudson. *Wyclif and His Followers: An Exhibition to Mark the 600th Anniversary of the Death of John Wyclif, December 1984-April 1985.* Oxford: Bodleian Library, 1984.

384. Chadwick, Dorothy. *Social Life in the Days of Piers Plowman.* Cambridge: Cambridge Univ. Press, 1922.

385. Chambers, R.W. "On the Continuity of English Prose from Alfred to More and His School." in *The Life and Death of Sr. Thomas More . . . by Nicholas Harpsfield.* Ed. E.V. Hitchcock. EETS o.s. 186. London: Oxford Univ. Press, 1932. xlv-clxxiv.

386. Chaplin, W.N. "Lollardy and the Great Bible." *Church Quarterly Review* 128 (1939): 210–37.

387. Chapman, W. *The Life and Times of John Wyclif, the Herald of the Reformation.* London, 1884.

388. Cheyney, Edward P. "The Recantation of the Early Lollards." *American Historical Review* 4 (1899): 423–38.

389. Christianson, Gerald. "Wyclif's Ghost: The Politics of Reunion at the Council of Basel." *Annuarium Historiae Conciliorum* 17 (1985): 193–208.

390. Cigman, G. "The Preacher as Performer: Lollard Sermons as Imaginative Discourse." *Literature and Theology* 2 (1988): 69–82.

391. ——. "*Luceat Lux Vestra*: The Lollard Preacher as Truth and Light." *Review of English Studies* 40:160 (1989): 479–96.

392. ——. "'The Keyes of Kunnynge': Unlocking the Texts." *Die deutsche Predigt im Mittelalter.* Ed. V. Mertens and H-J. Schiewer. Tubingen: Max Niemeyer, 1992. 256–67.

393. ——. "Bounden as a Sheep." *Notes and Queries* 41 (239):1 (1994): 15.

394. Clark, John P.H. "Walter Hilton in Defense of Religious Life and the Veneration of Images." *Downside Review* 103 (1985): 1–25.

395. Clebsch, W.A. *England's Earliest Protestants 1520–1535*. New Haven: Yale Univ. Press, 1964.

396. Clopper, Lawrence. "Miracula and *The Tretise of Miraclis Pleyinge*." *Speculum* 65 (1990): 878–905.

397. ——. "Langland's Persona: An Anatomy of the Mendicant Orders." Justice and Kerby-Fulton 144–184.

398. ——. *"Songes of Rechelesnesse": Langland and the Franciscans*. Ann Arbor: Univ. of Michigan Press, 1997.

399. Cole, Andrew. "Trifunctionality and the Tree of Charity: Literary and Social Practice in Piers Plowman." *ELH: A Journal of English Literary History* 62 (1995): 1–27.

400. ——. "Chaucer's English Lesson." *Speculum* 77.4 (2002): 1128–67.

401. Coleman, Janet. *English Literature in History, 1350–1400: Medieval Readers and Writers*. London: Hutchinson, 1981.

402. ——. "Property and Poverty." *The Cambridge History of Medieval Political Thought*. Ed. J.H. Burns. Cambridge: Cambridge Univ. Press, 1988. 607–648.

403. Colledge, E. "*The Recluse*: A Lollard Interpolated Version of the *Ancren Riwle*." *Review of English Studies* 15 (1939): 1–15, 129–45.

404. Collette, Carolyn. *Species, Phantasms, and Images: Vision and Medieval Psychology in The Canterbury Tales*. Ann Arbor: Univ. of Michigan Press, 2001.

405. Collinson, P. "The English Conventicle." Sheils and Wood, *Voluntary Religion* 223–59.

406. Conetti, M. "The Radical Dissenter John Wyclif's Challenge to the Constantin Church." *Studi Medievali* 38.1 (June, 1997): 139–201.

407. Constable, Giles. "Opposition to Pilgrimage in the Middle Ages." *Studia Gratiana* 19 (1976): 123–146.

408. Conti, Alessandro D. "Essenza ed essere nel pensiero della tarda scolastica (Burley, Wyclif, Paolo Veneto)." *Medioevo* 15 (1989): 235–67.

409. ——. "Logica intensionale et metafisica dell'essenza in John Wyclif." *Bullettino dell'Instituto Storico Italiano per il Medio Evo e Archivio Muratoriano* 1993 (99): 159–219.

410. ——. "Analogy and Formal Distinction: the Logical Basis of Wyclif's Metaphysics." *Medieval Philosophy and Theology* 6.2 (1997): 133–65.

411. Cook, William R. "John Wyclif and Hussite Theology, 1415–1436." *Church History* 42 (1973): 335–49.

412. Coleman, Janet. *Piers Plowman and the Moderni*. Rome: Edizioni di Storia e Litteratura, 1981 [should be listed after 401].

413. Cooke, James H. "Trevisa's Translation of the Bible." *Notes and Queries* 5th ser. 10 (1878): 261–62.

414. Copeland, R. "Vernacular Translation and Instruction in Grammar in Fifteenth-Century England." *Papers in the History of Linguistics*. Ed. H. Aarsleff et al. Amsterdam: Benjamins, 1987. 143–54.

415. ——. "Rhetoric and Vernacular Translation in the Middle Ages." *Studies in the Age of Chaucer* 9 (1987): 41–75.

416. ——. *Rhetoric, Hermeneutics, and Translation in the Middle Ages: Academic Traditions and Vernacular Texts*. Cambridge Studies in Medieval Literature 11. Cambridge: Cambridge Univ. Press, 1991.

417. ——. "Why Women Can't Read: Medieval Hermeneutics, Statutory Law, and the Lollard Heresy." *Representing Women: Law, Literature, and Femin-*

ism. Ed. Susan Heinzelman and Zipporah Wiseman. Durham, NC: Duke Univ. Press, 1994. 253–86

418. ——. "William Thorpe and His Lollard Community: Intellectual Labor and the Representation of Dissent." Hanawalt and Wallace 199–221.

419. ——. "Rhetoric and the Politics of the Literal Sense in Medieval Literary Theory: Aquinas, Wyclif, and the Lollards." *Interpretation: Medieval and Modern*. Ed. A. Torti and P. Boitani, eds. Cambridge: D.S. Brewer, 1992. 1–23. Rpt. in *Rhetoric and Hermeneutics in Our Time: A Reader*. Ed. W. Josh and M.J. Hyde. New Haven: Yale Univ. Press, 1997. 335–57.

420. ——. "Childhood, Pedagogy, and the Literal Sense: From Late Antiquity to the Lollard Heretical Classroom." Scase, Copeland, and Lawton 125–156.

421. ——. "Toward a Social Genealogy of Translation Theory: Classical Property Law and Lollard Property Reform." Beer 173–183.

422. ——. *Pedagogy, Intellectuals, and Dissent in the Later Middle Ages: Lollardy and Ideas of Learning*. Cambridge: Cambridge Univ. Press, 2001.

423. ——. "Sophistic, Spectrality, Iconoclasm." Dimmick, Simpson, and Zeeman 112–130.

424. Corsani, Bruno. "Il Discorso della montagna nella Biblia wycliffita e nel N.T. di W. Tyndale." *John Wyclif* 103–142.

425. Cottret, Bernard. "Traducteurs et Divulgateurs Clandestins de la Reforme dans l'Angleterre Henrecienne." *Revue d'Histoire Moderne et Contemporaire* 28 (July-Sept. 1981): 464–80.

426. Courtenay, William J. *Adam Wodeham*. Leiden: E.J. Brill, 1978.

427. ——. "Augustinianism at Oxford in the Fourteenth Century." *Augustiniana* 30 (1980): 58–70.

428. ——. "The Effect of the Black Death on English Higher Education." *Speculum* 55.4 (1980): 696–714.

429. ——. "Force of Words and Figures of Speech: The Crisis over *Virtus Sermonis* in the Fourteenth Century." *Franciscan Studies* 44 (1984): 107–28.

430. ——. "The Bible in the Fourteenth Century: Some Observations." *Church History* 54.2 (June 1985): 176–87.

431. ——. "The Reception of Ockham's Thought in Fourteenth Century England." Hudson and Wilks 89–107.

432. ——. *Schools and Scholars in Fourteenth Century England*. Princeton: Princeton Univ. Press, 1987.

433. ——. "*Antiqui* and *Moderni* in Late Medieval Thought." *Journal of the History of Ideas* 48.1 (1987): 3–10.

434. ——. "Inquiry and Inquisition: Academic Freedom in Medieval Universities." *Church History* 58 (1989): 168–181.

435. ——. "Theology and Theologians From Ockham to Wyclif." Catto and Evans 1–34.

436. Crane, Susan. "The Writing Lesson of 1381." Hanawalt 201–221.

437. Cré, Marleen. "Authority and the Compiler in Westminster Cathedral Treasury MS 4: Writing a Text in Someone Else's Words." *Authority and Community in the Middle Ages*. Ed. D. Mowbray, R. Purdie, and I.P. Wei. Phoenix Mill: Sutton, 1999. 153–176.

438. Crompton, James J. "*Fasciculi Zizaniorum*." *Journal of Ecclesiastical History* 12 (1961): 35–45, 155–65.

439. ——. "John Wyclif: A Study in Mythology." *Transactions of the Leicestershire Archaeological and Historical Society* 42 (1966–67): 6–34.

440. ——. "Leicestershire Lollards." *Transactions of the Leicestershire Archae-ological and Historical Society* 44 (1968–9): 11–44.

441. Cronin, Harry S. "John Wycliffe, the Reformer, and Canterbury Hall." *Transactions of the Royal Historical Society* 3rd. ser., vol. 8 (1914): 55–76.

442. ——. "Wycliffe's Canonry at Lincoln." *English Historical Review* 35 (1920): 564–9.

443. Cross, Claire. "Popular Piety and the Records of the Unestablished Churches 1460–1660." Baker, *Materials* 269–92.

444. ——. "'Great Reasoners in Scripture': The Activities of Women Lollards 1380–1530." *Medieval Women*. Ed. Derek Baker. Studies in Church History, Subsidia 1. Oxford: Basil Blackwell, 1978. 359–80.

445. ——. *Church and People: England 1450–1660*. 2nd ed. Oxford: Basil Black-well, 1999.

446. Cutts, Cecilia. "The Croxton Play: an Anti-Lollard Piece." *Modern Lan-guage Quarterly* 5 (1944): 45–60.

447. Dahmus, Joseph H. "Further Evidence for the Spelling 'Wyclyf.'" *Speculum* 16 (1941): 224–25.

448. ——. "Did Wyclif Recant?" *Church Historical Review* 29 (1943): 155–68.

449. ——. *The Prosecution of John Wyclyf*. New Haven: Yale Univ. Press, 1952.

450. ——. "Wyclyf Was a Negligent Pluralist." *Speculum* 28 (1953): 378–81.

451. ——. "Richard II and the Church." *Church Historical Review* 39 (1954): 408–33.

452. ——. "John Wyclif and the English Government." *Speculum* 35 (1960): 51–68.

453. ——. *William Courtenay: Archbishop of Canterbury 1381–1396*. University Park: Pennsylvania State Univ. Press, 1966.

454. Daly, Lowrie J. *The Political Theory of John Wyclif*. Chicago: Loyola Univ. Press, 1962.

455. ——. "Walter Burley and John Wyclif on Some Aspects of Kingship." *Mélanges Eugène Tisserant*. Vol. 4. Vatican: Biblioteca Apostolica Vaticana, 1964. 163–84.

456. ——. "Wyclif's Political Theory: A Century of Study." *Medievalia et Humanistica* n.s. 4 (1973): 177–187.

457. David, Daniell. *William Tyndale: A Biography*. New Haven: Yale Univ. Press, 1994.

458. Davidson, Clifford. "Wyclif and the Middle English Sermon." *Universitas* 3 (1966): 92–99.

459. Davies, Richard G. "Thomas Arundel as Archbishop of Canterbury, 1396–1414." *Journal of Ecclesiastical History* 14 (1973): 9–21.

460. ——. "Lollardy and Locality." *Transactions of the Royal Historical Society* Sixth Series, vol. 1 (1992): 191–211.

461. ——. "Richard II and the Church." *Richard II: The Art of Kingship*. Ed. Anthony Goodman and James L. Gillespie. Oxford: Oxford Univ. Press, 1998. 83–106.

462. Davis, D. G. "The Bible of John Wyclif: Production and Circulation." *Bibliotheca Sacra* 128 (1971): 16–26.

463. Davis, E. Jeffries. "Authorities for the Case of Richard Hunne." *English Historical Review* 30 (1915): 477–88.

464. Davis, John F. "Lollards, Reformers, and St. Thomas of Canterbury." *University of Birmingham Historical Journal* 9 (1963–4): 1–15.

465. ——. "Lollard Survival and the Textile Industry in the Southeast of

England." *Studies in Church History* 3. Ed. G.J. Cuming. Oxford: Basil Blackwell, 1966. 191–201.

466. ——. "John Wyclif's Reformation Reputation." *Churchman* 83 (1969): 97–102.

467. ——. "The Trials of Thomas Bylney and the English Reformation." *Historical Journal* 24 (1981): 775–90.

468. ——. "Lollardy and the Reformation in England." *Archiv für Reformationsgeschichte* 73 (1982): 227–32.

469. ——. "Joan of Kent, Lollardy, and the English Reformation." *Journal of Ecclesiastical History* 33 (1982): 225–33.

470. ——. *Heresy and Reformation in the South-East of England, 1520–1559.* London: Royal Historical Society, 1983.

471. Davis, Nicholas. "Another View of *The Tretise of Miraclis Pleyinge*." *Medieval English Theatre* 4 (1982): 48–55.

472. ——. "*The Tretise of Miraclis Pleyinge*: On Milieu and Authorship." *Medieval English Theatre* 12 (1990): 124–51.

473. Dawson, James D. "Richard Fitzralph and the Fourteenth Century Poverty Controversies." *Journal of Ecclesiastical History* 34.3 (July, 1983): 315–344.

474. Deane, David S. *John Wicleffe, the Morning Star of the Reformation.* London, 1884.

475. Deanesly, Margaret. *The Lollard Bible and other Medieval Biblical Versions.* Cambridge: Cambridge Univ. Press, 1920.

476. ——. "Vernacular Books in England in the Fourteenth and Fifteenth Centuries." *Modern Language Review* 15 (1920): 349–58.

477. ——. "Arguments Against the Use of Vernacular Bibles, Put Forward in the Controversy over their Lawfulness." *Church Quarterly Review* 91 (1921): 59–77.

478. ——. "The Significance of the Lollard Bible: The Ethel M. Wood Lecture Delivered before the University of London on 13 March, 1951." Pamphlet. London: Athlone, 1951.

479. de Boor, Frederick. *Wyclif's Simoniebegriff: Die theologischen und kirchenpolitischen Grundlagen der Kirchenkritik John Wyclifs.* Halle: Niemeyer, 1970.

480. de Lapparent, Pierre. "Un Précurseur de la Réforme Anglaise: L'Anonyme d'York." *Archives d'Histoire Doctrinale et Littéraire du Moyen Âge* 15 (1946): 149–168.

481. De La Torre, Bartholomew R., O.P. *Thomas Buckingham and the Contingency of Futures.* Publications in Medieval Studies. The Medieval Institute, vol. 25. South Bend: Univ. of Notre Dame Press, 1987.

482. Despres, Denise. *Ghostly Sights: Visual Meditation in Late-Medieval Literature.* Norman, OK: Pilgrim Books, 1989.

483. de Vooght, Paul. "Les indulgences dan la theologie de Jean Wyclif et de Jean Huss." *Recherches de theologie religieuse* 41 (1953): 481–518.

484. ——. *Les Sources de la Doctrine Chretienne.* Bruges: Desclee De Brouwer, 1954.

485. ——. "La doctrine et les sources du sermon 'Dixit Martha ad Jesum' de Jean Huss." *Revue des Sciences Religieuses* 31 (1957): 20–33.

486. ——. *Hussiana.* Louvain: Publications Universitaires de Louvain, 1960.

487. ——. "L'heresie de Taborites sur l'Eucharistie (1418–21)." *Irenikon* 35 (1962): 340–50.

488. ———. "Wyclif et la 'scriptura sola.'" *Ephemerides Theologicas Lovanienses.* 39 (1963): 50–86.

489. ———. *L'hérésie de Jean Huss.* 2nd rev. ed. 2 vols. Louvain: Publications Universitaires de Louvain, 1975.

490. Dickens, A.G. "Heresy and the Origins of English Protestantism." *Britain and the Netherlands, vol. 2.* Ed. J.S. Bromley and R.H. Kossmann. Groningen: J.B. Wolters, 1964. 47–66.

491. ———. *The English Reformation.* London: Batsford, 1964.

492. ———. *Lollards and Protestants in the Diocese of York, 1509–1558.* Oxford: Oxford Univ. Press, 1959.

493. ———. "The Shape of Anti-Clericalism and the English Reformation." *Politics and Society in Reformation Europe: Essays for Sir Geoffrey Elton.* Ed. E.I. Kouri and T. Scott. New York: St. Martin's, 1987. 378–410.

494. Diemer, Stefan. *John Wycliffe und seine Rolle bei der Entstehung der modernen englischen Rechtschreibung und des Wortschatzes.* Frankfurt: Lang, 1998.

495. Dillon, Janette. *Language and Stage in Medieval and Renaissance England.* Cambridge: Cambridge Univ. Press, 1998.

496. Dinshaw, Carolyn. *Getting Medieval: Sexualities and Communities, Pre- and Post-Modern.* Durham: Duke Univ. Press, 1999.

497. ———. "Queer Relations." *Essays in Medieval Studies: Proceedings of the Illinois Medieval Association* 16 (1999): 79–99.

498. Dipple, Geoffrey L. "Uthred and the Friars: Apostolic Poverty and Clerical Dominion between Fitzralph and Wyclif." *Traditio* 49 (1994): 235–58.

499. Dolnikowski, Edith. "Fitzralph and Wyclif on the Mendicants." *Michigan Academician* 19:1 (1987): 87–100.

500. ———. *Thomas Bradwardine: A View of Time and a Vision of Eternity in Fourteenth-Century Thought.* Studies in the History of Christian Thought, vol. 65. Leiden: E.J. Brill, 1995.

501. ———. "The Encouragement of Lay Preaching as an Ecclesiastical Critique in Wyclif's Latin Sermons." *Models of Holiness in Medieval Sermons.* Ed. Beverly M. Kinzie et al. Louvain–la-Neuve: Fédération Internationale des Institutes d'Etudes Médiévales, 1996. 193–209.

502. ———. "Preaching at Oxford: Academic and Pastoral Themes in Wyclif's Latin Sermon Cycle." *Medieval Sermons and Society: Cloister, City, University.* Ed. J. Hamesse et al. Louvain–la-Neuve: Fédération Internationale des Institutes d'Etudes Médiévales, 1998. 371–86.

503. Doyle, A.I. "Books Connected with the Vere Family and Barking Abbey." *Essex Archaeological Society's Transactions* n.s. 25 (1958): 222–43.

504. ———. "University College, Oxford, MS 97 and its Relationship to the Simeon Manuscript (British Library Add. 22283)." Benskin and Samuels 265–82.

505. ———. "English Books In and Out of Court from Edward III to Henry VII." *English Court and Culture in the Later Middle Ages.* Ed. V.J. Scattergood and J.W. Sherbourne. London, Duckworth, 1983. 163–81.

506. ———. "The European Circulation of Three Latin Spiritual Texts." *Latin and Vernacular: Studies in Late-Medieval Texts and Manuscripts.* Ed. A.J. Minnis. Woodbridge: Boydell and Brewer, 1989. 129–146.

507. ———. "The Study of Nicholas Love's *Mirror,* Retrospect and Prospect." *Nicholas Love at Waseda.* Ed. Shoichi Oguro, Richard Beadle, and Michael Sargent. Cambridge: D.S. Brewer, 1997. 163–74.

508. Doyle, Eric, O.F.M. "A Manuscript of William Woodford's *De Dominio Civili Clericorum.*" *Archivum Franciscanum Historicum* 62 (1969): 377–81.

509. ——. "William Woodford, O.F.M. and John Wyclif's *De religione.*" *Speculum* 52.2 (April 1977): 329–36.

510. Doyle, Robert. "The Death of Christ and the Doctrine of Grace in John Wycliffe." *Churchman* 99.4 (1985): 317–35.

511. Drees, Clayton J. *Authority and Dissent in the Medieval Church: The Prosecution of Heresy and Religious Non-Conformity in the Diocese of Winchester, 1380–1547.* Lewiston, NY: Edwin Mellon, 1997.

512. Duffy, Eamon. *The Stripping of the Altars: Traditional Religion in England 1400–1580.* New Haven: Yale Univ. Press, 1992.

513. Dunnan, D.S. "A Note on John Gough's *The Dore of Holy Scripture.*" *Notes and Queries* 36 (234).3 (Sept, 1989): 309–310.

514. ——. "A Note on the Three Churches in the *Lantern of Lyght.*" *Notes and Queries* 38:1 (1991): 20–22.

515. Dyson, A.H., and S.H. Skillington. *Lutterworth Church and its Associations, With a Chapter on John Wycliffe.* Leicester, 1916.

516. Dyson, Thomas. "Wyclif Reviewed." *Church Quarterly Review* 168 (1967): 423–433.

517. Dziewicki, M.H. "An Essay on John Wyclif's Philosophical System." *Johannis Wyclif Miscellanea Philosophica.* London, 1902. Vol. 1, v–xxvii.

518. Easson, D.E. "The Lollards of Kyle." *Juridical Review* 48 (1936): 123–28.

519. Eckermann, Willigis. "Augustinus Favaroni von Rom und Johannes Wyclif: Der Ansatz ihrer Lehre uber die Kirche." *Scientia Augustiniana: Studien uber Augustinus, den Augustinismus und den Augustinerorden.* Ed. Cornelius Mayer, Willigis Eckermann, and Coelestin Patock. Wurzburg: Augustinus, 1975. 323–48.

520. Edden, Valerie. "'And my boonus had dried vp as critouns': The History of the Translation of Psalm 101.4." *Notes and Queries* 28 (226).5 (1981): 389–92.

521. Eldredge, L. "The Concept of God's Absolute Power at Oxford in the Later Fourteenth Century." *By Things Seen: Reference and Recognition in Medieval Thought.* Ed. D.L. Jeffrey. Ottawa: Univ. of Ottawa Press, 1979. 211–26.

522. Emblom, Margaret. "'I Herd an Harping on a Hille': Its Text and Context." *Proceedings of the Illinois Medieval Association* 1 (1984): 49–61.

523. Emden, A.B. *An Oxford Hall in Medieval Times.* Oxford: Oxford Univ. Press, 1927.

524. Emerson, Everett H. "Reginald Pecock: Christian Rationalist." *Speculum* 31 (1956): 235–42.

525. Erickson, Carolly. "The Fourteenth-Century Fransciscans and their Critics, Part 1: The Order's Growth and Character." *Franciscan Studies* 8 (1975): 107–35.

526. ——. "The Fourteenth Century Franciscans and their Critics, Continued." *Franciscan Studies* 14 (1976): 108–47.

527. Erler, Mary. *Women, Reading, and Piety in Late Medieval England.* Cambridge: Cambridge Univ. Press, 2002.

528. Evans, Gillian R. "Wycliffe the Academic." *Churchman* 98.4 (1984): 307–18.

529. ——. *The Language and Logic of the Bible: The Road to the Reformation.* Cambridge: Cambridge Univ. Press, 1985.

530. ——. "Thomas of Chobham on Preaching and Exegesis." *Recherches de Theologie Ancienne et Medievale* 52 (1985): 159–70.

531. ——. "Wyclif's Logic and Wyclif's Exegesis: the Context." Walsh and Wood 287–300.
532. ——. "Wyclif on Literal and Metaphorical." Hudson and Wilks 259–66.
533. ——. "Wyclif on Ecclesiology: Issues of Perspective." *Anvil* 11.1 (1994): 45–55.
534. ——. *Fifty Key Medieval Thinkers*. New York: Routledge, 2002.
535. Evans, Nesta. "William Thorpe: An Early Lollard." *History Today* 18 (1968): 495–503.
536. ——. "Bishop Reginald Pecock and the Lollards." *Studies in Sussex Church History*. Ed. M.J. Kitch. London: Leopard's Head, 1981. 57–75.
537. ——. "The Impossibility of Tracing Dissent Through Time in Thirty-six Parishes on the Essex, Cambridgeshire, and Suffolk Borders." Spufford 397–400.
538. ——. "The Parishes Investigated for Details of the Genealogies of the Nineteen Families Searched for in the Chilterns." Spufford 401–30.
539. Everett, Dorothy. "The Middle English Prose Psalter of Richard Rolle of Hampole." *Modern Language Review* 17.3 and 17.4 (Oct. 1922): 217–227, 337–350; 18.4 (Oct. 1923): 381–393.
540. Farr, William. *John Wyclif as Legal Reformer*. Leiden: E.J. Brill, 1974.
541. Fairfield, Leslie P. "John Bale and the Development of Protestant Hagiography in England." *Journal of Ecclesiastical History* 24.2 (April, 1973): 145–60.
542. ——. *John Bale, Mythmaker for the English Reformation*. West Lafayette, IN: Purdue Univ. Press, 1976.
543. Fewer, Colin. "The 'Fygure' of the Market: The N-Town Cycle and East Anglian Lay Piety." *Philological Quarterly* 77 (1998): 117–47.
544. Figgis, J. N. "John Wyclif." *Typical English Churchmen*, Series 2. The Church Historical Society, 78. London: Society for the Promotion of Christian Knowledge, 1909.
545. Fines, John. "The Post-Mortem Condemnation for Heresy of Richard Hunne." *English Historical Review* 78 (1963): 528–31.
546. ——. "Heresy Trials in the Diocese of Coventry and Lichfield, 1511–12." *Journal of Ecclesiastical History* 44 (1963): 160–74.
547. ——. "An Unnoticed Tract of the Tyndale-More Dispute?" *Historical Research: The Bulletin of the Institute of Historical Research* 42 (1969): 220–30.
548. Finucane, Ronald. *Miracles and Pilgrims: Popular Belief in Medieval England*. London: Dent, 1977.
549. Fischer, H. *Über die Sprache J. Wicliff's*. Halle, 1880.
550. Fischler, David S. "The Political Philosophy of John Wyclif." *Church Divinity 1981*. Ed. John H. Morgan. Notre Dame: Church Divinity Monograph Series, 1981. 56–65.
551. Fisher, John H. "Wyclif, Langland, Gower, and the Pearl-Poet on the Subject of Aristocracy." *Studies in Medieval Literature in Honor of Professor Albert Croll Baugh*. Ed. MacEdward Leach. Philadelphia: Univ. of Pennsylvania Press, 1961. 139–157.
552. Fleming, John V. "Chaucer and Erasmus on the Pilgrimage to Canterbury." *The Popular Literature of Medieval England*. Ed. Thomas J. Heffernan. Tennessee Studies in Literature 28. Knoxville: Univ. of Tennessee Press, 1985. 148–166.

553. Fletcher, Alan J. "John Mirk and the Lollards." *Medium Aevum* 56.1 (1987): 217–224.

554. ——. "The Preaching of the Pardoner." *Studies in the Age of Chaucer* 11 (1989): 15–35. Rpt. in Fletcher 249–65.

555. ——. "The Topical Hypocrisy of Chaucer's Pardoner." *Chaucer Review* 25:2 (1990): 110–26. Rpt. in Fletcher 266–80.

556. ——. "A Hive of Industry or a Hornet's Nest? MS Sidney Sussex 74 and Its Scribes." Minnis, *Late-Medieval Religious Texts* 131–155. Rpt. in Fletcher 119–142.

557. ——. "The Summoner and the Abominable Body of Antichrist." *Studies in the Age of Chaucer* 18 (1996): 91–117.

558. ——. "Langland on Preaching." Fletcher 201–214.

559. Fletcher, John M. "Inter-Faculty Disputes in Late Medieval Oxford." Hudson and Wilks 331–42.

560. Forde, Simon. "Theological Sources Cited by Two Canons of Repton: Philip Repyngdon and John Eyton." Hudson and Wilks 419–428.

561. ——. "New Sermon Evidence for the Spread of Wycliffism." *De Ore Domini.* Ed. Thomas Amos et al. Kalamazoo: Medieval Institute, 1989. 169–83.

562. ——. "Social Outlook and Preaching in a Wycliffite Sermones Dominicales Collection." *Church and Chronicle in the Middle Ages: Essays Presented to John Taylor.* Ed. Ian Wood and G.A. Loud. London: Hambledon, 1991. 179–91.

563. ——. "The 'Strong Woman' and 'The Woman who Surrounds a Man': Perceptions of Woman in Wyclif's Theological Writings." *Revue D'Histoire Ecclesiastique* 88.1 (1993): 54–87.

564. ——. "La predication, les Lollards et les laics (diocese de Norwich, 1428–1429)." *La Parole de Predicateur.* Ed. R.M. Dessi and M. Lauwers. Nice: Centre d'Etudes Medievales, 1997. 457–78.

565. ——. "Lay Preaching and the Lollards of Norwich Diocese, 1428–1431." *Leeds Studies in English* 29 (1998): 109–26.

566. Foreville, R. "Manifestation de Lollardisme a Exeter, en 1421?" *Le Moyen Âge* 69 (1963): 691–706.

567. Forni, Kathleen. "The Chaucerian Apocrypha: Did Usk's 'Testament of Love' and the 'Plowman's Tale' Ruin Chaucer's Early Reputation?" *Neuphilologische Mitteilungen* 98.3 (1997): 261–72.

568. Förster, Erich. "Wiklif als Bibelübersetzer." *Zeitschrift für Kirchengeschichte* 12 (1891): 494–518.

569. Foss, David B. "'Overmuch Blaming of the Clergy's Wealth': Pecock's Exculpation of Ecclesiastical Endowments." Sheils and Wood, *Church and Wealth* 155–66.

570. Fountain, David. *John Wycliffe: The Dawn of the Reformation.* Southampton: Hampshire, 1984.

571. Fowler, David C. "John Trevisa and the English Bible." *Modern Philology* 58 (1960): 81–98.

572. ——. *The Life and Times of John Trevisa, Medieval Scholar.* Seattle: Univ. of Washington Press, 1995.

573. Fox, M. "John Wyclif and the Mass." *The Heythrop Journal* 3 (1962): 232–40.

574. Frantzen, Allen J. *Before the Closet: Same-Sex Love from Beowulf to Angels in America.* Chicago: Univ. of Chicago Press, 1998.

575. Freemantle, W.H. *John Wycliffe.* London, 1898.

576. Frere, Walter H. "Lollardy and the Reformation." *Church Quarterly Review* 69 (1910): 426–39.

577. Fristedt, Sven L. *The Wycliffe Bible*. 3 vols. Stockholm Studies in English 4, 21, 28. Stockholm: Almqvist and Wiksell, 1953–73.

578. ———. "The Dating of the Earliest Manuscript of the Wycliffite Bible." *Studier i modern språkvetenskap* n.s. 1 (1960): 79–85.

579. ———. "A Weird Manuscript Enigma in the British Museum." *Studier i modern språkvetenskap* n.s. 2 (1964): 116–121.

580. ———. "New Light on John Wycliffe and the First Full English Bible." *Studier i modern språkvetenskap* n.s. 3 (1970): 61–86.

581. ———. "A Note on Some Obscurities in the History of the Lollard Bible." *Studier i modern språkvetenskap* n.s. 4 (1972): 38–45.

582. ———. "Spanish Influence on Lollard Translation." *Studier i modern språkvetenskap* n.s. 5 (1975): 5–10.

583. Fürstenau, Hermann. *Johann von Wiclifs Lehren von der Einteilung der Kirche und von der Stellung der weltlichen Gewalt*. Berlin, 1900.

584. Gairdner, James. "Bible Study in the Fifteenth Century." *Fortnightly Review* 1 (1865): 710–20; 2 (1865): 59–78.

585. ———. *Lollardy and the Reformation in England: An Historical Survey in Four Volumes*. London: Macmillan, 1908–13.

586. Galloway, Andrew. "Chaucer's *Former Age* and the Fourteenth-Century Anthropology of Craft: The Social Logic of a Premodernist Lyric." *ELH* 63 (1996): 535–53.

587. Gasquet, F.A. *The Eve of the Reformation*. London: Kennikat, 1900.

588. Gasner, E. *Über Wyclifs Sprache*. Göttingen, 1891.

589. Gellrich, Jesse. *Discourse and Dominion in the Fourteenth Century: Oral Contexts of Writing in Philosophy, Politics, and Poetry*. Princeton: Princeton Univ. Press, 1995.

590. Genet, Jean-Phillippe. "Wyclif et Les Lollards." *Historiens et géographes* 294 (1983): 869–96.

591. ———. "Ecclesiastics and Political Theory in Late Medieval England: the End of a Monopoly." Dobson 23–44.

592. ———. "The Dissemination of Manuscripts Relating to English Political Thought in the Fourteenth Century." *England and her Neighbours, 1066–1453: Essays in Honour of Pierre Chaplais*. Ed. Michael Jones and Malcolm Vale. London: Hambledon, 1989. 217–37.

593. Gethyn-Jones, J.E. "John Trevisa – An Associate of Nicholas Hereford." *Transactions of the Woolhope Naturalists' Field Club* 40.2 (1971): 241–44.

594. Gewirth, Alan. "Philosophical and Political Thought in the Fourteenth Century." *The Forward Movement of the Fourteenth Century*. Ed. F.L. Utley. Columbus: Ohio State Univ. Press, 1961. 125–164.

595. Ghosh, Kantik. "Contingency and the Christian Faith: William Woodford's Anti-Wycliffite Hermeneutics." *Poetica* 49 (1998): 1–26.

596. ———. "Eliding the Interpreter: John Wyclif and Scriptural Truth." Copeland, Lawton, and Scase 205–24.

597. ———. "Manuscripts of Nicholas Love's *The Mirror of the Blessed Life of Jesus Christ* and Wycliffite Notions of 'Authority.'" *Prestige, Authority, and Power in Late Medieval Manuscripts and Texts*. Ed. Felicity Riddy. York: York Medieval Press, 2000. 17–34.

598. ———. *The Wycliffite Heresy: Authority and the Interpretation of Texts*. Cambridge: Cambridge Univ. Press, 2002.

599. Gifford, William A. "Wyclif and the Independence of the Church in England." *American Society of Church History*, ser. 2, vol. 7 (1923): 133–55.
600. Gilbert, Neal Ward. "Ockham, Wyclif, and the 'Via Moderna.'" Zimmerman 85–125.
601. Gilchrist, J. "The Social Doctrine of John Wyclif." *Canadian Historical Association, Historical Papers 1969*. 157–65.
602. Gillespie, Vincent. "Idols and Images: Pastoral Adaptations of the *Scale of Perfection*." *Langland, the Mystics, and the Medieval Religious Tradition: Essays in Honour of S.S. Hussey*. Ed. Helen Phillips. Cambridge: D.S. Brewer, 1990. 97–123.
603. ——. "Vernacular Books of Religion." Griffiths and Pearsall 317–344.
604. ——. "Thy Will be Done: *Piers Plowman* and the Pater Noster." Minnis, *Late Medieval Religious Texts* 95–119.
605. Gilpin, William. *The Lives of John Wicliff, and of the most Eminent of his Disciples, Lord Cobham, John Hus, Jerome of Prague, and Zizca*. London, 1765.
606. ——. *The Life of John Wyclif*. London, 1821.
607. Goheen, R.B. "Peasant Politics? Village Community and the Crown in Fifteenth-Century England." *American Historical Review* 96 (1991): 42–62.
608. Gradon, Pamela. "Langland and the Ideology of Dissent." *Proceedings of the British Academy* 66 (1980): 179–205.
609. ——. "Punctuation in a Middle English Sermon." Stanley and Gray 39–48.
610. Green, Richard F. "John Ball's Letters: Literary History and Historical Literature." Hanawalt 176–200.
611. ——. *A Crisis of Truth: Literature and Law in Ricardian England*. Philadelphia: Univ. of Pennsylvania Press, 1999.
612. Green, Samuel G. *John Wycliffe, the First of the English Reformers*. London, 1885.
613. Green, Vivian H.H. "Bishop Pecock and the English Bible." *Church Quarterly Review* 129 (1939–40): 281–95.
614. ——. *Bishop Reginald Pecock*. Cambridge: Cambridge Univ. Press, 1945.
615. Grimm, F. *Das syntaktische Gebrauch der praepositionen bei Wyclif und Purvey*. Marburg, 1891.
616. Gurevich, Aaron. "Heresy and Literacy: Evidence of the Thirteenth-century Exempla." Biller and Hudson 104–111.
617. Gwynn, A. *The English Austin Friars in the Time of Wyclif*. Oxford: Oxford Univ. Press, 1940.
618. Haigh, Christopher. *English Reformations*. Oxford: Clarendon, 1993.
619. Hailey, Arthur A. "'Geuyng light to the reader': Robert Crowley's Editions of *Piers Plowman* (1550)." *Papers of the Bibliographical Society of America* 95 (Dec 2001): 483–502.
620. Haines, R.M. "'Wilde Wittes and Wilfulnes': John Swetstock's Attack on those 'poyswunmongeres,' the Lollards." *Popular Belief and Practice*. Ed. G.J. Cuming and D. Baker. Studies in Church History 8. Oxford, Basil Blackwell, 1972. 143–53.
621. ——. "Church, Society, and Politics in the Early Fifteenth Century as Viewed from the English Pulpit." *Church, Society, and Politics*. Ed. Derek Baker. Studies in Church History 12. Oxford: Basil Blackwell, 1975. 143–57.
622. ——. "Reginald Pecock: A Tolerant Man in an Age of Intolerance." *Persecution and Toleration*. Studies in Church History 21. Ed. W.J. Sheils. Oxford: Basil Blackwell, 1984. 125–137.

623. Halasey, Steven Douglas. "Interview with Anne Hudson." *Comitatus* 13 (1982): 5–15.

624. Hall, L.B. *The Perilous Vision of John Wyclif.* Chicago: Nelson Hall, 1983.

625. Hammond, Gerald. "What was the Influence of the Medieval English Bible upon the Renaissance Bible?" *Bulletin of the John Rylands Library* 77.3 (1995): 87–95.

626. Hankey, Wayne John. "'*Magis . . . Pro Nostra Sentencia*': John Wyclif, His Mediaeval Predecessors and Reformed Successors, and a Pseudo-Augustinian Eucharistic Decretal." *Augustiniana* 45, fasc. 3–4 (1995): 213–245.

627. Hanna III, Ralph. "The Text of the *Memoriale Credencium*." *Neophilologus* 67:2 (1983): 284–92.

628. ——. "The Origins and Production of Westminster School MS. 3." *Studies in Bibliography* 41 (1988): 197–218. Rpt. in Hanna 35–47.

629. ——. "The Difficulty of Ricardian Prose Translation: The Case of the Lollards." *Modern Language Quarterly* 51:3 (1990): 319–40.

630. ——. "Two Lollard Codices and Lollard Book Production." *Studies in Bibliography* 43 (1990): 49–62. Rpt. in Hanna 48–59.

631. ——. "Some Norfolk Women and Their Books." *The Cultural Patronage of Medieval Women*. ed. June Hall McCash. Athens: Univ. of Georgia Press, 1996. 288–305.

632. ——. "'*Vae Octuplex*,' Lollard Socio-textual Ideology, and Ricardian-Lancastrian Prose Translation." Copeland 244–263.

633. ——. "Will's Work." Justice and Kerby-Fulton, 23–66.

634. Hanna, William. *Wycliffe and the Huguenots; or, Sketches of the Rise of the Reformation in England, and of the Early History of Protestantism in France.* Edinburgh, 1860.

635. Hanrahan, T.J. "John Wyclif's Political Activity." *Mediaeval Studies* 20 (1958): 154–66.

636. Hansen, H.M. "The Peasant's Revolt of 1381 and the Chronicles." *Journal of Medieval History* 6 (1980): 393–415.

637. Hansford-Miller, F. *The Diocesan Changes of King Henry VIII, and the Friars and the Lollards.* A History and Geography of Western Religion 7. Canterbury-Yanchep, Western Australia: Abcado Publishers, 1992.

638. Happé, Peter. *John Bale.* New York: Twayne, 1996.

639. Harding, W.H. *The Morning Star of the Reformation: John Wycliffe.* London, 1913.

640. Hargreaves, Henry. "The Latin Text of Purvey's Psalter." *Medium Aevum* 24 (1955): 73–90.

641. ——. "An Intermediate Version of the Wycliffite Old Testament." *Studia Neophilologica* 28 (1956): 130–47.

642. ——. "The Marginal Glosses to the Wycliffite New Testament." *Studia Neophilologica* 33 (1961): 285–300.

643. ——. "From Bede to Wyclif: Medieval English Bible Translations." *Bulletin of the John Rylands Library* 48.1 (1965): 118–140.

644. ——. "Wyclif's Prose." *Essays and Studies* 19 (1966): 1–17.

645. ——. "The Wycliffite Versions." *The Cambridge History of the Bible*, vol. 2. Ed. G.W.H. Lampe. Cambridge: Cambridge Univ. Press, 1969. 387–415.

646. ——. "Sir John Oldcastle and Wycliffite Views on Clerical Marriage." *Medium Aevum* 42 (1973): 141–46.

647. ——. "Popularising Biblical Scholarship: The Role of the Wycliffite Glossed

Gospels." *The Bible and Medieval Culture*. Ed. W. Lourdaux and D. Verhelst. Leuven: Leuven Univ. Press, 1979. 171–89.

648. ——. "The Wycliffite Glossed Gospels as Source: Further Evidence." *Traditio* 48 (1993): 247–51.

649. Harper-Bill, Christopher. *The Pre-Reformation Church in England, 1400–1530*. Revised ed. New York: Longman, 1996.

650. Harriss, G.L. *Cardinal Beaufort: A Study of Lancastrian Ascendancy and Decline*. Oxford: Clarendon, 1988.

651. Hartel, Helmar. "Sermon Literature." Edwards 177–207.

652. Harvey, Margaret. "The Case for Urban VI in England to 1390." *Genèse et débuts du Grand Schisme d'Occident*. Ed. Jean Favier et al. Paris: Éditions du Centre national de la recherche scientifique, 1980. 541–60.

653. ——. *Solutions to the Great Schism: A Study of Some English Attitudes, 1378 to 1409*. Kirchengeschichtliche Quellen und Studien, b. 12. St. Ottilien: EOS Verlag, 1983.

654. ——. "Lollardy and the Great Schism: Some Contemporary Perceptions." Hudson and Wilks 385–96.

655. ——. "The Diffusion of the *Doctrinale* of Thomas Netter in the Fifteenth and Sixteenth Centuries." *Intellectual Life in the Middle Ages: Essays Presented to Margaret Gibson*. Ed. L. Smith and B. Ward. London: Hambledon, 1992. 281–94.

656. ——. *England, Rome, and the Papacy, 1414–1464: The Study of a Relationship*. Manchester: Manchester Univ. Press, 1993.

657. ——. "Adam Easton and the Condemnation of John Wyclif." *English Historical Review* 113 (April 1998): 321–35.

658. ——. *The English in Rome 1362–1420: Portrait of an Expatriate Community*. Cambridge: Cambridge Univ. Press, 1999.

659. Havens, Jill. "A Curious Erasure in Walsingham's *Short Chronicle* and the Politics of Heresy." Given-Wilson 95–106.

660. Healey, J.E. "John of Gaunt and John Wyclif." *Canadian Catholic Historical Report* (1962): 41–75.

661. Hearnshaw, F.J.C. "John Wycliffe and Divine Dominion." *The Social and Political Ideas of Some Great Medieval Thinkers*. Ed. F.J.C. Hearnshaw. New York: Barnes and Noble, 1923. 192–223.

662. Heidtmann, P. "Wycliffe and the Lollards: A Reforming Heretical Sect at the End of the Fourteenth Century." *History Today* 29 (1970): 724–32.

663. Henry, Desmond P. *Medieval Mereology*. Amsterdam: Grüner, 1991.

664. Herold, Vilém. "Wyclif's Philosophy and Platonic Ideas." *Filozoficky Casopis* 33 (1985): 47–96.

665. ——. *Pražská univerzita a Wyclif: Wyclifovo učeni o ideách a geneze husitského revolučniho myšelni*. [*Prague University and Wyclif: Wyclif's Teachings about Ideas and the Beginning of the Hussite Revolutionary Thought*]. Prague: Univ. of Karlova, 1985.

666. ——. "Wyclif Polemik gegen Ockhams Auffassung der platonischen Ideen und ihr Nachklang in der tschechischen hussitischen Philosophie." Hudson and Wilks 185–216.

667. ——. "Platonic Ideas and 'Hussite' Philosophy." David R. Holeton, ed. *The Bohemian Reformation and Religious Practice*, vol. 1. Papers from the 17th World Congress of the Czechoslovak Society of Arts and Sciences. Prague: Academic of Sciences of the Czech Republic, Main Library, 1994. 13–18.

668. ——. "Wyklif als Reformer: Die philosophische Dimension." Seibt 39–47.

669. ——. "How Wycliffite was the Bohemian Reformation?" Zdenek V. David and David R. Holeton, eds. *The Bohemian Reformation and Religious Practice*, vol. 2. Papers from the 18th World Congress of the Czechoslovak Society of Arts and Sciences. Prague: Academic of Sciences of the Czech Republic, Main Library, 1998. 25–38.

670. ——. "Zum Prager philosophischen Wyclifismus." Šmahel and Müller-Luckner 133–146.

671. ——. "Philosophy in Prague University in the Pre-Hussite Period: Schola Aristotelis or Platonis Divinissimi?" *Filosoficky Casopis* 47 (1999): 5–14.

672. Heseltine, George C. "The Myth of Wyclif." *Thought* 7 (1932): 108–21.

673. Heymann, Frederick G. *John Žižka and the Hussite Revolution*. Princeton: Princeton Univ. Press, 1955.

674. Heyworth, P.L. "The Earliest Black-Letter Editions of Jack Upland." *Huntington Library Quarterly* 30 (1967): 307–14.

675. ——. "*Jack Upland's Rejoinder*: A Lollard Interpolator and *Piers Plowman* B.X.245f." *Medium Aevum* 36 (1967): 242–48.

676. Hill, Christopher. "From Lollards to Levellers." *Rebels and their Causes: Essays in Honour of A.L. Morton*. Ed. M. Conforth. London: Lawrence and Wishart, 1978. 49–67.

677. Hollack, E. *Vergleichende Studien zu der Hereford, Wyclif, und Purvey Bibelübersetzung und der lateinischen Vulgata*. Leipzig, 1903.

678. Holmes, George. "Cardinal Beaufort and the Crusade against the Hussites." *English Historical Review* 88 (1973): 721–50.

679. ——. *The Good Parliament*. Oxford: Clarendon, 1975.

680. Holt, Emily Sarah. *John de Wycliffe, The First of the Reformers and What He Did for England*. London, 1884.

681. Hope, Andrew. "Lollardy: the Stone the Builders Rejected?" *Protestantism and the National Church in the Sixteenth Century*. Ed. P. Lake and M. Dowling. London: Croom Helm, 1987. 1–35.

682. ——. "The Lady and the Bailiff: Lollardy among the Gentry in Yorkist and Early Tudor England." Aston and Richmond 250–277.

683. Horner, Patrick J. "Benedictines and Preaching in Fifteenth-century England: the Evidence of Two Bodleian Library Manuscripts." *Revue Benedictine* 99 (1989): 313–22.

684. ——. "'The King Taught us the Lesson': Benedictine Support for Henry V's Suppression of the Lollards." *Mediaeval Studies* 52 (1990): 190–220.

685. Houlbrooke, R.A. "Persecution of Heresy and Protestantism in the Diocese of Norwich under Henry VIII." *Norfolk Archaeology* 35 (1972): 308–26.

686. Howard, Donald. *Chaucer: His Life, His Works, His World*. New York: Random House, 1987.

687. Hudson, Anne. "A Lollard Quaternion." *Review of English Studies* n.s. 22 (1971): 451–65. Rpt. in Hudson 192–200.

688. ——. "A Lollard Sermon-Cycle and its Implications." *Medium Aevum* 40 (1971): 142–56.

689. ——. "The Expurgation of a Lollard Sermon Cycle." *Journal of Theological Studies* n.s. 22 (1971): 435–42. Rpt. in Hudson 201–15.

690. ——. "A Lollard Compilation and the Dissemination of Wycliffite Thought." *Journal of Theological Studies* n.s. 23 (1972): 65–81. Rpt. in Hudson 13–29.

691. ——. "Some Aspects of Lollard Book Production." Baker, *Schism* 147–57. Rpt. in Hudson 181–191.

692. ——. "A Lollard Mass." *Journal of Theological Studies* n.s. 23 (1972): 407–19. Rpt. in Hudson 112–123.

693. ——. "Contributions to a History of Wycliffite Writings." *Notes and Queries* 218 (1973): 443–53. Rpt. in Hudson 1–12.

694. ——. "The Examination of Lollards." *Bulletin of the Institute of Historical Research* 46 (1973): 145–59. Rpt. in Hudson 124–140, with an Appendix.

695. ——. "A Lollard Compilation in England and Bohemia." *Journal of Theological Studies* n.s. 25 (1974): 129–40. Rpt. in Hudson 30–42.

696. ——. "The Debate on Bible Translation, Oxford 1401." *English Historical Review* 90 (1975): 1–18. Rpt. in Hudson 66–84.

697. ——. "A Neglected Wycliffite Text." *Journal of Ecclesiastical History* 29 (1978): 257–79. Rpt. in Hudson 43–65.

698. —— "A Lollard Sect Vocabulary?" Benskin and Samuels 15–30. Rpt. in Hudson 164–180.

699. ——. "Some Problems of Identity and Identifications in Wycliffite Writings." Edwards and Pearsall 81–90.

700. ——. "John Purvey: A Reconsideration of the Evidence for his Life and Writings." *Viator* 12 (1981): 355–80. Rpt. in Hudson 85–110.

701. ——. "Lollardy: The English Heresy?" *Religion and National Identity*. Ed. Stuart Mews. Studies in Church History 18. Oxford: Basil Blackwell, 1982. 261–83. Rpt. in Hudson 141–63.

702. ——. "'No Newe Thing': The Printing of Medieval Texts in the Early Reformation Period." *Middle English Studies Presented to Norman Davis*. Ed. Douglas Gray and Eric Stanley. Oxford: Oxford Univ. Press, 1983. 153–74. Rpt. in Hudson 227–48.

703. ——. "Observations on a Northerner's Vocabulary." Stanley and Gray 74–83. Rpt. in Hudson 217–26.

704. ——. *John Wyclif and his Influence in England: A Commemorative Exhibition Held in Lambeth Palace Library June 4-July 26, 1984*. London: Lambeth Palace Library, 1984.

705. ——. "Wycliffite Prose." Edwards 249–70.

706. ——. "A New Look at the Lay Folk's Catechism." *Viator* 16 (1985): 243–258.

707. ——. "A Wycliffite Scholar of the Early Fifteenth Century." Walsh and Wood 301–315.

708. ——. "Wyclif and the English Language." Kenny 85–103.

709. ——. "Wycliffism in Oxford 1381–1411." Kenny 67–84.

710. ——. "Biblical Exegesis in Wycliffite Writings." *John Wyclif* 61–79.

711. ——. "The Lay Folk's Catechism: A Postscript." *Viator* 18 (1988): 307–309.

712. ——. "The Legacy of *Piers Plowman*." Alford 251–266.

713. ——. *The Premature Reformation: Wycliffite Texts and Lollard History*. Oxford: Clarendon, 1988.

714. ——. "William Thorpe and the Question of Authority." *Christian Authority: Essays in Honour of Henry Chadwick*. Ed. G.R. Evans. Oxford: Clarendon, 1988. 127–37.

715. ——. "Lollard Book Production." Griffiths and Pearsall 125–142.

716. ——. "The Mouse in the Pyx: Popular Heresy and the Eucharist." *Trivium* 26 (1991): 40–53.

717. ——. "The King and Erring Clergy: A Wycliffite Contribution." Wood, *Church and Sovereignity* 269–78.

718. ——. "John Wyclif." *The English Religious Tradition and the Genius of Anglicanism*. Ed. Geoffrey Rowell. Wantage: Ikon, 1992. 65–78.

719. ——. "The Variable Text." Minnis, *Crux and Controversy* 49–60.

720. ——. "Aspects of the 'Publication' of Wyclif's Latin Sermons." Minnis, *Late Medieval Religious Texts* 121–29.

721. ——. "The Hussite Catalogues of Wyclif's Works." Pánek, Polívka, and Rejchrtová 401–18.

722. ——. "*Laicus Litteratus*: The Paradox of Lollardy." Biller and Hudson 222–236.

723. ——. "*Piers Plowman* and the Peasant's Revolt: A Problem Revisited." *Yearbook of Langland Studies* 8 (1995): 85–106.

724. ——. "Trial and Error: Wyclif's Works in Cambridge, Trinity College MS B.16.2." *New Science out of Old Books: Studies in Manuscripts and Early Printed Books in Honour of A.I. Doyle*. Ed. Richard Beadle and A.J. Piper. Aldershot: Scolar, 1995. 53–80.

725. ——. "William Taylor's 1406 Sermon: A Postscript." *Medium Aevum* 64:1 (1995): 100–06.

726. ——. "Lollardy and Eschatology." Patschovsky and Smahel 99–113.

727. ——. "From Oxford to Prague: The Writings of John Wyclif and his English Followers in Bohemia." *Slavonic and East European Review* 75 (Oct. 1997): 642–58.

728. ——. "*Hermofodrita* or *Ambidexter*: Wycliffite Views on Clerks in Secular Office." Aston and Richmond 41–51.

729. ——. "Poor Preachers, Poor Men: Views of Poverty in Wyclif and his Followers." Šmahel and Müller-Luckner 41–54.

730. ——. "Cross Referencing in Wyclif's Latin Works." Biller and Dobson 193–216.

731. ——. "*Accessus ad auctorem*: The Case of John Wyclif." *Viator* 30 (1999): 323–44.

732. ——. "*Peculiaris regis clericus*: Wyclif and the Issue of Authority." *The Growth of Authority in the Medieval West*. Ed. M. Gosman, A.J. Vanderjagh, and J.R. Veenstra. Groningen: Mediaevalia Groningana, 1999. 63–81.

733. ——. "Wyclif and the North: The Evidence from Durham." Wood, *Life and Thought* 87–103.

734. ——. "Wyclif's Latin Sermons: Questions of Form, Date and Audience." *Archives d'Histoire Doctrinale et Littéraire du Moyen Âge* 68 (2001): 223–48.

735. Hudson, Anne, and Helen L. Spencer. "Old Author, New Work: The Sermons of MS Longleat 4." *Medium Aevum* 53 (1984): 220–238.

736. Hughes, Jonathan. *Pastors and Visionaries: Religious and Secular Life in Late Medieval Yorkshire*. Woodbridge: The Boydell Press, 1988.

737. Hunt, Alison M. "Maculating Mary: The Detractors of the N-Town Cycle's 'Trial of Joseph and Mary.'" *Philological Quarterly* 73.1 (Winter, 1994): 11–30.

738. Hurley, Michael. "'Scriptura Sola': Wyclif and His Critics." *Traditio* 16 (1960): 275–352.

739. ——. "A Pre-Tridentine Theology of Tradition: Thomas Netter of Walden (d. 1430)." *Heythrop Journal* 4 (1963): 348–66.

740. Irvine, Annie Sowell. "The Participle in Wycliffe, with Especial Reference to his Original English Works." *University of Texas Bulletin: Studies in English* 9 (1929): 5–68.

741. ——. "The *To Comyng(e)* Construction in Wyclif." *PMLA* 45 (1930): 468–500.

742. Ives, Doris. "A Man of Religion." *Modern Language Review* 27 (1932): 144–48.

743. Jacob, E.F. "Reynold Pecock, Bishop of Chichester." British Academy Ralegh Lecture of 1951. *Publications of the British Academy* 37 (1951): 121–53.

744. ——. *The Fifteenth Century, 1399–1485.* Oxford: Clarendon, 1961.

745. ——. *Henry Chichele.* London: Thomas Nelson, 1967.

746. ——. "The Canterbury Convocation of 1406." *Essays in Medieval History Presented to Bertie Wilkinson.* Ed. T.A. Sandquist and M.R. Powicke. Toronto: Toronto Univ. Press, 1969. 345–53.

747. Jäger, Oskar. *John Wycliffe, und seine Bedeutung für die Reformation.* Halle, 1854.

748. Janssen, V.F. "Die four sects und die sect of Christ bei Wiclif." *Zeitschrift für Kirchengeschichte* 56 (1937): 354–360.

749. Jeauneau, Edouard. "Plato apud Bohemos." *Mediaeval Studies* 41 (1979): 161–214.

750. Jeffrey, David Lyle. "Chaucer and Wyclif: Biblical Hermeneutic and Literary Theory in the xivth Century." *Chaucer and Scriptural Tradition.* Ed. D.L. Jeffrey. Ottawa: Univ. of Ottawa Press, 1984.

751. ——. "John Wyclif and the Hermeneutics of Reader Response." *Interpretation* 39.3 (July, 1985): 272–87.

752. ——. "False Witness and the Just Use of Evidence in the Wycliffite 'Pistel of Swete Susan.'" *The Judgment of Susanna: Authority and Witness.* Ed. Ellen Spolsky. Atlanta: Scholars, 1996. 57–71.

753. ——. "Victimization and Legal Abuse: The Wycliffite Retelling of the Story of Susannah." *Retelling Tales: Essays in Honor of Russell Peck.* Ed. T. Hahn and A. Lupack. Cambridge: D.S Brewer, 1997. 161–78.

754. Jenkins, Claude. "Cardinal Morton's Register." *Tudor Studies Presented . . . to Albert Frederick Pollard.* Ed. R.W. Seton-Watson. 1924. Rpt. Freeport, NY: Books for Libraries Press, 1969. 26–74.

755. Johnson, Ian. "Vernacular Valorizing: Functions and Fashionings of Literary Theory in Middle English Translation of Authority." Beer 239–54.

756. Johnston, Alexandra. "The Plays of the Religious Guilds of York: The Creed Play and the Pater Noster Play." *Speculum* 50.1 (1975): 55–90.

757. Jones, Edmund D. "The Authenticity of Some Works Ascribed to Wycliffe." *Anglia* 30 (1907): 261–8.

758. Jones, W.R. "Lollards and Images: The Defense of Religious Art in Later Medieval England." *Journal of the History of Ideas* 34 (1973): 27–50.

759. Jurkowski, Maureen. "Lancastrian Royal Service, Lollardy, and Forgery: The Career of Thomas Tykhill." *Crown, Government and People in the Fifteenth Century.* Ed. Rowena E. Archer. New York: St. Martin's, 1995. 33–52.

760. ——. "New Light on John Purvey." *English Historical Review* 110 (Nov. 1995): 1180–91.

761. ——. "Lawyers and Lollardy in the Early Fifteenth Century." Aston and Richmond 155–182.

762. ——. "Heresy and Factionalism at Merton College in the Early Fifteenth Century." *Journal of Ecclesiastical History* 48 (Oct. 1997): 658–81.

763. ——. "The Arrest of William Thorpe in Shrewsbury and the Anti-Lollard Statute of 1406." *Historical Research* 75 (2002): 273–295.

764. Justice, Steven. "Inquisition, Speech, and Writing: A Case from Late Medieval Norwich." *Representations* 48 (1994): 1–29; rpt. in Copeland 289–322.

765. ——. *Writing and Rebellion: England in 1381.* Berkeley: Univ. of California Press, 1994.

766. ——. "Lollardy." Wallace 662–689.

767. Kalidova, Robert. "Joannus Wyclifs Metaphysik des extremen Realismus und ihre Bedeutung im Endstadium der mittelalterlichen Philosophie." *Die Metaphysik im Mittelalter*, ed. Paul Wilpert. Miscellanea Medievalia, vol. 2. Berlin: de Gruyter, 1963. 717–23.

768. ——. *Revolution und Ideologie: Der Hussitismus.* Trans. H. Thorwart and M. Glettler. Cologne: Böhlau Verlag, 1976.

769. Kaluza, Zenon. "Late Medieval Philosophy, 1350–1500." *Routledge History of Philosophy, Vol. III: Late Medieval Philosophy.* Ed. John Marenbon. New York: Routledge, 1998. 426–451.

770. Kamerick, Kathleen. *Popular Piety and Art in the Later Middle Ages: Image Worship and Idolatry in England, 1350–1550.* London: Palgrave, 2002.

771. Kaminsky, Howard. "Wyclifism as Ideology of Revolution." *Church History* 32 (1963): 57–74.

772. ——. *A History of the Hussite Revolution.* Berkeley, Univ. of California Press, 1967.

773. Kaňák, M. *John Viklef. Život a dílo anglického Husove předchůdce.* Prague: Blahoslav, 1970. Trans. *Der Ketzer von Oxvord. Leben un Wirkungen John Wiklefs.* [*John Wyclif: The Life and Work of the English Precursor of Hus.*] Prague: Blahoslav, 1973.

774. Keen, Maurice. *England in the Later Middle Ages: A Political History.* London: Methuen, 1973.

775. ——. "Wyclif, the Bible, and Transubstantiation." Kenny 1–17.

776. ——. "The Influence of Wyclif." Kenny 127–145.

777. Kennedy, Leonard A. *The Philosophy of Robert Holcot: A Fourteenth Century Sceptic.* Lewiston: Edwin Mellen Press, 1993.

778. Keleman, Erick. "Drama in Sermons: Quotation, Performativity, and Conversion in a Middle English Sermon and the *Tretise of Miraclis Pleyinge.*" *ELH* 69 (2002): 1–19.

779. Kellogg, A.L., and Ernest W. Talbert, "The Wycliffite Pater Noster and Ten Commandments, with Special Reference to English Mss. 85 and 90 in the John Rylands Library." *Bulletin of the John Rylands Library* 42 (1960): 345–377.

780. Kelly, Henry Ansgar. "Lollard Inquisitions: Due and Undue Process." *The Devil, Heresy, and Witchcraft in the Middle Ages: Essays in Honor of J.B. Russell.* Ed. Alberto Ferreiro. Leiden: E.J. Brill, 1998. 279–303.

781. ——. "Trial Procedures against Wyclif and Wycliffites in England and at the Trial of Constance." *The Huntington Library Quarterly* 1999 (61): 1–28.

782. Kemp, Anthony. *The Estrangment of the Past: A Study in the Origins of Modern Historical Consciousness.* Oxford: Oxford Univ. Press, 1991.

783. Kendall, Ritchie D. *The Drama of Dissent: The Radical Poetics of Nonconformity, 1380–1590.* Chapel Hill: Univ. of North Carolina Press, 1986.

784. Kenny, Anthony. *Wyclif.* Past Masters Series. Oxford: Oxford Univ. Press, 1985.

785. ——. "The Realism of the *de Universalibus.*" Kenny 17–30.
786. ——. "Wyclif: A Master Mind." *Proceedings of the British Academy* 72 (1986): 91–113. Rpt. in *The Heritage of Wisdom.* Ed. A. Kenny. Oxford: Blackwell, 1987. 68–92.
787. ——. "Realism and Determinism in the Early Wyclif." Hudson and Wilks 165–178.
788. ——. "The Accursed Memory: The Counter-Reformation Reputation of John Wyclif." Kenny 147–68.
789. Kerby-Fulton, Kathryn. "Prophecy and Suspicion: Closet Radicalism, Reformist Politics, and the Vogue for Hildegardiana in Ricardian England." *Speculum* 75 (2000): 318–341.
790. Kerby-Fulton, Kathryn, and Denise Depres. *Iconography and the Professional Reader: The Politics of Book Production in the Douce Piers Plowman.* Minneapolis: Univ. of Minnesota Press, 1998.
791. King, John N. *English Reformation Literature.* Princeton: Princeton Univ. Press, 1982.
792. Klassen, John. *The Nobility and the Making of the Hussite Revolution.* Boulder: East European Quarterly, 1978.
793. ——. "Hus, the Hussites, and Bohemia." *New Cambridge Medieval History, vol. 7: c. 1415-c.1500.* Ed. Christopher Allemand. Cambridge: Cambridge Univ. Press, 1998. 367–91.
794. Knapp, Ethan. *The Bureaucratic Muse: Thomas Hoccleve and the Literature of Late Medieval England.* University Park: Penn State Univ. Press, 2001.
795. Knapp, Peggy. "Wyclif as Bible Translator: The Texts for the English Sermons." *Speculum* 46 (1971): 713–20.
796. ——. "John Wyclif and the Horned Patriarchs." *American Notes and Queries* 14 (1976): 66–67.
797. ——. *The Style of John Wyclif's English Sermons.* The Hague: Mouton, 1977.
798. ——. *Chaucer and the Social Contest.* New York: Routledge, 1990.
799. ——. "The Words of the Parson's 'Vertuous Sentence.'" *Closure in the Canterbury Tales: The Role of the Parson's Tale.* Ed. David Raybin and Linda Tarte Holley. Kalamazoo: Medieval Institute, 2000. 95–113.
800. ——. *Time-Bound Words: Semantic and Social Economies from Chaucer's England to Shakespeare's.* New York: St. Martin's, 2000.
801. Knowles, David. *The Religious Orders in England.* 3 vols. Cambridge: Cambridge Univ. Press, 1961.
802. ——. "The Censured Opinions of Uthred of Boldon." *The Historian and Character and Other Essays.* Ed. D. Knowles. Cambridge: Univ. of Cambridge Press, 1963. 129–70.
803. Kolesnyk, Alexander. "Hussens Eucharistiebegriff." Seibt 193–202.
804. Kolve, V.A. *The Play Called Corpus Christi.* Stanford: Stanford Univ. Press, 1966.
805. Krapp, J.P. *The Rise of English Literary Prose.* Oxford: Oxford Univ. Press, 1916.
806. Kras, Paweł. "Hussitism and the Polish Nobility." Aston and Richmond 183–198.
807. Kretzmann, Norman. "Continua, Indivisibles, and Change in Wyclif's Logic of Scripture." Kenny 31–65.
808. Krey, Philip. "Many Readers but Few Followers: The Fate of Nicholas of

Lyra's 'Apocalypse Commentary' in the Hands of his Late Medieval Admirers." *Church History* 64 (June 1995): 185–97.

809. Kristeller, Paul Oskar. "The Thomist Tradition." *Medieval Aspects of Renaissance Learning.* Durham: Duke Univ. Press, 1974.

810. Krofta, Kamil. "John Hus." *Cambridge Medieval History*, vol. 8. Ed. C.W. Previté and Z.N. Brooke. Cambridge: Cambridge Univ. Press, 1936. 45–64.

811. Krummel, Leopold. "Die Vorreformatoren Wycliffe und Hus und ihr Verhältnis zu den scholastischen Systemen des Realismus und Nominalismus." *Theologische Studien und Kritiken* 44 (1871): 297–317.

812. Kuhl, E. P. "Chaucer and the Church." *Modern Language Notes* 40.6 (1925): 321–38.

813. Kuczynski, Michael. *Prophetic Song: The Psalms as Moral Discourse in Late Medieval England.* Philadelphia: Univ. of Pennsylvania Press, 1995.

814. ——. "Rolle among the Reformers: Orthodoxy and Heterodoxy in Wycliffite Copies of Richard Rolle's *Psalter.*" *Mysticism and Spirituality in Medieval England.* Ed. W. F. Pollard and R. Boenig. Cambridge: D.S. Brewer, 1997. 177–202.

815. ——. "The Earliest English Wyclif Portraits?: Political Caricatures in Bodleian Library, Oxford, MS Laud Misc. 286." *Journal of the Early Book Society* 5 (2002): 121–139.

816. Kurze, D. "Die festländischen Lollarden: zur Geschichte der religiösen Bewegungen im ausgehenden Mittelalter." *Archiv für Kulturgeschichte* 47 (1965): 48–76.

817. Kybal, V. "Étude sur les origines du mouvement Hussite in Bohemia. Matthias de Ianov." *Revue Historique* 103 (1910): 1–31.

818. Lahey, Stephen. "Wyclif and Toleration." *Difference and Dissent.* Ed. Carey Nederman and John Laurson. New York: Rowman and Littlefield, 1996. 39–66.

819. ——. "Wyclif on Rights." *Journal of the History of Ideas* 58 (Jan. 1997): 1–21.

820. ——. "Wyclif and Lollardy." *The Medieval Theologians: An Introduction to the Theology of the Medieval Period.* Ed. Gillian R. Evans. Oxford: Blackwell, 2001. 334–54.

821. Lambert, Malcolm. *Medieval Heresy.* 2nd ed. Oxford: Basil Blackwell, 1992.

822. Landi, Aldo. "John Wyclif nella storia." *John Wyclif* 15–44.

823. Lares, Micheline. "Les traductions bibliques: l'exemple de la Grande Bretagne." Riche and Lobrichon 123–40.

824. Larsen, Andrew E. "The Oxford 'School of Heretics': the Unexamined Case of Friar John." *Vivarium* 37.2 (1999): 168–77.

825. Laun, Justus F. "Thomas Bradwardina, der Schüler Augustins und Lehrer Wiclifs." *Zeitschrift für Kirchengeschichte* 47 (1928): 333–56.

826. ——. "Recherches sur Thomas de Bradwardin, précursor de Wyclif." *Revue d'Histoire te de philosophie religieuses* 9 (1929): 217–33.

827. Lawton, David. "Lollardy and the *Piers Plowman* Tradition." *Modern Language Review* 76 (1981): 780–93.

828. ——. *Faith, Text, and History: The Bible in English.* Charlottesville: Univ. of Virginia Press, 1990.

829. ——. "Voice, Authority, and Blasphemy in the *Book of Margery Kempe.*" *Margery Kempe: A Book of Essays.* Ed. Sandra J. McEntire. New York: Garland, 1992. 93–115.

830. ——. "Englishing the Bible, 1066–1549." Wallace 454–482.

831. Lechler, Gotthard. *Johann von Wiclif und die Vorgeschichte der Reformation.* 2 vols. Leipzig, 1873. English trans. by Peter Lorimer as *John Wycliffe and His English Precursors.* 2 vols. London: Religious Tract Society, 1884.

832. Leff, Gordon. *Bradwardine and the Pelagians.* Cambridge: Cambridge Univ. Press, 1957. 32.

833. ——. *Richard Fitzralph: Commentator on the Sentences.* Manchester: Manchester Univ. Press, 1963.

834. ——. "John Wyclif: The Path to Dissent." *Proceedings of the British Academy* 52 (1966): 141–80.

835. ——. "The Apostolic Ideal in Later Medieval Ecclesiology." *Journal of Theological Studies* n.s. 18 (1967): 71–82.

836. ——. *Heresy in the Later Middle Ages: The Relation of Heterodoxy to Dissent, c. 1250-c. 1450.* 2 vols. Manchester: Manchester Univ. Press, 1967.

837. ——. "Wyclif and Hus: A Doctrinal Comparison." *Bulletin of the John Ryland's Library* 50 (1967): 387–410; revised rpt. in Kenny 105–25.

838. ——. "Wyclif and the Augustinian Tradition, with Special Reference to His *De Trinitate.*" *Medievalia et Humanistica* n.s. 1 (1970): 29–39.

839. ——. *The Dissolution of the Medieval Outlook.* New York: Harper and Row, 1976.

840. ——. "Ockham and Wyclif on the Eucharist." *Reading Medieval Studies* 2 (1976): 1–13.

841. ——. "John Wyclif as a Religious Reformer." *Annual Report of the Friends of Lambeth Palace Library* (1984): 21–29.

842. ——. "John Wyclif's Religious Doctrines." *Churchman* 98.4 (1984): 319–28.

843. ——. "The Place of Metaphysics in Wyclif's Theology." Hudson and Wilks 217–232.

844. ——. "John Wyclif." *Medieval Life* 6 (1997): 19–25.

845. Lepow, Lauren. *Enacting the Sacrament: Counter-Lollardy in the Towneley Cycle.* Cranbury, NJ: Fairleigh-Dickinson Univ. Press, 1991.

846. Lerner, Robert. *Heresy of the Free Spirit in the Later Middle Ages.* Notre Dame: Univ. of Notre Dame Press, 1991.

847. Lerner, Robert. "Le communautes heretiques." Riche and Lobrichon 597–614.

848. Levy, Ian C. "John Wyclif and Augustinian Realism." *Augustiniana* 48 (1998): 87–106.

849. ——. "*Christus Qui Mentiri Non Potest*: John Wyclif's Rejection of Transubstantiation." *Recherches de Theologie et Philosophie Medievales* (1999): 316–334.

850. ——. "Was John Wyclif's Theology of the Eucharist Donatistic?" *Scottish Journal of Theology* 53 (2000): 137–153.

851. ——. "Useful Foils: Lessons Learned from Jews in John Wyclif's Call for Church Reform." *Medieval Encounters* 7 (July 2001): 125–145.

852. Lewis, Ewart. *Medieval Political Ideas.* 2 vols. New York: Knopf, 1954.

853. Lewis, John. *The History of the Life and Sufferings of the Reverend and Learned John Wiclif, D.D.* London, 1720; new ed. 1820. Rpt. New York: AMS, 1973.

854. Lindberg, Conrad. "The Manuscript and Versions of the Wyclif Bible." *Studia Neophilologica* 42 (1970): 333–47.

855. ——. "The Break at Baruch 3:20 in the Middle English Bible." *English Studies* 60 (1979): 106–10.

856. ——. "The Language of the Wyclif Bible." *Medieval Studies Conference*

1983: Language and Literature. Ed. W. D. Bald and H. Weinstock. Frankfurt: Peter Lang, 1984. 103–110.

857. ——. "Who Wrote Wiclif's Bible?" *Stockholm Studies in Modern Philology* n.s. 7 (1984): 127–35.

858. ——. "A Note on the Vocabulary of the Middle English Bible." *Studia Neophilologica* 57:2 (1985): 129–31.

859. ——. "Reconstructing the Lollard Versions of the Bible." *Neuphilologische Mitteilungen* 90:1 (1989): 117–23.

860. ——. "Towards an English Wyclif Canon." *Essays on English Language in Honour of Bertil Sundby.* Ed. L.E. Breivik et al. Oslo: Novus, 1989. 179–84.

861. ——. "From Jerome to Wyclif, An Experiment in Translation: The First Prologue." *Studia Neophilologica* 63:2 (1991): 143–45.

862. ——. "Literary Aspects of the Wyclif Bible." *Bulletin of the John Rylands Library* 77.3 (1995): 79–85.

863. Lindsay, T.M. "A Literary Relic of Scottish Lollardy." *Scottish Historical Review* 1 (1903–04): 260–73.

864. Lindsay, Philip, and Reginald Groves. *The Peasant's Revolt, 1381.* London: Hutchinson, 1950.

865. Lipton, Emma. "Performing Reform: Lay Piety and the Marriage of Mary and Joseph in the N-Town Cycle." *Studies in the Age of Chaucer* 23 (2001): 407–435.

866. Little, A.G. and F. Pelster. *Oxford Theology and Theologians.* Oxford: Clarendon, 1934.

867. Little, Katherine C. "Catechesis and Castigation: Sin in the Wycliffite Sermon Cycle." *Traditio* 54 (1999): 213–44.

868. ——. "Chaucer's Parson and the Specter of Wycliffism." *Studies in the Age of Chaucer* 23 (2001): 225–253.

869. Lloyd, M.E.H. "John Wyclif and the Prebend of Lincoln." *English Historical Review* 61 (1946): 388–94.

870. Loades, David, ed. *John Foxe and the English Reformation.* Aldershot: Scolar, 1997.

871. Lochrie, Karma. *Margery Kempe and Translations of the Flesh.* Philadelphia: Univ. of Pennsylvania Press, 1991.

872. Logan, F. Donald. *Excommunication and the Secular Arm in Medieval England.* Toronto: Pontifical Institute, 1968.

873. ——. "Another Cry of Heresy at Oxford: The Case of Dr. John Holand, 1416." Cuming 99–113.

874. ——. "Archbishop Thomas Bourgchier Revisited." *The Church in Pre-Reformation Society.* Ed. C.M. Barron and C. Harper-Bill. Woodbridge: The Boydell Press, 1985. 170–85.

875. ——. *Runaway Religious in Medieval England, c. 1240–1540.* Cambridge: Cambridge Univ. Press, 1996.

876. Long, John D. *The Bible in English: John Wycliffe and John Tyndale.* Lanham, MD: Univ. Press of America, 1998.

877. Loomis, Roger. "Was Chaucer a Laodicean?" *Essays and Studies in Honor of Carleton Brown.* Ed. Percy W. Long. New York: New York Univ. Press, 1940. 129–48. Rpt. in Richard J. Schoeck and Jerome Taylor, eds. *Chaucer Criticism: The Canterbury Tales.* Notre Dame: Univ. of Notre Dame Press, 1960. 291–310.

878. Loserth, Johann. *Wycliffe and Huss.* Trans. M.J. Evans. London, 1884.

879. ———. "Zur Verpflanzung der Wiclifie nach Böhmen." *Mittheilungen des Vereins für die Geschichte der Deutschen in Böhmen* 22 (1884): 220–25.

880. ———. "Über die Versuche wiclif-husitische Lehren nach Österreich, Polen, Ungarn und Croatien zu verpflanzen." *Mittheilungen des Vereins für die Geschichte der Deutschen in Böhmen* 24 (1886): 97–116.

881. ———. "Wiclif's Buch 'Von der Kirche' (*De Ecclesia*) un die Nachbildungen desselben in Böhmen." *Mittheilungen des Vereins für die Geschichte der Deutschen in Böhmen* 24 (1886): 381–418.

882. ———. "Urkunden und Traktate betreffend die Verbreitun des Wiclifismus in Böhmen." *Mittheilungen des Vereins für die Geschichte der Deutschen in Böhmen* 25 (1887): 329–46.

883. ———. "Simon von Tischnow. Ein Beitrag zur Geschichte des böhimschen Wyclifismus." *Mittheilungen des Vereins für die Geschichte der Deutschen in Böhmen* 26 (1888): 221–45.

884. ———. "Die lateinischen Predigten Wiclif's, die Zeit ihrer Abfassung und ihre Ausnützung durch Hus." *Zeitschrift fur Kirchengeschichte* 9 (1888): 523–564.

885. ———. "Über die Beziehungen zwischen englischen und böhmischen Wiclifiten in den beiden ersten Jarhzehnten des 15. Jahrhunderts." *Mittheilungen des Instituts für öesterreichische Geschichtsforschung* 12 (1891): 254–69.

886. ———. "Die Wiclif'sche Abendmahlslehre und ihre Augname in Böhmen." *Mittheilungen des Vereins für die Geschichte der Deutschen in Böhmen* 30 (1892): 1–33.

887. ———. *Die kirchliche Reformbewegung in England im XIV. Jahundert und ihre Aufnahme und Durchführung in Böhmen.* Leipzig, 1893.

888. ———. "Das vermeintliche Schrieben Wiclif's an Urban VI, und einige verlorene Flugschriften Wiclif's aus seinen letzten Lebenstagen." *Historische Zeitschrift* 75.2 (1895): 476–80.

889. ———. "The Beginnings of Wyclif's Activity in Ecclesiastical Politics." *English Historical Review* 11 (1896): 319–28.

890. ———. *Geschichte des späteren Mittelalters von 1197 bis 1492.* Handbuch der mittlealterlichen und neueren Geschichte, Abt. 2. Berlin, 1903.

891. ———. "Wyclifs Lehre vom wahren und faslchen Papsttum." *Historische Zeitschrift* 96 (1907): 237–55.

892. ———. "Die ältesten Streitschriften Wiclifs. Studien über die Anfänge der kirchenpolitischen Tätigkeit Wiclif un die Überlieferung seiner Schriften." *Sitzungsberichte der kaiserlichen Akademie der Wissenschaften, Wien, philosophisch-historische Klasse* 160.2 (1909): 1–74.

893. ———. "Wiclifs Sendschreiben, Flugschriften, und kleinere Werke kirchen-politischen Inhalts." *Sitzungsberichte der kaiserlichen Akademie der Wissenschaften, Wien, philosophisch-historische Klasse* 164 (1910): vi, 1–96.

894. ———. "Zur Geschichte des Wyclifismus in Mähren." *Zeitschrift des Vereins für Geschichte Mährens und Schlesiens* 17 (1913): 190–205.

895. ———. "Studien zur Kirchenpolitik Englands im 14. Jahrhundert. II. Die Genesis von Wiclifs *Summa Theologiae* und seien Lehre vom wahren und falschen Papsttum." *Sitzungsberichte der kaiserlichen Akademie der Wissenschaften, Wien, philosophisch-historische Klasse* 180 (1916) vi, 1–118.

896. ———. "Johann von Wyclif und Guilelmus Peraldus: Studien zur Geschichte der Entstehung von Wiclifs Summa Theologie." *Sitzungsberichte der königlichen Akademie der Wissenschaften, Wien, philosophisch-historische Klasse* 180.3 (1916): 1 – 101.

897. ——. "Zur Kritik der Wiclifhandschriften." *Zeitschrift des deutschen Vereins für die Geschichte Mährens und Schlesiens* 20 (1916): 247–71.

898. ——. "Johann von Wiclif und Robert Grosseteste, Bischof von Lincoln." *Sitzungsberichte der bayrischen Akademie der Wissenschaften, Wien, philosophisch-historische Klasse,* 186 (1918): ii, 1–83.

899. ——. "Die kirchenpolitischen Schriften Wiclifs und der englische Bauernauftstand von 1381." *Mittheilungen des Instituts für öesterreichische Geschichte-Forschung.* 38 (1920): 399–422.

900. ——. *Huss und Wyclif: Zur Genesis der hussitischen Lehre.* 2nd ed. München: R. Oldenburgh, 1925.

901. Lupton, Lewis. *Wyclif's Wicket: Sign of a Credible Faith.* History of the Geneva Bible 16. London: Olive Tree, 1984.

902. ——. *Trodden Thyme: Lollard Aftermath.* History of the Geneva Bible 17. London: Olive Tree, 1985.

903. Luscombe, David. "Wyclif and Hierarchy." Hudson and Wilks 233–244.

904. Lutton, Rob. "Connections between Lollard Townsfolk and Gentry in Tenterden in the Late Fifteenth and Early Sixteenth Centuries." Aston and Richmond 199–228.

905. Luxton, I. "The Lichfield Court Book: A Postscript." *Bulletin of the Institute of Historical Research* 44 (1971): 120–25.

906. Lytle, Guy Fitch. "John Wyclif, Martin Luther, and Edward Powell: Heresy and the Oxford Theology Faculty and the Beginning of the Reformation." Hudson and Wilks 465–79.

907. Maass, M. "Die Wicliff'sche Bibelübersetzung im vergliech mit der recipirten englischen aus dem anfange des 17. jhrdts." *Archiv* 29 (1861): 221–30.

908. MacCulloch, Diarmid. *Thomas Cranmer: A Life.* New Haven: Yale Univ. Press, 1996.

909. MacNab, T.M.A. "Bohemia and the Scottish Lollards." *Records of the Scottish Church History Society* 5 (1935): 10–22.

910. Maitland, Frederic William. "Wyclif on English and Roman Law." *The Collected Papers of Frederick William Maitland.* Vol. 3. Ed. H.A.L. Fisher. Cambridge: Cambridge Univ. Press, 1911. 50–53.

911. Mallard, William. "John Wyclif and the Tradition of Biblical Authority." *Church History* 30 (1961): 50–60.

912. ——. "Dating the *Sermones Quadraginta* of John Wyclif." *Medievalia et Humanistica* o.s. 17 (1966): 86–104.

913. ——. "Clarity and Dilemma: The *Forty Sermons* of John Wyclif." *Contemporary Reflections on the Medieval Christian Tradition: Essays in Honor of Ray C. Petry.* Ed. G.H. Shriver et al. Durham: Duke Univ. Press, 1974. 19–38.

914. Mann, J. *Chaucer and Medieval Estates Satire.* Cambridge: Cambridge Univ. Press, 1973.

915. Manning, Bernard L. *The People's Faith in the Time of Wyclif.* Cambridge: Cambridge Univ. Press, 1919.

916. ——. "Wyclif and the House of Herod." *Cambridge Historical Journal* 2 (1926): 66–67.

917. ——. "Wyclif." *Cambridge Medieval History,* vol. 7. Ed. J.R. Tanner et al. Cambridge: Cambridge Univ. Press, 1932. 486–507.

918. Mantello, F.A.C. "The Endleaves of Trinity College Cambridge MS O.4.43 and John Wyclif's *Responsiones ad Argumenta Cuiusdam Emuli Veritatis.*" *Speculum* 54 (1979): 100–03.

919. Marti, Oscar A. "John Wyclif's Theory for the Disendowment of the English Church." *Anglican Theological Review* 11 (1929): 30–44.

920. Martin, C. "Walter Burley." Southern 193–230.

921. Martin, C.A. "The Middle English Versions of The Ten Commandments, with Special Reference to Rylands English MS 85." *Bulletin of the John Rylands Library* 64.1 (Autumn, 1981): 191–217.

922. ——. "Middle English Manuals of Religious Instruction." Benskin and Samuels 283–98.

923. Martin, Carol. "Alys as Allegory: The Ambivalent Heretic." *Comitatus* 21 (1990): 52–71.

924. Martin, Geoffrey. "Knighton's Lollards." Aston and Richmond 28–40.

925. Martin, Geoffrey, and J.R.L. Highfield. *A History of Merton College, Oxford.* Oxford: Oxford Univ. Press, 1997.

926. Martinet, Marie-Madeleine. "Wyclif et *Piers Plowman* sous le petit Josias: Le radicalisme médiéval transmis par Robert Crowley au temps d'Edouard VI." *Radicaux à l'anglaise.* Ed. Olivier Lutaud. Paris: Centre d'histoire des idées dans les îles Britanniques, 1984. 1–16.

927. Matthew, F.D. *The Life of John Wycliffe.* London, 1884.

928. ——. "The Date of Wyclif's Attack on Transubstantiation." *English Historical Review* 5 (1890): 328–30.

929. ——. "On the Authorship of the Wycliffite Bible." *English Historical Review* 10 (1895): 91–99.

930. Mattingly, Joanna. "Lollards Stop Play? A Curious Case of Non-Performance in 1505." *Medieval English Theatre* 22 (2000): 100–111.

931. Maxfield, E.K. "Chaucer and Religious Reform." *PMLA* 39 (1924): 64–74.

932. McCue, James F. "The Doctrine of Transubstantiation from Berengar through the Council of Trent." *Lutherans and Catholics in Dialogue 1–3.* Ed. P.C. Empie and T.A. Murphy. Minneapolis: Augsburg, 1965. 89–124.

933. McFarlane, K.B. *John Wycliffe and the Beginnings of English Nonconformity.* London: English Universities Press, 1953.

934. ——. *Lancastrian Kings and Lollard Knights.* Oxford: Clarendon, 1972.

935. McGrade, A.S. "Somersaulting Sovereignty: A Note on Reciprocal Lordship and Servitude in Wyclif." Wood 261–78.

936. ——. "Rights, Natural Rights, and the Philosophy of Law." *The Cambridge History of Later Medieval Philosophy, from the Rediscovery of Aristotle to the Disintegration of Scholasticism, 1100–1600.* Ed. Norman Kretzmann, Anthony Kenny, and Jan Pinborg. Cambridge: Cambridge Univ. Press, 1982. 738–756.

937. McGrath, Alister E. *A History of Reformation Thought: an Introduction.* 3rd ed. Oxford: Basil Blackwell, 1999.

938. McHardy, A.K. "Bishop Buckingham and the Lollards of Lincoln Diocese." Baker, *Schism* 131–45.

939. ——. "John Wycliffe's Mission to Bruges: A Financial Footnote." *Journal of Theological Studies* 24 (1973): 521–22.

940. ——. "The Dissemination of Wyclif's Ideas." Hudson and Wilks 361–68.

941. ——. "De Heretico Comburendo, 1401." Aston and Richmond 112–126.

942. McKisack, May. *The Fourteenth Century, 1307–1399.* Oxford: Oxford Univ. Press, 1959.

943. McNeill, John Thomas. "Some Emphases in Wyclif's Teaching." *Journal of Religion* 7 (1927) 447–466.

944. McNiven, Peter. "The Men of Cheshire and the Rebellion of 1403."

Transactions of the Historic Society of Lancashire and Cheshire 129 (1980): 1–29.

945. ———. *Heresy and Politics in the Reign of Henry IV: The Burning of John Badby.* Woodbridge: Boydell, 1987.

946. McShane, Eduardo. *A Critical Appraisal of the Antimendicantism of John Wyclif.* Romae: Officium Libri Catholici, 1950.

947. McSheffrey, Shannon. "Women and Lollardy: A Reassessment." *Canadian Journal of History* 26 (1991): 199–223.

948. ———. "Literacy and the Gender Gap in the Late Middle Ages: Women and Reading in Lollard Communities." *Women, the Book, and the Godly: Selected Proceedings of the St. Hilda's Conference, 1993.* Ed. Jane H.M. Taylor and Lesley Smith. Cambridge: D.S. Brewer, 1995. 157–70.

949. ———. *Gender and Heresy: Women and Men in Lollard Communities 1420–1530.* Philadelphia: Univ. of Pennsylvania Press, 1995.

950. McVeigh, T.A. "Chaucer's Portraits of the Pardoner and Summoner and Wycliff's *Tractatus de simonia.*" *Classical Folia* 29 (1975): 54–58.

951. Middleton, Anne. "William Langland's 'Kynde Name': Authorial Signature and Social Identity in Late Fourteenth Century England." Lee Patterson, ed. *Literary Practice and Social Change in Britain, 1380–1540.* Berkeley: Univ. of California Press, 1990. 15–82.

952. ———. "Acts of Vagrancy: The C Version 'Autobiography' and the Statute of 1388." Justice and Kerby-Fulton 208–317.

953. Milligan, William. "Wyclif and the Bible." *Fortnightly Review* 37 (1885): 788–98.

954. Milsom, S.F.C. "Richard Hunne's 'Praemunire.'" *English Historical Review* 76 (1961): 80–82.

955. Minnis, Alastair J. "'Authorial Intention' and 'Literal Sense' in the Exegetical Theories of Richard Fitzralph and John Wyclif: An Essay in the Medieval Theories of Biblical Hermeneutics." *Proceedings of the Royal Irish Academy* 75, Section C, no. 1 (1975): 1–30.

956. ———. "Late-Medieval Discussions of Compilatio and the Role of the Compilator." *Bietrage zur Geschichte der Deutschen Sprache und Literatur* 101 (1979): 385–201.

957. ———. *Medieval Theory of Authorship.* 2nd ed. Aldershot: Wildwood House, 1988.

958. ———. "The Author's Two Bodies? Authority and Fallibility in Late-Medieval Textual Theory." *Of the Making of Books: Medieval Manuscripts, Their Scribes and Readers. Essays Presented to M.B. Parkes.* Ed. P.R. Robinson and Rivkah Zim. Aldershot: Scolar, 1997. 259–79.

959. Molnár, Amadeo. "L'evolution de la théologie hussite." *Revue d'histoire et de philosophie religieuses* 43 (1963): 133–71.

960. ———. "Les responses de Jean Huss aux quarante-cinq articles." *Recherches de theologie medievale et ancienne* 31 (1964): 85–99.

961. ———. "Apocalypse XII dans l'interprétation hussite." *Revue d'histoire et de philosophie religieuses* 45 (1965): 212–31.

962. ———. "Der alternde Wyclif und die Logik der Heiligen Schrift." *Communio Viatorum* 28.3–4 (Winter, 1985): 161–76.

963. Molnar, Enrico Selley. "Marsilius of Padua, Wyclyf, and Hus." *Anglican Theological Review* 44 (1962): 33–43.

964. ———. "Wyclif, Hus and the Problem of Authority." Seibt 167–82.

965. Moore, Robert I. "Literacy and the Making of Heresy." Biller and Hudson 19–37.
966. Morrison, Stephen. "Lollardy in the Fifteenth Century-The Evidence of Some Orthodox Texts." *Cahiers Elisabethains: Late Medieval and Renaissance Studies* 52 (1997): 1–24.
967. Morrison, Susan Signe. "Don't Ask, Don't Tell: The Wife of Bath and Vernacular Translations." *Exemplaria* 8.1 (1996): 97–123.
968. Mozley, J.F. *John Foxe and his Book.* New York: Macmillan, 1940.
969. Mudroch, Vaclav. "John Wyclyf and Richard Flemyng, Bishop of Lincoln: Gleanings from German Sources." *Bulletin of the Institute of Historical Research* 37 (1964): 239–45.
970. ——. "John Wyclyf's Postilla in Fifteenth-Century Bohemia." *Canadian Journal of Theology* 10.2 (1964): 118–23.
971. ——. *The Wyclyf Tradition.* Ed. A. Compton Reeves. Athens, Ohio: Ohio Univ. Press, 1979.
972. Mueller, Ivan J. "A 'Lost' Summa of John Wyclif." Hudson and Wilks 179–83.
973. Mueller, Janel. *The Native Tongue and the Word.* Chicago: Univ. of Chicago Press, 1984.
974. Muir, Lawrence. "The Influence of the Rolle and Wyclifite Psalters upon the Psalter of the Authorized Version." *Modern Language Review* 30 (1935): 302–10.
975. Muldoon, James. "John Wyclif and the Rights of the Infidels: The 'Requerimiento' Re-examined." *Americas* (Academy of American Franciscan History) 6.3 (1980): 301–16.
976. Mullett, Charles F. "Cant Language, Common Language, and Ambiguity: English Churchmen, Linguistics, and Social Change." *Historical Magazine of the Protestant Episcopal Church* 40.3 (1971): 447–59.
977. Murray, Thomas. *The Life of John Wycliffe.* Edinburgh, 1829.
978. Nelson, Janet L. "Society, Theodicy, and the Origins of Heresy: Towards a Reassessment of the Medieval Evidence." Baker 65–77.
979. Nevanlinna, Saara. "The Occurrence of Glosses in Three Late Middle-English Texts: Lexical Variation." *Historical Linguistics and Philology.* Ed. Jacek Fisiak. Berlin: Mouton de Gruyter, 1990. 273–89.
980. ——. "Distribution of Glosses in MSS of the Wycliffite Gospel of John: The Class of Paraphrase." *Neuphilologische Mitteilungen* 102.2 (2001): 173–83.
981. Ng, Su Fang. "Translation, Interpretation, and Heresy: The Wycliffite Bible, Tyndale's Bible, and the Contested Origin." *Studies in Philology* 98.3 (Summer, 2001): 315–39.
982. Nichols, Ann E. "Books for Laymen, The Demise of a Commonplace: Lollard Texts and the Justification of Images as a Continuity of Belief and Polemic." *Church History* 56.4 (1987): 457–73.
983. ——. "Lollard Language in the Croxton Play of the Sacrament." *Notes and Queries* 36:1 (1989): 23–25.
984. ——. *Seeable Signs: The Iconography of the Seven Sacraments, 1350–1544.* Woodbridge: The Boydell Press, 1997.
985. Niezen, R.W. "Hot Literacy in Cold Societies: A Comparative Study of the Sacred Power of Writing." *Comparative Studies in Society and History* 33 (1991): 225–54.
986. Nissé, Ruth [Ruth Shklar]. "Cobham's Daughter: *The Book of Margery*

Kempe and the Power of Heterodox Thinking." *Modern Language Quarterly* 56:3 (1995): 277–304.

987. ——. "Reversing Discipline: *The Tretise of Miraclis Pleyinge*, Lollard Exegesis, and the Failure of Representation." *Yearbook of Langland Studies* 11 (1997): 163–94.

988. ——. "Staged Interpretations: Civic Rhetoric and Lollard Politics in the York Plays." *Journal of Medieval and Early Modern Studies* 28.2 (Spring, 1998): 427–73.

989. ——. "Grace under Pressure: Conduct and Representation in the Norwich Heresy Trials." *Medieval Conduct.* Ed. K. Ashley and L.A. Clark. Minneapolis: Univ. of Minnesota Press, 2001. 207–25.

990. ——. "Prophetic Nations." *New Medieval Literatures IV.* Ed. W. Scase, R. Copeland, and D. Lawton. Oxford: Oxford Univ. Press, 2001. 95–115.

991. Nuttall C. "Bishop Pecock and the Lollard Movement." *Transactions of the Congregational History Society* 13 (1937–9): 82–6.

992. Oberman, Heiko A. *Archbishop Thomas Bradwardine, A Fourteenth-Century Augustinian: A Study of his Theology in its Historical Context.* Utrecht: Kemink and Zoon, 1958.

993. ——. *The Harvest of Late Medieval Theology: Gabriel Biel and Late Medieval Nominalism.* 3rd ed. Durham: Labyrinth Press, 1983.

994. Ocker, Christopher. *Biblical Poetics Before Humanism and Reformation.* Cambridge: Cambridge Univ. Press, 2002.

995. Odložilík, Otakar. "Wyclif's Influence upon Central and Eastern Europe." *Slavonic Review* 7 (1928–9): 634–48.

996. ——. *Wyclif and Bohemia, Two Essays.* Prague: published by the author, 1937.

997. ——. *The Hussite King: Bohemia and European Affairs, 1440–1471.* New Brunswick: Rutgers Univ. Press, 1965.

998. O'Donovan, Joan Lockwood. *Theology of Law and Authority in the English Reformation.* Atlanta: Scholars, 1991.

999. ——. "Natural Law and Perfect Community: Contributions of Christian Platonism to Political Theory." *Modern Theology* 14.1 (1998): 19–42.

1000. Ogle, Arthur. *The Tragedy of the Lollard's Tower.* Oxford: Pen-in-Hand, 1949.

1001. ——. *The Canon Law in Medieval England; an Examination of William Lyndwood's "Provinciale" in reply to the Late Professor Maitland.* Rpt. New York: Burt Franklin, 1971.

1002. Olson, Paul A. *The Canterbury Tales and the Good Society.* Princeton: Princeton Univ. Press, 1986.

1003. Orme, Nicholas. *English Schools in the Middle Ages.* London: Methuen, 1973.

1004. Ortmann, Franz J. *Formen und Syntax des Verbes bei Wycliffe und Purvey.* Berlin: Mayer und Müller, 1902.

1005. Östermann, A. "'There' Compounds in Early English Bible Translation." *Neuphilologische Mitteilungen* 99.1 (1998): 71–82.

1006. Overstreet, Samuel A. "'Grammaticus Ludens': Theological Aspects of Langland's Grammatical Allegory." *Traditio* 40 (1984): 252–96.

1007. Owst, G.R. *Preaching in Medieval England.* Cambridge: Cambridge Univ. Press, 1926.

1008. ——. *Literature and Pulpit in Medieval England.* 2nd rev. ed. Oxford: Oxford Univ. Press, 1961.

1009. Pantin, William A. "A Benedictine Opponent of John Wyclif." *English Historical Review* 43 (1928): 73-7.

1010. ——. "The *Defensorium* of Adam Easton." *English Historical Review* 51 (1936): 675-80.

1011. ——. *The English Church in the Fourteenth Century*. Cambridge: Cambridge Univ. Press, 1955.

1012. ——. "The Fourteenth Century." *The English Church and the Papacy in the Middle Ages*. Ed. C.H. Lawrence. New York: Fordham Univ. Press, 1965. 157-94.

1013. Parker, Douglas H. "*A Proper Dyaloge Betwene A Gentillman and a Husbandman*: The Question of Authorship." *Bulletin of the John Rylands Library* 78.1 (1996): 63-75.

1014. Parker, G.H.W. *The Morning Star: Wycliffe and the Dawn of the Reformation*. Exeter: Paternoster, 1965.

1015. Partridge, A.C. *English Biblical Translation*. London: André Deutsch, 1973.

1016. Patrouch, Joseph F. *Reginald Pecock*. New York: Twayne, 1970.

1017. Patschovsky, Alexander. "The Literacy of Waldensianism from Valdes to c. 1400." Biller and Hudson 112-136.

1018. ——. "Ekklesiologie bei Johannes Hus." *Lebenslehren und Weltentwürfe im Übergang vom Mittelalter zur Neuzeit: Politik – Bildung – Naturkunde – Theologie*. Ed Hartmut Boockmann et al. Abhandlungen der Akademie der Wissenschaften in Göttingen, Philologisch-Historische Klasse 3, Folge 179. Goettingen, 1989. 370-399.

1019. ——. "'Antichrist' bei Wyclif." Patschovsky and Smahel 83-98.

1020. Patterson, Annabel. *Reading Holinshed's Chronicles*. Chicago: Univ. of Chicago Press, 1994.

1021. ——. "Sir John Oldcastle as a Symbol of Reformation Historiography." *Religion, Literature, and Politics in Post-Reformation England, 1540-2688*. Ed. Donna B. Hamilton and Richard Strier. Cambridge: Cambridge Univ. Press, 1996. 6-26.

1022. Patterson, Lee. "The 'Parson's Tale' and the Quitting of the 'Canterbury Tales.'" *Traditio* 34 (1978): 331-380.

1023. ——. "Chaucer's Pardoner on the Couch: Psyche and Clio in Medieval Literary Studies." *Speculum* 79.3 (July, 2001): 638-80.

1024. Pauli, R. *Bilder aus Alt-England*. 2nd ed. Gotha, 1876. Trans. E.C. Otté. Cambridge, 1861.

1025. Paull, M.R. "Mahomet and the Conversion of the Heathen in *Piers Plowman*." *English Language Notes* 10 (1972): 1-8.

1026. Pearsall, Derek. "Lunatyk Lollares in *Piers Plowman*." *Religion in the Poetry and Drama of the Late Middle Ages in England: the J.A.W. Bennett Memorial Lectures*. Ed. Piero Boitani and Anna Torti. Cambridge: D.S. Brewer, 1990. 163-78.

1027. ——. *The Life of Geoffrey Chaucer: A Critical Biography*. Oxford: Basil Blackwell, 1992.

1028. Peck, Russell. "Social Conscience and the Poets." *Social Unrest in the Later Middle Ages*. Ed. Francis X. Newman. Binghamton: Medieval and Renaissance Texts and Studies, 1986. 113-148.

1029. Peikola, Matti. "On the Trail of Wycliffite Discourse: Notes on the Relationship Between Language Use and Identity in the Wycliffite Sect." *Topics and Comments: Papers from the Discourse Project*. Ed. S.K. Tanskanen and B. Warvik. Turku, Finland: Univ. of Turku, 1994. 75-88.

1030. ——. "'Whom Clepist Thou Trewe Pilgrims?': Lollard Discourse on Pilgrimages in the Testimony of William Thorpe." *Essays and Explorations: A "Freundschrift" for Lisa Dahl.* Ed. M. Gustafsson. Turku, Finland: Univ. of Turku, 1996.

1031. ——. *Congregation of the Elect: Patterns of Self-Fashioning in English Lollard Writings.* Anglicana Turkuensia 21. Turku, Finland: Univ. of Turku, 2000.

1032. Penn, Stephen. "Antiquity, Eternity, and the Foundations of Authority: Reflections on a Debate between John Wyclif and John Kenningham, O. Carm." *Trivium* 32 (2000): 107–119.

1033. Penny, D. Andrew. *Freewill or Predestination: The Battle over Saving Grace in Mid-Tudor England.* London: The Royal Historical Society, 1991.

1034. Peschke, Erhard. "Die Bedeutung Wiclefs für die Theologie der Böhmen." *Zeitschrift für Kirchengeschichte* 54 (1935): 464–83.

1035. Petit-Dutaillis, Charles. "Le Prédications Popularies: Les Lollards et le soulèvement des travailleurs angalis en 1381." *Études d'histoire du Moyen-Âge dédièes à Gabriel Monod.* Ed. L. Cerf et al. Paris, 1896. 373–88.

1036. Phillips, Heather. "John Wyclif and the Optics of the Eucharist." Hudson and Wilks, 245–58.

1037. ——. "John Wyclif and the Religion of the People." *A Distinct Voice: Medieval Studies in Honor of Leonard E. Boyle, O.P.* Ed. Jacqueline Brown and William P. Stoneman. Notre Dame: Univ. of Notre Dame Press, 1997. 561–590.

1038. Phythian-Adams, Charles. *Desolation of a City: Coventry and the Urban Crisis of the Late Middle Ages.* Cambridge: Cambridge Univ. Press, 1979.

1039. Plumb, Derek. "The Social and Economic Spread of Rural Lollardy: A Reappraisal." Sheils and Wood, *Voluntary Religion* 111–129.

1040. ——. "The Social and Economic Status of Later Lollards." Spufford 103–31.

1041. ——. "A Gathered Church? Lollards and their Society." Spufford 132–63.

1042. Poole, Kristen. "Saints Alive! Falstaff, Martin Marprelate, and the Staging of Puritanism." *Shakespeare Quarterly* 46.1 (Spring 1995): 47–76.

1043. Poole, Reginald L. "Wycliffe's Birthplace." *The Athenaeum* 2960 (July 19, 1884): 82.

1044. ——. "On the Intercourse between English and Bohemian Wycliffites in the Early Years of the Fifteenth Century." *English Historical Review* 7 (1892): 306–11.

1045. ——. *Wycliffe and Movements for Reform.* New ed. London: Longmans, Green, 1911.

1046. ——. "Wycliffe's Doctrine of Dominion." *Illustrations of the History of Medieval Thought and Learning.* 2nd ed. Ed. R.L. Poole. London, 1920. 246–68.

1047. Pope, Hugh. "The Lollard Bible." *Dublin Review* 168 (1921): 60–72.

1048. Potkay, Monica B. "*Cleanness* on the Question of Images." *Viator* 26 (1995): 181–93.

1049. Powell, Susan. "Lollards and Lombards: Late Medieval Bogeymen?" *Medium Aevum* 59:1 (1990): 133–39.

1050. Pyper, Rachel. "An Abridgement of Wyclif's *De Mandatis Divinis.*" *Medium Aevum* 52:2 (1983): 306–10.

1051. Rae, H.R. *John Wycliffe – His Life and Writings.* London, 1903.

1052. Ransom, M. "The Chronology of Wyclif's English Sermons." *Research Studies of the State College of Washington* 16 (1948): 67–114.
1053. Rapallo, Umberto. "Ermeneutica e tradizione da Wyclif a Tyndale." *John Wyclif* 81–102.
1054. Rashdall, Hastings. "John Wycliffe." *Dictionary of National Biography*, vol. 21. Ed. L. Stephen and S. Lee. Oxford: Oxford Univ. Press, 1917. 1117–38.
1055. Read, Stephen. "'I Promise a Penny that I do not Promise': The Realist/Nominalist Debate Over Intentional Propositions in Fourteenth Century British Logic and Its Contemporary Relevance." *The Rise of British Logic*. Ed. P.O. Lewry. Toronto: Pontifical Institute, 1985. 335–59.
1056. Reeves, Marjorie. *The Influence of Prophecy in the Later Middle Ages*. Oxford: Clarendon, 1969.
1057. Reeves, W. Peters. "A Second MS. of Wyclif's *De Dominio Civili*." *Modern Language Notes* 50.2 (1935): 96–98.
1058. Reid, E.J.B. "Lollards at Colchester in 1414." *English Historical Review* 29 (1914): 101–04.
1059. Renna, Thomas. "Wyclif's Attacks on the Monks." Hudson and Wilks 267–80.
1060. ——. "Augustine's *De Civitate Dei* in John Wyclif and Thomas More." *Collecteana Augustiniana*. New York: Peter Lang, 1990. 261–71.
1061. Rex, Richard. *The Lollards*. London: Palgrave, 2002.
1062. Richardson, H.G. "Heresy and the Lay Power under Richard II." *English Historical Review* 51 (1936): 1–28.
1063. ——. "John Oldcastle in Hiding, August-October 1417." *English Historical Review* 40 (1940): 432–8.
1064. Robbins, R.H. "Dissent in Middle English Literature: The Spirit of (Thirteen) Seventy-Six." *Medievalia et Humanistica* n.s. 9 (1979): 25–51.
1065. Robertson, Edwin. *John Wycliffe: Morningstar of the Reformation*. Basingstoke: Marshall, 1984.
1066. Robertson, Kellie. "Common Language and Common Profit." *The Postcolonial Middle Ages*. Ed. Jeffrey J. Cohen. New York: St. Martin's, 2000: 209–28.
1067. Robson, J. A. *Wyclif and the Oxford Schools: The Relation of the "Summa de Ente" to Scholastic Debates at Oxford in the Later Fourteenth Century*. Cambridge: Cambridge Univ. Press, 1961.
1068. ——. "John Wyclyf." *Reformers in Profile*. Ed. B.A. Gerrish. Philadelphia: Fortress, 1967. 12–39.
1069. Roth, Francis. *The English Austin Friars 1249–1538*. 2 vols. New York: Augustinian Historical Institute, 1961–66.
1070. Rouse, Richard, and Mary. "The Franciscans and their Books: Lollard Accusations and the Franciscan Response." Hudson and Wilks 364–84. Rpt. in *Authentic Witnesses: Approaches to Medieval Texts and Manuscripts*. Ed. Richard and Mary Rouse. Notre Dame: Notre Dame Univ. Press, 1991. 409–24.
1071. Rubin, Miri. *Corpus Christi: The Eucharist in Late Medieval Culture*. Cambridge: Cambridge Univ. Press, 1991.
1072. ——. "Small Groups: Identity and Solidarity in the Late Middle Ages." *Enterprise and Individuals in Fifteenth-Century England*. Ed. Jennifer Kermode. Wolfeboro Falls, NH: Alan Sutton, 1991. 132–150.
1073. Russell, H.G. "Lollard Opposition to Oaths by Creatures." *American Historical Review* 51 (1946): 668–84.

1074. Russell, J.B., ed. *Religious Dissent in the Middle Ages*. New York: John Wiley, 1971.

1075. Russell-Smith, J.M. "Walter Hilton and a Tract in Defence of the Veneration of Images." *Dominican Studies* 7 (1954): 180–214.

1076. Salter, Elizabeth. "Manuscripts of Nicholas Love's *Myrrour of the Blessed Lyf of Jesu Christ* and Related Texts in Middle English Prose." Edwards and Pearsall 115–127.

1077. Salter, Herbert E. "John Wyclif, Canon of Lincoln." *English Historical Review* 35 (1920): 98.

1078. Samuels, M.L. "The Dialects of MS Bodley 959." Appendix 1 in item 111, vol. 5. Rpt. in *Middle English Dialectology: Essays on Some Principles and Problems*. Ed. A. McIntosh, M.L. Samuels, and M. Laing. Aberdeen: Aberdeen Univ. Press, 1989. 136–149.

1079. Sargent, Michael B. "Minor Devotional Writings." Edwards and Pearsall 147–175.

1080. Scanlon, Larry. *Narrative, Authority, and Power: The Medieval Exemplum and the Chaucerian Tradition*. Cambridge Studies in Medieval Literature 20. Cambridge: Cambridge Univ. Press, 1994.

1081. Scase, Wendy. *Piers Plowman and the New Anticlericalism*. Cambridge: Cambridge Univ. Press, 1989.

1082. ——. *Reginald Pecock*. Authors of the Middle Ages vol. 8.3. Aldershot: Variorum, 1996.

1083. ——. "Reginald Pecock, John Carpenter and John Colop's 'Common-Profit' Books: Aspects of Book Ownership and Circulation in Fifteenth-Century London." *Medium Aevum* 61.2 (1992): 261–74.

1084. ——. "'Strange and Wonderful Bills': Bill-Casting and Political Discourse in Late Medieval England." Copeland, Lawton, and Scase 225–48.

1085. Scattergood, V. John. *Politics and Poetry in the Fifteenth Century*. New York: Barnes and Noble, 1972.

1086. ——. "*Pierce the Ploughman's Crede*: Lollardy and Texts." Aston and Richmond 77–94.

1087. Schaff, D. *Jan Hus*. New York, 1915.

1088. Scherb, Victor. "Conception, Flies, and Heresy in Skelton's 'Replycacion.'" *Medium Aevum* 62 (1993): 51–60.

1089. Schlauch, Margaret. "A Polish Vernacular Eulogy of Wycliff." *Journal of Ecclesiastical History* 8 (1958): 53–73.

1090. Schofield, A. "An English Version of Some Events in Bohemia During 1434." *Slavonic and East European Review* 47.99 (1964): 312–31.

1091. ——. "England and the Council of Basel." *Annuarium Historiae Conciliorum* 5 (1973): 1–117.

1092. Scoufos, A.L. "Nashe, Jonson, and the Oldcastle Problem." *Modern Philology* 65 (1968): 307–24.

1093. Sedlak, J. M. *Jan Hus*. Prague, 1915.

1094. Sell, Alan. "John Wyclif (d. 1384): Anniversary Reflections." *Reformed World* 38.5 (1985): 290–300.

1095. Sergeant, Lewis. *John Wyclif: Last of the Schoolmen and First of the English Reformers*. New York, 1893. Rpt. New York: AMS, 1978.

1096. Shettle, G.T. *John Wycliffe, of Wycliffe, and Other Essays*. Leeds: Jackson, 1922.

1097. Siberry, Elizabeth. "Criticism of Crusading in Fourteenth-Century

England." *Crusade and Settlement*. Ed. Peter W. Edbury. Cardiff: Univ. College Cardiff Press, 1985. 127–34.

1098. Siebert, Georg. *Untersuchungen über An Apology for Lollard Doctrines, einen Wycliffe zugeschriebenen traktat*. Königsberg, 1905.

1099. Simon, H. "Chaucer a Wiclifite." *Essays on Chaucer* 3. Chaucer Society 2nd. Series 16, 1876. 227–92.

1100. Simonetta, Stefano. "Una singolare alleanza: Wyclif e Lancaster." ["A Singular Alliance: John Wyclif and the Duke of Lancaster: A Study of Ecclesial Politics in the 14th-Century English Church."] *Studi Medievali* 36.2 (1995): 797–837.

1101. ———. "John Wyclif between Utopia and Plan." *Société et Église: Textes et discussions dans les universités de l'Europe centrale pendant le moyen âge tardif*. Ed. Sophie Wlodek. Turnhout: Brepols, 1995. 65–86.

1102. ———. "La maturazione del progetto riformatore di Giovanni Wyclif: dal *De Civili Dominio* al *De Officio Regis*." *Medioevo* 22 (1996): 225–58.

1103. ———. "Una riforma prematura? Realizzabilita del progetto di Wyclif." *Pensiero Politico: Rivista di Storia della Idee Politiche e Sociali* 29.3 (1996): 343–73.

1104. ———. "Two Parallel Trains of Anti-Hierocratic Thought in the Fourteenth Century: Marsilius of Padua and John Wyclif." *Rivista Di Storia Della Philosophia* 1997 (52.1): 91–110.

1105. ———. "The Concept of Two Churches in the Religious Philosophy of the English Reformer, John Wyclif." *Studi Medievali* 40 (1999): 119–37.

1106. Skeat, W.W. "On the Dialect of Wyclif's Bible." *Philological Society Transactions* (1895–8): 212–19.

1107. Skinner, Quentin. *The Foundations of Modern Political Thought*. 2 Vols. Cambridge: Cambridge Univ. Press, 1978.

1108. ———. "Political Philosophy." *The Cambridge History of Renaissance Philosophy*. Ed. C.B. Schmitt and Q. Skinner. Cambridge: Cambridge Univ. Press, 1990. 395–452.

1109. Šmahel, František. "'Doctor Evangelicus super omnes evangelistas': Wyclif's Fortune in Hussite Bohemia." *Bulletin of the Institute of Historical Research* 43 (1970): 16–34.

1110. ———. "Hus und Wyclif: 'Opinio Media de Universalibus in Re.'" *Studia Mediewistyczne* 22:1 (1983): 531–37.

1111. ———. *La révolution hussite, une anomalie historique*. Paris: Presses Universitaires de France, 1985.

1112. ———. *Husitska revoluce*. 4 Vols. Prague, 1993.

1113. ———. "Literacy and Heresy in Hussite Bohemia." Biller and Hudson 237–54.

1114. Smalley, Beryl. "John Wyclif's *Postilla super totam Bibliam*." *Bodleian Library Record* 5 (1953): 186–205.

1115. ———. "Problems of Exegesis in the Fourteenth Century." *Antike und Orient im Mittelalter*. Ed. Paul Wilpert. Berlin: Walter de Gruyter, 1962. 266–74.

1116. ———. "Wyclif's *Postilla* on the Old Testament and his *Principium*." Southern 253–96.

1117. ———. *The Study of the Bible in the Middle Ages*. Notre Dame: Univ. of Notre Dame Press, 1964.

1118. ———. "The Bible and Eternity: John Wyclif's Dilemma." *Journal of the Warburg and Courtauld Institutes* 27 (1964): 73–89. Rpt. in *Studies in Medieval Thought and Learning from Abelard to Wyclif*. Ed. Beryl Smalley. London: Hambledon, 1981. 399–415.

1119. Smart, Stefan J. "John Foxe and 'The Story of Richard Hun, Martyr.'" *Journal of Ecclesiastical History* 37.1 (1986): 1–14.

1120. Smeeton, Donald D. *Lollard Themes in the Reformation Theology of William Tyndale.* Kirksville, MO: Sixteenth Century Journal Publishers, 1986.

1121. ——. "Holy Living and the Holy Ghost: A Study in Wycliffite Pneumatology." *Evangelical Quarterly* 59 (Apr. 1987): 139–46.

1122. ——. "The Wycliffite Choice: Man's Law or God's." *William Tyndale and the Law.* Ed. John Dick and A. Richardson. Kirksville, MO: Sixteenth Century Journal Publishers, 1994. 31–40.

1123. Smith, Herbert. "Syntax der Wycliffe-Purveyschen Übersetzung und der 'Authorised Version' der vier Evangelien." *Anglia* 30 (1907): 413–500.

1124. Smith, Herbert M. "Lollardy." *Church Quarterly Review* 119 (1934): 30–60.

1125. Smith, K.S. "An English Conciliarist?: Thomas Netter of Walden at the Councils of Pisa and Constance." *Popes, Teachers, and Canon Law in the Middle Ages.* Ithaca: Cornell Univ. Press, 1989. 290–9.

1126. Snape, M.G. "Some Evidence of Lollard Activity in the Diocese of Durham in the Early Fifteenth Century." *Archaeologia Aeliana,* 4th ser., 39 (1961): 355–61.

1127. Somerset, Fiona. "Vernacular Argumentation in the *Testimony of William Thorpe.*" *Mediaeval Studies* 58 (1996): 207–41.

1128. ——. "Answering the *Twelve Conclusions*: Dymmok's Halfhearted Gestures Towards Publication." Aston and Richmond 52–76.

1129. ——. *Clerical Discourse and Lay Audience in Late Medieval England.* Cambridge: Cambridge Univ. Press, 1998.

1130. ——. "'As just as is a squyre': The Politics of 'Lewed Translacion' in Chaucer's *Summoner's Tale.*" *Studies in the Age of Chaucer* 21 (1999): 187–207.

1131. —— "'Mark him wel for he is on of tho': Training the 'Lewed' Gaze to Discern Hypocrisy." *English Literary History* 68 (2001): 315–34.

1132. ——. "Excitative Speech: Theories of Emotive Response from Richard Fitzralph to Margery Kempe." *The Vernacular Spirit.* Ed. Renate Blumenfeld-Kosinski, Duncan Robertson, and Nancy Bradley Warren. London: Palgrave, 2002. 59–79.

1133. Spencer, Helen Leith. *English Preaching in the Late Middle Ages.* Oxford: Clarendon, 1993.

1134. ——. "The Fortunes of a Lollard Sermon Cycle in the Later Fifteenth Century." *Mediaeval Studies* 48 (1986): 352–396.

1135. Spinka, Matthew. *Jan Hus and the Czech Reform.* Chicago: Univ. of Chicago Press, 1941.

1136. ——. "John Wyclif, Advocate of Radical Reform." Spinka 21–31.

1137. ——. "Paul Kravař and Lollard-Hussite Relations." *Church History* 26 (1956): 16–26.

1138. ——. *Jan Hus's Concept of the Church.* Princeton: Princeton Univ. Press, 1964.

1139. ——. *Jan Hus: A Biography.* Princeton: Princeton Univ. Press, 1968.

1140. Spufford, P. "The Comparative Mobility and Immobility of Lollard Descendants in Early Modern England." Spufford 309–31.

1141. Stacey, John. "The Character of John Wyclif." *London Quarterly and Holborn Review* 184 (1959): 136–39.

1142. ——. "The Piety of John Wyclif." *The Expository Times* 73 (1962): 327–29.

1143. ——. *John Wyclif and Reform.* London: Lutterworth, 1964.

1144 ——. "John Wyclif and the Ministry of the Word." *London Quarterly and Holborn Review* 190 (January 1965): 50–54.

1145. ——. "Wyclif and the Preaching Art." *Expository Times* 93 (1982): 139–42.

1146. ——. "John Wyclif as Theologian." *Expository Times* 101 (1990): 134–41.

1147. ——. "Six Wyclif Sermons." *Epworth Review* 24 (1997): 86–92.

1148. Stackhouse, Ian. "The Native Roots of Early English Reformation Theology." *Evangelical Quarterly* 66 (1994): 19–35.

1149. Stanbury, Sarah. "The Vivacity of Images: St. Katherine, Knighton's Lollards, and the Breaking of Idols." Dimmick, Simpson, and Zeeman, 131–50.

1150. Stein, I.H. "Another 'Lost' Chapter of Wyclif's *Summa de Ente*." *Speculum* 3 (1928): 254–55.

1151. ——. "The Wyclif Manuscript in Florence." *Speculum* 5 (1930): 95–97.

1152. ——. "Two Notes on Wyclif." *Speculum* 6 (1931): 465–68.

1153. ——. "The Vatican Manuscript Borghese 29 and the Tractate *De Versuciis Anti-Christi*." *English Historical Review* 47 (1932): 465–8.

1154. Steiner, Emily. "Inventing Legality: Documentary Culture and Lollard Preaching." *The Letter of the Law: Legal Practice and Literary Production in Medieval England*. Ed. Emily Steiner and Candace Barrington. Ithaca: Cornell Univ. Press, 2002. 185–201.

1155. Stevenson, Joseph. *The Truth about John Wyclif, His Life, Writings, and Opinions*. London: Burns and Oates, 1885.

1156. Strohm, Paul. *Social Chaucer*. Cambridge: Harvard Univ. Press, 1989.

1157. ——. "Chaucer's Lollard Joke: History and the Textual Unconscious." *Studies in the Age of Chaucer* 17 (1995): 23–42.

1158. ——. "Counterfeiters, Lollards, and Lancastrian Unease." Scase, Copeland, and Lawton, 31–58.

1159. ——. *England's Empty Throne: Usurpation and the Language of Legitimation, 1399–1422*. New Haven: Yale Univ. Press, 1998.

1160. ——. *Theory and the Premodern Text*. Medieval Cultures 26. Minneapolis: Univ. of Minnesota Press, 2000.

1161. Sturges, Robert S. "Anti-Wycliffite Commentary in Richardson MS 22." *Harvard Library Bulletin* 34.4 (Fall, 1986): 380–395.

1162. Summers, William H. *Our Lollard Ancestors*. London: National Council of Evangelical Free Churches, 1904.

1163. ——. *The Lollards of the Chiltern Hills: Glimpses of English Dissent in the Middle Ages*. London: Francis Griffiths, 1906.

1164. Summerson, Henry. "An English Bible and Other Books Belonging to Henry IV." *Bulletin of the John Rylands Library* 79.1 (1997): 109–15.

1165. Swanson, R.N. *Church and Society in Late Medieval England*. Oxford: Basil Blackwell, 1989.

1166. ——. *Religion and Devotion in Europe, c. 1215–c. 1515*. Cambridge: Cambridge Univ. Press, 1995.

1167. ——. "A Small Library for Pastoral Care and Spiritual Instruction in Late Medieval England." *Journal of the Early Book Society* 5 (2002): 99–120.

1168. Swiderska, H.M. "A Polish Follower of John Wyclif in the Fifteenth Century." *University of Birmingham Historical Journal* 6 (1957–58): 88–92.

1169. Szittya, Penn R. *The Antifraternal Tradition in Medieval Literature*. Princeton: Princeton Univ. Press, 1986.

1170. Talbert, Ernst W. "The Date of the Composition of the English Wycliffite Collection of Sermons." *Speculum* 12 (1937): 464–74.

1171. ——. "A Fifteenth-Century Lollard Sermon Cycle." *University of Texas Studies in English* 19 (1939): 5–30.

1172. ——. "A Note on the Wycliffite Bible Translation." The University of Texas, *Studies in English* 20 (1940): 29–38.

1173. Tanner, Norman P. *The Church in Late Medieval Norwich 1370–1532.* Studies and Texts 66. Toronto: Pontifical Institute, 1984.

1174. ——. "Penances Imposed on Kentish Lollards by Archbishop Warham 1511–12." Aston and Richmond 229–249.

1175. Tatlock, J.S.P. "Chaucer and Wycliffe." *Modern Philology* 14 (Sept. 1916): 257–68.

1176. Tatnall, Edith Comfort. "John Wyclif and Ecclesia Anglicana." *Journal of Ecclesiastical History* 30 (1969): 19–43.

1177. ——. "The Condemnation of John Wyclif at the Council of Constance." *Councils and Assemblies.* Ed. G.J. Cuming and D. Baker. Studies in Church History 7. Oxford: Basil Blackwell, 1971. 209–18.

1178. Tavard, George H. *Holy Writ or Holy Church.* London: Burns and Oates, 1959.

1179. Taylor, Andrew. "'To Pley a Pagyn of the Devyl': *Turpiloquium* and the *Scurrae* in Early Drama." *Medieval English Theatre* 11:1–2 (1989): 162–74.

1180. ——. *Textual Situations: Three Medieval Manuscripts and their Readers.* Philadelphia: Univ. of Pennsylvania Press, 2002.

1181. Terasawa, Yoshio. "A Rhetorical Spoken Style of M.E.: The Case of Wyclif's Sermon Translation." *Studies in English Literature* (1968): 61–81.

1182. ——. "The Epistle to the Ephesians in a Manuscript of the Wycliffite Bible (EV)." *Seisho to Eibungaku o Megutte.* Ed. T. Yamamoto. Tokyo: Pedilavium, 1982.

1183. ——. "Wyclif to Lollard Bible: Kenkyu no Genkyo to Kadai." *Eigo Seinen* 130 (1984): 374–376.

1184. Tew, Tony, dir. *John Wycliffe: The Morning Star.* Perf. John Howell. Gateway Films, 1984.

1185. Thamm, Walter. *Das Relativpronomen in der Bibelübersetzung Wyclifs und Purveys.* Berlin, 1908.

1186. Thomas, Alfred. *Anne's Bohemia: Czech Literature and Society, 1310–1420.* Minnesota: Univ. of Minnesota Press, 1997.

1187 Thomson, J.A.F. "A Lollard Rising in Kent: 1431 or 1438?" *Bulletin of the Institute of Historical Research* 37 (1964): 100–02.

1188. ——. "John Foxe and Some Sources for Lollard History: Notes for a Critical Reappraisal." *Studies in Church History* 2. Ed. G.J. Cuming. London: Nelson, 1965. 251–57.

1189. ——. *The Later Lollards, 1414–1520.* Oxford: Oxford Univ. Press, 1965.

1190. ——. "Orthodox Religion and the Origins of Lollardy." *History* 74 (1989): 39–55.

1191. ——. "Knightly Piety and the Margins of Lollardy." Aston and Richmond 95–111.

1192. Thomson, S. Harrison. "Three Unprinted *Opuscula* of John Wyclif." *Speculum* 3 (1928): 248–253.

1193. ——. "Some Latin Works Erroneously Ascribed to Wyclif." *Speculum* 3 (1928): 382–391.

1194. ——. "The Order of Writing of Wyclif's Philosophical Works." *Českou Minulostí.* Ed. O. Odložilík et al. Prague, 1929. 146–165.

1195. ———. "The Philosophical Basis of Wyclif's Theology." *Journal of Religion* 11.2 (January 1931): 86–116.

1196. ———. "A Gonville and Caius Wyclif Manuscript." *Speculum* 8 (1933): 197–204.

1197. ———. "Pre-Hussite Heresy in Bohemia." *English Historical Review* (1933): 23–42.

1198. ———. "Unnoticed Manuscripts and Works of Wyclif." *Journal of Theological Studies* 38 (1937): 24–36, 139–48.

1199. ———. "Wyclif or Wyclyf?" *English Historical Review* 53 (1938): 675–8.

1200. ———. "Unnoticed Manuscripts of Wyclyf's *De Veritate Sacre Scripture.*" *Medium Aevum* 12 (1943): 68–70.

1201. ———. "A Note on Peter Payne and Wyclyf." *Medievalia et Humanistica* o.s. 16 (1964): 60–3.

1202. ———. "Later Medieval Reform: John Wyclyf." *Reformers in Profile.* Ed. B.A. Gerrish. Philadelphia: Fortress, 1967. 12–39.

1203. Thomson, Williell R. "An Unknown Letter by John Wyclyf in Manchester, John Rylands University Library MS. Eng. 86." *Mediaeval Studies* 43 (1981): 531–37.

1204. ———. "*Manuscripta Wyclifiana Desiderata*: The Potential Contribution of Missing Latin Texts to our Image of Wyclif's Life and Works." Hudson and Wilks 343–351.

1205. Thompson, A. Hamilton. *The English Clergy and their Organisation in the Later Middle Ages.* Oxford: Oxford Univ. Press, 1947.

1206. Thompson, E. M. *Wycliffe Exhibition at the King's Library.* London: British Museum, 1884.

1207. Thompson, J. Radford. *The Life and Work of John Wiclif.* London, 1884.

1208. Tierney, Brian. "'Sola Scriptura' and the Canonists." *Collectanae Stephan Kuttner I, Studia Gratiana Post Octava Decreti Saecularia XI.* Ed. I. Forchielli and A.M. Stickler. Bologna, 1967. 347–66.

1209. ———. *Religion, Law, and the Growth of Constitutional Thought 1150–1650.* Cambridge: Cambridge Univ. Press, 1982.

1210. ———. "Tuck on Rights: Some Medieval Problems." *History of Political Thought* 4.3 (Winter, 1983): 429–411.

1211. ———. "Origins of Natural Rights Language: Texts and Contexts 1150–1250." *History of Political Thought* 10.4 (Winter, 1989): 615–646.

1212. ———. "Marsilius on Rights." *Journal of the History of Ideas* 52 (1991): 3–17.

1213. ———. *The Idea of Natural Rights: Studies on Natural Rights, Natural Law, and Church Law 1150–1625.* Emory University Studies on Law and Religion 5. Atlanta: Scholars, 1997.

1214. Töpfer, Bernhard. "*Lex Christi, dominum* und kirchliche Hierarchie bei Johannes Hus im Vergleich mit John Wyklif." Seibt 157–65.

1215. ———. "Die Wertung der weltlich-staatlichen Ordnung durch John Wyclif und Jan Hus." Šmahel and Müller-Luckner 55–76.

1216. Trapp, Damasus. "Unchristened Nominalism and Wycliffite Realism at Prague in 1381." *Recherches de Theologie ancienne et medievale* 24 (1957): 320–60.

1217. Treschow, Michael. "On Aristotle and the Cross at the Center of Creation: John Wyclif's *De Benedicta Incarnacione*, Chapter Seven." *Crux* 33 (1977): 28–37.

1218. Tresko, Michael. "John Wyclif's Metaphysics of Scriptural Integrity in the *De Veritate Sacrae Scripturae.*" *Dionysius* 13 (Dec. 1989): 153–96.

1219. Trevelyan, G.M. *England in the Age of Wycliffe*. New Edition. London: Longmans, Green, 1909.

1220. Trivedi, Kalpen. "The *Pore Caitif*: Lectio through Compilatio. Some Manuscript Contexts." *Framing the Text*. Ed. K.L. Boardman, Catherine Emmerson, and A.P. Tudor. *Medievalia* 20 (2001): 129–52.

1221. Trtik, Zdenek. "Jan Hus als philosophischer Realist." *Theologische-Zeitschrift* 28 (1972): 263–75.

1222. Tuck, Anthony J. "Carthusian Monks and Lollard Knights: Religious Attitudes at the Court of Richard II." *Studies in the Age of Chaucer* 1 (1984): 149–61.

1223. Tuck, Richard. *Natural Rights Theories: Their Origin and Development*. Cambridge: Cambridge Univ. Press, 1979.

1224. Twemlow, J.A. "Wycliffe's Preferments and University Degrees." *English Historical Review* 15 (1900): 529–30.

1225. Tyler, C. *Tares and Wheat: A Memorial of John Wycliffe*. London, 1897.

1226. Utz, Richard J. "'For All That Comth, Comth by Necessitee': Chaucer's Critique of Fourteenth-Century Boethianism in *Troilus and Criseyde* IV, 957–58." *Arbeiten aus Anglistik und Amerikanistik* 21.1 (1996): 29–32.

1227. Vale, M.G.A. *Piety, Charity, and Literacy Among the Yorkshire Gentry, 1370–1480*. York: Borthwick Papers, no. 50, 1976.

1228. van Engen, John. "Anticlericalism among the Lollards." *Anticlericalism in Late Medieval and Early Modern Europe*. Ed. Peter Dykema and Heiko A. Oberman. Leiden: E.J. Brill, 1993. 53–63.

1229. Varley, H. *John Wyclif: A Chapter from English Church History*. London, 1884.

1230. Vasold, Manfred. *Fruhling im Mittelalter: John Wyclif und sein Jahrhundert*. Munich: List, 1984.

1231. Vassilev, Georgi. "Bogomils and Lollards: Dualistic Motives in England during the Later Middle Ages." *Etudes Balkaniques* 1 (1993): 97–111.

1232. ——. "Traces of the Bogomil Movement in English." *Etudes Balkaniques* 3 (1994): 85–94.

1233. ——. "Bogomils, Cathars, Lollards, and the High Social Position of Women during the Middle Ages." *Facta Universitatis. Series Philosophy and Sociology* 2.7 (2000): 325–36.

1234. Vattier, Victor. *John Wyclyff, D.D.: Sa Vie, Ses Oeurvres, Sa Doctrine*. Paris: Ernest Leroux, 1886.

1235. Vaughan, Robert. *The Life and Opinions of John De Wycliffe D. D.* 2 vols. 2nd ed. London: Holdsworth and Ball, 1831.

1236. —— *John De Wycliffe: A Monograph*. London: Seeleys, 1853.

1237. Vidmanova, Anezka. "Autoritaten und Wiclif in Hussens homiletischen Schriften." Zimmermann 383–93.

1238. Voegelin, Eric. *The Collected Works of Eric Voegelin*. Ed. David Walsh. Volume 21. The History of Political Ideas, Volume III: The Later Middle Ages. Columbia: Univ. of Missouri Press, 1998.

1239. Volz, Carl A. *The Medieval Church: From the Dawn of the Middle Ages to the Eve of the Reformation*. Nashville: Abingdon, 1997.

1240. von Nolcken, Christina. "Some Alphabetical Compendia and How Preachers Used Them in Fourteenth-Century England." *Viator* 12 (1981): 271–88.

1241. ——. "An Unremarked Group of Wycliffite Sermons in Latin." *Modern Philology* 83 (1986): 233–49.

1242. ——. "Another Kind of Saint: A Lollard Perception of John Wyclif." Hudson and Wilks 429–43.

1243. ——. "*Piers Plowman*, the Wycliffites, and *Pierce the Plowman's Creed*." *Yearbook of Langland Studies* 2 (1988): 71–102.

1244. ——. "Wyclif in Our Times: The Wyclif Sexcentenary, 1984." *Yearbook of Langland Studies* 2 (1988): 143–54.

1245. ——. "Richard Wyche, A Certain Knight, and the Beginning of the End." Aston and Richmond 127–154.

1246. ——. "Lay Literacy, the Democritization of God's Law, and the Lollards." *The Bible as Book: The Manuscript Tradition.* Ed. K. Van Kampen and John L. Sharpe III. London: British Library, 1998. 177–95.

1247. ——. "Notes on Lollard Citation of John Wyclif's Writings." *Journal of Theological Studies* n.s. 39.2 (October, 1998): 411–37.

1248. ——. "A 'Certain Sameness' and our Response to it in English Wycliffite Texts." R. Newhauser and John Alford, eds. *Literature and Religion in the Later Middle Ages: Philological Studies in Honor of Siegfried Wenzel.* Binghamton: Medieval and Renaissance Texts and Studies, 1995. 191–208.

1249. Wager, Charles A. "Pecock's *Repressor* and the Wiclif Bible." *Modern Language Notes* 9 (1894): 97–9.

1250. Walker, G. "Saint or Schemer? The 1527 Heresy Trial of Thomas Bilney Reconsidered." *Journal of Ecclesiastical History* 40.2 (1989): 219–38.

1251. ——. "Heretical Sects in Pre-Reformation England." *History Today* 43 (May, 1993): 42–48.

1252. Wallace, David. "Dante in Somerset: Ghosts, Historiography, Periodization." Lawton, Copeland, and Scase 9–38.

1253. Walsh, Katherine. "The Manuscripts of Archbishop Richard Fitzralph of Armagh in the Österreichische Nationalbibliothek, Vienna." *Römische historiche Mitteilungen* 18 (1976): 67–75.

1254. ——. *A Fourteenth Century Scholar and Primate: Richard FitzRalph of Oxford, Avignon, and Armagh.* Oxford: Oxford Univ. Press, 1981.

1255. ——. "Vom Wegestreit zur Häresie: Zur Auseinandersetzung um die Lehre John Wyclifs in Wien un Prage an der Wende zum 15. Jahrhundert." *Mitteilungen des Instituts für österreichische Geschichtsforschung* 94 (1986): 25–47.

1256. ——. "Wyclif's Legacy in Central Europe in the Late Fourteenth and Early Fifteenth Centuries." Hudson and Wilks 397–417.

1257. ——. "Die Rezeption der Schriften des Richard Fitzralph (Ardmacanus) im lollardisch-hussistischen Milieu." *Das Publikum politischer Theorie im 14. Jahrhundert*, ed. Jürgen Miethke. Munich: Oldenbourg, 1992. 237–53.

1258. ——. "Die englische Universität nach Wyclif: Von geistiger Kreativität zur Beamtenausbildung?" *Die Universität in Alteuropa*, ed. Alexander Patschovsky and Horst Rabe. Constance: Universitätsverlag Konstanz, 1994. 85–110.

1259. ——. "*Ecce arbor in medie terre*. Ein irische Prälat an der Prager Juristenuniversität, das 'Purgatorium sancti Patricii,' und die Dbatta um das Fegefeuer." Pánek, Polívka, and Rejchrtová 167–90.

1260. ——. "Lollardisch-hussitische Reformbestrebunge im Umkreis und Gefolgschaft der Luxemburgerin Anna, Köningin von England (1382–1394)." Šmahel and Müller-Luckner 77–108.

1261. Warner, Anthony. "Infinitive Markings in the Wyclifite Sermons." *English Studies* 56 (1975): 207–14.

1262. ——. *Complementation in Middle English and the Methodology of Historical Syntax: a Study of the Wyclifite Sermons*. University Park: Pennsylvania State Univ. Press, 1982.

1263. Watkinson, W.L. *John Wicklif*. London, 1884.

1264. Watson, Nicholas. *Richard Rolle and the Invention of Authority*. Cambridge: Cambridge Univ. Press, 1991.

1265. ——. "Censorship and Cultural Change in Late-Medieval England: Vernacular Theology, The Oxford Translation Debate, and Arundel's Constitutions of 1409." *Speculum* 70.4 (October 1995): 822–864.

1266. ——. "Conceptions of the Word: The Mother Tongue and the Incarnation of God." Scase, Copeland, and Lawton 85–124.

1267. Waugh, W.T. "Sir John Oldcastle." *English Historical Review* 20 (1905): 434–56, 637–58.

1268. ——. "The Lollard Knights." *Scottish Historical Review* 11 (1913–14): 55–92.

1269. Wawn, Andrew N. "The Genesis of *the Plowman's Tale*." *Yearbook of English Studies* 2 (1972): 21–40.

1270. ——. "Chaucer, Wyclif, and the Court of Apollo." *English Language Notes* 10 (1972): 15–20.

1271. ——. "Chaucer, *The Plowman's Tale*, and Reformation Propoganda: The Testimonies of Thomas Godfray and *I Playne Piers*." *Bulletin of the John Rylands Library* 56 (1973–74): 174–92.

1272. Welch, E. "Three Sussex Heresy Trials." *Sussex Archaeological Collections* 95 (1957): 59–70.

1273. ——. "Some Suffolk Lollards." *Proceedings of the Suffolk Institute of Archaeology* 29 (1962): 154–65.

1274. Wenzel, Siegfried. *Verses in Sermons*. Cambridge, MA: Medieval Academy of America, 1978.

1275. ——. *Macaronic Sermons: Bilingualism and Preaching in Late Medieval England*. Ann Arbor: Univ. of Michigan Press, 1994.

1276. ——. "Academic Sermons at Oxford in the Early Fifteenth Century." *Speculum* 70.2 (April, 1995): 305–329.

1277. ——. "A New Version of Wyclif's 'Sermones Quadraginta.'" *Journal of Theological Studies* 49 (April, 1998): 154–60.

1278. ——. "Robert Lychlade's Oxford Sermon of 1395 (Lollard Sympathies and Heretical Teachings in England)." *Traditio* 53 (1998): 203–30.

1279. Westin, Gunnar. *John Wyclif och has Reformidéer*. 2 vols. Uppsala: Almqvist & Wiksell, 1936.

1280. White, Helen C. *Social Criticism in Popular Religious Literature of the Sixteenth Century*. New York: Macmillan, 1944.

1281. Whitney, James P. "A Note on the Work of the Wyclif Society." *Essays in History Presented to Reginald Lane Poole*. Ed. Henry W.C. Davis. Oxford: Clarendon, 1927. 98–114.

1282. Wiegand, Friedrich. *De Ecclesiae Notione quid Wiclif docuerit*. Leipzig, 1892.

1283. Wilks, Michael. "The Apostolicus and the Bishop of Rome." *Journal of Theological Studies* n.s. 13 (1962): 290–317; 14 (1963): 311–54.

1284. ——. *The Problem of Sovereignty in the Later Middle Ages*. Cambridge: Cambridge Univ. Press, 1963.

1285. ——. "Predestination, Property, and Power: Wyclif's Theory of Dominion and Grace." Baker 220–236. Rpt. in Wilks 16–32.

1286. ——. "The Early Oxford Wyclif: Papalist or Nominalist?" Cuming 69–98. Rpt. in Wilks 33–62.

1287. ——. "*Reformatio Regni*: Wyclif and Hus as Leaders of Religious Protest Movements." Baker, *Schism* 109–130. Rpt. in Wilks 63–84.

1288. ——. "Misleading Manuscripts: Wyclif and the Non-Wycliffite Bible." Baker, *Materials* 147–61. Rpt. in Wilks 85–100.

1289. ——. "Royal Priesthood: The Origins of Lollardy." *The Church in a Changing Society: Conflict – Reconciliation or Adjustment?* CIHEC Conference in Uppsala, 1977. Uppsala: Uppsala Univ., 1978. 63–70. Rpt. in Wilks 101–116.

1290. ——. "Royal Patronage and Anti-papalism from Ockham to Wyclif." Hudson and Wilks 135–164. Rpt. in Wilks 117–146.

1291. ——. "*Thesaurus Ecclesiae* [Wyclif's Views on Wealth]." Sheils and Wood, *Church and Wealth* xv–xlv. Rpt. in Wilks 147–178.

1292. ——. "Wyclif and the Great Persecution." *Prophecy and Eschatology*. Ed. Michael Wilks. Studies in Church History, Subsidia 10. Oxford: Basil Blackwell, 1994. 39–63. Rpt. in Wilks 179–204.

1293. ——. "Wyclif and the Wheel of Time." *The Church Retrospective*. Ed. R.N. Swanson. Studies in Church History 33. Oxford: Basil Blackwell, 1997. 177–93. Rpt. in Wilks 205–222.

1294. ——. "Thomas Arundel of York: The Appellant Archbishop." Wood, *Life and Thought* 57–86. Rpt. in Wilks 223–252.

1295. ——. "John Wyclif, Reformer, c. 1327–1384." Wilks 1–15.

1296. ——. "Roman Candle or Damned Squib? The English Crusade of 1383." Wilks 253–72.

1297. Wilkins, H.J. *Was John Wyclif a Negligent Pluralist? Also John de Trevisa, His Life and Work*. London: Longmans, Green, 1915.

1298. Williams, Arnold. "Chaucer and the Friars." *Speculum* 28.3 (1953): 499–513.

1299. Williams, C.H. *William Tyndale*. London: Thomas Nelson, 1969.

1300. Wilson, John Laird. *John Wycliffe, Patriot and Reformer, The Morning Star of the Reformation*. New York, 1884.

1301. Wlodek, Zofia. "Les Idees Theologico-politiques dans l'ecclesiologie de Thomas Netter Waldensis." *Soziale Ordnungen im Selbstverständnis des Mittelalters*. Ed. Albert Zimmermann. Berlin: Walter de Gruyter, 1980. 439–448.

1302. ——. "Der Begriff des Seins bei Thomas Netter von Walden." *Salzburger Jahrbuch für Philosophie* 26–7 (1981–82): 103–16.

1303. ——. "Les Idees Cles de la Philosophie d L'etre chez Thomas Netter de Walden." *Studia Mediewistyczne* 27:1 (1990): 1–30.

1304. Wood, Douglas C. *The Evangelical Doctor: John Wycliffe and the Lollards*. Welwyn, Hertfordshire: Evangelical Press, 1984.

1305. Wood, Rega, and Gideon Gál. "Richard Brinkley and his Summa Logica." *Franciscan Studies* 40 (1980): 59–102.

1306. Woolf, Rosemary. *The English Mystery Plays*. London: Routledge and Kegan Paul, 1972.

1307. Workman, Herbert B. "The First English Bible." *London Quarterly Review* 135 (1921): 187–99.

1308. ——. *John Wyclif: A Study of the English Medieval Church*. 2 vols. Oxford: Clarendon, 1926.

1309. Wray, J.J. *John Wyclif: A Quincentenary Tribute*. London, 1884.

1310. Wunderli, R. "Pre-Reformation Summoners and the Murder of Richard Hunne." *Journal of Ecclesiastical History* 33 (1982): 209–24.

1311. Wurtele, Douglas J. "The Anti-Lollardy of Chaucer's Parson." *Mediaevalia* 11 (1989, for 1985): 151–68.

1312. Yonekura, H. *The Language of the Wycliffite Bible: The Syntactic Differences between the Two Versions.* Tokyo: Aratake Shuppan, 1985.

1313. ——. "John Purvey's Version of the Wycliffite Bible: A Reconsideration of His Translation Method." *Studies in Medieval English Language and Literature* 1 (1986): 67–91.

1314. Young, Robert F. "Bohemian Scholars and Students at the English Universities from 1347–1750." *English Historical Review* 38 (1923): 72–84.

1315. Zuckerman, Charles. "The Relationship of Theories of Universals to Theories of Church Government in the Middle Ages: A Critique of Previous Views." *Journal of the History of Ideas* 35 (1975): 579–594.

Part B: Introductions to Selected Topics

These paragraphs are intended to introduce current arguments in the field, to enable researchers to uncover connections between Lollardy and various specific issues, and to make Part A accessible to those unfamiliar with the field or some aspect of it. They are keyed to the numbers in Part A. The references, especially those in sections 1–12 and 16, are designed to give a breadth of coverage which can lead to further bibliography. It cannot be emphasized enough therefore that these paragraphs are not prescriptive, definitive, or exhaustive; they merely provide a start. They do not include all of the references in Part A on any given topic, nor do they provide a historical retrospective of arguments in the field (on this, see the essays in this volume by Geoffrey Martin and Anne Hudson). References are also not made to essays in this volume. There is some repetition since it assumes that readers will dip in for specific topics. Ultimately this Bibliography, and especially this section, cannot help but be somewhat idiosyncratic, yet hopefully this arrangement will nevertheless provide stimulation for further work, especially across traditional disciplinary boundaries.

1. General Introductions

The most important of these is Hudson's *The Premature Reformation* (713), an immensely important study of Lollard texts, history, thought, culture, and influence. This book could be cited under every section, and so with that notable caveat will be cited only to note specifics of its arguments. Chapters in McKisack (942) on medieval history, Haigh (618) and Jacob (744) on Tudor and Reformation history, and Lambert (821) on medieval heresy provide good, general introductions. Other general discussions of Wyclif and the movement include Catto (375), Justice (766), Kenny (784), Rex (1061), and Thomson (1190). Initial reference should also be made to the essay collections by Aston (43–44), Aston and Richmond (45), Hudson (67), Hudson and Wilks (68), Kenny (73), and Wilks (92).

Several editions of primary texts are vital. Wyclif's Latin works (236–54) are mostly untranslated, and are not all edited – Thomson (39) provides a full index. Of vernacular texts, the most prominent edition is Hudson and Gradon's *English Wycliffite Sermons* (158), not only for the sermons, but also for the introductory essays and notes. Other editions of sermons are listed in Section 7. The Lollard Bible has not been edited in its entirety since Forshall and Madden (106), who inevitably did not know of many manuscripts; see Section 6 for newer editions. For shorter texts, see Hudson (155) first; Matthew (182) and volume three of Arnold (100) are helpful though over a century old. Other editions of avowedly Lollard texts include the *Lantern of Liȝt* (174), Lindberg's two volumes entitled *English Wyclif Tracts* (177–78), the *Tractatus de Regibus* (145, a translation of Wyclif's *De Officio Regis*), and the texts preserved in the *Fasciculi zizaniorum* (139). There are editions of other texts listed in Section 3 of Part A, and more still exist in unpublished dissertations and theses. Much, however, remains only in manuscript.

2. Biographies of Wyclif

Von Nolcken (1242) notes two different approaches to Wyclif's life: academic and hagiographic. Both are included since both are relevant to the study of Lollard history. Hagiographies and apologies include Burrows (360), Bushill (361), Chapman (387), Deane (474), Figgis (544), Freemantle (575), S. Green (612), Harding (639), Holt (680), Jäger (747), Lupton (901–02), Milligan (953), Rae (1051), Tew (1184, a video), J.R. Thompson (1207), Tyler (1225), Varley (1229), Vattier (1234), R. Vaughan (1235–36), Watkinson (1263), Wilson (1300), and Wray (1309). Crompton (439) has written on this "mythology."

In academic studies, Workman (1308) marks a watershed in Lollard studies, though many of its points large and small have been modified by later scholarship. Entries in Emden (6), G.R. Evans (534), and the *Dictionary of National Biography* by Rashdall (1054) are helpful introductions (and the *DNB* should soon be updated with a new entry by Hudson and Kenny). Other critical work on his life includes Benrath (311), Catto (378), Dahmus (447–52), Hudson (718), Kenny (784, 786), Leff (834, 844), Lytle (906), McFarlane (933), and Wilks (1295). Hudson (733) comments on his possible place of origin. Two informative exhibition catalogues on Wyclif and his works are by Catto, Gradon, and Hudson (383) and Hudson (704).

3. Biographies of Other Figures

For figures which precede Wyclif: Fitzralph (often "Ardmacan") is the subject of a biography by Walsh (1254) and figures prominently in Szittya (1169); also see Section 5 below. On Uthred (or Uhtred) of Boldon, who preceded Wyclif at Oxford, see Catto (378, with bibliography) and Hudson (733).

Nicholas Hereford was named as a possible translator of the Later Version (LV) of the Wycliffite translation by Deanesly (475) and, more recently, Lindberg (109–10, 112, 114, 116). Lindberg also names Wyclif as a translator of the Early Version (EV) and Trevisa as a collaborator on the LV, though Hudson (713) sees no conclusive evidence of this, arguing that virtually no extant vernacular Lollard texts can be with confidence ascribed to a known author. On Hereford also see Catto (378), Hudson (709), Forde (151), and on Hereford and Trevisa see Fowler (572).

Peter Payne, who began in Oxford and traveled to Bohemia, is the subject of a hagiographical biography by Baker (291); more recently see S.H. Thomson (1201), and in Catto (378), Emden (523), and Hudson (696).

John Purvey was considered by Deanesly (475) to be a possible translator of the Bible and the author of the General Prologue; this view is assumed by many including, for instance, Carr (369), Grimm (615), Hargreaves (640), and Yonekura (1313). Again, Hudson (713) finds no concrete evidence of his involvement, though see Jurkowski (760).

Philip Repingdon (sometimes Repton), an early Lollard who later recanted and became bishop of Lincoln, is discussed by Archer (267), Catto (378), Forde (560), Martin's edition of Knighton (165), and Hudson (709).

William Thorpe's and William Taylor's works are edited by Hudson (156). Thorpe's life and works are commented on by Aers and Staley (263), Copeland (418), Hudson (714), Jurkowski (763), Peikola (1030), Somerset (1129), and Steiner (1154).

The so-called "Lollard Knights" first figured in Waugh (1268), which McFarlane (934) takes as the starting point for his well-known essay; on them see also Catto (372, 377) and Tuck (1222). Clanvowe's literary works are edited by Scattergood (129).

Sir John Oldcastle, his rebellion, and his later status as Lollard martyr are discussed by Aston (269), Brooks (355), Hargreaves (646), A. Patterson (1021), K. Poole (1042), Richardson (1063), Strohm (1159–60), and Waugh (1267). Also see Section 9, below, on Hoccleve's "Remonstrance against Oldcastle."

For mention of other Lollard figures, see, for example, McNiven (944) and Strohm (1160) on John Badby; Aston (275) on William White; Trefnant's *Register* (213) for material on Swinderby and Brut (among others); Bostick (335), Hudson (722), and Nissé (990) also on Brut; Jurkowski (759, 761) on Tykhill and other lawyers; and von Nolcken (1245) on Wyche. See section 15 for studies of women and Lollardy.

For opponents to Lollardy, see Aston (273) and essays by R.G. Davies (459), Watson (1265), and Wilks (1294) on Archbishop Arundel; Dahmus' biography of Courtenay (453) and Jacob's of Chichele (745) discuss two other involved Archbishops; also see McHardy (183) for Courtenay's *acta* as Archbishop. Trefnant's *Register* (213) and McHardy's article on Buckingham (938) detail the work of other bishops. On Richard II, see especially Aston (279, in a volume of essays on his reign), Bennett (305), R.G. Davies (461, in another essay collection on his reign), and Dahmus (451); on Henry IV and V see especially Catto (374, in a volume of essays on Henry V), Horner (684), McNiven (945) and Strohm (1159).

Academic opponents include Ullerston, a faculty member at Oxford who wrote a determination against translation; on him see Bühler (126), Catto (378), Deanesly (475, who thought his tract was by Purvey), and Hudson (696). Woodford's works are edited and discussed in Brown (125, vol. 1), E. Doyle (508–09), and Ghosh (598). On Netter, see Ghosh (598), Harvey (655), Hurley (739), K.S. Smith (1125), and Somerset (1129).

Work on Reginald Pecock is proliferating; see, e.g., Brockwell (354), Emerson (524), N. Evans (536), Foss (569), V.H.H. Green (614), Haines (622), Jacob (743), Patrouch (1016), and Scase (1082–83). On John Trevisa, see Fowler (572) and Somerset (1129).

The "later Lollards" are the subject of J.A.F. Thomson (1189). Mudroch (971) contains brief discussion of intellectual followers through the eighteenth century. On Tyndale see David (457); on Cranmer see MacCulloch (908); on Bale see Fairfield (541) and Happé (638). On Hus and central Europe see Section 15.

4. History

For a general historical introduction see the studies cited in Section 1, above. Harper-Bill (649) and Swanson (1165 with 206) provide introductions to the period which place Lollardy in context with contemporary documents as illustrations. Hansford-Miller (637) and Trevelyan (1219) draw geographical maps of Lollard influence.

On the 1381 Peasants' Revolt see Aers (259), Aston (269), Barr (296), Crane (436), Green (610), Hansen (636), and Justice (765). Dean (133) and Dobson (135) collect contemporary documents. Gower refers to it (148–49). Chroniclers attribute it to Lollards – see Knighton (165) for example – though this is, as Aston argues, most likely revisionist history. Also see the references to John Ball, above in Section 3. On other peasant movements see Goheen (607) and J.A.F. Thomson (1187); on Oldcastle, see above in Section 3.

Trial proceedings have been edited by Tanner for Norwich (208) and Kent (209). Discussions of trials include Arnold (268), Copeland (417, 422), Justice (764), Nissé (989) and Steiner (1154) on Norwich, and Fines (546) on Lichfield. Hudson (694) writes on the process of interrogation. Trefnant's *Register* (213) contains information on Hereford diocese, and Jenkins (754) quotes several abjurations in Canterbury from Morton's *Register*. McSheffrey (949) appends lists of those prosecuted for Lollardy in heresy trials.

For discussions of chronicles and other historical documents, see introductions to the editions, as well as Crane (436), Havens (659), Justice (765), Martin (924), and R.F. Green (610–11).

Religious history: on English relations with the Papacy, see Harvey (652–58), who includes work on Adam Easton, and Pantin (1009–12). On popular religious culture see Brown (356), Cross (443, 445), Duffy (512), Hudson (701, 716), Rubin (1071–72), Swanson (1165–66), and texts edited in Shinners (202), Shinners and Dohar (203), and Swanson (206). Also see Sections 10, 11, 13, and 14.

Studies of Lollardy in specific regions of Britain include McNiven (944) on Cheshire; N. Evans (538) on the Chiltons; Reid (1058) on Colchester; McSheffrey (949) on Coventry in one chapter, though she discusses communities all over England; Dickens (492), Hudson (733) and Snape (1126) on Durham, York, and the north; N. Evans (537), Hanna (631), Houlbrooke (685), and Tanner (1173) on Norwich and East Anglia; Foreville (566) on Exeter; Lutton (904), Tanner (1174), and J.A.F. Thomson (1187) on Kent; Crompton (440) on Leicestershire; McHardy (938) on Lincoln diocese; Jurkowski (759, 761) on Derbyshire; Brown (356) on Salisbury; Welch (1272–73) on Sussex and Suffolk; and Easson (518), T.M. Lindsay (863), and McNab (909) on Scotland. Davies (460) discusses the importance of local and familial connections for the spread of Lollardy.

General discussions of Lollardy during the Tudor period and Reformation include Aston (271), Brandt (349), Dickens (490–93), and Haigh (618). Kenny (788) projects forward to the Counter-Reformation.

Two specific reformation trials have gained importance. On Richard Hunne see St. Thomas More (187), E.J. Davis (463), Fines (545), Milsom (954), Ogle (1000), Smart (1119), and Wunderli (1310); on Thomas Bilney see Walker (1250) and in Erler (527). Skelton's "Replycacyon," edited by Scattergood (204), is about Bilney.

5. Philosophy and Theology

For general introductions and discussions of Wyclif's thought which pertain to many or all of the sections below, see de Vooght (484), Kenny (784), Lahey (820), the chapter in Leff (836), Rex (1061), and Robson (1067). Discussions the broader context of the history of philosophy are Beonio-Brocchieri Fumigalli (313) and Kaluza (769). The essays in Hudson and Wilks (68) discuss various aspects of the philosophical movements from Ockham's nominalism to Wyclif's realism. Courtenay (432) and Catto and Evans (53) provide the best introductions to the contemporary state of philosophical and theological learning at Oxford. Readers are also referred to the introductions to editions.

On anti-clericalism, see work on Fitzralph in Section 3; also de Boor (479), Clopper (398), Dickens (493), Dipple (498), Dolnikowski (499, 501), Erickson (525–26), Renna (1059), Wilks (1290), and van Engen (1228).

On Wyclif's realism, universals, and implications of his realism, see Spade's preface to the edition of *On Universals* (250), Carre (370), Kemp (782), Kenny (785), Krummel (811), Levy (848), Oberman (993), Robson (1067, including a discussion of realist precursors), Read (1055), Trapp (1216), Wilks (1286), and Zuckerman (1315).

On the Eucharist, see Aers (261–62), Bowman (339), Catto (373), Hudson (716), Keen (775), Leff (840), Levy (849–50), McCue (932); Phillips (1036), and Rubin (1071).

For political theory, Black (324) provides a general introduction. On specific topics, including dominion, ecclesiology, and disendowment, see Aston (281, 287), Bertelloni (318), Coleman (402), Conetti (406), Dahmus (449–50, 452), Daly (454), G.R. Evans (533), Farr (540), Fischler (550), Fisher (551), Gellrich (589), Genet (590–92), Gewirth (594), Lahey (818–19), Leff (835), Luscombe (903), McGrade (935–36), Simonetta (1100–05), and Wilks (esp. 1284–85). Many of these discuss political ramifications as well as theory.

On metaphysics, see Conti (408–10), De La Torre (481), Leff (843), and Tresko (1218).

On the theory and interpretation of scripture, see Copeland (419), G.R. Evans (529, 531–32), Ghosh (598), Hudson (696, 710), Hurley (738), Kretzmann (807), Levy (254, a translation of the *De Veritate*), Minnis (955–58), Molnár (962), and Smalley (1114–18).

On connections to Hussite theology, see Section 16.

6. The Bible

This is one of the oldest areas of interest in Lollardy. Many older works cited in the Bibliography are not mentioned here. No new complete edition of the Late Version of the Wycliffite Bible has been edited since Forshall and Madden in 1850, though Lindberg has edited the Early Version (109–10) and has begun the Late Version (112–14, 116), both based on specific manuscripts rather than a full collation. For possible translators, see work on Hereford, Purvey, and Trevisa in Section 3, above. Two facsimiles (113, 115) and one modern translation (117) exist.

Wycliffite tracts on translation are numerous; many appear in unpublished dissertations. Lindberg (111) separately edits Jerome's Prefaces that are included in the WB. Bühler (126) edits one tract on translation; Ker (161) edits a summary of the Bible; Kuhn (166) and McIntosh (184) in fact edit the same tract as each other, the preface to a concordance of the New Testament – Kuhn with a much more extensive discussion. The "General Prologue" appears in its entirety in Forshall and Madden (106), though excerpts appear in Hudson (155) and Dean (133).

On the translation itself, including comparison to other versions, see Bobrick (330), Deanesly (475, though many of her points have been modified by later scholarship), Fowler (572), Hammond (625), Hargreaves (643, 645), Lawton (828, 830), and Ng (981).

On the textual and manuscript history, see Forshall and Madden (106); for more recent work, see Breeze (352), Fristedt (577–82), Lindberg (854–62), and Wilks (1289).

On the *Glossed Gospels* commentary see Copeland (420, 422); Ghosh (597); Hargreaves (647–48), Hudson (719), and (briefly) Swanson (1167).

On the Psalms and its commentaries see Edden (520), Everett (539), Kuczynski (813–14), and Muir (974).

For philology and linguistics, see Section 12.

7. Sermon Studies

Recent editions of sermons aside from Hudson and Gradon (158) have been edited by Cigman (128), Forde (151), Hudson (157), Parkes (189, some fragments), and Wenzel (180). Also see Wimbledon's "Sermon" (225). Hartel (651) is a brief overview of literature on medieval sermons.

Spencer (1133) is the most comprehensive study since Owst (1007–08). Also see especially Catto (382), Cigman (390–93), A. Fletcher (553–58), Forde (560–65), Haines (620–21), Hudson (688–89, 725), Hudson and Spencer (735), Little (867), Vidmanova (1237), and Wenzel (1274–75, 1278). Fletcher (553) and Spencer (1134) suggest that Mirk's cycle (186) may have been composed specifically to counter the popular Lollard cycle.

On style and delivery see Auksi (289), Hudson (705), P. Knapp (795, 797), Mueller (973), Peikola (1029, 1031), Stacey (1145), and Terasawa (1181); also see Section 12 on philology and linguistics.

On Wyclif's and Wycliffite Latin sermons see Dolnikowski (501–02), Hudson (734), Mallard (912–13), von Nolcken (1241), and Wenzel (1276–77). Gradon's essay in volume three of the sermons (158) discusses connections between the English cycle and Wyclif's Latin sermons.

8. Langland and Chaucer

On *Piers* itself, the essays in Alford (42 – see 256, 257, 292, and 712) discuss various connections to Lollardy. Other discussions are by Bowers (336), Clopper (397–98), Cole (399), Gillespie (604), Gradon (608), and Pearsall (1026).

Hudson's essay in Alford (712) provides an introduction to Langlandian texts aside from *Piers*. For editions see Barr (103), Dean (132–33) and Parker (198); for commentary see Hudson (702, on print history), Lawton (827), Scattergood (1085–86), Somerset (1129), and von Nolcken (1243).

Section 2 of Bisson (323) provides the most current evaluation of the relationship between Chaucer and Lollardy; also see the biographies by Howard (686) and Pearsall (1027), and J.A.W. Bennett (304) on the university towns. Among other general considerations of Chaucer's relation to Lollardy are Ames (266), P. Knapp

(798, who also comments on several of the *Canterbury Tales*), Olson (1002), and Strohm (1157). The belief that Chaucer was a Lollard has been out of critical favor for well over a century, as Kuhl's critical summary makes clear (812). Simon (1099) tried to make this case in 1876; in 1940 Loomis (877) backed off from a clear statement for his Lollardy, but just barely.

Most work on Chaucer and Lollardy has focussed on *The Canterbury Tales*, though see Cole (400) and Galloway (586). On the Nun's Priest's Tale, see Barr (296). On the Pardoner, see A. Fletcher (554–55), McVeigh (950), and L. Patterson (1023). On the Parson, see Collette (404, also on the Physician's Tale), P. Knapp (799), Little (868), Maxfield (931), L. Patterson (1022), Scanlon (1080), and Wurtele (1311). On the Summoner and Friar see Fletcher (557), McVeigh (950), Somerset (1130–1), Szittya (1169), and Williams (1298). On the Wife of Bath see Besserman (320), Blamires (327), Martin (923), and S.S. Morrison (967).

On the apocrypha, see Forni (567) and Wawn (1269–71), and editions by Bowers (123), Dean (132–33), and McCarl (196).

9. Drama

The *Tretise of Miraclis Pleyinge* is edited by Davidson (214), and discussed by Clopper (396), Davis (471–72), Keleman (778), and Nissé (987). Relevant book length studies of medieval and renaissance drama, and anti-dramatic sentiment, include Barish (294), Beckwith (300, 302), Dillon (495), Kendall (783), and Lepow (845); discussion also appears in Kolve (804) and Woolf (1306).

On Lollardy and N-Town see W.F. Bennett (306), Fewer (543), and Hunt (737). On Lollardy and York see Beckwith (301–02), Johnston (756), and Nissé (988). The "Croxton Play of the Sacrament" has been written about by Cutts (446) and Nichols (983); on this also see studies listed in Section 6 on the Eucharist. On Oldcastle and Shakespeare, see Section 3.

10. Other Literary Texts

Aside from work on the literary texts already cited, book-length studies relevant to Lollardy which reach more widely into English and Latin literary culture are many. They are hard to categorize aside from the attention they pay to texts and writing. They include Aers (261), Aers and Staley (263), Barr (296), Bowers (338, on *Pearl*), Coleman (401), Copeland (416, 422), Dinshaw (496), Gellrich (589), R.F. Green (611), Hughes (736), Justice (765), King (791), P. Knapp (800), Minnis (957), Nichols (984), Somerset (1129), Strohm (1159), Szittya (1169), and White (1280). Readers should also attend to the "Collections of Articles" in Section 2 of Part A.

For specific writers or texts: on Hilton see Clark (394), Gillespie (602), and Russell-Smith (1075); on the *Ancrene Riwle* see Colledge (403) and Zettersten's edition (96); Hoccleve's "Remonstrance against Oldcastle" is edited by Seymour (153), on which also see Barr (296) and E. Knapp (794); on Nicholas Love see A.I. Doyle (507), Salter (1076), and Sargent's edition (179); Dunnan writes on Gough (513) and the *Lantern of Liȝt* (514); on Kempe see section 14, below; on the *Pearl*-poet see Aers (261), Barr (296), Bowers (338), and Potkay (1048); on Skelton see Scherb (1088); on Rolle see Allen (265), Everett (539), Kuzcynski (813–14), Muir (974), and Watson (1264); and on the *Upland Series* see Dean (132), Heyworth (159, 674–75) and Somerset (1129).

11. Manuscript Studies, Book Production, and Book History

Most paleographical and codicological work done in the last half-century has been in the context of editing texts; readers are therefore referred to the introductions to editions. Hudson's introduction to volume one of the Sermons (158) makes a crucial argument for Lollard book production. For studies of manuscripts of major texts, see the appropriate section.

Studies of vernacular manuscripts include Brady (342–45, on the *Pore Caitif*), Cré (437), A.I. Doyle (503–06), Fletcher (556), Hanna (627–28, 630–31), Hudson (706, 711, 715), Kellogg and Talbert (779), Kuczynski (815), C.A. Martin (921), Nichols (982), Sturges (1161), Trivedi (1220), and von Nolcken (1248). On common-profit books and Lollardy in particular, see H.S. Bennett (303), A.I. Doyle (506), Robertson (1066) and Scase (1083).

On Latin manuscripts, especially of Wyclif's works, see Banning (101), Breck (350), Catto (376), E. Doyle (508, on Woodford), Genet (592), Hudson (721, 724, 727, 730–31); Mantello (918), Reeves (1057), Stein (1150–53), S.H. Thomson (1192–94, 1196, 1198, 1200) and W.R. Thomson (1203–04).

12. Philology and Linguistics

Much philological work was done during the nineteenth century; see, for example, Fischer (549), Gasner (588), Grimm (615), Ortmann (1004), and Skeat (1106), H. Smith (1123) and Thamm (1185). Many studies are in monographs and dissertations, especially German, not all of which are included. For specific information about manuscripts, readers are referred to editions. Lindberg's work has developed out of his editions of the Bible (854–862). Aside from these, recent work includes Aita (264), Bergs (315), M. Black (325), Diemer (494), Irvine (740–41), Nevanlinna (979–80), Östermann (1005), Samuels (1078), Warner (1261–62), and Yonekura (1312–13).

Barr (296), Hudson (698, 703), P. Knapp (800), Mueller (973), Mullett (976), and Peikola (1029–31) have commented on the uniqueness of Lollard vocabulary and discourse.

13. Lollardy and Images

The *Tretise of Miraclis Pleyinge* (214) contains a fundamental Lollard argument against images; see Section 10. Margaret Aston, in work published in her essay collections (43–44), is a seminal critic. Phillips (1036) notes that Wyclif, in his *Sermones*, confesses to an early interest in optics.

Other recent work includes Kamerick (770) and the essays in Dimmick et al. (57). Connecting Lollardy to other contemporaries, see Clark (394), Gillespie (602), and Russell-Smith (1075) on Hilton's defense of images; Collette (404) on Chaucer; Despres (482) on devotional literature; E. Knapp on Hoccleve (794); and Potkay (1048) on *Cleanness*. Jones (758) and Nichols (984) discuss refutations of Lollard iconoclasm. Kerby-Fulton and Depres discuss iconography and manuscript culture (790).

14. Lollardy and Literacy

Aston (276–78) argues explicitly for Lollardy's connection with literacy, and both Aston (283) and Hudson (701, 708) have written on Lollardy and the vernacular.

General studies of literacy and heresy have since taken note. Coleman (401) discusses the range and valence of literature. The texts and essays in Wogan-Browne et al. (234) demonstrate the range of medieval conceptions of literacy. Biller and Hudson's collection (50) includes relevant essays on literacy's importance to Lollard, Waldensianism, and Hussitism.

For discussions of conflicts over literacy in more specific arenas, R.F. Green (611) discusses Lollard literacy in the conflict between a dying oral and an incipient literate culture; Crane (436) and Justice (765) argue for the role of lay resentment of literacy in the Peasants' Revolt; Copeland's work (415–17, 420, 422) on pedagogy and dissent identifies literacy and hermeneutics as areas of conflict in the classroom and in commentaries; Steiner discusses legal documentary culture (1154) in an essay collection on the topic; and several essays on Chaucer's Parson, including most recently Little (868), L. Patterson (1022), and Scanlon (1080), have discussed how his didacticism recalls Lollard ideals.

15. Lollardy and Women

Recent work begins, again, with Aston (274) and the fact that Lollards apparently permitted women to lead conventicles. Since her essay, Cross (444–45) and McSheffrey (947–49) have written specifically on the role of women in the movement. J.F. Davis (469) writes on Joan of Kent. Blamires (327) argues for Lollard sympathy in Chaucer's Wife of Bath. Blamires and Marx (119) and Copeland (417) discuss arguments over the roles for women, as preachers and commentators. Hanna (631) and Steiner (1154) discuss the women in the Norwich heresy trials. Forde (563) discusses women in Wyclif's theological writings. Erler (527) writes on women's book ownership and reading – mostly orthodox, but with Lollard connections. Margery Baxter specifically has been commented on in, *e.g.*, Hanna (631), Steiner (1154) and J.A.F. Thomson (1189).

For discussions and editions of women's testimony in heresy trials, see Fines (546) and Tanner (208–09). The confession of Hawisia Mone, from the Norwich trials, is also edited in Hudson (155); she is also commented upon in Hanna (631).

Margery Kempe is not considered to be a Lollard, though discussions of her in relation to Lollardy appear in Boyd (340), Lawton (829), Lochrie (871), Nissé (986), and Staley (in her edition, 121, with bibliography).

16. Lollardy and Central Europe

Studies included cover the debate over the nature and extent of the influence Wyclif and Lollardy had on Hus and Hussitism; these will also include further bibliography. On Hus's life, see Krofta (810) and Spinka (1139). On Peter Payne, see Section 3. Thomson (211) edits several brief texts by Hus formerly ascribed to Wyclif.

On general and historical influence see Betts (321), Cannon (367), Herold (665–66, 669), Hudson (695, 721), Kaminsky (771–72), Klassen (792–93), Leff (837), Šmahel (1109, 1111–12), Spinka (1135–39), Walsh (1255–60), and Wilks (1287). On theological influence more specifically see Cook (411), de Vooght (483–89), Herold (667–68, 670), Kolesnyk (803), Molnár (963–64), Patschovsky (1018), Šmahel (1110), Spinka (1138), Töpfer (1214–15), Trapp (1216), and Trtik (1221).

For Lollardy and other areas of central Europe, see Schlauch (1089), S.H. Thomson (1197), and Vassilev (1231–33).

Index of Manuscripts

Detailed analysis of contemporary documentary sources is mainly confined to Jurkowski's essay where many are mentioned only once and are, therefore, not included here. Readers are referred to her essay. Printed government rolls and calendars, and printed and unprinted episcopal registers, are included in the general index. Page numbers given for notes refer to the page of text to which the note belongs.

General Index

Most scholars in the field now use the terms "Lollard" and "Wycliffite" synonymously, and such has been the case in this volume. For the purposes of the index, the terms have similarly been treated as interchangeable, but "Lollard" has been preferred to "Wycliffite" as an indexing term in order to provide a comprehensive entry without reduplications under "Lollard." Works with known authors are indexed under author even if less is said of the author in the text. All anonymous works are indexed under title. Individual texts are indexed under author or title, but not under editor. Modern authorities are cited as well as original materials, but more selectively, with a focus on those that are extensively discussed or that provide important background information. Page numbers given for notes refer to the page of the text to which the note belongs. Page numbers in italics refer to plates or maps in the volume.

Breinigsville, PA USA
13 March 2011
257519BV00002B/15/P